Integrated Content Literacy

Fifth Edition

Ray Wolpow
Western Washington University

Marian Tonjes
Professor Emeritus, Western Washington University
and
Adjunct Professor, University of New Mexico

KENDALL/HUNT PUBLISHING COMPANY
4050 Westmark Drive   Dubuque, Iowa 52002

Book Team

Chairman and Chief Executive Officer   Mark C. Falb
Senior Vice President, College Division   Thomas W. Gantz
Director of National Book Program   Paul B. Carty
Editorial Development Manager   Georgia Botsford
Developmental Editor   Angela Willenbring
Vice President, Production and Manufacturing   Alfred C. Grisanti
Assistant Vice President, Production Services   Christine E. O'Brien
Prepress Editor   Angela Puls
Permissions Editor   Renae Horstman
Designer   Jenifer Chapman

Front cover: Top left, top right, and lower left images © 2005
JupiterImages Corporation. Lower right image courtesy Creatas.
Back cover: Top and middle images © 2005 JupiterImages Corporation.
Lower image courtesy Creatas.

Part Opener images © 2005 by JupiterImages Corporation.

This book is dedicated to . . .

my wife Diane, sons Jesse and Sol,
(R.W.)

and my children, Jeff, Ken, and Nancy
(M.J.T.)

Brief Contents

Part I ◆ Setting the Stage 1

Chapter One: A Toolbox of Reading and Learning Strategies 3

Taking and Making Notes, Teaching Outlining Skills, Skills Needed for Good Note Taking and Making, Abbreviations and Symbols, Listening and Following Directions

Chapter Two: Reading Rate Adaptability 39

Levels and Rates, The Eye and Mind Connection, The Multiple Reading Process (MRP), The Eight Steps to Previewing a Large Text, *A Weekend with My Grandfather*

Chapter Three: A Frame of Reference: Literacy, Diversity, Censorship, and the Mature Reader 75

Schemata for the Concept of Literacy, Learning to Read vs. Reading to Learn, Introduction to Diversity, Censorship Concerns, Qualities of the Mature Reader, *Evangelina Can Read*

Chapter Four: Promoting Affective Dimensions: The Engaged Reader 111

Taxonomy of the Affective Domain, Attitudes and Interests, Assessing Atttitudes and Interests, Values Clarification, Engaging All Students: Concerns and Opportunities, Strategies for Engagement, *Sharing Is Healing*

Part II ◆ The Process of Comprehension and Its Assessment 149

Chapter Five: Matching Print with Reader: Part One—Text Assessment 151

Plain Language Laws, Readability Defined, Textual Factors: What Makes Something Easy or Difficult to Read?, Levels of Understanding, Tools for Measuring Readability, Readability Checklists, Qualitative Assessment of Text Difficulty, Student Input/Personal Factors, The Readability Assessment Triangle, Textbook Analysis: More Than Just Readability

Chapter Six: Matching Print with Reader: Part Two—Authentic Reader Assessment 195

Definitions and Standards, Standards for the Assessment of Reading and Writing, Classroom Assessments: Standardized Tools, Informal Whole-Class Assessment, Student, Parent, and Community Input

Chapter Seven: Making Meaning, Reflecting, and Remembering 231

The Process of Making Meaning, Taxonomies, Directed Reading-Thinking Activities: The Multiple Reading Process Revisited, Setting the Stage: Pre-Reading Strategies, During-Reading Strategies, Post-Reading, Strategies to Enhance Retention of What Is Read

Chapter Eight: Writing Process, Traits, and Patterns for Content Area Learning 277

The Writing Process, The Link Between Assessment and Writing to Learn, Analytic Traits of Writing, Content-Area Writing Tasks, Assignments, and Activities, *Writing My Way to My Family's History*

Part III Specialized Tools for Content Needs 319

Chapter Nine: Vocabulary: Building Blocks to Understanding and Enjoyment 321

Language Acquisition and Word Study, Specifics Types of Word Study, CSSD for Attacking New Words in All Content Areas, Teaching Strategies: Before, During, and After, Playing with Words: Fun for All!, Ten Things to Remember When Teaching Vocabulary, Vocabulary Tools and Games on the Internet

Chapter Ten: Study Learning 351

Search and Locate Information, Receive and Organize Information, Interpret and Apply Information, Special Strategies, Check/Recall/Monitor Information, Pulling It All Together, Testing

Chapter Eleven: Classroom Organization and Approaches 389

Organizational Concerns, Teaching Formats, Approaches, Organizing for Diversity Responsive Instruction, Approaches to Bilingual Education, Technology: Organizing Instruction with Old Friends, *My High School's Transformational Power*

Chapter Twelve: Integrating Literature into Content Classrooms 409

Rosenblatt's Efferent and Aesthetic Reading: Reader Response Theory, Motivating and Restorative Qualities of Literature, Importance of Reading Rate Adaptability, Multicultural Literature for Understanding and Transformation, Locating Appropriate Materials, Other Sources of Help in Selecting Appropriate Trade Books, Content Classroom Activities, *The Truth, Whispered or Shouted. . .*

Appendix A: Directed Reading/Thinking Activity 443

Appendix B: Content IRI Report 447

Appendix C: CIRI for Chemistry and Math: For Use in Triangulation of Assessments 455

Appendix D: Structural Analysis: Words and Affixes 471

Appendix E: Word Study References 475

Appendix F: Religion in the Public School Curriculum: Questions and Answers 477

Appendix G: Using Advance Organizers to Enhance the Processing of Texts 483

Glossary 491

Author Index 499

Subject Index 501

Contents

From the Pages of Our Lives   xiv

Preface   xv

Acknowledgments   xix

About the Authors   xx

Part I ◈ Setting the Stage   1

Chapter One: A Toolbox of Reading and Learning Strategies   3

Outline   3

Anticipatory and Review Questions   4

A Sampling of National Performance Standards   4

Introduction   5

From the Content Classroom: Johnny's Story   5

Taking and Making Notes   6

  Cornell Notes   6

  Ferndale and Harvard Notes   7

    Applications   9

From the Content Classroom: A Suggestion   13

  Recall Diagramming or Thought Mapping   13

    Overcoming Roadblocks   14

    Applications   15

  Notes as Connection Constructors   17

  Elsner's DaNOTES: Student Self-Evaluation of Notes   19

    Workshop 1.1: Note Taking and Making Practice   20

  Outlining   20

Teaching Outlining Skills   22

From the Content Classroom: Notes Required   23

  Using Technology to Improve Notes   23

Skills Needed for Good Note Taking and Making   25

  Paraphrasing: Saying It in Your Own Words   25

  Summarizing with G.I.S.T.   25

  Learning to Summarize: Changing Narrative to Lyrical   26

    Workshop 1.2: Summarizing by Changing Narrative to Lyric   26

Abbreviations and Symbols   27

From the Content Classroom: Conspiracy Days   28

Listening and Following Directions   28

  The Need   28

  Explicit Instruction in Listening Skills   29

    Workshop 1.3: Constructing Listening Puzzles   33

    Workshop 1.4: Give One, Get One   34

Cinquain as Summary   34

Summary   34

References and Recommended Readings   36

Chapter Two: Reading Rate Adaptability   39

Anticipatory and Review Questions   40

A Sampling of National Performance Standards   40

Introduction   41

Levels and Rates   41

  The Sprockets and Gears   41

    The Sprockets: Adler's Levels of Reading   41

    The Gears: Zintz's Reading Rates   42

  Why Read Faster?   43

  Misconceptions That Hold Us Back   43

From the Content Classroom: Reading Elephants   44

The Eye and Mind Connection   45

  Reading Depends Upon What Readers Already Know   45

  Reading Requires Continual Rapid Eye Movements   45

  When Scanning, Readers Must Be Fast and Selective   45

  Lessening Eye Fatigue   46

    Workshop 2.1: Word Recognition   47

    Workshop 2.2: Word Discrimination and Phrase Recognition   51

  Visual Discrimination   55

    Workshop 2.3: Phrase Comprehension   55

The Multiple Reading Process (MRP)   57

Stage One: Previewing or Pre-Reading   57
Stage Two: Reading   57
Stage Three: Post-Viewing or Post-Reading   57
From the Content Classroom: Reading Love Letters   58
Workshop 2.4: The MRP Applied—"Quality Not Quantity," by Mary Gillette   58
The Eight Steps to Previewing a Large Text   60
Using the Eight-Step Preview Method to Teach for Multicultural Understanding   61
From the Content Classroom: MRP in Action   62
Surveying Student Texts   62
Workshop 2.5: A Preview Guide for This Book—ICL 5   65
Cinquain as Summary   67
Summary   67
From the Pages of Our Lives: *A Weekend with My Grandfather*, by Ray Wolpow   68
Answer Keys   71
References and Recommended Readings   72

Chapter Three: A Frame of Reference: Literacy, Diversity, Censorship, and the Mature Reader   75

Outline   75
Anticipatory and Review Questions   76
A Sampling of National Performance Standards   76
Introduction   77
Schemata for the Concept of Literacy   77
Evolution of the Word *Literacy*   77
Survival and Functional Schemata of Literacy   78
Workshop Activity 3.1: Reaching Consensus on the Meaning of Literacy   79
My Father's Hands   81
Cognitive, Purposeful, and Critical Schemata of Literacy   82
History of the Schema of Content Literacy   84
Learning to Read vs. Reading to Learn   85
Workshop 3.2: Comparing Purpose and Skills   89
Introduction to Diversity   91
A Schema for Cultural Diversity   91
Censorship Concerns   94
When Teachers Are Confronted with Censors   94
Censored Books   95
Qualities of the Mature Reader   96
Workshop 3.3: Self-Assessment of Reading Maturity   97
Cinquain as Summary   103
Summary   103
From the Pages of Our Lives: *Evangelina Can Read*, by Leila Flores-Dueñas   104
References and Recommended Readings   107

Chapter Four: Promoting Affective Dimensions: The Engaged Reader   111

Outline   111
Anticipatory and Review Questions   112
A Sampling of National Performance Standards   112
Introduction   113
Workshop 4.1: Pre-reading Activity: A Quick Personal Inventory   115
Workshop 4.2: Engaged Readers   117
Workshop 4.3: Anticipation   117
From the Content Classroom: Strong Memories   119
Taxonomy of the Affective Domain   119
Workshop 4.4: Using Krathwohl's Taxonomy to Assess Your Own Level of Engagement   120
Language of Feelings   120
Emotional Intelligence: Emotional Quotient (EQ)   120
Motivation and Distracted Students   122
From the Content Classroom: Gail's Story   123
Attitudes and Interests   123
Building Positive Attitudes and Interests   123
Changing Poor Attitudes by Promoting Interests   123
Workshop 4.5: Readers' Bill of Rights   124
Assessing Attitudes and Interests   124
General Reading Attitude Survey   125
Tonjes Interest Inventory (TII)   127
Personal Reading Interest Inventory   129
Workshop 4.6: Creating Interest Inventories   130
Values Clarification   130
Twenty Things I Like to Do   130
Rank Order   131
Understanding Self and Others   131
Engaging All Students: Concerns and Opportunities   132
Religion in the Schools   132
English Language Learners   133
Aliteracy   133
From At-Risk to Resiliency   134
Bibliotherapy and the Restorative Qualities of Reading and Writing   136
Attention Deficit Hyperactivity Disorder (ADHD) and Literacy   136
Gender-Role Stereotyping   137
Strategies for Engagement   137
What Not to Do: Literacy Activities That Turn Students Off   137
Think-Pair-Share   138
Discussion Web   138
Informational Books, Trade Books, and Magazines   139
Integrate Content   139
Gender: Dual-Voiced Journals   140
Giraffe Talk: Nonviolent Communication   140

Cinquain as Summary   142

Summary   142

From the Pages of Our Lives: *Sharing Is Healing*, by Noémi Ban   143

References and Recommended Readings   146

Part II ◆ The Process of Comprehension and Its Assessment   149

Chapter Five: Matching Print with Reader: Part One—Text Assessment   151

Outline   151

Anticipatory and Review Questions   152

A Sampling of National Performance Standards   152

Introduction   153

Plain Language Laws   153

Readability Defined   154

   Workshop 5.1: Speculating on Reading Ease/Difficulty   155

Textual Factors: What Makes Something Easy or Difficult to Read?   157

  Concept Load and Abstractness   157

  Format and Length of Text   157

  Vocabulary (Lexical Complexity)   158

  Sentence Length and Structure (Syntactical Complexity)   159

  Inclusiveness   159

Levels of Understanding   160

Tools for Measuring Readability   161

  Formulae   161

    Workshop 5.2: Using a Fry Graph   165

  Evaluating Shorter Passages with the Fry Graph   167

  Caveat: Why Readability Formulae Do Not Work with Most Math Books   167

  Flesch Reading Ease and Flesch-Kincaid Grade Level Scores   168

    Workshop 5.3: Estimating the Grade Level of Your Own Writing   169

  Other Formulae: Dale-Chall, Lexile, DRP, and ATOS   169

  Summary of the Strengths and Weaknesses of Readability Formulae   171

Readability Checklists   171

  Marshall's Checklist   171

  The ICL Checklist Buffet   172

  Summary of Strengths and Weaknesses of Checklists   175

Qualitative Assessment of Text Difficulty   175

Student Input/Personal Factors   176

  Informal Assessments   177

Summary of Strengths and Weaknesses of Student Input   178

The Readability Assessment Triangle   178

From the Content Classroom: Matching the Readability of Textbooks with the Reading Abilities of Students Who Must Read Them   180

    Workshop 5.4: Should All School Texts Be Written at or Below Grade Level?   183

Textbook Analysis: More Than Just Readability   185

    Workshop 5.5: Schaefer's Textbook Analysis Assignment   187

Cinquain as Summary   189

Summary   189

References and Recommended Readings   191

Chapter Six: Matching Print with Reader: Part Two—Authentic Reader Assessment   195

Outline   195

Anticipatory and Review Questions   196

A Sampling of National Performance Standards   196

Introduction   197

Definitions and Standards   197

  Authentic Assessments   197

  Formative and Summative Assessments   198

  Performance-Based or Criterion-Referenced Assessments   198

  Rubrics   198

  High-Stakes, Standardized, and Norm-Referenced Assessments   198

  Aggregating and Disaggregating Data   199

Standards for the Assessment of Reading and Writing   200

    Workshop 6.1: Discussing Assessment Standards   202

  Triangulating Assessment Data   202

Classroom Assessments: Standardized Tools   202

  Individual Quick Classroom Screening   203

    Wide Range Achievement Test: Reading   203

    The San Diego Quick Assessment (SDQA)   203

    Caveat: Quick Screening Tools May Be Unfair to English Language Learners   206

    Summary of Strengths and Weaknesses of Quick Screening Tools   206

    Workshop 6.2: Practice in Administering and Scoring the SDQA   207

    Basic Reading Inventory   207

Informal Whole-Class Assessment   207

  The Art of Writing Comprehension Questions   208

  The Content IRI   210

    Part I: The Comprehension Section   211

    Part II: Subject-Specific Reading Skill Subtests   214

    Part III: Displaying and Using CIRI Data   220

CLOZE Procedure 221
    Constructing a CLOZE 221
    Administering and Scoring a CLOZE 221
    Other Uses 222
    Summary of Strengths and Weaknesses of Informal Assessments 223
    Workshop 6.3: Developing a Content IRI and CLOZE 223
Student, Parent, and Community Input 223
    Portfolios: A Framework for Ongoing Collaborative Assessment 224
    A Sample Portfolio Record Sheet 225
    Summary of Strengths and Weaknesses of Student, Parent, and Community Input through Portfolio Assessment 226
    Workshop 6.4: Creating a Triangulation Diagram 227
Diamante as Summary 227
Summary 227
References and Recommended Readings 227

Chapter Seven: Making Meaning, Reflecting, and Remembering 231
Outline 231
Anticipatory and Review Questions 232
A Sampling of National Performance Standards 232
Introduction 233
    Workshop 7.1: Ideas to Ponder 233
The Process of Making Meaning 234
    The Comprehending Process vs. the Comprehension Product 235
    Narrative vs. Expository Comprehension 236
Taxonomies 237
From the Content Classroom: Peggy's Story 238
    Gardner's Ways of Knowing—Eight Ways of Comprehending 238
From the Content Classroom: Jeremy's Story 240
    Workshop 7.2: Applying the Eight Ways of Knowing 240
Directed Reading-Thinking Activities: The Multiple Reading Process Revisited 240
Setting the Stage: Pre-Reading Strategies 241
    Workshop 7.3: The Importance of Background Knowledge: What Is the Topic? 243
    Parts of the Text Pre-Reading Guides 245
    Advance Organizers 246
    Guidelines for Writing and Teaching with Advance Organizers 247
    Graphic Representations 247
    Workshop 7.4: Using Cognitive Maps 247
    Guidelines for Constructing and Teaching with Structured Overviews 248

List-Group-Label 248
    Guidelines for Preparing and Teaching with List-Group-Label 249
    Anticipation/Reaction Guides 250
    Guidelines for Preparing and Teaching with an Anticipation/Reaction Guide 251
    Collateral Pre-Reading 252
    Workshop 7.5: Using Pre-Reading Strategies 252
During-Reading Strategies 252
    Glossing or Gloss Booklets 253
    During-Reading Guides 255
    ReQuest 255
    Guidelines for Preparing and Teaching Using the ReQuest Procedure 258
    Slicing: A Technique for Modeling Questioning 258
    Metacognitive Scripts 260
    Workshop 7.6: Using During-Reading Strategies 261
Post-Reading 262
    Workshop 7.7: What Do We Learn from Answering Comprehension Questions 263
    Cinquains as Summaries 265
    Analyze This!: Plus, Minus, Interesting (PMI) 265
    Guidelines for Teaching with a PMI 265
    Classroom Discussion 266
    Simulations/Role-Playing 267
From the Content Classroom: Poor Use of Simulation/Role-Playing 267
    Imaging 267
    Workshop 7.8: The Power of Imaging 268
    Collateral (Reiterative) Post-Reading/Viewing 268
    Workshop 7.9: Using Post-Reading Strategies 268
Strategies to Enhance Retention of What Is Read 268
    Mnemonics 269
    Putting Them All Together 270
    K-W-L Plus 270
    PLAN 271
Cinquain as Summary 271
Summary 272
Answers to Workshop 7.3 272
References and Recommended Readings 272

Chapter Eight: Writing Process, Traits, and Patterns for Content Area Learning 277
Outline 277
Anticipatory and Review Questions 278
A Sampling of National Performance Standards 278
Introduction 279
    Why We Teach Writing Within and Across the Disciplines 279
    The Reading and Writing Connection 280
    Teaching Writing: Teacher as Writer 280

The Writing Process   281
  Product Writing vs. Process Writing   281
  Writing Forms   282
    Workshop 8.1: Using Writing Forms to Enhance Content Learning   282
  The Five Stages of Process Writing   283
    Pre-writing   283
    Drafting   283
    Revising   284
      Language, Culture, and Writing   284
    Editing   285
      The Importance of Correct Punctuation   285
    Publishing   286
The Link Between Assessment and Writing to Learn   286
Analytic Traits of Writing   287
  Ideas and Content (Details, Development, and Focus)   287
  Organization (Internal Structure)   288
    Workshop 8.2: Practice in Assessing Writing for Ideas and Organization   288
  Voice (Tone, Style, Purpose, and Audience)   289
  Word Choice (Precise Language and Phrasing)   289
    Workshop 8.3: Practice in Assessing Writing for Voice and Word Choice   290
  Sentence Fluency (Correctness, Rhythm, and Cadence)   290
  Conventions (Mechanics)   290
    Workshop 8.4: Practice in Assessing Writing for Sentence Fluency and Conventions   291
    Nonstandard Dialects and Conventions   291
    Workshop Activity 8.5: Errors in Conventions or Cultural Sensitivity?   292
From the Content Classroom: "Each Has Its Proper Time and Place"   293
  Electronic Connections: To Six-Traits and More   293
Content-Area Writing Tasks, Assignments, and Activities   293
  Low-Stakes Writing Activities   293
    Admit Slips, Quick-Writes, and Exit Slips   293
    Free Writing, Journals (Personal, Dialogue, and Double-Entry), and Learning Logs   295
From the Content Classroom: Learning Notebooks in a Middle School Science Classroom   296
    Biopoems, Diamante Poems, RAFT, and Alphabet Books   296
    Key Pals, Blogs, and Digital Stories   298
    One More Thought on Technology and Content Writing   300
  High-Stakes Writing   300
    The Five-Paragraph Essay   300
      An Alternative Approach to the Five-Paragraph Essay for Struggling Writers   301
    The Research Paper   301

TER: A Technique for Helping Students Select Topics for Essays   302
Writing and Second Language Learners in the Content Classroom   303
  Risky Writing   304
Cinquain as Summary   305
Summary   305
From the Pages of Our Lives: *Writing My Way to My Family's History*, by Kie Relyea   306
References and Recommended Readings   308
Chapter 8 Appendices   311
  Appendix 8A: Answer Keys for Workshops 8.2, 8.3, and 8.4   311
  Appendix 8B: Five-Paragraph Essay Rubric   314
  Appendix 8C: TER Worksheet and Instructions   315

Part III ◆ **Specialized Tools for Content Needs**   319

Chapter Nine: Vocabulary: Building Blocks to Understanding and Enjoyment   321
Outline   321
Anticipatory and Review Questions   322
A Sampling of National Performance Standards   322
    Workshop 9.1: Getting a Mental Set   323
From the Content Classroom: Benefits of Teaching Vocabulary   323
Introduction   323
From the Content Classroom: Values Voting and Vocabulary   324
    Workshop 9.2: Words with Multiple Meanings   324
From the Content Classroom: Adventures of the CIMTE 538 Class by a Graduate Student   325
    Workshop 9.3: Key Words   325
Language Acquisition and Word Study   325
  Some Potential Stumbling Blocks   325
  Levels of Knowing a Word   326
  Definitions vs. Meanings   326
  Size and Type of Vocabulary   327
  Etymology (Word Origins and Histories)   327
    Workshop 9.4: Spectre   328
  Home Economics for Food Lovers   329
  Amelioration and Pejoration   329
  Denotations and Connotations   330
  Coining New Words   330
Specific Types of Word Study   331
CSSD for Attacking New Words in All Content Areas   333
  Context (The Intelligent Guess)   333
  Structural Analysis (Meaningful Word Parts)   335
  Sound (Phonics—Symbols, Syllables, and Sounds)   335

The Dictionary: A Multipurpose Tool   336
Thesaurus: A Storehouse of Information   337
    Workshop 9.5: Strategy Selection   338

From the Content Classroom:
Antidisestablishmentarianism   338

Teaching Strategies: Before, During, and After   338
  Before   338
    Word-of-the-Day   338
    Synonym Clusters   339
    List/Group/Label Concept Development   339
    Cognitive Maps   340
    Student-Selected Key Words   340
  During (While Reading)   340
    Modified CLOZE Technique   340
    Think-Alouds   341
  After (To Confirm, Clarify Meanings, Extend)   341
    OPIN   341
    Semantic Feature Analysis (SFA)   342
    TOAST: A Vocabulary Study System   342

Playing with Words: Fun for All!   343
  Collective Nouns   343
  Mistaken Clichés   343
  Palindromes, Pangrams, Anagrams, and
  Spoonerisms   344
  Different Definitions   344
  Word Pairs   345

Ten Things to Remember When Teaching Vocabulary   345
Vocabulary Tools and Games on the Internet   345
Cinquain as Summary   346
Summary   346
References and Recommended Readings   346

Chapter Ten: Study Learning   351

Outline   351
Anticipatory and Review Questions   352
A Sampling of National Performance Standards   352
Introduction   353
    Workshop 10.1: Study Learning Checklist   353
Search and Locate Information   354
  General and Specific References   354
  Internet Search Form   355
  Library Scavenger Hunt   355
Receive and Organize Information   356
Interpret and Apply Information   356
  Written Language   356
  Graphics   356
    Types of Graphics   357
    Charts and Diagrams   357
    Graphs   359
    Tables   360

    Maps   360
    Pictures/Illustrations   361
    Cartoons   362
    Graphic Information Lesson   363
    Teaching Tips   364
      Workshop 10.2: Interpreting Charts   364
      Workshop 10.3: Interpreting Maps   365
Special Strategies   366
  Scaffolding Strategies in General   366
SQ3R/SQ4R   367
PARS   367
    Workshop 10.4: Preparing a Learning Center   368
K-W-L   369
    Workshop 10.5: K-W-L   370
REAP   370
Guided Reading and Summary Procedures:
GRASP   371
Check/Recall/Monitor Information   372
  Establishing Study Habits for Better Concentration   372
  Physical Conditions   372
  Frame of Mind   372
  Efficient Use of Time   373
  Time Schedules   373
  Memory: Forgetting and Remembering   375
  Memorizing: Some Personal Reminiscences   375
  Retention   376
  Concentration Aids   376
    Workshop 10.6: Practicing Concentration   378
Pulling It All Together   378
  Thematic Teaching Units   378
  Predict, Verify, Judge, and Extend   379
Testing   380
  Preparing for Tests   380
  Writing Essay Tests   381
  Objective Tests   382
  Taking the Objective Test: A Worksheet for Students   383
    Workshop 10.7: Teaching Test-Taking Skills   383
Cinquain as Summary   384
Summary   384
References and Recommended Readings   384

**Chapter Eleven: Classroom Organization
and Approaches**   389

Outline   389
Anticipatory and Review Questions   390
A Sampling of National Performance Standards   390
Introduction   391
Organizational Concerns   391
  Time   391
  Space   392

Materials 392
> *Workshop 11.1: Flexible Time Plans, Designing Space, and Organizing Materials* 393

Teaching Formats 393
  Total Class 393
  Flexible Small-Group Instruction 394

From the Content Classroom: The Freedom of Using Small Groups 395
  Triads or Buddy System 395
  Peer-Tutoring or Pairs 396

Approaches 396
  Individualized/Personalized Learning 396
  Language Experience Approach (LEA) 396

From the Content Classroom: Dream Car 397
  Learning Centers for Content Areas 397
    Workshop 11.2: Mini-Learning Centers 398
  Cooperative Learning 399

Organizing for Diversity Responsive Instruction 399
  Planning for a Responsive Environment 399
  Planning What We Teach 400
  Planning How We Teach 400

Approaches to Bilingual Education 400

Technology: Organizing Instruction with Old Friends 401
    Workshop 11.3: Old Technology at Wegotnonewtechno High 402

Cinquain as Summary 403

Summary 403

From the Pages of Our Lives: *My High School's Transformational Power*, by Carole H. Tyson 404

References and Recommended Readings 405

Chapter Twelve: Integrating Literature into Content Class 409

Outline 409

Anticipatory and Review Questions 410

A Sampling of National Performance Standards 410

Introduction: Looking at Literature 411
    Workshop 12.1: In the Beginning 411

Rosenblatt's Efferent and Aesthetic Reading: Reader Response Theory 411

Motivating and Restorative Qualities of Literature 412

Importance of Reading Rate Adaptability 412

Multicultural Literature for Understanding and Transformation 413

From the Multicultural Classroom: The Correct Answer Is Wrong 413
  Empowering Minority Students 413

From the Multicultural Classroom: The Tree of Life 413
  Two Poems: "The Beads of Life" and "We Wear the Mask" 414
  Integrating Folklore into a Middle School Cross-Cultural Unit 416

Workshop 12.2: A Classroom Visit 416
Workshop 12.3: Sharing Multicultural Understandings 417

Locating Appropriate Materials 417
  Text vs. Trade Books 417
  Using Trade Books in Content Classrooms 417
  Leveled Books 418

Other Sources of Help in Selecting Appropriate Trade Books 419
  A Guide to Locating Content-Specific Literature 419
  A Guide to Locating Multicultural Literature 420
  A Guide to Locating Young Adult Literature 422
  An Annotated Literature Bibliography: Some Personal Choices 424
  Content-Specific Websites with Literature Resources 426
  A Guide to Trade Book Selection Guides 427
  Graphic Novels, Fandom, and Anime 427

Content Classroom Activities 428
  Read-Alouds 428
  Book Talks 429
  Text Walk 430
  Picture Books for Adolescents 430
  Sustained Reading and Writing 431

From the Content Classroom: Promoting SSR 431
  Study Reading Circles (Literature Circles) 432
  Response Journals (RJ) 433
  Curriculum-Based Readers Theatre (CBRT) 433
    Workshop 12.4: Select a Strategy 434
  Here's a Checklist for You 434

Cinquain as Summary 435

Summary 435

From the Pages of Our Lives: *The Truth, Whispered or Shouted . . .*, by Janice Brendible 436

References and Recommended Readings 438

Appendix A: Directed Reading/Thinking Activity 443

Appendix B: Content IRI Report 447

Appendix C: CIRI for Chemistry and Math: For Use in Triangulation of Assessments 455

Appendix D: Structural Analysis: Words and Affixes 471

Appendix E: Word Study References 475

Appendix F: Religion in the Public School Curriculum: Questions and Answers 477

Appendix G: Using Advance Organizers to Enhance the Processing of Texts 483

Glossary 491

Author Index 499

Subject Index 501

From the Pages of Our Lives

Ban, Noémi   *Sharing Is Healing*   143

Brendible, Janice   *The Truth, Whispered or Shouted . . .*   436

Flores-Dueñas, Leila   *Evangelina Can Read*   104

Relyea, Kie   *Writing My Way to My Family's History*   306

Tyson, Carole   *My High School's Transformational Power*   404

Wolpow, Ray   *A Weekend with My Grandfather*   68

Preface

 Integrated Content Literacy—Why This Title? What Does It Mean?

Most will agree that as secondary-level teachers, we teach because we have a passion for our content area. We know that the central concepts, structure, and tools used to acquire content expertise bring meaning into our lives. Having dedicated a significant portion of our lives to the study of our subject area, and with the intention of continuing to do so, we want to share what we know, and what we continue to learn, with others.

It is that desire to share that made us become teachers. We who teach middle and high school-aged learners want to be more than experts in subject knowledge. We find fulfillment in empowering others to learn. There is something very special, perhaps magical, that occurs each time the look on our students' faces. They tell us that we helped bridge the gap between confusion to understanding. Those smiles, those bright eyes, they are a major part of why we teach.

However, highly qualified content teachers need more than subject knowledge and the desire to find better ways to teach content. Effective teaching requires the qualities of integrity, respect, kindness, courage, and responsibility. These become manifest when we take the time to create caring and inclusive lessons and learning environments that are relevant and responsive to the diverse backgrounds, perspectives, and needs of our students and their families. When we take the time to integrate content and strategies, heart and mind, and difference and wholeness, we foster the connections we choose to call integrated content literacy.

 What's New?

As the readers of the previous editions of this book attest, integrating content instruction with literacy methods improves achievement and empowers student learning. In the revised and updated chapters that follow you will find numerous tried-and-true examples of ways that you and your students may read and write to learn in your content area. We've expanded the chapters on assessment, reading to make meaning, writing to learn, and developing content vocabulary. We've added a chapter on content and literature. Content from the chapter on technology and literacy has been infused throughout the text and we've expanded the glossary at the end of the text. Finally, this edition includes a new and unique feature, a series of essays that appear at the end of several chapters, entitled *From the Pages of Our Lives*. The authors of these essays are teachers who come from diverse backgrounds and provide heart-felt perspectives that add meaning to the concepts introduced in the chapters that precede them.

For Whom Is This Book Intended?

This text is intended primarily for college classes in content-area reading for middle and secondary teachers, either preservice or in-service, across the curriculum. Because of its practical emphasis and because each chapter is complete in itself, this text should also prove useful in staff development workshops in school districts.

Most important, however, this book is intended for individual content teachers who wish to improve their knowledge and skills in the areas of reading and writing to learn. We don't start this book with a definition of literacy. Instead, we acknowledge that you are embarking on the challenging task of learning from this new text and your instructor. In the first two chapters we provide you with a toolbox of reading, writing, and learning strategies that you will be able to use to get the most out of the ten chapters that follow. No matter what order you read this text, three helpful suggestions follow:

Suggestions for Our Readers

Before Reading—(5 minutes max!) Always preview a text chapter before reading it to get an overview of main points. First, look over the cognitive map found on the first page of each chapter. Next, read the questions written for various levels of thought, which will alert you to some key ideas to be found when reading. You need not try to answer them at this point. Now rapidly skim the pages, glancing at major subheadings and graphics. Read cinquains and summary at the chapter's end. Ask yourself, what are the major points and how are they organized. What do I already know about these? What do I need to learn? What vocabulary is unique to this chapter and where might I find their meanings. You have a road map in your mind now, so you are ready to read.

During Reading—Either use a highlighter for parts you think are important or take brief notes as you proceed. You are beginning to process the information when you do this. Jot any questions that occur as you read for later reference.

After Reading—Return to the cognitive map and questions at the beginning of the chapter. Review these important points and check your understanding by answering the text questions posed. Were your own questions answered satisfactorily? What do you still need to know? Go back and reread the parts of the text that might answer your remaining questions. This layered approach to understanding will aid your long-term memory.

How Are We Different?

One way to get more out of a textbook is to have a sense of how it is different than others. Here are a few:

First	We begin the text by situating you the reader as learner. The tool box of literacy and learning strategies can help you throughout the course and may be used with your students as well.
Second	We model teaching strategies in each chapter of the book. For example, we begin each chapter with cognitive maps that are creative and artistic representations of the concepts and methods that follow. We ask

anticipatory/review questions about personal attitudes, creative interests, and values, thereby integrating affect and cognition. We embed workshops within chapters so that readers may pause to reflect and react before moving on to the next major topic. We end each chapter with a cinquain and a summary to express key facets of that chapter.

Third Recently individual states have established specific measurable literacy standards, derived from those established by national and international professional associations. Each chapter includes a sampling so that readers can connect the concepts and methods within to the components of these standards.

Fourth Throughout the text you will find unique chapter sections entitled *From the Pages of Our Lives*. These are written by educators across cultures and speak from the heart. Their courage, personal commitment, and love of learning add perspective to the concepts presented in chapters that precede them.

Fifth Our own model of study skills—what we call "study learning," which has appeared in prior editions—is interactive in that it moves in a sequence through all aspects of this important content strategy.

Sixth To date we are the only text that has a separate chapter on reading rate adaptability—so important to good comprehension.

Seventh We have come to believe it is time to return to an area that appeared in our third edition—"religion in the public school curriculum," which outlines what *can* be taught about religions and why it should be included. Sponsoring organizations listed in Appendix F can be approached for further clarification or information.

Eighth This is a practical text based on current theory. It is chock-full of innovative strategies that can be used in your classroom tomorrow.

Finally, several key beliefs from authors Ray Wolpow, Marian Tonjes, and former coauthor Miles Zintz.

◆ We Believe . . .

1. in integrating knowledge—blurring borders between subjects and bringing a fresh perspective to learning.
2. that reading, thinking, writing, and studying are not separate subjects or entities but flow across the entire curriculum.
3. in cooperative teaching and learning, allowing for freedom of choice when feasible.
4. that everyone has the potential for creativity, but that for many it has been downplayed in early years; to flourish it must be encouraged and practiced often.
5. in creating a nonthreatening, stimulating classroom environment in which students feel free to risk, experiment, and make mistakes without fear of ridicule or shame.
6. in the innate dignity and worth of every human being.
7. that the process—or keys to opening avenues of learning—is as important or even more so than the product or knowledge gained. When we feel comfortable with how and when to perform the process, we will be more apt to continue learning on our own, and then the knowledge gained will be more personally meaningful.

8. in modeling or practicing what we preach, using exemplars when possible. We should not, for example, just tell our students to take notes, we should first remind or show them how.

9. that because we organize, store, and retrieve knowledge by categorizing data into patterns, we should make it a common practice to construct a cognitive map of our learnings.

10. that teaching is not just telling, nor is it an easy task, if performed properly; that it takes continuous effort, study, and willingness to try the unknown; that it takes a caring heart.

11. that teaching is a mutually transformative process.

12. that cognitive and affective developments are complementary co-requisites for achievement. Self-esteem is built when we both know and feel that we can do something.

Acknowledgments

We wish to express our gratitude to the following people who so graciously assisted us in producing this text:

- To our students, for your thoughtful suggestions and ideas, many of which are now integrated into these pages. Your desire to find better ways to teach your students is what inspires us.
- To Noémi Ban, Janice Brendible, Leila Flores-Dueñas, Kie Relyea, and Carole Tyson, for the moving essays you wrote for this text. Your integrity and love for literacy speak from every page.
- To our colleagues for your scholarly support and excellent suggestions. A special thank you to Christine Schaefer and Lauren McClanahan, for all the time you took to read and comment on chapters; and to Stephanie Salzman, for your pervasive encouragement.
- To Western Washington University, Bureau of Faculty Research, for your support for manuscript preparation, and especially to Paula Ronquillo for typing and retyping to tight deadlines.
- To our editor, Angela Willenbring, for your creative energy, thoroughness, and persistence; Lisa Zenner for introducing us to the Kendall/Hunt family; and Paul Carty, for your excellent suggestions.

About the Authors

Ray Wolpow is associate professor and chair of the Department of Secondary Education at Western Washington University, in Bellingham, where he also serves as the director of the Northwest Center for Holocaust Education.

For twenty years, Ray taught classes in reading, special education, social studies, music, math and English in public and private K-12 schools in New York, Arizona, California and Washington State. His work with inner-city and rural underachieving students inspired him to develop a nationally recognized program for teaching reading and study skills across the curriculum. He received the Christa McAuliffe Award for Excellence in Education and certificates of recognition and appreciation from Washington State's Association for Supervision and Curriculum Development and from the Tribal Council of the Lummi Nation.

Ray returned to university in 1993 to study the role that teachers could play in meeting the needs of at-risk students. His study of the teaching methodologies of three outstanding educators, each a survivor of pervasive and prolonged trauma, won first prize in "Research in Behavior and Social Sciences" at the 1994 Pennsylvania State University Graduate Research Exhibition.

Over the last eleven years Dr. Wolpow has received highly positive evaluations from his university students and from in-service participants. His university level classes and workshops include content reading, writing and learning; instruction, evaluation and management; and enhancing the resiliency of at-risk students. In addition, he supervises student teachers, and chairs a talented department of secondary teacher-educators. In 1999, the President of Western Washington University presented Dr. Wolpow with their university's Excellence in Teaching Award.

Ray's work with the Northwest Center of Holocaust Education includes facilitating teacher in-service about Holocaust/genocide/ethnocide education and maintaining a resource center with appropriate grade-level materials. Two years ago he helped Holocaust survivor and retired teacher Noémi Ban author and publish her story as a book for elementary students.

Dr. Wolpow has an M.A. degree in special education from Teachers College, Columbia University and a Ph.D. in curriculum and instruction from the Pennsylvania State University. Ray's personal interests include sports, hiking, and organic vegetable gardening.

Marian J. Tonjes is a Professor Emerita from Western Washington University, Bellingham and currently Adjunct Professor, University of New Mexico, Albuquerque. Author of many articles and texts, Dr. Tonjes has won a number of awards over the past years, and the one she treasures most is the "Distinguished Teaching Award" for the University, presented to her by Western's president in 1981, with the highest student evaluations up to that time. She is known internationally for her work and has been an invited speaker throughout the United Kingdom as well as Argentina, Australia, Canada, China, Estonia, Germany, Guam, India, Hungary, the Netherlands, Sweden and the Philippines. She was the first invited guest in Reading from the U.S. to speak for eight days in Moscow to educators across Russia and the USSR. She is serving her sixth year as a trustee of the secondary White Mountain School in Bethlehem, N.H., and is an honorary trustee of the Lomononov School in Moscow. She has served as an international advisor for Vantage Deluxe Travel. From 1976-1993, she developed and was Director of Western's "Summer Study in England" program at Oriel College, Oxford University, and has recently been made an honorary Oxonian as well as a Friend of Oriel. In 2002 she designed and with her sister, Caroloyn Grant, led a study tour group "In the Footsteps of Dickens" throughout England. She was the first elected chair of the American Reading Forum and has never missed the annual conference. She is also active today in ARF, IRA, PEO, Tri Delta and Circumnavigators. As listed in "Who's Who" her avocations are tennis, bridge, art appreciation, theatre and miniature collecting. In 2005 she was nominated by McDaniel College (formerly called Western Maryland College) as their outstanding professional alumna.

Note: The first edition of this text, 1981, with coauthor Miles Zintz, was titled *Teaching Reading/Thinking/Study Skills in Content Classrooms*, William C. Brown.

PART

I

Setting the Stage

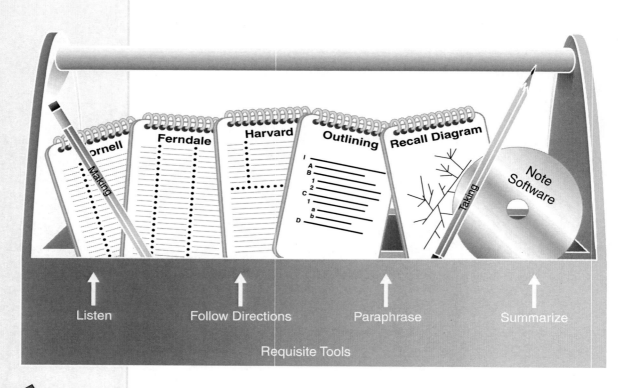

FIGURE 1.1

A Toolbox of Reading/Learning Strategies: A Cognitive Map

A Toolbox of Reading and Learning Strategies

Outline

- Anticipatory and Review Questions
- A Sampling of National Performance Standards
- Introduction
- From the Content Classroom: Johnny's Story
- Taking and Making Notes
  - Cornell Notes
  - Ferndale and Harvard Notes
    - Applications
- From the Content Classroom: A Suggestion
  - Recall Diagramming or Thought Mapping
    - Overcoming Roadblocks
    - Applications
  - Notes as Connection Constructors
  - Elsner's DaNOTES: Student Self-Evaluation of Notes
  - *Workshop 1.1: Note Taking and Making Practice*
  - Outlining
- Teaching Outlining Skills
  - Using Technology to Improve Notes

- From the Content Classroom: Notes Required!
- Skills Needed for Good Note Taking and Making
  - Paraphrasing: Saying It in Your Own Words
  - Summarizing with G.I.S.T.
    - Learning to Summarize: Changing Narrative to Lyrical
    - *Workshop 1.2: Summarizing by Changing Narrative to Lyric*
  - Abbreviations and Symbols
- From the Content Classroom: Conspiracy Days
- Listening and Following Directions
  - The Need
  - Explicit Instruction in Listening Skills
    - *Workshop 1.3: Constructing Listening Puzzles*
    - *Workshop 1.4: Give One, Get One*
- Cinquain as Summary
- Summary
- References and Recommended Readings

"It is the province of knowledge to speak
And it is the privilege of wisdom to listen."

Oliver Wendell Holmes

"Note, n. [from L. *nota*, a mark, a sign . . . from *notus* pp of *nonscere* to know] . . . a brief statement of a fact, experience, etc., written down for review, as an aid to memory, or to inform someone else; a memorandum."

Webster's New Universal Unabridged Dictionary

Anticipatory and Review Questions

Literal

1. What are four formats that a student might use to take and make notes?

2. What is the difference between hearing and listening?

Interpretive/Applied

3. Select one method of teaching note taking/making that you believe will be useful in improving student learning. Explain why you chose it.

4. Using abbreviations makes note taking more efficient. List five abbreviations from your content area that can save the note taker time.

Evaluative/Critical

5. What do most strategies in this chapter have in common and how do they differ?

6. Justify time taken away from content instruction to help your students become better listeners or note makers.

Creative/Personal

7. Develop a customized note taking/making evaluation system like DaNOTES. Decide criteria for scoring and develop lesson plans to teach this system.

8. Who taught you how to take or make notes? Was it one of your content teachers? Did you appreciate this instruction at the time? Why, or why not? How did this instruction help you to succeed in high school and/or college?

A Sampling of National Performance Standards

- The professional educator understands and uses a variety of instructional strategies to encourage students' development of critical thinking, problem solving, and performance skills (Council of Chief State School Officers, 2005).
- Students conduct research on issues and interests by generating ideas and questions, and by posing problems. They gather, evaluate, and synthesize data from a variety of sources (e.g., print and non-print texts, artifacts, people) to communicate their discoveries in ways that suit their purpose and their audience (International Reading Association/National Council of Teachers of English, 1996, p. 38).

Introduction

Imagine a basketball coach meeting the team for the first time. Her students are excited about the possibilities of playing for the school's team. All players have some skills they bring to the squad but their mastery of these skills varies. Most can dribble, pass, shoot, and rebound, but their experience, especially in game situations, differs from player to player.

Now imagine the coach simply bouncing the ball a couple of times, showing a video in which she "demonstrates" a few plays, giving a short lecture on the fundamentals of basketball, and then concluding with the explanation: "The object of this game is to get the ball through the hoop as often as possible. By the way," she adds, "do your best to keep the other team from scoring. The first game is on Monday, so make sure you practice." Were the coach to leave at this point, she would be failing to provide students with explicit practice in the necessary skills and strategies to compete successfully.

As teachers, we are academic coaches. We must provide our students explicit instruction in skills and strategies necessary to learn content. We allow time for guided practice and give feedback to assure their success. It is not enough to tell our students what they need to know and when they need to know it. We must coach them every step of the way.

This chapter introduces different ways to take and make notes as well as applications to help students use their notes to learn content. A portion of this chapter is dedicated to instructing students in requisite tools for using these note methods: listening, outlining, paraphrasing, following directions, and self-evaluating as well as ways to overcome reading roadblocks. The chapter on study skills will delineate further skills in this area.

 ## FROM THE CONTENT CLASSROOM

Johnny's Story

Having failed his second history test in as many tries, his teacher called Johnny's parents to ask for help. "John is a very likable student," the teacher shared with the mother. "He often comes into my classroom before or after school to visit. However, " the teacher explained, "despite my continued encouragement, it appears Johnny does not do the reading or studying necessary to prepare adequately for tests."

His mother's voice became defensive, "Neither Johnny's father nor I are high school graduates, so I hate to disagree with you. However, I must defend my Johnny. The Friday before your test he came home, sat down at the kitchen table, and organized his books and notes. Two hours of study later I hugged him and told him I was impressed that he was already spending so much time preparing for his Monday test. He told me he had done poorly on the first test and he had to show you

that he could do much better. Later that weekend he was back at the table studying and once again I complimented him for his efforts. Johnny didn't hang out with his friends; instead he must have studied 10 to 12 hours for your test. He said that he really liked you and didn't want to let you or us down."

The next day John's eyes avoided his teacher. The teacher didn't return his paper with the rest. Instead, he asked him to stay after school for a tutorial session. During that session the teacher and Johnny agreed to study together each day after school. His teacher told him when they were done, Johnny would have much more than a knowledge of history. He would also have a toolbox full of ways to learn and study. The teacher then started the task of helping John learn how to use his notes to organize, focus his attention, and study effectively.

◆ Taking and Making Notes

Why give students explicit instruction in taking and making notes? The following are four good reasons. During note taking/making student must: (1) read or listen attentively; (2) discriminate among key thoughts; (3) be able to organize, paraphrase, and process ideas; and (4) condense or summarize those ideas. Empowering students to improve upon their note taking/making abilities can quickly result in improved reading and listening comprehension.

There is a difference between *taking* notes from a book or during a lecture and *making* notes afterward. *Taking* notes involves writing down the main ideas and supportive details. *Making* notes involves reviewing, analyzing, and reflecting upon the information noted. Like Johnny, most students spend the majority of their time taking notes. They do not spend enough time discerning what they do or don't understand. It is very difficult to retain what we do not comprehend fully.

Several approaches to note taking and making are Cornell Notes, Ferndale Notes, and Harvard Notes. No single approach will work for everyone. Think of them as tools in a toolbox. (See Figure 1.1.) Encourage your students to pick the appropriate tool for the task at hand. Listening strategies, paraphrasing, outlining, and methods for following directions are needed to effectively take and make notes. Whichever method students use, DaNOTES (pronounced dahh NOTES) can be one effective way to evaluate their notes.

Cornell Notes

Of the note taking procedures developed over the years, one of the most practical is Walter Pauk's Cornell System (1989). It is uncomplicated, efficient, and logical. There are three stages:

Stage 1—*Preparing:* Use a large loose-leaf notebook or spiral. Draw a vertical line about 2.5 inches from the left edge of several sheets. (See Figure 1.2.) When students *take* notes from class, discussion, lecture, or textbook, they write on

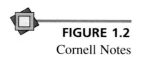

FIGURE 1.2
Cornell Notes

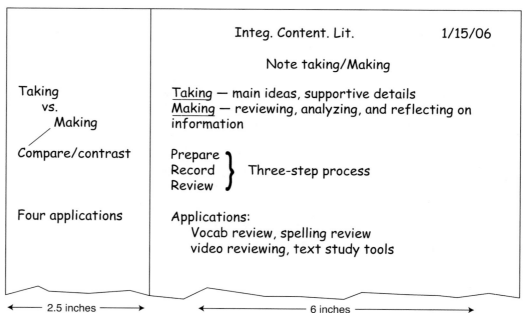

Integ. Content. Lit.   1/15/06

Note taking/Making

Taking — main ideas, supportive details
Making — reviewing, analyzing, and reflecting on information

Taking
  vs.
    Making

Compare/contrast

Prepare
Record   } Three-step process
Review

Four applications

Applications:
  Vocab review, spelling review
  video reviewing, text study tools

←— 2.5 inches —→   ←——————— 6 inches ———————→

the right-hand side of the line. Later students *make* notes, in the form of key words and phrases in the left-hand margin.

Before each note taking/making session, students should review the previous day's notes in order to reconnect mentally with the content. This can be done easily by overlapping each page so that only the key word columns (left) are uncovered.

Stage 2—***Recording:*** Notes are taken in simple list or paragraph form, making them as complete and clear as possible. Elaborate outlines and Roman or Arabic numerals should not be used here. These may be filled in later when notes are reviewed. Emphasize major ideas. Use abbreviations. (Abbreviations are especially helpful for that teacher who talks too fast.) Writing should be legible so that time will not be wasted recopying or typing notes. Recopying notes is a mechanical process that does little to enhance learning or retention.

Stage 3—***Reviewing:*** Soon after taking notes, students should make notes their own. Fill out abbreviations and/or add thoughts to the blank spaces. Underline or highlight key thoughts. Draw diagrams or illustrations.

Another important way to *make* these notes their own is to use the left-hand column. Reduce the extensive notes on the right side of the page by writing key words and phrases on the left side. Think of these words as "clues." When studying, cover the right-hand column and these key words can be used to "test" recall. After reciting these aloud, the student should uncover the notes and check for accuracy. Tell students to highlight (in a different color ink) those ideas that they find difficult to recall so that they may review them more frequently.

Ferndale and Harvard Notes

Two systems of formatting notes that are adaptations of the Cornell System are Ferndale and Harvard notes. The Ferndale System creates a third column by adding a right-hand column. A two inch/ five inch/ one and one/half inch format is used. (See Figure 1.3.) The left and center column are the same as in the Cornell system. The right

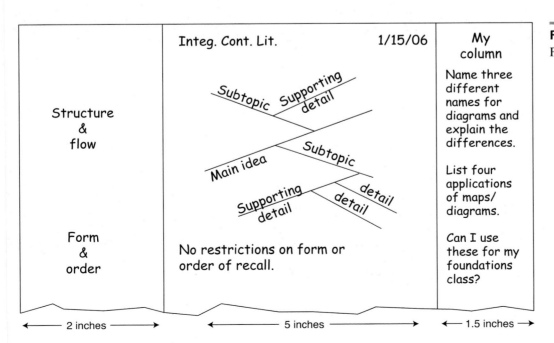

FIGURE 1.3
Ferndale Notes

column is called the "My" column. Here students are asked to reflect and personalize their notes. They are encouraged to write their unanswered questions (to ask friends or the teacher), construct sample test questions, crack jokes, or draw illustrations.

The Harvard System is similar to the Ferndale System except the third column is added to the bottom of the page. (See Figure 1.4.) This seems to be especially advantageous to students whose handwriting is large and for students in math classes where equations tend to extend across the page.

FIGURE 1.4
Harvard Notes

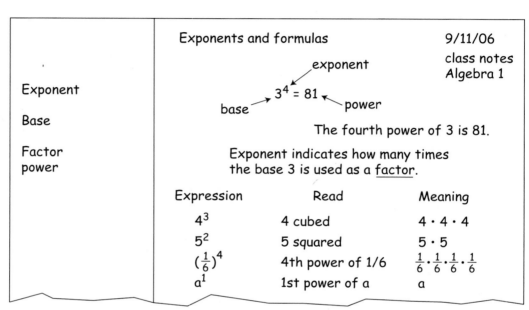

Exponent	Exponents and formulas	9/11/06
		class notes
Base		Algebra 1
Factor power	

exponent
$3^4 = 81$
base → power

The fourth power of 3 is 81.

Exponent indicates how many times the base 3 is used as a <u>factor</u>.

Expression	Read	Meaning
4^3	4 cubed	$4 \cdot 4 \cdot 4$
5^2	5 squared	$5 \cdot 5$
$(\frac{1}{6})^4$	4th power of 1/6	$\frac{1}{6} \cdot \frac{1}{6} \cdot \frac{1}{6} \cdot \frac{1}{6}$
a^1	1st power of a	a

4^5 5th power of y $y \cdot y \cdot y \cdot y \cdot y$

Order of operations

① (*)

② a*

③ x ÷ →

④ + − →

① Perform operations within parentheses or grouping symbols.

② Evaluate powers.

③ Do multiplications and divisions in order from left to right.

④ Do additions and subtractions in order from left to right.

Example

$\frac{1}{5}(8a - b)^2$ $a = 3$ $b = 4$

(see bottom for answer)

$\frac{1}{5}(8a - b)^2 = \frac{1}{5}(8 \cdot 3 - 4)^2$

$= \frac{1}{5}(24 - 4)^2$ Rule 1

$= \frac{1}{5}(20)^2$

$= \frac{1}{5}(400)$ Rule 2

$= 80$ Rule 3

APPLICATIONS

Several applications for these three note taking/making systems are vocabulary review, spelling review, participation in video viewing, and textbook study tool.

1. **Vocabulary Review**: (Ferndale Notes) Have students use the left-hand column to write the vocabulary word. Use the center column to write the definition of the word. Use the "My" column to create a clue that facilitates memory of the word and definition. (See Figure 1.5.) Take a second sheet of paper and fold it into three equal parts. Use the folded page to cover the left-hand column. Have students look at the definition and clue columns and then write the vocabulary word that is being covered. (Take no more than 2 minutes for a list of 10 to 15 words.) When students are done, have them check for correct answers. Advise them that they need to make additions to the clues of any words they missed. Encourage them to get ideas from their classmates. Repeat. Next, cover the middle section and give students 3 to 4 minutes to write paraphrased definitions of the words by looking at the word and clue columns. When they are finished, have them check for correct answers once again, making additions to the clues of any words they missed. Continue with variations (e.g., cover all but the right-hand column, cover all but the left-hand column, cover all but the center column, etc.).

	Vocabulary 9/25	
Word	Definition	Clue
barracks	a long building used to house soldiers	RR
agitate	to excite, disturb, or upset	
vitality	strength, energy, force	BAM!

FIGURE 1.5
Vocabulary Review

2. **Spelling Review**: (Ferndale Notes) This exercise is very much like the vocabulary review, with the exception that the right-hand column features that part of the spelling of the word that creates the most difficulty for the student. (See Figure 1.6.)

FIGURE 1.6

Spelling Review

	Spelling notes 9/26	
Word	Definition	Trouble Spot
clientele	customers	ien ele
erroneous	containing or marked by error	err
vulnerable	capable of being wounded or hurt	vul
cache	hidden supply	che
ecstacy	an overpowering emotion of excitement	ecs

3. **Participation in Video Viewing**: Today's student is an expert at "watching" television without paying attention. Given the intensity of most advertisements, perhaps this behavior is a survival mechanism. However, most teachers want students to participate more actively in the viewing of educational programming. Inform students that they will be given 3 minutes at the end of the video to add information to the note making columns of their notes. This means students are also encouraged to take notes during the video when they see or hear anything that they want to remember. (See Figure 1.7.)

FIGURE 1.7
Video Participation Notes

	World History, Video Period 6 "Cry Freedom" 2/6/06	
Crossroads settlement 11/75 Cape Province S. Africa	very poor people ambush of people cops are black, commanders are white	How can police act this way?
James Donald Wood - editor for U.S.A. newspaper	radio tells only the white side of the story James Wood - white, liberal newspaper editor; doesn't believe black witnesses	Isn't banning unconstitutional?
Steve Biko Banning	Steve Biko - black leader; befriends Wood - takes him into a clinic. Has to do this with care because he is banned, which means he may not visit with others Married couples unable to live in same township	What law gives the minority whites control over majority blacks?

4. **Textbook Study Tool**: Instead of (or in addition to) answering end-of-chapter questions for homework, have students create two to three pages of Harvard or Ferndale Notes on their reading. Then, using a list of higher-level thinking verbs such as those in Figure 1.8, create at least three questions in the "My" column. Collect these and compliment those students who create questions that you might use on a future test. Encourage students to use these questions as a means to review for tests.

FIGURE 1.8

My Column Words

Good answers to essay questions depend in part on the meaning of the directive words. If you are asked to *compare* the events in Rwanda to those during the Holocaust, you will get little or no credit if you merely *describe* them. If you are asked to *criticize* the way that we elect a president, you are not answering the question if you merely *explain* how a president gets elected. If your teacher asks you to *compare* and *contrast*, make sure that you know what she means. (Be polite when you point out that she may be asking you to be reduntantly redundant.)

Here are words that are frequently used in essay questions. Learn their meanings and use them to construct questions and answers in your right-hand "my" column.

Word	Meaning	"My"
enumerate	Name over—one after another; list in concise form.	
evaluate	Give the good and bad points; appraise; give an opinion regarding the value of.	
contrast	Bring out the points of difference.	
explain	Make clear; interpret; make plain; tell how to do; tell the meaning of.	
describe	Give an account of; tell about; give a word picture of.	
define	Give the meaning of a word or concept; place it in the class to which it belongs, and set it off from other items in the same class.	
compare	Bring out the points of similarity and the points of difference.	
discuss	Talk over; consider from various points of view; present the different sides of.	
criticize	State your opinion of the correctness or merits of an item or issue; criticism may approve or disapprove.	
justify	Show good reasons for; give your evidence; present facts to support your opinion.	
illustrate	Use a word picture, diagram, chart, or concrete example to clarify a point.	
summarize	Sum up; give the main points briefly.	
list	Present an itemized series or tabulation, always in concise form; listing is similar to enumeration.	
outline	Present information in a systematic arrangement or classification; an outline answer is an organized description in which you give main points and essential supplementary materials omitting minor details.	
state	Give, state, present, or ask the writer to express the high points in a clear, brief, narrative form.	
prove	Establish the truth of something by giving factual evidence or logical reasons.	

FROM THE CONTENT CLASSROOM

A Suggestion

There is a tendency to assume that students who are in "special needs classes" are the students who will benefit most from note taking and making instruction. One veteran high school reading teacher conducted interviews of students throughout a typical suburban high school. While interviewing students in an advanced physics class, an honor's student shared the following:

"I am an honor roll student and I know how to take notes from an English, social studies, biology, or math textbook. But when it comes to taking notes out of my advanced physics book, I wind up copying everything down. And I know better!! Perhaps you could suggest to our teacher that he show us how he does it. Maybe when he assigns the next chapter, he could take out the book and use the overhead to show us how he takes notes."

It is indeed probable that this student lacked the background knowledge needed to differentiate between major concepts and minor details in physics. Many students may be the first in their families to study what we are teaching. They are therefore dependent upon their teachers to model and teach these skills. Although these skills and abilities may not be part of the curriculum, they should be.

Recall Diagramming or Thought Mapping

A recall diagram is a schematic method for relating associated remembrances. The objective is to encourage students to remember information in the order that works best for each of them. Therefore, there should be *no restrictions on form or order of recall.* The following example is but one model of a recall diagram. Encourage each student to use it as a blueprint to develop the method that works best for them.

One way to construct a diagram or thought map is to turn a piece of paper lengthwise. Draw a slanted line from a point near the bottom left corner diagonally across the page. On this line write any idea or point that comes to mind. This idea will work like a magnet for other ideas. It is helpful if this idea is the main idea; however, it does not have to be. (See Figure 1.9.)

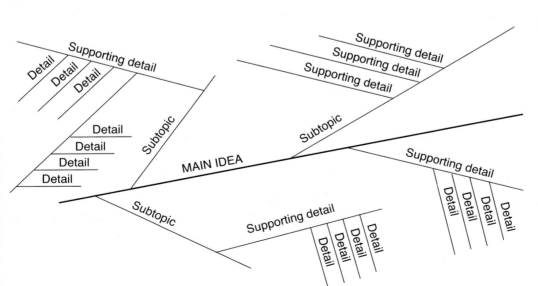

FIGURE 1.9
Mapping/
diagramming

Then starting at the bottom, have them draw slash lines alternately on either side of the diagonal line. On these have them write related subtopic ideas they remember. Do not expect them to be able to write all the first time, but just whatever comes to mind.

Branching off from these lines they can draw shorter lines. These are for the details that they remember that relate to the subtopics. After a while the diagram will look like the branch of a tree. Some people like to think that these lines are like those on highway maps. The main branch is a interstate highway; each exit leads eventually to a neighborhood of local thoughts.

Overcoming Roadblocks

From time to time the note maker will encounter roadblocks. That is, it may be difficult to recall what needs to be added next to the diagram. Here are three solutions to such roadblocks:

1. Suggest they rotate from one branch or road to another. Often thinking about a different subtopic will help them start to remember again.

2. Suggest they visualize what they are trying to remember. This is especially helpful for visual thinkers. As they bring up an image, they will see things they may want to add to their diagram.

3. Suggest they use the Eight Trigger Questions. They will probably know these from the Yellow Pages advertisement. After looking at each branch of the recall diagram they should ask these questions. There is an excellent chance they will recall another significant piece of information.

Eight Trigger Questions

Who? What?	Persons or things
When? Where	Times, dates, seasons, past, present, future, locations, and places
Why? How?	Reasons and methods
Numbers?	How many, how much?
Feelings?	(Emotions are the glue of recall.)

APPLICATIONS

Here are a few examples of how these study tools may be used in content classrooms:

1. **Two-Color Diagram:** Often students waste time reviewing that which they already know. This was the case in the scenario about Johnny. The teacher taught Johnny to use the two-color diagram study method. After studying from his textbook and notes for 15 to 20 minutes, students should close their books. Then have them take 5 to 10 minutes to construct (in blue ink) a recall diagram of all they can remember. Pick up a red pen, open the textbooks, and have them find the information that they knew might be on the test but had trouble recalling. Then take 5 to 10 minutes to review the red ink. Make sure the students understand that what they have written in red is what they must spend most of their time studying. Repeat this process. (See Figure 1.10.)

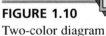

FIGURE 1.10
Two-color diagram

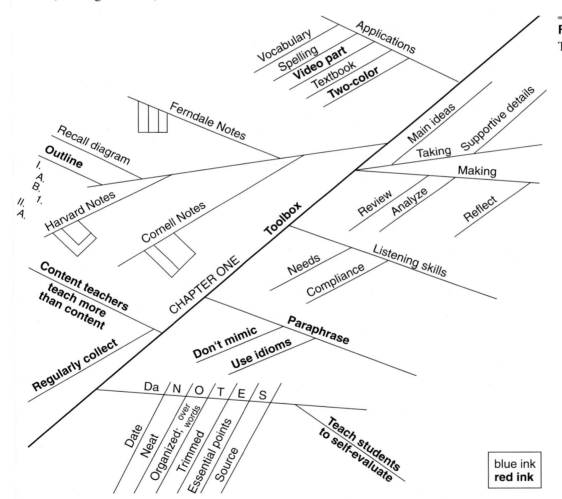

blue ink
red ink

2. **Organizational Essay Test**: Many students use recall diagrams before each question on an essay test. Taking 3 minutes to create a diagram before starting to answer the essay question helps them organize information. This method is especially helpful if students have been using the two-color diagram as a study tool. Many of these students report that their instructors tend to grade these preplanned essays more favorably. Perhaps this is because instructors can see, at a glance, how much students know about what they are writing.

3. **Pre/Post Individual Student Evaluation**: Many business people report that a recall diagram is a good system for organizing their thoughts before or after a business meeting. Teachers can use the same principle. During the first 5 minutes of class have students construct a recall diagram on assigned readings. Collect these before starting class activities. This can help the teacher sort out the students who are coming unprepared. It can also give the teacher a clear grasp of what information students have gained from their independent reading. The same idea may be applied after a lecture or Sustained Silent Reading (SSR) session. Give students 3 to 5 minutes to construct a recall diagram. Collect these. The instructor will gain valuable insights into what students are or *are not* retaining.

Note: Remember the coach at the beginning of the chapter? The point of collecting students' recall diagrams is to provide the teacher with information about how best to support them.

4. **Note Taking for Report Writing**: Given the assignment to complete a one- or two-page report using three sources, it is not unusual for students to copy directly from each source. Teachers reading these reports know when the student has changed sources; the writing style has changed. This plagiarism may be overcome by encouraging students to make notes that mesh the information from each of the three sources (in three different colors) on a single recall diagram. (See Figure 1.11.) By the way, there is software that can help students go from this diagram to an outline. If you are interested in learning more about this, turn ahead to Figure 1.12 (page 24).

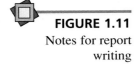

FIGURE 1.11

Notes for report writing

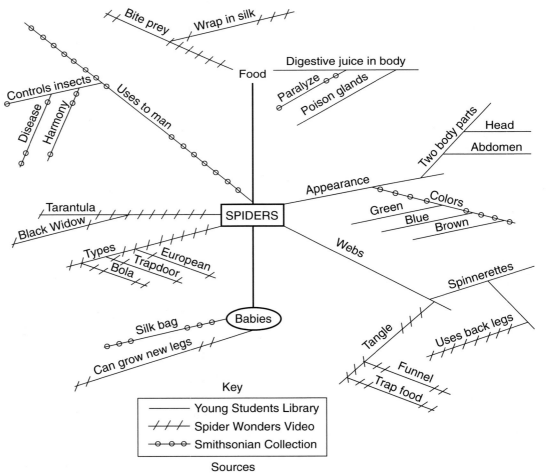

5. **Participation in Video Viewing**: As mentioned earlier, most students are experts at "watching" television without paying attention. However, most teachers want students to participate more actively in the viewing of educational programming. One way to do this is to inform students that they will be given 3 minutes at the end of the video to construct a recall diagram. Encourage them to start the diagram during the video if they see or hear anything that they wish to remember. At the end of the video, give students 5 minutes to complete their notes.

6. **Small-Group Discussion Facilitator**: Not all students feel comfortable verbally sharing their ideas in class or even in small discussion groups. One way to get them to listen and to use input from each other, thereby facilitating small-group discussion, is a modification of the two-color diagram. Each student should use their first color to create a recall diagram independently. Then, students share in small groups. Additional information from group members is recorded in the second color. The teacher can encourage participation by giving additional credit for lines in the second color ink. This provides students with a visual representation of the value of listening to each other's ideas.

7. **ELL/Foreign Language Practice**: Many teachers of English language learners (ELLs) as well as teachers of foreign languages use maps or diagrams to help students cluster words that are meaningful to each other. For example, a teacher of ELL might have students write the word *dog* on the main branch of their diagrams. Then the teacher gives students 3 to 5 minutes to diagram as many words as they can that are related to *dog*. These might include leash, paw, mouth, teeth, etc. Students can then share their answers and, in a second color of ink (see Figure 1.10), add input from their peers.

Note: Returning to the metaphor of teacher as coach, one role of the coach is to build confidence. There are several ways in which recall diagrams can build such confidence. Students feel better about themselves when they are allowed freedom in determining the organization and content of their diagrams. Often students will be negative about what they remember or what they read or hear in a lecture without really giving themselves the opportunity to find out what they have really gained. The diagram/map can be used as a tool to facilitate students' recall in an unthreatening way and build their confidence.

Notes as Connection Constructors

Sometimes students have trouble figuring out what belongs in the "My" column of their notes. Other times, students need additional help in making connections between the ideas in the notes they *take* and the reflection and analysis they *make* in their notes. Tovani (2000) explicitly directs students to make these connections. Here is an example of a note taking/making worksheet:

Text-to-Self Connection Constructors

Directions: Use the space provided to copy an important sentence or two from your text. Then write down the connection you made between the quotations and your own life. If you are confused by the quotes, try to explain what is confusing.

1. Text quote(s) and page number(s):

This reminds me of . . .
(Or) This confuses me because . . .

2. Text quote(s) and page number(s):

This reminds me of . . .
(Or) This confuses me because . . .

Elsner's DaNOTES: Student Self-Evaluation of Notes

Students need a means to self-evaluate the quality of their notes. Barbara Elsner, a teacher of English and Native American history at a local Washington state high school, developed the following system to help her students. Typically, students were encouraged to check each other's notes before submitting them to the teacher for further evaluation. Each component was worth one point. (Elsner originally named this "DNOTES," pronounced deeNOTES. However, her students affectionately renamed them "daaaahNOTES.")

Date

Neat Enough to Be Read After Three Days
If being checked by another person, the note maker must be able to say what was written.

Organized in an Acceptable Format
In many classes this means notes must either be taken as maps, diagrams, Cornell, Ferndale, or Harvard notes or as outlines or own words (paraphrased).

Trimmed
The notes contain only information that will be used; unnecessary words have been left out. This criterion was added to highlight the need to be selective about what students write down.

Essential Points Highlighted
Notes are underlined, circled, stars, highlighter/different color pen.

Source
This includes name of class, text, pages, or other source of information.

Scoring Recall Diagrams

As mentioned earlier, those teachers who teach their students how to take, make, and evaluate their notes, and **regularly collect** these notes, obtain invaluable input into their students' learning. Notes may be scored for form, quantity of ideas, and value of content. The students do the scoring for form and quantity. The teacher quickly scores for content accuracy and to get information about student understanding.

Scoring for Form: Students exchange their notes and use DaNOTES as a means for quick evaluation. Each element of the diagram is worth one point, for a total of six. For example, the students will get one point if they have the date, one point if their notes are neat enough to be read in 3 days, one point for organizing in their own words, one point for trimming down to only important information, one point for highlighting the essential points, and one point for the source.

Scoring for Quantity: While students are exchanging papers and grading for the above six points, have them count the number of slash lines beyond the main branch. All slash lines, whether a subordinate topic or supportive details, are to be counted. Have them write this number somewhere on the page and then circle it. Provide the following matrix (based upon 3 to 5 minutes of diagramming) for scoring:

Scoring Matrix for a 3–5 Minute Recall Diagram

4th–6th grade	7th grade + up	Rating	Points
12 + lines	20+ lines	Superior	4 points
9–11 lines	15–19 lines	Excellent	3 points
5–8 lines	10–14 lines	Good	2 points
2–5 lines	5–10 lines	Fair	1 point

This makes for a possible 10 points (6 points for DaNOTES and 4 points for quantity) per notes assignment. Notes then need to be evaluated by the teacher for content accuracy.

Scoring for Content: Once students have completed the above, the teacher is left the simple but important task of evaluating the content of the diagrams. This may be done by checking for essential content. Keep in mind that if nearly all the students are missing an important idea, this is an indication that it should be retaught in subsequent lessons.

Workshop 1.1

Note Taking and Making Practice

1. Individually create a page of notes on the content in this chapter.
2. Check your work using the DaNOTES strategy.
3. Share results with a classmate. Use a second-color pen to add ideas you have learned from this neighbor.
4. After whole-class discussion of problems and/or questions raised, have volunteers put their notes on the board or overhead.
5. Realize that everyone's notes will be different.

Outlining

Outlining is a way of logically organizing or categorizing information. It is the dual process of dividing and classifying that forces the reader to ferret out main ideas and their supporting details. Basically, there are three types of notations used in outlining: (1) a standard system of indentation using Roman numerals, capitals, and Arabic numbers; (2) a newer form that uses a numbering system; and (3) a simple bulleted system. In all three types, items closer to the left margin will be superordinate (above in importance) to items further from the margin, the subordinate ones. Learning to outline should begin in primary grades when students find the topic sentence for a short paragraph, then identify several items subordinate to the topic sentence. (Keep in mind that this may not always be the case.) Have students look over the whole category, then read the label and the topic sentence carefully, deciding on the logical order of items, and finally choosing a topic for the paragraph.

Standard Outline:

I. Main topic
- A. Subtopic
  - 1. Supporting detail
  - 2. Supporting detail
- B. Subtopic
- C. Subtopic
  - 1. Supporting detail
    - a. Explanatory detail
      - i. Further support
      - ii. Further support
    - b. Explanatory detail
  - 2. Supporting detail

II. Main topic, etc.

Numbering System:

1.0 Main topic
1.1 Subtopic
1.1.1 Supporting detail
1.1.1.1 Explanatory detail
1.1.1.1.1 Further support
2.0 Main topic

Bulleted System:

- Main topic
- Subtopic
  - Supporting detail
  - Supporting detail
- Subtopic
- Subtopic
  - Supporting detail
    - Explanatory detail
      - Further support
      - Further support
    - Explanatory detail
  - Supporting detail

- Main topic, etc.

The advantage of the standard system is that in appearance it is neater and less cluttered. An advantage of the numbering system is that it makes it easier to note outline headings on note cards. The bulleted system removes the need to use a numbering system at all.

For the body of the outline, there are two major styles: the sentence outline, which records complete sentences, and the topic outline, which uses only words and phrases.

Teaching Outlining Skills

Content teachers might wish to use the following sequence of steps to help their students outline what they have read in their texts:

1. First, provide students with a complete outline for one part of their text chapter. Have them compare the outline to the text, noting the relationships among the elements and the major ideas versus their supporting details. Encourage their questions. (This should be followed in all note taking/making methodologies as a first step.)

2. Next, give students another outline that has only labels for major sections (main and subtopics) and the number of subordinate details in the text. Have them fill in the missing points from the book. For example:

Chapter One: A Toolbox of Reading and Learning Strategies

    I. Taking and Making Notes

       A. Cornell Notes

          1.

          2.

       B. Ferndale and Harvard Notes

          1.

          2.

       C. Applications

          1.

    II. Recall Diagrams

       A. Overcoming Roadblocks

          1.

          2.

       B. Applications

          1. Two-Color Diagram

          2. Organizational Essay Test

          3.

          4.

3. From the next section of a chapter, supply students with a list of main topic headings and supporting information from their text. Have them place these in outline form. Go over the results in class.

4. From the next section of the chapter, supply students with outline form and numbers only. Have them fill in the blanks.

5. Have students outline the next section on their own. Make sure to leave time to compare these with others in class. Then compare with a teacher-made outline for the same section. This can be done on the board or overhead projector.

Those students who are unable to do the first two activities will need additional help with prerequisites for outlining: (1) Have students organize a series of objects into specific categories and explain their reasons for that organization; (2) find three or four main ideas in a section or chapter; and (3) return to the section or chapter and list or group details around these main ideas.

FROM THE CONTENT CLASSROOM

Notes Required

After taking the time to model and practice several note taking/making methods, a tenth grade honors biology teacher announced to class that from this date on, all students would be required to complete and turn in notes for each reading assignment she gave. This assignment earned a very large collective groan. In order to soothe student concerns, she announced that anyone who earned an "A-" or better on the next unit exam would be excused from this requirement.

Three weeks, several sets of notes, and one exam later, this teacher notified several students that their high scores on the exam earned them the right to no longer complete these notes. To her surprise all but one continued to complete notes for each reading. When asked why, one student responded, "I might want to be lazy, but not at the price of good grades. This method works, so I plan to continue to use it."

Using Technology to Improve Notes

Inspiration 7.0™ is a handy software tool (www.inspiration.com/) that combines the functions of a thought map and a standard outline. This software permits students to switch between the two formats. Students may begin their brainstorming in either view, moving back and forth as needed.

The thought-mapping application is helpful for visual learners or those who are just trying to throw thoughts onto the page and think about organizing them later. Once all the students' ideas are mapped out, they can add additional thoughts, notes, visual clues, and link-related information. If they get stuck within the current view, the program has several formats to organize their information, or they can switch into the outline view and work from there. Switching between views is as easy as the click of a button; there is no need to recopy all the information. (See Figure 1.12.)

The software has over 1,200 symbols and shapes to differentiate between main ideas, subpoints, and details. Students may make all the ideas from each level have the same shape or use picture icons for visual clues that reinforce their ideas.

Students may also import graphics and pictures from other sources. The program even offers a function to add text to the links between symbols to clarify the type of link it is. If students have web access, they can connect to the Internet directly from Inspiration and display active hyperlinks to other related information.

FIGURE 1.12

A Toolbox of Reading/Learning Strategies: A Cognitive map

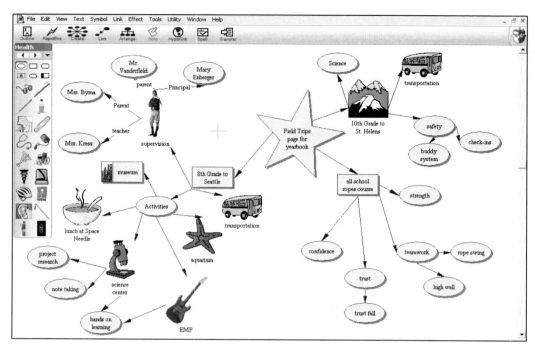

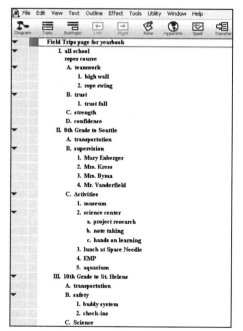

The outline view has options for adding topics, subtopics, and supporting details, changing the levels of importance or rearranging the order of the information. After working in Inspiration to brainstorm, organize, and outline, the software has a one-click option to transfer outlines into a Microsoft Word or Apple Works document. Students will appreciate that they need not recopy any of the data they have entered.*

---

*Authors would like to acknowledge the assistance from Eric Canfield for constructing the Inspiration diagrams in this chapter.

Teachers with access to a projection device could use this as a brainstorming tool with their students. Working in the thought-map view, teachers could enter student input and link their ideas and suggestions.

 ## Skills Needed for Good Note Taking and Making

Paraphrasing: Saying It in Your Own Words

As students advance through school, the content they learn becomes more substantial. Many teachers are frustrated because their students tend to copy and memorize. Often this is because students have not had explicit instruction and practice in paraphrasing. Paraphrasing can be divided into three steps: (1) reading or listening; (2) asking oneself what was read or heard; and (3) putting the above into one's own words.

Many teachers introduce and practice paraphrasing as a "sponge" or warm-up activity using idioms and/or proverbs as a means of demonstrating the difference between copying and paraphrasing. Here are some sample sentences teachers might read to their students with the understanding that the students' job was to put the meaning of the idioms into their own words.

---

1. Jane has a big job to do. Her dad asks her to stack a big pile of wood. She calls her friends to ask for help. After all, **many hands make light work.**

   (Answer: Work is easier if many people help.)

2. John is frustrated because the other members of his club are not trying very hard. He tells his dad who tells him, **"You can lead a horse to water but you can't make it drink."**

3. Mary's mother told her that she couldn't go to the 8:00 p.m. movie unless she finished all of her homework first. Mary finished her homework, but she did it **by the skin of her teeth.** When she got to the movie and found out that her friend had a date with the school athletic star, she became **green with envy.**

4. Daniel's dad took him to the store for an ice cream cone. There were so many flavors that Daniel couldn't decide. His dad was in a hurry. Finally Daniel's dad said, "Son, we have to go. **You have to fish or cut bait."**

5. Diane's father had died last year. Her mother worked two jobs and cared for Diane and her little brother. Diane's mother was prone to complain that she often **"could not see the forest for the trees"** and that she felt as if she was **"burning the candle at both ends."**

Once students understand the difference between copying and paraphrasing, the teacher should pause from time to time and ask students to paraphrase what she or another student has just said or read.

Summarizing with G.I.S.T.

One reason students tend to copy an entire paragraph into their notes is because they haven't been taught to summarize. Summarizing is not an easy task. To summarize a student must first determine if information needs to be included or excluded. Content must then be paraphrased and organized concisely. Here are two ways to teach students how to summarize.

G.I.S.T., which stands for Generating Interactions between Schemata and Text (Cunningham, 1982), is a method for teaching students to write progressively more condensed summaries of a selection. Here are the steps to follow:

- Choose a series of paragraphs from which to work. (To start, a series of five or six paragraphs with three to five sentences in each work best.)
- Ask the students to read the first sentence of the first paragraph and tell you what it says in 15 words or less. Write their summary on the board or project it onto a screen.
- Have students read the second sentence of the paragraph. Erase the first summary and ask students to summarize both sentences in 15 words or less.
- Repeat this with the third and fourth paragraphs. Discuss the idea of representing all important information in summary sentences.
- If students are getting the hang of this, have them read the last paragraph as a whole and summarize it in a sentence of no more than 15 words. If they aren't getting it, provide extra practice before going to this stage.
- Finally, when students are proficient at this as a group, ask them to provide summaries individually.

Learning to Summarize: Changing Narrative to Lyrical

One way to help students learn to summarize is to compare the process of summarizing to that of changing narrative text (a story) to lyrical text (poem, either free verse or rhymed). For example:

> I woke up to 20 degree below zero weather and dreaded the thought of the long blustery two-hour drive on the twisting New Hampshire roads. With the recent snow and icy roads I knew I needed to be especially careful. I carefully walked from my hotel lobby to the rental car. I was bundled to the hilt and saw that all the car windows were completely iced up. My door was frozen shut! I took the ice scraping tool given to me by the hotel and started the extensive brushing and scraping process. Brrr! I wish I had never left Florida.

101 words

> Waking up to 20 below
> Dreading the long drive on twisting roads
> With recent snow and ice
> Bundled to the hilt
> Carefully made my way to my car
> Windows iced, doors frozen
> Brushing, scraping—Brrr!
> Wish I never left Florida.

41 words

Workshop 1.2

Summarizing by Changing Narrative to Lyric

Get into pairs to complete this exercise:

- Write a paragraph about something that recently happened to you.
- Now look at that paragraph and remove any and all unnecessary words. (Our language is often very redundant.)
- Convert your narrative into a poem—either free verse or rhymed.

Abbreviations and Symbols

In elementary school students are often discouraged from using abbreviations. Perhaps this is because it is important to demonstrate that they know the correct spelling of the entire word or phrase. Or perhaps they feel that students are not truly learning how to read and write unless they know how to write the entire word or phrase.

The rigors of note taking require that students be able to use abbreviations. Many content teachers will create a bulletin board display of acceptable abbreviations and symbols for their content area. Students should know that they can also use their own abbreviations if explained the first time.

Here are a few suggestions for such a bulletin board:

1. Use symbols for commonly recurring connective or transitional words:

& → and	w/ → with	w/o → without	vs → against
∴ → therefore	= → equals	≠ → does not equal	

2. Whenever possible, use an apostrophe with the abbreviation:

gov't → government	am't → amount	educat'l → educational

3. Form the plural of a symbol or abbreviated word by adding "s":

chpts → chapters	co-ops → cooperatives	f s → frequencies

4. Use "g" to represent "ing" endings.

Decrg → decreasing	ckg → checking	estg → establishing

5. Eliminate final letters. Use just enough of the beginning of a word to form an easily recognizable abbreviation.

Biol → biological	info → information	intro → introduction
max → maximum	chem → chemistry	rep → repetition

FROM THE CONTENT CLASSROOM

Conspiracy Days

As part of a reading and study skills across the curriculum program (Simmers-Wolpow, Farrell, & Tonjes, 1991), teachers endeavored to teach several reading/study skills by means of an attention-grabbing device, "conspiracy days." On designated days, all faculty members "conspired" to teach and reinforce the same study skill in each area.

In a student survey, 82% of students valued knowing ways to take good notes, but only 42% expressed sufficient confidence in this skill. To address these concerns, the reading specialist and school principal created a series of skeletal lesson plans in all disciplines and then met with teachers during their preparation periods for assistance.

On five selected days, teachers took the first 10 minutes of each period to introduce and then reinforce paraphrasing, mapping, abbreviations, Ferndale and Harvard notes, and DaNotes. At the end of the week, the principal delivered a 10-minute talk to the entire school over the intercom while students took notes. Teachers then collected these notes, which they and the reading specialist evaluated, and feedback was given to students, teachers, and parents. Teaching these lessons, although repetitive, resulted in 91% of the student body achieving mastery in this skill. Just imagine—students coming to class on a conspiracy day and finding all classes teaching the same skill but using their own content area! It worked.

Listening and Following Directions

"If we were meant to talk more than listen we'd have two mouths."

—Anonymous

The Need

Students can take notes from a textbook without listening skills. However, taking notes during a lecture is contingent on being able to listen well. A longitudinal "Study Skills Needs Assessment" was completed by students, grades 8 through 12, and consistently indicated that students held the perception that success in secondary school was contingent on their ability to listen effectively and follow oral and written directions (Simmers-Wolpow, Farrell, & Tonjes, 1991). Occupational advisory groups in most secondary schools stress the importance of having high school graduates who can listen carefully, ask relevant questions, and then follow directions.

Reading and listening have similar subskills that include reading/listening to follow directions, finding main ideas, finding supporting details, distinguishing fact from opinion, visualizing, asking questions, making inferences, and/or determining point of view. However, comprehending what we have heard is often more difficult because the listener does not have the opportunity to reread.

Listening skills are often not taught explicitly as part of the regular school curriculum. Instead, most teachers have been trained to "tell them what we are going to tell them, tell them, and then tell them what we have told them." Teachers are often heard in faculty lunchrooms lamenting their students' inability to "follow a simple set of directions." If the solution to students' poor listening skills was repetition, would not the problem have been solved years ago?

Explicit instruction in listening skills, with specific application to content areas, is a necessary requisite for student learning in the classroom. These same skills can then be used by students as they read from their textbooks.

There is a saying: "Hearing is not listening; listening is not compliance." Whereas hearing is a natural ability and a physical process, listening requires the listener to focus his or her attention on what is being heard. Webster (1994) defines listening as the "conscious effort to hear; to listen closely." Listening also implies connecting with the speaker by attempting to make personal meaning from what is being said.

In some cultures, the process of telling and listening is sacred. Katz (1991), professor of Indian Social Work at Saskatchewan Indian Federated College, has eloquently described the connection between teller and listener as "symbolized by the process of listening to stories told by the elders so intently that the elders can 'hear' the listening and, therefore, fully tell the stories." Communication requires community. Telling requires listening, listening requires telling.

Often, when disciplining their children for not complying with their wishes, parents and teachers will ask: "Are you listening to me?" Is this what they mean to ask? Good listening is a skill that can and should be taught explicitly. While careful choice of words by the parent or teacher can lessen ambiguity for students, listening does not always mean compliance or agreement. In fact, careful listening sometimes leads to disagreement. When we ask, "Were you listening to me?" are we really meaning to ask "Why did you disobey me?" or, "Why don't you agree?" A great deal may be learned by listening intently to our students' answers to those questions.

Explicit Instruction in Listening Skills

The acquisition of skills should include an element of fun. Teachers can devise a series of listening skills/direction following puzzles. Puzzles should allow students to progress from the less intricate to the more complex. One such puzzle is provided in this chapter. (See Figure 1.13.) Within this format teachers can provide instruction and describe their expectations. This listening skills puzzle has the reader give each part of the directions one time and one time only. This is essential! The teacher may choose to alternate puzzles that require students to follow written directions.

FIGURE 1.13
Listening Skills
Puzzle #1: Teacher's
Instructions

Directions *(teacher reads to class)*

Directions: Please listen carefully. You will be given some oral directions to follow. The directions will be given once and only once. You must get them the first time.

The directions will be given in thirteen parts. If you miss or don't understand any one part of the directions, keep going. You may be able to fill in the missing part later. Are there any questions? (Teacher does not repeat directions but does answer questions relative to worksheet or directions.)

Part 1: Print the letter on the left side of the three-toed sloth in box number 9.

Part 2: Print the letter that is above the California condor in box 15.

Part 3: Print the letter that is between the addax's horns in box 7.

Part 4: Print the letter that is above the spotted owl in box 16.

Part 5: Print the letter to the left of the larger of the two brown hyenas in box 19.

Part 6: Lightly shade boxes 1 and 12.

Part 7: Lightly shade boxes 20, 21, and 22.

Part 8: Print the letter on the left side of the kakapo in boxes 5, 13, and 17.

Part 9: Print the letter to the right of the smaller of the two brown hyenas in boxes 4 and 11.

Part 10: Print the letter on the right side of the spotted owl in boxes 3, 6, and 14.

Part 11: Print the letter on the right side of the three-toed sloth in boxes 2, 8, and 10.

Part 12: Print the letter to the left of the California condor in box 18.

Part 13: Print your first and last name on top of the line above the larger of the two brown hyenas.

Discussion questions:

1. Did you guess what the phrase was going to be before it was finished?

2. Did unfamiliar words like "addax" and "kakapo" make it harder to follow the directions?

3. What did you learn from this puzzle about following directions?

Listening Skills Puzzle #1: Student Worksheet

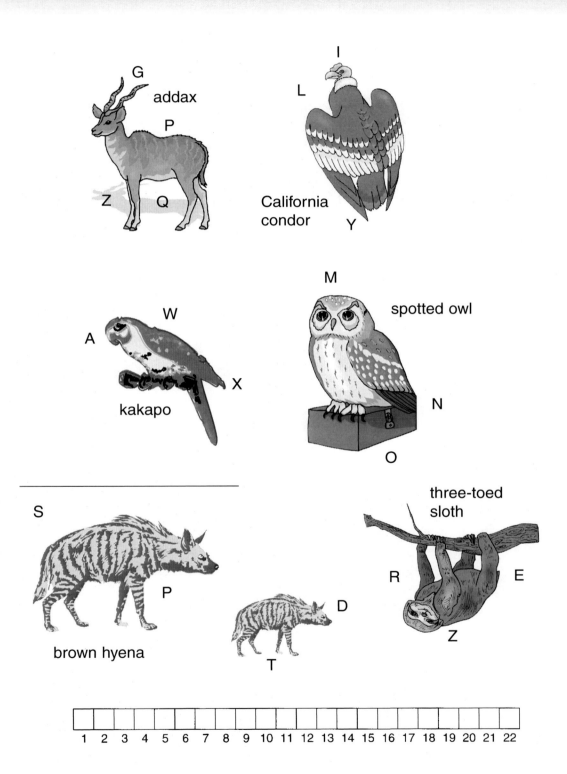

Once students demonstrate mastery of this type of puzzle, try giving short lectures. Prior to beginning the lecture, inform students that they may take notes, and at the conclusion of the lecture, they will have an "open-note" quiz. Start with a lecture on the differences between "skillful and unskilled listeners." Here are some ideas to include in your lecture:

Skillful Listeners	Unskilled Listeners
Watch for the speaker's nonverbal cues while speaker is talking.	Watch to see what other classmates are wearing while the speaker is talking.
Get motivated. They listen for the reason that something is being said.	Don't care. The reason the speaker is speaking is not important.
Anticipate what the speaker may say next.	Think about what they will say after the speaker is done.
Maintain eye contact, nod, and/or smile to let the speaker know that they are listening.	Stare into space, nod off, smile at the wrong times, and give the speaker the impression that they aren't listening.
Suspend their own opinions until they feel they understand the viewpoint of the speaker.	Form opinions before hearing the entire argument of the speaker.
Take/make notes to remember what has been said.	Send notes to friends about what they will be doing after school.

Once you have given a lecture about listening, try a short lecture on something they need to know for the next test. Follow this short lecture with an open note quiz so that students begin to connect these two skills with success in your classroom. A strategy to help students practice listening and note taking skills while reviewing the content of a chapter or lesson is Give One, Get One. (See Workshop 1.4.)

When giving students practice in following oral or written directions, include tasks that require them to experiment, assemble, and/or perform. **Experimental** directions require students to make or solve a problem or practice the application of a principle. (One example of this is setting up a lab experiment in a science class or learning an algorithm in a math class.) **Assembling** directions require students to make or create an object. (Having students assemble something to eat is usually a big favorite. Following the printed directions to assemble a crib has confounded more than one soon-to-be parent.) **Performing** directions require students to focus on the performance of a task rather than its product. Most oral directions in PE classes are given in this manner as is following the directions given to use Inspiration software.

Constructing Listening Puzzles	**Workshop 1.3**
Form small groups according to content interests. Construct one listening and one written directions puzzle to be solved in each of your disciplines. Make sure one of each of the puzzles involves following directions to conduct and experiment, assemble something, or perform a task. Try these out on another group for feedback.	

Workshop 1.4

Give One, Get One

This workshop activity works best in groups of 10 or more. It provides excellent opportunities to practice note taking/making, paraphrasing, summarizing, and listening skills.

1. Take 5 to10 minutes and review the content of this chapter.
2. Turn to Figure 1.14 (page 35). Think of an idea or application that you believe is worthy of remembering or using from this chapter. It might be an idea that you already knew was helpful. It might be an application that you would like to try. Or it might be something you want to make sure to integrate into your content instruction with your students.
3. Paraphrase or summarize that idea and write it into one of the boxes. Now think of a second idea and write it into another box. Continue with as many ideas into as many boxes as you can for a total of 10 minutes.
4. Now it is time to visit with your class colleagues. Taking your worksheet with you, take 10 to 15 minutes and approach a colleague. *Give* them one of your ideas; that is, share an idea from your page. If your colleague doesn't already have that idea, then encourage them to write it down.
5. Now it is time to practice your listening and note taking strategies. *Get* an idea from a colleague; that is, listen to the ideas that they have written and then write one into one of your empty boxes.
6. Continue these processes until you have talked with each of your colleagues or your page is full.

Cinquain as Summary

Notes
Recording Meanings
Listening, Anticipating, Connecting
Capable, Thorough, Determined, Confident
Learning Tools

Summary

National standards call for educators to understand and use "a variety of instructional strategies to encourage students' development of critical thinking, problem solving, and performance skills." They also call for educators to help students learn how "to gather, evaluate, and synthesize data from a variety of sources." Techniques for taking and making notes are essential to reach these standards. So are the requisite skills of paraphrasing, summarizing, and listening attentively.

Different ways to make and take notes include Cornell, which uses a left-hand column for writing key words and phrases that serve as clues for later review; the Ferndale System, which adds a right-hand column labeled "My" column, where students reflect and personalize notes; and the Harvard System, where the third column is added to the bottom of the page. Connection constructor worksheets may be used to help students make text-to-reader connections for the "My" column. Recall Diagrams are study tools to organize and recall information. They are most effective when students are encouraged to record what they recall in whatever structure works best for them. When roadblocks appear on these thought maps, note makers may either rotate from one side to another, visualize or ask "trigger questions." DaNOTES is a self- or peer-evaluation

 **FIGURE 1.14**

Give One, Get One

Note taking/making, paraphrasing, summarizing, and listening skills.

system that helps students to assess the quality of their own notes, looking at form and quality. If the solution to students' poor listening skills was repetition, teachers would have solved this problem years ago. Instead, explicit instruction in this skill, tied to clearly stated expectations and relevant content, can provide a solution.

References and Recommended Readings

Alvermann, D. (1991). The discussion web: A graphic aid for learning across the curriculum. *The Reading Teacher, 45,* 92–99.

Alvermann, D., & Hayes, D. (1986). Instructional strategies that induce useful study skills. In E. Dishner, T. Bean, J. Readance, & D. Moore (Eds.), *Reading in the content areas: Improving classroom instruction.* Dubuque, IA: Kendall/Hunt.

Amos, N., & Waters, G. (1985). A nation at risk: The imperative for effective communication. *Journal of Business Education, 60* (5), 184–187.

Amundson, K. (1995). *Brush up your study skills: Tips for students and parents.* Arlington, VA: American Association of School Administrators.

Anderson, T. H., & Armbruster, B. (1984). Studying. In P. D. Pearson, R. Barr, M. L. Kamil, & P. Mosenthal (Eds.), *Handbook of reading research* (pp. 657–679). New York: Longman.

Anderson-Inman, L. (1996). Computer-assisted outlining: Information organization made easy. *Journal of Adolescent and Adult Literacy, 39* (4), 316–320.

Armbuster, B. (2000). Taking notes from lectures. In R. Flippo & D. Caverly (Eds.), *Handbook of college reading and study strategy research* (pp. 175–179). Mahway, NJ: Erlbaum.

Berne, J. E. (2004). Listening comprehension strategies: A review of the literature. *Foreign Language Annals, 37* (4), 521–533.

Burkle, C., & Marshak, D. (1980). *HM study skills program, level I: Student text.* Arlington, VA: National Association of Elementary School Principals.

Castallo, R. (1976). Listening guide—A first step towards notetaking and listening skills. *Journal of Reading, 19* (4), 289–290.

Council of Chief State School Officers. (2005). INTASC Standards. Retrieved March 21, 2005, from http://www.ccsso.org/projects/Interstate_New_Teacher_Assessment_and_Support_Consortium/

Cunningham, J. (1982). Generating interactions between schemata and text. In J. Niles & L. Harris (Eds.), *New inquiries in reading research and instruction, Thirty-first Yearbook of the National Reading Conference* (pp. 42–47). Washington DC: National Reading Conference.

Devine, T. (1978). Listening: What do we know after fifty years of research and theorizing. *Journal of Reading, 21,* 296–304.

Fishman, S. (1997). Student writing in philosophy: A sketch of five techniques. *New Directions for Teaching and Learning, 69,* 53–66.

Hoover, J. (1993). Helping parents develop a home-based study skills program. *Intervention in School and Clinic, 28* (4), 238–245.

Hughes, C., & Suritsky, S. (1993). Notetaking skills and strategies for students with learning disabilities. *Preventing School Failure, 38* (1), 7–11.

International Reading Association/National Council of Teachers of English (1996). *Standards for the English language arts.* Urbana, IL: Authors.

James, A., & Kratz, D. (1995). *Effective listening skills.* Boston: McGraw-Hill.

Katz, R., & St. Dennis, V. (1991). Teacher as healer. *Journal of Indigenous Studies, 2* (2), 24–36.

Lazarus, B. (1996). Flexible skeletons: Guided notes for adolescents with mild disabilities. *Teaching Exceptional Children, 28* (3), 36–40.

Lim, P. L., & Smalzer, W. (1996). *Noteworthy: Listening and note taking skills (*2nd ed.). Boston: Heinle & Heinle Publications.

Luckie, W., Smethurst, W., & Huntley, S. (1999). *Study power workbook: Exercises in study skills to improve your learning and your grades.* Cambridge, MA: Brookline Books.

Lynch, T. (2004). *Study listening student's book: A course in listening to lectures and note taking.* Cambridge, UK: Cambridge University Press.

Maida, P. (1995). Reading and note-taking prior to instructions. *Mathematics Teacher, 88* (6), 470–473.

Novak, J. D. (1998). *Learning, creating and using knowledge: Concept maps as facilitative tools in schools and corporations.* Mahway, NJ: Erlbaum.

Pauk, W. (1989). *How to study in college* (4th ed.). Boston: Houghton Mifflin.

Simmers-Wolpow, R., Farrell, D., & Tonjes, M. (1991). Implementing a secondary reading/study skills program across the disciplines. *Journal of Reading, 34* (8), 590–594.

Tovani, C. (2000). *I read it, but I don't get it: Comprehension strategies for adolescent readers.* Portland, ME: Stenhouse.

Wiekel, B. (1991). High school review: Listening skills. *Social Studies Review, 30* (2) 28–30.

Wood, J. (1991). Study skills: Enhancing success. *Ohio Reading Teacher, 26* (1), 18–21.

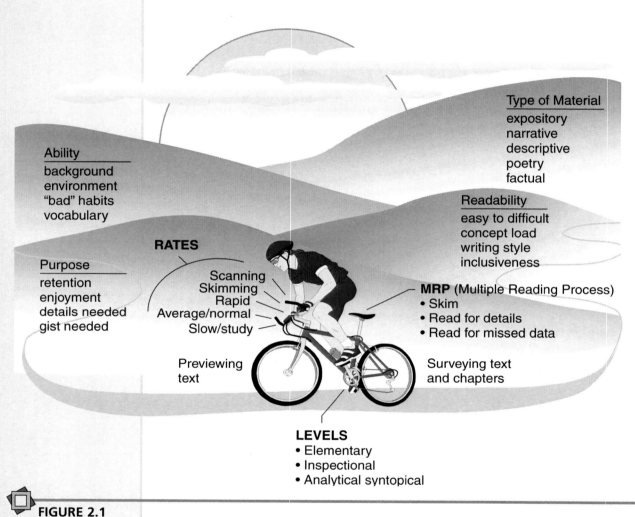

Ability
background
environment
"bad" habits
vocabulary

Purpose
retention
enjoyment
details needed
gist needed

RATES
Scanning
Skimming
Rapid
Average/normal
Slow/study

Previewing
text

Type of Material
expository
narrative
descriptive
poetry
factual

Readability
easy to difficult
concept load
writing style
inclusiveness

MRP (Multiple Reading Process)
• Skim
• Read for details
• Read for missed data

Surveying text
and chapters

LEVELS
• Elementary
• Inspectional
• Analytical syntopical

FIGURE 2.1
Reading Rate Adaptability: A Cognitive Map

Reading Rate Adaptability

Outline

- Anticipatory and Review Questions
- A Sampling of National Performance Standards
- Introduction
- Levels and Rates
  - The Sprockets and Gears
    - The Sprockets: Adler's Levels of Reading
    - The Gears: Zintz's Reading Rates
  - Why Read Faster?
  - Misconceptions That Hold Us Back
- From the Content Classroom: Reading Elephants
- The Eye and Mind Connection
  - Reading Depends Upon What Readers Already Know
  - Reading Requires Continual Rapid Eye Movements
  - When Scanning, Readers Must Be Fast and Selective
  - Lessening Eye Fatigue
    - *Workshop 2.1: Word Recognition*
    - *Workshop 2.2: Word Discrimination and Phrase Recognition*
  - Visual Discrimination

- *Workshop 2.3: Phrase Comprehension*
- The Multiple Reading Process (MRP)
  - Stage One: Previewing or Pre-Reading
  - Stage Two: Reading
  - Stage Three: Post-Viewing or Post-Reading
- From the Content Classroom: Reading Love Letters
  - *Workshop 2.4: The MRP Applied—"Quality Not Quantity" by Mary Gillette*
- The Eight Steps to Previewing a Large Text
  - Using the Eight-Step Preview Method to Teach for Multicultural Understanding
- From the Content Classroom: MRP in Action
  - Surveying Student Texts
    - *Workshop 2.5: A Preview Guide for This Book—ICL 5*
- Cinquain as Summary
- Summary
- From the Pages of Our Lives: *A Weekend with My Grandfather*
- Answer Keys
- References and Recommended Readings

"Some books are to be tasted, others to be swallowed, and some few to be chewed and digested."

Sir Francis Bacon

"I am not a speed reader. I am a speed understander."

Isaac Asimov

Anticipatory and Review Questions

Literal

1. What are the three stages of the Multiple Reading Process?

2. According to Adler, what are the four levels of reading?

Interpretative/Applied

3. How might you integrate the three stages of the Multiple Reading Process into reading assignments for one of your classes?

Evaluative/Critical

4. A student must write a paper on a controversial topic on which she has gathered a wealth of material, including more than one dozen books and magazine articles. The opinions in each of these texts vary greatly. Finally, she finds one thick book that presents a number of points of view. Should she read the one book that contains multiple viewpoints? Or should she pre-read the more than one dozen books and choose sections to read thoroughly? What do you think? Why?

5. Explain why the following three statements are interdependent:
   a. Reading comprehension depends upon what the reader already knows.
   b. Reading requires continual rapid eye movements.
   c. When scanning, reading must be fast and selective.

Creative/Personal

6. How might the ability to rapidly skim and scan a number of books on a subject add meaning to or improve the quality of your life?

7. Have you ever decided not to read a book for pleasure because it was too thick (too many pages)? How might having strong rate adaptability skills have changed your decision?

A Sampling of National Performance Standards

- Students read a wide range of print and nonprint texts to build an understanding of texts, of themselves, and of the cultures of the United States and the world; to acquire new information; to respond to the needs and demands of society and the workplace; and for personal fulfillment. . . . (International Reading Association/National Council of Teachers of English, 1996, p. 27).
- The teacher uses multiple teaching and learning strategies to engage students in active learning opportunities that promote the development of critical thinking, problem solving, and performance capabilities and that help students assume responsibility for identifying and using learning resources (Council of Chief State School Officers, 2005).
- The student understands and uses different skills and strategies to read. To meet this standard, the student will read fluently, adjusting reading for purpose and material (Office of the Superintendent of Public Instruction, 2005).

Introduction

Have you ever ridden a one-speed bike? Push down on the pedals and you go forward; push back and you apply the brakes. These one-speed bikes are excellent for riding leisurely on the beach or on level terrain. However, an 18-speed bike is far more easily adapted to riding on a mountain trail. The experienced rider can shift sprockets (the small wheels with tooth-like projections attached to the pedal to engage the links of the chain) and gears (the small wheels attached to the rear axle) to adjust the amount of force needed to pedal the most challenging of mountain grades. One might say that an 18-speed bike is more *adaptable* to difficult terrain because the amount of pressure needed to push the pedal can be adjusted easily to suit the purpose of the rider. (See Figure 2.1.)

Readers who shift sprockets and gears to adapt to changes in the terrain of their text employ **reading rate adaptability**. Thus, reading rate adaptability is the ability to adjust levels and rates of reading in order to respond to the purpose, type, and difficulty of the text. In the pages that follow, you will become familiar with four "sprockets"—Mortimer Adler's levels of reading, and five commensurate "gears"—Zintz's reading rates. Through the completion of a series of workshop activities, you will be given the opportunity to experiment with pedaling in various combinations of these levels and rates, thus increasing your abilities to handle the changing terrain of text more easily. Next you will be introduced to the concept of the "multiple reading process" and strategies for previewing a book. The importance of these approaches to your work with diverse student populations will be explained. Finally, these methods of reading rate adaptability will be applied to the content reading challenges that your students face on a daily basis.

 Levels and Rates

The Sprockets and Gears

The Sprockets: Adler's Levels of Reading

In the classic *How to Read a Book*, Adler (1940) describes four levels of reading: elementary, inspectional, analytical, and syntopical. Here is a synopsis of the essence of each level:

1. *Elementary:* Also called rudimentary, basic, or initial reading, elementary reading is the type of reading that is taught in the primary school. When we read on the elementary level we use word attack skills to decode symbols, blending their sounds to form words. When we don't know the meaning of new words, we take time to study the context in which they appear. More proficient readers resort back to elementary reading whenever we encounter new vocabulary. This is most likely to happen when we are reading with content with which we have a very limited background.

Note: Remember, many English language learners must resort to this reading level when they are reading in English. Adler's higher levels of reading are dependent on language skills that ELL students may have when reading in their first language, but are just beginning to develop in English.

2. *Inspectional:* Also called skimming and scanning, speed reading, pre-reading, previewing, and/or rapid reading, inspectional reading involves searching text for

main ideas and then organizing these ideas to activate prior knowledge about the text. When reading in this gear, readers search the entire text quickly. While reading in the inspectional mode, students do not stop to look up those words or ideas they don't understand. This allows them to get the big picture of the meaning. What they do comprehend, even if less than 50%, will help later when reading in the analytic gear.

3. *Analytical:* Whereas inspectional reading is the best and most complete reading one can do in a limited time, analytical reading is the best and most complete reading that is possible given unlimited time. Analytical reading is done for the sake of understanding. Good books need to be read and reread analytically because their meaning changes as readers develop insight from experience and rereadings. Perhaps analytical reading is what Sir Francis Bacon meant when he said that some few books are to be "chewed and digested."

4. *Syntopical:* Also called comparative reading, syntopical reading requires the reader to creatively relate the concepts of several works to one another and to the subject about which they revolve. When reading at the syntopical gear, readers construct an analysis of the text that is not present in any individual book.

The Gears: Zintz's Reading Rates

Reading rates are determined in part by the material itself and the purpose for which it is being read. The ideal is not merely to be able to read faster, but to be able to read at different speeds and adjust speed in order to most efficiently understand the material. As Asimov explains, "I am not a speed reader, I am a speed understander."

"Speed understanders" adjust their rate to the terrain of the text. Every book, no matter how difficult, contains interstitial (filler) material that can and should be read quickly. Every good book also contains content that is difficult to understand and should therefore be read more slowly, and read several times. Most important, good literature should be read slowly to savor the language and imagery.

The various rates of reading can be arbitrarily broken into five types. Reading rates are measured in words per minute (wpm). Actual rates are only approximations.

1. Analytic/evaluative reading   50–250 wpm
2. Personal reading   250–350 wpm
3. Rapid reading   350–800 wpm
4. Skimming   800 wpm–up
5. Scanning   1,000 wpm–up

Skimming involves a very rapid form of overviewing to get the gist, in which unneeded information is skipped. Scanning is the rapid search of text for specific details. Obviously, at rates of 800 words per minute the reader does not consciously focus on every word.

When effective readers come to an "incline" in reading material (a place where the text becomes difficult), they shift to a lower gear and slow their rate. New vocabulary may cause them to shift sprockets as well from the analytic to the elementary level. However, as soon as these readers come to a downhill portion (which is easier to understand and thus less demanding of their energy) they quickly "shift up" to higher rates and levels.

Commercial software companies that advertise that their programs will "double or triple" one's average rate of reading often use a misleading ploy. Average word-per-minute (wpm) rates are found by dividing the total number of words read by the total number of minutes. However, this computation only includes time spent reading. It does not include time to think about what has been read, or time spent answering comprehension questions. Many of these programs help readers learn to skim and scan more effectively, however, time will still be needed to reflect upon what has been read. In the end, for a program to be effective, it must be able to help the reader learn to adjust gears and sprockets to travel through text efficiently.

While we're on the topic of misleading ploys, mechanical devices, such as pacing machines, or software that shows text on the screen at different rates, have been shown to be problematic for several reasons:

1. Although reading rate may be increased, gains are not necessarily lasting. Once the pacing device is removed, speed tends to decrease.

2. An increased rate using a machine does not automatically transfer to regular print material.

3. Motivated reading with a clear purpose in mind can improve rate as much as any mechanical device.

Why Read Faster?

We all have a wealth of reading material that we are required to read each day. Being able to read faster when we choose, or slower when it is appropriate, is an important skill to have. Here are a few of the reasons why adaptability is so important:

1. *Saves time.* If students who read 2 hours a day increase their efficiency by just 25%, it will give each of them 3 extra hours of free time per week. This is an excellent motivator.

2. *Helps in remembering.* Readers who let themselves get bogged down in word-by-word reading may, with longer paragraphs, take so long to reach the end of a passage that they forget what was written at the beginning.

3. *Improves comprehension.* This comes with continual practice with a variety of texts. The very slow reader is often the one who opts not to read for pleasure because of the time and effort it takes, and thus gets little practice.

4. *Improves concentration.* When driving, have you ever noticed that if you drive at exactly the same speed for a long period of time you start to lose concentration or become drowsy? Being stuck in one routine can affect your concentration. On the other hand, varying your reading rate can help you concentrate on the task at hand.

Misconceptions That Hold Us Back

1. *True Reading Must Be Done Word-for-Word.* We may have started to learn to read by learning letters. Then we may have learned to read whole words. Then someone told us that we had better not skip any words. It is only natural to read in phrases, because this is how we make sense of groups of words like "ice cream" and "peanut butter."

2. *All Parts of a Book Are of Equal Value.* Perhaps they are of equal value to the author, but are they to you, the reader? Efficient readers make conscious choices about which parts of a book they will read several times analytically, and which parts are only worthy of a quick skim and scan. These choices are based on the purpose for reading.

3. *If We Want to Get Good Comprehension, We Need to Read a Book or Chapter from Beginning to the End.* This may be true if the purpose of our reading is pleasure.

On the other hand, if our goal is to learn content from a nonfiction book, we should read a book the same way an author writes it. Start with an outline (table of contents), skim the ending chapters first, the introductory chapters next, and then choose to read carefully from the parts that match your purpose.

4. *I'm Not a Good Reader Unless I Understand All of What I Read the First Time I Read It.* Some readers define a good book as one that needs to be read many times to get it all. If it is a good book, you will never get it all. A good book merits many readings.

FROM THE CONTENT CLASSROOM

Reading Elephants

One group of middle school students asked their teacher why they should have to learn to read materials in several different ways. They said that their teachers had taught them to read every word and make sure they pronounced them correctly. They felt that inspectional reading was cheating and that only by reading a book from beginning to end could they really understand what the writer intends. Their teacher responded with this parable, probably an adaptation of John Godfrey Saxe's (1899) "The Blind Men and the Elephant":

> A special education teacher once took six blind students to the zoo. Upon arrival, the zookeeper offered to introduce them to a very docile elephant. Having never experienced such an animal, the children were very excited. The first child was led to the front of the elephant where she touched its trunk. After a few exhilarating moments this student ran back to her teacher exclaiming that an elephant was very much like a "big fire hose." The second child was escorted to the elephant by the zookeeper and happened upon the elephant's legs. When he returned to his teacher, he claimed that an elephant was very much like a tree. The third child was escorted to the elephant and happened to brush against the elephant's massive and sturdy side. She returned to her teacher claiming that an elephant was like a wall. The fourth child felt the elephant's ear and returned to claim that an elephant was like a huge fan. The fifth child touched the elephant's tusk and returned to claim that an elephant was very much like a spear. The sixth child felt the elephant's tail and returned asserting that an elephant was like a rope.

Having shared this story, the middle school teacher asked: "How can the special education teacher help her blind children to understand what an elephant really is?" Her middle school students agreed that the blind children needed to learn that an elephant was the sum of all of its parts. Misunderstanding was the result of the blind students guessing what an elephant was before they had all of the information.

The middle school teacher explained that the same problem could happen when they are asked to read a long passage from a book. When first starting to read an elephant-sized chapter, they may think they are reading about fire hoses, then about trees, walls, fans, and ropes. It is by using the inspectional reading sprocket that they can truly understand what the elephant, or their book, is about.

Image © Clipart.com

The Eye and Mind Connection

No single chapter can provide a comprehensive physiology of the visual system, nor can it provide a comprehensive list of characteristics of eye-mind function that make critical differences when reading. For a summary of these, see Smith (1988, pp. 64-86).

However, three important implications from such studies pertain to reading effectively:

- Reading depends on what readers already know (their background knowledge).
- Reading requires continual rapid eye movements.
- When scanning, reading must be both fast and selective.

Reading Depends Upon What Readers Already Know

With our eyes we look at the world. We collect information for our minds. However, it is in our minds that decide what we are to look for and how we see it. Our minds' perceptual decisions are based only in part on the information provided by our eyes. The mind also depends greatly upon the knowledge that we already possess about a subject. The less background information available in the mind, the more visual information is required. For example, it is easier to read letters on a street sign when they are arranged into meaningful words and phrases than the same size letters arranged in a meaningless order on an optometrist's eye chart. Given the above, can you see why a computer game enthusiast might be able to read a "cheat sheet" faster than an engineer who has never seen one? Or why a Tejano music enthusiast could read the jacket of a Salina album more quickly than an expert on Mozart?

Consider what is involved in learning to read piano music. At first, we tend to focus on one clef at a time, but with time, we are able to read two lines of music at the same time. Orchestra conductors learn to sight-read entire pages of music at a glance. When a reader is first learning to read in elementary school, he or she must focus on one word at a time. However, as readers' skills develop, they are able to train themselves to scan larger areas of print, that is, to learn to read on the inspectional level, shifting back and forth between levels as needed.

Reading Requires Continual Rapid Eye Movements

Picture in your mind da Vinci's famous painting the *Mona Lisa*. Close your eyes and look at the features of her face—her eyes, nose, hair, her famous smile, etc. Do it now.

Having done so, consider how you looked at her face. Most probably, your eyes did not systematically scan one line at a time from left to right. Nor did they roll about uncontrollably. Nor did they lock in exclusively on any one point or feature for an excessive amount of time.

Those who study the physiology of vision tell us that motion is essential for seeing. If the same image is held on the retina for too long a time, perception disappears. Hence, rapid eye jumps, or fixations, from one position or focus to another, are necessary for accurate perception of the words that we read. Spending too much time per fixation can lead to poor perception.

When Scanning, Reading Must Be Fast and Selective

Eye fixations are guided by the information our minds receive by processing the images on the periphery of the point of focus. When skilled individuals read from the narrow columns of a newspaper, you would see they rarely make more than one fixation per line and may skip lines while reading down the page. Were these same readers to fix-ate on a few letters or even a whole word at a time, not only would perceptual accura-cy be compromised, but the meaning of the text would be reduced. Individuals with strong reading skills, who choose to read slower than 200 words per minute, are reduc-ing words to isolated units rather than meaningful sentences and paragraphs. Limitations of memory can prevent comprehension of these isolated words. Hence, the sage old advice to "slow down and be careful to examine every word closely" often leads to confusion, not comprehension. However, just moving our eyes faster does not help either.

When presented with multiple pages of text, the mind can easily become inundat-ed by visual information. One secret to successful reading rate adaptability is not to read indiscriminately but to sample from the text. The mind must make maximum use of what it already knows to direct the eyes to locate the parts of the text that convey the meaning. Where mature readers will employ but one or two fixations to comprehend the four word phrase "The United States of America," beginning readers will require five or six fixations to read the same phrase. The mature readers require fewer fixations because of the prior knowledge they bring to the task. (Interestingly enough, many spe-cial needs students, with trouble maintaining attention over longer periods of time, experience high levels of success when rapidly scanning for information. Perhaps this is due, in part, to their abilities to remember in small chunks of time. Imagine the impact of helping such a student build on this strength!)

If you are like most adult readers, the formal instruction you received in reading was primarily at the elementary levels. Practice in reading at the inspectional level was rare. What follows are a number of practice exercises designed to help develop your abilities to read at the inspectional level. We hope you will approach them as fun oppor-tunities to practice shifting sprockets and gears.

Lessening Eye Fatigue

Speed without accuracy is dangerous. Before undertaking the next workshop in which you are asked to discriminate among similar-looking words, let us examine the nature of print in English.

Look at the sentences written in Figure 2.1. They are the same, except, that in one sentence the top half of the print has been blotted out, and in the second, the bottom half has been blocked. Which half of the sentence (top or bottom) contains the most dis-criminative stimuli that you the reader needs to decode the phrase?

Yes, most of the discriminative stimuli are in the top half of the line of print. This is why it is important to place books on an incline when reading. It is important to locate the part of the line that has the most important information closest to the point of focus of the reader. This will decrease eye fatigue.

FIGURE 2.1

Frank's little brother attends high school.

Frank's little brother attends high school

Name _____   Date _____

 Workshop 2.1

Word Recognition

This workshop is divided into parts "A" and "B." Use part "A" to establish a baseline for yourself.

Part A—Skimming and Scanning for Word Recognition

Directions: For each group of words in this exercise there is a key word. For the first group the word is ***density***. Scan the two lines of words to the right of ***density*** and count how often it occurs. Write this number in the right-hand margin. In the next group, do the same for the word ***format*** and so on. Don't forget that the key word may appear several times. Remember that there is a new key word for each group.

You need to recognize the number of times a word is repeated. There is no content to "comprehend." Hence, you needn't limit yourself to reading solely from left to right, or one line at a time. When you are done, check your answers with the answer key at the end of the chapter.

Goal Time: 2 minutes or less

density
cabin, dense, person, density, rotten, poster, rat, board, instrument, poor,
density, ready, floor, wheel, city, density   _____

format
first, format, mat, hound, formula, anger, format, cat, matter, rug, fortress,
system, actually, factual, absence, poster   _____

readability
possible, finally, kindly, maybe, readability, further, confusion, readability,
ready, ignition, person, moderate, contradiction, middle, effrontery, readability _____

lexical
plain, obvious, grammar, lofty, left, pest, chevron, lexical, people, knife,
pencil, sample, age, asterisk, stairs, bring   _____

criteria
criteria, cafeteria, orange, circus, fortunate, extra, talk, criteria, taught, lesson,
criteria, perfect, slack, genius, mildly, criteria   _____

reader
speed, car, book, lamp, compare, action, figment, draw, child, hide, word, seek,
reader, normal, courage, reader   _____

syntax
revenue, rhetoric, aural, indigenous, system, gravity, world, syntax, syncopate,
security, belief, season, type, detective, celebrate, taxing   _____

cloze
settle, cloze, bridge, cream, close, tenable, team, cloze, zip, reckon, collate,
clap, floral, senile, bushel, cloze   _____

diagnosis

> defective, diagnosis, hypnosis, celebration, artificial, disguise, algebra, diagnosis, detail, chosen, limpid, diagram, genial, diagnosis, crystal, mend _____

validity

> clarity, informal, normal, levity, select, canine, hospitality, decimate, floral, validity, purify, city, validity, measure, pure, nonsense _____

equivalent

> equal, reliable, quality, cringe, vengeance, charter, value, destroy, tradition, type, equivalent, throat, quiver, democracy, valet, wisdom _____

assessment

> access, mental, assessment, willing, happy, assessment, assess, taxes, attitude, test, assessment, mediate, friendly, mild, encampment, assessment _____

acronyms

> hymnal, sad, acrid, acronyms, etymology, ability, fictions, acronyms, rat, rugged, acronyms, select, computer, acronyms, foal, brother _____

amelioration

> three, amelioration, strategies, happy, west, paper, change, radio, handy, corruption, amelioration, cup, instruct, time, budget, second _____

denotations

> connotate, caption, seasons, marvelous, beware, excise, action, ordinary, allowed, time, denotations, controllable, black, endure, often, black _____

connotations

> misery, security, connotations, favor, destroy, pencil, connotations, crystal, brick, connotations, mediation, foam, integrate, diagnosis, derange, fair _____

pejoration

> perfection, sicken, mutilate, decimal, fictive, tiny, dimple, fortress, mediation, effect, infringe, barter, pejoration, computation, less, every _____

End of part "A." Use the answer key at the end of the chapter to check your answers.

Part B—Skimming and Scanning for Word Recognition

Directions: The objective of this exercise is the same as the one that precedes it. Scan to enumerate the number of times a word appears in the line after the word and note this number in the margin. This time take a different tact. Since you are already holding a pen or pencil, you may want to use it to guide your eyes across the lines. Use your hand or a pencil to frame the area being scanned. Consider scanning both lines at the same time or going from right to left instead of left to right. Always double-check to ascertain that you haven't missed any of the words for which you are scanning. When you are done, check your answers using the answer key at the end of the chapter.

Goal time: 2 minutes or less

graphic

> elevate, contradiction, kindliness, orange, expedient, time, book, affective, fatalistic, fellowship, graphic, actual, house, graphic, knife, evil _____

concentration

        uppermost, confusion, marvelous, go, concentration, middle, believe, concentration, ignition, caution, concentration, ready, problem, concentration, battery, grand   _____

facilitator

        masked, about, detach, crystal, history, facilitator, sinful, derange, gym, facilitator, levity, develop, defend, facilitator, methods, distend   _____

proactive

        typical, genial, chervil, feather, type, exegete, frantic, friendly, writer, fall, ability, fortuitous, proactive, mildly, decimal, harbor   _____

interference

        faction, mutilate, ferocious, fictional, destruction, brute, foot, figment, traction, ridge, brought, interference, broil, spinster, darn, truthful   _____

testing

        spell, frozen, taste, midwife, effort, equate, banter, superfluous, testing, frightened, testing, forcing, budge, treachery, testing, fertile   _____

mapping

        mapping, running, correspond, archives, banning, superb, table, mapping, natural, medium, forsake, spinal, tiny, pestle, comfort, disease   _____

system

        disagree, clam, system, disqualify, inactive, cloister, system, squeeze, aching, cleft, system, study, skill, using, time, system   _____

study

        management, disrobe, fiction, exterminate, collate, dumb, mother, furtive, forceful, backing, spell, treason, study, offend, baking, study   _____

mnemonic

        allude, askew, future, window, belief, remains, techniques, bred, payment, devoid, false, unread, devices, mnemonic, strawberry   _____

barriers

        barriers, planes, new, object, born, hasty, esteemed, barriers, festering, love, premise, payment, barriers, photo, blood   _____

habits

        student, good, picture, mossy, habits, foolish, research, insane, habits, after, for, have, habits, gerbil, poor, closed   _____

outline

        of, joy, days, old, guided, feeling, private, token, shuttered, beauty, outline, coffee, reception, recent, words, outline   _____

devices

        white, mailed, glad, phrase, illustration, graphic, interrelationships, using, model, content, devices, apply, written, tables, cartoon, technical   _____

advance

        study, advance, diamond, comforts, home, away, edge, rest, reached, revival, veto, advance, agronomy, carted, advance, wasted   _____

question

previous, best, heart, comic, fine, question, answer, idea, all, final, nearly, point, question, youth, premise, fount _____

textbook

maternal, act, out, discussion, role, written, defend, partner, locate, read, guidance, earn, ready, anticipate, search, matter, textbook _____

End of part "B." Check your answers at the end of the chapter. Discuss the strategies that you found most effective for quick and efficient scanning with your colleagues.

Workshop 2.2

Word Discrimination and Phrase Recognition

Continue to experiment with ways to improve your skimming and scanning abilities. This workshop is also divided into parts "A" and "B." Part "A" provides practice in discrimination from among similar looking words. Part "B" provides practice in recognizing phrases.

Mind and Eye Exercise 2A: Word Discrimination

Directions: The objective of this exercise is the same as the one that precedes it. Scan to enumerate the number of times a word appears in the line after the word and note this number in the margin. When you are done, use the answer key at the end of the chapter to check your answers.

Goal Time: 2 minutes or less

similes
silvery, similes, simian, similar, simmer, simony, simper, similes, sly, similitude, simpleton, simply, simulcast, simulation, smile, similes _____

dictionary
dictator, diazotize, dichondra, dichotomy, dichroic, dictionary, diesis, dietitian, dickcissel, diction, dictionary, dieseling, diorama, dimity, dilute, diner _____

receptive
reflection, reform, regardant, regency, redpoll, reference, receptive, redound, recycle, receptive, red, redeem, receptive, redolent, receptive, repent _____

pivotal
pivotal, pickle, picket, physician, piano, pimple, pitiful, pitch, pittance, pivot, pivotal, place, plafond, pithy, pivotal, placer _____

thesaurus
third, theta, they, thigh, thesaurus, these, thesis, thievish, thespian, thesaurus, thing, thanage, thankless, the, thesaurus, theocracy _____

structure
string, stripper, structure, struggle, strontianite, strontium, stroke, stroganoff, stroud, struck, stravage, straw, straight, stratify, strafe, strawberry _____

expressive
express, espresso, experimental, expert, eutectoid, euonymus, eye, extraversion, extrovert, exudation, expressive, expectancy, exhibit, existential, expectorate, expressive _____

gloss
glory, glockenspiel, glogg, glitter, gluconic, glue, glum, global, globe, gizzard, glacial, ginger, gloss, gimmick, giraffe, glom _____

inquiry

informer, infraction, intaglio, instinct, inquiry, inspect, inrem, insanity, inquiry, inspection, innate, inpatient, inquiry, inquest, injure, inland _____

capstone

capacitance, cap, canyon, canzone, cantabile, capstone, canvas, canning, capstone, cannoli, captain, carnival, capstone, careful, cardiology, cardiac _____

thinking

thought, thinking, thank, tinker, tough, take, taipan, thermoperiodic, theorem, thinking, there, thousand, thirty, thoracic, thorn, thinking _____

mode

moan, modality, mobile, mockery, mode, module, monkey, mode, monism, monitor, mommy, mode, monandry, moon, moorage, mode _____

schematic

scissors, sclaff, scoop, scoter, scherzo, scary, schematic, schedule, scapegoat, schema, schism, schematic, scotoma, sconce, sclerotic _____

cinquain

cinnamon, cinematize, cinquain, ciborium, cicada, chump, chute, cinquain, cingulum, clam, cinquain, citation, cite _____

euphemisms

eugenics, eunuch, eureka, euphoria, evasion, evasive, evacuate, euthenics, euphemisms, evangelize, eventful, evening, even, euphemisms, eventual, everyone _____

metaphor

metallic, metaphor, metamorphosis, metaphysical, metastasis, mete, metaphor, meteor, methane, method, methanol, metaphor, metric, meter, metaphor, metrication _____

oxymoron

oxbow, oxidizer, oxygen, oxymoron, oyster, ozone, oxyacetylene, oxygenate, owe, owl, oxblood, ovoviviparous, oxford, oxidant, ovule, ox _____

End of part "A." When you are done, use the answer key at the end of the chapter to check your answers.

Mind and Eye Exercise 2B: Phrase Recognition

Directions: Your task is to find matches for the topic phrases. Before starting, ask yourself if you believe that recognizing word phrases will be easier or more difficult than recognizing single words. Be prepared to explain your answer.

Goal Time: 2 minutes or less

Fry readability

strange to say, up and away, bird in hand, glad hand, quick reader, final stage, devoid of charm, Fry readability, hasty plan, natural beauty, Fry readability, French fry _____

reader interaction

drug interaction, university scholarship, perfect job, sheep pasture, gently slap, bold heart, radiant dawn, reader interaction, bold and beautiful, strawberry shortcake, still in doubt, reader interaction _____

personal factors
> personal factors, serious composer, only in jest, in high time, personal factors, in the pink, frightened child, delayed action, pure crystal, personal account, polio vaccine, books and breakfast

_____

lexical complexity
> sooner or later, tell a story, religious vows, lexical complexity, crystal glasses, lexical complexity, file and store, secret rendezvous, seen and heard, lexical complexity, find a friend, high mountain

_____

syntactical complexity
> eat an apple, syntactical complexity, complete one's work, out of touch, syntactical complexity, freely chosen, crawl into bed, churning butter, syntactical complexity, federal courts, syntactical complexity, hunting bears

_____

concept load
> chicken in a bisquit, in the fire, travel guide, good chance, work hard, stagnant water, breeding place, suicidal warfare, concept load, cloudy water, load the truck, fence post

_____

format factor
> format factor, informal meeting, begin anew, strange to say, moon over fields, focal point, sheep for sale, brink of disaster, hot weather, format factor, open house

_____

Marshall's readability checklist
> shuttered window, grocery list, checkbook balance, friend to all, shout of joy, raging river, free choice, cheerful smile, Marshall's readability checklist, character reference, subtle distinctions, middle of the road

_____

cloze procedure
> cloze procedure, kill time, printed matter, afraid to be, out of touch, complete silence, police car, cloze procedure, strained expression, in the house, cloze procedure, the free and the brave, take a minute, cloze procedure

_____

content IRI
> horse-drawn carriage, coddled child, cruelly punished, graduating class, content IRI, frustrated attempts, modern house, finely made, auto dealer, white paint, electric motor, bar scene

_____

criterion-referenced tests
> green foliage, happy days, stars at night, criterion-referenced tests, true or false tests, multiple choice tests, criterion-referenced tests, full figure, in the nick of time, guessing game, criterion-referenced tests, foolish haste

_____

Cornell note taking system
> church and state, modern phenomenon, work hard, young children, good roads, large cities, Cornell note taking system, antique store, few bargains, American diet, any city, particularly rich

_____

mnemonic devices
> more strength, tile roof, rainy day, quiet country roads, deep rivers, first settlers, lengthy poems, first day, out of the car, mnemonic devices, lots of fun, nail together

_____

notes facilitator

bird's feathers, notes facilitator, noisy frogs, notes facilitator, past times, chocolate brownies, plains of the west, seriously injured, run fast, notes facilitator, choose a prize, notes facilitator

_____

outlining systems

outlining systems, write your answers, piece of paper, hot dog bun, outlining systems, classified advertisement, nasty cough, pink pad, color the rainbow, mouse pointer, ream of paper, presentation quality

_____

interference theory

plaid shorts, green blanket, closet door, hot afternoon, day to clean, folding chair, small lamp shade, interference theory, girls like to play, couch cushions are big, collect newspapers, answer the policeman

_____

study habits

study habits, joystick, cellular phone, race car track, study habits, use the library, school lunches, study habits, make a list, ask the students, study habits, sharpen your pencil

_____

End of part "B." When you are done, use the answer key at the end of the chapter to check your answers. Which was easier: single words or larger phrases? Why? Discuss your findings with your colleagues.

Visual Discrimination

Are you wondering how the idea of "speed reading" got started? Many teachers of reading rate adaptability attribute the beginnings of this type of training to the American Navy. During World War II, antiaircraft gunners had to make rapid discrimination between friendly and enemy aircraft. Sometimes these aircraft would appear from between the clouds for less than a second. Speed and accuracy were life-and-death matters. Hence, Navy personnel were trained using tachistoscopes, machines that flashed images of the silhouettes of aircraft. As the gunner became increasingly accurate in identification of different aircraft, the speed of the flash increased and the time the gunner had to identify the silhouettes decreased. Eventually the images were flashed for but a fraction of a second. At these speeds gunners could not say that they had seen any image at all. However, when asked to use their intuition to guess, accuracy still remained very high. Ensuing studies led to an understanding of subliminal perception, which was later exploited by advertisers in movie theaters and then later outlawed.

Meanwhile, the Army started using tachistoscopes to train clerks to see words more quickly. Unfortunately, removal of the machines resulted in subsequent decreases in speed and accuracy. Commercial reading teachers, most notably, Evelyn Wood, addressed this problem by training readers to use their hand to frame the area of text to be focused upon. More importantly, reading teachers realized that when scanning, students did not have to hear themselves subvocalize (say each word to themselves) to know what they had seen. Much like the Navy gunners, parts of what are seen can be processed subliminally. Efficient use of background knowledge can guide scanning and thus help the reader find those words that contain the essential content.

The next workshop exercise will give you an opportunity to see how this works.

Phrase Comprehension

Workshop 2.3

Directions: This exercise requires the reader to scan lines of print to locate phrases that are synonymous with the key phrase. For example, in the first group "inquire about" is the same as "find out." Writing the answer in the margin will require extra time; hence, the goal time has been expanded to 2.75 minutes.

Most readers find that they can locate the phrase with the same meaning with only minimal amount of subvocalization. That is, they can scan across the line in a similar fashion to the way they located phrases in the previous exercise.

Goal Time: 2.75 minutes

inquire about
   sorted papers, kind words, shortly after, parking ticket, climb the stairs,
   cautious procedure, find out, fold up, certainly evident, final event   _____

ice cream
   church and state, bicameral legislature, frozen dairy dessert, California
   gold rush, bookshelves of books, comfortable chairs, ear wax,
   desk lamp   _____

fall down
   practical skill, hear and see, find out, take a minute, cause an obstruction,
   fall flat, shortly after, good books, hit the sack, play baseball,
   listen to music   _____

ice cubes
   crystal mountain, complete control, cubes of ice, spools of thread,
   stained by grass, whistle in the distance, historical events, strike three,
   ballet slippers   _____

kill time
> shortage of food, find a book, waste time, see a friend, attend a concert, field and stream, cost of living, Alabama Avenue, gross national product _____

rough weather
> shortening for bread, giggling girls, showcase exhibit, front deck, soft couch, Apple computer, Roget's Thesaurus, stormy climatic conditions _____

nonalcoholic beverage
> liquid refreshment, steak and potatoes, favorite photograph, cost of living, pencil sharpener, wooden box, metal case, silver candelabra _____

laughing lads
> churning butter, frying eggs, among the best, hollow walls, light a fire, go to bed, stained with wine, giggling guys, healthy climate, atmospheric pressure _____

pay a visit
> short funds, trying troubles, legal redress, horrified by the sight, strained expression, modern art, quite empty, spend time with a friend, to the brink _____

complete one's work
> enter one's house, tell a story, crystal glasses, halogen lamp, change of heart, finish the job, complete control, morning newspaper, consumer price index _____

money on loan
> stained with ink, cost of living, office desk, borrowed cash, plaster sculpture, jazz musician, dinner date, folding chair, printer cable, wicker basket _____

government lawmaker
> ranch style house, legislative representative, automatic pencil, frost-free refrigerator, microwave oven, automatic pencil sharpener, post office mailbox _____

fully loaded
> filled to the brim, empty of contents, night telescope, collection of books, in the house, hit the sack, cautious procedure, seldom heard, climatic conditions _____

take one's time
> take a minute, hurry up, land of the free and the brave, constitutional amendments, encouraging results, simple problems, move slowly _____

tall skyscraper
> small monument, towering building, burning matches, ringing bells, change of heart, strained expression, find the right book, sort mail, play monopoly _____

family photograph
> governmental scandal, snapshot of parents and offspring, deck of playing cards, monthly mail, leather briefcase, green wastepaper basket, heat vent _____

lock the door
> eat an apple, burning matches, lock up, from a tree, vegetable garden, whistle as you work, afraid to be late, historical events, artistic advantage _____

sports event
> stained with ink, cost of living, office desk, borrowed cash, plaster sculpture, jazz musician, dinner date, folding chair, athletic competition, wicker basket _____

piece of luggage
> index cards, computer mouse, overnight bag, rate adaptability, introduced to a concept, grading scale, required textbooks, favorite photograph _____

This concludes the third workshop exercise. When you are done, check your answers using the answer key at the end of the chapter.

The Multiple Reading Process (MRP)

Now that you have demonstrated your ability to skim and scan for specific information, it is time to use these skills in a reading strategy that enables you to adapt reading rate for maximum efficiency. One such strategy is the *Multiple Reading Process* (*MRP*). The underlying principle of this strategy is that comprehension is a layered process. Each time we read something we add to our prior knowledge. Hence, repetition enhances comprehension, rate, and retention. For example, given a limited time to read a passage, one may choose to read it only once, but very thoroughly. On the other hand, the same reader may choose to read the passage three times, using each reading to build on prior understanding. One need but remember the story of the elephants in the classroom to see the inherent dangers in the first strategy.

The three stages of the MRP are (1) previewing or pre-reading; (2) reading; and (3) post-viewing or post-reading. Definitions and sample student learning objectives for each stage are listed below:

Stage One: Previewing or Pre-Reading

Pre-reading serves the four objectives. After a quick preview of the reading material students will be able:

- to locate main ideas, identify the structure and organization, and locate key vocabulary and sources of their definitions in the text to be read.
- to activate prior knowledge of the content so as to be able to use this as a scaffold for new learning.
- to identify passages that will require closer attention.
- to locate sources to help with comprehension problems.

Stage Two: Reading

After carefully reading material from beginning to end, students will be able to demonstrate an understanding of the meaning of the text by:

- listing important ideas and details.
- expanding upon comprehension by analyzing, interpreting, and synthesizing information and ideas.
- critically thinking about authors' use of language, style, purpose, and perspective.
- listing important information not yet fully understood from the passage.

Stage Three: Post-Viewing or Post-Reading

It is during this stage of reading that readers shift sprockets and gears most frequently in search of the missing information needed for comprehension. Rapid inspectional reading is usually employed to locate missing information. Slower analytical reading is employed once the information is located. The objectives of Stage Three are the same as those of Stage Two; however, criterion for mastery are raised to a higher level.

FROM THE CONTENT CLASSROOM

Reading Love Letters

"Read the same passage three times. You've got to be kidding," blurted a group of middle school students who had already heard the story of the blind children and the elephants. Their teacher needed to reach into her treasure chest of examples to remake her point.

"Tell me," she asked, "How many of you have ever received a love letter?" Slowly and cautiously a handful of students raised their hands. "Those of you whose hands are up, please tell me, how many times did you read your letter?"

Nearly everyone who indicated having received a love letter smiled. Their teacher re-explained the importance of the multiple reading process: "When you want to make sure that you fully understand something, you read it at least three times. The first time read through quickly to find out what is in the letter. The second time you read more slowly, savoring each turn of the word to make sure that you understand what you have been told. The third time you skim through looking for meaning that you may have missed in the first two readings."

Workshop 2.4

The MRP Applied—"Quality Not Quantity" by Mary Gillette

You are now familiar with skimming and scanning techniques and the Multiple Reading Process. Now it is time to try to put them together.

Read "Quality Not Quantity" by Mary E. Gillette, who was the great-great aunt of coauthor Marian Tonjes. This piece was originally published more than 100 years ago (March 1901) in the Cortland, New York, *Normal News*. As you preview, read and post-view this essay, consider how reading, writing, and language have changed over time. Also consider whether or not you think Ms. Gillette would have supported the idea of using the Multiple Reading Process.

We recommend that you read the essay in the following way:

Preview: (Goal time: approximately 3 minutes plus 1 minute for recall diagram)

- Quickly read the first and last paragraph.
- Starting at the second paragraph, read the topic sentence of each paragraph and then skim through the remainder of the paragraph locating main ideas, vocabulary, and structure.
- Complete a recall diagram that includes background information activated by this preview.

Read: (Goal time: approximately 4 to 6 minutes plus 2 minutes for recall diagram additions)

- Read the entire article from beginning to end. Accelerate reading speed during first and last paragraph and topic sentences. Slow down when you encounter information that you need to process more thoughtfully.
- Add to your recall diagram. Consider any information that you may have seen but not fully understood. Make sure to look for this information in your post-read.

Post-View: (Goal time: approximately 2 minutes plus 1 minute to add to diagram)

- Skim through the entire article looking for information you might have missed and/or passages that you may not have fully comprehended. Read these sections more carefully.
- Add to your recall diagram. Share your results with others.

Quality Not Quantity

by Mary Gillette

The dawn of a new century naturally causes one to look back over the pages of history to note the changes that have taken place. Nowhere is a change more manifest, than in the amount of literature produced.

No less than twenty-five thousand volumes were issued from the press last year, to say nothing of the newspapers and magazines that were published in addition. If all these books measured up to, or even approached the standard of true literature, the people of this century would have a great advantage over those of preceding centuries. Some one has said, "Real books in the multitude of new publications are as rare as real persons in a fashionable assembly."

Such a vast amount of reading matter necessitates a careful and wise selection. Provision to meet such a demand is being made by the introduction of the classics in the lower grades. A child, thus early brought in contact with nobler sentiments, will never care for such books as constitute a larger portion of the reading of today. The test of a book is its enduring power. A book that outlives generations of men must have something in it worthwhile.

Some friends are the gift of God to us, and some the gift of man through his creative imagination. Some of the latter seem as real to us as our human companions, and as such exert as great an influence over us. Whether this influence shall be for our good or not, depends upon the character of these people of fancy. Another danger that we encounter is reading so much that we retain nothing. Lincoln, in his early life, had very few books to read. These he mastered so thoroughly, that they became a part of his very being. Through the careful study of a few good books he attained a mastery of language. Thus, though uneducated in the sense that we use the term, he was able to write the great emancipation proclamation, while his second inaugural has become a classic.

In our efforts to read everything new, we are apt to forget that the oldest is sometimes the best. There is one book that has stood the test of time. It surpasses the thousands in its literary merit. All great men, whether poet, statesman, or philosopher, have united in its praise. Daniel Webster acknowledged his indebtedness to it. Lord Bacon said, "There is no philosophy like it." "Bring me the book," said Walter Scott upon his death bed. "What book? There is but one—the Bible."

If we remember that the character of the books we read has its influence upon us, that here as everywhere else thoroughness has its reward, and that the oldest is sometimes the best, we may feel that our lives are made better and more complete by contact with the best of literature.

How did you do with this three step process?

Mary Gillette thought that there was a vast amount of literature published at the turn of the twentieth century. With the number of volumes published today, not to mention what is published on the Internet, one can't help but wonder what she would think today.

Skill in previewing provides the reader with the information needed to make an informed decision as to whether a printed text is "worthwhile." What is more, in the event that one decides that it is indeed worthy, the information gathered in the preview becomes background knowledge that can assure that the reader will understand and retain more of what they read.

The preview is analogous to studying a map in preparation for a journey of unfamiliar terrain. If we really want to understand, we had best read the text multiple times, and build upon our prior understanding.

Now let us see how we might use previewing to scan through an entire text.

The Eight Steps to Previewing a Large Text

As in all previewing exercises, the purpose of previewing a large text is fourfold:

- to locate main ideas, identify the structure and organization, and locate key vocabulary and sources of their definitions in the text to be read.
- to activate prior knowledge of the content so as to be able to use this as a scaffold for new learning.
- to identify passages that will require closer attention.
- to locate sources to help with comprehension problems.

This task is a bit more challenging with a larger text; however, most expository books provide text features to make this process easier.

Here are eight steps to preview book-length expository text:

1. *Examine the front and back covers.* Start with the title and the subtitle. What do they mean? What is the theme of the book? Skim and scan through the publisher's blurbs looking for summaries of the main points of the book itself. Once you find these, downshift your gears and read them carefully. If the book is a hardcover, read the leaves of the jacket to learn about the authors and their affiliations. What studies and life experiences did they draw upon to author this book? If the book is a paperback, this information will usually appear either on the first or last inside pages of the book.

2. *Skim through the copyright dates, preface, introduction, words from the author, and other inside page materials.* The copyright date helps you to place the content of the book in context with the time it was written. A book with an old copyright may not have current information; however, it might provide other valuable insights. For example, a book written shortly after the American Civil War might provide the reader with important perspectives about that time period. Skim through the other materials inside the cover. These often contain more than credits. The authors may explain why the book was written, suggest ways to read it, and what you might expect to gain from studying it. Frequently, the authors will give pointers on how the book is organized. A second party who knows the author, or an expert on the topic, usually writes the introduction or foreword. Pre-reading objectives can be found in this person's insights.

3. *Study (note the use of the word "study" as opposed to "read") the table of contents of expository text to obtain a general sense of its structure.* When publishers request proposals from authors, they almost always ask for the table of contents. It is, after all, an outline of the content of the book. Is the book divided into sections? Does it progress sequentially? Examining chapter titles allows readers to reconstruct prior knowledge, discern the structure and organization of the book, and detect relationships between topics. If a chapter title is perplexing, skim and scan parts of that chapter to get a sense of its contents.

4. *Study the index and bibliography.* It is a daunting task to try to understand a large book on any subject. Books with many hundreds of pages sometimes take the author years to assemble. How can we get a sense of the "lay of the land"? The index and the bibliography are good places to start. The index has listed, in alphabetical order, all the important information contained in the book. In fact, the most important content will have the most page numbers and often the most subtitles. The index can be used to reconstruct prior knowledge and to plant seeds of curiosity for reading. In the same respect, the bibliography of a book lists the authors'

sources. When you know what authors have read, you will have a good idea of what they will write about.

5. *If a book has summaries at the end of its chapters, and/or a last chapter entitled "conclusion," read them, and/or it, first.* This is the quickest way to make sure that you know how parts will fit the whole. There are some notable exceptions to this rule. You may want to avoid this when reading literary works such as mysteries or horror stories.

6. *Study the pictures, graphs, tables, and illustrations.* These graphic aides provide readers with visual representations of thoughts used by the authors to clarify or augment the text. Attend to them carefully because authors put them in for a purpose. Read the captions, but don't forget, a picture may be worth a thousand words.

7. *Skim and scan through the entire text to identify main ideas, structure and organization, and key vocabulary.* When we skim milk, we take out the richest part, the cream. When skimming and scanning, we look at each page in order to locate and read the headings, subheadings, topic sentences, and key words. What pages or chapters will merit further attention when we read them in Stage Two? This step is analogous to walking through all of the rooms in a house before considering it for purchase. One must look in every chapter (room) to have a sense of what is in it to grasp the whole of the book.

8. Once you have completed the seventh step, *summarize the main ideas, structure, and organization of the book.* Take time to organize your thoughts. Complete a recall diagram, create an outline, or write a summary. Consider the following questions:

   • What is the main idea of the book?

   • What do you know about the background of the authors?

   • What bearing does the copyright date have on the information in the book?

   • What is its structure and organization?

   • Upon what sources do the authors rely for their work?

   • What pictures, graphs, tables, and illustrations are most helpful in understanding the concepts given?

   • What parts of the book deserve more of your time? What sections of the book deserve less attention?

Most experienced readers will agree that an eight-step preview of a book should take less than an hour. This time will enable the reader to read faster and with more comprehension during the second stage of the Multiple Reading Process. However, this is not always the case. Sometimes, after a one-hour preview of a book, readers discover their book doesn't deserve any more of their time. In the past, these very same readers may have spent hours reading from the first few chapters just to discern that the book didn't have what they wanted.

Using the Eight-Step Preview Method to Teach for Multicultural Understanding

Finding relevant curricula and responsive methods to reach children from all cultures is essential for successful content literacy instruction. One means to help students develop competency in this book previewing method is to incorporate culturally relevant books in the process. For example, Dorothy and Thomas Hoobler (1994a, 1994b, 1995a, 1995b, 1996, 1997, 1998a, 1998b, 1998c, 1998d) have authored a series of short

FROM THE CONTENT CLASSROOM

MRP in Action

A high school junior learned how to apply the Multiple Reading Process to his school readings. Shortly thereafter, he enrolled in advanced placement history at his local community college.

Given a long list of readings he chose to spend the first week of the course previewing all the assigned readings. He created a series of recall diagrams (as shown in Chapter One) with the essential content of each reading. The day before specific assignments were due, this conscientious student read the assignment thoroughly.

When the unit exam was announced, he reviewed his notes from class and then post-read the assignments. He earned an "A" on the exam, and when he was asked how he did it, he replied, "By previewing all of the materials early in the course I knew what I needed to know

for the final. By rereading the material before class I knew what needed careful attention. And by post-reading the materials I found additional information that I would have missed if I had only read the material one time. I guess the third time is the charm."

This student was demonstrating his ability to meet the International Reading Association's literacy standards to ". . . read a wide range of print and non-print texts to build an understanding of texts, [and] of themselves . . . to acquire new information; to respond to demands of society and the workplace . . . " In addition to helping him read to learn "independently," this student now has a strategy he can use throughout his learning career.

books with parallel formats that are designed like family albums (African, Chinese, Cuban, German, Irish, Italian, Jewish, Japanese, Mexican, and Scandinavian American Family Album). Students may be asked to preview (not read) three or four of these books and then complete a worksheet comparing the contributions of each family.

Surveying Student Texts

Whenever a group of students receive a new text, it is important for them to get a notion of its content, structure, and organization. It is also important for teachers to ascertain how well their students can use the aids provided within the text. In order to plan reading instruction, students can complete a written inventory. Following are some possible components for a student inventory activity. Then you will have a chance to do the same with this book.

Title Page: What is this book going to be about? Who wrote it? What kinds of things can you expect to find in this book?

Copyright Date: When was this book most recently published? Is it up to date?

Preface: Why did the authors write the book? What emphasis or bias can you expect? What clues do the authors give you as to how the book is organized? (For example: From a keyboard text, "What do the authors tell you about using this book for Apple computers?")

Table of Contents: How many units, sections, chapters are there? What do they tell you about the content, structure, and organization of this book? Looking at the Table of Contents, where might you be able to find information about _____? (For example: In an economics book, "In which chapter might you find information about the Gross National Product?")

Index: Where can you find information on _____? Which five topics have the most entries listed? Where can you find a map or illustration of _____?

Glossary: What is the definition of _____? If a person has a _____, what do you think you should do?

Maps, Graphs, Diagrams, Tables, and Other Illustrations: Have students turn through the book locating these important visual aids. Ask them questions about what different figures represent in the visual aid. (For example: From a math book: Turn to page 70. Which terms are explained on this page? From a history book: Turn to the map on page 19. What is the name of the country shaded in red ink?)

Appendices and Bibliography: Turn to these sections of the book. (From a keyboarding text: "Turn to the appendix on page 212. Looking at the fingering chart, which finger do you use to type the number 2?")

This same procedure of surveying may be used prior to reading a chapter. Read to answer questions from the following sections of the chapter:

- Titles and Subtitles
- Introduction and Summary
- Vocabulary words from that chapter
- Maps, Graphs, Diagrams, Tables, and Other Illustrations

👥 Workshop 2.5: A Preview Guide for This Book—ICL 5

Instructions: Complete this worksheet individually and then compare your answers with a colleague.

1. Title of Text: *Integrated Content Literacy*, 5th edition. What do you think the title may mean?
   _____

2. Copyright Date: Is it new enough to be up-to-date? What topics, if any, might not be up-to-date?
   _____

3. Now turn to the Preface: What information pertinent to the organization and/or relevant to reading from this book is provided in this section? _____
   _____
   _____
   _____

4. Next turn to the **Brief** Table of Contents:

   How many chapters are there in this text? _____

   Into how many sections have these chapters been divided? _____

   Are there any appendices? How many? _____

5. Now turn to the **Detailed** Table of Contents: Study it to answer these questions:

   a. Outlining can be a difficult skill to teach. Which chapter contains instructions on how to teach outlining?
   _____

   b. At the end of six of the chapters in this book you will find sections entitled: *From the Pages of Our Lives*. Which chapter has an essay written by a survivor of the Holocaust explaining how sharing can be healing? _____ By a Native American educator who talks about how the truth is the truth, whether whispered or shouted? _____By a Hispanic American professor who worked with a seventh grade English language learner named Evangelina? _____ By an Asian American journalist who used writing to get to know the history of her family? _____ By an African American diplomat who speaks to the transformative power of her high school? _____ By the coauthor of this text who writes about a weekend he had with his grandfather? _____

   c. There is a difference between learning to read and reading to learn. In which chapter might you find an explanation of the distinction between the two? _____

   d. In which chapter will you find information about tools that you may use to figure out how hard a textbook will be to read? _____

   e. The issue of what materials may or may not be used in the classroom (censorship) can become volatile. In which chapter will you find a guide for teachers to use when confronted by censors? _____

   f. Understanding what we read is a process. In which chapter might you find information on the differences between the process of comprehending and comprehension? _____

   g. There are six traits that may be used to assess student writing. In which chapter will you find information on what they are? _____

h. In which chapter might you find information on using the CSSD process to figure out the meaning of new words? _____

i. SQRR, PARS, and REAP are all acronyms for study strategies. In which chapter could you learn more about them? _____

j. In which chapter might you find information on how to reach the hard to engage reader? _____

k. In which chapter will you find out what a Content Informal Reading Inventory is? _____
In which appendix(ces) are there samples of these? _____

6. There is both an author index and a subject index for this book. Please turn to the subject index to answer these questions:

a. The Fry Readability Graph is a tool used to assess the approximate grade level at which a text is written. On what pages can you find information about this tool? _____

b. The San Diego Quick Assessment is a tool that teachers may use to estimate the approximate reading level of a student. On what pages can you find information about this tool? _____

c. It is important to help students develop the strategies needed to remember what they have read. On what pages can you find information on three or more memory strategies? _____

d. One authentic means for students to write about what they are learning is by journaling. On what pages can you find information about journaling? _____

7. Next, please turn to the glossary to answer these three questions:

a. What is the difference between illiteracy and aliteracy? _____
_____

b. What does one's E.Q. measure? _____
_____

c. What is the difference between one's independent and instructional reading levels? _____
_____

8. Finally, please take a quick turn through your text, from beginning to end, to answer these questions:

a. What three text features are at the beginning of every chapter?
_____
_____
_____

b. Why do you think these are there? _____
_____

We're guessing that you had no problems with this preview exercise. However, if you hand out a similar exercise, written for your content area class textbook, you may find that your students don't have the skills to complete some of these questions. The skills that many students lack can become teaching points during the term.

Cinquain as Summary

Rate Adaptability
Gears Sprockets
Skimming, Adjusting, Analyzing
Empowering Efficient Rewarding Able
Selective

Summary

The reading skills necessary to acquire new information, respond to the demands of society and workplace, and fulfill personal ambitions are all requisites of national standards. Selecting, reading, and studying from large quantities of text require students to read with efficiency and adapt their reading rates to their ability level as well as the purpose, type of material, and format of the text.

Reading a text is very much like riding an 18-speed bike. The better the reader is at shifting gears and sprockets, the easier it will be to negotiate varying terrain. The sprockets of this analogous bike are Adler's levels of reading: elementary, inspectional, analytical, and syntopical. The gears are Zintz's reading rates: slow/study, average, rapid, skimming, and scanning. Although no single chapter can provide a complete physiology of the visual system, four important implications need to be considered. These are: (1) reading depends on what readers already know; (2) reading requires continual rapid eye movements; and (3) when scanning, reading must be both fast and selective.

The Multiple Reading Process (MRP) is a strategy that improves comprehension through a layered reading process. Text is previewed, read, and then post-viewed. Repetition enhances comprehension, rate, and retention. There are eight steps to previewing a book: (1) examining the front and back covers; (2) skimming through copyright dates, preface, introduction, words from the author, and other inside page materials; (3) studying the table of contents; (4) studying the index and bibliography; (5) reading summaries and conclusions; (6) studying pictures, graphs, tables, and illustrations; (7) flash previewing the text for content and structure; and (8) summarizing the main idea and structure of the text as a whole. This same method may be used to survey textbooks, and introduce culturally relevant curriculum into content studies. One final note, if you read the essay that follows, entitled *A Weekend with My Grandfather*, you will learn how reading rate adaptability skills may help us make personal connections with those we love.

FROM THE PAGES OF OUR LIVES
A Weekend with My Grandfather

by Ray Wolpow

Dr. Ray Wolpow, coauthor of this text, taught secondary school history, English, and reading for 20 years during which time he received several awards for excellence in teaching. Since returning to school to receive his doctorate, he has taught university literacy methods courses. In this essay Wolpow describes how his grandfather, a man with but a fourth grade education, helped him learn the real value of reading and writing as well as how to be a better teacher.

Hearing the telephone, I hurriedly unlock my apartment door. Yet-to-be graded papers slip from my arms and scatter onto the floor. Stepping over them and the cat, I snatch the receiver on what could have been its last ring. "Hello" I say, hoping there is still someone on the line. It's my Grandpa Sol. His normal gruff demeanor is overshadowed by uncharacteristic vulnerability, but his English remains, as always, flawless—no accent, neither shtetl-Russian nor Brooklyn-American. His tone of voice is tinged with urgency: "It's time for you to come for a visit. I know you're busy . . . . Two or three days. . . . Just the two of us. . . . Please." Concerned about his failing health, I try to hide my alarm, "I'll be there soon. . . . I love you, plenty, Grandpa." During the next 48 hours I arrange for a sub, prepare lesson plans, muddle through a six-hour transcontinental flight and, finally, a nighttime taxi ride to his apartment building with its view of the New York harbor. Glancing across the water, I envision Grandpa Sol arriving in the New World. It's 1916 . . . an overcrowded dilapidated cattle-ship named the Patricia with 500 Russian immigrants aboard has just arrived at Ellis Island. . . .

Stepping into the closet-sized elevator, I push the button for the fourth floor. My stomach gurgles; I am both worried and hungry. Finally, the heavy doors open on a windowless hallway and I follow the black-and-white checkered linoleum down to Grandpa Sol's apartment. Before ringing the bell, I hesitate for a moment to collect myself, take a deep breath, and suddenly identify the familiar aroma of Grandpa's cooking: my favorite—spaghetti with fresh meat sauce. Within minutes Grandpa takes me into the kitchen and serves me dinner; Grandpa understands the need for a good meal after a long trip. First we talk about my flight and then about his failing health. With equal portions of humor and frustration he remarks, "Don't grow old if you can help it." Hearing his folk-witticism reminds me of what he used to tell me when, as a high school student, I groused about my homework: "Complaining is part of getting the job done . . . as long as you are getting the job done." Now that I am with him, what does Grandpa need to say to me, and, what do I want to say to him? Our life-

time together is drawing to an end. Suddenly at a loss for words, we each avert our eyes. After a few minutes that feel like hours, we clear the table. Summoning my courage, I walk over to his collection of books. Nervous but resolute, I ask, "Grandpa, what do you have here that you think I should read?"

Eight years earlier, during one of our "just the two of us" visits, I had announced plans to leave college. Education wasn't "my thing." I couldn't "handle" my classes. There was just "too much reading" and I read "painfully slow." Surely Grandpa would understand: after all, he had made it no further than the fourth grade in Russia and that was enough to support himself and his family in the New World as a shipyard riveter, union organizer, merchant and businessman. I even recalled his stories of when, as an immigrant dockworker, he had to protect himself from "tough guys who picked fights" with Jews. His powerful left hook had earned him the moniker of "Wolpow-the-walloper." Perhaps this was why his response to my announcement to quit school caused me to flinch. Grandpa moved aggressively towards me, and then stopped, calmed himself and said, "Raymond, your real education will begin when your formal education ends. On the shelves of any library you will find all the knowledge, insight and compassion you need. Before you leave school, if you do nothing else, learn how to learn better from books."

I knew Grandpa was right. I stayed in school, and my focus changed. I took a reading improvement course and started applying what I learned there to the assignments in my other classes. I had thought my learning problem was that I was a slow reader. Not so—my deliberate, analytic reading style had its place. But I read everything at the same speed. I soon learned to skim and scan and then to adapt my reading rate to the specific needs dictated by the changing terrain of the text before me. In so doing, I discovered that few books are actually meant to be read from cover to cover; that good books need to be read several times; and that most books contain interstitial content. Most significantly, however, I found that a methodic "pre-reading" of difficult texts allowed me to organize my time

Wolpow, Ray, "First Person: The Pages from Our Lives," *Journal of Adolescent & Adult Literacy*, 48(1). Copyright ©2004 by the International Reading Association.

to concentrate on those passages that were the most important and/or most difficult to grasp. With time, I learned how to learn from books . . . and I became good at it.

Now, standing in front of Grandpa's bookshelves in his New York apartment, I finally have the chance to share what I have learned. So I repeat my question: "Grandpa, what do you have here that you think I should read?" I don't know which surprises him more: the tone of my voice or my question. With one eyebrow unconsciously raised and a bit of an uncertain smile, Grandpa turns toward the section of his library with his oldest volumes and makes his choice: Alexander Kuprin's *Yama: The Pit*. I watch him open the book and leaf through several pages. Then I witness something I have never before seen in his eyes: a flood of emotion—nearly tears. Recomposing himself, Grandpa closes the book, and challenges me, "I bet you can't tell me what this book is about." I take the book and, stalling for time, ask him to fix our favorite dessert.

To his sounds of opening cabinet doors, banging baking pans, and clanking liqueur bottles, I quickly start to skim through *Yama*. Its cracked binding and brown, worn pages merit cautious handling. I read from the dedication: "I know that many will find this novel immoral and indecent; never the less [sic.] I dedicate it with all my heart to mothers and youths" and then, hurriedly, from the preface: "No evil is ever met by shutting it out of sight. In time the world will learn that facing facts is the beginning of progress. Ignorance is the greatest evil. Bigotry is never justified." I find Kuprin's stilted language irritatingly sermonic, but I read on. From the postscript: "The real psychological success of this book cannot be attributed to an unwholesome curiosity on the part of its readers; I am deeply convinced of the fact that *Yama* has compelled many people to reflect, with sincere sympathy, about prostitution." Now I'm the one with the uncertain smile. Why did Grandpa pick specifically this book? And who else has read this copy? My father? My uncles? I use the remaining few minutes to skim its nine or ten chapters for plot, characters and setting. The language and descriptions strike me as graphic for a book published in the 1920s.

Ten minutes later Grandpa returns with two highly flammable desserts, each multi-layered, and topped with a dollop of whipped cream, liberally infused with honey. I never learned what he called this concoction, but I later came to recognize it as a Russianized version of an English trifle, only there was never anything trifling about its calories. After the first spoonfuls find their way into my mouth, I begin talking about several of the women characters, of the cruel and inhuman treatment they received from men, and of the author's decision to write about prostitution. Grandpa is impressed. Looking down at my empty dessert

bowl, he quips, "You seem to have changed your mind about reading. You don't just read books now, you gobble them up like a dessert." Soon we are talking about why he chose *Yama* to share with me. With affection Grandpa tells me about his first wife, Rae, my namesake, who died of tuberculosis when their son — my father — was only six. After Rae's death and during the years he was a single father, Grandpa made several poor choices. There were times when he drank, womanized, and was far too rough in disciplining his children. Grandpa tells me of finding love and self-respect again with his second wife, Alice. If she hadn't come along . . . "who knows?" Listening to Grandpa, I reflect on my own recent divorce and the mistakes I keep making in the transition. There is plenty for us to talk about and share. Although we've finished our desserts, I want to read and talk more.

I ask Grandpa for another book. He doesn't hide his pleasure. As he returns to his bookcase, I ask, "Grandpa, you only had four years of school. How is it that you became such an avid reader?" Taking my question as a compliment, he reminds me that evenings "weren't always filled with movies and television entertainment." No, back in Russia, "gathering around the table to talk and read by kerosene lamplight" was common fare for the day's end. Sometimes, the older children occupied themselves with books of their own, but most often, Father read to them all. "Your great-grandfather was a hard man, but around the table he had an open heart. When he read, we heard more than his words, we heard his love." As the evening progressed, mother suckled the newest-born to sleep. The next youngest, a year or so older, was Father's responsibility. When the toddler became squirrelly, a drop of honey on Father's fingertip, placed lovingly on the child's lips, helped Father compensate for what nature hadn't provided. Grandpa Sol rests his hand on mine to finish his answer, "You asked me, Raymond, why I became such an avid reader. Perhaps I learned in my father's arms that with an open heart, a good book, and a drop of honey, you could give a soul a melody."

Grandpa returns to the table, picks up a small dish of candies, places it between us, then hands me a second novel and encourages me to "gobble it up." While he reads *The New York Times*, I skim through the story of a gang of immigrant, adolescent "hoodlums" living in poverty and trying to make sense of the "New World." When I am done, I ask him why he chose this book for discussion. "Like your father before you, you are a teacher. I will tell you what I told him. Children are not empty vessels to be filled with knowledge. They have inherent talents and abilities that need to be nurtured. Doing so requires a teacher to be a mirror. . . ." Grandpa explains that when students, like the characters in this novel, look at their teachers, they should see their own qualities reflected back at them. He tells me, "The English verb to educate comes from the Latin word *educare;* it means to lead forth." Two college degrees and I had never considered the etymology of the root word of my profession. "How do you think a teacher should 'lead forth'?" I ask. Tonight, a man with a fourth grade education is my mirror. His heart open, Grandpa answers, "The most important pages we must learn to read and write are the pages of our own lives. . . ."

For more than thirty years I've "led forth": twenty years with middle- and high-school youth and eleven as a university professor. So many under-performing students seem to lack both desire and skill to read the printed pages of their history, science, or math books. For far too many of these students, reading is a school activity; something they are "not good at" and consequently something they have learned to dislike. To address these concerns, I have, for many years, integrated literacy skill instruction (like the methodic pre-reading described above) with content knowledge instruction. However, I soon learned that knowledge and method were not enough. My teaching lacked sufficient connections to qualities of heart, both my students', and mine. Yes, I could teach cognitive concepts brilliantly, but in practice my courses were devoid of this important "affec-

tive" dimension. Thank goodness, a man, with nothing more than a fourth grade education, modeled for me the courage, commitment and vulnerability needed to read both from printed books and the pages of my life. I've learned that cognitive and affective developments are complimentary co-requisites of achievement. Carefully observe the avid readers in your classroom and you will see exactly what I mean.

Twenty-five years later, I leaf through the cracked and decaying pages of *Yama*, one of several books given to me by my grandfather a month before he passed away. Ignorance, denial and bigotry are still ever-present. However, so is Grandpa's confident message of the power of sharing a good book. So, dear reader, as you prepare to digest the last of this chapter on Reading Rate Adaptability, please consider the following challenge: Go to your grandmother, grandfather, great-aunt or uncle, son or daughter, and ask her or him for a book worth reading. Take twenty minutes, skim its pages using the methods on the pages that follow, and then engage the book's owner in a meaningful conversation. If you get a fraction of what I got from my grandfather the night we read and talked, from dessert until dawn, you may taste a sweetness that could stay with you forever.

Questions for Reflection and Discussion

1. Consider the problems Wolpow had "handling" the reading for his classes. How did his development of reading rate adaptability skills eventually help him to improve in school? Connect with his grandfather?

2. Was Wolpow "cheating" when he previewed *Yama* instead of reading it a word at a time from cover to cover?

3. Consider the ways that Wolpow's grandfather convinced his grandson that reading and teaching were of great value. Do elders share their wisdom and values about reading and/or teaching in the culture in which you grew up?

4. Have you ever had a teacher use reading and writing as a means to get closer to you? If so, how? Have you ever used books or reading and writing to get closer to someone you love? Why, or why not? If so, how was this done?

Answer Keys:

Workshop 2.1, Exercise A

density (3), format (2), readability (3), lexical (1), criteria (4), reader (2), syntax (1), cloze (3), diagnosis (3), validity (2), equivalent (1), assessment (4), acronyms (4), amelioration (2), denotations (1), connotations (3), pejoration (1).

Workshop 2.1, Exercise B

graphic (2), concentration (4), facilitator (3), proactive (1), interference (1), testing (3), mapping (2), system (4), study (2), mnemonic (1), barriers (3), habits (3), outline (2), devices (1), advance (3), question (2), textbook (1).

Workshop 2.2, Exercise A

similes (3), dictionary (2), receptive (4), pivotal (3), thesaurus (3), structure (1), expressive (2), gloss (1), inquiry (3), capstone (3), thinking (3), mode (4), schematic (2), cinquain (3), euphemisms (2), metaphor (4), oxymoron (1).

Workshop 2.2, Exercise B

Fry readability (2), reader interaction (2), personal factors (2), lexical complexity (3), syntactical complexity (4), concept load (1), format factor (2), Marshall's readability checklist (1), cloze procedure (4), content IRI (1), criterion-referenced tests (3), Cornell note taking system (1), mnemonic devices (1), notes facilitator (4), outlining systems (2), interference theory (1), study habits (4).

Workshop 2.3

inquire about	find out
ice cream	frozen dairy dessert
fall down	fall flat
ice cubes	cubes of ice
kill time	waste time
rough weather	stormy climatic conditions
nonalcoholic beverage	liquid refreshment
laughing lads	giggling guys
pay a visit	spend time with a friend
complete one's work	finish the job
money on loan	borrowed cash
government lawmaker	legislative representative
fully loaded	filled to the brim
take one's time	move slowly
tall skyscraper	towering building
family photograph	snapshot of parents and offspring
lock the door	lock up
sports event	athletic competition
piece of luggage	overnight bag

References and Recommended Readings

Aaronson, D., & Ferres, S. (1986). Reading strategies for children and adults: A quantitative model. *Psychological Review, 93* (1), 89–112.

Adler, M. J. & Van Doren, C. (1940). *How to read a book: The classic guide to intelligent reading.* New York: Simon & Schuster.

Beers, P. (1986). Accelerated reading for high school students. *Journal of Reading, 29* (4), 311–315.

Bell, T. (2001). Extensive reading: Speed and comprehension. *Reading Matrix: An International Online Journal 1* (1). Retrieved March 21, 2005 from http://www.readingmatrix.com

Bowers, P., & Newby-Clark, E. (2002). The role of naming speed within a model of reading acquisition. *Reading and Writing: An Interdisciplinary Journal, 15* (1), 109–126.

Breznitz, Z. (1997). Enhancing the reading of dyslexic children by reading acceleration and auditory masking. *Journal of Educational Psychology, 89* (1), 103–113.

Buehl, D. (1996). Improving students' learning strategies through self-reflection. *Teaching and Change, 3* (3), 227–443.

Carver, R. (1987). Teaching rapid reading in the intermediate grades: Helpful or harmful? *Reading Research and Instruction, 26* (2), 65–76.

Council of Chief State School Officers. (2005). INTASC Standards. Retrieved March 21, 2005 from http://www.ccsso.org/projects/Interstate_New_Teacher_Assessment_and_Support_Consortium/

Davis, S. (1989). Nonfiction book scans. *Journal of Reading, 33* (3), 222.

Drake, B., Acosta, G., & Smith, R. (1997). An effective technique for reading research articles—The Japanese KENSHU method. *Journal of Chemical Education, 74* (2), 186–188.

Dyson, M., & Haselgrove, M. (2001). The influence of reading speed and line length on the effectiveness of reading from a screen. *International Journal of Human-Computer Studies, 54* (4), 585–612.

Frank, S. (1994). *The Evelyn Wood seven day speed reading and learning program.* New York: Barnes and Noble.

Hirai, A. (1999). The relationship between listening and reading rates of Japanese EFL learners. *Modern Language Journal, 83* (3), 367–384.

Hoobler, D., & Hoobler, T. (1994a). *The Italian American family album.* Oxford, UK: Oxford University Press.

Hoobler, D., & Hoobler, T. (1994b). *The Mexican American family album.* Oxford, UK: Oxford University Press.

Hoobler, D., & Hoobler, T. (1995a). *The African American family album.* Oxford, UK: Oxford University Press.

Hoobler, D., & Hoobler, T. (1995b). *The Jewish American family album.* Oxford, UK: Oxford University Press.

Hoobler, D., & Hoobler, T. (1996). *The German American family album.* Oxford, UK: Oxford University Press.

Hoobler, D., & Hoobler, T. (1997). *The Scandinavian American family album.* Cambridge UK: Cambridge University Press.

Hoobler, D., & Hoobler, T. (1998a). *The Chinese American family album.* Oxford, UK: Oxford University Press.

Hoobler, D., & Hoobler, T. (1998b). *The Cuban American family album.* Oxford, UK: Oxford University Press.

Hoobler, D., & Hoobler, T. (1998c). *The Irish American family album.* Oxford, UK: Oxford University Press.

Hoobler, D., & Hoobler, T. (1998d). *The Japanese American family album.* Oxford, UK: Oxford University Press.

International Reading Association/National Council of Teachers of English. (1996). *Standards for the English language arts.* Urbana, IL: Authors.

Kaakinen, J., Hyoenae, J., & Keenan, J. (2003). How prior knowledge, WMC, and relevance of information affect eye fixations in expository text. *Journal of Experimental Psychology: Learning, Memory and Cognition, 29* (3), 447–457.

Kawakami, A. (1991). Reading processes of English sentences in Japanese and Canadian students. *Reading and Writing: An Interdisciplinary Journal, 3* (1), 31–41.

Kelly-Vance, L., & Schreck, D. (2002). The impact of a collaborative family/school reading programme on student reading rate. *Journal of Research in Reading, 25* (1), 43–53.

Krischer, C. (1994) Gliding text: A new aid to improve the reading performance of poor readers by subconscious gaze control. *Educational Research, 36* (3), 271–283.

Lai, F-K. (1993). The effect of a summer reading course on reading and writing skills. *System, 21* (1), 87–100.

Lewis, N. (1978). *Read better and faster.* New York: TY Crowell.

Memory, D., & Moore, D. (1981). Selecting sources in library research: An activity in skimming and critical reading. *Journal of Reading, 24* (6), 469–74.

Millis, K., & King, A. (2001). Rereading strategically: The influences of comprehension ability and prior reading on the memory for expository text. *Reading Psychology, 22* (1), 41–65.

Mounsteven, J. (1990). Speed reading: A technique for developing fluent readers. *Teaching Exceptional Children, 22* (3), 69–71.

Office of the Superintendent of Public Instruction. (2005). Essential academic learning requirements: Reading. Retrieved October 2, 2005 from http://www.k12.wa.us/curriculumInstruct/reading/ealrs.aspx

O'Reilly, R., & Walker, J. (1990). An analysis of reading rates in college students. *Reading Research and Instruction, 29* (2), 1–11.

Roberts, R. (1996). The basic information processing (BIP) unit, mental speed and human cognitive abilities: Should the BIP R.I.P? *Intelligence, 23* (2), 133–135.

Samuels, S., & Naslund, J. (1994) Individual differences in reading: The case for lexical access. *Reading and Writing Quarterly, 10* (4), 285–296.

Saxe, J. G., (1899). The blind men and the elephant. In *The poetic works of John Godfrey Saxe.* Boston: Houghton Mifflin.

Sherrill, M. (1994). Urban readers spring ahead (open to suggestion). *Journal of Reading 37* (8), 687–688.

Shimoda, T. (1993). The effects of interesting examples and topic familiarity on text comprehension, attention and reading speed. *Journal of Experimental Education, 61* (2), 93–103.

Skinner, C. (1993). A comparison of fast-rate, slow-rate, and silent previewing interventions on reading performance. *Journal of Learning Disabilities, 26* (10), 674–681.

Smith, F. (1988). *Understanding reading: A psycholinguistic analysis of reading and learning to read.* Hillside, NJ: Erlbaum Associates.

Sovik, N., Arntzen, O., & Samuelstuen, M. (2000). Eye movement parameters and reading speed. *Reading and Writing: An Interdisciplinary Journal, 13* (3–4), 237–255.

Stein, H. (1978). The visual reading guide. *Social Education, 4* (6), 534–535.

Stoddard, K. (1993). Increasing reading rate and comprehension: The effects on repeated readings, sentence segmentation and intonation training. *Reading Research and Instruction, 32* (4), 53–65.

Tonjes, M. (1980). Adaptable rates and strategies for efficient comprehension. In G. Ray & A. Pugh (Eds.), *The reading connection,* London: Ward Locke Publishers (pp. 144–153).

Weintraub, S. (1978). Summary of investigations relating to reading. *Reading Research Quarterly, 14 (*3), 287–466.

Wepner, S. (1990). Do computers have a place in college reading courses? *Journal of Reading, 33* (5), 348–354.

Wolpow, R. (1978). *Adventures in the world of reading: A complete reading development program.* San Jose, CA: Adventures in Reading Inc.

Young, A. (1996). Effects of prosodic modeling and repeated reading on poor readers' fluency and comprehension. *Applied Psycholinguistics, 17* (1), 59–84.

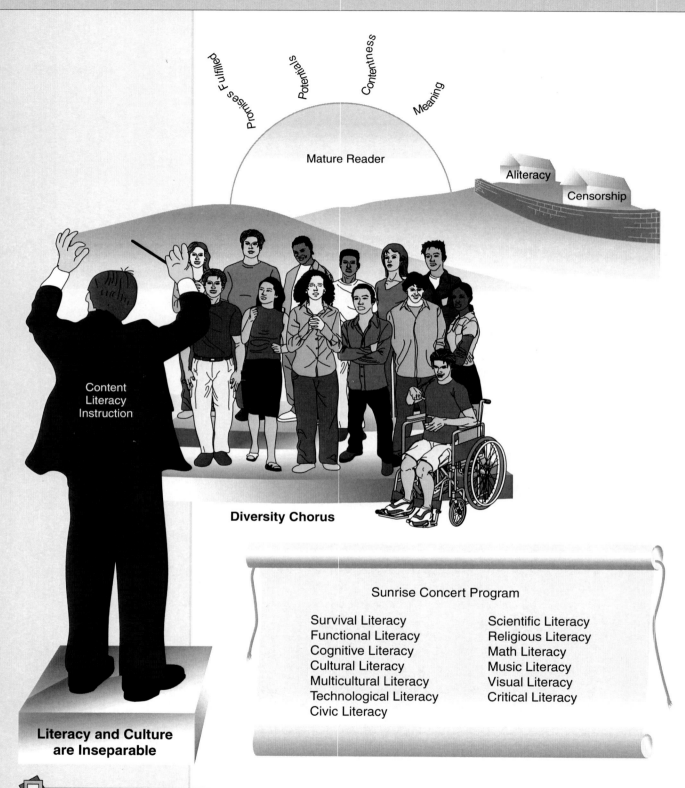

Promises Fulfilled

Potentials

Contentness

Meaning

Mature Reader

Aliteracy

Censorship

Content
Literacy
Instruction

Diversity Chorus

Sunrise Concert Program

Survival Literacy
Functional Literacy
Cognitive Literacy
Cultural Literacy
Multicultural Literacy
Technological Literacy
Civic Literacy

Scientific Literacy
Religious Literacy
Math Literacy
Music Literacy
Visual Literacy
Critical Literacy

**Literacy and Culture
are Inseparable**

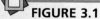

FIGURE 3.1

A Frame of Reference: Literacy, Diversity, Censorship, and the Mature Reader—A Cognitive Map

A Frame of Reference: Literacy, Diversity, Censorship, and the Mature Reader

3

Outline

- Anticipatory and Review Questions
- A Sampling of National Performance Standards
- Introduction
  - *Workshop 3.1: Reaching Consensus on the Meaning of Literacy*
- Schemata for the Concept of Literacy
  - Evolution of the Word *Literacy*
  - Survival and Functional Schemata of Literacy
    - My Father's Hands
  - Cognitive, Purposeful, and Critical Schemata of Literacy
  - History of the Schema of Content Literacy
- Learning to Read vs. Reading to Learn
- *Workshop 3.2: Comparing Purpose and Skills*
- Introduction to Diversity
  - A Schema for Cultural Diversity
- Censorship Concerns
  - When Teachers Are Confronted with Censors
  - Censored Books
- Qualities of the Mature Reader
  - *Workshop 3.3: Self-Assessment of Reading Maturity*
- Cinquain as Summary
- Summary
- From the Pages of Our Lives: *Evangelina Can Read,* by Leila Flores-Dueñas.
- References and Recommended Readings

"Public and educational attention has long been focused on the beginning of literacy, planting seedlings and making sure they take root, but without careful cultivation and nurturing seedlings may wither and their growth become stunted."

International Reading Association Commission on Adolescent Literacy

"Once you learn to read you will be forever free!"

Frederick Douglas

"I do not want my house to be walled in on all sides and my windows to be stuffed. I want the cultures of all the lands to be blown about my house as freely as possible. But I refuse to be blown off my feet by any."

Mahatma Gandhi

Anticipatory and Review Questions

Literal

1. What are two prominent dimensions of culture in American schools?

2. What is the difference between learning to read and reading to learn?

Interpretive/Applied

3. Compare the purpose and skills needed to read in two different content areas.

4. Should the teaching of reading and writing be the responsibility of all secondary teachers or just those who teach English? Give an example to illustrate your answer.

Evaluative/Critical

5. Do you have the qualities of a mature reader? (Before you answer this question you may want to evaluate your own level of reading maturity based on the aspects delineated in Workshop 3.2.)

6. Do you agree or disagree with the statement that literacy and culture are inseparable? Explain your answer.

7. List at least three textual items that might be considered censorable by members of the community in which you teach, or hope to teach. Would you defend these items? If so, how and why? If not, why not?

Creative/Personal

8. How did you feel after reading "My Father's Hands"? Have you ever known someone who couldn't read? Have you ever kept a secret about a skill you lacked or something you were unable to do? Why?

A Sampling of National Performance Standards

- Students participate as knowledgeable, reflective, creative, and critical members of a variety of literacy communities. (International Reading Association/National Council of Teachers of English, 1996, p. 45)

- The professional educator understands how students differ in their approaches to learning and creates instructional opportunities that are adapted to diverse learners. (Council of Chief State School Officers, 2005)

- Students develop an understanding of and respect for diversity in language use, patterns, and dialects across cultures, ethnic groups, geographic regions, and social roles. (International Reading Association/National Council of Teachers of English, 1996, p. 44)

Introduction

Without debate, most would accept the suggestion that we educate our children so they demonstrate high levels of literacy. We might also agree that illiteracy fosters continued poverty and the inability to pursue happiness. However, some scholars point out that words like literacy, liberty, justice, and happiness are "autopositive terms." When we get past our initial positive thoughts about them and attempt to define exactly what they mean, we find that they are complex and illusive (Venezky, Wagner, & Ciliberti, 1990). The terms *literacy* and *illiteracy* can mean different things to different people, as you may discover by completing Workshop 3.1 on page 79. On the pages that follow we provide definitions of these words along with a relevant history of their meaning. Before we do, let's work toward developing appropriate schemata for literacy.

Schemata for the Concept of Literacy

Schemata (the plural of schema) can be defined as a series of ideas or concepts in a framework into which new information can be assimilated or categorized, which in turn facilitates comprehension. Let us start to construct a series of schemata of literacy by first looking at the history of this word.

Evolution of the Word Literacy

Literate and *illiterate* come from the Latin *literatus* which, for Cicero, meant a learned person. In the Middle Ages a "literatus" was someone who could read Latin. Writing was not included as it required manipulating parchment, ink, and quills (Venezky, 1991). During the Middle Ages, a breakdown of learning occurred, which combined with the spread of vernacular languages led to a new meaning for this word. After the Reformation, a "literatus" was someone who could read and write minimally in their own native language (Clancy, 1979). The word *illiterate* found its way into the English language during the last half of the sixteenth century, when Lord Chesterton wrote that an illiterate was one ignorant of Greek and Latin (Simpson & Weiner, 1989).

However, the actual term *literacy* did not appear in the English language until the 1880s, first appearing in the *New England Journal of Education*. As you might know from your study of the history of education, during this time period many states started requiring children to go to school. This wasn't entirely popular, especially in agricultural areas where farmers wanted their children home to help gather the harvest. Realizing this was costing him votes, Governor Butler, a shrewd and ambitious Massachusetts statesman, found a way to justify the large amount of money spent on compulsory education. He proudly stated that, according to this most recent census, the "literacy" of the "native population" of his state was the best in the Union. For the record, the "native population" of which he spoke excluded all foreign-born inhabitants and all people of color (Bicknell, 1883). How did they know how many people were literate? In 1870, those who conducted interviews for the United States census asked whether any member of the household was "deaf, dumb, blind, insane, idiotic or illiterate" (Walker, 1872). Illiteracy then was the inability to read or write in any language. No tests were administered, a verbal response was sufficient.

Survival and Functional Schemata of Literacy

The National Literacy Act of 1991 of the United States defines literacy as ". . . an individual's ability to read, write, and speak in English, and compute and solve problems necessary to function on the job and in society, to achieve one's goals, and develop one's knowledge and potential" (Public Law 102-73, Sec. 3). This law was passed in response to concerns that there were many citizens of the United States who could not:

- read help wanted ads;
- fill out social security forms or driver's license forms;
- read instructions relating to the workplace; and/or
- understand directions on a bottle of medicine.

The skills needed to do this kind of reading and writing is called ***survival literacy.*** Think of the mother, distraught because her little girl has started to bring home books from school, books that she wanted her mother to read to her, but . . . she could not do it. Think of the 40-year-old maintenance man who all his life wanted to be a truck driver, but could not read signs or road maps. Think of the woman who bought canned dog food for her family, thinking it was beef stew. "My Father's Hands" is yet another poignant example (Figure 3.2).

Sadly, stories such as "My Father's Hands" are not isolated cases. It has been estimated that millions of adults in our country are not functioning at a level of survival literacy. Figure 3.3, Hagar the Horrible, makes a similar point.

The term ***functional literacy*** is usually equated with school attainment levels. Today the level of school attainment required has risen dramatically. If students completed 3 or more years of schooling in 1930 they were considered functionally literate. In 1950, the criterion was 5 or more years, in 1960 8 or more years; and in 1980 graduation from high school constituted that level of attainment (Stedman, 1996).

Name _____   Date _____

Workshop 3.1

Reaching Consensus on the Meaning of Literacy

This is a whole-class activity. First, individually write your answer to question one, moving on to the next four activities as time permits. After comparing the final groups' definitions, staying with your group of eight, discuss the seven questions (5. a–g) below. This activity takes approximately 50 minutes. The sequence is as follows:

1. On a sheet of paper, write your own definition of literacy. Describe what you mean when you say someone is literate or illiterate. (Time 3–5 minutes)

2. Form into pairs to share what you both have written. Your goal is to settle on one definition upon which you both can agree. You may either select the better of the two definitions or combine them in some way. (Time 5–10 minutes)

3. Find a second pair, thus forming groups of four. Once again, your goal is to agree upon a definition that represents the whole group. You may either select the better of the two definitions or combine them in some way to form a new version. (Time 8–10 minutes)

4. Combine with another group of four to make a group of eight. Once again, your goal is to agree upon a definition that represents the whole group. (Time 8–10 minutes)

5. Designate someone from each group of eight to write their definition on the board. As a class decide on common threads and differences. Then discuss each of the following—either total class or in small groups. (Time 10–15 minutes)

   a. If a woman has a Ph.D. in literature or composition from a Russian university, but she is unable to read and write English, is she literate or illiterate? Why, or why not?

   b. If a Native American can tell the history of his people to the highest level as attributed by his tribal elders, but cannot write it, is he literate or illiterate? Why, or why not?

   c. Does your definition include a quarterback's ability to "read" the defense? How about a kayaker's ability to "read" the whitewater of a rushing river? Why, or why not?

   d. What about the ability of a trial lawyer to "read" the body language of a defendant during a cross-examination? Why, or why not?

   e. Does your definition include the musician's and artist's ability to "read" (view and listen) and "write" (create) music or art? Why, or why not?

   f. What about reading and understanding the culturally specific knowledge needed to be productive members or society? Why, or why not?

   g. Is the ability to read and interpret mathematical symbols to quantify objects an aspect of your definition? Operating a graphing calculator or computer? Why, or why not?

6. Was your group able to arrive at a consensus from the various definitions? If so, pat yourselves on the back. The process you just completed is not unlike the process that professional organizations undergo to establish standards in literacy.

FIGURE 3.2
My Father's Hands

"My Father's Hands"
A Reader's Digest Story

Condensed from *New York Sunday News Magazine,* Nov. 30, 1978. Calvin R. Worthington

His hands were rough and exceedingly strong. He could gently prune a fruit tree or firmly wrestle an ornery mule into harness. He could draw and saw a square with quick accuracy. He had been known to peel his knuckles upside a tough jaw. But what I remember most is the special warmth from those hands soaking through my shirt as he would take me by the shoulder, and, hunkering down beside my ear, point out the glittering swoop of a blue hawk, or a rabbit asleep in its lair. They were good hands that served him well and failed him in only one thing: they never learned to write.

My father was illiterate. The number of illiterates in our country has steadily declined, but if there were only one I would be saddened, remembering my father and the pain he endured because his hands never learned to write.

He started in the first grade, where the remedy for a wrong answer was ten ruler strokes across a stretched palm. For some reason, shapes, figures and recitations just didn't fall into the right pattern inside his six-year-old towhead. Maybe he suffered from some type of learning handicap such as dyslexia. His father took him out of school after several months and set him to a man's job on the farm.

Years later, his wife, with her fourth-grade education, would try to teach him to read. And still later I would grasp his big fist between my small hands and awkwardly help him trace the letters of his name. He submitted to the ordeal, but soon grew restless. Flexing his fingers and kneading his palms, we would declare that he had had enough and depart for a long, solitary walk.

Finally, one nigh when he thought no one saw, he slipped away with his son's second-grade reader and labored over the words, until they became too difficult. He pressed his forehead into the pages and wept, "Jesus—Jesus—not even a child's book!" Thereafter, no amount of persuading could bring him to sit with pen and paper.

From the farm to road building and later factory work, his hands served him well. His mind was keen, his will to work unsurpassed. During World War II, he was a pipefitter in a shipyard and installed the complicated guts of mighty fighting ships. His enthusiasm and efficiency brought an offer to become line boss—until he was handed the qualification test. His fingers could trace a path across the blueprints while his mind imagined the pipes lacing through the heart of the ship. He could recall every twist and turn of the pipes. But he couldn't read or write.

After the shipyard closed, he went to the cotton mill, where he labored at night, and stole from his sleeping hours the time required to run the farm. When the mill shut down, he went out each morning looking for work—only to return night after night and say to Mother as she fixed his dinner, "They just don't want anybody who can't take their tests."

It had always been hard for him to stand before a man and make an X mark for his name, but the hardest moment of all was when he placed "his mark" by the name someone else had written for him, and saw another walk away with the deed to his beloved farm. When it was over, he stood before the window and slowly turned the pen he still held in his hands—gazing, unseeing, down the mountainside. I went to the springhouse that afternoon and wept for a long while.

Eventually, he found another cotton-mill job, and we moved into a millhouse village with a hundred look-alike houses. He never quite adjusted to town life. The blue of his eyes faded; the skin across his cheekbones became a little slack. But his hands kept their strength, and their warmth still soaked through when he would sit me on his lap and ask that I read to him from the Bible. He took great pride in my reading and would listen for hours as I struggled through the awkward phrases.

Once he had heard "a radio preacher" relate that the Bible said, "The man that doesn't provide for his family is worse than a thief and an infidel and will never enter the Kingdom of Heaven." Often he would ask me to read that part to him, but I was never able to find it. Other times, he would sit at the kitchen table leafing through the pages as though by a miracle he might be able to read the passage should he turn to the right page. Then he would sit staring at the Book, and I knew he was wondering if God was going to refuse him entry into heaven because his hands couldn't write.

When Mother left once for a weekend to visit her sister, Dad went to the store and returned with food for dinner while I was busy building my latest homemade wagon. After the meal he said he had a surprise for dessert, and went out to the kitchen, where I could hear him opening a can. Then everything was quiet. I went to the doorway, and saw him standing before the sink with an open can in his hand. "The picture looked just like pears," he mumbled. He walked out and sat on the back steps, and I knew he had been embarrassed before his son. The can read "Whole

FIGURE 3.2
Continued

White Potatoes," but the picture on the label did look a great deal like pears.

I went and sat beside him, and asked if he would point out the stars. He knew where the Big Dipper and all the other stars were located, and we talked about how they got there in the first place. He kept that can on a shelf in the woodshed for a long while, and a few times I saw him turning it in his hands as if the touch of the words would teach his hands to write.

Years later, when Mom died, I tried to get him to come live with my family, but he insisted on staying in his small frame house on the edge of town with a few farm animals and a garden plot. His health was failing and he was in and out of the hospital with several mild heart attacks. Old Doc Green saw him weekly and gave him medication, including nitroglycerine tablets to put under his tongue should he feel an attack coming on.

My last fond memory of Dad was watching as he walked across the brow of a hillside meadow, with those big, warm hands—now gnarled with age—resting on the shoulders of my two children. He stopped to point out, confidentially, a pond where he and I had swum and fished years before. That night, my family and I flew to a new job and new home, overseas. Three weeks later, he was dead of a heart attack.

I returned alone for the funeral. Doc Green told me how sorry he was. In fact, he was bothered a bit, because he had just written Dad a new nitroglycerine prescription, and the druggist had filled it. Yet the bottle of pills had not been found on Dad's person. Doc Green felt that a pill might have kept him alive long enough to summon help.

An hour before the chapel service, I found myself standing near the edge of Dad's garden, where a neighbor had found him. In grief, I stopped to trace my fingers in the earth where a great man had reached the end of life. My hand came to rest on a half-buried brick, which I aimlessly lifted and tossed aside, before noticing underneath it the twisted and battered, yet unbroken, soft plastic bottle that had been beaten into the soft earth.

As I held the bottle of nitroglycerine pills, the scene of Dad struggling to remove the cap and in desperation trying to break the bottle with the brick flashed painfully before my eyes. With deep anguish I knew why those big warm hands had lost in their struggle with death. For there, imprinted on the cap, were the words, "Child-Proof Cap—Push Down and Twist to Unlock." The druggist later confirmed that he had just started using the new safety bottle.

I knew if was not a purely rational act, but I went right downtown and bought a leather-bound pocket dictionary and a gold pen set. I bade Dad good-by by placing them in those big old hands, once so warm, which had lived so well, but had never learned to write.

These higher expectations are not surprising when we consider the kinds of materials citizens and workers need to read in their daily lives, such as directions accompanying the IRS tax forms or information that comes with a microwave oven or a DVD player. Technological advances require new and often more sophisticated literacy skills. Functional illiteracy can take a devastating toll—unemployment, poverty, alienation. To maintain a competitive edge in the global workplace, we need to improve our reading, writing, and computing abilities.

Cognitive, Purposeful, and Critical Schemata of Literacy

Cognitive psychologists have described literacy as an observable skill. For them, reading involves decoding and encoding. Think of letters and words as inkblots that make a code. ***Decoding*** requires readers to recognize letters and other word parts and then assemble them into wholes. Doing so requires the cognitive abilities of recognizing the shapes and associating them with their sounds. Once words are decoded, the reader encodes them. ***Encoding*** is making meaning of what these symbols represent. Higher-level cognitive skills are needed in order to integrate and associate these words with meanings.

As a content teacher, you will probably agree that there is more to reading to learn than just decoding and encoding. Literacy comes with a purpose and that purpose may provide the definition of the type of literacy itself. Here are some *simplified* examples

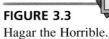

of purposeful conceptions of literacy. ***Cultural literacy*** (Hirsch, 1987) involves knowledge of concepts, items, or facts a person needs to succeed in a cultural context. Some argue that these facts that are so crucial that the person who does not know them will not succeed in society. Advocates of ***multicultural literacy*** recognize that there are many cultures in each society and call for reading and writing that provides a "broad perception in the formulation" of knowledge (Banks, 1991).

In the same vein, those who argue for ***technological literacy*** assert that as society and its technologies continue to change we must be in a continuous process of redefining our definition of literacy (Martorella, 1996).

Other purposeful concepts of literacy include ***civic literacy***, referring to knowledge and ability to read about government and ways of acting in the political sphere. ***Computer literacy*** refers to knowledge about and capacity to use computers for a variety of purpose. ***Scientific literacy*** involves the ability to access and process core knowledge in science. ***Math literacy*** (also called ***numeracy***) is the ability to quantify or express oneself with numbers and mathematics. ***Religious literacy*** is the ability to read and understand the scriptural teachings of a religion. ***Visual literacy*** is the ability to view and create art by recognizing and analyzing different elements, relating them to each other and thus creating meaning (Eubanks, 1997). ***Musical literacy*** is similar to visual literacy, except its medium is auditory (Brophy, 1996; McPherson, 1994).

Critical theorists take a broader view on the purposeful definition of literacy, saying that reading and writing, by its very nature, includes the practice of representation as "a means of organizing, inscribing and containing meaning" (Giroux, 1991). For those who take this approach, literacy is how we make meaning of and transform the world. Take for example Friere's popular understanding of the reading process. "Reading the world always precedes reading the word, and reading the word implies continually reading the world. . . . In a way, however, we can go further and say that reading the [world is preceded] by a certain form of writing it or rewriting it, that is, of transforming it by means of conscious practical work" (Friere, 1991, p. 144). The schema of ***critical literacy*** may be the sum of two questions: (1) What is it like to read the world; and (2) What is it like to rewrite the world by reading the world?

History of the Schema of Content Literacy

McKenna and Robinson (1990) defined ***content literacy*** as the "ability to use reading and writing for the acquisition of new content in a given discipline" (p. 184). Content literacy is therefore a purposeful literacy. First, a short history of how educators came to realize that literacy instruction specific to each content area is needed for most students to be successful across all disciplines. Then, we will look to see how the skills required for content literacy may vary from discipline to discipline.

In 1917, Thorndike observed that many children learned to read because they found reading of stories, especially those related to history, geography, and the like, of interest. In the 1920s the U. S. Bureau of Education acknowledged that each subject matter area contributes directly to the development of reading competency (Gray, 1925). Professor Gray helped popularize the slogan "Every teacher should be, to a certain extent, a teacher of reading" (Moore, Readence, & Rickelman, 1983). It was Gray who provided content teachers with direction as to how to include reading instruction in their curricula.

In 1941, Bond and Bond (1941) authored a methods text on developmental reading in the high school stating that every subject demands specialized and complicated reading skills, which must be developed in that subject itself. In the early 1970s research in content reading emerged as a focus and in 1973 eight states required coursework in content reading instruction for secondary teacher certification. Ten years later, 31 states had this requirement. Those who integrated content reading strategies into their instruction reported greater confidence in their teaching (Pearce & Bader, 1986), and that their lessons were better organized for student success (Conley, 1986). Furthermore, the research of Alvermann and Swafford (1989) indicated improved learning on the part of students who were taught and who used content reading instruction.

In the 1990s, national standards for performance were established in almost all subjects; high-stakes performance tests were mandated; and issues of second-language learning got renewed attention. Since 2001, the push for high test scores in reading and writing has renewed an interest in teaching reading and writing in many secondary classrooms.

Learning to Read vs. Reading to Learn

There is a difference between learning to read and reading to learn. When learning to read we learn letters, the sounds they make, how to blend them together to make words, and how to read sentences and paragraphs. We usually learn to read in elementary school; unfortunately, it is not unusual for secondary teachers to be faced with the challenge of students who haven't yet learned how to read. Methods to do this are the subject for another book.

In the area of integrated content literacy we are concerned with helping students learn to read to acquire new content in a given discipline. We usually start reading to learn in the fifth or sixth grade when presented with our first content area textbooks.

As the purposes for reading in the content areas vary, so do the skills required to read with understanding. The left-hand column of Table 3.1 gives a summary of some of the purposes required to read from textbooks in different content areas. The right-hand column lists some of the specific reading skills needed to accomplish these purposes.

As you review this table, ask yourself the following:

1. What specific content reading skills must my students use in order to read to learn in my discipline?
2. How are these skills the same as those required in other content area classes? How are they different?

This table is by no means complete. Make notes of other ideas that need to be included so that you may share them with your colleagues.

TABLE 3.1 Reading to Learn: Purposes and Skills

Purposes for reading from textbook	Reading skills required to meet these purposes
English	
• Comparing actions and motivation; exploring the influence of setting and of characters on each other; and/or seeing recurring patterns in literature and human behavior. • Explaining human characteristics and behavior. • Seeing personal and real-world connections; and/or developing imagination.	• Ability to recognize plot, character, conflict, setting, and theme. • Ability to read descriptive language; to interpret creatively; and/or to make literal, inferential, and critical interpretations. • Ability to adapt reading rate to changes in passage difficulty. • Ability to read in many voices and discern meaning with few graphics.
Math	
• Attaching meaning to symbols; giving reasons for procedures; and/or evaluating the reasonableness of answers. • Using mathematical knowledge to see real-world applications. • Engaging in quantitative reasoning as a reasonable rather than arbitrary activity.	• Ability to read compact and precise language including horizontal and vertical text. • Ability to make critical inferences and deductions. • Ability to preview, read slowly and thoroughly and know when rereading is needed. • Ability to read quantitative graphics and visuals. • Ability to use words, pictures, or numbers to explain thinking.
Social Studies	
• Making facts and concepts meaningful within a social/historical context. • Explaining social and historical patterns. • Exploring chronological patterns and causation. • Defining socially responsible behavior.	• Ability to read through larges volumes of text, including source and interpretative documentation. • Ability to use inferential reasoning, think critically and objectively (e.g., cause and effect, chronology, fact from opinion.). • Ability to adapt reading rate (e.g., skimming as well as careful slow reading, and rereading as required). • Ability to interpret graphics and visuals unique to social/historical content.
Science	
• Describing real-world objects, systems, or phenomena. • Explaining laws or theories in a scientific context. • Predicting future observations. • Defining scientifically responsible behavior.	• Ability to read to classify, measure, and examine systems and subsystems. • Ability to understand compact and precise language. • Ability to make inferences, deductions, and separate facts from opinions. • Ability to locate explanation, to follow written directions, to understand detailed statements of fact, to recognize patterns, and to link cause and effect. • Ability to recognize and interpret abbreviations, symbols, charts, equations, and text with diagrams.

TABLE 3.1 Continued

Purposes for reading from textbook	Reading skills required to meet these purposes
Physical Education	
• Developing exercise, health, and moral concepts. • Illustrating competitive and non-competitive skills. • Encouraging lifelong health and fitness.	• Ability to read to classify, measure, and examine systems and subsystems. • Ability to understand compact and precise language. • Ability to make inferences, deductions, and separate fact from opinion. • Ability to locate and understand explanations, to follow directions, to understand detailed statements of fact, to recognize patterns, and to link cause and effect. • Ability to recognize, interpret, and understand diagrams and illustrations. • Ability to associate words with specific concepts of physical motion.
Vocational Education	
• Learning the names and functions of tools. • Interpreting a work situation or job and responding with the appropriate knowledge and skill. • Building the ability to learn more in the face of changing work conditions.	• Ability to understand compact and precise language. • Ability to make inferences, deductions, and separate fact from opinion. • Ability to locate and interpret explanation, to follow directions, to understand detailed statements of fact, to recognize patterns, and to link cause and effect. • Ability to visualize the internal workings of a machine described in text. • Ability to follow diagrams and illustrations. • Ability to associate words with specific physical motion.
Foreign Languages	
• To learn how languages are structured. • Building the ability to use languages to make meaning. • Making connections between language and culture.	• Ability to decode symbols that may have different sound associations than native language. • Ability to discern differing cultural context of words and phrase than in native language. • When reading any content in a foreign language, each of the skills mentioned above.
Visual Arts	
• To read the compositional sources of all kinds of visual materials, messages, objects, and experiences. • Ability to understand the meaning and components of an image.	• To understand relationships among dots, lines, shapes, direction, texture, hue, saturation, value, scale, dimension, and motion.

Name _____ Date _____

 ## Workshop 3.2

Comparing Purpose and Skills

Form a triad with colleagues who teach, or plan to teach, different subjects than your own. Refer to Table 3.1. Let your colleagues know what you added or amended in each column of the table. Once you have done so, answer these questions:

1. How are the skills required to read in one content area the same as those required to read in the other content areas? How are they different? Where do they overlap with each other? You may list these, or use the diagram provided below.

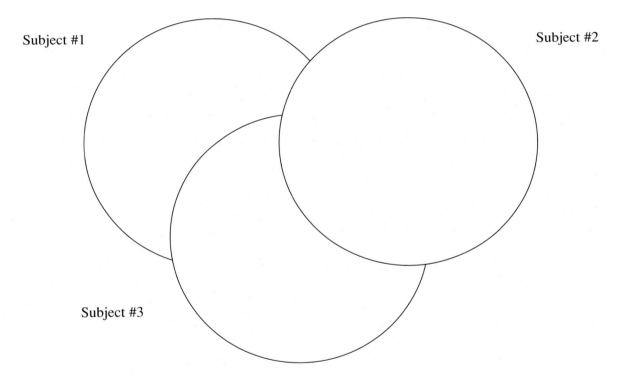

Subject #1

Subject #2

Subject #3

2. Often secondary teachers will assume that teaching of reading and writing is the *sole* responsibility of the English teachers. Given the answers you provided to the first question, is it reasonable to expect English teachers to teach the skills necessary to read in all content areas? Why, or why not?

Introduction to Diversity

Today, more than 54 million students attend American elementary and secondary schools. Of these, 62% are white, 38% are from minority groups, 25% live in poverty, and 13% have special needs (National Center for Educational Statistics, 2005; United States Bureau of the Census, 2005; United States Department of Education, 2005). When we look at the reading and writing scores of those students who are minorities and those who live in poverty, we see that these groups of students are significantly lower than their peers (Campbell, Hombo, & Mazzeo, 2000). What can we do to help improve these scores?

A significant part of the answer to this question is in recognizing that literacy and culture are inseparable. If we want to teach all of our students how to acquire new content knowledge we must include the knowledge and experiences our students use to make meaning. This is what we mean when we say that content literacy instruction must be relevant and responsive to the cultural diversity of our individual students.

Appropriate methods to effectively assess and teach diverse students are presented throughout this text. However, since this chapter introduces schemata for literacy, let us define some of the dimensions of diversity. While doing so, we will describe several misconceptions that may prevent us from being responsive to the needs of all students.

A Schema for Cultural Diversity

Every culture is a blend of cultural influences from dozens of outside peoples and places. However, a number of dimensions have achieved prominence in today's schools. These dimensions include, but are not limited to the following:

- Ethnicity
- People with disabilities
- Religion
- Language minorities
- Gender
- Sexual orientation
- Socioeconomic status (class)
- Family structure

Learning more about diversity can be a first step towards responsive teaching. Here are definitions of some of these dimensions based on the work of Guldin (2002). With these definitions are some examples of false interpretations reinforced by stereotypes. (Stereotypes assume that everyone in a group is alike based on information that is not true or only partly true.)

Ethnicity: A group of people who believe that they have a common origin, and believe they have some distinctive cultural patterns that distinguish them from others, may be called an ethnic group. Ethnic groups include Whites, Hispanics, Blacks, Native Americans, Asians, and Pacific Islanders, to name a few. In using these ethnic categories we can hide the diversity amongst them. For example, the term *White* might refer to those who are Russian, Irish, Italian, French, Dutch, Polish, Slovak, Danish, Swedish, English, Norwegian, Romanian, Hungarian, Czech, etc. The term *Hispanics* is often used to refer collectively to all Spanish speakers. However, it connotes a cultural heritage from Spain. Many Spanish speakers believe they are Chicano or Mexican American, Cuban American, Puerto Rican, etc. Native Americans may identify with any one of hundreds of tribes with distinct cultures of their own. Note that we are not using the term *race*. Most scientists who study human variation have rejected this term as having little biological validity. They tell us that humans vary physically; however, the whole species cannot be broken into a few types. Despite the fact that these divisions are social constructs, they are still used to make very real decisions that can result in real discrimination.

Stereotypical misconceptions around ethnicity and literacy run rampant. Here are but a few:

- *Native American students are "nonverbal." They often refuse to talk before the entire class, avoid eye-contact with teachers, and refuse to answer questions.* This stereotype misses the fact that some Native cultures expect children to listen respectfully, avoid eye contact with elders, and avoid answering questions deemed inappropriate because their answers could embarrass the questioner.

- *African Americans speak Ebonics, an inferior and incorrect form of English.* This stereotype misses the fact that dialects like Ebonics have highly developed phonological and structural rules that include metaphoric language, rhythm, alliteration, and word play, which may be signs of high linguistic intelligence.

- *Asian American students are "model" students who don't need extra academic attention.* Some Asian cultures value and foster demeanor, quietness, and complicity. However, these characteristics should not be confused with academic achievement. Often viewed as a "model minority," many Asian American children who need help are overlooked.

- *Mexican American immigrant parents are easily confused about education and reading and writing assignments.* Actually, the confusion runs both ways. What most English speakers call "education" is school or book learning. What many Mexican immigrants call "educación" has a much broader meaning and includes both manners and moral values. Many Mexican parents think of reading as decoding and encoding and think of "dando conselos," as spontaneously improvised stories, a way to teach comprehension of ways to act in the world.

People with disabilities: While there are many people with disabilities who do not require any assistance, there are also disabled individuals whose limitations do not allow them to function in school without additional support or accommodation. Students with disabilities comprise about 12% of the school population. They include students who have a cognitive disability, Down syndrome, a learning disability, a physical disability, an emotional disability, and/or those who have autism. The content texts we read and the language we use in discussions about them should portray people with disabilities in respectful and realistic ways. When talking about or with people with disabilities, we do not use disability labels to define human beings. Instead we use "person-first" language. Here are a few examples: Individuals wear glasses; they are not myopic. People have cerebral palsy; they are not spastic. Students have autism; they are not autistic. Finally, it is not uncommon to confuse the disabilities students have with their abilities to learn. For example, because a person has cerebral palsy does not mean that they have less than normal intelligence.

Religion: Religious diversity in America has increased over the past two decades. The United States is now about 60% Protestant and 24% Catholic. Jews and Muslims are now approximately 2% each; Buddhists, Hindus, and other religions add to the mix. The number of people not affiliating with any religious grouping has increased significantly. The topic of religion in the schools has been a controversial issue for some time. Discussion about religion and the role it plays in society is not banned from schools; however, literacy activities that overtly endorse one religion over another most certainly are. We address the challenge teachers face in reconciling their personal beliefs with their responsibility to create a learning environment that makes all students feel welcome and valued in Chapter Four and provide further clarification in Appendix F. Finally, the culture of religion may determine how health and illness are viewed. For example, Western medicinal procedures do not address the spiritual nature of some health problems, and hence physical explanations and treatments may be considered entirely inappropriate within these cultures.

Language minorities: By the year 2000, there were 18% of all children in American schools who spoke a language other than English at home, up from 11% in 1980. Spanish is the mostly widely spoken second language. The numbers of children speaking Chinese, Korean, Vietnamese, Thai, Laotian, Farsi, Russian, Asian Indian, and Filipino languages have each doubled or more than doubled since 1980. Students whose daily language at home is not English are more likely to be economically disadvantaged, report difficulty with the English language, have lower graduation rates, and/or higher dropout rates. Some common rules for communicating with limited-English speakers include: (a) speak slowly (not louder) and articulate clearly; (b) avoid slang expressions/proverbs; (c) stay with the main point and avoid peripheral items; and (d) avoid repeating the question, "Do you understand?" Perhaps from observing others following these rules some teachers have developed the misconception that English language learners learn slowly and must therefore be presented "lower-level" academic challenges. Nothing could be further from the truth. English language learners have the same cognitive and affective developmental needs as their English-speaking peers. Finally, it is not uncommon to confuse language challenges with learning disabilities. Exposure to or use of a non-English language in and of itself never causes any handicapping condition, including communication disorders (Barrera, 1993).

Gender: Sex refers to the two major biological reproductive forms (male and female) that occur in living things. *Gender*, on the other hand, refers to the social, cultural, and psychological constructs (masculine and feminine) that society has assigned to these biological differences. *Gender roles* refer to the notions of how men and women should behave because they are male or female. Gender roles have led to inequalities. For example, in the past, females were often discouraged from excelling in mathematical, science, and/or technological literacy, which, in part, led to a "gender gap" in achievement in these areas. Teachers should ask themselves, "Do we treat boys and girls differently in the classroom? Why?" Equity should be the goal. As many writers have noted, equity does not mean everyone gets the same treatment. Equity means that everyone gets what they need, not that one gender gets more or less than the other.

Sexual orientation: The way in which people view and express the sexual component of their personality is their sexual orientation. *Heterosexual* is the term used for those who are attracted to members of the opposite sex. *Homosexual* is the term used for those who are attracted to people of the same sex. *Bisexual* is the term used for people attracted to people of both sexes; *asexual* is the term for those with no attraction to members of either sex. In many of today's classrooms, students who are angry and/or trying to shame each other use the same terminology that describes sexual minorities (e.g., "homo," "queer"). This compounds the hostile reception that sexual minorities receive in many schools. The challenge for teachers is to provide environments in which all students feel safe and respected.

Family and family structure: Family is a concept that varies across cultures. For example, in many cultures it is not unusual to have strong bonds and loyalty to members who have not lived under the same roof for many years. Other cultures value physical proximity. Childrearing practices reflect cultural context. For example, it is appropriate in some cultures for grandparents to be the primary caregivers; in other cultures, it is older siblings who are expected to assume this role. Difference in family structure should be taken into account when creating assignments that require students to share their family backgrounds. For example, students whose parents are undergoing a divorce, students who recently experienced a death in the family, and/or students who may have a parent in prison, all need to feel safe and respected.

There is an affective, very personal element to teaching content literacy in ways that are relevant and responsive to the diverse cultures in the classroom. In an attempt to integrate this perspective, this edition of *Integrated Content Literacy* includes a new and unique feature, a series of essays at the end of several chapters, entitled *From the Pages of Our Lives.* The authors of these essays are teachers who come from diverse backgrounds and provide heartfelt stories that add meaning to the content literacy concepts and methods introduced in the chapters that precede them. These include: *A Weekend with My Grandfather,* at the end of Chapter Two, *Evangelina Can Read,* at the end of this chapter, *Sharing Is Healing* at the end of Chapter Four, *Writing My Way to My Family's History* at the end of Chapter Eight, *My High School's Transformational Power* at the end of Chapter Eleven, and *The Truth, Whispered or Shouted. . . ,* at the end of Chapter Twelve. Since all of these essays deal with dimensions of diversity, you may want to preview them at this point in time.

Censorship Concerns

A chapter on schemata of literacy and diversity is not complete without reference to a serious problem in today's education world—censorship (Durban, 2005; Neuman, 1986; Oboler, 1981; Pipkin & Lent, 2002). Censors can wield great power over what publishers dare to print and can object to ideas and materials presented in content classrooms. In America, censors generally look for nine items:

1. Sex (risqué, filthy, indecent, too explicit)
2. Patriotism (un-American, anti- or pro-war)
3. Religion (atheist, irreligious, un-Christian)
4. Magic
5. Civil rights (bias)
6. Offensive or sexist language (profane, unfit for human eyes or ears)
7. Secular humanism (a nonreligious movement)
8. Violent (gratuitous, lengthy, explicit)
9. Defamation of our historical personalities

When Teachers Are Confronted with Censors (Tonjes, 1991)

1. Make sure every book selected for classroom study or on supplementary reading lists meet solid educational objectives. Know every book on your list in order to talk about it intelligently if challenged. Also preview every film.

2. Play the devil's advocate when reviewing your school's material selection policy. Challenge each statement as if you were a censor. Then work together to strengthen the policies.

3. No one should have the authority to remove a book without a review and recommendation of a special committee. Make sure any person lodging a complaint has a chance to talk informally with the teacher or librarian responsible for the work in question.

4. Make sure your school system has informed citizens of its philosophy, curriculum, goals, policies, and procedures.

5. Give anyone with a complaint a fair hearing. Do so in public, when possible. One of the largest protest groups in our country was formed by a parent who was "put down" by a teacher when asking about a book.

6. Become acquainted with protest groups' publications, learning their buzz words, and be prepared to refute their challenges.

7. Be certain you and your principal are on the same page as to censorship concerns.

8. Help form a support group of citizens such as ministers who believe in intellectual freedom. Do your best job possible and you will have many to rally around you in your time of need.

Censored Books

The following partial list of books have either already been censored or are likely to be soon. How many have you read? Which category of censorship do they fall under? Check the familiar ones and be ready to discuss.

The Catcher in the Rye	*One Flew Over the Cuckoo's Nest*
Go Ask Alice	*The Sun Also Rises*
Of Mice and Men	*For Whom the Bell Tolls*
The Grapes of Wrath	*A Farewell to Arms*
Catch-22	*The Great Gatsby*
Brave New World	*Animal Farm*
Lord of the Flies	*Adventures of Huckleberry Finn*
To Kill a Mockingbird	*The Outsiders*
Slaughterhouse Five	*The Pigman*
Forever	*Harry Potter* series
My Darling, My Hamburger	*Our Town*
Are You There, God? It's Me Margaret	*1984*
The American Heritage Dictionary	*Death of a Salesman*
Romeo and Juliet	*Othello*
The Wizard of Oz	*Merchant of Venice*
The Glass Menagerie	*Summer and Smoke*
I Know Why a Caged Bird Sings	*Bridge to Terabitha*
The Giver	*Goosebumps* series
The Color Purple	*A Wrinkle in Time*
A Light in the Attic	*Bless Me, Ultima*

And on . . . and on . . . and on . . .

Qualities of the Mature Reader

Those who have achieved a high and wide degree of literacy are fortunate indeed, for not only are they able to read necessary material efficiently, but also finding pleasure in doing so. Mature readers have the capacity to lose themselves in a good story, travel around the world without leaving their armchair, and can fill their minds with ideas not actually seen.

Even though the formal teaching of reading is usually discontinued after sixth grade, whether students fully develop into mature readers is a hit-or-miss proposition. You may wish to self-assess your own reading maturity by completing Workshop 3.3. Remember that awareness is the first step to change and improvement.

Whatever your personal definition of literacy, or perspectives on diversity, and no matter how mature a reader you are, it would be helpful for you to turn back to the cognitive map (Figure 3.1) at the beginning of this chapter. It shows how you, as teacher, may direct (empower) your students toward engagement in literacy learning, a process that is culturally responsive and relevant to everyone in the choir (your class).

Reading, writing, speaking, listening (the language arts) are the basis for making meaning and thinking. When integrated with specific content literacy it allows for better construction of meaning, to better master the content area studied.

Readers comprehend by taking in concepts and processing them in a variety of ways. Connected to this taking in is the other side of the coin—writing to learn, which involves generating concepts and processing them by writing. By learning how to best use these processes students become more proficient in all content areas.

Now, in the 21st century, we are faced with difficult decisions as to assessment, school climate, curriculum changes, discipline, and the need to learn more about diverse cultures so that we may meet the needs of all of our students. Just knowing our subject matter is not enough. We must be able to empower our students with the tools they need to master the various disciplines with an attitude of engagement—motivated to continue learning.

Name _____ Date _____

Part I
Self-Assessment of Reading Maturity

How Mature a Reader Are You? Here are general reading factors as they relate to the behavior of mature readers. Check those that apply to you.

General Factors	Behaviors
Interest, attitude, and valuing	_____ 1. Show enjoyment and appreciation of reading.
	_____ 2. Choose to read at times over other pleasant options.
	_____ 3. Use reading to satisfy and extend personal interests through a wide variety of topics and materials.
	_____ 4. Willingly state a commitment to reading as a lifetime adventure.
Purpose	_____ 5. Read for specific purposes.
	_____ 6. Use a wide range of purposes.
	_____ 7. Use their own purposes as well as assigned ones.
	_____ 8. Are always ready to change purposes when the need directs.
Rate adaptability	_____ 9. Read at rates determined by their purpose and the difficulty of the material.
	_____ 10. Have a variety of rates for whole selections or within selections.
Study learning	_____ 11. Have mastered locational, reference skills.
	_____ 12. Are adept at organizing information through listening, outlining, and note taking.
	_____ 13. Interpret graphics of all types.
	_____ 14. Apply study-learning strategies for immediate recall and long-term retention.
Comprehension	_____ 15. Use thinking strategies at the literal, interpretive, and critical/creative levels.
	_____ 16. Reflect on ideas presented.
	_____ 17. Predict outcomes.
	_____ 18. Tap into the writer's organizational plan.
	_____ 19. Relate new ideas to old.
	_____ 20. Use mental imagery when reading narrative, descriptions, etc.
	_____ 21. Perceive paragraph organization.
	_____ 22. Read like a writer.
Vocabulary	_____ 23. Use several strategies for identifying words and establishing meanings, including context, structural analysis, phonics, and/or dictionary.
	_____ 24. Consistently enlarge technical and general vocabulary.
	_____ 25. Recognize multiple meanings and connotations in context.
	_____ 26. Maintain a positive attitude toward word study.

Part II

Few of us can claim honestly to be mature readers in *all* aspects. It is actually possible to spend an entire life-time refining our reading, thinking, writing, and study skills. Attitude about these matters is an important determinant to successful mature reading. The following activities, then, have two main purposes: (1) to give you the opporutnity to assess for yourself your specific areas of strengths and weaknesses; and (2) to introduce you to a sampling of the vairety and scope of skills to be explored in this text. These exercises should be taken objectively, and any sharing of results in class should be optional.

The following activity is a form of *advance organizer* in that it includes categories of questions representing areas of skills deemed appropriate for a mature reader. Because *no one* is an ideal reader, you should expect to find some areas that are not as strong as others. Again this survey should be considered private information, with sharing on a voluntary basis only.

Quick Survey for Adult Readers: How Mature a Reader Are You?

Directions: Note the organization of this survey. The left-hand side indicates the terminology in the field of reading to which this activity refers; the middle column asks you a question about how you think you function in reading with respect to this category; and a third column is provided for you to write a response to that question. Obviously, this preassessment presupposes no preparation for any given set of answers. Please respond rapidly to the questions. These may be referred to in later class sessions.

Category	Question	Response
Motivation	1. List two books you have read lately (*not* work-required or study-related) for pure pleasure, inspiration, or general expansion of your knowledge of the world.	
Interests/ attitudes/ values	2. If you have the choice between reading a story or watching it on television, which would you choose most often?	
	3. How much time each day do you put aside for recreational or pleasure reading?	
Variety of interests	4. Put a "+" by all those read regularly, a "0" by those read occasionally, and a "–" by those read rarely.	

Fiction
1. Romance ___
2. Adventure ___
3. Mystery ___
4. Historical ___
5. Poetry ___
6. Other ___

Nonfiction
7. Autobiography ___
8. Biography ___
9. Political ___
10. Historical ___
11. Other (specify) ___
_____

Newspaper
12. Sports ___
13. Front page ___
14. Editorial ___
15. Financial ___
16. Other ___

Magazines
17. Women's/Men's ___
18. News ___
19. Literary ___
20. Sports ___
21. Other ___

Category	Question	Response

5. Look at your responses to item 4 (variety of interests) on the previous page. Would you say that you read widely with a broad range of interests?

Circle one of the following:

Very much so   Somewhat
Not as much as I should   Not at all
I'm not sure

Vocabulary

6. Describe your own system for building up vocabulary. If you have none, leave this blank.

7. List and define three new words that you have encountered through reading in the past three months.

    1. _____ _____

    2. _____ _____

    3. _____ _____

8. Circle strategies you use for identifying unfamiliar words while reading.

configuration   phonics
context clues   dictionary
structural analysis   other: _____

9. List two technical content terms you have learned recently and give exact definitions.

    1. _____ _____

    2. _____ _____

Syntax

10. Write the meaning of the italicized nonsense words in the following context:

    a. Jerry was *glongering* the data. _____

    b. The man *galurned* the *troper.* _____ _____

Rate adaptability

11. At what rate do you read the following?

    a. very rapid   b. rapid   c. average   d. slow

    1. Novels   _____   4. Magazines   _____
    2. Newspapers   _____   5. Textbooks   _____
    3. Poetry   _____   6. Other   _____

Category	Question			Response

12. Can you skim a text chapter in three minutes and recite the main ideas?

   (Yes/No/Maybe/Don't know)

   Do you read everything at the same rate?

   (Yes/No/Maybe/Don't know)

Category	Question	Very Easy	Somewhat Easy	Difficult
Getting the gist of the topic (liberal comprehension)	13. How easy is it for you to:			
	a. spot the topic sentence in a paragraph?	___		
	b. read to follow directions?	___		
	c. identify a pattern or a sequence of ideas?	___		
	d. relate supporting details to main ideas?	___		
Thinking about what you read	14. How easy is it for you to:			
	a. spot cause and effect?	___		
	b. see comparison and contrast?	___		
	c. identify the mood, time, and place?	___		
Critical/ creative comprehension	15. How easy is it for you to:			
	a. use what you have learned in new situations?	___		
	b. combine concepts into new and innovative ideas?	___		
	c. make judgments about your reading while stating your own criteria for judgment?	___		

Study skills   16. List strategies you use for mastering text reading in content fields.

1. _____
2. _____
3. _____
4. _____

	Very	Average	Not at All	Don't Know
17. How well do you interpret graphics?				
18. How efficient are you in your use of the library to locate hard-to-find materials?				
19. How easily do you identify key points in a lecture from your notes after several months?				
20. How well do you remember material over a period of time?				

Category	Question	Response
Self-assessment	Now that you have finished this survey, look back over your responses and identify those categories that you believe need immediate improvement. Set a few goals for yourself for improving at least two or three of these categories by the end of the term. Write here the areas you have selected (e.g., vocabulary):	

1. _____

2. _____

3. _____

At the end of the term look back through this self-assessment to reevaluate yourself in terms of how much change, growth, or enjoyment there has been.

I have changed in the area of _____

_____

_____

I have grown most in _____

_____

_____

I enjoy much more than I did _____

_____

_____

Cinquain as Summary

Literacy
Integrating content
Censorship—crucial concern
Diversity, engagement, mature readers
Reading/writing

 ## Summary

National standards suggest that educators should understand how students differ in their approaches to learning and create learning opportunities that are adapted to diverse learners and that teachers should help students become knowledgeable, reflective, creative, and critical members of a variety of literacy communities. To do so we must understand what we mean by "literacy" and "diversity." We began by examining the historical origins and definitions of literacy with special attention given to content area literacy. Other definitions we explored included survival, functional, cognitive, critical, cultural, multicultural, civic, computer, scientific, visual, and musical literacies. There is a tremendous span between the functionally illiterate to the mature reader. Qualities constituting a mature reader include interest, attitude, valuing, purpose, rate adaptability, study learning, comprehension, and vocabulary.

Literacy and culture are inseparable. Effective content literacy instruction must be relevant and responsive to the cultural diversity of the individual. Doing so requires the development of a schema for cultural diversity. Cultural dimensions include, but are not limited to ethnicity, disabilities, language, gender, socioeconomic status, religion, and sexual orientation. Problems and possible solutions to censorship were addressed, as the world today requires knowledgeable teachers who are aware of their options.

FROM THE PAGES OF OUR LIVES

Evangelina Can Read

by Leila Flores-Dueñas

Dr. Leila Flores-Dueñas is a professor at the University of New Mexico. Her areas of expertise include language and literacy, sociocultural studies, and teacher education. Her research interests include understanding the role of culture in text comprehension and literacy learning of minority students. In this essay Dr. Flores-Dueñas tells of Evangelina's needs to negotiate the culturally different literacy expectations of school and home and how teachers can help their students do so.

She seemed to always wear long tee shirts beneath her never-been-cut coarse hair that hid her dark complexion and round face. She was friends with the newly arrived immigrant girls, more so than any other students. With other *Mexicana* girls Evangelina spoke mostly Spanish. They giggled a lot when they had the opportunity to be together. Perhaps she identified with them because she, too, was born in Mexico. Evangelina had come to the United States with her family at the end of her 5TH grade year. Now in the 7TH grade, her ESL teacher, Ms. C., described Evangelina as a "shy and nice student who needed help in reading." Ms. C. went on to explain that Evangelina switched between Spanish and English easily but it was hard for her to determine whether or not she could maintain a conversation in one language or the other.

At the time I was working on a research project in Evangelina's school. I wanted a better understanding of how the process of reading comprehension might be different for Latino students in English, their second language. I got to know Evangelina in one of our after-school focus groups, a group of five students who met twice a week over the spring semester of that year. In our meetings together, Evangelina mostly spoke English unless the whole group spoke in Spanish. Most of the texts we read were written in English, with the exception of a few with occasional words or phrases in Spanish.

Ms. C. indicated that even though Evangelina had been working below grade level in English early in the school year, she was still making progress in her literacy learning. For example, she stated that each week Evangelina understood more vocabulary than most other ESL students in her class. She attributed this to Evangelina's level of native language literacy development.

Evangelina was fortunate enough to have had access to schooling in Mexico, where she reportedly performed well in all subjects. Theoretically, Evangelina's language learning reflected what research in bilingual education tells us: The more second language learners have the opportunity to develop literacy in their native language, the more they are able to transfer language skills and academic concepts into another language. Even so, Evangelina did not feel that she was a good reader. She felt that she needed to improve in reading. That is why she chose to meet with me, and four other English language learners, after school twice weekly.

Evangelina reported that she did not read for pleasure. However, she very much wanted to like reading. She told me that although she sounded like she could read, she had little faith in her reading abilities to really comprehend what she was reading. Like many other Latino second language learners who do not read for pleasure, she preferred to talk. This form of communication was much more meaningful since it was how her family shared and had fun together. When she thought about the way that her family and friends preferred to communicate, and the opposing way that people in the American school wanted students to communicate, Evangelina was left with the message that she was the one who would need to change. When in school, she would *not* be able to use what she had learned from her family and community about good story telling. This opposition of expectations made it difficult for Evangelina to have a *healthy literate identity*. Understanding that was half of the battle.

Desiring to know more about the home-school relationship, I visited Evangelina's home. During those interviews I attempted to get a better picture of the family's expectations for Evangelina and their perspectives on her literacy learning. At home, Evangelina's reading was more communal than at school. She regularly read aloud to her three younger siblings. The school had required nightly reading to her younger brothers, and she was in charge of that.

I interviewed her father about her literacy experiences and he explained to me that he and his wife help their children with school work as much as they can but they were limited because of their nighttime jobs and because they only had a third grade education from Mexico. When I asked Evangelina's father about the kinds of things he and his wife talk about with Evangelina, he stated that they talk with her a lot about the future and about doing well in school. The following narrative illustrates the commitment that Mr. Valdes demonstrated to his children:

Le hablamos mucho del futuro, de que sin la escuela uno no es nada, y que hay que estudiar para ser algo. Yo le digo que tiene que estudiar por que quiero, que cuando sea grande, que sea algo. Y que si no hace su tarea, pues no va a terminar . . . entonces, ella se va a quedar siempre en bajas calificaciones. Y que yo quiero, bueno, uno quisiera que sus hijos fueran los mejores, ¿verdad? Y este, a veces también a uno le afecta, la razón del trabajo y como ahorita estamos los dos trabajando de noche, siempre tenemos que estar por el teléfono, hable y hable, "que hagan la tarea, duérmanse temprano" y que esto y lo otro. Pero estoy luchando. A veces me cambian pa'llá o me cambian en la mañana para que me quede en la tarde ya con ellos (los niños) para remediar, y aunque es en la mañana, siempre les reviso su tarea y todo.

Translated into English, he said:

We talk to her a lot about the future, that without school you are nothing, and that you have to study to be something. I tell her that she has to study because I want for her, when she is older, to be something (important). And that if she does not do her homework, well, she will never finish (school) and she will keep low grades. And that I want, well, one would want for one's children to be the best, right? Well, sometimes, too, things affect what you do, because of work and like right now, we are both working at night, so we always have to be calling on the telephone, talking and talking, "you need to do your homework, go to sleep early" and this and that. But I'm working hard (for them). Sometimes they change (my schedule) one way or they make me work in the morning so I can be with them in the afternoons but at least I can correct (their work . . . and even if it's in the morning, I always check their homework and everything else.

I've included Evangelina's father's words here because his family's way of working with their children, the hopes they had for them, and the many struggles they were having are different than what is often portrayed in the general media. Teachers also misinterpret immigrant parent involvement often describing it a being non-caring, or worse, non-existent, when it comes to helping their children with the academic work.

Evangelina's father is a gentle man. He reported that he had much more patience with the children than his wife. At the time of our interview he was working the night shift and taking care of the youngest boy during the morning. He shared many of the younger children's books with me and told me about how he expected Evangelina to be an example for her four younger brothers. He also introduced me to Evangelina's 16 and 17-year-old aunts who lived with them. Both of them had hair teased high above their heads and faces heavy with make-up. At the time of this interview, neither of the teenagers attended school. Evangelina did not

have many role models to show her how to succeed in American schools.

Unfortunately, many secondary teachers haven't had the preparation required to improve their teaching in ways that will meet the needs of these students. Knowing little about students like Evangelina, they are often susceptible to public perceptions of minority families and this in turn may influence their own expectations for these students. Learning more about the complex socio-cultural context in which Evangelina and her peers use literacy skills is a necessary step that we must take to be able to make informed decisions about what we teach and how we teach it. Doing so requires us to consider the complexities of conflicting home and school "worlds" that send mixed messages about literate identity. As teachers, it is our job to figure that part out for our students. I discovered this as we read, retold and discussed particular stories and the literacy learning experiences that accompanied them.

Throughout our focus group discussions that semester, we read stories from the approved 7TH grade curriculum, and others that seemed more culturally relevant to the Latino students (mostly Mexican descent). First we would read chapters from selected books. Then we would retell these stories in writing. Finally we would engage in conversations about the reading processes they used to make sense of the text. Evangelina was the hardest to hear because of her soft voice; but when she did speak up, she surprised the members of our group with her insightful comments.

Over time, Evangelina articulated her theory about what goes on in her mind when she is reading from a text that she, and others in the group, considered difficult. Some of her observations are especially noteworthy. For example, Angelina insisted that she needed to read out loud to have the best understanding of the story. The other English language learners agreed. So we tested the theory to see if indeed they did comprehend better if they read aloud compared to reading the same text silently. Using "think-alouds" we examined the processes they used for reading comprehension such as use of visualization or context clues. [Editor's note: Think-alouds are very much like the reading procedures described in Chapters Seven and Twelve of this book.]

I would first model what they were to do and then, as a group, they would practice voicing what they understood about what they had read aloud, or silently. They would also discuss their thoughts about the story itself. Next I set up individual think-aloud sessions and asked each of them to answer general and detailed questions about the material they were reading. In all, we looked at the quality of their responses. Together, we came to the conclusion that all students had difficulty with pronunciation, and this, as Evangelina explained, "got in the way of comprehending the story." Therefore, they found out that they did understand texts much better if they read them silently. Silent reading also provided opportunities to visualize more, use context clues, and thereby make better sense of the text. They also found that reading "hard words" was easier because in silent reading they were not so focused on "sounding right," so they were free to try to make sense about what they were reading.

As secondary teachers we often require students to read the classics we were required to read when we were in middle and high school. Knowing that only some students comprehend or are motivated by the content of these texts, we should begin to rethink how we go about selecting reading materials for students such as Evangelina. Here's how we did this in our focus groups: The five Latino students read materials that were selections deemed "important" because they were traditional literature. Most of these stories, several of which had won prestigious awards, reflected White, middle-class values and morals. I chose to supplement these with stories written by Latino/a writers, labeled appropriate for 7–9TH grade students. These included works by Sandra Cisneros, David Rice and Rudolfo Anaya. After reading several of these, Evangelina voiced the sentiments of the group: "Wow, we CAN read. . . . it's just that all this time we have been reading things that don't interest us." After all, it is easier to understand the main ideas of literature in which we are interested, literature with topics and people who reflect our lives. Indeed, these students found that when they read mostly European American novel chapters, they worried so much about whether or not they were "getting it" that the extra thinking they had to do got in the way of their comprehension. Culturally familiar literature allowed them to focus " . . . less on their reading and more on understanding the story."

Traditional texts, especially those that have won awards, often reflect the values of the authors of those texts. Minority students like Evangelina need to be introduced to these materials, however, they also need to be introduced to materials written by and about their own cultures so that they will be able to realize that they can read both. As Evangelina explained, "We need to know that we CAN read. Reading can make us travel in our minds. But sometimes we don't get to even find out that we are good readers because they [teachers] always give us stuff to read that is boring and has nothing to say about us [Mexicans]." She, and the others, suggested that teachers should give them readings that are more compelling. In Evangelina's words, ". . . just like adults, they read stories that are interesting to them, not because they are 'good' for them. That way, we can go on and read other stories to find out why others are so interested in them." It's hard to argue with her logic. Stories that are relevant to their lives are of higher interest. Higher interest promotes more reading. More reading leads to the skills necessary to tackle other texts. In Evangelina's words: "When we find out that we can read . . . then we want to read more, like what we have to read in school."

Questions for Reflection and Discussion

1. What conflict made it difficult for Evangelina to have a "healthy literate identity"? Why was understanding this conflict "half the battle"? What was the other half?

2. Flores-Dueñas made adjustments in the content (books selected) in order make it more relevant. She also made adjustments in her teaching so that she could be more responsive to the needs of her students. What adjustments did she make and why do you think they worked?

3. Think of one or two content area texts you plan to teach with your students. What supplement texts might you use that would be more relevant to the students who read them?

4. Reread the sampling of standards that are at the beginning of Chapter Three. In what ways are these addressed by the teacher and students described in this essay? In what ways are they not addressed?

Janice Brendible's essay *The Truth, Whispered or Shouted* . . tells the story of an Alaskan Native young woman struggling to negotiate the culturally different literacy expectations of school and home. If you have the time and inclination, you may want to turn to the end of Chapter Twelve and read it. Comparing the two essays may yield insights worthy of further thought and discussion.

References and Recommended Readings

Agree, J. (1999). There it was, that one sex scene: English teachers on censorship. *English Journal, 89,* 61–69.

Akamatsu, N. (2003). The effects of first language orthographic features on second language reading in text. *Language Learning, 53* (2), 207–231.

Alexander, P. A., & Jelton, T. L. (2000). Learning from text: A multidimensional and developmental perspective. In M. J. Kamil, P. B. Mosenthal,. P. D. Pearson, & R. Barr (Eds.). *Handbook of reading research,* pp. 111, 285–310. Mahwah, NJ: Lawrence Erlbaum Associates.

Alvermann, D., & Swafford, J. (1989). Do content area strategies have a research base? *Journal of Reading, 32,* 388–394.

Au, K. (1998). Social constructivism and the school literacy learning of students of diverse backgrounds. *Journal of Literacy Research, 30,* 297–310.

Banks, J. (1991). Multicultural literacy and curriculum reform. *Educational Horizons, 69,* 135–140.

Baron, D. (2002 February 11). Will anyone accept the good news on literacy? *The Chronicle of Higher Education, 78,* B10.

Barrera, I. (1993). Effective and appropriate instruction for all children: The challenge of cultural/linguistic diversity and young children with special needs. *Topics in Early Childhood Special Education, 13* (4), 461–487.

Bean, T. W., Bean, S. K., & Bean, K. F. (1999). Intergeneration conversations and two adolescents multiple literacies: Implications for defining content area literacy. *Journal of Adolescent and Adult Literacy, 42,* 438–448.

Beers, K. (1996). No time, no interest, no way: The three voices of aliteracy. *School Library Journal, 42,* 110–113.

Bicknell, J. (1883). First fruits of Butler's inaugural. *New England Journal of Education, 17* (4), 54.

Bigelow, M., & Tarone, E. (2004). The role of literacy level in second language acquisition: Doesn't who we study determine what we know? *TESOL Quarterly, 38,* 689–708.

Binkley, M., & Williams, T. (1997). *Reading literacy in the United States.* Washington, DC: U.S. Department of Education.

Bond, G., & Bond, E. (1941). *Developmental reading in the high school.* New York: MacMillan.

Brophy, T. (1996). Building literacy with guided composition. *Music Educators Journal,* 15–18.

Campbell, J., Hombo, C., & Mazzeo, J. (2000). *NAEP trends in academic progress: Three decades of student performance.* Jesup, MD: U.S. Department of Education.

Clancy, M. (1979). *From memory to written record: England, 1066–1307.* Cambridge, MA: Harvard University Press.

Conley, M. (1986). Teachers conceptions, decision and changes during initial classroom lessons containing content reading strategies. In J. Niles & R. Lalik (Eds.), *Solving problems in literacy: Learners, teachers and searchers. Thirty-five yearbook of the National Reading Conference* (pp. 120–126). Oak Creek, WI: National Reading Conference.

Council of Chief State School Officers. (2005). INTASC Standards. Retrieved March 21, 2005 from http://www.ccsso.org/projects/Interstate_New_Teacher_Assessment_and_Support_Consortium/

Donelson, K. (1987). Six statements/censors from the censors. *Phi Delta Kappan,* 208–214.

Dunne, J., & Khan, J. (1998). The crisis in boys' reading. *The Library Association Record, 100* (8), 408–410.

Durbin, K. (2005). Books under fire. *Teaching Tolerance,* 47–53.

Education Commission to the States. (2005). Mandates and graduation requirements for state reports. Retrieved June 12, 2005, from: http://www.ecs.org

Eubanks, P. (1997). Art is a visual language. *Visual Arts Research, 23,* 31–35.

Friere, P. (1991). The importance of the act of reading. In C. Mitchell & K. Weiler (Eds.) *Rewriting Literacy: Culture and the discourse of the other* (pp. 139–145). New York: Bergin & Garvey.

Friere, P., & Macedo, D. (1987). *Literacy: Reading the word and the world.* New York: Bergin & Garvey.

Garcia, E. E., & Gonzalez, R. (1995). Issues in systemic reform for culturally and linguisitically diverse students. *Teachers College Record, 96* (3), 418–428.

Gee, J. P. (2000). Teenagers in new times: A new literacy studies perspective. *Journal of Adolescent and Adult Literacy, 43,* 412–426.

Giroux, H. A. (1991). Literacy, difference and the politics of border crossing. In C. Mitchell & K. Weiler (Eds.), *Rewriting literacy* (pp. ix–xvi). New York: Bergen and Garrey.

Gray, W. (1925). *Summary of investigations related to reading.* Supplementary Educational Monographs, No. 28. Chicago: University of Chicago Press.

Greenleaf, C., Schoenbah, R., Cziko, C., & Mueller, F. (2001). Apprenticing adolescent readers to academic literacy. *Harvard Educational Review, 71,* 79–129.

Guldin, G. E. (2002). *Cultural diversity in school: A guide for school board members and school administrators.* Olympia, WA: Washington State School Directors' Association.

Gutierrez, K. D., & Stone, L. (1997). A cultural-historical view of learning and learning disabilities: Participating in a community of learners. *Learning Disabilities Research and Practice, 12* (2), 123–131.

Heath, S. B. (1986). The functions and uses of literacy. In S. de Castell (Ed.), *Literacy, society and schooling: A reader* (pp. 15–25). New York: Press Syndicate of the University of Cambridge.

Herber, H. (1970). *Teaching reading in content areas.* Englewood Cliffs, NJ: Prentice Hall.

Hirsch, E. (1987). *Cultural literacy: What every American needs to know.* New York: Vintage Books.

Hull, G., & Schultz, K. (2001). Literacy and learning out of school: A review of theory and research. *Review of Educational Research, 71* (4), 571–611.

International Reading Association. (1999). *Position statement on adolescent literacy.* Retrieved July 2005, from http://www.reading.org/downloads/positions/ps1036_adolescent.pdf

International Reading Association/National Council of Teachers of English. (1996). *Standards for the English language arts.* Urbana, IL: Authors.

Jones, T. G., & Fuller, M. L. (2003). *Teaching Hispanic children.* Boston: Pearson Education Inc.

Kamil, M., & Bernhardt, E. (2004). The science of reading and the reading of science: Successes, failures, and promises in search for prerequisite reading skills for science. In E. Saul (Ed.), *Crossing borders in literacy and science instruction.* (pp. 123–139). Newark, DE: International Reading Association.

Klug, B., & Whitfield, P. (2003). *Widening the circle: Culturally relevant pedagogy for American Indian children.* New York: RoutledgeFalmer.

Langer, J. (2001). Beating the odds: Teaching middle and high school students to read and write well. *American Educational Research Journal, 38* (4), 837–880.

Lev, D. J. (2002). The new literacies: research on reading instruction with the Internet. In A. Farstrup & S. J. Samuels (Eds.), *What research has to say about reading instruction* 3rd ed., (pp. 310–336) Newark, DE: International Reading Association.

Luke, A., & Elkin, J. (2000). Special themed issue: Remediating adolescent literacies. *Journal of Adolescent and Adult Literacy, 45,* 396–398.

Manzo, A. V. (2003, May). Literacy crisis or cumbrian period? Theory, practice, and public policy implications. *Journal of Adolescent and Adult Literacy, 46,* 654–661.

Martorella, P. (1996, October). The degathering of society: Implications for technology and educators. *NASSP Bulletin,* 34–41.

McKenna, M. C., & Robinson, R. D. (1990). Content literacy: A definition and implications. *Journal of Reading, 34,* 184–186.

McPherson, G. (1994). Factors and abilities influencing sight-reading skills in music. *Journal of Research in Music Education, 42,* 217–231.

Meachum, S. (2001). Literacy at the crossroad: Movement, connection, and communication within the research literature on literacy and cultural diversity. *Review of research in education, 25,* 181–208.

Moore, D. W., Bean, T. W., Birdyshaw, D., & Rycik, J. R. (1999). Adolescent literacy: A position statement. *Journal of Adolescent and Adult Literacy, 43,* 97–112.

Moore, D. W., Readance, J., & Rickelman, R. (1983). An historical exploration of content area reading instruction. *Reading Research Quarterly, 28*, 419–438.

National Center for Educational Statistics. (2005). Public school student, staff and graduate counts by state: School year 2001–2002. Retrieved June 7, 2005, from http://nces.ed.gov/pubs2003/snf_report03/#4

Neuman, S. (1986). Rethinking the censorship issue. *The English Journal, 75*, 46–50.

Oboler, E. (1981). *Censorship and education.* Bronx, NY: Wilson.

Pearce, D., & Bader, L. (1986). The effect of unit construction upon teachers' use of content area reading and writing strategies. *Journal of Reading, 30*, 130–135.

Pipkin, G., & Lent, R. C. (2002). *At the schoolhouse gate: Lessons in intellectual freedom.* Portsmouth, NH: Heinemann.

Reese, L., Balzano, S., Gallimore, R., & Goldenberg, C. (1995). The concept of educación: Latino family values and American schooling. *The International Journal of Educational Research, 23* (1), 57–81.

Simmons, J. S., & Dresong, E. T. (2001). *School censorship in the 21st century: A guide for teachers and school library specialists.* Newark, DE: International Reading Association.

Simpson, J. A., & Weiner, E. S. (1989). *The Oxford English dictionary* (2nd ed.). Oxford, England: Clarendon Press.

Stedman, L. (1996). An assessment of literacy trends, past and present. *Research in Teaching English, 30* (3), 383–402.

Tatum, A.W. (2005). *Teaching reading to Black adolescent males: Closing the achievement gap.* Portland, ME: Stenhouse.

Tonjes, M. J. (1980). Adaptable rates and strategies for efficient comprehension: The effective reader. In J. Ewing (Ed.), *Reading and new technologies* (pp. 41–48). London: Heinemann Educational Books.

Tonjes, M. J. (1991). *Secondary reading, writing and learning.* Needham Heights, MA: Allyn & Bacon.

United States Bureau of the Census. (2005). *Census Bureau reports.* Retrieved March 21, 2005, from http://www.census.gov/

United States Department of Education. (2005). *No Child Left Behind Act of 2001.* Retrieved June 7, 2005, from http://www.ed.gov/legislation/ESEA02/

Unrau, N. (2004). *Content area reading and writing: Fostering literacies in middle and high school cultures.* Upper Saddle River, NJ: Pearson Education.

Vacca, R. T. (1998). Literacy issues in focus: Let's not marginalize adolescent literacy. *Journal of Adolescent and Adult Literacy, 44*, 604–609.

Valdés, G. (1996). *Con respeto: Bridging the distances between culturally diverse families and schools.* New York: Teachers College Press.

Valdés, G. (1998). The world outside and inside schools: Language and immigrant children. *Educational Researcher, 27*, 4–18.

Venezky, R., Wagner, D., & Ciliberti, B. (1990). *Toward defining literacy.* Newark, DE: International Reading Association.

Venezky, R. L. (1991). The development of literacy in the industrialized nations of the west. In R. Barr, M. Kamil, & P. D. Pearson (Eds.), *Handbook of reading research.* (pp. 46–67). White Plains, NY: Longman.

Vygotsky, L. S. (1962). *Thought and language.* Cambridge. MA: MIT Press.

Walker, F. (1872). *The ninth census—Volume 1: The statistics of the population of the United States embracing the tables of race, nationality, sex, selected ages and occupations to which are added the statistics of school attendance and illiteracy, of schools, libraries, newspapers and periodicals, churches, pauperism and crime, and of areas families and dwellings.* Washington, DC: Government Printing Office.

Willinsky, J. (1987). The paradox of text in the culture of literacy. *Interchange, 18* (1/2), 147–162.

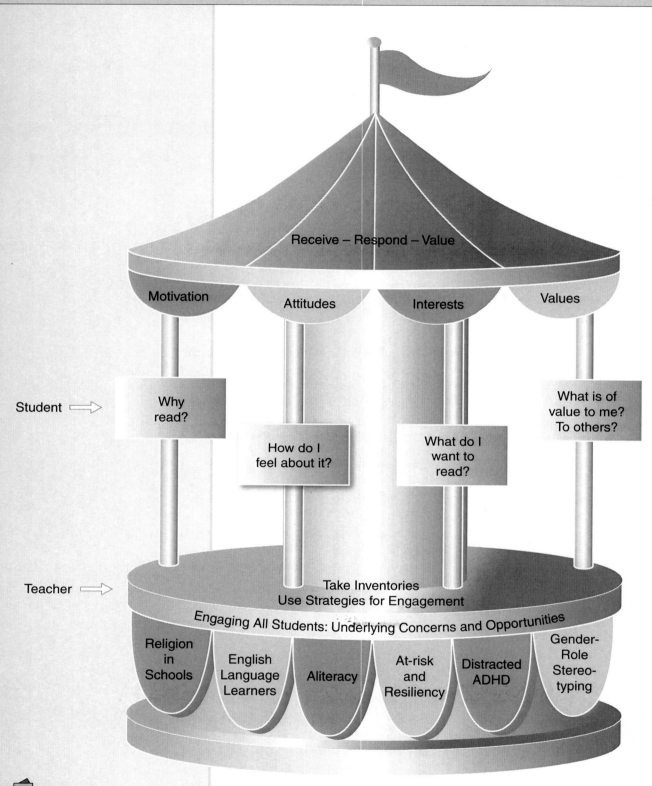

Receive – Respond – Value

Motivation   Attitudes   Interests   Values

Student ⇨

Why read?

What is of value to me? To others?

How do I feel about it?

What do I want to read?

Teacher ⇨

Take Inventories
Use Strategies for Engagement

Engaging All Students: Underlying Concerns and Opportunities

Religion in Schools | English Language Learners | Aliteracy | At-risk and Resiliency | Distracted ADHD | Gender-Role Stereo-typing

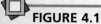

FIGURE 4.1

Promoting Affective Dimensions: The Engaged Reader—A Cognitive Map

Promoting Affective Dimensions: The Engaged Reader

4

Outline

- Anticipatory and Review Questions
- A Sampling of National Performance Standards
- Introduction
  - *Workshop 4.1: Pre-reading Activity: A Quick Personal Inventory*
  - *Workshop 4.2: Engaged Readers*
  - *Workshop 4.3: Anticipation*
- From the Content Classroom: Strong Memories
- Taxonomy of the Affective Domain
  - *Workshop 4.4: Using Krathwohl's Taxonomy to Assess Your Own Level of Engagement*
- Language of Feelings
- Emotional Intelligence: Emotional Quotient (EQ)
- Motivation and Distracted Students
- From the Content Classroom: Gail's Story
- Attitudes and Interests
  - Building Positive Attitudes and Interests
  - Changing Poor Attitudes by Promoting Interests
    - *Workshop 4.5: Readers' Bill of Rights*
- Assessing Attitudes and Interests
  - General Reading Attitude Survey
  - Tonjes Interest Inventory (TII)
  - Personal Reading Interest Inventory
    - *Workshop 4.6: Creating Interest Inventories*

- Values Clarification
  - Twenty Things I Like to Do
  - Rank Order
  - Understanding Self and Others
- Engaging All Students: Concerns and Opportunities
  - Religion in the Schools
  - English Language Learners
  - Aliteracy
  - From At-Risk to Resiliency
  - Bibliotherapy and the Restorative Qualities of Reading and Writing
  - Attention Deficit Hyperactivity Disorder (ADHD) and Literacy
  - Gender-Role Stereotyping
- Strategies for Engagement
  - What Not to Do: Literacy Activities That Turn Students Off
  - Think-Pair-Share
  - Discussion Web
  - Informational Books, Trade Books, and Magazines
  - Integrate Content
  - Gender: Dual-Voiced Journals
  - Giraffe Talk: Nonviolent Communication
- Cinquain as Summary
- Summary
- From the Pages of Our Lives: *Sharing Is Healing*, by Noémi Ban
- References and Recommended Readings

"All sorrows can be born if you put them into a story, or tell a story about them."

Isak Dinesen

"The text is here, in our hearts. The most important text for us to read and write is the ongoing story of our own lives."

G. Kenneth Fox

"Perhaps one of the greatest problems in education today is not illiteracy, but aliteracy."

Eugene Cramer and Marrietta Castle, 1994

Anticipatory and Review Questions

Literal

1. What is the difference between illiteracy and aliteracy? What is the difference between a dormant and an uncommitted reader?

2. Is it legal to teach about religion in the schools?

Interpretive/Applied

3. Specifically, how will you help your students to become more engaged as readers/writers?

4. From your experiences of observing students in classrooms, give examples of student engagement that could be categorized as receiving, responding, and valuing.

Evaluative/Critical

5. Why do you suppose that many students at higher grade levels are less motivated to read and write?

6. How will you tilt the balance from vulnerability to resiliency with at-risk students?

Creative/Personal

7. What would you respond to a colleague in your subject area department who claims that teachers are there to dispense knowledge, not to act as nursemaids to kids who don't want to learn?

A Sampling of National Performance Standards

- The professional educator is a reflective practitioner who continually evaluates the effects of his or her choices and actions on others (students, parents, and other professionals in the learning community) and who actively seeks out opportunities to grow professionally (Council of Chief State School Officers, 2005).
- Students participate as knowledgeable, reflective, creative, and critical members of a variety of literacy communities (International Reading Association/National Council of Teachers of English, 1996, p. 44).
- Accomplished science teachers create stimulating and safe learning environments that foster high expectations for the success, of all students, in which students experience the values inherent in the practice of science (National Board for Professional Teaching Standards, 2005).

Introduction

It is unfortunate that too often our schools concentrate solely on cognitive concerns, giving mostly lip service to affective dimensions. The cognitive map, Figure 4.1, shows the carousel effect of these four affective dimensions: motivation, attitudes, interests, and values. The affective literacy questions we want our students to answer are: Why should I read and write? How do I feel about reading and writing? Why? What do I want to read? Why? How does reading help me to figure out and pursue those things that are of value to me and to others?

Goals of integrated content literacy instruction include creating and enhancing positive feelings and engagement in literacy learning. There are tools we can use to assess and compile data on students' interests, attitudes, and values. We may then use this data to design activities that will increase feelings that motivate students to participate in content area literacy learning. At the same time, there are underlying affective concerns and opportunities. These include how we may use literacy to move students from at-risk to resiliency, addressing aliteracy, helping students who are easily distracted, engaging students who value their religious upbringings and want to discuss these in school, responding to the needs of English language learners as well as other diverse learners who need literacy learning content that is relevant to their needs. Ways to address these concerns and opportunities are described in this chapter; but first, let's take a few minutes to assess our own attitudes towards literacy.

Workshop 4.1

Pre-reading Activity: A Quick Personal Inventory

1. Take a few moments to reflect on your own attitude towards literacy and literacy skills. How much then do you really value being able to read and write? For example, are there times when you would rather read than watch television? Why do you read? What are your preferences? How about writing? Do you enjoy corresponding by e-mail or surface mail or both? Look at the list of writing forms on Table 8.2, page 282. Decide which of these give you pleasure or satisfaction upon completion. Jot some thoughts in the space below.

2. Next, write the title of one book you have read purely for fun in the last 3 months. Leave this space blank if you don't have one to list.

3. Have you read a magazine article of interest in the last 3 months? Write down what it was about.

4. What is your favorite section of the newspaper?

5. Name one book that has made a difference in your life. Why?

6. Is there a book you would recommend today to colleagues, friends, or family that you consider a "must read"? Why?

7. How often do you write to your friends?

              Often   Seldom   Rarely   Never

8. Do you keep a personal journal? Why, or why not?

9. Do you enjoy writing articles or papers about your subject area? Have any of them ever been published?_____ If so, what are the titles?

10. When you go on vacation or holiday, do you bring along something to read? If yes, what and why? If not, why not?

    After you have completed this chapter you may want to look again at the answers you wrote above. Your attitude is important to successful teaching. Students will see right through a teacher who says, "Do as I say, not as I do." It will be hard to convince your students of the importance of reading and writing in your field if you don't do it yourself. Students are usually quite aware of their teacher's real attitudes towards reading and writing.

Workshop 4.2

Engaged Readers

As a class, brainstorm ideas on how to assist content area students in becoming engaged readers—those with increased positive reading attitudes and interest. Recollect strategies used effectively by teachers in your past and situations that brought you pleasure and satisfaction. Share these ideas with your colleagues by having a volunteer write these ideas in a list to be shared as handouts for others in the class.

Workshop 4.3

Anticipation

Read the following statements. With which do you agree or disagree? How strongly do you feel? Discuss with a partner.

_____ 1. As a content area teacher it is my job to motivate and encourage positive attitudes and interests in my students.

_____ 2. It matters little if we teach students to be better readers. After all, given the choice, most will choose not to read.

_____ 3. There are so many pressures today on teachers to help their students to meet standards. There is so much content to teach that there isn't enough time in the day to deal with the affective dimensions or reading and writing.

_____ 4. Trust is the by-product of communication. The purpose of reading and writing is to enhance communication.

_____ 5. Pleasure reading is not usually connected directly to subjects like math, history, science, or physical education.

FROM THE CONTENT CLASSROOM

Strong Memories

A high school social studies teacher wanted to encourage his students to read more. As part of an assignment, he asked students if they had any good memories of reading or having someone read to them. One Native American student, who rarely spoke up in class, wrote the following:

> I have strong memories of my great-grandfather. He used to read to me out of the Bible. My great-grandfather is dead now, but he read to me one last time. I was in the hospital with him. I got there right after school and I had just got a new book. It was *Where the Red Fern Grows*. Grandpa asked to see it. He read the first chapter to me. It was just the two of us. He stopped and said, "I love you my great-grandson." When I went home that night I finished the book. He died the next day. That book will be special to me forever.

After class the teacher talked to the tall young man who had written this paragraph. "This is an excellent essay," the teacher said. "You really do understand the value of books and reading." Avoiding eye contact, the student smiled and said, "I remembered that story because just the other day I read the first chapter of that book to my little brother. I told him the story of how our great-grandfather read the first chapter to me. I'm helping my little brother learn to read. I know my great-grandfather is proud of both of us."

Taxonomy of the Affective Domain

Krathwohl, Bloom, and Masia (1964) developed a taxonomy of the affective domain, which may serve as a guide to content teachers in assessing levels of student involvement. The first three levels are appropriate for content classrooms. When students are below the first level, they are not receiving information and are not effectively involved; daydreamers are examples of this. When students value reading to acquire content, they do more of it.

1. *Receiving:* At the lowest level students are dutifully sitting in class, paying attention, are receiving, but not with enthusiasm. ("Tell me, I'll listen and consider it, but this isn't important to me.")

2. *Responding:* A step higher means first of all responding only when asked to do so. ("I'll answer if called upon."); volunteering to respond ("I want to answer."); showing satisfaction and interest in responding voluntarily. ("I'm glad I answered.") Often responding may be for the purpose of showing respect for the teacher or an established set of rules rather than because of genuine personal interest.

3. *Valuing:* Seeing the relevance and significance of what they are learning to the point that it becomes an important part of one's life. This will include making time to make an activity or using a skill a regular part of what they are doing. Those who value something are often willing to state this in public. ("I value this activity/information; it's important to me and I'll continue to be involved and share this with others.")

Students who are completing skill exercises at the receiving level are wasting their time and yours. Cognitive and affective developments are complementary co-requisites for learning. One without the other simply does not work.

Those of you who read *Evangelina Can Read* (at the end of the previous chapter), will remember her words: "Wow, we CAN read . . . It's just that all this time we have been reading things that don't interest us." For Evangelina, the establishment of affective and cognitive connections required relevant materials and responsive teaching.

Culturally familiar literature and a teacher who used methods tailored to their needs enabled Evangelina and her peers to go from the "responding level" to the "valuing level" and to make the significant progress in reading that she wanted. As she said, "When we find out that we can read . . . then we want to read more, like what we have to read in school."

Workshop 4.4	**Using the Krathwohl's Taxonomy to Assess Your Own Level of Engagement**

Let us pause for a moment to reflect on our own levels of engagement in this text. Read the descriptions below to determine your own level of engagement. Share your findings with a colleague.

LEVELS

Receiving
1. I am concentrating on reading the chapter and sometimes writing notes. I keep my eyes on the page, take some notes, but I'm very easily distracted.

Responding
2. I am concentrating on reading. I voluntarily take and make notes on the reading because I think I might be called on in class or have to answer questions on a quiz.

Valuing
3. I have to admit, I'm interested. Evangelina's story really got me thinking about what I want to do the next time I am in class with English language learners. Also, I believe it is important to show your students that you walk your own talk. When we get into a small-group discussion I'm going to share my thoughts and feelings about that. I also might take the time to read ahead.

Language of Feelings

With training, most teachers become highly competent in using language to describe what they are thinking. However, when it comes to expressing how we feel, many of us are at a loss for words. Whether we are receiving, responding, or valuing, we do so with feeling. Figure 4.2 displays categories of affect. Each category has a list of words that may be used to describe how we feel, what we may be thinking when we feel that way, and how we may act when we are having these feelings. Refer to it when you are reflecting on the affective dimensions of your teaching and learning.

Emotional Intelligence: Emotional Quotient (EQ)

Brain research has suggested that emotions may be a significant measure of human intelligence, as important, if not more important than IQ. Emotional intelligence is a controversial and provocative topic. Our *emotional quotient*—if it can truly be measured—is a measure of how well we understand our own feelings, our empathy for others' feelings, and our ability to regulate emotions for enhanced living. This certainly belongs in the realm of the affective domain.

Goleman (1995) says it is time to provide preventative medicine in schools. For example, Public School 75 in New York City adopted an emotional literacy program to help students manage anger, frustration, and loneliness. One measurable result was that fights during lunch time became almost nonexistent.

The general thinking in education is that anger and depression interfere with concentration when reading, listening, and learning. Some researchers, however, warn that

FIGURE 4.2

Category	Feeling	Thinking	Acting
Apathy	Cut off, defeated, despairing, discouraged, disillusioned, futile, overwhelmed, tired, and/or resigned.	I can't. It doesn't matter. I give up. It will never work. It's too hard. No matter what I do, it won't make a difference. What's the use? Why bother?	Careless, disassociated, forgetful, inattentive, indecisive, lazy, listless, negative, passive, stuck, and/or unresponsive.
Fear	Anxious, caged, confused, distrusting, doubtful, exposed, frantic, nervous, skeptical, tense, terrified, threatened, and/or vulnerable.	It's not safe. Disaster is looming and I've got to protect myself. What if I fail? What will they think? It's so confusing that I just can't move. I don't want anything to change.	Agitated, traumatized, scared, irrational, distraught, defensive, disturbed, mistrustful, nervous, timid, shady, secretive, and/or self-sabotage.
Pride	Vain, uncompromising, smug, judgmental, aloof, above it all, righteous, holier than thou, cool, and/or condescending.	I'm in a better place than you. I'm smarter than everyone else. It's your fault, not mine. I knew that. I would never associate with those kinds of people. I'm not like them. I know this already. I'm better . . .	Patronizing, putting others down, dogmatic, sanctimonious, stoic, aloof, hypocritical, closed, false humility, boastful, and/or distant.
Anger	Frustrated, vengeful, perturbed, sizzling, violent, upset, resentful, jealous, hateful, agitated, disturbed, full of rage, livid, and/or mad.	I'll get them. I'm not going to do what they want. Not a chance! Now you'll pay for that. I'll get even. Drop dead! Who do you think you are? I won't be pushed around like that!	Stubborn, sarcastic, pushy, resistant, abusive, aggressive, belligerent, blinded, destructive, ferocious, fierce, inflexible, malevolent, merciless, nasty, offensive, and/or passive aggressive.
Tranquility	Serene, free, fulfilled, full of awe, complete, centered, aware, quiet, and/or peaceful.	This is just perfect. I am just fine with what is happening now. Everything is unfolding as it should. I'm enjoying this!	Balanced, serene, connected, centered, composed, quiet, and/or whole.

there is a danger in trying to teach a "correct" emotional response to different situations. Without a moral compass, EQ can be used for either good or evil. What do you think?

Motivation and Distracted Students

Motivation refers to processes that arouse and give direction or purpose to behavior. Students aren't necessarily lazy; many are unmotivated while others are distracted. As they progress through the grades, why is it that many students seem to become less interested in school learning? What is it they don't want to learn? Could it be that what interests them, and what the curriculum provides, do not seem to correspond? We *all* want to learn *something*, but when we find reading and learning not relevant, our reaction is boredom. Then again, no one really wants to be bored either.

Most will agree that it is hard to concentrate on your chess game if you are in a hurricane. Students distracted by traumatic events in their lives may not be able to focus on school assignments. Does this mean they do not want to learn? Could it be that what they most need to learn at this time lies outside the classroom? In this case, schoolwork may seem irrelevant to their lives. Many teachers have found that if they support students through a personal crisis, later, when these students are ready to catch up, significant accomplishments often follow. Content teachers must pay attention to both student motivation and needs to deal with these problems.

Willingness and enthusiasm go hand in hand with attention and involvement. Attentive, involved students will learn more, remember longer, and make better use of their learning. They are much less likely to be discipline problems in the classroom or community.

A wise man once said to his teenage daughter as she took off for college far away from home, "Don't forget who you are. My hope for you is that by time you finish your college education you will want, more than ever, to continue to learn."

Initially many content teachers may see few reasons to motivate their students to read widely for pleasure and appreciation. They think it's the job for English or language arts teachers. Consider whether some of the following arguments might help to convince them.

1. A particular subject such as science or physical education may be the only one students care about at the time. Having collateral reading materials available such as biographies of famous scientists or sports figures, science fiction or novels of young people in sports not only increases their pleasure but also can expand and reinforce their subject matter knowledge.

2. Students who are "turned-off" to a subject, such as history, may become more motivated when reading light fiction in the same setting and time period. This helps with visual imagery of historical facts and may flesh out important concepts. After all, who buys textbooks to read for pleasure?

3. Popular teachers in any subject can serve as role models and convince reluctant readers to read; not just because it is good for them, but because they may find pleasure in doing so. The teacher/coach is a good example.

Here are some motivating techniques and activities.

   - Set aside a regular block of time each week for self-selected, content-oriented, and uninterrupted reading.
   - Provide a wide variety of collateral material in the classroom from magazines and newspaper articles to trade books and serious reference books.
   - Discover interests and attitudes through inventories and apply these to your chosen curriculum and classroom.

- When assigning text to read, tell students *why* they are being asked to read it. Give them reasons beyond the fact that they have to read it for the test on Friday. Instead, give them examples of how this content may truly be relevant to their lives.
- Assign reading tasks that meet varied ability levels, easier to read materials for those with less literacy skills, and more challenging materials for those greater ability. (More on this in Chapters Five and Six.)
- Integrate more art, music, drama, and interpretive movement into subjects such as social studies, math, and science.
- Use reading logs or response journals instead of book reports for keeping track of assigned reading. (More on this in Chapters Seven and Eight.)
- Shift focus to effort and improvement as may be shown in portfolios. (See Chapter Six.)
- When students seem to have trouble concentrating, approach them privately and sincerely ask them if there is anything you can do to help them do better in your class. When they answer, listen with love and respect.
- Use more group-cooperative rather than individual-competitive learning.
- Allow students more autonomy in planning and evaluating.
- Let students assist in creating an aesthetically pleasing classroom environment reflecting changing units in student work.

FROM THE CONTENT CLASSROOM

Gail's Story

An eighth-grade girl, Gail, kept asking for permission to look at her teacher's grade book. The teacher had asked the class to contract for the grade they wished to work toward. Better grades required more and higher-quality work. Gail, usually a poor student, had contracted for an "A," which was written by her name in the grade book.

When the teacher asked why she kept asking to see the grade book, Gail replied that never before had there been an "A" by her name. Her teacher realized this was a turning point, and during those days, weeks, and months that she helped Gail reach her goal, they built a relationship that lasted for many years.

Attitudes and Interests

Building Positive Attitudes and Interests

Along with motivating students in content classrooms there are ways to enhance positive attitudes and interests. We all know that successful experiences in reading can breed positive attitudes. For that reason we must take into consideration text readability, levels, and student interests. Allowing time for sustained silent reading (SSR) of student-selected reading materials during class time can also have a positive effect. (See Chapter Twelve for more on SSR.) However, it is the enthusiasm we share about the reading we, as learners enjoy doing, that makes the biggest difference.

Changing Poor Attitudes by Promoting Interests

As mentioned earlier, not all students will respond to teachers' attempts to inspire, encourage, and stimulate their reading. Other important considerations can influence student motivation and achievement. Nevertheless, in order to promote students' interests, teachers must exhibit appropriate attitudes themselves. These include showing empathy, being sensitive and caring while still firm, and holding high expectations for our students.

In the words of one elementary principal, "Long after your students have forgotten everything they learned from you, they will remember how you treated them." We praise when appropriate, but not overdoing it. Authentic praise should always precede criticism. When we choose to point out errors, we do so in respectful and helpful ways. We actively listen to their comments reflecting upon the relevance of what they have told us. We remember that it takes trust for students to ask a question about something they do not understand. We talk with them, not at them, and never down to them.

Teachers can support family efforts to encourage reading in the home. After all, the family that reads together is one that sets the stage for engaged readers in school. When parents, or grandparents, model how important reading is for them, their children will reflect its importance in their own lives. A mother sits reading a novel. Her young daughter races in breathlessly to ask her a question. "Just a minute, dear, I am right in the middle of an exciting story." This communicates something to the youngster that speaks louder than any advice she gives her about what reading she should do herself.

Workshop 4.5	**Readers' Bill of Rights**

In 1994, Pennac wrote about the Readers' Bill of Rights—rights that we grant ourselves and what he says we must also grant young readers. Here is an abbreviated version.

All young readers have the right to do the following:

1. Not read
2. Skip pages
3. Not finish
4. Reread
5. Read anything

6. Escape through reading
7. Read anywhere
8. Browse
9. Read aloud or not
10. Not defend tastes

As a teacher and/or parent, do you agree with all of them? Why, or why not? Discuss opinions with a colleague.

Assessing Attitudes and Interests

Assessing student reading attitudes and special interests is a first step in making a classroom one where students enjoy learning and who participate eagerly. Remember, simple observation by the teacher is often the best way to discover students' interests. However, the following examples can be adapted to fit your goals.

One other possible general inventory on interests is the Tonjes Interest Inventory (TII) on pages 127–128. If there are English language learners in your class, and if you or someone can translate the survey into their first language(s), doing so can yield valuable information.

Name _____ Date _____

General Reading Attitude Survey

This survey will show your present attitude toward books and reading. Do **not** put your name on it. The scale is:

1. strongly agree	3. sometimes agree	5. never agree
2. usually agree	4. rarely agree	

Put the appropriate number by each item.

_____ 1. Reading is a waste of time.

_____ 2. I like hard, challenging books.

_____ 3. Books are dull.

_____ 4. I'm a better reader than my classmates.

_____ 5. I don't learn much from reading texts.

_____ 6. I like to read in class.

_____ 7. Teachers ask us to read too much.

_____ 8. It's important to me to be a good reader.

_____ 9. SSR is a waste of time.

_____ 10. I would enjoy having my teacher read to my class.

_____ 11. I dislike having to go to the library.

_____ 12. I think students should have a say in choosing books to read in class.

Note to the teacher: The even numbered statements are positive statements; the odd numbered statements are negative statements. This can be given at the beginning of the term and again at the end to note overall class growth in positive attitudes toward books and reading. The reason for instructing students not to put their name on the paper is to get a more honest response; students often lie if they think this will affect their grade.

Name _____   Date _____

Tonjes Interest Inventory (TII)

A. Circle each activity that you enjoy.

1. football	26. fishing	50. motorcycling
2. baseball/softball	27. hunting	51. square dancing
3. basketball	28. bicycling	52. card games
4. soccer	29. backpacking	53. packaged games, e.g. Trivial Pursuit, Monopoly
5. hockey	30. archery	54. chess
6. volleyball	31. gymnastics	55. parties
7. tennis	32. reading newspapers	56. picnics
8. badminton	33. reading magazines	57. singing
9. racketball	34. reading novels	58. playing a musical instrument
10. golf	35. reading nonfiction	59. listening to music
11. track	36. ping pong	60. raising animals or pets
12. wrestling	37. pool, billiards	61. gardening
13. jogging	38. bowling	62. jigsaw puzzles
14. surfing	39. movies	63. crossword puzzles
15. skin diving, scuba	40. watching television	64. drawing, painting
16. water skiing	41. acting in plays	65. attending plays
17. swimming	42. attending museums	66. sculpturing
18. roller blading	43. concerts	67. writing
19. ice skating	44. ballet	68. composing
20. skiing	45. cooking	69. photography
21. horseback riding	46. sewing	70. videogames
22. mountain climbing	47. ham radio	71. line dancing
23. sailing	48. carpentry	72. other _____
24. canoeing	49. auto remodeling	
25. power boating		

B. List any other recreational activities not on this list you have engaged in and enjoyed during the past year.

73. _____

74. _____

75. _____

76. _____

C. Look over the activities you have selected and decide which three you most prefer. List in order of preference.

    1. _____

    2. _____

    3. _____

D. Add up the number of activities you enjoy.

What is one thing you learned about yourself from taking this interest inventory?

I learned that _____

_____

_____

_____

_____

What will you do with this information now to enhance learning? Explain _____

_____

_____

_____

_____

_____

_____

_____

After asking students to complete one of these interest inventories, follow up with a specific inventory based on your subject content. That way you can begin to tie student interests into your curriculum.

For example, in one English class students could read different short stories of their choice or choose from a long list. They then could share common characteristics. In history class, popular music could show the spirit of the times—with students researching music of the era studied and comparing it to the music of today. With a unit coming up on measurement, teachers may ask students to decide which they would like to read: articles favoring the metric system; the history of measurement in the United States; how different cultures helped develop ideas of measurement; Olympic contests involving measurement; or how-to books on constructing items of interest.

The two previous inventories asked students for input regarding their reading attitudes. The next inventory is designed to measure student interest.

Personal Reading Interest Inventory

Check answers that are true for you. There are no wrong answers.

1. What kind of reading do you do most often outside of school work?

   _____ newspaper   _____ novels   _____ science fiction

   _____ magazine   _____ nonfiction   _____ mysteries

   _____ comic book   _____ poetry   _____ horror

   _____ short stories   _____ history   _____ other _____

2. Where do you do most of your personal reading?

   _____ study hall   _____ at home

   _____ school library   _____ other: _____

   _____ town library   _____ I don't do any personal reading.

3. When do you most often read for pleasure?

   _____ weekday evenings   _____ any time

   _____ weekends   _____ other: _____

   _____ vacations   _____ It's never a pleasure.

4. When reading do you prefer background music or complete silence?

5. How long at a stretch do you usually read for pleasure?

   _____ fifteen minutes   _____ one hour

   _____ thirty minutes   _____ longer (how long?) _____

6. How long does it take you to read all of your homework each day? _____

7. Which do you prefer, reading or writing, and why?_____

8. Do you usually finish what you start to read? _____

9. Do you prefer reading a story or watching it on TV or at the movies? _____

10. When reading for pleasure do you read as slowly and carefully as you do for class-work?

11. Have you ever felt proud of something you wrote and wanted to share it with others?

Workshop 4.6	**Creating Interest Inventories** In pairs or triads create a content-specific attitude and interest inventory. When completed, meet with another pair or triad, exchanging inventories for feedback. You may wish to have final drafts typed and duplicated for all class members for further discussion.

Values Clarification

Thus far, we have talked about motivation, attitudes, and interests. The fourth rail on the carousel is values. How are teachers to know what students value? Just as important, how can we help our students clarify what it is that they value?

Values clarification (Simon, Howe, & Kirschenbaum, 1992) is a technique used to help identify, reflect, and clarify values. This technique is *not* intended to teach students any one set of values, but instead to help participants better understand what they value.

The process includes:

1. prizing one's behaviors and beliefs;
2. choosing from alternatives after consideration of consequences; and
3. acting on one's beliefs with a pattern, consistency, and repetition.

Upon completion of this process, students have a better understanding of why they prize certain things, why they consistently choose those things over others, and why they are willing to stand up for and act in accordance with those beliefs. What follows are three exercises to explore using this process.

Twenty Things I Like to Do

Adolescence is a time when it is the job of young people to take greater responsibility for their own choices. When it comes to school, deciding that we value learning, our work, or our grades can act as a strong incentive. Ask students to "take a sheet of paper and number 1 to 20 down the middle of the page. Then quickly jot down the 20 things they like most to do in this world, knowing they will not have to share responses."

When finished, ask them to "go back over your list to do some categorizing with symbols to the left of the items." Have them put a "$" sign by all items that would cost you at least $10.00 every time you do it, put an "S" by all items that could easily and appropriately be done in school. Put an "A" by items you usually do alone, an "R" by those requiring some risk, an "M" by those your mother might have done at your age, an "F" for father.

Those who wish may share one thing they learned from this exercise. This should be strictly voluntary.

Rank Order

Tell students they are shipwrecked alone on a desert island and can have only one of the following. Encourage students to add one additional book or set of books. Then, rank them from #1, the most desired, to #4, for the least desired.

_____ Complete Works of Shakespeare

_____ The Bible

_____ The Encyclopedia Britannica

_____ (Other) _____

Voluntarily defend your choice with reasons why. (This should provide a dynamic discussion, even with the most reticent class.)

Understanding Self and Others

Each student completes the first column with a yes or no. Then, thinking of family, friends, or other important people in their lives, the student completes columns for four other people. When done, the students can write a paragraph explaining how they are the same or different than the important people in their lives.

1 Self	2	3	4	5	This person . . .
					1. likes to get the highest grade on an exam;
					2. puts things off to the last minute;
					3. prefers reading to sports activities;
					4. will do it yourself when it needs doing;
					5. could be happy watching sports all day;
					6. is eager to participate in discussions;
					7. sees life as an exciting adventure;
					8. judges people at first just by appearance;
					9. prefers reading to watching TV; and/or
					10. is willing to risk new things.

Items in the right-hand column may be adapted to a specific content area.

Engaging All Students: Concerns and Opportunities

Religion in the Schools

Inevitably, when students think about values or read from books of their own choosing, one or several students will want to discuss their religion, or their activities as members of a religious group. Teaching about religion in public schools is legal and educationally sound when it is a part of the academic program of the school. Commitment to comprehensive education requires the inclusion of religious studies for knowledge *about* and for understanding *of* religions in the school curriculum. Twenty years ago the National Council for the Social Studies (1985) wrote that "Knowledge about religion is not only a characteristic of an educated person, but also absolutely necessary for understanding and living in a world of diversity."

Religious quotations are prevalent in the literature of many cultures. For example, students reading Dr. Martin Luther King's "I Have a Dream" speech will encounter this quote: "I have a dream that one day every valley shall be exalted and every hill and mountain shall be made low, the rough places will be made plain, the crooked places will be made straight and the glory of the Lord shall be revealed and all flesh shall see it together." King was quoting parts of Isaiah 40:4 and 5 in the Hebrew Scriptures. Dr. King's insights on equality and freedom emerged out of his faith and the religious texts he studied.

Religion in the Public School Curriculum: Questions and Answers, a paper issued by a coalition of 17 major religious and educational organizations*, describes the importance of religion in the curriculum:

> Because religion plays a significant role in history and society, study about religion is essential to understanding both the nation and the world. Omission of facts about religion can give students the false impression that the religious life of humankind is insignificant or unimportant. Failure to understand even the basic symbols, practices, and concepts of the various religions makes much of history, literature, art, and contemporary life unintelligible.
>
> Study about religion is also important if students are to value religious liberty, the first freedom guaranteed in the Bill of Rights. Moreover, knowledge of the roles of religion in the past and present promotes cross-cultural understanding essential to democracy and world peace.

Education about religion is an integral part of American education. As Goodlad (1984) suggests, the role of the school is to press toward a

> . . . common identification with diversity and a sense of homogeneity which encompasses and integrates diverse elements. Schools created to assure reinforcement of only one set of values or to serve only my race, my neighborhood, and my economic class, fail this function.

Respectful study and/or discussion that does not denigrate the practices of any religion or promote one religion over others is not only appropriate, but it is necessary in a democratic society. Respectful is the key word here. If teachers or students promote one religion over others, then the spirit, if not the letter, of the law is being neglected.

---

*More questions and answers from the paper *Religion in the Public School Curriculum: Questions and Answers* sections of which may be found in Appendix "F" of this text. The entire document may be viewed by visiting http://www.freedomforum.org/publications/first/findingcommon ground/B07.inPublicSchool.pdf

English Language Learners

Imagine moving to another country, hundreds if not thousands of miles away from your home, where they don't speak English. Now imagine having to attend school the next day. Imagine what it would be like to walk into a science, social studies, reading and writing, math, art, or health class, in which not a word of the language you know is spoken.

Only those who have faced this challenge can speak to the courage, tenacity, and character needed to succeed. Obviously, the suggestions we provide below are no substitute for training in teaching second language learners. However, here are several general suggestions that can help students feel more welcome in your classroom. By the way, each of these suggestions may be appropriate for English speakers as well:

1. Always greet your students with a smile. A welcoming, warm smile needs no translation.
2. When possible, have new students work with other English language learners who speak their language and have developed proficiency in English.
3. When presenting, speak slowly, use deliberate enunciation and simple language. Avoid figurative language and idioms.
4. Use visual aids, gestures, facial expressions to make language more meaningful.
5. Show as well as tell.
6. Wait a few extra seconds for response. Reward effort to speak English with patience and affirmations.
7. Encourage students to discuss content in their own language as well as English.
8. Ask students to teach you important subject area words in their language. For example, have you ever said the "Pledge of Allegiance" in Spanish, Russian, or Vietnamese? Ask a student to help you learn how to do so.
9. Use prompts such as "tell me more," or "how can you explain that?"
10. Allow extra time for discussion of procedures and findings, especially in small groups.
11. Allow students to demonstrate knowledge in a variety of ways such as drawing a diagram, conducting an experiment, or making a project.

Aliteracy

Illiteracy is the inability to read and write well enough to meet current standards. *Aliteracy* has been defined as a "lack of reading habit; especially, such a lack in capable readers who choose not to read" (Harris & Hodges, 1981). In other words, an aliterate person is one who has little or no desire to read. An aliterate person either does not read at all or reads only what is minimally necessary (Cramer & Castle, 1994). This has created an issue for educators. Is it enough that we teach students to read in our content areas, or must we also create ways to increase their motivation to choose to read on their own?

Beers (1996) completed a yearlong study with seventh graders. She was interested in categorizing the levels of motivation they had for reading. Based on the data collected, Beers found that students fit into three groups:

- *Dormant:* Students who like to read but don't often make the time to do it.
- *Uncommitted:* Students who don't like to read but say they may read in the future.
- *Unmotivated:* Students who don't like to read and don't ever expect to change their mind.

Beers then compiled information from students in each of the groups about the reading activities they "like and loath." Here is a summary of the findings:

Dormant readers say they want to:

- Choose their own books
- Listen to the teacher read a few pages aloud
- Compare a movie to a book
- Meet authors
- Buy books at a book fair
- Keep a reading journal
- Go to the library
- Take part in book discussions
- Share books with friends

Uncommitted and unmotivated readers say they want to:

- Choose books from a narrowed selection on their own
- Listen to teacher read an entire book aloud
- Compare a book to a movie
- Read illustrated books
- Do book-related art activities
- Read nonfiction

Dormant readers say they do *not* want to:

- Write book reports
- Do a lot of art activities
- Listen to a teacher read an entire book aloud

Uncommitted and unmotivated readers say they do *not* want to:

- Meet authors
- Buy books at a book fair
- Go to the library
- Keep a reading journal
- Take part in book discussion
- Share books with friends

As you can see, dormant aliterates and uncommitted and unmotivated aliterates do not follow the same path. Individualized solutions yield better results.

From At-Risk to Resiliency

Most of us would agree that healthy child development results from family, school, and community environments that support and elicit a resiliency or "self-righting mechanism" within every person. This ability to withstand difficulty is essential for survival when children reach a teenage world that may include broken homes, drug and alcohol abuse, physical abuse, date rape, teen pregnancy, gang violence, homelessness, drug- and alcohol-related violence, sexual abuse, and teen suicide pacts.

The reason students are not reading and writing effectively may have nothing to do with their reading abilities. In the words of one teacher of at-risk students, "It is hard to concentrate on your grammar homework assignment when your father is throwing empty beer bottles at you. It can be difficult to read about the history of the Vietnam War when your own home is a war zone. It is equally difficult to read any text when one is being abused on a daily basis" (Fox, 1999).

Research indicates that resilient children possess four important personality characteristics that define them as resilient (Benard, 1993). These characteristics and abilities include: (a) social competence, (b) problem-solving skills, (c) autonomy, and (d) a sense of purpose and future. In addition, several qualities of the educational environment of resilient youth tend to predict positive life outcomes. These include: (a) a caring and supportive relationship with another person, (b) high family and community expectations for the youth's behavior, and (c) opportunities to participate in meaningful activities.

How might content teachers provide students with such an environment? Guidelines for an appropriate learning environment can be found in a study of three teachers who were themselves survivors of pervasive trauma (Simmers-Wolpow, 1995). Conclusions of this study encourage:

- Eliminating possible systems of testing, classification, or categorization that might tend to exacerbate the traumatized students' vulnerability.
- Replacing inflexible curricula and instructional methodology with student-centered activities, shifting control to the traumatized student.

Many significant professional implications exist within these guidelines. If at-risk students discern, correctly or incorrectly, that they may have to expose themselves to increased risk for abuse, the likelihood of self-protective behaviors increases. These self-protective behaviors interfere with learning. What then of the accepted practice of administrating a test that a student knows she or he will fail? The assessment standards of the International Reading Association and the National Council of Teachers or English (1994, p. 25) are clear:

> The consequences of an assessment procedure are the first, and the most important, consideration in establishing the validity of an assessment. . . . No matter what attributes an assessment procedure has, its consequences for students are primary. Any assessment that does not contribute positively to teaching and learning should not be used.

Some teachers find this recommendation contrary to their beliefs about discipline. Perhaps these same teachers might consider instead, how they as teachers might help to tilt the balance from vulnerability to resiliency. Experts in resilience argue that, when dealing with the at-risk youth, one can and should change the three R's from Reading, wRiting, and aRithmetic to Reason, integrity in Relationship, and Respect (Fox, 1999). Teachers can do this by acting in the following ways:

- Accept students temperamental idiosyncrasies and allow them some experiences that challenge, but do not overwhelm, their coping abilities.
- Convey to students a sense of responsibility and caring, and, in turn, helpfulness and cooperation.
- Encourage a student to develop a special interest, hobby, or activity that can serve as a source of gratification and self-esteem.
- Model, by example, a conviction that life makes sense despite the inevitable adversities that each of us encounters.
- Encourage students to reach out beyond their nuclear family to a beloved relative or friend (Werner, 1984).

Bibliotherapy and the Restorative Qualities of Reading and Writing

The origins of the idea of bibliotherapy go back to the library at ancient Thebes, which, according to legend, bore the inscription "The Healing Place of the Soul." In more modern times, Dr. William Menniger hired librarians to create a library at his clinic that would provide patients with well-chosen books to ease their suffering and aid in their healing. There are several journal articles and books with suggestions of titles of books that teachers might use to help their students find comfort (Pardeck, 1993; Tillman, 1984). However, some critical reviews question the efficacy of this way of using books and reading (Heitzmann, & Heitzmann, 1975).

Students who have been through significant traumas such as violent assault or sexual abuse need to work with trained mental health professionals, not simply be given books by teachers to read (Wolpow & Askov, 1998, 2001). Nonetheless, reading and writing may bring comfort to those dealing with problems ranging from the death of a pet, the difficulties resulting from moving to a new community, or the death of a loved one. As long as teachers remember that they are *not* therapists and remain teaching professionals, they can share books or suggest ideas to write about.

Noémi Ban's essay, *Sharing Is Healing*, which appears at the end of this chapter, provides an example of how literacy may be healing. The ways in which Mrs. Ban and her father used reading and writing to help heal their wounds is testimony to the restorative qualities of literature and journaling. For more on writing to heal, see the section entitled "Risky Writing" in Chapter Eight.

Attention Deficit Hyperactivity Disorder (ADHD) and Literacy

Attention deficit hyperactivity disorder (ADHD) is one of the most common mental disorders among students. The National Institute of Mental Health (1997) estimates that on the average at least one child in every classroom in the United States needs help for ADHD. Once called *hyperkinesis* or *minimal brain dysfunction*, ADHD affects 3 to 5% of all students, perhaps as many as two million American students. It is possible for people to have constitutional impairments in their "attentional mechanism" without the accompanying hyperactivity. In this case, their behavior is simply labeled attention deficit disorder (ADD).

Frequent shifts of attention, which are characteristic of ADHD, can interfere with acquisition of content during classroom instruction. Fluctuations in attention can also affect a student's ability to synthesize ideas during reading and study time, thus diminishing comprehension and retention. Subsequent stress and embarrassment experienced by the student may lead to inappropriate behavior that only exasperates the problem. What follows is a brief discussion of the effects of medications prescribed to treat students with ADHD on reading achievement and a list of practical suggestions teachers may employ to improve the learning of students with this problem.

In theory, the young people with ADHD or ADD have the perception that stimuli are not as intense, and are not coming quickly enough. Therefore, three medications in the class of drugs known as *stimulants* are frequently prescribed for those exhibiting hyperactive behavior, poor attention span, and/or distractibility. These are methylphenidate (Ritalin), dextroamphetamine (Dexedrine or Destrostat), and pemoline (Cylert). While significant improvement in classroom social behavior has been noted in higher doses of Ritalin, the positive effects on academic performance are less clear (Gittelman, Klein, & Feingold, 1983; Sprague & Sleator, 1997). Researchers (Cotter, 1987) found that higher doses of Ritalin do not appear appropriate for improving academic performance and may, in fact, have a detrimental effect on performance on cognitive tasks such as reading. Given these findings, content teachers would seem well advised to work in close cooperation with a student's parents and physician to help determine the optimum dosage.

Hallowell (1994), a physician with ADHD himself, reminds teachers that "ADD people are highly imaginative and intuitive. They have a 'feel' for things, a way of seeing right to the heart of matters while others have to reason their way along methodically." He provides a number of practical suggestions that classroom teachers can employ to improve learning with this problem.

- Color coding: Many people with ADHD are visually oriented. Virtually anything in black and white can be made more memorable, arresting, and therefore attention-getting, with color.
- Make frequent use of lists, reminders, notes to self, rituals, and files.
- Break down large tasks into smaller ones. Attach deadlines to the smaller parts.
- Prioritize: Procrastination is one of the hallmarks of ADHD.
- Add mini-breaks to leave time to gather thoughts; transitions are difficult for people with ADHD.
- Encourage! More so than the average person, those with ADD positively light up like a Christmas tree when given encouragement. They will often work for another person in a way they won't work for themselves.

Gender-Role Stereotyping

Gender-role stereotyping has been an issue for the past 35 years. In 1994, Cassidy and colleagues developed the Sexist Intelligence Quotient (SIQ) test to expand our knowledge of gender bias and sex-role stereotyping as related to literacy education. The SIQ-R is a newly revised version. Interestingly, even provocative true-and-false statements such as the following are included:

- Books that teachers read aloud to elementary children tend to be mostly about male protagonists.
- Women's organizations like the National Organization for Women (NOW) have rarely focused on textbook images of women.

This new edition also contains assessment standards and recommendations for the classroom teacher. In the next chapter, "Matching Print with Reader: Text Assessment," we will further examine the issue of inclusiveness.

Strategies for Engagement

What Not to Do: Literacy Activities That Turn Students Off

Before considering several effective strategies, let us look at some literacy activities that turn students off. Please never consider doing these things. As you read, check items that remind you of your past schooling. Please consider the reasons why you should not perpetuate these with your own students.

1. Ask the class to read aloud in a round-robin fashion, one by one, up and down the rows. Correct all mispronunciation. (Students should never be asked to read aloud, for an audience, text they have not first read silently nor had the opportunity to practice.)

2. After a silent reading assignment ask only low-level (I've got the facts) literal questions, never allowing for personal inference, criticism, or creative embellishment. Ask "guess what's in my head" kinds of questions. (There is only one correct answer, the one the teacher is looking for. These questions create the student tendency to duck behind another's head to get out of the teacher's "line of fire.")

3. Use reading or writing as punishment for misbehavior such as having a student write something 50 times or read in the detention room with all its negative connotations. (We want our students to associate reading and writing with pleasant experiences, so they will choose to do so on their own, voluntarily.)

4. Refuse to accept reading of current best-sellers in school during free reading time, or telling students who finish an assignment early that there is more content-related work to be done.

5. Ridicule students openly because you have discovered they are hiding one of their own books inside a cover instead of the prescribed assignment. Yes, this embarrasses them, but it teaches them a lesson (—to hate reading!).

6. Insist that every unknown word be looked up immediately in the dictionary or glossary and written down on a vocabulary sheet. (Giving students long lists of words to look up, copy definitions and then use in a sentence is *the* most effective turn-off related to improving one's vocabulary.)

7. Assign silent reading to the class, but don't do it yourself. Instead, talk to the neighbor across the hall in a voice loud enough to disturb concentration.

What other things have teachers done in the past to turn off students to reading or writing?

Think-Pair-Share (McTighe & Lyman, 1988)

The think-pair-share strategy encourages full participation without putting any one student on the spot. Before or after reading, give students a prompt. Students think about it for a few moments and jot a response. Then ask them to get into pairs and share the ideas that they were thinking about. Finally, bring the class together to share their ideas. This strategy allows time for thinking and responding—whether to a partner or to the class.

Discussion Web (Alvermann, 1991)

A discussion web incorporates reading, writing, speaking, and listening with cooperative learning and provides many opportunities for students to interact. This is especially effective with texts that involve opposing points of view.

- First, students read the assigned material
- Next, students form into pairs. Each pair is given a graphic organizer in the shape of a web. (Graphic representations are explained in Chapter Seven.) A focus question is written on the board and students copy it onto a line in the center of the web. Each pair then returns to the reading to locate arguments and information supporting "yes" and "no" answers. They are told to keep an open mind at this point.
- When each pair has completed the evidence for both sides of the question, they form a quad with a second pair. These four must try to reach consensus on the question.

- Finally, having had many chances to discuss their points of view, students share with the whole class.

Informational Books, Trade Books, and Magazines

A good strategy to deal with impending insomnia is to keep a mind-numbing textbook on your nightstand. Few of us choose to keep a textbook on the nightstand to read for pleasure. Information books, trade books, and magazines make for much more pleasant reading, on just about any topic. Chapter Twelve has lists of books in various content areas and additional ideas on how to use them in class. However, to get your thinking started, here are some suggestions for how to use these types of materials in your content classroom.

- Start to read an excerpt from a book telling just enough to whet their appetite. Stop at a provocative spot. Ask them if they would like to hear more.
- Have a variety of books available. Allow students to make their own selections. Let them know that once they have selected a book that they may return it without having to complete it first.
- Remember the lesson you learned in the chapter on reading rate adaptability? Show your students how to "preview" rather than read a book.
- Students will automatically be more interested in a book recommended by other students. Get a list of books from your students that they have enjoyed in the past. Check these out of the library and then have students "sell" their favorites to the class. For example, instead of a book report, have students act out a 60-second commercial promoting their book.
- Magazines can also serve as interesting sources for content information. They are available in all content areas.

Integrate Content (Katz, Brown, Braun, Massie, & Kuby, 2003)

Instruction that integrates subject matter like English, drama, history, and science can be extremely motivating. Take as an example Armstrong's (1998) award-winning non-fiction narrative *Shipwreck at the Bottom of the World: The Extraordinary True Story of Shackleton and the Endurance*. This could be the focus of a unit that could allow students to do an in-depth study and may motivate reluctant readers to discover further information.

Such a unit could be partly traditional and the rest innovative. Before reading the book, students could be asked to activate their prior knowledge by either agreeing or disagreeing with a series of statements. The teacher could have the students divide up the work. For example, for each chapter the teacher could assign four or five questions to answer. Each question could be asked from a different content area angle. Instead of having students answer all the questions, they could choose one. The next day they meet with the others who have chosen the same question. Together they try to forge a consensus before reporting to the class.

Or if you prefer, choose four or five characters from the book to profile, and assign one group of students to each character. Each group could then be assigned one of these characters and asked to imagine themselves as that character. They could act-out scenes. Integrating drama enables students to display emotions contained in the book. As they read on, they may feel closer to events because they have related so closely to them.

Gender: Dual-Voiced Journals (Styslinger, 2004)

How do gender roles influence response to text? Styslinger devised a duel-voiced journal assignment that requires readers to respond in two voices—male and female. When the reader is male, he first responds in his own voice. After writing his ideas, he then predicts what someone might feel as a woman, hence he writes a response in a female voice. If the reader is female, she does the reverse of this process. For example, Styslinger described her 12th graders' response to Shakespeare's Lady Macbeth. One male student contended that Lady Macbeth was personally motivated because of her desire for power, that she manipulated Macbeth for her own ends. A female student argued that Lady Macbeth only wanted power for the sake of her husband, that she influenced Macbeth for his own best interests. When responses are shared in this way, a stimulating and lively classroom discussion can take place about gender roles.

Giraffe Talk: Nonviolent Communication (Rosenberg, 2003)

Earlier, in the section on the language of feelings, you read about the importance of being able to find words to describe your feelings. What then are students to do when reading about something brings to the surface their own feelings of anger and frustration? Books do that sometimes. When we read about how someone was mistreated and we realize that the same kind of thing is happening to us, we may share the feelings of the victim.

Rosenberg believes that students learn with fewer discipline-related problems when they have been taught to be assertive. This technique is called "giraffe talk" because asserting oneself nonviolently requires one to stick their neck out.

Giraffe talk is done in four steps:

1. *When I observe . . .*

   Describe events without using evaluative judgments, labeling, or name-calling.

2. *I feel . . .*

   Name the feelings that were stirred up within you. (The language of feeling chart on page 121 may be helpful here.) Was it fear, sadness, anger, hurt, excitement . . . ?

3. *Because I imagine . . .*

   A statement of what I think you are thinking (or believe) about me.

4. *Would you please . . .*

   A request for a concrete, specific action that the other person can do to help you meet your needs. This request needs to be positively framed and should not be a demand, threat, or guilt-shaming manipulation. The listener has the right to say "no."

Here are examples of violent talk, in the left-hand column, paired with contrasting examples of giraffe talk in the right-hand column.

When I observe . . .

Violent Talk	Giraffe Talk
You "dissed" me . . .	When I observed you saying that I was the one who broke the science lab rule . . .
You flunked me.	When I saw that I received a "0" on my test for using pen instead of pencil . . .

I feel . . .

Violent Talk	Giraffe Talk
You must hate my guts!	I feel hurt and ashamed . . .
You made me feel "pissed-off".	I felt sad and angry.

Because I imagine . . .

Violent Talk	Giraffe Talk
You are so mean to me!	Because I imagine that you haven't noticed how hard I have been trying to improve.
You keep doing things like that over and over again.	Because I imagine that you must think that I am not very bright and I don't study.

Would you . . .

Violent Talk	Giraffe Talk
Stop yelling at me or I'll do something we both regret!	When you see me doing something you think I shouldn't, would you talk to me about it, privately and in a softer tone of voice?
I guess I'm just going to have to flunk this class. It won't be the first time I failed English.	Would you grade my paper so that I at least know that you know that I am learning something in your class?

Once violent talk has been changed to assertive "giraffe talk," students can be encouraged to write a note to the person involved. Here are the two examples:

Violent Talk:

You "dissed" me! You must hate my guts! You are so mean to me. Stop yelling at me or I'll do something we both regret!

Giraffe Talk Letter:

Dear Science Teacher,

When I observed you saying that I was the one who broke the science lab rule, I feel hurt and ashamed. This is because I imagine that you haven't noticed how hard I have been trying to improve. When you see me doing something you think I shouldn't, would you be willing to talk to me privately and in a softer tone of voice?

Violent Talk:

You flunked me. You make me feel "pissed-off." You keep doing things like that over and over again. I guess I'll have to flunk this class. It won't be the first time I failed English.

Giraffe Talk Letter:

Dear English Teacher,

When I saw that I received a "0" on my test for using pencil instead of pen, I felt sad and angry because I imagined that you must think I am not very bright and I don't study. I know you don't count grades on papers that are in pencil, but will you grade my paper so that I at least know that you know that I am learning something in your class?

Cinquain as Summary

Affective
Feelings, Attitudes
Motivated to read
Valuable to me always
Engaged-Reader

 Summary

National standards call for educators to: (a) reflect upon the effects of their choices on a variety of diverse literacy communities, (b) create stimulating and safe learning environments, and (c) help students learn the values inherent in their subject matter. Each of these standards speaks to the affective domain, which is concerned with personal feelings, motivation, attitudes, interests, and values. The first three levels of Krathwohl's Taxonomy of the Affective Domain, a tool that may be used to assess levels of engagement, include: (1) receiving information, (2) responding to it, and (3) valuing learning this content beyond school and in their lives.

Teachers must learn to use the language of feelings so that they may teach their students to do the same. Emotional intelligence may be as significant measure of human intelligence as IQ. By attending to students' reactions to what is occurring in our classrooms we can find better ways to motivate, change negative attitudes, select materials of interest, and help clarify values. There are several tools for assessing attitudes and interests and to help students learn to identify and articulate their values. Engaging all students provides concerns and opportunities as we figure out how to best deal with religion in the schools, assist English language learners, struggle with aliteracy, guide students who are at-risk to resiliency, attend to the needs of those with ADHD, and help our students learn to avoid gender-role stereotyping. Effective strategies for student engagement include think-pair-share, discussion webs, information books, integrating content, dual-voiced journals, and giraffe talk.

FROM THE PAGES OF OUR LIVES
Sharing Is Healing
by Noémi Ban

Mrs. Noémi Ban is the recipient of numerous awards for excellence in teaching and author of the book *Sharing Is Healing: A Holocaust Survivor's Story*. In this essay Mrs. Ban shares ways in which she and her father used reading and writing to heal wounds that most of us cannot even imagine. Now retired from teaching, Mrs. Ban still speaks at scores of schools each year. Her message to embrace love and life—especially in the face of grief, humiliation, and despair—can inspire and inform students and teachers alike.

When Nazi troops entered Debrecen, Hungary, in March of 1944, they rounded up all the Jewish men and deported them to work at forced labor camps. The Nazis met little resistance because the Jewish community hoped that compliance might assure the safety of those who remained behind. I remember my mother crying all day and saying, "I will never see him again." Unfortunately, her premonition was correct.

At the end of the war, when my father returned to Debrecen, he learned that his mother, wife, two daughters and son had all been deported to Auschwitz. Had any of us survived? From the ruins of what had once been his home he managed to unearth a small appointment book which he used as his personal diary. Its pages are stained with tears of love and sadness. Let me read to you an entry, translated from Hungarian:

14 August '45

Every night I dream about what has happened to you. I can find comfort only in remembering.

I remember seeing Anyu (my mother) at the Sabbath table. She is reading in a very quiet atmosphere after dinner. And then, Noémi, I see you sitting opposite me. While you read, you comb your hair with your fingers. I also see little Elizabeth sitting next to you. We are family, and we are very much in love as we do our reading.

Even today, sixty years later, these words bring the whole picture back to me. Before lighting the candles, each of us was immersed in our own world. But after the blessings and our meal, we sat together and read. This was a time of quiet, shared enjoyment and love. We sat together, honoring each other's privacy, and read. There was a strength, a unity, a harmony. Most important, we were not alone. It was not isolation or routine. It was a celebration . . . a quiet way to show love and to enjoy each other. Even in the most terrible times, my father would remember who sat where . . . and I remember it too.

I grew up in a very warm, loving and nurturing family. My family in Hungary then, just as my family in America now, used reading and writing to connect with each other and to make sense of the events of our lives. My mother and I went frequently to the local library to find the books to share. We must have read hundreds of them. One of them was *The Forty Days of the Musah Dagh* by Franz Werfel, the tragic story of the Turkish genocide against the Armenians during World War I. I did not know then that I myself would one day be involved in a similar struggle.

One night, several months after my father left, the SS announced that we had to line up in our backyard the next morning. We were not allowed to take any valuables with us, only one change of underwear, and a small package of dry food. We talked to each other that night and agreed not to attempt to take any valuables.

Just a few days later we were in a cattle car. The doors were locked from the outside and people screamed all night long. Suddenly my grandmother shouted "Nobody can take it away from me!" "Take, what, Grandma," I asked. "My Shabbos candlesticks" she answered. Doing my best to comfort her I said, "Grandma, don't worry about them, they are back home. We hid them there." "No! No! No!'" she said, 'They're here, I have them." She had taken them, somehow, under her three layers of skirts. She handed them to me and I tucked them away in my package.

One week later, we arrived at Auschwitz. By that time my mom, sister, baby brother and grandma were all in a daze. We were ordered to leave everything in the cattle car. I asked the man, in the striped prison outfit who helped us get out of the cattle car, if I could take with me the formula and diapers for my little brother. I pleaded with him, "What will happen if he gets no food to eat?" In German he said, "Schade," which means "I'm sorry." I still remember his face. He was really sorry. But I did not yet know why.

There is not enough space in this short essay to tell you the details of what happened next. My grandmother, my mother, my thirteen-year-old sister, and my six-month-old brother were all killed in the gas chambers. I had to breathe their ashes, and the ashes of thousands of others incinerated in the crematoria. Three months later I was transported, with one thousand other young women, to a forced labor munitions factory near Buchenwald. After liberation I was nursed back to health and returned home. My father and I were reunited. A month later I married Earnest, also a slave-labor camp survivor whom I had known before the war. We both became teachers. We had two children and persuaded my father to move with us to Budapest.

After the 1956 Soviet invasion of Hungary, Earnest and I moved our family to America. One dictatorship in a lifetime was enough. My father decided to stay behind. At first Earnest and I worked as laborers in factories but we hungered to return to teaching. In order to do so we had to acquire college-level reading and writing skills in English. I used my training in education to fashion a solution to this problem.

As a child I had read Hungarian translations of several books by Mark Twain. To improve my English, I went to the library and brought home my old friends, Tom Sawyer and Huck Finn. I already knew the characters and the plot, so I could focus on learning the English. With my trusty *English/Hungarian, Hungarian/English Dictionary* and *Webster's New Ideal Dictionary* by my side, I reread dozens of books that I had read as a child and adolescent. One of those books was *The Forty Days of the Musah Da*gh. As I reread it, I became one with the Armenians. I felt their pain. This book is a testimony that such inhumanity could happen for 40 days and my life was now a testimony that this could happen for 19 months. In 1939, when Hitler was about to invade Poland, I heard him on the radio giving a speech to his soldiers. He said, "Who, after all, speaks today of the annihilation of the Armenians?" Can you see why it is so important to remember?

I learned English, returned to college and I got a job teaching 6TH grade. During this time, I read to fill in the missing spaces. I read about the Nazis: Hitler, Goring, Goebbels, and Himmler. In the camps, many times, we wondered if the world had forgotten about us. I read about the Western world to try to figure out why they didn't do more. I read about American politics, and more.

During my first five years of teaching in America I was afraid to say I was a Jew, let alone share my Holocaust experience with students, colleagues or parents. No longer did I wear a yellow star on my blouse, but I still wore it inside my head. However, when I started teaching the history and geography of Europe, I began to share pieces of my story. Telling was healing for me, especially seeing the faces of my children as I would tell.

They listened and they wanted to hear more. What had happened to me was big in their eyes. Then, if something happened to their cat, or a parent divorced, or there was a death in their family, or their father was alcoholic, these children knew they could come to me. I had a treasure chest to share. I would listen with love and show them it was important to remember. I would show them that whatever happened to them there was always hope.

In the late sixties and early seventies teachers were called upon to teach special education students who never attended "mainstream" classes. I attended workshops on special methods to teach these children the subject matter but soon discovered my own common denominator. The most important thing that I had to do was help them regain their self-respect. You cannot teach children to do anything until they feel they are able. Once they achieve that, the subject matter can be fitted to their interest and ability.

I constantly strove to put into practice my belief that talking down to any student for any reason was wrong. Perhaps this was because of the time that I had been treated as if I were less than a human being. When I taught social studies, I would take time to talk about prejudice. I would tell them of what Americans did to American-born Japanese families during the Second World War and then describe for them the feeling of having to give up my home and my possessions to live behind barbed wire because my family was of Jewish heritage. When we learned about slavery, I would ask them how they thought it would feel to be kidnapped and separated from their families and forced to live and work in squalor as a slave. Then I would tell them of my experiences in the forced labor camps. I would ask, "Do you see what prejudice does?" I asked them to think of the tragedies in my story as a "stop sign." I implored them, as I implore you, whenever you experience prejudice, to stop and think of what even a little prejudice can do.

I started this essay by sharing words from my father's diary, the diary he kept when he returned from the slave labor camps. I have his journal because he gave it to me when Earnest, my sons and I moved to the United States. At that time he asked that I not read it right away but instead "save for some quiet reading moments." If you have a few quiet moments, and you are willing, I will translate them for you.

On the first few pages he compares his head to a boiler building up steam from imaginings of the deadly gas of Auschwitz. He explains that he is using this writing as a "safety valve," so that "he will not explode." He has no idea how many of us, if any have survived.

1945 May 29

My friends are reminding me that I look terrible. They remind me that I should take care of myself, because if all of you come back I will be gone. But how can I do that? . . . How can you say to a river to change its course and flow backwards? . . .

Are you alive? I don't know? Who is among you that I might see again? . . . Why, and for how long? . . . How terrible [it is] just to write this down.

"Why? And for How Long?" is the title of a poem that he originally wrote to the woman who would be his wife. He wrote it in 1918 while imprisoned in a P.O.W. camp during the first great war. In this journal entry he was reconstructing it in a new context. Here are his words:

I wrote this poem in Siberia . . . Small fractions of it are in my mind as I wait for you. This afternoon I was able to recall the whole poem . . . as I wrote I clearly visualized you and our future together. But today these words are even timelier.

Can I dream of our future again? Are you alive?
Without you what will I do?

Why? And for How Long?

Do you know?
You the beauty of my world,
Do you feel it?
You the most beautiful on this earth,
Why? The yearning hurts, it is burning.
Why? And for how long?

Did you notice, dear soul?
Did you comprehend, you, the wish of my heart?
Do you feel the hope, my yearning?
Why? And for how long?

I will always wait for you
My yearning is limitless
Where is the end of my sorrow?
Why? And for how long?

On the wings of my yearning
I fly towards you
But to arrive, to get to you
I have not the strength any more
Maybe you have forgotten me?
Why? And for how long?

My soul is tired
My body is weak
I am standing at the edge of my grave
My grave is waiting for me with its Peace
Without you, why would I want to live?
Why? And for how long?

He wrote this poem during one great war, and then rewrote it at the end of a second. I had just been liberated. When he learned I was alive he couldn't wait to see me, but then again, he knew I might bring to him a final statement about the rest of our family. That double feeling was tearing him apart.

I can still see, in my mind's eye, his coming up the steps to me. He was walking as if in a dream—wanting to and not wanting to come. Finally, he broke down; I just rushed to him and hugged him. We held each other for minutes and minutes and minutes. He was sobbing, terribly. Then we went into the living room and sat down. He wanted to hear the details from beginning to end. He wanted to know as much as I knew. I was hardly recovered myself. I too was hurt. What I had to say came from really deep down.

I decided ahead of time, if he asked, I would tell him all the details. It was much more merciful to tell him all, right then. So I told him it all: About the cattle cars; about arriving at Auschwitz; and about the look in my mother's eyes as the Nazis separated me from the rest of the family. In her eyes I could see she was saying, "Take care . . . I love you . . . " I told him how for weeks I asked the guards where my family was, and how finally one pointed to the sky and said, "Do you see the ash-colored clouds? Do you see them? There are your relatives!" I never saw any of them again. I told him it all.

He was crying terribly. So was I. I now realize that at that time, it was almost life-saving for me to tell him. I was holding such terrible pain in myself. My father was the first person I told, and there are many reasons I continue to tell it. The most important reason is the title of this essay and of my book: *Sharing Is Healing*. When I tell my story I look into the eyes of the people who are listening to me. I see respect, sympathy and love. Seeing this is healing. The pain is still there, but each time I see the respect, sympathy, and love in their eyes, the pain gets less and less.

Thank you for reading about my story. May teaching bring as much joy and fulfillment into your life as it has in mine.

Questions for Reflection and/or Discussion

1. In what ways did Mrs. Ban and her father use reading and writing to heal their wounds?

2. Please think back to a time in your life when you were experiencing hard times (death of a loved one, threat of death due to illness, loss of health or property due to an accident or natural disaster, pervasive emotional, physical or sexual abuse, contentious separation or divorce, etc.). What role did (or could have) reading and/or writing play(ed) in your recovery?

3. In Chapter Four the authors suggest we should change the three R's from Reading, wRiting, and aRithmethic to Reason, integrity of Relationship, and Respect. What examples of these new three R's are evident in Mrs. Ban's teaching?

4. Mrs. Ban writes about being trained to work with special education students who were "mainstreamed" into her classes. She writes:

"The most important thing that I had to do was help them regain their self-respect. You cannot teach children to do anything until they feel they are able."

Why might the students with whom you work feel like they have lost their self-respect? As their teacher, how might you use reading and writing to help restore it?

References and Recommended Readings

Alvermann, D. (1991). The discussion web: A graphic aid for learning across the curriculum. *The Reading Teacher, 45*, 92–99.

Alvermann, D., & Muth, K. D. (1990). Affective goals in reading and writing. In G. G. Duffy (Ed.), *Reading in the Middle School*, (pp. 97–110). Newark, DE: International Reading Association.

Armstrong, J. (1998). *Shipwreck at the bottom of the world: The extraordinary true story of Shackleton and the Endurance*. New York: Random House.

Athey, I. (1985). Reading research in the affective domain. In H. Singer & R. Ruddell (Eds.), *Theoretical models and processes of reading*, (3rd ed., pp. 527–557). Newark, DE: International Reading Association.

Baines, L., & Kunkel, A. (Eds.). (2000*). Going Bohemian: Activities that engage adolescents in the art of writing well*. Newark, DE: International Reading Association.

Ban, N., & Wolpow, R. (2003). *Sharing is healing: A Holocaust survivor's story*. Bellingham, WA: Holocaust Educational Publications.

Beers, K. (1996). No time, no interest, no way: The three voices of aliteracy, part 2. *School Library Journal, 42,* (3), 110–113

Benard, B. (1993). Fostering resiliency in kids. *Educational Leadership, 51,* (3), 44–48.

Bitz, M. (2004, April). The comic book project: Forging alternative pathways to literacy, *Journal of Adolescent and Adult Literacy, 47*, 574-586.

Cassidy, J., Smith, N., Winkeljohann, R., Ball, R., & Blouch, K. (1994). The SIQ-R test: Assessing knowledge of gender issues in literacy education. *Journal of Reading, 38,* (2), 104–108.

Cotter, R. & Werner, P. (1987). Ritalin update: Implications for reading teachers. *Reading Psychology, 8*, 179–187.

Council of Chief State School Officers. (2005). *INTASC Standards*. Retrieved March 21, 2005, from http://www.ccsso.org/projects/Interstate_New_Teacher_Assessment_and_Support_Consortium/

Cramer, E. H., & Castle, M. (1994). Developing lifelong readers. In E.H. Cramer & M. Castle (Eds.), Fostering the love of reading: The affective domain in reading education (pp. 3–9). Newark, DE: International Reading Association.

DeLorenzo, R. (1999). When hell freezes over: The approach to develop student interest and communication skills. *Journal of Chemical Education, 16*, 503.

Friere, P. (1995). *Pedagogy of hope: Reliving the pedagogy of the oppressed*. New York: Continuum.

Fox, K., & Serlin, I. (1996). High-risk youth and the transition to adulthood. *The Humanistic Psychologist, 24,* (3), 349–363.

Fox, K. (1999). Personal communication, May 1, 1999.

Gittleman, R., Klein, D., & Feingold, I. (1983). Children with reading disorders: Effects of methylphenidate in combination with reading remediation. *Journal of Children, Psychology, and Psychiatry, 24,* (2), 193–212.

Goleman, D. (1995). *Emotional intelligence: Why it can matter more than IQ*. New York: Bantam Books.

Golup, J. N. (2000). *Making learning happen: Strategies for an interactive classroom*. Portsmouth, NH: Boynton/Cook.

Guthrie, J. T., & McCann, A. S. (1997). Characteristics of classrooms that promote motivations and strategies for learning. In J. T. Guthrie & A. Wigfield (Eds.), *Reading engagement: Motivating readers through integrated instruction*, (pp. 128–148). Newark, DE: International Reading Association.

Hallowell, E., & Ratey, J. (1994). *Driven to distraction*. New York: Pantheon Books.

Harris, T., & Hodges, R. (Eds.). (1981). *A dictionary of reading and related terms*. Newark, DE: International Reading Association.

Heath, S. B. (1995). *Children of promise*. Washington, DC: National Education Association.

Heitzmann, K. A., & Heitzmann, W. R. (1975). The science of bibliotherapy: A critical review of research findings. *Reading Improvement, 12*(2), 120-124.

Horsman, J. (2000). *Too scared to learn: Women, violence, and education*. Mahway, NJ: Lawrence Erlbaum Associates, Inc.

International Reading Association/National Council of Teachers of English. (1996). *Standards for the English language arts*. Urbana, IL: Authors.

Ivey, G., & Broadolus, K. (2001). Just plain reading: A survey of what makes students want to read in middle school. *Reading Research Quarterly, 36*, 350–377.

Katz, C., Brown, K., Braun, T. J., Massie, M. J., & Kuby, S. A. (2003). The importance of being with Sir Ernest Shackleton at the bottom of the world. *Journal of Adolescent and Adult Literacy, 47*, 38–49.

Krashen, S. (1991). Sheltered subject matter teaching. *Cross Currents, 18*, 183–189.

Krathwohl, D., Bloom, B., & Masia, B. (1964). *Taxonomy of educational objectives: Handbook II*. New York: David McKay.

Ladsen-Billings, G. (1994). *The dream keepers: Successful teachers of African American children*. San Francisco: Jossey-Bass.

Lamberg, W. J. (1983). Helping reluctant readers help themselves: Interest inventories. *The English Journal, 66*, 139–144.

Lugones, M. (1997). Playfulness world traveling and loving perception. In D. T. Meyers (Ed), *Feminist social thought—A reader,* (pp.148–159). New York: Routledge.

Marlett, P. B., & Gordon, C. J. (2004). The use of alternative texts in physical education. *Journal of Adolescent and Adult Literacy, 48,* (3), 226–237.

McKenna, M. C. (2000). Development of reading attitudes. In L. Verhoeven & C. Snow (Eds.), *Literacy and motivation,* (pp. 135–158). Mahwah, NJ: Erlbaum.

McTighe, J., & Lyman, F. T. (1988). Cueing thinking in the classroom: The promise of theory—embedded tools. *Educational Leadership, 45*, 18–24.

National Board for Professional Teaching Standards. (2005). *Adolescents and young adult/science* (2nd ed.). Retrieved June 20, 2005, from http://www.nbpts.org/standards/stds.cfm

National Council for the Social Studies. (1985). *Study about religions in the social studies curriculum: Prepared by the Religion in the Schools Committee and approved by the NCSS Board of Directors, 1984*. Retrieved July, 3, 2005, from http://www.socialstudies.org/positions/religion/

National Reading Association/National Council of Teachers of English. (1994). *Standards for the assessment of reading and writing*. Newark, DE: Authors.

Nell, V. (1988). The psychology of reading for pleasure: Needs and gratification. *Reading Research Quarterly, 18*, 6–50.

Panofsky, C., Eanet, M., & Wolpow, R. (2001). Literacy and the affective domain: Three perspectives. In *Multiple perspectives in the millennium, Yearbook of the American Reading Forum, 21*, 45–79.

Pardeck, J. (1993). *Using bibliotherapy in clinical practice: A guide to self-help books*. Westport, CT: Greenwood Press.

Pennac, D. (1994). *Better than life*. Toronto: Coach House Press.

Powell-Brown, A. P. (2003–2004). Can you be a teacher of literacy if you don't love to read? *Journal of Adolescent and Adult Literacy, 47*, 284–288.

Purkey, W. W., & Novak, J. M. (1996). *Inviting school success: A self concept approach to teaching, learning and the democratic practice,* (3rd ed.). Belmont, MA: Wadsworth.

Raths, L., Harmin, M., & Simon, S. (1966). *Values and teaching*. Columbus: Charles Merrill, 1966.

Rosenberg, M. (2003) *Nonviolent communication: A language of compassion.* Chicago, IL: Puddledancer Press.

Sanacore, J. (2000). Promoting the lifetime reading habit in middle school students. *The Clearing House, 73,* 157–161.

Simmers-Wolpow R. (1995). *Trauma, literacy and the pedagogy of hope.* Unpublished doctoral dissertation, Pennsylvania State University.

Simon, S., Howe, L., & Kirschenbaum, H. (1992). *Values clarification: A handbook of practical suggestions for teachers and students.* Lebanon, IN: Warner Books.

Singer, J., & Hubbard, R. (2002–2003, December–January). Teaching from the heart: Guiding adolescent writers to literate lives. *Journal of Adolescent and Adult Literacy,* 326–336.

Sprague, R. L., & Sleator, E. K. (1977). Methylphenidate and thioridazine: Learning, reaction time, activity, and classroom behavior in disturbed children. *American Journal of Orthopyschiatry, 40,* (4), 615–628.

Stone, N. R. (1984). Accentuate the positive: Motivation and reading for secondary students. *Journal of Reading, 27,* 684–690.

Styslinger, M. (2004, May). Chasing the albatross: Gendering theory and reading with dual-voiced journals. *Journal of Adolescent and Adult Literacy, 47,* 628–637.

Tillman, C. E. (1984). Bibliotherapy for adolescents: An annotated review. *Journal of Reading, 27,* (8), 713–719.

Tonjes, M. J. (1991). *Secondary reading, writing and learning.* Needham Heights, MA: Allyn & Bacon.

Triplett, C. F. (2004, November). Looking for a struggle: Exploring the emotions of a middle school reader. *Journal of Adolescent and Adult Literacy, 48,* 214–222.

Verhoeven, L., & Snow, C. (Eds.). (2001). *Literacy and motivation.* Mahwah, NJ: Erlbaum.

Werner, E. (1984). Resilient children. *Young Children, 39,* 68–72.

Williams, B. T. (2004–2005). Are we having fun yet? Students, social class and the pleasures of literacy. *Journal of Adolescent and Adult Literacy, 48,* 338–342.

Wolpow, R. (1999). Wirklichkeitswund und wirklichkeit suchend (stricken by and seeking reality): Literacy conversations which restore families, schools and communities. *Yearbook of the American Reading Forum, 19,* 131–138.

Wolpow, R. (2001). Canaries in the literacy learning coalmine: Lessons about the affective dimensions of literacy instruction culled from darkness. *Yearbook of the American Reading Forum, 21,* 56–71.

Wolpow, R., & Askov, E. (1998). Strong at the broken places: Literacy instruction for survivors of pervasive trauma. *Journal of Adolescent and Adult Literacy, 34,* 50–57.

Wolpow, R., & Askov, E. (2001). School violence and trauma demand widened frameworks and practice. From bibliotherapy to the literacy of testimony and witness. *Journal of Adolescent and Adult Literacy, 44,* (7), 606–609.

Wolpow, R., Neff, G., & Neff, S. (2002). High tech—high touch: Utilizing technology to foster meaningful intergenerational literacy connections. *Yearbook of the American Reading Forum, 22.* Retrieved June 15, 2005 from http://www.fd.appstate.edu/arfonline/02_arfyearbook/volume02 toc.htm#wolpow

Worthy, J., Moorman, M., & Turner, M. (1999). What Johnny likes to read is hard to find in school. *Reading Research Quarterly, 34,* (1), 12–27.

Zintz, M. V. (1986). A rationale for teaching students with limited English proficiency. *American Reading Forum Yearbook,* 1–5.

PART

II

The Process of Comprehension and Its Assessment

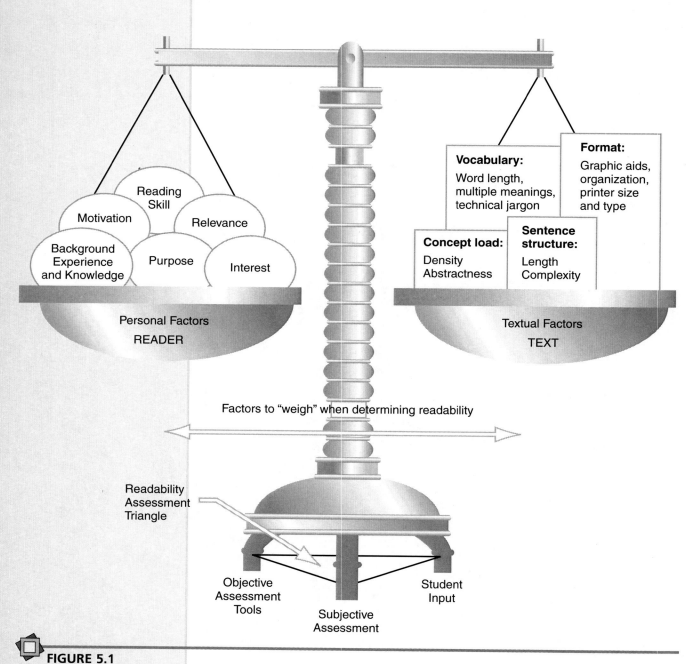

FIGURE 5.1

Matching Print with Reading—A Cognitive Map

Matching Print with Reader: Part One— Text Assessment

Outline

- Anticipatory and Review Questions
- A Sampling of National Performance Standards
- Introduction
- Plain Language Laws
- Readability Defined
  - *Workshop 5.1: Speculating on Reading Ease/Difficulty*
- Textual Factors: What Makes Something Easy or Difficult to Read?
  - Concept Load and Abstractness
  - Format and Length of Text
  - Vocabulary (Lexical Complexity)
  - Sentence Length and Structure (Syntactical Complexity)
  - Inclusiveness
- Levels of Understanding
- Tools for Measuring Readability
  - Formulae
    - *Workshop 5.2: Using a Fry Graph*
  - Evaluating Shorter Passages with the Fry Graph
  - Caveat: Why Readability Formulae Do Not Work with Most Math Books
  - Flesch Reading Ease and Flesch-Kincaid Grade Level Scores
    - *Workshop 5.3: Estimating the Grade Level of Your Own Writing*
  - Other Formulae: Dale-Chall, Lexile, DRP, and ATOS

- Summary of the Strengths and Weaknesses of Readability Formulae
- Readability Checklists
  - Marshall's Checklist
  - The ICL Checklist Buffet
  - Summary of Strengths and Weaknesses of Checklists
- Qualitative Assessment of Text Difficulty
- Student Input/Personal Factors
  - Informal Assessments
  - Summary of Strengths and Weaknesses of Student Input
- The Readability Assessment Triangle
- From the Content Classroom: Matching the Readability of Textbooks with the Reading Abilities of Students Who Must Read Them
  - *Workshop 5.4: Should All School Texts Be Written at or Below Grade Level?*
- Textbook Analysis: More Than Just Readability
  - *Workshop 5.5: Schaefer's Textbook Analysis Assignment*
- Cinquain as Summary
- Summary
- References and Recommended Readings

> "The key point here is that the research has well demonstrated the need for students to have instructional texts that they can read accurately, fluently, and with good comprehension if we hope to foster academic achievement. The evidence also suggests that for large numbers of students this recommendation has been routinely ignored."
>
> *Richard Allington*

> "There is no such thing as a moral or an immoral book. Books are well written or badly written."
>
> *Oscar Wilde*

Anticipatory and Review Questions

Literal

1. Describe five or six factors that make a text difficult or easy to read.

2. Name at least two advantages and two disadvantages of using textbooks that students can read easily.

Interpretive/Applied

3. Compare the importance of personal vs. textual factors in determining the readability of a text. Explain why each is important.

4. At what grade level should a voter's information pamphlet be written? Why?

Evaluative/Critical

5. What do the readability tools in this chapter have in common? In what significant ways do they differ?

6. You are asked by your school's principal to form a committee to evaluate a prospective textbook. Given the high cost of this purchase, the principal wants to make sure this text will be useable by the majority of students. Which readability measuring tools would you use? How would you use them? Who would you ask to serve on the committee? Why?

Creative/Personal

7. Think of a difficult form or contract that you had to read and sign. Perhaps it was the lease for an apartment or the medical permission form prior to a surgery. Did you read it? Did you ask someone to explain it to you first? Or did you just sign? Why? How did this process feel to you? Why?

8. If you could have only one set of textbooks available to you in your classroom, would you choose a set that reads at grade level, or a set that reads above grade level? Why? More important, once you made this decision, how would you use those textbooks? Why?

A Sampling of National Performance Standards

- The assessment process should involve multiple perspectives and sources of data. . . . The more consequential the decision, the more important it is to seek diverse perspectives and independent sources of data. . . . A single measure is likely to be misleading or erroneous for individuals and groups. Multiple sources of data . . . can allow for "triangulation" . . . (International Reading Association/National Council of Teachers of English, 1994, pp. 29–30).
- Accomplished Adolescents and Young Adulthood/Science teachers employ a deliberately sequenced variety of research-driven instructional strategies and select, adapt, and create instructional resources to support active student exploration and understanding of science (National Board for Professional Teaching Standards, 2005).

Introduction

No two wooden baseball bats are exactly alike. It is the job of the hitting instructor to help players choose the "right" bat. Variations in the hitter's size and strength may make a bat too light or too heavy, too long or too short. One thing is for certain: The hitter who is well matched with a bat will find it easier to "make contact" with the pitched ball.

Many student reading problems may be attributed to the textbooks their teachers assign to them. If the book is not a match, an unnecessarily high percentage of students will "strike out." Students who do not wish to be embarrassed by revealing their lack of reading strength may display negative attitudes including apathy or acting-out behaviors. As frustration builds, students are sure to find ways to let their teachers know that they have lost interest in a game they have no hope of winning. Conversely, students capable of reading and understanding more challenging materials will find a way to display their boredom and frustration. Good hitters will not be happy playing Wiffle-ball when they are capable of playing in the big leagues.

In the past, many content teachers would select only the strongest hitters/readers for the team. Using the excuse that they were content experts, not reading teachers, some teachers ignored and/or blamed students who couldn't meet the challenge of the text. In some cases, the poorest readers were sent to remedial classes. Remedial tracks proved to be both expensive and ineffective. The bottom line is all students benefit when their teachers are able to integrate their passion and knowledge for the subject area with instruction in the literacy skills needed to read and write about it.

As illustrated by the cognitive map at the beginning of this chapter, matching print with reader is a delicate balancing act. In order to learn how to do so, we will look first at the intent of plain language laws and then at the many factors that determine how easy or difficult a text is to read. Next we will examine formulae and checklists that teachers may use to assess these factors. We will complete the triangulation of data, as recommended by assessment standards, by considering ways to gather data from our students about the personal preferences they bring to the text. Finally, we will apply what we have learned about readability by discussing ways that teachers can analyze their textbooks to determine if they are also a good match for the content they plan to teach.

Plain Language Laws

Plain language laws differ from state to state but their basic goal is to require that consumer contracts be written in language that is easy to understand. Take, for example, a residential lease. "Lessor" and "lessee" may be changed to "landlord" and "tenant." "Commencement date" and "expiration date" can be changed to "beginning date" and "ending date." "The addendum attached hereto" may be changed to "part two." Plain language laws suggest reducing jargon and providing explanations in plain English whenever technical language is used. Shorter words, sentences, and paragraphs are also recommended. The citizens of New York, New Jersey, Pennsylvania, Hawaii, Connecticut, and Minnesota have passed these laws to guarantee that they wouldn't have to hire a legal expert in order to read a common contract (Millus, 1983; O'Matz, 1994; Siegel, 1981).

The need for plain language has also extended into the field of medicine. Take, for example, the "Notice of Privacy Act" passed in 2003. This federal law was designed to protect the privacy of the patient. By law, people who provide medical service must inform their patients how the medical information they gather is protected. To prove they have done so, medical providers must have their patients read and sign a form, "written in plain language," explaining how this information is used. One study of these handouts found that 80% of patients had difficulty understanding what they had "read" and signed. The researchers noted these forms were lengthy, printed in small font size, and contained complex language appropriate for a medical journal, not for a common patient (Breese & Burnman, 2005). Similar concerns have been voiced by physicians who found that their patients were unable to understand the permission forms required before a surgical procedure.

In Oklahoma, the State Department of Education checks ballot propositions for ease of reading. The problems Florida had with voters reading its ballot in 2000 attest to the wisdom of Oklahoma's practice. The Department of Motor Vehicles, in Arizona, rewrote its driver's manual when they discovered the text was too difficult for the majority of citizens to read with understanding. Most will agree that a 16-year-old applying for a license should not be required to read at the level of a graduate student in college!

Why then are so many important documents hard to read? Perhaps it is because they are written by experts. After all, they became experts by reading and writing volumes of technical text. No wonder these experts have trouble writing about what they know in plain language!

Like the documents listed above, many school textbooks were written by experts. While the content may be accurate and thorough, many are not written in plain language. Many textbooks, from fourth grade through high school, are written at higher levels than the abilities of the students using them. For example, the typical 10th-grade biology textbook has several chapters written at the graduate school level. A typical sixth-grade social studies textbook may have one chapter written at the sixth-grade level and then the next written at the eleventh-grade level.

Readability Defined

Research has demonstrated that academic achievement requires that students have instructional texts that they can read accurately, fluently, and with good comprehension (Allington, 2001). **_Readability_** is the term used to describe the overall difficulty or ease with which material can be read by a given audience. Assessing the readability of texts is crucial to lesson planning because it allows teachers to anticipate and instructionally compensate for the reading problems their students might experience. In other words, teachers who know how to evaluate the readability of a text can do a better job of matching text with reader. When they know that a text is difficult for their students to read, they can use instructional reading enhancing strategies (Chapter Seven) to help their students comprehend.

Readability, as defined above, is a property of a text. It is a measure of the physical aspects of text that contribute to its level of difficulty. When we assess the readability of a text, we are determining how easy or difficult that text is to read for the "average" reader who has the skills to read at that level. However, material written at a 10th-grade level can be easy for some people and harder for others. For example, a high school sophomore who loves to play video games will find a video game magazine easier to read than a professor who doesn't know an Xbox from a PlayStation. Personal factors like motivation, relevance, background knowledge, and experience can offset textual factors. In the end, matching text with reader is as much an art as it is a science. Before we examine the factors involved, let us speculate about physical characteristics of text that would make reading materials easy or difficult to read.

Workshop 5.1

Speculating on Reading Ease/Difficulty

A. What factors do you believe contribute to the ease with which you read something? Think of texts, novels, or magazines that you have read. With a partner or alone, list as many factors as you can that affect your ability to comprehend written materials.

1.   6.

2.   7.

3.   8.

4.   9.

5.   10.

B. Take a guess as to the overall reading grade level of any of the following:

1. *Silas Marner* _____

2. *Shogun* _____

3. *Time Magazine* _____

4. *Reader's Digest* _____

5. *Psychology Today* _____

6. *Popular Mechanics*_____

7. A big city newspaper _____

8. A small town newspaper _____

9. *The Diary of Anne Frank* _____

C. Which section of a newspaper generally has the highest readability level?

a. Front Page

b. Sports Page

c. Financial Page

d. Comics

e. Editorial

D. At which level do you think you would write

1. a letter to a friend? _____

2. a term paper? _____

3. a study guide for your students? _____

Answers to sections B and C are at the end of the chapter.

Textual Factors: What Makes Something Easy or Difficult to Read?

The discussion that follows focuses on five textual factors. They are (1) concept load and abstractness, (2) format and length of text, (3) vocabulary, (4) sentence length and structure, and (5) inclusiveness.

Concept Load and Abstractness

The **concept load,** also called density, refers to the number of concepts that are introduced in each paragraph. A paragraph with a heavy concept load will have many new words introduced with little explanation, repetition, or examples.

The **abstractness** of a text will vary with the nature of the people, objects, events, phenomena, or concepts being described. For example, a sentence telling us that Thomas Jefferson drafted the Declaration of Independence and that 56 representatives of 13 colonies signed it on July 4, 1776, is far less abstract than the first sentence of that document: "When in the course of human events, it becomes necessary for one people to dissolve the political bands which have connected them with another, and to assume among the powers of the earth, the separate and equal station to which the Laws of Nature and of Nature's God entitle them, a decent respect to the opinions of mankind requires that they should declare the causes which impel them to the separation."

Format and Length of Text

Suppose you were asked to read a 3-page legal document, all single-spaced and in fine print. Suppose there were no pictures or diagrams. Suppose all the material was small print. How would this format affect your ability to read with understanding?

Format refers to the way the page is laid out. Spacing and lettering should serve as a guide to the reader. Most readers will need help in separating the main ideas from the supporting details. They will also need help in understanding how all the pieces form the whole.

Textbooks that use format to enhance readability will include the following:

a. *Graphic Aids* (pictures, maps, graphs, charts, and diagrams) and use of color: A picture can be worth a thousand words. So can flowcharts, diagrams, or maps. Creative use of color assists readers with understanding. However, not all graphic aids are easy to read.

b. *Headings and Subheadings*: Do you ever glance over the headlines of your newspaper to get an idea of what there is to read? When reading a web page, do you ever scan through the hyperlinks to determine what part of the document you want to read? The headings and subheadings in a document should help you in the same way. They should guide the reader through the text providing a sense of coherence and unity.

c. *Print Size*: The size of print and the style of type can influence the legibility of text and the ease of reading. This may be especially true for readers with vision problems. In case you had trouble reading the last two sentences, here they are again, this time in a bigger font and easier-to-read type face: The size of print and the style of type can influence the legibility of text and the ease of reading. This may be especially true for readers with vision problems.

d. *Length of Text:* Students with reading problems will be the first to tell you that the longer a text is, the harder it is for them to read. Longer text will usually contain greater elaboration. However, ability to maintain concentration may become a factor here.

Vocabulary (Lexical Complexity)

Vocabulary is one of the most easily identifiable characteristics of text difficulty. As a general rule, longer words (with many syllables) are harder to read. Perhaps this is because sounding out long words requires more cognitive memory, which interferes with comprehension. If you know that many of your students read slowly and struggle with new words, you will have to make sure they have been introduced to the vocabulary before they read. If you don't have time to do this, then students should not be asked to read it independently.

If there is limited use of longer words (a controlled vocabulary), look to see how the material has been written. All readers are entitled to read rich, provocative well-written text. The important variable is the quality of the writing, not the sophistication of the vocabulary. Look to see if common words are used instead of words of Latin or Greek origin. For example, "go" may sometimes be used instead of "proceed" and "safe" can sometimes be used instead of "secure."

Using computers, millions of pages of text have been studied revealing that longer, multisyllabic words appear less frequently than shorter ones. This has led researchers to believe that many longer words are harder to read because readers see them less often. Therefore, a difficult longer word should be introduced in a manner that makes it easier to learn and remember. For example:

- Newly introduced words should be in **bold face** or <u>underlined</u>.
- Multisyllabic words should be followed by *syllabification* (syl lab i fi ca tion) or phonetic spelling (si lab əfi ka shən) to help the reader unlock their sounds. Doing so may help the reader get the meaning.
- Finally, and most important, the new word should be defined and used in context. For example:

> **Syllabification** is the process of dividing words into their syllables. For example, the word syllabification may be divided into six syllables (syl lab i fi ca tion). Each of these syllables is a part of the word. Syllabification is a synonym for the more common term "syllabication." Syllabification is necessary in order to complete the Fry Graph.

Furthermore, the odds of students remembering the meaning of vocabulary words improve if the words appear again on the same page and later in the chapter. Repetition is a key to remembering. Look to see how often the same vocabulary is repeated on a page or in a chapter.

Jargon is the specialized or technical vocabulary of a subject area. Sometimes the subject of a chapter requires technical jargon and in most cases, this terminology contains many long words. There is no way to avoid them. In fact, teaching technical vocabulary is an important part of teaching content literacy.

Well-written text does not introduce too many technical terms at one time. This aspect of text is called **lexical density**. Lexical density is the proportion of technical words per sentence. Look at the lexical density of the sentence that follows. Wouldn't it be difficult for a first-time biology student to understand?

> The process of **photosynthesis** takes place in the chloroplasts, specifically using chlorophyll, the green **pigment** involved in photosynthesis.

A word to the wise: The more reading you have done in your subject area, the more need for input about lexical complexity. For example, if you completed several university courses in biology, the sentence above is easy to read. However, if you have studied only a little biology, and it was a long time ago, this same sentence will have to be read with a dictionary. If you are a highly qualified educator, you have extended practice in reading in your discipline(s). When trying to judge the lexical density of a text, make sure to ask someone who doesn't have your expertise. Ask if they think the vocabulary is presented in a way that will be easy for all students to learn.

Finally, when looking at the vocabulary in a text, look to make sure that words with **multiple meanings** (also called polysemy) are used carefully. For example, read these two sentences from a student textbook on landscaping design:

> The *root* of the problem is in the *root* system. If you want to *root* out this problem, leave plenty of extra space for *root* expansion.

Readability may be improved by changing these sentences to the following:

> The main reason for the problem is in the *root* system of the plant. To solve this problem, leave plenty of extra space for the *roots* to grow.

Sentence Length and Structure (Syntactical Complexity)

Lengthy sentences will often be more difficult to comprehend than shorter ones. This may be especially true for the slow reader. The longer the sentence, the longer you must keep track of the subject, verb, and predicate agreement to get the meaning. In other words, the distance between words or phrases and their modifiers can determine a sentence's complexity.

For example: (spaces have been inserted to simulate the difficulty a struggling reader experiences)

> By the time that slow readers get to the end of a very long sentence, a sentence that may have several clauses as well as many multisyllabic words to sound out, the readers may forget what it is that they were reading about in the first place.

Although longer sentences may be harder to read, nothing is less stimulating than a long series of short choppy sentences. Short sentences hit home because they provide emphasis and are easier to understand. Longer sentences provide description, link ideas, establish qualifications, or express reservations. Text with sentences varying in length is easier to read. For example:

a. Farmer Brown's wife needed to see the doctor. But they didn't go to town. That would be a greater risk. She was ill. His tires were old. The roads were icy. Old tires don't get adequate traction. Better to wait a day or two.

b. Rather than take the risk, Farmer Brown stayed home with his wife. Even though she needed to see the doctor, driving on the icy roads, with old tires that didn't get adequate traction, was a greater risk than waiting a day or two to see the doctor.

Inclusiveness

It is easier for readers to understand a text when they have reason to believe the author is try to include them in the reading audience. If the reader's culture, gender, or ethnicity is not represented fairly, comprehension will be lessened. When turning through a book, check for inclusiveness and balance. Ask: Are people of color represented? How? Which ethnic or racial groups are included? Are both males and females represented? How? Are they accurate portrayals? Is one group always in the background and the other always in the foreground? Is the linguistic pattern suitable to most populations? Are male pronouns used to describe both males and females? Are uncomplimentary adjectives used to describe any one group? Are there stereotypes? If religion is discussed, ask: Is one religion presented as "superior" to another?

Texts that portray the cultures of students with respect and realism are easier to read because they reflect what is true for the reader. Texts that are exclusive are harder to read because identity and personal safety may be compromised. (To get a better sense of how language may be used to make a student feel included or excluded, read *The Truth, Whispered or Shouted*, at the end of Chapter Twelve, and/or *Evangelina Can Read*, at the end of Chapter Three.

Levels of Understanding

When students read assigned materials, their ability to understand what they read will vary from text to text. In fact, sometimes the readers' abilities will vary within the very same text. When matching students with texts, teachers should take steps to find out how the text relates to the students' abilities. There are three levels of understanding: (1) independent reading level, (2) instructional reading level, and (3) frustration level.

The ***independent reading level*** is the level at which readers can read text for understanding without outside help. Hence, the science teacher who asks students to read a new chapter and answer the questions before the next class is assuming that students can read this chapter at the independent reading level. Such independent reading assignments assume that each student is familiar with the vocabulary, has the necessary reading skills to get the ideas, and has the prior knowledge to understand the concepts described.

Independent level

Readers Have ⟷	Author Expects
Vocabulary	Vocabulary
Skills	Skills
Ability to Grasp Concepts	Ability to Grasp Concepts

The ***instructional reading level*** is the level at which the readers' vocabulary, skills, and/or conceptual awareness fall slightly below the writer's expectations. At this level readers are able to learn but not with complete thoroughness or ease. Text that is at the instructional level is challenging to readers, but not beyond their grasp. Often the teacher can provide instruction geared to helping them read with greater ease or understanding. This instruction and/or instructional aid may be seen as a bridge over the gap between the students' abilities and those necessary to read for full understanding.

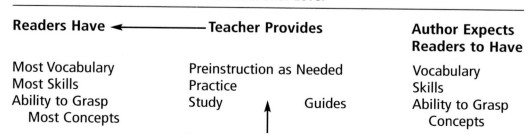

Instructional Level

Readers Have ⟵	Teacher Provides		Author Expects Readers to Have
Most Vocabulary	Preinstruction as Needed		Vocabulary
Most Skills	Practice		Skills
Ability to Grasp Most Concepts	Study	Guides	Ability to Grasp Concepts

The *frustrational level* is that level at which no reasonable amount of instructional assistance is sufficient to bridge the gap between readers' abilities and author's expectations. When students are asked to read material at their frustration level, they can be expected to manifest behavior from denial to anxiety and/or tears to anger. If assigned to read this material independently, they can be expected to show up for class without having done the reading.

Frustrational Level

Readers Have	Teacher Provides	Author Expects
Limited Vocabulary	Preinstruction	Vocabulary
Limited Skills	Support During Reading	Skills
Limited Grasp of Concepts	Support After Reading	Ability to Grasp Concepts

 ## Tools for Measuring Readability

Since 1852 reading authorities have been designing and refining tools to analyze and predict how easy or difficult text will be to read. There are many different tools that may be used and each has its own strengths and weaknesses. The material and the intended audience should determine which tool you choose. There are three corners of the readability measurement triangle: (1) formulae, (2) teacher checklists, and (3) student input.

Formulae

Formulae usually measure vocabulary and sentence difficulty. Their biggest advantage is in their objectivity. Teachers can agree to rules for counting words, sentences, and syllables. They may then double-check to make sure that they have the same numbers. Once they have done so, they can agree on a readability score from a formula or chart that has been standardized to the reading levels of normative samples of students or reading books. Computer software can be used to simplify this process.

The Fry Readability Graph is one of the most widely used formulas for estimating readability in both business and education (Fry, 1977). It has been validated on all levels of material for grades one through seventeen. Fry's graph estimates the reading ability needed to comprehend somewhere between the frustration and instructional levels. (See Figure 5.2.)

Expanded Directions for Working the Readability Graph

1. Randomly select three sample passages and count out exactly 100 words each, starting with the beginning of a sentence. Do count proper nouns, initializations, and numerals.

2. Count the number of sentences in the 100 words, estimating the length of the fraction of the last sentence to the nearest one-tenth.

3. Count the total number of syllables in the 100-word passage. If you don't have a hand counter available, an easy way is to simply put a mark above every syllable over one in each word, then when you get to the end of the passage, count the number of marks, and add 100. Small calculators can also be used as counters by pushing numeral 1, then push the + sign for each word or syllable when counting.

FIGURE 5.2

Edward B. Fry's graph for estimating readability—extended. *From Fry's Readability Graph: Clarification, Validity, and Extensions to Level 17," by Edward B. Fry, Journal of Reading, December 1977, p. 249.*

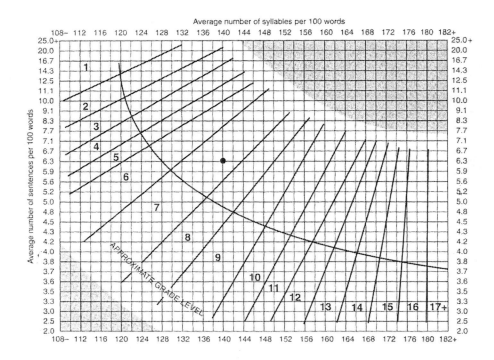

4. Enter graph with *average* sentence length and *average* number of syllables; plot dot where the two lines intersect. Area where dot is plotted will give you the approximate grade level.

5. If a great deal of variability is found in syllable count or sentence count, putting more samples into the average is desirable.

6. A word is defined as a group of symbols with a space on either side; thus, *Joe, IRA, 1945,* and *&* are each one word.

7. A syllable is defined as a phonetic syllable. Generally, there are as many syllables as vowel sounds. For example, *stopped* is one syllable and *wanted* is two syllables. When counting syllables for numerals and initializations, count one syllable for each symbol. For example, *1945* is four syllables, *IRA* is three syllables, and *&* is one syllable.

Fry developed this graph for his work in Africa in 1968 and it has undergone revisions since that time. He did not retain copyrights, so it can be duplicated and used without permission.

Hints for avoiding mistakes with the Fry graph:

- Read the directions carefully.
- If your findings fall in the gray area, they are not valid and other samples will need to be taken.
- When counting syllables, remember that each syllable has one vowel sound. *Bi-cy-cle* has three sounds and therefore three syllables. It is what you hear, rather than what you see. *Count-ed* has two syllables, but *skipped* has only one. This is because you hear only the one sound. Also note that people from different regions may have accents that would cause them to syllabicate differently. For example, "stairs" and "more" each have two syllables in the southeastern United States.

- Remember, you are to find the mean of a *minimum* of three 100 words samples. As a rule, more is always better.

Example	Syllables	Sentences
First Hundred Words	124	6.6
Second Hundred Words	141	5.5
Third Hundred Words	158	6.8
Total	3)423	3)18.9
Average (total divided by 3)	141	6.3

Readability is approximately seventh grade, a range of sixth to eighth grade (see dot plotted on the graph in Figure 5.2). The range is established by going from one level below to one level above. Some refer to this as the "true range" reflecting variability that is inherent in text.

When in doubt, take additional samples. For example:

- From time to time it may appear that one of the scores is an outlier. An outlier is a sample with numbers that are much larger or smaller than the numbers in the other samples. Outliers create variability that can be remedied with additional samples.

- If you discover that your findings fall in the gray area, they are not valid. You will need to take additional samples.

- Many content textbooks have different authors for different chapters. Hence one chapter may read four to five grade levels higher than another. In these cases, it would be wise to take samples from each chapter that students will be asked to read.

Remember, the Fry graph measures *only* vocabulary in terms of the number of syllables per 100 word passage. Consider the sentence, "To be or not to be, that is the question." There aren't many syllables. However the concept load and density are enormous.

The Fry graph is well liked because it is "quick and dirty." However, be on the look out for ***readability cheating***. Readability cheating is when an author writes text to the formula. Purposeful shortening of sentences can increase the number of sentences in a 100 word passage. Replacing longer words with shorter words can reduce syllable count. These actions will lower the readability score on the Fry graph. They will not, however, improve the readability. Short, choppy sentences may, in fact, make the text hard to read. (Remember Farmer Brown, his sick wife, his bad tires, and the icy road!)

Workshop 5.2

Using a Fry Graph

Here are data from three samples taken from a book used by the Private Industry Counsel. PIC provides training for high school dropouts whose earnings are below the poverty level. Students are asked to look through this book about occupations and then choose occupations to discuss with a counselor.

The data are from two samples using the Fry method. A third sample is provided for you to practice. Count the syllables and sentences in the sample text that follows. In the space provided below, write in your data, and then use the graph in Figure 5.2 to ascertain the readability level. Remember, Fry requires three 100-word samples.

Finally, write brief recommendations for the people at PIC about this material. Keep in mind the limited data you have available. After completing this exercise, pair off with another student to compare answers.

Sample	Syllables	Sentences
One	206	6.8
Two	189	6.2
Three	Use text below	

Automobile Mechanics: _____ (Start counting your 100 words here; place a slash line after the 100th word.)

// They examine the automobile and discuss the type and extent of the malfunction with the customer. They plan how the work is to be done. Using hand tools, they remove the part, repair it, or replace it if necessary. They then reinstall the part and check their work. Some mechanics specialize in one type of repair. Front-end mechanics align wheels, frames, and steering wheels. Transmission mechanics disassemble, adjust, and repair manual and automatic transmissions. Tune-up mechanics adjust the ignition, timing, and valves and adjust or replace spark plugs, distributor, and points. They also test and repair carburation and fuel injection systems. Mechanics can also use computers for diagnostic checks of electronic parts.

FRY GRAPH EXAMPLE AND WORKSHEET

Your turn	Syllables	Sentences
First 100 words	_____	_____
Second 100 words	_____	_____
Third 100 words	_____	_____
Total	_____	_____
Average (total divided by 3)	_____	_____

Now plot these coordinates on the graph. Indicate the range. Consider any other factors that should go into your recommendation for the teacher who uses this book.

Readability _____   True Range _____

See answer key at the end of the chapter.

Evaluating Shorter Passages with the Fry Graph

It is often important to be able to determine the difficulty level of passages shorter than 100 words, such as those found in directions or essay questions. Forgan and Mangrum (1981) outlined procedures for doing this using the Fry graph. Keep in mind that these are rough approximations:

1. Count the total number of words in the passage. For example, the total might be 69 words.
2. Always round down to the nearest 10. In this case you would round down the 69 words to 60.
3. Use this number (in this case, 60) when counting the number of sentences and syllables.
4. Multiply the number of sentences and the number of syllables by the corresponding number found in the conversion chart below. With our example of a 69 word passage rounded down to 60, you would multiply the number of sentences by 1.67 and then the number of syllables by 1.67.
5. Use these numbers to enter Fry's graph to find your readability estimate.

Conversion Chart

Number of Words in Selection (less than 100)	Multiply by
30	3.3
40	2.5
50	2.0
60	1.67
70	1.43
80	1.25
90	1.1

From *Teaching Content Area Reading,* by Harry Forgan and Charles Mangrum II, 1981, Columbus, OH: Charles E. Merrill Publishing Company. Copyright 1981. Used with permission.

Caveat: Why Readability Formulae Do Not Work with Most Math Books

The language in most mathematics textbooks is very different than in other content areas (Weist, 2003). Unlike other content areas, math uses symbolic language and prepositions in ways that can invalidate readability results.

Symbols place special demands on readers in the concise language of mathematics. Math is rich in symbols for operations (e.g., +, -, x, ÷, and $\sqrt{}$), relational symbols (e.g., <, ≤, >, and ≥) and procedural symbols such as brackets and parentheses (e.g., $3^3[(6+2)3]$). The order in which these symbols appear (syntax) is vital to comprehension. The Fry graph was not designed to account for the use of this many symbols in sentences.

A preposition is a linking word that shows the relationship of a noun or pronoun to some another word in the sentence (e.g., I bought this book *from* him). Most often prepositions are short words (e.g., "of," "at," "with," "into"). A formula usually rates one-syllable words as easy to read. However, in the concise language of math, these small but powerful words place significant demands on the reader. For example, check out the prepositions in this sentence:

Find 3/4 *of* 16, and divide it *by* the number *of* items *in* the box.

Powerful little words, aren't they? Now look at this mathematical equation:

8/2 = 4

How would you read it? 8 divided by 2 equals 4. Or divide 8 *by* 2 and this equals 4. Or 2 divided into 8 equals 4? Or 8 divided in half equals 4? Are the symbols in this equation a complete sentence? Fry tells you to assign one syllable to each symbol. When estimating readability do you count this equation as a sentence? Or do you just skip it and find a passage that contains "normal" text?

If that weren't enough, remember math also has its own technical vocabulary (numerator, quadratic, hypotenuse, and exponent). It also uses many common words in ways that are unique to math (e.g., expression, product, negative, odd, rational). The meanings of some math vocabulary even change with context (e.g., words like "base" and "square" have different meanings in a spatial context than in a number context). Therefore this warning: Math formulae do *not* work with *most* math text. Therefore, teachers assessing math text depend heavily on the other two corners of the readability triangle: checklists and student input.

However, note the qualifying word "*most.*" There are still times when you would be well advised to use formulae to check readability. For example, look this passage from a popular sixth-grade math book:

Patterns When multiplying numbers that end in zeros, multiply the non-zero parts and annex one zero to your answer for each zero in the problem. When dividing a number that ends in zeros, subtract the number of zeros in the divisor from the number of zeros in the dividend to find the number in the quotient.

The readability of this passage, according to Flesch-Kincaid, is 12th grade. And, in case you are interested, the readability of the preceding section of this text, with all of its symbols, equations and expressions, is 9.8, high ninth grade!

Flesch Reading Ease and Flesch-Kincaid Grade Level Scores

Completing word and sentence counts for the Fry graph provides the teacher with chances to detect the reasons that text may score high or low when using a formula. However, counting and dividing syllables is time-consuming. Fortunately, a wide variety of computer software programs is available for calculating readability estimates. One of the most popular of these software programs comes free with Microsoft Word 5.0 and higher. When Microsoft Word finishes checking spelling and grammar, it can display information about the reading level of the document. This includes two formulae: (1) the Flesch Reading Ease Score and (2) the Flesch-Kincaid Grade Level Score. Each readability score bases its rating on the average number of syllables per word and words per sentence.

The Flesch Reading Ease Score rates text on a 100-point scale. The higher the score, the easier it is to understand the document. No grade level score is given. Hence, scores from any one passage may be used only for comparative purposes.

Kincaid et al. (1975) modified the Flesch Reading Ease formula and created the *Flesch-Kincaid Grade Level Scores*. This score is stated in U.S. school grade levels 1 through 12. Before you use this tool, here are three advisories:

1. No matter how difficult a text passage is to read, it will not be scored above 12th grade. Flesch-Kincaid Grade Level Scores do not go above 12th grade. (Fry goes up to grade 17.)

2. Kincaid standardized the scores with 531 Navy enlisted personnel and the comprehension section of the Gates-McGinitie reading test. The subjects were mostly male and recent high school graduates. Since very few of the subjects were women and none were of middle school age, scores may not be a valid representative of these populations.

3. When using this or any other computerized program, you must still look at the words, sentences, and symbols that are in the body of the text. This will help you discover reasons that the book might score higher or lower than it should have.

Despite these warnings, you can't beat the cost (free with your copy of MS Word) or the convenience of this tool. To enable this option, click on "tools," then "options," then "spelling and grammar," and then check "show readability statistics." Highlight the passage you want checked, and then run the spell check. At the end of the sequence you will be provided with scores.

Estimating the Grade Level of Your Own Writing

Take a sample of your own expository writing. This might be a portion of a paper you wrote in college or a handout you regularly give to your students. Using the Fry Graph and/or the Flesch-Kincaid Grade Level Score, estimate the readability of your own writing. Do the same with a personal letter or a long e-mail. Which is higher? Why do you suppose that is? Now take one of these samples and try to rewrite it so that it will score two or three grade levels lower.

The next time you meet with your colleagues, share your findings about your writing. Also, share your rewritten passages. Ask your colleagues: Which passage is easier to understand? Why? When I rewrote this to score lower on the readability scale, did I make it easier or more difficult to understand? Why? If your rewritten passage is harder to understand, you have an example of "readability cheating."

Workshop 5.3

Other Formulae: Dale-Chall, Lexile, DRP, and ATOS

The Fry Readability Graph and the Flesch-Kincaid Grade Level Score are the most popular of the readability formulae for secondary texts. This is mostly because they are easy to get and easy to use. Both measure the number of syllables per word as the means to assess the difficulty of vocabulary. Wouldn't it be great if there was a formula that would recognize shorter words that are hard to read and longer words that a reader should already know? One way to do this would be to compile a list of commonly known words at a specific grade level. Then the words in any text could be compared to the list of commonly known words.

The *New Dale-Chall Readability Formula* (Chall & Dale, 1995) is a carefully validated word list formula. It can be used to estimate the difficulty of a text based on average sentence length and the number of words not found on its 3,000 word list of words known by fourth-grade students. This formula is most valid for materials in the 3rd to 12th grade range; however, it does provide scores for grades 1 to 16. At the time of this book's publication, there was no software available for this formula. Therefore the comparison of words to the list of known words must be gathered and calculated manually.

There are also three popular readability information systems available on the web: (1) the Lexile Scale, (2) the DRP or Degrees of Reading Power, and (3) the ATOS™ Readability Formula. All three are available from for-profit corporations. Each can help provide some information that may be helpful in matching text with reader for a fee.

The Lexile Scale (Smith, Stenner, Horabin, & Smith, 1989) is a computerized method that estimates the difficulty of text by comparing sentence length to "word frequency." Word frequency is measured by comparing the words that appear in the text to a database of 600 million words. Using the Lexile Scale to find out how difficult a text is to read will require their software program, the Lexile Analyzer, is available from Metametrics Inc. (http://www.lexile.com). However, if the book you want to analyze is a novel, trade book, or one several textbooks, there is a good chance that it has already been assessed. To find out, go to the Lexile Book Database (at the same website) and type in the title and author. More than 30,000 books have been rated using Lexile scores ranging from 200L (beginning readers) to 1,700L (advanced text).

Metametrics Inc. (owner of Lexile) has also assigned Lexile scores to items on several standardized reading tests. Based on their performance on these tests, students can be given individualized Lexile scores of their reading abilities. The teacher can thereby, at least in theory, match the students' individualized reading Lexile scores with the individualized Lexile scores of potential books. However, buyers beware. All formulae have their shortcomings. For example, at the time of this writing, we entered John Grisham's novel *The Firm* and E.B. White's *Charlotte's Web* into the Lexile Book Database. Both had the same Lexile book score of 680L!

One other problem with the way that Metametrics reports readability data is the Lexile score is for the entire book. Textbooks frequently have significant variations in readability from chapter to chapter. For example, we typed in the title of a popular high school biology textbook. It came out at 1050L. Shortly thereafter, we completed Fry checks on five of the chapters of this textbook. The overall score for all five chapters was 12th grade (range of 11–13). However, multiple checks revealed that the introductory chapter scored 10th grade (range 9–11), the chapters on chemical compounds and cell energy each scored 11th grade (range 10–12), a chapter on genetics scored 14th grade (range 13–15), and the chapter on mosses and ferns scored 10th grade (range 9–11).

DRP or Degrees of Reading Power, operated by Touchstone Applied Science Associates Inc. (http://tasaliteracy.com), reports the ease or difficulty of a book using DRP units that comprise a scale from 30–70. These DRP units are determined by measuring the average sentence length, comparing words to The Dale List of words that students should know, and calculating the average numbers of letters per word. DRP unit scores for content textbooks can be found by going to the website above and clicking on the "Readability of Textbooks Online" button. This company also offers a series of their own reading comprehension tests. Student test scores from these tests may be assigned DRP values that can be matched with the DRP unit scores of books. We typed in the names of three commonly used high school books into the DRP Database. None of the three were listed.

The ATOS™ Readability Formula is a product of Renaissance Learning, the same company that created Accelerated Reader (AR). The company developed the ATOS formula so that students could be matched with books at their skill levels, as determined by scores on reading tests. ATOS uses the number of words per sentence, characters per word, and average grade level of words to determine the reading level of the book. The company claims to use the entire text when making this determination. Readability is reported in grade level equivalents. Hence, if you want a rough estimate of the reading level of a book, their website (http://www.renlearn.com/) may be helpful. This website claims to contain readability estimates for more than 40,000 trade books. Three thousand of these books are published in Spanish.

Summary of the Strengths and Weaknesses of Readability Formulae

Strengths

- They are objective and therefore not prone to teacher bias.
- Any two people checking the same passages and using the same formula will come up with the same result.
- Results provide standardized grade level or unit level scores that fit within a comparative range. Computerized versions are quick and easy to use.
- Formulae provide one of the three corners of the readability triangle.

Weaknesses

- Formulae don't factor in student interest or the background knowledge that the reader brings to the book.
- Formulae don't assess concept load, abstractness, textual features, or vocabulary problems such as multiple meanings.
- Formulae don't factor in elements of writer style such as inclusiveness and sentence structure.
- Symbols and prepositions make them ineffective for math text.
- Different formulae can yield different levels.

Readability Checklists

A second corner of the readability triangle is **checklists**. Before a commercial plane taxis to the runway, pilots and mechanics run through a series of long checklists. These lists provide them with a reminder of everything they must check before the plane leaves the gate. *Readability checklists* are designed to serve a similar function. Before a book is assigned to a student, teachers should carefully check several features for ease of student reading. A readability checklist requires teachers to closely examine several key components of the text. However, unlike an airplane checklist, the criteria for judgment are not as precise. No grade level scores can be assigned.

Given the subjective nature of a checklist assessment, results are most valuable when several teachers (from differing disciplines) and/or students rate the same material. These small groups may then choose to average or compare their results.

Marshall's Checklist

Nancy Marshall (1979) developed one of the first published checklists for readability and comprehensibility. It is relatively short and easy to use with nonfiction textbooks.

TABLE 5.1 Marshall's Readability Checklist for Comprehensibility

		Well Done + Average 0 Poor –
Main ideas	1. a. Are major points stated clearly? b. Are chapter titles and headings meaningful? c. Do titles outline major points clearly?	_____ _____ _____
Vocabulary	2. a. Are key vocabulary terms defined clearly when the subject is new? b. Are these terms used in a variety of contexts meaningful to the reader?	_____ _____
Concepts	3. a. Are new concepts introduced in the context of familiar concepts? b. Are they well-defined in the text?	_____ _____
Related ideas	4. a. Are ideas clearly related to each other? b. Will the reader be able to understand relationships among ideas? c. Could the reader illustrate these graphically?	_____ _____ _____
Referents	5. a. Are pronouns used unambiguously? b. Do they usually refer to referents no more than one sentence away?	_____ _____
Audience	6. Has the author addressed the audience intended?	_____

Adapted from Marshall, Nancy. (March 1979). "Readability and Comprehensibility." *Journal of Reading,* 22(6): 542–544. Copyright © 1979 by the International Reading Association.

The ICL Checklist Buffet

We developed the ICL Checklist Buffet to assist teachers in the assessment of a wide variety of textbooks. It is called a "buffet" because teachers get to decide what belongs on a text's assessment plate. For example, format is far more important in a history book than in a novel. Literary devices are more important in a novel than a science text.

If you have a book that you wish to assess, your job, individually or as a member of a group, is to design your own assessment checklist that may be used for your book. Choose any and all items you feel are relevant. If you wish, place two or three items together rephrasing them as one. When working in a group, each member should start with the list as a whole and then reach a consensus on those items that should be skipped.

Readability Buffet Items	Place Check Mark in Appropriate Column			
	n/a	Evident Throughout	Somewhat Evident	Poorly Done
Concept Load/Abstractness				
Conceptual level generally appropriate to the intended audience. (Appropriate assumptions made regarding the prior level of reader concept knowledge.)				
The author introduces new ideas with sufficient explanation, illustration, repetition, and/or examples.				
Author limits the number of concepts introduced in each paragraph. (Says a lot about a few ideas rather than a little about many ideas.)				
Concepts are presented intuitively and/or concretely.				
Literary techniques employed by the author are appropriate to the readers.				
Format and Organization				
The overall layout helps readers understand the text.				
Titles, headings, and subheadings guide the reader through the text. (Provide and outline of major points.)				
Captions tie the visual aids to the text.				
Table of contents, index, and glossary present content clearly.				
Well-written introductory and summary paragraphs provide overview and summary.				
Topic sentences of paragraphs can be easily inferred or identified.				
Print size and type easy to read.				
Purpose of graphic information is clear.				
Pictures/illustrations/charts are appealing.				
Pictures/illustrations/charts are consistent with text information.				
Pictures/illustrations/charts clarify or extend the textual information.				
Questions provided at the end of each chapter/unit emphasize important aspects of the chapter. In fact, they could be used as a reading guide.				
Questions span levels of reasoning from literal to evaluative.				
Is the length of the text and/or chapters within the text, appropriate for the attention span of the readers?				

(Continued)

Readability Buffet Items	Place Check Mark in Appropriate Column			
	n/a	Evident Throughout	Somewhat Evident	Poorly Done
Vocabulary				
Longer (multisyllabic) words are used judiciously (only when necessary).				
Words with multiple meanings are not used within the same sections of the text.				
Word choice is appealing and appropriate.				
Vocabulary used in this work (fictional) is familiar to readers of this age and maturity.				
Newly introduced words are highlighted (boldface/italics/underline).				
New vocabulary words are syllabicated.				
New vocabulary words are defined in context.				
Definitions are provided in footnotes, at the end of the chapter, or in a glossary and are consistent with how the word is used in the text.				
Sentence Length and Structure				
Longer sentences are used judiciously.				
Sentence structure varies providing fluency.				
Pronouns are used unambiguously and refer to referents no more than a sentence away.				
Inclusiveness				
The text is inclusive and balanced.				
There is no evidence (in text or illustrations) of sexual, racial, economic, cultural, religious, or political bias.				
The linguistic pattern is suitable to most populations.				
The text portrays cultures of students with respect and realism.				
Individuals featured in the text (especially expository text) have human qualities that are believable and real.				
Tone and manner of expression are appealing to intended readers.				

Summary of Strengths and Weaknesses of Checklists

Strengths

- May be used to help remember to check for concept load, abstractness, format, organization, use of visuals, audience, and use of referents.
- May be used to help remember to check for inclusiveness and writing style.
- May be used to check for vocabulary (e.g., how new words are introduced, word choice, length, and multiple meanings).
- Especially helpful in assessing text for which formulae may be ineffective (e.g., math, and text about music and art).
- Can facilitate meaningful discussion among colleagues as to the strengths and weaknesses of a text to meet the needs of the student audience.
- Checklists provide data for one of the three corners of the readability triangle.

Weaknesses

- No grade level scores are provided.
- Assessment is subjective.
- Background experience on the part of the teacher can lead to bias.
- Assessment is time-consuming. This is especially the case if a group must discuss each item on the checklist.

Qualitative Assessment of Text Difficulty

Formulae are quick and easy; some even computerized. They provide objective data and grade level scores. Unfortunately they don't factor in the background knowledge or interest that the reader may bring to the text. As important, they don't assess concept load, abstractness, inclusiveness, or textual features. They also don't identify words with multiple meanings or poorly constructed sentences. While checklists do help teachers assess many of these features, they do have significant shortcomings: (1) they are generic, (2) they do not give grade level scores, and (3) they are subjective, thereby subject to teacher bias. Wouldn't it be nice if there were a tool that incorporated features of both?

With the idea in mind that different subject area texts require different kinds of background knowledge as well as different applications of reading strategies, a group of researchers developed the *Qualitative Assessment of Text Difficulty* (QATD). This tool consists of six scales for making assessments specific to subject areas. There is a literature scale, a popular fiction scale, a life sciences scale, a physical sciences scale, a narrative social studies scale, and an expository social studies scale. Each scale then has a series of nine or ten passages ranging in difficulty from grade 1 through college. Passages serve as grade level benchmarks and each level has a distinct change in language, concepts, structure, and difficulty of thought.

To use the QATD, one must first borrow or purchase a copy of the instruction manual (Chall, Bissex, Conard, & Harris-Sharples, 1996). You then decide which of the six scales best matches the text you wish to assess. For example, if you want to assess a short novel, you would use the popular fiction scale. Next you would select a series of samples from your novel. The number of samples depends on the length of the text. The authors recommend one 100-word sample from every 50 pages of text. If your novel has 200 pages, you would select four samples from the book. Using the worksheet provided, you would then match each of your samples with the passages on the popular fiction scale. By averaging the scores of the four samples, you would then be able to ascertain the reading level for the book.

Is the QATD a formula or a checklist? Neither. The QATD is a qualitative tool to assess grade level scores. It allows the teacher to compare levels of difficulty of passages from their texts to benchmarked grade level passages. If you choose to use this tool as one of the corners of the assessment triangle, note that there are several checklist factors that are not assessed such as format, organization, and inclusiveness. Also note that there are no rating scales for several disciplines.

Often preservice teachers will tell us they don't have experience identifying text that is readable at respective grade levels in their subject areas. One advantage of becoming familiar with the readings in this scale is that its format provides validated examples that may be used to make better judgments.

Student Input/Personal Factors

Please take a moment and turn back to the cognitive map on the first page of this chapter. Look again at the left-hand side of this balance. Textual factors may be offset by personal factors. These factors include reading skill, motivation, relevance, background knowledge and experience, reader purpose, and interest. Reader interest or purpose can motivate students to read texts that are extremely difficult. On the other hand, students who are not motivated to read a text or who find a book irrelevant will find reading difficult. For example, a young person who has traveled around the world will have the background experience to best understand a geography text. Personal experiences can significantly change students' abilities to interact with written ideas.

One may therefore conclude that some of the most important input on the readability of a text must come from the students who will be assigned to read from it. To gather this input, we must ask the students. We want their honest opinion as to how well the author introduces new ideas and vocabulary. Is there sufficient explanation, repetition, and/or examples? Are the chapters they will be asked to read independently easy enough for them to go it alone? Are the pictures, maps, graphs, diagrams, and charts helpful? Is the format of the text appealing? Does the layout make it easier for them to separate main ideas from supporting details? Most secondary teachers have too many students to engage in conversation with each student individually. Instead, consider returning to the ICL Readability Buffet to construct a checklist for students to complete. Hand out copies of the text and your checklist. Make sure to explain each item you wish them to assess as well as why you will value their input.

Chapter Four includes several tools that may be used by teachers to gather information on student interest and attitude towards reading. Before you turn back to those pages, take a moment to look at your subject text from your own personal perspective. Ask yourself: Is the topic of particular interest to me? Am I motivated to read about it with enthusiasm? Do I have a compelling purpose for reading from this book? Are the topics presented in a way that is relevant to my life? Do I have the necessary background experience and knowledge of the subject? What were those experiences? Are my reading skills adequate for this task? A "no" response to one or more of these personal questions will hamper the ease with which you read from your own subject area textbook. If that is the case, where will this leave your students? In what way can you supplement the text to make it more personally meaningful?

With this in mind you may now want to return to the materials in Chapter Four to adapt and administer a survey or inventory. Use student responses to gather information on the personal factors relevant to reading.

Informal Assessments

Often, for reasons of pride or shame, students who have trouble reading will be hesitant to honestly respond to checklist questions about the challenge of a text. In other cases, students may respond to checklist items in ways that either over- or underestimate the challenge of a text. We regret to add that there are some students (not many, but some) who deliberately report that a text is harder so that the teacher will "make it easier" to complete assignments. For these reasons many teachers prefer to gather informal performance data from their students. Here are two tools to gather this data:

Allington (2001) suggests a *Quick Check* for appropriateness of reading materials. He asserts that a quick way to find out how difficult a book is for students is to check if they can read with *fluency*. Fluency is the ability to read with accuracy, expression, phrasing, and appropriate rate. Allington's quick check procedure presents logistic problems for secondary teachers, and has been therefore adapted below for the secondary level:

1. Select six students from the class—two each from students whose grades from the previous year indicate they are high, middle, and low achievers.

2. Make time available to sit for 10 minutes with each student individually. Since some students may be embarrassed by reading out loud in front of peers, choose a time and location that provides a degree of privacy.

3. Have each student read about 100 words from one to five different chapters of the text.

4. Listen to how fluently the student reads. Rate their reading as good, fair, or poor as based on the guidelines below.

5. Note the number of passages each student reads with good, fair, and poor ratings. This will give you a quick estimate as to whether students will be able to read these chapters at the independent, instructional or frustration levels.

Good Reads in phrases, with intonation. Knows all or nearly all the words.

Fair Reads in phrases mostly, but often lacks intonation. Is unable to decode or pronounce several words.

Poor Reads mostly word by word. Is unable to decode or pronounce more than one quarter of the words.

In the chapter that follows we suggest the use of a *content informal reading inventory* (CIRI) to match text with reader. A CIRI is a content-specific assessment that evaluates students' abilities to read with comprehension from a specific test. Typically a CIRI starts by having the students silently read a 250 to 400 word passage from the text and then answer a series of 10 comprehension questions. A CIRI will also present questions on tasks related to reading the book, such as interpreting graphics or other text features, using parts of the text (glossary, index, and reference tables), interpreting formulas and symbols, and/or background knowledge of content specific vocabulary. Please see Chapter Six for more information on how to construct this valuable assessment tool.

Summary of Strengths and Weaknesses of Student Input

Strengths

- Students can provide valuable insights into text features, graphics, and organization.
- Informal assessments provide hard data specific to the group that will read from these books.
- Background experiences and subject interest gathered is useful for instructional planning.

Weaknesses

- Students may be hesitant to respond to checklist questions, or may over- or underestimate their abilities to handle the challenges of a text.
- On checklists, surveys, or informal assessments, some students may intentionally mislead the teacher.
- Gathering and compiling data from these tools can be time-consuming.

The Readability Assessment Triangle

Children learn to ride on tricycles because they are so steady to the ground. Surveyors always pick three points to make sure their readings are accurate. The three branches of government provide checks and balances. Assessment also requires triangulation.

The 8th assessment standard of the International Reading Association (1994) advises that an assessment ". . . should involve multiple perspective and sources of data [because] . . . a single measure is likely to be misleading or erroneous for individuals and groups. Multiple sources of data . . . allow for triangulation." Figure 5.3 shows how each of the three corners of the readability triangle contribute to a balanced assessment.

OBJECTIVE ASSESSMENT

These tools typically measure the difficulty of vocabulary and sentence structure.

The use of formulae and graphs can be extremely helpful because they are standardized to the reading levels of normative samples, and can offset the bias teachers have due to content familiarity.

The drawback to these measures is they can overlook important factors like concept load, clarity of format, and inclusivity. Symbols and prepositions make them ineffective with most math text.

SUBJECTIVE ASSESSMENT

These tools measure components such as clarity of text format, use of supporting graphics, concept load, and use of definitions.

Checklists help flesh out and assess components of reading difficulty standardized formulae miss. They are most valuable when several teachers, especially from other disciplines, rate the material together.

This form of assessment is quite subjective, and does not provide grade level estimates. Background experience on the part of the teacher can lead to biased assessments.

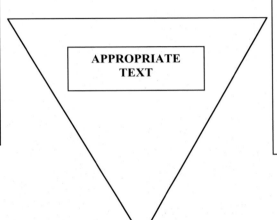

APPROPRIATE TEXT

STUDENT ASSESSMENT

Students can provide valuable insights into the readability of text materials. After all, they are the intended audience. Checklists, surveys, and informal assessments may be used. Students may be asked to complete sample readings and then scored for reading fluency and comprehension of facts and concepts. Surveys may provide invaluable information about student background and interest in the subject matter.

This type of assessment may be compromised when students don't feel safe to reveal their lack of skill or when they choose not to participate honestly.

IMPORTANCE OF BALANCE

Without either objective or subjective assessment tools, important components may be left out and a balanced evaluation of text readability cannot be made. Further, if these assessments are not firmly centered on the student audience for which the text is intended, the selection loses credibility.

FIGURE 5.3
The Reliability Assessment Triangle

Matching the Readability of Textbooks with the Reading Abilities of Students Who Must Read Them

The teachers and administration at a rural high school were concerned about a high failure rate of students in their ninth-grade social studies classes. They decided to create special history classes for those students who were poor readers. These classes were smaller and featured special "remedial" activities. The high failure rate persisted. Many teachers suggested that the content had to be "watered-down" or the majority of these students would never pass.

The reading teacher did a readability check on the text. According to the Fry, it read at about the eleventh grade. Some chapters read at ninth-grade level, but just as many read at the college level. He also noted that there were problems with concept density and the way that new vocabulary was introduced to the reader.

It would be several years until funding would be available to replace or supplement the text. With the principal's approval, he rewrote the difficult-to-read chapters. Students received the same content but at their instructional level. Particular attention was given to lessening concept load, improving format, introducing vocabulary, and overall shortening of sentence length.

For example, here is a segment of original text with the question that followed:

What Was the Provisional Government?[1]

    The Champoeg committee . . . presented these laws to the community on July 5, 1843 . . . The whole code was called "The Organic Act of the Provisional Government of Oregon." (The word "organic" shows that this act created a new government. The word "provisional" means temporary. American settlers believed this government would last only until Oregon became a U.S. territory.)

15. Define these terms: "organic laws," "provisional government."

Here is the same text rewritten with corresponding questions:

The Organic Act of the Provisional Government of Oregon

    The Champoeg committee . . . presented these laws to the community on July 5, 1843. . . . The whole

[1]Pelz, R. (1979). *The Washington story: A history of our state.* Seattle: Seattle Public Schools, p. 85.

code was called "The Organic Act of the Provisional Government of Oregon." There are a lot of new words here. Let's go over them.

    You probably know what a government is. **Organic** comes from the word "organize." So organic means to organize or get started. An act is a set of laws. So what is an "organic act" of government? It is the set of laws that organize or start a government.

    Provisional means temporary. American settlers believed their government would be temporary. They would get a permanent government later. They figured this provisional (temporary) government would end when Oregon became a U.S. territory.

    So, what was the "Organic Act of the Provisional Government of Oregon"? It was an organizing set of laws. These laws set up the temporary government of Oregon.

15. What does "organic" mean? What is an "organic act" of government?

16. What does "provisional" mean? When would the provisional government end?

17. In your own words explain what "The Organic Act of the Provisional Government of Oregon" was.

The reading specialist was determined to prove that rewriting the text was not the same thing as "watering it down." He wanted to prove that making the content accessible to poor readers would result in comparable learning with the mainstream classes. So he also rewrote the final exam, which was given to all students. The questions were the same, but the sentences were shortened and pronouns were used more judiciously.

Mainstream and remedial students both took the rewritten exam as a pre-test (before the history course) and as a post-test (after completing the course). Here are the results:

Students	Pre-Test Scores	Post-Test Scores	Improvement
Mainstream Classes	46.9%	67.1%	up 20.2%
Class for Poor Readers	34.4%	76.7%	up 42.3%

Conclusion: Use of low readability materials in class for poor readers resulted in a significant improvement of mastery of materials.

The history teacher reported that a higher percentage of students in his "special" classes read the assignments than he would have normally expected. He also noted improvements in student self-image and group participation. He was able to spend less time reviewing the basic content of each chapter in the "special" classes and consequently used more class time to teach critical thinking about the concepts involved.

However, not all the results were positive. Some students complained that they were given more pages to read than in other history classes. The teacher was concerned that several students who might have been able to handle the more challenging reading did not. Finally, he noted that making the transition back to the regular history text was difficult for many of the students.

Finding the "right bat" for each reader in a class is a tricky business. In this case, the history teacher eventually went back to teaching with the regular textbook, but not exclusively. He used to rewritten versions to help students who were interested in history but did not have the reading skills to read the more difficult text.

Workshop 5.4

Should All School Texts Be Written at or Below Grade Level?

You have read about student success made possible when texts are accessible (written or rewritten at their grade level). Earlier, you read about the movement towards plain language laws. In small groups, consider this question:

Should all school texts be written at or below grade level?

As you discuss your opinions consider any/all of the following questions. However, end by discussing the last bulleted question in the series:

- The example given above shows how students might do better in history with text that is easier to read. Aren't history textbooks rewritten versions of primary source documents? If this is so, shouldn't we choose text that is written at the grade level of our students?

- If we choose easier-to-read texts, what will happen when students get to college and discover that their textbooks are even harder to read? Don't all students, including those not going to college, need to be challenged to read harder materials? Don't all students deserve to be spared from "watered down" text?

- What about music? Would an orchestra teacher insist that students play only from the original score of a great composer like Tchaikovsky? Or would they use music that was rewritten at the students' levels?

- What about literature? Hawthorne wrote sentences and paragraphs that go on forever. Should these be rewritten? Why, or why not?

- What about Russian, Spanish, French, or other world literature? These have been carefully translated. Is this different from carefully rewriting a text at a lower grade level? Some might argue that a cultural context gets lost in any translation. Why don't we translate literature so it is easier to understand?

- The Hebrew Bible was originally written in Aramaic. Then it was translated to Hebrew, Greek, Latin, English, etc. There are versions of the Bible that have been translated so that young people can read it. If this can be done so school age students can understand the Bible, why don't we do so with school textbooks?

- What about art, specifically the appropriation art of artists like Warhol, Levine, Koons, and Kruger? By placing other images in a new artistic context, the original meaning is altered and the intention of the original artist is made clear. If this is done with art, shouldn't it also be done with written text?

- If you could have only one set of textbooks available to you in your classroom, would you choose a set that reads at grade level, or a set that reads above grade level? Why? More important, once you made this decision, how would you use those textbooks? Why?

Textbook Analysis: More Than Just Readability

Our discussion about readability has focused primarily on textbooks. Textbooks are the primary source of reading material in most secondary-level classrooms. They have long been the topic of much discussion and debate. Some have argued that textbooks are too long, or too heavy, or that they have been "dumbed-down." Others argue that they are too expensive, or that their publishers are more concerned with writing for the broadest possible market rather than meeting the needs of individual schools. Some teachers advocate for getting rid of textbooks altogether, but this may be shortsighted and ill-advised.

While many good textbooks are available, teachers are often disappointed by how these books are organized, how content is treated, inaccuracies in the content, or incomplete information. Readability of text is an important factor, but not the only factor. Even a book with an appropriate readability will have deficiencies.

Textbooks are tools. Teachers are well-advised to learn how to use those tools in the best possible ways. Good teachers recognize and find ways to overcome deficiencies. Doing so requires them to examine textbooks closely so as to develop an awareness of a text's strengths and weaknesses.

What follows is a textbook analysis assignment developed by Schaefer (2005). It provides readers with an opportunity to examine and analyze a secondary-level textbook in their own fields of teaching.

Workshop 5.5

Schaefer's Textbook Analysis Assignment

Working with the *Teacher's Edition* of a textbook from your discipline, do the following, explaining fully what you have found.

Big Picture Items:

1. Identify the grade level(s) for which the book is intended. (Note: Sometimes it is difficult to find this information.)

   _____

   _____

2. Look at the basic organization of the text material in the table of contents. Are you comfortable with what has been included? With the arrangement of the information? Is there anything that you think should be there? Explain and give examples.

   _____

   _____

3. Identify the parts of the book. Are there appendices, an index, glossary, maps, answers, etc.? How useful do these appear to be? Are they well-organized, easy to use, etc.? Explain and give examples.

   _____

   _____

Chapter Items:

1. Evaluate the content of the chapters in depth.

   a. Evaluate the content. Is it accurate, appropriate, and well placed in the text? Are the concepts explained well? _____

   _____

   b. Examine the book for diversity and balance: Are people of color represented? How? Which ethnic or racial groups? Are both males and females represented? How? Are they accurate portrayals? Stereotypes? Add-ons? Could these portrayals be done better? How? _____

   _____

   c. Explain what, if anything, you would add to the text to make the content more suitable. Is there anything you would skip? Would you rearrange the information? If you like it the way it is, explain why.

   _____

   _____

   d. Use examples from the text to illustrate your points.

   _____

   _____

2. Examine the graphic representations. What are their roles? Are they helpful, useful, and consistent with text information? Do they illuminate the text? Extend it? Do they provide examples to clarify text information? Is it easy to determine the purposes of the graphic information? Give examples and illustrate your points.

_____

_____

_____

3. Are there any study aids in the text to help students understand and remember the material? If so, what are they, and are they useful?

_____

_____

_____

4. Examine the questions that accompany the chapters and evaluate them. Consider the following:

> Are they good questions?
> Do they represent several levels of comprehension?
> Do they ask the readers to think deeply?
> Do they emphasize the important aspects of the chapters?
> Do they lead or mislead?
> Are there other considerations that are appropriate to discuss?
> Cite examples to illustrate your points.

_____

_____

_____

5. Are there enough activities and projects to give you good choices? Are there any identified for enrichment and remediation? If yes, are they appropriate for advanced students and for those who need more help? Give examples to illustrate your points.

_____

_____

_____

6. What have you learned from formulaic, checklist, and student input readability assessments of this text?

_____

_____

_____

7. Go back to item #1. Based on your entire analysis, do you think that this book is appropriate for the grade level for which it is intended? Why, or why not? If not, is it salvageable with expansion, clarification, and revision of the text? Explain and give examples.

_____

_____

_____

Cinquain as Summary

Readability
Easier? Harder?
Formulae, Checklists, Students
Frustration, Instructional, Independent, Unchallenging
Accessibility

 Summary

Readability is the difficulty or ease with which material can be read by a given audience. Factors affecting readability fall into two categories that must be weighed: textual and personal. Textual factors include vocabulary, sentence length, concept load or density, format, and length. Personal factors are found in readers and include their reading skill, motivation, relevance, knowledge and background experience, purpose, and interest. National standards call for teachers to be able to select, adapt, and create instructional resources that are appropriate for active learners. Good teachers use readability assessment tools to gather information on the reading challenges that a text provides. These teachers then adjust instruction to meet those challenges.

The difficulty of text may be categorized into three reading levels: independent, instructional, and frustration. The same text might be at any of the three levels for different students in the class, and it might vary from chapter to chapter. Two categories of tools for measuring readability are formulas and checklists. Formulas generally measure vocabulary and sentence difficulty and are objective measures. Software is now available to estimate readability and there now is a qualitative means to assess readability. Checklists help teachers examine the many other factors that affect readability, but they are far more subjective. When assessing textbooks teachers should also gather student input as to the appropriateness of a text. Once teachers have formulaic, checklist, and student input they can triangulate their findings, as recommended by IRA standards.

There is more to analyzing a text than just readability. Teachers will also want to check into the support materials a textbook might provide. Sometimes rewriting portions of the difficult text may be helpful to students who have trouble reading it. The better teachers become at matching text readability with students' reading abilities, the more success students will have reading to learn in the subject areas. Success increases when teachers combine their expertise in the subject matter, their knowledge of students' capabilities, and their skills at assessing the reading challenges provided by the texts they assign to their students.

Answers to Workshop 5.1

Part B: 1. ninth, 2. eighth, 3. ninth, 4. eighth to twelfth, 5. tenth, 6. twelfth, 7. tenth to twelfth, 8. sixth to eighth, 9. seventh to eighth
Part C: a. Sports Page

Answers to Workshop 5.2

Automobile Mechanics: ⟵ start counting your 100 words here

|| ||| | | 7
//They examine the automobile and discuss the type and extent of the

|| || | 5
malfunction with the customer$_0$[1] They plan how the work is to be done$_0$[2] Using

| | | ||| 6
hand tools, they remove the part, repair it or replace it if necessary$_0$[3] They then

|| || || 6
reinstall the part and check their work$_0$[4] Some mechanics specialize in one type of

| | || | | 6
repair$_0$[5] Front-End Mechanics align wheels, frames and steering wheels$_0$[6]

|| || ||| | | || ||| 14
Transmission Mechanics disassemble, adjust and repair manual and automatic

|| | || | || | 9
transmissions$_0$[7] Tune-Up Mechanics adjust the ignition, timing and valves and

| | ||| | | 7
adjust or replace spark plugs, distributor and points$_0$[8] They also test and repair

||| || 100 9/10 5
carburetion and fuel injection/systems. Mechanics may also use computers for   ——

65
diagnostic checks of electronic parts. $8\frac{9}{10}$ + 100
                                                                                ——
                                                                                165

Fry Graph Example and Worksheet:

Your turn:	Syllables	Sentences
First Hundred Words	206	6.8
Second Hundred Words	189	6.2
Third Hundred Words	165	8.9
Total	560	21.9
Average (total divided by 3)	186.6	7.3

Now plot these coordinates on the graph. Indicate the range. Consider any other factors that should go into your recommendation for the teacher who uses this book.

The three samples given show the readability of this text as 17th grade, a range of 16th–18th grade. These three sample passages have significant variability. (See the difference in the number of syllables and sentences between the first and third samples.) Therefore, additional samples should be taken. Nevertheless, this point of the readability triangle appears to indicate that this text is above the skill level of those who would read it. (17th grade is graduate-level university studies.)

However, evaluating a book solely on the scores of a readability formula is not appropriate. The 8th assessment standard of the International Reading Association advises that assessment ". . . should involve multiple perspectives and sources of data [because] . . . a single measure is likely to be misleading or erroneous for individuals and groups. Multiple sources of data . . . allow for triangulation." Hence I recommend that this text also be assessed with a checklist and with a student input device. Sentences like "Transmission Mechanics disassemble, adjust and repair manual and automatic transmissions. Tune-Up Mechanics adjust the ignition, timing and valves and adjust or replace spark plugs, distributor and points." contain longer words that drive up the score on the Fry graph. The subjective input received from students and the teacher may reveal that these are words with which the readers are very familiar. Furthermore, the sample above does not reveal how formatting may help or hinder comprehension.

References and Recommended Readings

Afflerbach, P., & Vansledright, B. (2001). Hath! Doth! What? Middle graders reading innovative history text. *Journal of Adolescent and Adult Literacy, 44,* 696–707.

Allington, R. (2001). *What really matters for struggling readers: Designing research based programs.* New York: Longman.

Allington, R. (2002). You can't learn much from books you can't read. *Educational Leadership, 60* (3), 16–19.

Armbruster, B. (1996). Considerate texts. In D. Lapp, J. Flood, & N. Farnan (Eds.), *Content area reading and learning instructional strategies* (2nd ed.) pp. 47–57. Boston: Allyn & Bacon.

Armbruster, B., Osborn, J., & Davidson, A. (1985). Readability formulas may be dangerous to your textbooks. *Educational Leadership, 42* (7), 18–20.

Barba, R., Pang, V., & Santa Cruz, R. (1993). User friendly text: Keys to readability and comprehension. *The Science Teacher, 60* (5), 14–17.

Breese, P., & Burman, W. (2005). Readability of notice of privacy forms used by major health care institutions. *Journal of the American Medical Association, 293* (13), 1,593–1,594.

Chall, J., Bissex, G., & Conard, S. (1991). *Should textbooks challenge students?* New York: Teachers College Press.

Chall, J., Bissex, G., Conard, S., & Harris-Sharples, S. (1996). *Qualitative assessment of text difficulty: A practical guide for teachers and writers.* Cambridge, Mass.: Brookline Books.

Chall, J. & Dale, E. (1995). *Readability revisited: The new Dale-Chall readability formula.* Cambridge, MA: Brookline.

Chavkin, L. (1997). Readability and reading ease revisited: State-adopted science textbooks. *Clearing House, 70* (3), 151–154.

Fitzgerald, G. (1980). Reliability of the Fry sampling procedure. *Reading Research Quarterly, 15,* 489–503.

Forgan, H., & Mangrum, C. (1981). *Teaching content area reading* (2nd ed.). Columbus OH: Charles E. Merrill Publishing Company.

Fry, E. (1977). Fry's readability graph: Clarification, validity and extension to level 17. *Journal of Reading, 21,* 242–251.

Fry, E. (1989). Reading formulas—maligned but valid. *Journal of Reading, 33,* 292–297.

Fusaro, J. (1998). Applying statistical rigor to a validation study of the Fry Readability Graph. *Reading Research and Instruction, 28,* 44–48.

Giles, T. (1990). The readability controversy: A technical writing review. *Journal of Technical Writing and Communication, 20,* 131–138.

Gray, W., & Leary, B. (1935). *What makes a book readable?* Chicago: University of Chicago Press.

Gunning, T. (2003). *Building literacy in the content areas.* Boston: Pearson Education Inc.

Hare, V., & Lomax, R. (1985). Text effects on main idea comprehension. *Reading Research Quarterly, 24* (1), 72–88.

Hayes, D., Wolfer, L., & Wolfe, M. (1996). Schoolbook simplification and its relation to the decline in SAT-verbal scores. *American Educational Research Journal, 33,* 489–508.

International Reading Association and National Council of Teachers of English Joint Task Force on Assessment. (1994). *Standards for the assessment of reading and writing.* Newark, DE: International Reading Association.

Jones, K. (1995). Analysis of readability and interest of vocational education textbooks: Implications for special needs learners. *Journal of Vocational Education Research, 20* (1), 55–77.

Kincaid, J., Fishburne, R., Rogers, R. L., & Chissom, B. S. (1975). Derivation of new readability formulas (Automated Readability Index, Fog Count and Flesch Reading Ease formula) for Navy enlisted personnel. Branch Report 8–75. Millington, TN: Chief of Naval Training.

Long, R. (1991). Readability for science: Some factors which may affect the students' understanding of a work sheet. *School Science Review, 73* (262), 21–34.

MacGregor, M., & Price, E. (1999). An exploration of aspects of language proficiency and algebra learning. *Journal of Research in Mathematics Education, 30,* 449–467.

Marshall, N. (1979). Readability and comprehensibility. *Journal of Reading, 22,* 542–544.

Millus, A. (1983). Plain language laws: Are they working. *Uniform Commercial Code Law Journal, 16* (2), 147–159.

National Board for Professional Teaching Standards. (2005). *Adolescents and young adult/science* (2nd ed.). Retrieved June 20, 2005, from http://www.nbpts.org/standards/stds.cfm

Nielsen, G., & Mason, D. (2005, May 1). Inland views: State exams flunk the readability test. *The Press-Enterprise,* pp. D04.

O'Matz, M. (1994, June 24). How's that again? Contracts must be easier to understand under new "plain language" law. *The Morning Call,* pp. A04.

Schaefer, C. (June 3, 2005). Personal communication.

Siegel, A. (1981). The plain English revolution. *Across the Board, 18* (2), 19.

Smith, D., Stenner, A. J., Horabin, I., & Smith, M. (1989). *The Lexile scale in theory and practice: Final report.* Washington, DC: Metametrics. (ERIC Document Reproduction Service No. ED30757)

Touchstone Applied Science Associates. (1994). *DRP handbook.* Brewster, NY: Author.

Wood, T., & Wood, W. (1988). Assessing potential difficulties in comprehending fourth grade science textbooks. *Science Education, 72* (5), 561–574.

Weist, L. (2003). Comprehension of mathematical text. University of Nevada, Reno. Retrieved February 12, 2005, from http://www.ex.ac.uk/~PErnest/pome17pdf/lwiest.pdf.

Walpole, S. (1998–1999). Changing texts, changing thinking: Comprehension demands of new science textbooks. *The Reading Teacher, 52,* 358–369.

Zakuluk, B., & Samuels, S. (1988). *Readability: Its past, present and future.* Newark, DE: International Reading Association.

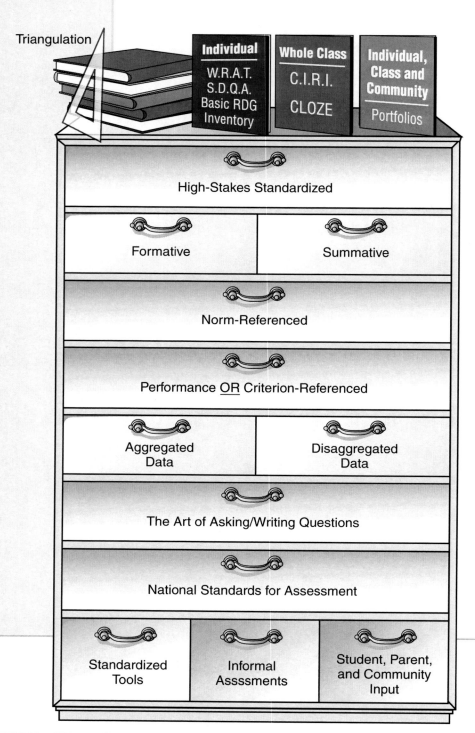

Triangulation

Individual	Whole Class	Individual, Class and Community
W.R.A.T. S.D.Q.A. Basic RDG Inventory	C.I.R.I. CLOZE	Portfolios

High-Stakes Standardized

Formative   Summative

Norm-Referenced

Performance OR Criterion-Referenced

Aggregated Data   Disaggregated Data

The Art of Asking/Writing Questions

National Standards for Assessment

Standardized Tools   Informal Assssments   Student, Parent, and Community Input

FIGURE 6.1

Matching Print with Reader: Part Two—Authentic Reader Assessment—A Cognitive Map

Matching Print with Reader: Part Two— Authentic Reader Assessment

6

Outline

- Anticipatory and Review Questions
- A Sampling of National Performance Standards
- Introduction
- Definitions and Standards
  - Authentic Assessments
  - Formative and Summative Assessments
  - Performance-Based or Criterion-Referenced Assessments
  - Rubrics
  - High-Stakes, Standardized, and Norm-Referenced Assessments
  - Aggregating and Disaggregating Data
- Standards for the Assessment of Reading and Writing
  - *Workshop 6.1: Discussing Assessment Standards*
  - Triangulating Assessment Data
- Classroom Assessments: Standardized Tools
  - Individual Quick Classroom Screening
    - Wide Range Achievement Test: Reading
    - The San Diego Quick Assessment (SDQA)
  - Caveat: Quick Screen Tools Unfair to Second Language Learners
  - Summary of Strengths and Weaknesses of Quick Screening Tools
  - Basic Reading Inventory
    - *Workshop 6.2: Practice in Administering and Scoring the SDQA*

- Informal Whole-Class Assessment
  - The Art of Writing Comprehension Questions
  - The Content IRI
    - Part I: The Comprehension Section
    - Part II: Subject-Specific Reading Skill Subtests
    - Part III: Displaying and Using CIRI Data
- CLOZE Procedure
  - Constructing a CLOZE
  - Administering and Scoring a CLOZE
  - Other Uses
  - Summary of Strengths and Weaknesses of Informal Assessments
    - *Workshop 6.3: Developing a Content IRI and CLOZE*
- Student, Parent, and Community Input
  - Portfolios: A Framework for Ongoing Collaborative Assessment
  - A Sample Portfolio Record Sheet
  - Summary of Strengths and Weaknesses of Student, Parent, and Community Input through Portfolio Assessment
    - *Workshop 6.4: Creating a Triangulation Diagram*
- Diamante as Summary
- Summary
- References and Recommended Readings

"The present emphasis upon assessment is not unwarranted. For too long schools have failed to effectively link what has been taught to what was tested. . . . We must engage in assessment activities that help prevent failure rather than just document it. This task is particularly important for students who are poor and/or minority."

Jerry D. Bamburg

"As accountability systems accelerate educators must prevent evaluation systems from eviscerating the curriculum."

John T. Guthrie

"There is considerable research that indicates that there is no culture-free test. In addition, it is clear that some tests (such as multiple choice testing) have linguistic demands that are inequitable for minority language students."

Washington Association for Bilingual Education

Anticipatory and Review Questions

Literal

1. Define authentic, formative, and summative assessment.

2. Name three content-specific reading skills that students need to succeed in your content area.

Interpretative/Applied

3. What is the difference between norm-referenced and criterion-referenced assessment? Why is it important for educators to understand this difference?

4. What skills must be used to answer a literal comprehension question? An inferential comprehension question?

Evaluative/Critical

5. Think of the process used to triangulate data when assessing a textbook. How is it the same or different than the process that should be used to triangulate assessment data of students' reading abilities? Why is this important?

6. Some content teachers gear their teaching towards what they know will be asked on high-stakes tests. Is this educationally sound? Why, or why not?

Creative/Personal

7. What experiences have you had with assessment? How was your ability to read and write assessed in secondary school?

8. Do you know someone who was negatively impacted by scores received on a standardized test? Was the use of this test appropriate? Was it in keeping with the IRA/NCTE reading and writing assessment standards? Why, or why not?

A Sampling of National Performance Standards:

- The teacher understands and uses formal and informal assessment strategies to evaluate and ensure the continuous intellectual, social, and physical development of the learner (Council of Chief State School Officers, 2005).
- Accomplished teachers employ a variety of assessment methods to obtain useful information about student learning and assist students in reflecting on their own progress (National Board for Professional Teaching Standards, 2005).

Introduction

To improve education it is necessary to assess student learning as well as our instructional programs. However, as most of us are well aware, researchers and educators have been deeply divided over assessment issues. Those who spend time in our schools know that assessment has become a pervasive part of schooling, and unfortunately, much of that assessment has been for the sake of accountability, not for improving classroom instruction. Classroom time taken up with accountability testing means teachers have less time to meet the individual learning needs of their students. We believe that assessment can and should be used to place more emphasis on investigating where students are in the *process* of learning, not just the *products* of their learning.

Hence, the major emphasis of this chapter will be on reading assessments that can be used to design instruction that improves student learning. To provide context we will first define some of the terms used in literacy assessment and then discuss the literacy assessment standards that should guide our work with students. These standards speak to the importance of triangulating data, so we will apply this paradigm to assessing the reading strengths and weakness of our students by visiting each of the three corners of the triangle. First, we will look at the standardized data available to us in student records, and in the event that this data is not available, we will recommend individual classroom screening instruments that can provide correlation data. Next, we will look at the second corner, informal assessments that assess the kind of reading students must do in their content areas. By assessing this kind of reading, content teachers can learn where explicit learning of literacy skills is needed to improve learning. Hence, we will dedicate several pages to the art of writing reading comprehension questions in the content areas. We will then detail the craft of designing content informal reading inventories, and the CLOZE procedure. Finally, we will close this chapter by visiting the third corner of the triangle, input gathered in portfolios and assessed in conferences with the students themselves, their families, and their communities.

Definitions and Standards

The art of assessment has specific vocabulary. Here are several terms and their definitions as they are used in this chapter.

Authentic Assessments

A test is **authentic** if it really measures what it claims to measure. In reading and writing, we think of an assessment as authentic if it requires students to read and write in "real-world" situations. From the title of this chapter you probably deduced that we place high value on authentic assessments. Tools used for authentic assessment are teacher-designed and specific to a real-life learning tasks. These include teacher observations, conferences, student journals, portfolios, essay questions, and content informal reading inventories. Teacher-designed assessments are usually informal. Evaluating these tasks can be difficult. Evaluation may be done by the teacher, the student, or both. When doing so, it is important to examine the *process* of reading as well as the *product* of that learning. Hence, authentic assessment may be *formative* or *summative*. Authentic assessments may work especially well with students of diverse backgrounds or with disabilities because they are easy to adapt to differing contexts and abilities.

Formative and Summative Assessments

Formative assessments are intended to help students to "form" or develop their skills. Data from formative assessments are used by teachers *while* students are working on projects and activities in order to give students feedback before they hand their work in to be graded. For example, a teacher may collect the notes students have taken on a book to provide formative feedback. No grade is assigned, but feedback is provided to help students improve their understanding of what they have read. Teachers may choose to provide formative feedback several times before a big project is due. *Summative assessments* are intended to "summarize" the accomplishments of projects and activities. Grades on assignments, tests, and projects are examples of summative assessments. Continuing the example above, when teachers collect assignments and assess projects to assign a final grade, this is summative assessment.

Performance-Based or Criterion-Referenced Assessments

Some authentic assessments are *performanced-based*. In these cases teachers, districts, or states have set the **criteria** needed for passing. These criteria are what students should know or be able to do. In content areas like science or physical education, performance assessment means students must show competence or knowledge by giving a response, creating a project, or performing a skill activity. Student scores on these tests are referenced against these criteria to determine whether they have been met. There are several different ways to do this. Student answers may be compared to *anchor* papers that educators agree meet levels of expectation. Or a *rubric* may be used to show what answers on papers must include in order to meet the criteria. Or the number of correct answers may be compared to an arbitrary number of correct answers designated as the "cutoff" point.

Rubrics

A *rubric* is a chart or table that describes the traits or characteristics of criteria for mastery of an objective. Generally speaking, rubrics provide lists of descriptors at several different levels of proficiency. Using rubrics, evaluators examine each piece of student work to find the level at which the descriptors best fit the skill level. Rubrics are becoming increasingly popular because they may be constructed to fit just about any authentic activity and because they can be used as a teaching tool as well. This is because the rubric explicitly articulates the learning objectives. Multiple samples of rubrics, as well as rubric generators, may be found at http://www.rubrician.com/general.htm

High-Stakes, Standardized, and Norm-Referenced Assessments

A *high-stakes* test is one that has a direct effect on the lives of those who take them. One's score on a high-stakes test is used as a decision point. For example, your score on a motor vehicle driver's test determines whether or not you get a driver's license. The score earned on a bar exam determines whether or not you may practice law in a state. Your score on the Praxis Exam may determine whether or not you get a teacher's license. For students, failing a high-stakes test may mean they will not be promoted to the next level or graduate from high school. For schools, high-stakes tests may be used to determine whether the school is making the "annual yearly progress" required to maintain federal funding.

A *standardized* test is usually prepared commercially and must be administered and interpreted in a uniform way. For example, all students taking a standardized test receive the same directions and the same amount of time to complete each section. Their papers are also scored and interpreted in exactly the same way. Most standardized tests are **norm-referenced**. This means that each student's score on a test is compared to a "norming" population—a large, representative cross-section of sample students who took the same test. Norm-referenced standardized tests are the most common form of large-scale testing.

For teachers, the difference between norm-referenced and criterion-referenced assessment is one of the most important concepts to understand. For example, suppose you took the SAT test. The scores from a large representative cross-section of students who took the test were used to establish the "norms." (Hence, the term "norm-referenced.") Scores on the SAT range from 200 to 800. Were you to score 200 on this test, this would mean that nearly everyone else in that "norming" group did better than you. A score of 800 would mean that that you did better than almost everyone else in the "norming" group. A score of 500 would mean that you did better than half the group. Note that your score doesn't in itself say anything about how many answers you got right or wrong. So getting a score of 800 doesn't mean that you got every answer correct. It means that your score on the test falls in the range achieved by the top 0.13% of test takers.

Now let's compare your SAT test scores to the scores you might receive on a criterion-referenced test. Let's say you took the WASL reading exam, a state-mandated criterion-referenced test. Your test answers would be scored by a trained team of teachers who would use a rubric aligned with grade-level expectations for readers in your grade, to determine how well each test answer you provide meets the criterion for mastery. (Hence, the term "criterion-referenced.") In the end, you will receive a total score, the total number of points you earned. The State Department of Education helped write and set standards for interpretation of these scores and then established cutoff scores. Whether or not you pass this criterion-referenced reading test is determined by whether or not your score is above or below the cutoff score.

Some parents, teachers, administrators, and policymakers have been convinced by the companies that write these tests, that norm-referenced test scores are easy to interpret and to use in planning instruction. Others argue that these tests have limited value because they oversimplify the complexities of literacy and that the test questions are not authentic. Many educators believe that these tests are being used to hold students and teachers accountable, not to help teachers plan ways to improve student learning.

Aggregating and Disaggregating Data

Sometimes we collect data from a large group of students and put it together. The processes of collecting data for the purpose of making a general statement is called *aggregating* data. For example, school districts aggregate the data of their students on standardized tests to determine whether or not they have met the requirements for "adequate yearly progress." On the classroom level, we might give all of our students a content informal reading inventory to see how well they can read from their textbook and then add together (aggregate) their scores to find the average performance of the class. Knowing that 80% of our students are at mastery level would be helpful in our lesson planning.

Unfortunately, aggregating data strips away the differences between our students. For this reason we will often *disaggregate* our data. To do so means to separate our data into piles for specific groups of students. For example, we might want to see how students who are English language learners or have special learning needs have done on a standardized test. School districts sometimes do this to make policy decisions. If the disaggregated data shows that English language learners are doing poorly, the district might allocate more resources to help these students. Classroom teachers may also disaggregate performance data by separating out scores on similar skills questions. For example, if we learn that a small group of students in one class has trouble reading timelines, we might group them together for the purpose of providing extra instruction in this skill.

Standards for the Assessment of Reading and Writing

The Joint Task Force of the International Reading Association and the National Council of Teachers of English (1994) developed standards to guide decisions for assessing reading and writing. These eleven standards, as well as brief summaries of key points, appear below. These standards will be referenced throughout this chapter.

1. **The interests of the student are paramount in assessment.** This standard refers to individual students, not students on average or students collectively. Assessment must serve, not harm, each and every student.

2. **The primary purpose of assessment is to improve teaching and learning.** Assessment is used in educational setting for a variety of purposes, such as diagnosing reading and writing difficulties, determining eligibility, evaluating programs, and reporting to others. Underlying all these purposes is a concern for improving teaching and learning. However, many times this concern is obscured by the format and process of assessment, and by the ways we use assessment information.

3. **Assessment must reflect and allow for critical inquiry into curriculum and instruction.** Sound educational practices do *not* result from a model in which assessment determines curriculum and instruction. Indeed, the more invasive the assessment, the less valuable the information. [Assessment should drive instruction and serve as an indicator of students' needs.]

4. **Assessments must recognize and reflect the intellectually and socially complex nature of reading and writing and the important roles of school, home, and society in literacy development.** For assessment purposes, it is essential to understand that the multiple influences involved in both reading and writing mean that students' behavior in one setting may not be at all representative of their behavior in another.

5. **Assessment must be fair and equitable.** Assessment plays an important part in ensuring fairness and equity. . . . Language itself involves social conventions that differ from culture to culture. Furthermore, words have different shades of meaning for different cultures, and the variation in life situations can be quite extreme. . . . The inevitability of bias notwithstanding, when tests must be used, as many biases as possible should be controlled, and multiple perspectives and sources of data should be brought to bear to help balance against one another those biases that will inevitably remain.

6. **The consequences of an assessment procedure are the first, and most important, consideration in establishing the validity of the assessment.** If a test has adverse motivational consequences for school communities, or segments of school

communities, then the procedure is invalid. Adverse consequences from assessment can arise from a variety of procedures . . . [such as] . . . publicly valuing only a narrow range of literacy activity . . . reporting procedures that make students or teachers defensive or unreflective, thus inhibiting learning . . . [or] . . . focus on ranking or rating rather than performance, thus drawing learners' attentions away from the process of learning . . . [and/or] . . . oversimplifying complex literacy behaviors or situations and consequently narrow the curriculum.

7. **The teacher is the most important agent of assessment.** . . . Teachers design, assign, observe, collaborate in, and interpret the work of students in their classroom. They assign meaning to interactions and evaluate the information that they receive and create in these settings; in short, they function as agents of assessment, and their assessments have enormous impact on students' lives . . . [T]eachers are in a unique position to engage in valid assessment. Because they are closest to students' learning they have the opportunity to make many detailed observations over time. . . .

8. **The assessment process should involve multiple perspectives and sources of data.** Perfect assessments and perfect assessors do not exist. . . . The more consequential the decision, the more important it is to seek diverse perspectives and independent sources of data. . . . A single measure is likely to be misleading or erroneous for individuals and groups. . . . The need for multiple indicators is particularly important in assessment of reading and writing because of the complex nature of literacy and its acquisition. Multiple sources . . . can allow for "triangulation" in problem solving.

9. **Assessment must be based in the school community.** . . . Assessment is value laden, and the ongoing participation of . . . [the members of the school community outside the schools] is necessary in a democratic society. . . .With the school community as a center of inquiry, diversity of perspective is possible, not only as a source of growth for individual classroom teachers but also among teachers and the larger school community.

10. **All members of the educational community—students, parents, teachers, administrators, policymakers, and the public—must have a voice in the development, interpretation, and reporting of assessment.** Each of the constituents named in this standard has a stake in assessment. . . . when policymakers develop assessment practices that drive local assessment and instructional processes, other stakeholders' voices are easily silenced, and assessment becomes dominated by procedures developed by people with little regular contact with students or teachers. . . . Since the teacher is the central agent of assessment, the teaching community is responsible for maintaining communication about the process of classroom assessment with other interested parties.

11. **Parents must be involved as active, essential participants in the assessment process.** . . . Parental involvement includes the following: (a) Becoming knowledgeable about assessment. . . . (b) Actively participating in the assessment process and all other aspects of governance. (c) Contributing their knowledge of their children. . . . (d) Seeing ways to become more knowledgeable about their children's development. . . . Teachers need the knowledge parents have of their children, and school communities need the diversity of perspectives that parents bring to school problem solving, including assessment.

Workshop 6.1

Discussing Assessment Standards

Take a few minutes to review the literacy assessment standards listed above. Can you think of times when these standards helped to protect the rights and needs of students? Can you think of times when these standards were ignored and students were harmed? For example, with regards to standard one, can you think of times when assessment was used to help your teachers do a better job of teaching? With regards to standard 6, can you think of a time when a student or group of students suffered adverse consequences because of a test that was biased or unfair? How about the other standards?

In small groups share your experiences. Then have one member of each group report back to the class as a whole.

Triangulating Assessment Data

As stated in the chapter on textbook assessment, children learn to ride on tricycles because they are steady to the ground. Surveyors always pick three points to make sure their readings are accurate. The three branches of government provide checks and balances. Assessment of student reading abilities also requires triangulation.

The need for triangulation is called for in the fifth and eighth assessment standards listed above. Furthermore, the American Educational Research Association, the nation's largest organization for the scientific study of education, advises that ". . . decisions that affect individual students' life chances or educational opportunities should not be made on the basis of test scores alone. Other relevant information should be taken into account to enhance the overall validity of such decisions" (Wilde, 2002, p. 107). We therefore recommend that when teachers are attempting to match readers with appropriate texts, or must make instructional decisions based upon data from reading and writing assessments that they first check to make sure these data have been triangulated.

The three points of the reader ability triangle should include: (1) results from standardized assessments (norm-referenced or criterion-referenced), (2) results from authentic teacher- and student-designed tools such as content informal reading inventories, and CLOZE assessments; and (3) input gathered in portfolios and assessed in conferences with the students themselves, their families, and their communities.

Classroom Assessments: Standardized Tools

One corner of the reading assessment triangle should include results from standardized assessments (norm-referenced or criterion-referenced). To gather these scores teachers may visit the school office and review the files of their students. Here we can find results of commercial standardized tests, such as the ITBS or CTBS. We also can find results from state-designed standardized criterion-referenced tests. The reading samples from these state tests have been aligned with the reading standards for that state.

These scores may reveal if a student's reading level is significantly above or below the grade level of the materials they will have to read. For example, if scores reveal that students are reading three grades or lower than the grade in which they are enrolled, these students will most likely have trouble reading the material in your classroom. If you find one or more of these students is having trouble in your classroom, you would be well advised to inquire with the school counselor to see if this student qualifies for help. On the other hand, students who are capable of reading three grades or higher may find the assigned materials unchallenging. In both cases, the poor match between text and reader can easily lead to academic and behavioral problems in the classroom.

Unfortunately, the scores from these tests are usually of limited value to content teachers when designing instruction for most of their students. This is because students' scores on a standardized reading test will not necessarily reflect their abilities to read content-specific materials in different subjects. In other words, the reading tasks on these tests are not authentic. As mentioned earlier, standardized tests are used more for accountability than for guiding content area instruction.

Sometimes, as in the case of special education students, student files will include the results of norm-referenced tests used to write Individual Education Plans (IEPs). IEPs describe students' abilities and disabilities and recommend ways to accommodate their needs. In the instance of students who are learning to speak English, test scores may reveal the level of that student's level of proficiency in English.

Oftentimes, students move from one school district to another. Sometimes, parent employment requirements and/or parental custody arrangements result in students moving many times in a 2 or 3 year period. When this happens students may be enrolled at your school for several months before their files catch up to them. What should you do if they don't have these records available? When the results of standardized tests are not available, teachers can use individual quick screening tools.

Individual Quick Classroom Screening

When it is helpful to obtain a rough estimate of one or more individual students' reading levels, there are two quick and dirty (5-minute) assessments that may be used. They are not reading tests. These assessments only require students to say the words on lists. They therefore don't measure reading comprehension. Nonetheless, student performance on these screening devices correlates highly with results they might get on rigorous tests of reading comprehension. That is why they are called screening tools. They may be used to screen for students who may need more extensive assessment. What follows is information on the *Wide Range Achievement Test—Reading* (WRAT) and the *San Diego Quick Assessment*.

Wide Range Achievement Test: Reading (Justak & Bijou, 1975)

This one-page word list is divided into two parts. Part one is "normed" for students under 12 and part two for those age 12-years or older. The individual student reads aloud to the teacher from a list of words across a page until twelve consecutive words are missed. Then, using the numbers at the end of each line the tester gets an immediate raw score by subtracting words missed. A box in the center of the page converts this into a reading grade level.

Several cautions should be mentioned: (1) When administering to older students, it is wise to warn them that words rapidly accelerate in difficulty up to 19th grade level, so they are not expected to complete the test; (2) the WRAT does not measure comprehension or knowledge of word meanings; (3) because WRAT is a standardized assessment, and since this same protocol may be used by another teacher at a later time, at no point should words be explained or pronounced by the teacher for the student.

The San Diego Quick Assessment (SDQA) (LaPray & Ross, 1969)

Similar to the WRAT, the *San Diego Quick Assessment* (SDQA) has been found useful and reliable by many teachers through the grades. This SDQA is presented in Table 6.1 (page 205). Directions for preparing, administering, and scoring the SDQA follow.

Preparing to Administer the SDQA

1. Prepare the cards. Do this by typing each list of 10 words onto index cards, one list to a card. Each card must either be printed (computer) or typed (typewriter). Handwritten cards should not be used. For younger children, type the first four lists in larger type.

2. Use only the words listed on Table 6.1. This is a standardized tool. Do not change the order of the words on each list. Check your spelling for accuracy. If you misspell or change a word on a card you invalidate the results. (Note: Yes, the word "certainly" does appear on both the fourth- and fifth-grade lists.)

3. *Do not* put the reading level on the cards. Do your own coding on the back of the card. For example, you might label the back of the cards by writing the names of a sequence of 11 freeway exits. Or you may list the names of the first 11 presidents. Or you may choose to color code the cards. Bottom line, you don't want students to know the grade level a card represents.

4. Make a photocopy of Table 6.1. Place it on a clipboard. You will use this copy to indicate whether or not the student pronounced the word correctly.

5. Make sure you know the correct pronunciation of each word. Look up the word in a dictionary if you are not sure.

Administering the SDQA

1. Arrange seating so that you are facing each other.

2. When administering to older students, it is wise to warn them that words rapidly accelerate in difficulty from one card to the next and that they may not be required to read the words on all the cards. The first few cards are easier, so they should take their time and not rush through them. Tell the student that not rushing will also make it easier for you to keep track of what they have read to you.

3. Hand the student the first card. Position your clipboard so that the student will not be able to see what you write. Ask students to read the words listed on the card. On your clipboard indicate whether they pronounced the word correctly (+) or incorrectly (-). Make sure that you make a mark after every word so that the student will not use your writing motions as indication of the correctness of their answers.

4. *Do not* help students sound out words. As with the WRAT, *do not* teach students how to pronounce words correctly. This is a standardized assessment, and since this same protocol may be used by another teacher at a later time, at no point should words be explained or pronounced by the teacher for the student.

5. If a student gets stuck on a word, encourage them to move on to the next word on the list. If a student pronounces a word several times, and the pronunciation changes, score only the last pronunciation.

6. As long as the students have not missed three or more words on a card give them the next card. Stop when three words are missed on any one list. If a student has missed three words on one card, *do not* give the student the next card. The SDQA is complete as soon as the student has missed three words from one list.

Two last ideas to remember when administrating the SDQA: (1) This is a standardized protocol. Follow it closely so that you don't invalidate your results. Creativity in administering this test is not appropriate. (2) If you already have experience administering the SDQA and have many students to assess in a short period of time, you need

TABLE 6.1 San Diego Quick Assessment

pp	Primer	1	2
see	you	road	our
play	come	live	please
me	not	thank	myself
at	with	when	town
run	jump	bigger	early
go	help	how	send
and	is	always	wide
look	work	night	believe
can	are	spring	quietly
here	this	today	carefully
3	**4**	**5**	**6**
city	decided	scanty	bridge
middle	served	certainly	commercial
moment	amazed	develop	abolish
frightened	silent	considered	trucker
exclaimed	wrecked	discussed	apparatus
several	improved	behaved	elementary
lonely	certainly	splendid	comment
drew	entered	acquainted	necessity
since	realized	escaped	gallery
straight	interrupted	grim	relativity
7	**8**	**9**	**10**
amber	capacious	conscientious	zany
dominion	limitation	isolation	jerkin
sundry	pretext	molecule	nausea
capillary	intrigue	ritual	gratuitous
impetuous	delusion	momentous	linear
blight	immaculate	vulnerable	inept
wrest	ascent	kinship	legality
enumerate	acrid	conservatism	aspen
daunted	binocular	jaunty	amnesty
condescend	embankment	inventive	barometer
11			
galore	exonerate		
rotunda	superannuate		
capitalism	luxuriate		
prevaricate	piebald		
risible	crunch		

From Lapray, Margaret Helen, & Ross, Ramon Royal. (January 1969). "The Graded Word List: Quick Gauge of Reading Ability," *Journal of Reading*, 12, 305–307. Reprinted with permission of the International Reading Association.

not begin with the first card in the set. Instead start with a card that is at least 3 years below the student's grade level. If the student misses any words on the card, move back one card. After the student reads all the words on one card correctly (the base level), skip the cards from which the student has already read, and give the student the next card. Proceed until the student misses three words on one card.

Scoring the SDQA

- The highest list from which students miss no more than one in 10 words is their independent reading level.
- Two errors per list indicate instructional level.
- Three or more identify frustration level.

(For more information on the difference between independent, instructional, and frustration reading levels see Chapter Five.)

Caveat: Quick Screening Tools May Be Unfair to English Language Learners

The rules of pronunciation of letter sound associations are different in many romance languages. For example, the correct pronunciation of the first word on the "pp" list of the SDQA, the word "see," has a long "e" sound. However, the same group of letters correctly pronounced in Spanish would be read "say," with the long "a" sound. Therefore, word pronunciation assessments like the WRAT and the SDQA may be biased against non-English speakers.

Summary of Strengths and Weaknesses of Individual Quick Classroom Screening Tools

Strengths

- A teacher without access to standardized reading data can get a quick and rough estimate of the reading level of a student.
- The results obtained from these quick assessments correlate very closely with the results from time-consuming standardized norm-referenced tests.
- The SDQA is inexpensive, easy to administer, and can done in 5 minutes or less.
- Results from these instruments provide one corner of the reader assessment triangle.

Weaknesses

- These are not reading tests. They do not measure comprehension. Scores on these assessments merely correlate closely with scores on more sophisticated reading assessments.
- These lists are not authentic reading tasks.
- The results of these quick list reading assessments exhibit bias against English language learners.
- The SDQA only tests up to grade 11. Hence, this assessment is of very limited value for high school juniors and seniors.

Practice in Administering and Scoring the SDQA

1. Administer the SDQA to a *willing* secondary student (grades 6 to 10). You may administer the test to an ESL student if you are confident she or he can read above a 4th-grade level, or to an 11th-grade student if you are certain he or she reads *below* grade level. Remember the "clipboard" method!

2. After you have administered the SDQA, address the points below in concise and clearly written paragraphs:

   • Describe the student and the test administration environment. (Grade, gender, school, background of student, where you administered the test, where each of you sat, how you handled the cards and recorded the information.)

   • Describe the test procedures and the results you obtained. (Provide detailed results and procedures. With which card did you begin? When did the student miss their first word? List words missed on each card. When did you stop? Why? Report the student's independent, instructional, and frustrational levels as prescribed above.)

   • Describe the conclusions you have reached based upon your data. Keeping in mind the NCTE/IRA standards concerning triangulation issues, is there a reason/need for further evaluation?

3. Return to class and share the results of this activity with your colleagues and instructor.

Basic Reading Inventory

A more sophisticated and a reasonably easy tool to determine the reading level of an individual student is the Basic Reading Inventory (Johns, 2001). The Basic Reading Inventory provides data on the independent, instructional, and frustration level of student reading grades pre-primer through 12. The BRI contains multiple word lists for students to pronounce. Errors in pronunciation may be used to analyze word attack skills. Once a score is obtained on the word lists, students are asked to read aloud from graded passages. By having the student read words in context, the teacher may obtain contextualized data about the oral reading errors made by the student. Finally, the student is asked to answer questions about the content of the passages read aloud. This provides information about levels of comprehension in context.

The Basic Reading Inventory does require some study on the part of the teacher in order to develop the familiarity needed to administer it effectively. However, it measures level performance scores in context through grade 12. Content teachers in smaller schools with limited support services will find this tool helpful.

Informal Whole-Class Assessment

The seventh IRA reading assessment standard states that "teachers are the most important agent of assessment." This is because ". . . teachers are in a unique position to engage in valid assessment. Because they are closest to students' learning they have the opportunity to make many detailed observations over time. . . ." Unfortunately standardized reading tests do not provide teachers with specific data about how well students can read from their content area texts. These formal tests, despite the time and expense they incur, do not provide student data on how effectively students can use reading skills specific to a content area.

More and more teachers are integrating literacy and subject area instruction to realize significant improvements in student achievement. However, to do so they need to know what literacy skills students bring to their texts, and what skills they need to teach along with the content. In an ideal world, teachers would sit with each student, one at a time, and have them read and discuss the content of their texts. The unfortunate reality that most secondary teachers meet three to five classes of 25 to 35 students per week makes this goal unrealistic. Hence, whole-class paper-and-pencil assessment is the next best choice. In either case, teachers must be skillful in the design of the questions they ask.

Designing whole-class assessments requires the honing of the craft of writing questions to measure student comprehension.

The Art of Writing Comprehension Questions

As content-area teachers, we know the content we want our students to be able to read. Well-written questions reveal more about what students have learned. Pearson and Johnson (1978) suggest it is helpful to think of question-and-answer relationships (QARs) when we write questions. They suggest it is helpful to think of these in two categories: *textually implicit/explicit* and *scriptally implicit*. For the sake of simplicity we will rename these two general categories **literal** (explicit/implicit) and **inferential** (connection/reflection).

Literal		Inferential	
The answer may be found in the text.		**The answer requires inference from the reader.**	
explicit	implicit	connection	reflection
Readers must find the exact words in text. Answers are either copied or paraphrased.	Readers must integrate information that is stated literally in different areas of the text. Answers require the combining or paraphrasing of ideas.	Readers must use their own experiences (prior knowledge) and facts from the text to derive a conclusion or consequence (induction/deduction).	Readers go beyond making connections between the book and their background knowledge. The text spurs the readers into new tracts of thought.
QAR	QAR	QAR	QAR
If students cannot answer these questions correctly, their reading from this text is at the frustration level.	If students can answer all literal questions correctly, they read at the instructional level. However, if they can answer explicit questions but cannot answer implicit questions, their reading is between the frustration and instructional level.	If students can answer all literal questions correctly but cannot answer inferential connection questions, their reading from this text is at the instructional level. If they can answer literal and inferential-connection questions, their reading is at the independent level.	If students can answer inferential-connection questions but cannot answer inferential reflection questions, their reading from this text is at the independent level. However, if students can answer all literal and inferential questions correctly, they may benefit from supplementary materials that will further challenge their reading abilities.

FIGURE 6.2

Literal and Inferential Questions and Their Question-and-Answer Relationships

The answers to ***explicit literal*** questions are stated word-for-word in the text. To answer this type of question readers need to find the exact words within the text that provide the answer. They can then either copy those words, or paraphrase them in their own. Now, let's look at the question-and-answer relationship (*QAR*). If students are unable to answer an explicit literal question, the student probably cannot read this part of the text at even the frustration level.

Here is a sample explicit literal question from the children's story, *The Three Little Pigs:*

Q. Why did the three little pigs build houses for themselves?

A. (copied) The three little pigs grew so big that their mother said to them, "You are too big to live here any longer. You must go and build houses for yourselves."

A. (paraphrased) Because their mother told them that they were growing up and it was time for them to build their own homes.

The answers to ***implicit literal*** questions may require readers to provide answers that can be understood but are not stated directly in any one section of the text. To do so, readers must integrate information that is stated literally in different areas of the text. Answers require the combining or paraphrasing of ideas. With regard to *QAR*, if students can answer all literal questions correctly, they read at the instructional level. However, if they can answer explicit questions but cannot answer implicit questions, their reading is between the frustration and instructional level.

Here is a sample implicit literal question from the same story:

Q. What happened to the pigs that lived in the straw and stick house?

A. (Depending on which version of the story you read) Both pigs were eaten by the wolf. (or) The first pig ran for shelter with the second pig, and then both pigs took shelter in the brick house of the third pig.

An ***inferential connection*** question requires readers to derive a conclusion or consequence from facts or premises in the text. However, to do so, readers must use their own experiences (prior knowledge) along with the facts in the book to infer their answers. With regard to *QAR*, if students can answer all literal questions correctly but cannot answer inferential connection questions, their reading from this text is at the instructional level. If they can answer literal and inferential-connection questions, their reading is at the independent level.

Once again, comprehension questions for *The Three Little Pigs*. This time an inferential connections question:

Q. What lessons do you think the writer of this story wants to teach the children who read it? Please explain your answer. (Note that the words "what do you think" cue readers that this is an inferential question. The sentence, "Please explain your answer." informs readers that the connections used to derive their conclusions should be explained.)

A. There are several lessons that the author may be trying to teach. First, if you want to have a safe home, you must choose sturdy building materials. Bricks are stronger than twigs or straw. Second, the writer tells the reader that the brick house "took a long time to build." The lesson here might be the hard work you do today will pay off tomorrow. Given that in the end, the third pig, described as "clever" outsmarts the hungry wolf, the lesson might be that hard work and clever thinking are a powerful way to preserve life and property.

An ***inferential reflection*** question requires readers to take their inferences to a higher level. To answer these questions students must use the text and their background knowledge to travel into new tracts of thought. Answers to these questions are personal and creative. In fact, any answer the student provides will be considered correct as long as the student provides evidence as to how their reflection may be inferred from the text. With regard to *QAR*, if students can answer inferential-connection questions but cannot answer inferential reflection questions, their reading from this text is at the independent level. However, if students can answer all literal and inferential questions correctly, they may benefit from supplementary materials that will further challenge their reading abilities.

Finally, an inferential/reflection question:

Q. The three pigs built houses out of different materials. Reflecting on the different places in which you have lived, what lessons might you offer in a story about using the right building materials?

A. I would definitely want a brick house if I lived in Florida because of the dangers of hurricanes. If a wolf could blow down a stick house, imagine what the hurricane could do. Brick is a very expensive building material. Where did the third pig get the money to pay for the bricks? Safe housing may *not* be affordable to young people who are just getting started in life. However, that wouldn't matter if I lived in California. When the ground starts to shake a house must be flexible. Bricks are not flexible. When bricks start to crumble, anyone in the house will be in terrible danger. However, if there were a great many wolves in the neighborhood, the safety of a brick house might be worth the risk.

In order to understand how well our students read to learn, it is important to see if they understand vocabulary words. Questions about vocabulary words may be literal or inferential.

The answers to **literal vocabulary questions** are explicitly or implicitly written into the text. To answer these questions students need only copy or integrate facts stated in the text. On the other hand, a **contextual vocabulary question** requires the student to use the context that surrounds the text to infer its meaning.

For example:

Q. In the story the pig goes to the carnival to ride on a *carousel*. What is a carousel?

A. (quoted from story) A carousel is a lot like a merry-go-round.

Q. The writer says, "The wolf was angry but he *pretended* not to be." What do you think the word *pretended* means?

A. I think that *pretended* means that the wolf was trying to fool the pig, so he acted as if he wasn't angry. To pretend is to act differently than you are feeling.

Now we are ready to construct a content informal reading inventory.

The Content IRI

A content informal reading inventory (also referred to as a Group IRI, CIRI or CARI) is an informal assessment tool designed by teachers to evaluate their students' abilities to read with comprehension from a content area book. In addition, it provides a way to measure students' abilities to use different literacy skills (e.g., locating reference materials, interpreting graphics, taking and making notes, etc.) for specific subject area texts. It is usually administered to the whole class during one sitting. Samples of two

CIRIs, one linked to a DRTA and the second used to establish the readability of a text may be found in Appendix B and Appendix C.

A CIRI is constructed in two parts. *Part I* focuses on reading with comprehension. A representative passage (250–400 words) is selected from near the beginning of the content area text. The passage is titled and an introductory paragraph provides context for the reader. After reading the passage independently, students are asked to answer 10 to 12 questions. These questions are designed to gauge how well the passage was understood. Questions for this part are designed to fall within one of three categories: literal (explicit and/or implicit), inferential (connection and/or reflection), and vocabulary (inferential).

Part II is designed to measure other literacy skills specific to the subject area. These may include, but are not limited to: interpreting graphics such as political cartoons, pie graphs, maps, and flow-charts; defining background vocabulary; translating symbols and formulae; reading a search engine home page; using a dictionary; taking and making notes from a lecture; and following written directions. The teacher may choose to use parts of the textbook for this purpose, or to use other resources (e.g., dictionary, Internet.) Teachers choose the three literacy skills they believe will be most important to read to learn in their classes. They provide an introduction for each subtest that proves a rationale and directions. After reading the passage students are asked to answer 5 to 10 questions. These questions should progress from literal to inferential.

Obviously, an informal inventory designed by an individual teacher is not a standardized test. Criteria for mastery for comprehension components and subtests are set by the teachers themselves. No normative data or grade level scores are provided. Instead, results from a CIRI are displayed on a *scoring profile*. The scoring profile provides information on the strengths and weaknesses of each student and also disaggregates the data by comprehension component or subtest skills. This scoring profile can then be used to plan whole-class instruction that meets the overall needs of the class and/or for small tutorial study groups. This profile can and should be shared with special-needs resource teachers so they may better support the needs of the students enrolled in your class.

The questions chosen for any CIRI should be guided by the goals that teachers have for their classes. These goals begin, of course, with the standards established by their school districts and/or their states. Therefore, many teachers who write CIRIs take time to align each question with the appropriate standard. For an example of this, see the Chemistry/Math CIRI Appendix C.

Finally, a CIRI *should not* be confused with the IRI (informal reading inventory) used widely by elementary teachers and reading specialists. An IRI is administered individually by the teacher. The student reads orally (sometimes silently) from a series of brief graded paragraphs and then answers questions.

Part I: The Comprehension Section

Here is a nine-step guide for constructing the Part I of your CIRI:

1. Select a short representative sample from near the beginning of the text. This excerpt should be somewhere around 250 to 400 words depending on the class grade level. While it may be relatively easy to find suitable excerpts from social studies, science, math, health, and English composition books, some courses do not have a required text. In those cases, consider the following:

Physical Education	Use a rule manual, the directions provided with a heart rate monitor, or the directions on a treadmill, elliptical, or weight machine. Use an article from a sports magazine or, with younger age groups, consider a story from *Sports Illustrated for Kids*.
Literature (novels)	Choose an excerpt from a novel that you will be teaching first.
Art	Safety directions for operation of a potters wheel, directions for mixing paints or cleaning paint brushes, or an article from an art magazine that describes the medium you will be using.
Music	Sheet music. Ask literal questions such as: "What is the key signature at the beginning of the piece?" Vocabulary questions such as: "If solo means for one person to sing that section, what do you think "tutti" (measure 32) means?" and ask inference questions such as, "Why do you think the composer chose to change the time signature at measure 81?" Or use articles from music magazines.
Classic and World Languages	If this is an advanced or emersion class, choose a passage in that language. If not, choose a passage that combines English and the new language.
Shop, Vocational Education	Procedural and repair manuals. Safety instructions.

2. If possible, type the selection into a word-processed document, or, use a scanner with an editable text feature. Do your best to format text as much like the original as possible. This may require you use a two-column format and/or to include pictures or illustrations (you may want cut and paste the old-fashioned way). One advantage of word processing the text is that you will be able to add features that make it easier for students to respond to questions (e.g., underlining or **boldfacing** vocabulary words within the text so they can go back to reread the surrounding context). A second advantage is easy access to the Flesch-Kincaid Readability Scores (see Chapter Five). If you choose not to type, you may ask students to read directly from the text. This might cause difficulties. For example, the definition of a vocabulary (inference) question may appear in the glossary. Or, the answer to an inference question may appear (literally) later in the book.

3. Compose a title and an introductory preparation/motivation paragraph. Be aware of the readability level of your own writing. You don't want students to do poorly on your CIRI because they couldn't read your directions. This paragraph should explain to the students what a CIRI is and how the results will be used.

*For example: This is **not** a test. It is a CIRI (content informal reading inventory). No grades will be given, but you will receive points for participation and completion. The results of this CIRI will be used to help me design better lessons. It will help me to know what reading strengths you can use when reading from our textbook. It will also help me figure out where some members of the class may need extra help.*

4. Write a two to three sentence paragraph that provides context for the passage to be read. This should include a frame of reference statement followed by a sentence telling the reader the purpose for reading it. Be sure to ask a question about this later.

For example: The following is from your text, <u>Magruder's American Government.</u> The text describes some of the many forms of government used throughout the world. This information will help your understanding of our American government. The United States uses a form of democracy. As you read this selection, look for the differences between direct and indirect democracy. Also, consider why the United States uses its current form of government.

5. Give directions for what students will need to do after completing the reading. Don't forget to tell the students that they may go back to the text as often as they need. Make sure to articulate your expectations regarding answers (e.g., complete sentences).

For example: *Read the short passage from the novel. Then answer the 10 questions about what you have read. You may look back if you wish. You need not answer in complete sentences. Please follow the directions carefully and do your best work.*

6. Next, compose 10 to 12 questions about your text passage. Preface your questions with a reiteration of the directions. The questions may be multiple choice, fill-ins, whatever. If you want complete sentences, remember to say so! If not, say that as well.

- Choose at least three questions of each: literal (L), vocabulary (V), and inferential (I). Your tenth (eleventh or twelfth) question(s) can be from any category.
- Start easy with a literal question. Be sure that the answers to literal questions are easily located in the passage. (You may choose to write a literal explicit or literal implicit question, but remember to start easy. You don't want to intimidate your students.)

For example: *Two forms of democracy are mentioned in the passage. Which one does the United States use?*

Another example: *Name the three types of musical shows described in this passage.*

7. Next, compose your inferential vocabulary questions. You will improve the likelihood that the readers understand your question if you repeat the word in context in your question (quoted directly from the passage). Students should be able to infer meanings by utilizing the surrounding text. Your question should ask readers: "What do you think _____ means? (If the definition for the word is contained in the text, this is a literal vocabulary question, not an inferential vocabulary question.)

For example: *In the first paragraph of the reading, it says, "The people hold the <u>sovereign</u> power, and the government is conducted only by and with the consent of the people." What do you think the word <u>sovereign</u> means?*

Another example: *In the passage we read: "No one ever mentioned it; the <u>disgrace</u> was unspeakable." In the context of this sentence, what does the word <u>disgrace</u> mean?*

8. Next compose your inference (connection/reflection) questions. Remember, students must infer the answer to these questions by combining what they learned from the passage with their own personal thoughts. With inferential questions, you're asking students what they think. Make sure to ask for elaboration. For example, "Why do you think," or, "Why do you suppose," and "explain your answer," or, "give two reasons why you think this is true." (Most CIRI inference questions are inferential connection

questions; however, an inferential reflection question will help you identify those students who need supplementary challenges.)

For example: *After reaching the ocean, Gandhi said that he was "shaking the foundations of the British empire." What do you think he meant by this? Explain your answer.*

Another example: *In the second line of the song, why do you suppose the word "Baltimore" is spelled (and sung) as "Baltimoe"? Explain your answer.*

Another example: *Our geometry text tells us that logical reasoning is required to support mathematical decisions. Reflect on the different ways that people use, or don't use, logical reasoning to make decisions. Give one example of a decision that you would <u>not</u> want to use logical reasoning to make. Explain your answer.*

9. At the end of the questions, be sure to include a word of encouragement before the students move on to Part II.

For example: *Congratulations on completing Part I. Take a breath, turn the page and move on to Part II.*

A CIRI is usually composed of both Parts I and II. However, some textbooks have dramatically different readability challenges from chapter to chapter. In this case, you might choose to write a second or third version of Part I and administer them prior to beginning the corresponding chapters.

Part II: Subject-Specific Reading Skill Subtests

Part II is an assessment of three needed skills from among those you believe are most important to reading with comprehension in your subject area. The following is a four-step guide to constructing this section. Once you have completed the four steps, you can construct your CIRI Scoring Profile Sheet.

1. Choose at least three skill areas from the list below. Read over this list. You may want to refer to the examples provided in step 4 below:

	Skill Area	Examples
A	Interpreting Graphics	Able to read and understand maps (e.g., political, topographical, weather, agricultural, historical, road, cognitive), charts (e.g., flow, position, conversion, musical fingering), tables (e.g., color, conjugation, comparison, rate, size, logarithmic), diagrams (e.g., for using a calculator, wiring, construction, sentence, recall), graphs (e.g., bar, line, circle), cartoons (e.g., political, gag, comic, poetic, illustrative) . . .
B	Outlining, Note Taking and Making	Able to use any of the following to effectively record and organize ideas from readings or lectures: Conventional outlines, bulleted outlines, recall diagrams, Cornell Notes, Ferndale Notes, Harvard Notes . . .
C	Parts of the Text	Able to efficiently locate and use text aids (table of contents, index, glossary, appendices, copyright, references . . .) to preview a text and find specific information.
D	Locating and/or Using Reference Materials	Able to locate and use information from dictionary, thesaurus, encyclopedias, almanacs, reader's guides, and search engines on the Internet.

	Skill Area	Examples
E	Following Directions	Able to follow written or oral directions in intermittent or concurrent sequences (test item, assembly of parts, operating machinery . . .).
F	Translating symbols	Able to recognize and use symbols ($\geq$, $\prod$, £, IV, #, ©, $\leftrightarrow$, ♪, ♀. . .) and formulae A = 1/2 bh.
G	Defining or Applying Content-Specific Vocabulary	Able to define and apply subject area content vocabulary (e.g., literary devices, words whose meanings are different in the subject areas).
H	Comprehension Skills	Beyond the passage used in Part I, able to read passages to determine the sequence of events, establish cause and effect, analyze, synthesize, or evaluate.
I	Survey of Study Habits	Aware of study strategies needed for specific reading tasks.
J	Reading Rate Adaptability	Able to efficiently scan a table of contents, index, or glossary for specific information.
K	Attitude/Interest Survey	Gathers interests, relevant background information.

2. Each subtest should have an introduction that includes a rationale, and directions.

For example: *In most history classes, you are asked to do research. This is true for our class as well. Finding sources outside of your textbook is an important skill. The next five questions have to do with your ability to locate reference materials. Write the answers to each question in the space provided. Please write in <u>complete</u> sentences.*

Another example: *The following symbols are commonly used in mathematics. You will have to use them frequently in our geometry text. Please write the meaning for each of the symbols. Use the space provided. You may already know some of these. Others may be new. Do the best you can.*

Another example: *An important tool to aid you in reading with understanding is the dictionary. Using the attached copy from Webster's' Dictionary, answer the following questions. Remember to use complete sentences.*

3. Include 5 to 10 questions for each skill area. When writing matching questions, in order to offset guessing, make sure to have at least three additional choices (outliers) that do not match.

4. If you are assessing the ability of your students to read graphic aids, questions should be sequenced from the very literal to the application. This will help you to discern the level of reading ability the student brings to the graphic. Remember, you first want to know if they can access the information in the graphic. Then you can ask what they can do with it. For example:

- What type of graphic is this?
- What is the title?
- Are there subheadings? If so, how are they labeled?
- What special devices of symbols are used?
- What kind of information might you be asked to find in this graphic?
- What is the significance of. . . ?

Sample Subtests

What follows are some examples of several subtests. We wish to thank the following students for their contributions to this section: Warren Brusick, Chris Fryer, and Lee Krancas.

An Example of a Graphics Subtest

The study of mathematics tends to involve a lot of data. There are many ways in which to organize and display data to make it easier to understand. One of the most common ways to display data is with the use of a graph. A graph takes many pieces of data and displays them visually, so we can learn about patterns, trends, and relationships between different factors. For example, the graph below shows the relationship between the distance a car travels and the time over which it travels. *Please inspect this graph, and then answer the questions that follow.*

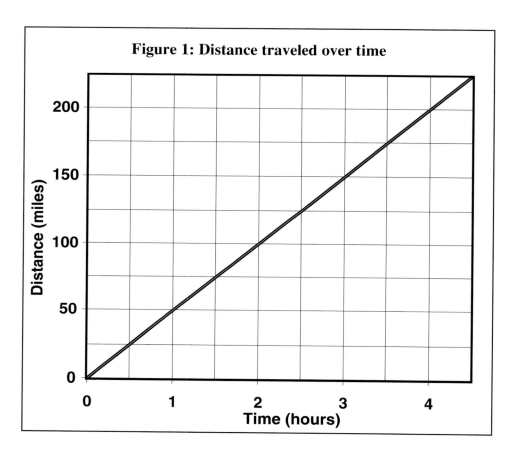

1. What is the title of this graph?

2. What two factors are being compared in the graph?

3. What units are being used to measure the two factors?

4. How much time is being shown on the graph?

5. According to the graph, how long does it take for the car to travel 50 miles?

Examples of Outlining, Taking, and Making Notes Subtests

Strong note taking and making skills are important to be able to pull out key points from a lecture or from your book. Either:

(a) Go back to Part I and quickly reread the passage. Next, use the space below to write notes on that passage that you would use to study. Your notes may be in whatever form works best for you (outline, recall diagram, Cornell notes, etc.). I will be looking to see if you have found the main ideas and then noted the supporting details. Or

(b) I will read you a short passage from our textbook. Use the space below to take notes on the key points in that passage. Your notes may be in whatever form works best for you (outline, recall diagram, Cornell notes, etc.). I will be looking to see if you have found the main ideas and then noted the supporting details.

An Example of a Parts of the Text Subtest

Your textbook can be an extremely helpful tool to learn world history. As with most tools, the more you know about the different parts of your textbook, the easier it will be for you to use it as a learning source. Please answer the following questions. You answers will help me to learn how well you can find information in your book.

Directions: The following questions may be answered by using the information copied for you into this booklet on pages 10-A (index), 10-B (glossary) and 10-C (table of contents). Please do the best you can.

1. Information on the ***diaspora*** may be found on page _____

2. I found the answer to this question by looking in the:
   a. Index
   b. Glossary
   c. Table of Contents

3. The authors define ***feudalism*** as _____

4. I found the definition for this word by looking in the:
   a. Index
   b. Glossary
   c. Table of Contents

5. On what page does the ***Spanish glossary*** start? _____

6. I found the answer to this question in the:
   a. Index
   b. Glossary
   c. Table of Contents

7. To find the chapter on the ***Middle East***, you would look in the:
   a. Index
   b. Glossary
   c. Table of Contents

8. On what page does the Middle East chapter begin? _____

An Example of a Locating and/or Using Reference Materials Subtest

When studying science we will often discover new words. One way to find out more about the meaning of a word is to use a dictionary. The questions that follow will help me to learn how well you can use a dictionary.

Directions: Please look at the attached page copied from *Webster's Dictionary;* then answer the following questions. You may look at the dictionary page as often as you wish. Write your answer in the space provided below each question. You need not write in complete sentences.

1. Find the word **monarch** on the dictionary page. Please copy the first definition of this word exactly how it appears on the page.
2. How many syllables are there in the word **monarch**?
3. Right after the word **monarch** there is a lowercase, italicized letter. In this case it looks like this: "n." What does the "n" mean?
4. There are two words at the very top of the dictionary page, above the three columns. The word on the right is **Monera**, where on the age does the entry and definition of this word begin?
5. According to the information in parenthesis, the word **monarch** comes from **monos** and **archein**. What does **monos** mean?

An Example of a Following Directions Subtest

An exercise that may be used to check to see how well students follow oral directions may be found in Chapter One. Here is an exercise in following written directions.

We will be doing a lot of fun activities in this class that require following directions closely. If the directions are not followed, you will not be successful, or worse, something dangerous could happen! Follow the directions written below to fill in the graph.

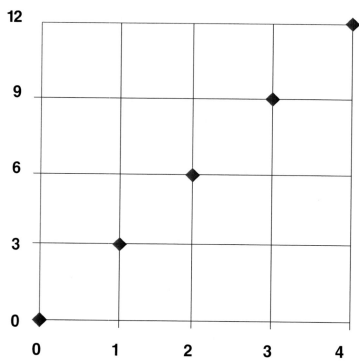

DIRECTIONS

1. Above the graph write the title: "Walking Distance vs. Time."
2. On left edge of the graph, label the vertical scale "Distance (miles)."
3. On the bottom edge of the graph, label the horizontal scale "Time (hours)."
4. There are five dots on the graph. Connect the dots with a straight line.
5. Next to the line you just drew, write: "Walking speed = 3mph."

An Example of a Translating Symbols and Formulae Subtest

Formulae are valuable science and math tools. They are used to represent relationships between factors. For example, the formula "S = D/T" can be used to represent the graph you studied in the previous exercise. The factors of speed, distance, and time are represented by the symbols, "R," "D," and "T." *Look at the formula and symbols below; then answer the questions that follow.*

=====

Formula: R = D/T
Symbols: R = Rate (in miles per hour)
D = Distance (miles)
T = Time (hours)

====

QUESTIONS

Please answer each question with a short answer. You do not need to use complete sentences.

1. In words, what do the symbols "R," "D," and "T" stand for? What are the units for each?

2. In words, what do the operation symbols "=" and "/" mean?

3. In words, how would you say the formula "R = D/T"?

4. If a car travels 20 miles in 2 hours, what is the rate? Include the units for your answer.

5. Which is faster: 20 miles in 2 hours, or 40 miles in 6 hours? Please explain how you found your answer.

An Example of a Defining or Applying Content-Specific Vocabulary Subtest

When reading and writing, it is important to understand how a word functions in a sentence. This is a senior-level English class and before I assume that you know each of the parts of speech, I want to check. Please read each sentence carefully. Using the words in the boxes below, tell me what part of speech you think the underlined word is.

Some answers may be used more than once. Others may not be used at all.

Write your answer underneath the underlined word.

Noun	Verb	Pronoun	Adjective
Adverb	Article	Preposition	Conjunction

1. My grandpa used to tell me that "I shouldn't <u>grow</u> old if I could avoid it."

2. Judy turned out for soccer practice <u>with</u> a dirty jersey and brand new cleats.

3. He turned <u>abruptly</u> to face his accuser.

4. Since <u>she</u> had already earned an "A," Cleo Esperanza was excused from detention.

5. He <u>ran</u> for the touchdown and then danced in the end zone.

6. Put the book <u>on</u> the table.

7. Samantha shined the <u>tarnished</u> trophy with silver polish.

Congratulations! You've completed Parts 1 and II of a content informal reading inventory that is geared specifically to your course and reading materials! Now you will want to create a profile sheet so that you may record and analyze data.

Part III: Displaying and Using CIRI Data

The following directions may be used to create a CIRI Class Profile Sheet:

1. To set up your grid, create a column for student names and then a set of columns for each component of Part I and each subtest of Part II. Note that this is how such data is normally aggregated and disaggregated; however, you can choose to disaggregate data in any fashion you see fit.

Below the title of each column establish criteria for mastery. Use your judgment to decide how many correctly answered questions constitute mastery. For example, if you know that one of the four vocabulary questions is especially difficult, you might decide to set the criteria as 3/4. If you know that you will be reviewing the content vocabulary terms in class, then 4/7 might be sufficient.

For example:

CIRI Scoring Profile

Student Name	Part I			Part II			Overall Individual Needs
	Vocabulary (3/4)	Literal (2/3)	Inferential (2/3)	Terms (4/7)	Dictionary (4/5)	Internet (4/5)	
1							
2							
3							
4							
5							
6							
7							
8							
9							
10							
Class Skill Needs							

2. Here is an explanation as to how you can use your data to plan individual and group instruction.

Scoring each section: A ✓ in one of the skill boxes indicates that a student has mastered that particular skill. To receive a ✓ for a section of the CIRI, a student must meet or exceed the minimum score indicated inside the parentheses at the top of each column.

Meeting overall class needs:	For all skills that are not mastered by more than half of the class, explicit class instruction in this skill should be integrated into lesson plans for that unit.
Meeting individual needs:	If a box in one of the columns does not have a ✓, the student has not mastered that skill and needs more instruction in that particular area. If a student has three or more boxes without a ✓, then that student is a candidate for individual skill instruction in those particular skill areas. This may be achieved through grouping or tutorial assistance.

CLOZE Procedure

The simplicity and relative accuracy of the CLOZE procedure makes it another potent tool for assessing the ability of students to read from a content text. Students may initially find CLOZE tests to be a frustrating experience. Some practice is therefore strongly recommended.

The idea behind this procedure was conceived by Wilson Taylor (1953) and much research has been carried out since then. Today CLOZE is considered a viable instrument for measuring reading levels and comprehension. The term comes from the Gestalt psychological term "closure" and means the tendency to anticipate completing a pattern—closing the gap.

We have a natural tendency to perceive things as whole. If someone said "Merry Christmas and Happy New ____," you would automatically supply the word "year." Viewing an incomplete portrait with one eye still missing you would mentally picture the missing eye.

In order to complete a CLOZE assessment, readers must know the meanings of words, their form or function (e.g., noun), as well as the combined meanings or how the words make sense together. English language learners, especially those whose native language is not a romance language, may find this exercise especially frustrating. In fact, using CLOZE with English language learners is not recommended.

Constructing a CLOZE

If you plan to use CLOZE to assess text the reading abilities of your student to read from a specific text, follow these guidelines.

1. Select a representative sample from the text of approximately 275 to 300 words that students have not seen before.
2. Leave the first and last sentence intact.
3. Start with the second sentence and delete every fifth word, substituting a standard length of twelve spaces _____, until fifty words are deleted. Science material may require every seventh word and young elementary every tenth word.
4. Do not number the blanks or give answer sheet.

Administering and Scoring a CLOZE

1. Explain that the purpose of CLOZE is to find out how easy the text is for them. Model the process of completing it for them. Gunning (2003) has suggested a list of tips that teachers should share with students as they model the process. These include:

- Read the whole exercise first.
- Use all the clues given in a passage.
- Read past the blank to the end of the sentence. Sometimes the best clues come after the blank.
- If necessary, read a sentence or two ahead to get additional clues.
- Spell as best as you can. You lose no points for misspelled words.
- Do your best, but do not worry if you cannot correctly complete each blank. Most readers will be able to fill in fewer than half the blanks correctly.
- After you have filled in as many blanks as you can, reread the selection. Make any changes you think are necessary.

2. Allow unlimited time to complete the typed passage.
3. When scoring allow only the exact word replacement. Each blank is worth two points. Table 6.2 shows how to interpret scores. Those falling within the instructional level are said to be equivalent to approximately 75% on a multiple choice test on the same material.
4. If you decide to allow for synonyms, the inventory will be much more difficult and time-consuming to score. If you use CLOZE for instruction, however, then synonyms are welcome.
5. Advantages include:
   - Easy to construct
   - No questions to create (and possibly misunderstood)
   - No special test development expertise needed
   - Quick and easy to administer
   - For those students who enjoy crossword puzzles or different challenges, CLOZE is like a game.

   Disadvantages include:
   - English language learners who speak an Asian, Slavic, Semitic, or other nonromance language are at a distinct disadvantage because they are not as familiar with the syntax and grammar.

TABLE 6.2 Reading levels Based on CLOZE Scores

Score	Level
58–100	Independent
44–57	Instructional
0–43	Frustration

Other Uses

CLOZE is also a good instructional strategy. If you want to practice general comprehension, just delete every fifth noun and verb—the meaning bearing words. CLOZE provides practice in noting significant details and making inferences. Synonyms are encouraged, deletions vary, and clues can be given such as the first letter of the deleted word, using dashes to indicate the number of letters.

Summary of Strengths and Weaknesses of Informal Assessments

Strengths

- These assessments are authentic. The materials used to measure students' reading comprehension are the very same materials read in the content classroom.
- Data may be aggregated for planning of whole-class instruction and disaggregated to identify students who should be grouped or sent to resource teachers for extra help.
- By writing and scoring questions for these assessments, teachers become more familiar with the content reading challenges faced by students. After addressing these challenges, teachers can include questions on content post-tests to document integrated literacy learning.

Weaknesses

- Authoring, administering, scoring, and interpreting are time-consuming tasks. This is yet one more test that students must complete, taking away time from instruction.
- No grade level scores are provided. Interpretation is subjective.
- The CLOZE puts English language learners at a disadvantage.

Developing a Content IRI and CLOZE
 	
After completing this chapter, construct a content IRI and a CLOZE using a text from your content area and level you plan to teach or are teaching. Rough drafts should be shared with your group for further refinement.
 	
    When your instructor is satisfied with your rough draft of the CIRI, it should be printed, copies run off, and administered to a content class or group of content students.
 	
    Optionally, if time allows, give the CLOZE to the same class or a different one.
	Workshop 6.3

Student, Parent, and Community Input

Students should be involved in the assessment of content literacy learning because, among other things, their concepts of themselves as literate people and the quality of their lives and careers may be at stake. Indeed, the very first IRA standard for assessment is that the interests of the student are paramount in assessment. The reason we integrate content with literacy is because we believe that reading, writing, and talking about subject area knowledge can have a significant impact on the lives of our students. The second IRA standard for assessment states that "The primary purpose of assessment is to improve teaching and learning." Hence, we need to gather input from our students to improve the assessment techniques used to help them success.

The eleventh IRA standard for the assessment of reading and writing reminds us that "parents must be involved as active, essential participants in the assessment process." Parents clearly have an investment in their children's learning and educational future. Parents can provide important information about their children's development as well as valuable insights to student challenges by sharing stories of their children's success and failures as readers and writers of content area knowledge. Let us not forget that parents provide the home environment that can reinforce and expand upon the skills our students acquire at school. Conversely, by learning from parents about the home and culture of our students, we can make reading and writing more authentic.

Finally, the community in which the students, parents, and teachers exist needs to be involved in the assessment of student literacy learning. There are experts in every community about nearly everything we read and write about in our classrooms. When our students complete content area projects, they should be presented to and/or assessed by community members.

Portfolios: A Framework for Ongoing Collaborative Assessment

One of the most powerful ways to involve students, parents, and community members in assessment is through the construction, display, and evaluation of portfolios. A portfolio is a collection of student work in progress. Sometimes referred to as "Literacy Albums," portfolios are now used widely to document and reflect learning. The contents of a portfolio are gathered over time. Each entry should be aligned with a learning objective, which in turn should be aligned with a state or national standard for learning in that content area. Most important, portfolios contain the reflective comments of students, their teachers, parents, and members of the community.

Portfolios encourage us all to look at student learning in terms growth: growth in performance, attitudes, behaviors, and experiences that are reflected in the artifacts placed into the literacy album. Portfolios empower students to be participants in assessing their own learning. Working together students and teacher establish criteria for selecting and evaluating work to be placed in the portfolio—from rough draft to completed work. Input from parents and other family and community members should be part of this process. Checklists and observations assess progress against established benchmarks, which are aligned with standards as determined by the teacher.

Portfolio construction is a three-step process:

Collect: Throughout the year students collect anything they may want to put in their portfolios.

Select: Later students select which of the collected pieces will actually go into the portfolio.

Reflect: Once pieces have been selected, the students write a short reflection introducing the artifact and describing why it is significant. They may also choose to explain how this piece has helped them meet a learning standard.

Portfolios may include any or all of the following depending on goals and purposes.

- artwork
- computer work
- conference forms
- content IRI results
- cooperative activity reports
- criteria for selecting and evaluating work
- graphic representations
- interest surveys
- interviews
- journal entries
- literature logs
- observational checklists
- project analysis
- records of voluntary reading
- "think alouds" (metacognitive scripts)
- video tapes
- vocabulary
- word attack strategies
- word problems
- writing samples
- parent comments
-community member comments

It is important to note that a portfolio is not just a collection of a student's best work, but a reflection of what the student considers to be meaningful progress. Some portfolios are graded using a rubric and this rubric should show progress along a continuum. Nonetheless, all portfolio entries need not be graded. Instead, they may be used for discussion and reflection.

To help students reflect upon the items they have selected, teachers may ask students:

- What makes this an example of your growth as a learner? Why?
- Tell your reader how you went about creating it.
- Did you encounter any problems when you started? What were they?
- Did you have to overcome a problem to finish this work?
- How did you solve these problems?
- Did you set any goals for yourself? How did you accomplish them?
- If you were to do this assignment again, what would you do differently?
- What suggestions do you have for a student who decides to try this same assignment?

Authentic assessment using portfolios should:

- support higher-level thinking
- incorporate authentic real-life tasks
- sample from a wide variety of student learning
- show collaboration between students and their teachers
- show collaboration between students and their families
- show collaboration between students and other members of their communities
- show continuous development, involvement, and integration with other assessment tools
- be a basis for dialogue and decision making

It takes an incredible amount of time and work for a student to create a portfolio. Consequently, it would be a shame if the teacher were the only person to view and assess its contents. Therefore, many schools hold special events to which parents and community members are invited. At these events students are given the opportunity to present the content of the portfolios to family and community members. Often, these guests are encouraged to write comments on assessment forms, which are later reviewed by the teacher and the student.

A Sample Portfolio Record Sheet
(for student/teacher reaction and assessment)

Name _____ **Class** _____ **Date** _____

1. *Writing*
   a. Choose your best writing, mark it a "1" and tell us why it's your best.

   _____

   b. Describe your prewriting activities. How did they help?

   _____

   c. How useful were classmates/comments? _____
   Which did you use?_____

   d. Any problems with mechanics? If so, which ones and what do you plan to do about it next time?_____

e. Anything else you would like me to know?_____

_____

2. *Response Journal (RJ)*

 a. Select two of your best entries to date, star them, and tell why they are your best.

 b. How does writing in your RJ help your learning of this subject?

 c. Have you summarized learnings?

 d. Have you expressed your feelings honestly?

 e. Will you continue using an RJ after this class? Why, or why not?

3. *Cooperative Learning*

 a. Which small group activity did you find to be most helpful? Most interesting? Least helpful? Most boring? Why?

 b. Which copy of a product from a small group activity will be placed in your portfolio as the best cooperative work? Why?

4. *Vocabulary and Word Attack List*

 a. Which words caused you the most difficulty?

 b. What word attack strategies worked best for you when meeting unknown words?

A Sample Unit Self-Assessment Checklist

_____ I cooperated with my small group.

_____ I actively participated in experiments.

_____ I voluntarily selected a collateral book to read on the unit topic.

_____ I responded daily to assignments in my response journal.

_____ I finished my research on my chosen topic.

Summary of Strengths and Weaknesses of Student, Parent, and Community Input through Portfolio Assessment

Strengths

- Student awareness and involvement in their own learning.
- Parent, family, and community involvement in student learning.
- Portfolios can provide detailed authentic samples of what students have learned.
- Family and community responses to portfolios can provide teachers with opportunities to reflect upon our curriculum and instructional practice.

Weaknesses

- The construction, display, and assessment of portfolios is a time-intensive process.
- Involvement of parents and other family members might constitute an infringement on privacy. If a student's family is going through a personal crisis (e.g., divorce, prison, health issue), public display of student readings and writing about these events may not be well received.
- Parents and community members have limited time during the school day to attend portfolio assessment sessions. These events may be held evenings, however, this may be seen as further infringement on valuable family time in the home.

Creating a Triangulation Diagram

Working individually, or in small groups, create a diagram that illustrates the process of triangulation of data when assessing student reading ability. Uses the model provided in Chapter Five, Figure 5.3, or create one of your own. Once done, share your results with colleagues.

Workshop 6.4

 ## Diamante as Summary

(For more about Diamante Poems, see Chapter Eight.)

Norm-referenced
Compared—Others
Formal, Summative, Expensive
Standardized, High-Stakes, Authentic, Formative
Informal, Relaxed, Timely
Compared—Criteria
Criterion-referenced

 ## Summary

Authentic reader assessment requires teachers to gather data about where students are in the process of reading to learn in each specific content area. Assessment should be formative and summative. With this data, teachers can decide about individual needs for instruction—standards that look at student interests and what each student needs to learn next. Standards to guide assessment decisions in reading and writing have been developed to look at student interests and must focus on improving teaching and learning and critical inquiry. Fairness and equity should guide assessment processes and decisions in reading and writing. All of these facets are only considered valid if they use many sources of data and involve parents and the community too.

There are three corners of the reading assessment triangle. The first is standardized test scores. When these are not available, teachers may use standardized test quick assessment tools such as the WRAT, SDQA, or the Basic Reading Inventory. The second corner of the triangle is informal teacher-designed assessment tools such as the content IRI or the CLOZE procedure. Finally, the third corner of the triangle is student, parent, and community input for which the portfolio is a powerful tool.

References and Suggested Readings

Alverman, D. E., & Commeyras, M. (1998). Feminist poststructuralist perspectives on the language of reading assessment: Authenticity and performance. In C. Harrison, M. Bailey, & A. Dewar (Eds.), *New paradigms in reading assessment* (pp. 50–60). London: Routledge.

Asby-Davis, C. (1985, April). CLOZE and comprehension: A qualitative analysis and critique. *Journal of Reading, 28,* 585–589.

Au, K. H., Scheu, J. A., & Kawakami, A. J. (1990). Assessment of students' ownership of literacy. *The Reading Teacher, 44,* 154–156.

Au, K. H., & Valencia, S. W. (1997). The complexities of portfolio assessment. In D. Hansen & N. Barbules (Eds.), *Teaching and its predicaments* (pp.123–144). Boulder, CO: Westview.

Barton, J., & Collins, A. (1993, May–June). Portfolios in teacher education. *Journal or Teacher Education, 44,* 200–210.

Bamburg, J. (Ed.). (1992). *Assessment: How do we know what they know?* Union, WA: Washington State Association for Supervision and Curriculum Development.

Bauer, E. (1999). The promise of alternative literacy assessments in the classroom: A review of empirical studies. *Reading Research and Instruction, 38,* 153–168.

Calfee, R. C., & Perfamo J. (April 1993). Student portfolios: Opportunities for a revolution in assessment. *Journal of Reading, 36,* 532–537.

Clariana, R. B. (1991). A computer administered CLOZE placement test and a standardized reading test. *Journal of Computers in Mathematics and Science Teaching, 10,* 107–113.

Council of Chief State School Officers. (2005). *INTASC standards.* Retrieved March 21, 2005, from http://www.ccsso.org/projects/Interstate_New_Teacher_Assessment_and_Support_Consorti um/

DeSanti, R. J. (1989, Winter). Concurrent and predictive validity of a semantically and syntactically sensitive CLOZE-scoring system. *Reading Research and Instruction, 28,* 19–40.

Ediger, M. (2000–2001). Assessing and improving reading in technical education. *ATEA Journal, 28*(2–3), 18–20.

Fuchs, L. S., Fuchs, D., Hosp, M. K., & Jenkins, J. R. (2001). Oral reading fluency as an indicator of reading competence. *Scientific Studies of Reading, 5*(3), 239–256.

Garcia, G., & Pearson, P. (1994). Assessment and diversity. *Review of Research in Education, 20,* 339–391.

Gillespie, C., Ford, K., Gillespie, R., & Leavell, A. (1996). Portfolio assessment: Some questions, some answers, some recommendations. *Journal of Adolescent and Adult Literacy, 39,* 480–491.

Glazer, S. M., & Brown, C. S. (1993). *Portfolios and beyond: Collaborative assessment in reading and writing.* Norwood, MA: Christopher-Gordon.

Gunning, T. G. (2003). *Building literacy in the content areas.* Boston: Pearson Education Inc.

Harp, B. (1996). *The handbook of literacy assessment and evaluation.* Norwood, MA: Christopher-Gordon.

Hoffman, J. V., Paris, S. G., Salas, R., Patterson, E., & Assaf, L. (2003). High stakes assessment in the language arts: The piper plays, the players dance, but who pays the price? In J. Flood, D. Lapp, J. Squire, & J. Jensen (Eds.), *Handbook of research on the teaching of the English language arts* (2nd ed., pp. 619–630). Mahwah, NJ: Erlbaum.

Hughes, A. (1993). Testing the ability to infer when reading a second or foreign language. *Journal of English as a Foreign Language, 10 & 11,* 13–20.

International Reading Association and National Council of Teachers of English Joint Task Force on Assessment. (1994). *Standards for the assessment of reading and writing.* Newark, DE: International Reading Association.

Jacobson, J. M. (1990, January). Group vs. individual completion of a CLOZE passage. *Journal of Reading, 33,* 244–251.

Johns, J. (2001). *Basic reading inventory,* (8th ed.). Dubuque, IA: Kendall/Hunt Publishing Company.

Justak, J. R., & Bijou, A. (1975). *Wide range achievement test: Reading (WRAT)*(rev. ed.). Wilmington, DE: Guidance Associates.

Kembo, J. A. (2001). Testing of inferencing behavior in a second language. *International Journal of Bilingual Education and Bilingualism, 4*(2), 77–96.

Lambdin, D. V., & Walker, V. L. (1994). Planning for classroom portfolio assessment. *Arithmetic Teacher,* 318–321.

LaPray, M., & Ross, R. (1969, January). The graded word list: Quick gauge of reading ability. *Journal of Reading,* 305–307.

McLaughlin, M., & Vogt, M. E. (1996). *Portfolios in teacher education.* Newark, DE: International Reading Association.

McNeil, L. M. (2000). *Contradictions of school reform: Educational costs of standardized testing.* New York: Routledge.

National Board for Professional Teaching Standards. (2005). *Adolescence and young adult/social studies standards* (2nd ed.). Retrieved June 20, 2005, from http://www.nbpts.org/standards/stds.cfm

Orlofsky, G. F., & Olson, L. (2001). The state of the states. In *Education Week* (Ed.), *A better balance: Standards, tests, and the tools to succeed* (Vol. XX, no. 17, pp. 86–108). Bethesda, MD: Author.

Pearson, P., & Johnson, D. (1978). *Teaching reading comprehension.* New York: Holt, Rinehart & Winston.

Reif, L. (1990). Finding the value of evaluation: Self assessment in the middle school classroom. *Educational Leadership, 47*(6), 24–29.

Ribrician.com. (2005). The official site for links to rubrics. Retrieved June 20, 2005, from http://www.rubrician.com/general.htm

Riddle Buly, M., & Valencia, S. (2002). Below the bar: Profiles of students who fail state reading assessments. *Educational Evaluation and Policy Analysis, 24(*3), 219–239.

Taylor, W. (1953, Fall). CLOZE procedure: A new tool for measuring readability. *Journalism Quarterly, 30*, 415–453.

Vacca, J. A., Vacca R. J., & Gove, M. K. (1995). *Reading and learning to read.* New York: Harper-Collins College Publishers.

Valencia, S. W., Hieger, E. H., & Afflerbach, P. P. (1994). *Authentic reading assessment: Practices and possibilities.* Newark, DE: International Reading Association.

Valencia, S. W., & Wixson, K. (2000). Policy-oriented research on literacy standards and assessment. In M. Kamil, P. Mosenthal, P. D. Pearson, & R. Barr (Eds.), *Handbook of reading research* (Vol. 3, pp. 909–935). Mahwah, HJ: Erlbaum.

Volands, S. R., Topping, K. J., & Evans, R. M. (1999). Computerized self-assessment of reading comprehension with the accelerated reader: Action research. *Reading and Writing Quarterly, 15*(3), 197–211.

Washington Association for Bilingual Education. (1992). Assessment and bilingual education. In J. Bamburg (Ed.), *Assessment: How do we know what they know* (p. 81). Union, WA: Washington State Association for Supervision and Curriculum Development.

Winne, P. H., Graham, L., & Prock, L. (1993). A model of poor readers' text-based inferencing: Effects of explanatory feedback. *Reading Research Quarterly, 28*(1), 53–75.

Wilde, S. (2002). *Testing and standards: A brief encyclopedia.* Portmouth, NH: Heinemann.

Wiggens, G. (1998). *Educative assessment: Designing assessments to inform and improve student performance.* San Francisco: Jossey-Bass.

Wolf, K. P. (1993, April). From informal to informed assessment: Recognizing the role of the classroom teacher. *Journal of Reading,* 518–523.

Wolf, K., & Sie-Runyon, Y. (1996). Portfolio purposes and possibilities. *Journal of Adolescent and Adult Literacy, 40*(1), 30–37.

Young, J. P., Mathews, S. R., Kietzmann, A. M., & Westerfield, T. (1997). Getting disenchanted adolescents to participate in school literacy activities: Portfolio conferences. *Journal of Adolescent and Adult Literacy, 40*(5), 348–360.

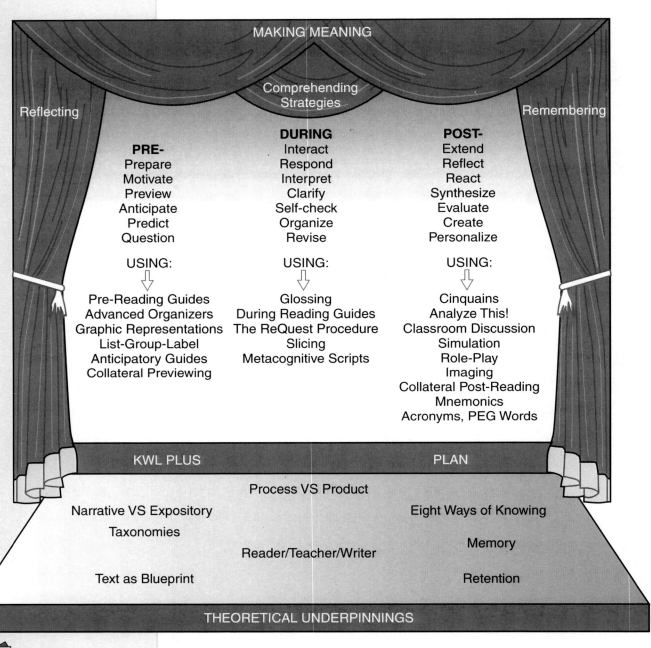

MAKING MEANING

Comprehending
Strategies

Reflecting

Remembering

PRE-
Prepare
Motivate
Preview
Anticipate
Predict
Question

DURING
Interact
Respond
Interpret
Clarify
Self-check
Organize
Revise

POST-
Extend
Reflect
React
Synthesize
Evaluate
Create
Personalize

USING:

USING:

USING:

Pre-Reading Guides
Advanced Organizers
Graphic Representations
List-Group-Label
Anticipatory Guides
Collateral Previewing

Glossing
During Reading Guides
The ReQuest Procedure
Slicing
Metacognitive Scripts

Cinquains
Analyze This!
Classroom Discussion
Simulation
Role-Play
Imaging
Collateral Post-Reading
Mnemonics
Acronyms, PEG Words

KWL PLUS

PLAN

Process VS Product

Narrative VS Expository

Eight Ways of Knowing

Taxonomies

Reader/Teacher/Writer

Memory

Text as Blueprint

Retention

THEORETICAL UNDERPINNINGS

FIGURE 7.1

Making Meaning, Reflecting, and Remembering—A Cognitive Map

Making Meaning, Reflecting, and Remembering

7

Outline

- Anticipatory and Review Questions
- A Sampling of National Performance Standards
- Introduction
  - *Workshop 7.1: Ideas to Ponder*
- The Process of Making Meaning
  - The Comprehending Process vs. the Comprehension Product
  - Narrative vs. Expository Comprehension
- Taxonomies
- From the Content Classroom: Peggy's Story
  - Gardner's Eight Ways of Knowing— Eight Ways of Comprehending
- From the Content Classroom: Jeremy's Story
  - *Workshop 7.2: Applying the Eight Ways of Knowing*
- Directed Reading-Thinking Activities: The Multiple Reading Process Revisited
- Setting the Stage: Pre-Reading Strategies
  - *Workshop 7.3: The Importance of Background Knowledge: What Is the Topic?*
- Parts of the Text Pre-Reading Guides
- Advance Organizers
  - Guidelines for Writing and Teaching with Advance Organizers
- Graphic Representations
  - *Workshop 7.4: Using Cognitive Maps*
  - Guidelines for Constructing and Teaching with Structured Overviews
- List-Group-Label
  - Guidelines for Preparing and Teaching with List-Group-Label
- Anticipatory/Reaction Guides
  - Guidelines for Preparing and Teaching with an Anticipation/Reaction Guide
- Collateral Pre-Reading

- *Workshop 7.5: Using Pre-Reading Strategies*
- During-Reading Strategies
  - Glossing or Gloss Booklets
  - During-Reading Guides
  - ReQuest
    - Guidelines for Preparing and Teaching Using ReQuest Procedure
  - Slicing: A Technique for Modeling Questioning
  - Metacognitive Scripts
    - *Workshop 7.6: Using During-Reading Strategies*
- Post-Reading
  - *Workshop 7.7: What Do We Learn from Comprehension Questions*
  - Cinquains as Summaries
  - Analyze This!: Plus, Minus, Interesting (PMI)
    - Guidelines for Teaching with a PMI
  - Classroom Discussion
  - Simulations/Role-Playing
    - From the Content Classroom: Poor Use of Simulation/Role-Playing
  - Imaging
    - *Workshop 7.8: The Power of Imaging*
  - Collateral (Reiterative) Post-Reading/Viewing
    - *Workshop 7.9: Using Post-Reading Strategies*
- Strategies to Enhance Retention of What Is Read
  - Mnemonics
  - Putting It All Together
  - K-W-L Plus
  - PLAN
- Cinquain as Summary
- Summary
- Answers to Workshop 7.3
- References and Recommended Readings

> "Such happiness as life is capable of, comes from the full participation of all our powers in the endeavor to wrest, from each changing situations of experience, its own full and unique meaning."
>
> *John Dewey*

> "It is clear that very little improvement may be expected from formal drill . . . unless at the same time, provision is made for the enrichment of experience, the development of language abilities, and the improvement of thinking."
>
> *Ernest Horn*

Anticipatory and Review Questions

Literal

1. What is the role of the reader, the teacher, and the writer in the process of comprehending meaning from text?

2. Name at least two pre-reading, during-reading, and post-reading strategies.

Interpretive/Applied

3. Explain the difference between comprehension and comprehending. In what ways might this distinction be significant to teachers when designing assessment and instruction?

4. Write a content assessment question for each of the four levels of comprehending listed in Figure 7.3.

Evaluative/Critical

5. Having analyzed the pre-reading, during-reading, and post-reading strategies described in this chapter, decide which could be used to help students comprehend a chapter in a biology text, a social studies selection about the Great Depression, a Shakespeare play, or an assigned reading from another of your classes.

Creative/Personal

6. Think of a challenging reading assignment you were given to complete independently in high school or college. What aspect of this reading challenge did you find most frustrating? Why? How did this affect your attitude towards reading text in this subject? What could your teacher have done differently?

7. How would you respond to a colleague who claimed that the teaching of reading (including reading for understanding in your content area) is the sole responsibility of those who teach English?

8. You have been assigned to serve on a school team planning and directing a workshop on teaching reading comprehension in the content areas. In 200 words or less, provide an "advanced organizer" of your plan that includes key topics, vocabulary, and organization.

A Sampling of National Performance Standards

- Students employ a wide range of strategies to comprehend, interpret, evaluate, and appreciate texts. They draw on their prior experience, their interactions with other readers and writers, their knowledge of word meaning and of other texts, their word identification strategies, and their understanding of textual features . . . (International Reading Association/National Council of Teachers of English, 1996, p. 31).
- Accomplished Adolescence and Young Adulthood/Science teachers employ a deliberately sequenced variety of research-driven instructional strategies and select, adapt, and create instructional resources to support active student exploration and understanding of science (National Board for Professional Teaching Standards, 2005).
- The professional educator understands and uses a variety of instructional strategies to encourage students' development of critical thinking, problem solving, and performance skills (Council of Chief State School Officers, 2005).

Introduction

Teaching students how to read to learn in the content areas is the essence of integrated content literacy. Hence, helping students to read with understanding, reflect upon, and remember what they have read is the focus of this entire textbook. Let us review what we have studied in the first six chapters in order to put the content of this chapter into context.

In the first two chapters, you, the reader, were situated as a learner and teacher. You were provided with a practical toolbox of note taking/making, listening, and reading rate adaptability strategies to help you read to learn about content literacy instruction. Having had the strategies modeled for you, each chapter then provided suggestions as to how you might incorporate these techniques into your own subject area teaching, thus helping your students read to learn.

More about the difference between learning to read and reading to learn followed in Chapters Three and Four as, you, the teacher-reader, were invited to wrestle with ever-changing definitions of literacy in order to see their evolution into current standards. We have used both evidenced-based research and stories from the pages of our lives to illustrate how literacy skills and attitudes are necessary for achievement. In other words, if teachers want their students to read and write with understanding, they must effectively engage their students in the affective dimensions of the content knowledge they are learning. They must read and write about issues that are relevant to their lives and in ways that are responsive to their realities as individual members of their family and community cultures.

Most teachers, especially those who have earned endorsements in specific content areas, are very knowledgeable about their subjects. Working with curriculum specialists, they strive to find textbooks that address content in relevant and responsive ways. Unfortunately, however, they often learn that their students cannot independently read the textbooks they have so carefully chosen. In Chapters Five and Six we examined methods by which teachers may determine how easy or hard texts are to read (text readability) as well as the means by which teachers may evaluate students' abilities to read, with comprehension, from their specific content-area textbooks (student reading abilities). These assessment data are an important starting point; however, what are teachers to do when the reading skills of our students are not a match for the texts they must read? What can content teachers do to help students, lacking sufficient content reading skills, make meaning from, reflect upon, and remember the content of challenging text?

In Chapter Seven we will address these questions by providing a selection of pre-reading, during-reading, and post-reading strategies that may be adapted to your subject areas to enhance reading to learn. As we did in Chapters One and Two, we will show you how these strategies may work for you as learner and then suggest ways you may want to use them in your classrooms. Before doing so, we will define our terminology and create a framework for the effective use of these strategies. In order to get ready, please take a few minutes to reflect on how you find meaning in what you read.

Ideas to Ponder

Take a few minutes to ponder the statements that follow. Jot down your response to one or more of these statements. Then, prior to a whole-class discussion, share your ideas with a colleague.

1. What we do or think about when reading a text can be more important than what actually exists on the page.
2. What we bring to the print has more effect on comprehension than the facts, action, or description on the page.
3. Meaning resides essentially in the reader, not in the text.

Workshop 7.1

The Process of Making Meaning

Not too many years ago, reading was thought to be text driven. Students, like empty vessels, decoded text in an attempt to fill themselves with the knowledge contained within each book's cover. It was thought that the author had placed meaning within the text, meaning that could best be transmitted through a literal interpretation of the author's choice of words.

The works of Vygotsky, Dewey, Piaget, and others led educators to understand that meaning is created through an interaction between the text and the reader. During this interaction the reader relates the text to personal experiences, to other ideas mentioned within the text, and in the world around them. The text is thus a metaphoric blueprint from which the reader "constructs" meaning.

For example, as you previewed (as discussed in Chapter Two) and then read this chapter you probably looked at the cognitive map, the outline, headings, subtitles, graphics, and boldfaced words. Certain titles may have triggered ideas and memories for you. At the same time you may have felt confused about concepts and methods described within. This confusion should guide your reading as you seek answers to your questions. Some parts of pages may still confuse you. Hopefully, ideas provided by your instructor and colleagues will help clarify your understandings. Thus, the reader, the teacher, and the writer(s) of the text play important roles in the process of making meaning. You may want to refer to Figure 7.2 as we define each of these roles.

The reader's role in this constructive process is one of active learner, using background knowledge or schemata and metacognition (denoting self-monitoring of task and process) to consciously assign personal meaning to the words on each page of a

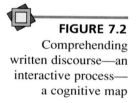

FIGURE 7.2
Comprehending
written discourse—an
interactive process—
a cognitive map

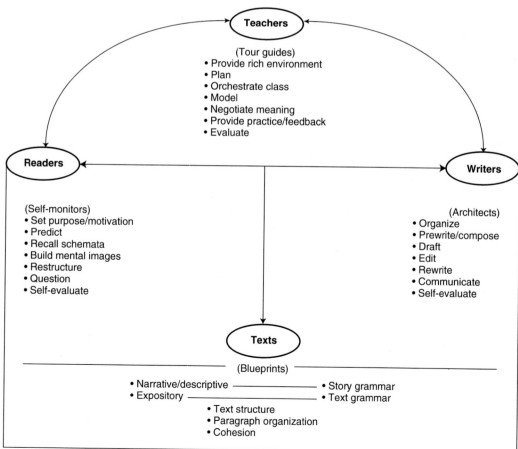

book. Active readers know when they are making sense of their reading and when they are confused. They acknowledge and identify areas from the text that create confusion, and choose from a selection of strategies to help themselves understand it. Less-skilled readers are more likely to be confused and assume that they don't understand the material. This creates a special need for careful support from the teacher.

Teachers play the role of tour guides, helping students negotiate the meaning of what they are seeing. Teachers are familiar with how and why the text is put together in the way it is. Their knowledge of where readers could or should be going (learning objectives of the curriculum), ability to measure understanding (authentic assessment), and sense of how best to help them get there (instructional methodologies) make challenging reading accessible for the reader. Most important, as experts in their content areas, teachers model effective reading comprehension strategies, provide guided practice, and share the joy to be found in connecting what they have read to what they know about themselves, other texts, and the world.

The **writer's role** is very much like that of an architect: organizing, designing, and building into the words and spaces the messages that will be interpreted by readers and teachers. Just as poorly designed buildings put a damper on comfort, poorly designed text can put a damper on the comprehending process. As you know from Chapter Five, the text itself—the style in which it is written, its level of difficulty, or the way information is organized—may also affect the reader's ability to make meaning. However, even a well-designed text can be confusing to those who don't have the background knowledge, strategies, and/or skills necessary to create meaning.

The Comprehending Process vs. the Comprehension Product

As our understanding of active reading evolves, so does our need to distinguish between the process of comprehending and comprehension products. The process of *comprehending* refers to how—not what—we comprehend. It is what we actually do to get at the needed meaning (Harvey & Goudvis, 2000; Pearson, Dole, Duffy, & Roehler, 1992). The process of comprehending may require the following:

- Focusing attention on the topic
- Connecting meanings to what we already know about the topic
- Searching for connections between what we know and the new information we encounter
- Distinguishing which ideas are more or less important in the text
- Predicting what will come later in the material
- Deciding what strategies or skills will serve the reader's needs
- Making inferences (reading between the lines) during and after reading
- Asking questions of ourselves, the authors we encounter, and the texts we read
- Revising predictions as necessary
- Correcting errors in our comprehension
- Monitoring the adequacy of our understanding
- Synthesizing ideas within and across texts
- Evaluating the worth of the message

Thus, comprehending is a complex interactive process that involves building a bridge between what is being read and what we already know about the real world. This building process requires predicting, interpreting, relating ideas into some sort of organizational pattern, deciding what strategies or skills are needed for a given text, revising ideas when necessary, and finally, evaluating the worth of the message. Readers who are good at comprehending move back and forth between concentrating on the message in the print and deciding on the processes needed to meet their purpose.

Comprehension is the end product of comprehending. The term *comprehension* refers to facts, meanings, knowledge, or feelings gained from reading. Comprehension, as measured in a test question, is a measurement of the comprehending process at a fixed point in time. There are those who believe that the overemphasis on testing for comprehension has led us to a generation of students who read to find "the teacher or test writer's answer." Unfortunately, those who are seeking the "the answer" may not be fully engaged in creating their own deeper understanding. While Durkin (1978–1979) and Smith (1978) were among the first to point out that teachers often regard comprehension as the result of learning rather than the basis for making sense out of anything, the surging popularity of educational books that focus on explicit instruction in comprehending strategies testify that some progress is being made.

By now you must be ready to read and explore strategies to teach comprehending. However, before doing so let us make sure we understand the theoretical underpinnings necessary to evaluate these strategies. First, we will discuss the challenge that readers in the intermediate grades face when attempting to read in the content areas. Then we will examine several taxonomies that are used to understand the dimensions of comprehending. Then we will discuss and illustrate several comprehending strategies.

Narrative vs. Expository Comprehension

Young children usually learn to read through contact with narrative material found in basal readers and children's literature. As much as 95% of what emerging readers read is narrative. Most children don't seriously encounter expository material until the third or fourth grade (Alverman & Boothby, 1982). Often little or no attempt is made to teach them how to read expository text. This may seriously impede their ability to use reading in order to learn in science, social studies, and other content areas.

Table 7.1 shows some major differences between narrative and expository writing. Content-area teachers should be familiar with basic writing patterns used in expository text. These include, but are not limited to: (a) classification, (b) compare/contrast, (c)

TABLE 7.1 Narrative versus Expository Writing: What Are the Differences?

Narrative *Trade books story grammar (literary)*	Expository *Textbooks schemata*
• Based on life experiences • Person-oriented (dialogue, familiar language) • Purposes: to entertain, give literary or aesthetic experience • Time—past tense or historical present ("There once was") • Vocabulary—Anglo-Saxon origin, related • Vocabulary—less essential • Chronological links ("first," "one day," "then") • Sentence complexity—sometimes less • Density of concepts—sometimes less • Thought patterns—less varied • Questions—"Who is the main character?" "What happened next?"	• Abstract concepts • Subject-oriented (little dialogue) • Purposes: to explain or present information, inform, persuade • Time—not focal, various tenses used • Vocabulary—Latinate, more complex structurally and semantically • Vocabulary—essential to comprehension • Logical links—(sentence topic and parallel structure keep discourse moving) • Sentence complexity—sometimes greater • Density of concepts—sometimes greater • Thought patterns—more varied • Questions—"What is the subject?" "Focus?" "Topic sentence?"

Source: Adapted from Carolyn Kent, "A Linguist Compares Narrative and Expository Prose," *Journal of Reading* 28 (December 1984): 232–236; and Sandra Stotsky, "A Proposal for Improving High School Students' Ability to Read and Write Expository Prose," *Journal of Reading* 28 (October 1984): 4–7.

explanation of a concept, (d) cause and effect, (e) enumeration of steps in a process, (f) following directions, (g) generalizations, (h) problem-solving diagrams, and (i) sequencing.

Taxonomies

In an effort to better understand the process of comprehending, numerous taxonomies have been developed. The "grandparent" of them all is *Bloom's Taxonomy of the Cognitive Domain* developed in the 1950s. Bloom (1956) sequenced comprehending on six levels: knowledge, comprehension, application, analysis, synthesis, and evaluation. Responding to concerns that "comprehension" should not be the name of the second to lowest level, Norris Sanders (1966) changed this category's name to "interpretation." Thomas Barrett (1968) revised the order somewhat and added "appreciation" at the top. The present authors' adaptation of these arbitrary levels, as seen in Figure 7.3, are "literal," "interpretive/applied," "evaluative/critical," and "creative/personal."

Levels	Skills/Behaviors	Tasks (Verbs)
1. *Literal:* Read lines as stated and recall or restate in own words	1. Determine explicitly stated details 2. Find explicit main ideas 3. Follow directions 4. Determine sequence	List, recall, restate, name, identify, locate, label, recognize, tell, explain, translate, measure, convert
2. *Interpretive/applied:* Thoughtfully read between lines, exercise judgment in selecting and relating relevant information to produce a conclusion or apply to new situation	5. Determine implicit main ideas and details 6. Identify cause/effect or effect/cause 7. Make inferences 8. Predict outcomes 9. Describe character, tone, mood, intent 10 Explain relationships 11. Draw conclusions	Classify, outline, organize, summarize, problem-solve, infer, compare, contrast, illustrate, select, demonstrate, perform, differentiate, analyze, explain, apply, conclude
3. *Evaluative/critical:* Pass personal judgment on truth, accuracy, worth of text and justify based on own stated criteria	12. Compare/contrast 13. Generalize 14. Make value judgments 15. Justify	Judge, justify, generalize, compare/contrast, rate, appraise, value
4. *Creative/personal:* Go beyond message to form personal extensions, develop new ways, show emotional response	16. Form own extensions 17. Explore similar problems 18. Synthesize 19. Find similarities in unrelated materials 20. Examine possible consequences 21. Suggest new solutions 22. Use visual imagery 23. Empathize with characters or situation 24. Appreciate	Create, design, synthesize, respond with feeling, stand up for, volunteer, empathize, image, appreciate

FIGURE 7.3

Comprehension Levels, Skills, Behaviors, and Tasks (An aid to writing objectives and questions)

Figure 7.3 shows the skills, behaviors, and tasks that might be connected to each level and can serve as a reference for teachers when developing lesson plans, objectives, and questions.

Regardless of the names used to list levels of comprehending, one possible misinterpretation of taxonomies is to think that they are developmental, assuming that academic content at each level has to be mastered before a student can move on to the next level. As a result, many at-risk students are tracked into remedial groups, which remain at the "knowledge" level until they have memorized their "facts." Consequently, our students who are struggling with reading may not be receiving enough crucial support or acknowledgment. They need explicit guidance in ways to interpret, evaluate, and creatively think about assigned readings. (For an example of this, read Peggy's story, described below.) Correctly used, taxonomies enable students and teachers to assess the level of thinking required for answering questions about content at all levels.

FROM THE CONTENT CLASSROOM

Peggy's Story

Peggy, a high school sophomore, was placed in remedial reading and social studies classes because of her poor performance in academic subjects that required reading and memorization. For example, in her freshman-level history class, she failed test after test because she had trouble remembering names, dates, and places.

One Friday, in an attempt to fill the remainder of Friday class period, the reading teacher drew the following symbol on the board. He then asked students, in groups, to generate a list of answers to these questions: (1) What is this? (2) What might it be a symbol for? (3) How might you describe it?

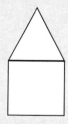

Within 15 minutes students generated lists totaling nearly 100 items. Some said it was a triangle on top of a square, a piece of cheese, a picture hanging from a wall, a symbol for a house or school, an upside-down ice cream cone with a square tab of ice cream, candy corn, etc. Confident that his students had thought of all but a few of the possibilities, their teacher offered one point extra credit for each group of five additional items they listed as homework over the weekend.

Peggy returned Monday with a list of 130 additional items. These included: (a) the rubber tip at the end of the toothbrush used for gum massage, (b) the shadow of a Klu Klux Klansman sitting on an orange crate, (c) a clown's hat, (d) the nose of a jack'o lantern, (e) a refrigerator magnet, (f) a backrest pillow, and (g) a mouse (she explained that you need to turn the object onto its side, add feet, a tail, and whiskers.)

How was it possible that this remedial reading and social studies student who was unable to pass history and English was able to generate such a long list of answers on the levels of application, synthesis, and evaluation? Is it possible that Peggy, who clearly can think divergently, is not being asked to do so very often? How could a teacher help Peggy use her creative thinking skills as she reads new material?

Gardner's Ways of Knowing—Eight Ways of Comprehending

According to Howard Gardner, intelligence refers to "the human ability to solve problems or make something that is valued in one or more cultures" (Gardner, 1983). Gardner believes that there are at least eight ways by which the human brain/mind system approaches these tasks. He calls these multiple intelligences the "Eight Ways of Knowing."

Each of the "Eight Ways of Knowing" are processes by which we "make meaning" or "comprehend" text. For the sake of improving your understanding of this chapter, you might want to call them "eight ways of *comprehending*." As you read these eight ways of knowing (comprehending), consider the many ways that you can plan and assess student learning.

Verbal/Linguistic: Demonstrated in the capacity to use language to express what is on your mind and to understand other people. Poets, orators, speakers, and lawyers rely on this intelligence. People use this type of thinking when they create metaphors, similes, write their own sequels to stories, participate in discussions, or keep personal journals. In the past, most Western literacy curricula have focused almost exclusively on this and the logical/mathematical way of demonstrating comprehension.

Logical/Mathematical: Most often associated with "scientific thinking," inductive reasoning and deductive reasoning. People with highly developed logical/mathematical intelligence understand the underlying principles of some kind of causal system, and/or how to manipulate numbers, quantities, and operations. People use this kind of thinking when they create outlines, provide rational explanations, or use the scientific method to quantify the answer to a question.

Note: Verbal/linguistic and logical mathematical ways of knowing form the basis for most current intelligence tests, standardized achievement tests, and college entrance exams used in our current system of education. There are at least six other ways for students to comprehend text, which should be included.

Visual/Spatial: The ability to represent the spatial world the way a sailor navigates the ocean, a pilot navigates space, a chess player visualizes the chess board, or a sculptor makes art from a large rock. People use this type of thinking to draw maps, timelines, and diagrams. This way of knowing usually requires the use of artistic media (paints, clay, markers, etc.). The challenge of this type of thinking is making sure that students elaborate sufficiently to show the depth of their understanding in their final products.

Bodily/Kinesthetic: The capacity to use the body or parts of the body to solve a problem, make something, or put on some kind of a production. The most evident examples of people who have developed this intelligence include athletes and performing artists, particularly dancers and actors. People use this type of thinking when they role-play an idea, opinion, or feeling. For example, students might be asked to physically demonstrate what a gnarly tree looks like.

Musical/Rhythmic Intelligence: The capacity to think in music, to be able to hear patterns, recognize, remember, and manipulate them. Many of us learned the alphabet through this intelligence and the "A-B-C" song. All of us are constantly bombarded by melodies from commercials that linger in our minds. Melody and rhythm may be used to inspire beliefs, intensify feelings, or express great loss or profound joy. One way to get students to use this kind of thinking is to have them borrow a common melody, such as "Old MacDonald" to construct a song that demonstrates an understanding of the concepts of a reading. Older students might be asked to write a "rap song" that carries a similar message.

Interpersonal: An individual's ability to understand other people, work cooperatively in a group, and/or communicate verbally and nonverbally with other people. This is an ability we all need; however, it is at a premium if you are a teacher, clinician, salesperson, or politician. People who use this kind of intelligence demonstrate genuine empathy for another's feelings, fears, anticipations, and beliefs. Rubrics used to evaluate cooperative learning can be helpful in assessing how students use this way of knowing to grasp the content of what appears in text.

Intrapersonal: How readers are able to demonstrate an understanding of themselves, who they are, what they can or can't do. Those who grasp the world through this way of knowing are capable of self-reflection and have a sense of or intuition about spiritual realities. This intelligence is the most private and requires use of the other intelligences to be expressed.

Naturalist: The human abilities to recognize and value the nature that is behind our thoughts and thus demonstrate awareness of the features of the natural world (clouds, rock configurations, etc.). This ability was clearly of value in our distant past when humans depended on hunting, gathering, and farming for their survival. People with this sort of intelligence understand the importance of considering cycles in nature or relating one aspect of nature to another. Plant identification, horticultural understanding, and the ability to recognize cultural artifacts may also depend on this way of knowing. To encourage students to use this way of thinking to develop understanding, ask students to make recommendations as to how to sort objects included as part of a text.

Proponents of using the "Eight Ways of Knowing" to plan and implement literacy instruction point out that everyone can develop their abilities for comprehending in each of the eight ways.

FROM THE CONTENT CLASSROOM

Jeremy's Story

Jeremy, a 16-year-old high school student, consistently received poor grades due to his poor behavior in class until he had a social studies teacher who placed a heavy emphasis on cooperative learning. At midterm he approached his social studies teacher to ask about his current grade. When he was told he had a "B," he smiled gratefully and told him, "I have never been able to get a good grade in social studies because I am constantly being criticized for being out of my seat and talking to others. You are the first teacher who understands that I need to talk with others to be able to comprehend what I am supposed to be reading."

His teacher complimented Jeremy. "Your ability to talk with others and get them to talk about what they are learning (interpersonal intelligence) makes you an asset to this class. My goal is to get you to teach other students how to think out loud with each other." From that day forward, when the teacher assigned small-group work, Jeremy was asked to roam from group to group to "stir-up" conversation about the topic. With time, groups that were "stuck" asked Jeremy to help them out. Jeremy became more knowledgeable, and went on to earn an "A-" in this class.

Workshop 7.2	**Applying the Eight Ways of Knowing** Divide into groups. Pick a chapter from a textbook from one of your content areas. Plan one activity in which students may comprehend the text with each of the "Eight Ways of Knowing." Share your findings with the class.

Directed Reading-Thinking Activities: The Multiple Reading Process Revisited

In Chapter Five we studied methods to determine how easy or hard a text is to read. In Chapter Six we studied ways to determine what reading abilities our students bring to these same texts. These assessment data are an important starting point; however, what are teachers to do when the reading skills of students are not a good match for the texts we want them to read? What can we do to help students who lack sufficient content reading skills make meaning from, reflect upon, and remember the content of challenging text? One answer is to design directed reading-thinking activities or DRTAs. A DRTA is an adaptation of directed or guided reading lessons used successfully at the elementary level.

Do you remember the MRP (multiple reading process) discussed in Chapter Two? A directed reading-thinking activity is an instructional application of the MRP. As you may recall, the three stages of the MRP are (1) previewing or pre-reading, (2) reading, and (3) post-viewing or post-reading. Definitions and sample student learning objectives for each stage are listed in Chapter 2. The DRTA is also divided up into three stages: pre-reading (readiness, anticipation, and preparation), during-reading (guided reading), and post-reading (reflections, reactions, applications, and extensions) as illustrated in Table 7.2.

TABLE 7.2 Strategies: Teacher/Student/Text

Prereading—Orient to Print	During Reading—Guided Reading	Postreading—Process the Reading
Build, activate, and enrich background information	Focus	Provide feedback
Preview/survey	Rehearse	Elaborate
Predict/question	Recite	Stimulate thinking by asking reflective questions
Motivate with concrete examples, objects, etc.	Guide reader/text interactions	Lead discussion
Preteach key vocabulary	Induce imagery	Summarize
Use analogies	Model self questions/adjunct questions	State major concepts and generalizations
State objectives	Provide notes facilitators/lesson frameworks	Use mapping
Provide pretests/prequestions	Gloss	Use cinquains as synthesizers
Use advance organizers	Provide study guides	Use English debates
Brainstorm	Guide writing	Use simulation/role play
Dress as a character		Use visual imagery
Provide attention-getting skit		Draw, illustrate
Write		Dramatize
		Integrate/synthesize with other subjects

The underlying principle of both the MRP and DRTA is that comprehension is a layered process. Each time we comprehend something we add to our prior knowledge. We use the assessment data we have to design lessons that help students to prepare to read the text, guide them through the reading, and/or provide them with opportunities to react, apply, and integrate this content after reading. Because no single strategy will meet the needs of all teachers or all students, teachers and readers need to select and adapt these ideas to fit their own teaching and reading needs.

Setting the Stage: Pre-Reading Strategies

In Chapter Two, we discussed the role pre-reading (previewing) plays in the multiple reading process. In summary, pre-reading serves five objectives.

While previewing, the reader does the following:

1. Establishes the purpose for reading
2. Activates background knowledge
3. Identifies the main ideas of the passage
4. Locates key vocabulary and sources for their definitions
5. Asks questions and sets goals for comprehension

Before going on, you may want to complete Workshop 7.3. This may be done individually, or as part of a group. This workshop will provide you with an opportunity to experience why identification of the main idea and activation of background knowledge are essential to reading with comprehension.

Workshop 7.3

The Importance of Background Knowledge: What Is the Topic?

Read the two passages that follow carefully. Your primary goal should be to identify the topic of each passage. A secondary goal will be to explain how the passage is organized (sequenced). You may read them as many times as you wish. Depending on your background and/or experiences, you may find one passage more comprehensible than the other.

Passage A

It really doesn't matter whether yours is black, brown, yellow or red. Most will agree, however, that those with red pigmentation gather more attention. From the inside, all maneuver in similar fashion; nonetheless, you will find that each is a bit different from the other. Make sure you are seated comfortably and that you can see where you are going. Engage the mechanism with your foot. Start up and go to number one. Now that you are ready, your first objective will to find the "sweet spot." Feed the monster with your right foot. No one can do it for you. You must do it on your own. The "sweet spot" is usually in the middle. If it is too close to the top, prepare to spend money. One, two, three, four . . . you will repeat this sequence thousands of times and it will get easier with practice. It is best to proceed in order on the way up; however, feel free to skip on your way down. If all this seems overwhelming, there is another more expensive option. Know that going that route will mean giving up some control.

Passage B

Some think they are like lice—irritating, pervasive, and lascivious. Before they start to get through, you would be wise to seek protection. You may try to filter them out, but it is inevitable that one or two will find their way into your habitat. Unfortunately, they tend to travel in waves: one or two today, one hundred-and-two tomorrow. It is difficult to foresee an end to them. You check in, and there they are. They go where you go. What is worse, some carry diseases that can tear your insides apart! Nonetheless, some people must welcome them, into their homes and offices. Someone—somewhere must enjoy them. Is it because of these few admirers that the rest of us must suffer? Who would have thought that our forefathers had this in mind when they wrote the First Amendment? Someone should pass a law.

Referring to Passage A and then Passage B, answer the following:

1. What is the topic of the passage? How many times did you have to read the passage to figure this out? Why?
2. How is the passage organized or sequenced? What vocabulary is used to describe content unique to the topic?
3. What background knowledge was necessary in order to comprehend this passage?
4. What group of people might be at a distinct disadvantage in comprehending the meaning of this passage?
5. Let us assume that a teacher is about to give these passages to students to read independently. Several students are at a distinct disadvantage because they lack background knowledge about the topic. Before students start to read, what should the teacher do to help their chances of comprehending?

The topics of Passage A and Passage B may be found at the end of the chapter.

Pre-Reading strategies described in this chapter include:

1. Parts of the Text Pre-Reading Guides
2. Advance Organizers
3. Graphic Representations (Cognitive Maps and Structured Overviews)
4. List-Group-Label
5. Anticipatory Guides
6. Collateral Pre-reading/showing/viewing

Please keep in mind that each of these strategies may fall under more than one category. Also remember that some students may already be familiar with some of these strategies.

Parts of the Text Pre-Reading Guides

With the guidance of their teacher (preferably in person, but if not, in the form of an easy-to-read and complete worksheet), students skim through their texts using text features such as the titles, subtitles, and graphics to answer questions. There are five reasons for doing this chapter preview:

1. We want to set our purpose for our reading. We can do this by turning through the chapter and skimming to see what is there.
2. We want to find out what the main ideas of this chapter are. This will help us to understand it better when we actually read it.
3. There are many things in this chapter that we already know. We want to find out what they are.
4. There may be new vocabulary words here. We want to locate them and find out where their definitions are located.
5. Once we know what we know, and know what the new vocabulary words are, we can set some goals for what we want to know when we are finished reading.

If this preview is done orally, dialogue should be encouraged. Here are some sample questions for a chapter pre-reading guide:

I. Look at the first page.

1. What is the title? What do you think this chapter will be about?
2. What do you think you might already know about this topic?
3. How does this chapter connect with the rest of the book? (Hint: What chapter did we read last? What chapter will we read next?)
4. What do you think we will find out as we read? What makes you think that?
5. Now look at the pictures on this page. Are there captions? What do they tell you about this chapter?
6. Are there any boldfaced words or words in italics on this page? Are definitions provided? Where?

II. Look at the last page of this chapter.

1. Are there questions at the end of the chapter? If so, let's read them to help figure out what we need to know when we are done.

2. Is there a summary at the end of the chapter? If so, let's read this to see if this answers any of our questions about this chapter.

3. What questions do you still have about this chapter?

III. Let's now turn through the chapter from beginning to end.

Let's go back to the first page.

1. Are there any subtitles? What do they tell you about this part of the chapter? Might the answer to one of your questions be on this page? Why do you think this is so?

2. Let's go to the next page. Look for subtitles, pictures, captions, and boldfaced words. What do they tell you about this page? What questions might be answered?

3. Now let's go to the next page.

IV. (After inspecting each page of a chapter.) Here are some questions we should be able answer:

1. What is the main idea of this chapter?

2. What do you already know about this?

3. How are the ideas of this chapter organized?

4. Are there new vocabulary words in this chapter? Where can you find their definitions?

5. What information in this chapter do you need/want to know? Where is it located?

6. If you have trouble with a specific part of this chapter, who might be able to help you?

Advance Organizers

Have you ever noticed that most articles in professional journals feature a 100- to 150-word abstract directly after the title? These abstracts help us determine whether or not we should read the rest of the article. (Reading the abstract can help us determine if its content serves our purpose for reading it.)

Think again, this time as a teacher who wants to help students pre-read a difficult article. Careful reading of an abstract may enable the reader to activate prior knowledge and set goals for comprehension. A well-written abstract provides readers with the main idea of the manuscript, key vocabulary, and hints about its organization.

An advance organizer (Ausubel, 1968) provides a brief summary, at a more abstract level, of the more detailed text material. Ideally, this pre-reading aide is 50 to 500 words in length and is written by content teachers in simple rather than complex language. Well acquainted with their students, content teachers may use advance organizers to relate new content to students' existing knowledge.

Ausubel describes two types of advance organizers: expository and comparative, an important distinction to keep in mind when constructing such an aid to pre-reading. An expository advance organizer is written for completely unfamiliar new material, providing an "idea" scaffold or summary that introduces what might be entirely new concepts. A comparative advance organizer is written for materials with which students are already familiar. A comparative advance organizer provides pre-readers with explicit suggestions on how to discriminate between the similarities and differences of the new text and the other readings they have already done on this topic.

Guidelines for Writing and Teaching with Advance Organizers

1. Read the chapter carefully, noting major ideas.

2. Reorder these ideas into a hierarchy that will show their relationship to each other from the superordinate (most general) to the subordinate (most specific).

3. Write a 50- to 300-word passage showing the relationship, or order, that the readers should understand while reading the chapter. Whether or not you intend to read this to your students, or have them read it independently, it is important that this passage be written.

4. Duplicate the written organizer, distributing it to students before they read the chapter. When time permits, read it aloud, pausing at key points to pose and answer questions with your students. Have students place their copies in their notebooks to use for future reference.

For more on this important pre-reading strategy, see Appendix G.

Graphic Representations

As Howard Gardner would be quick to point out, there are many more ways to learn about the world than verbal linguistic. Graphic representations (also called schematic organizers) are especially helpful to those who learn visually. The two we recommend for pre-reading are **cognitive maps** and **structured overviews.**

You are in a position to evaluate the effectiveness of **cognitive maps** for yourself. A cognitive map appears at the beginning of each chapter of this text. Hilda Taba (1967) believed that teachers should develop their own cognitive maps of content before attempting to facilitate class discussion. Cognitive maps use pictures and illustrations to symbolize meaning. Those who are visual learners and those whose English skills are emerging may benefit from the illustrations. Each cognitive map in this text took many tries to complete. The form or shape evolved over time with many revisions. Cognitive maps therefore tend to be more creative than outlines or flow diagrams.

Using Cognitive Maps

Join with others to form several small groups. Each group should pick a chapter they have already read from this book. Examine the cognitive map. Discuss its design. What ideas and vocabulary are introduced? What features were especially helpful to you? Why? After you are done, you might want to look at the cognitive map for this chapter and discuss ways it can help you in comprehending the rest of this chapter.

Workshop 7.4

Construction of cognitive maps provides creative opportunities for content teachers to introduce readers to the most important vocabulary in a chapter while helping them relate pertinent new information to their existing knowledge. Students should be told to examine them both before and after reading the chapter. Like recall diagrams (Chapter One), cognitive maps encourage students to fill in the gaps.

Barron & Stone (1974) conceived of the idea of a **structured overview**. While planning lessons for a difficult chapter of a biology class, he decided to use a diagram to show how several of the new vocabulary words in a chapter were related, and then how each concept represented by those words related to the content of the chapter as a whole. He then brought this diagram to his students and asked them to add words they already knew to his diagram. He continued this process during and after the students read the passage. Please see Figure 7.4 for an example of the teacher-constructed initial overview for a social studies lesson. Then see Figure 7.5 for what the same overview looked like once the class had given its input.

Guidelines for Constructing and Teaching with Structured Overviews

1. List representative vocabulary words that students will need to understand.
2. Play with the list, rearranging until you have a diagram that shows the interrelationships among the concepts they represent.
3. Simplify or amplify the list as needed.
4. Think of what icons or illustrations you might be able to use that will help students picture what the words and concepts mean. This will be helpful to all students, especially those with limited English skills.
5. Place on an overhead or on the board.
6. When introducing the structured overview, show students *only* initial attempts in diagramming. Explain your arrangement and then encourage them to add what they already know about the topic.
7. Continue to refer and add to the structured overview during and after reading.

List-Group-Label

Originally conceived of as a means to help students remember elementary social studies vocabulary, Massey and Heafner (2004) suggest that list-group-label (LGL) (Taba, 1967) may be used as a pre-reading instructional strategy to help students, who have some background knowledge on a topic organize what they already know. Keeping in mind Gardner's points about interpersonal intelligence, this strategy provides ample opportu-

FIGURE 7.4

An initial structured overview for social studies.

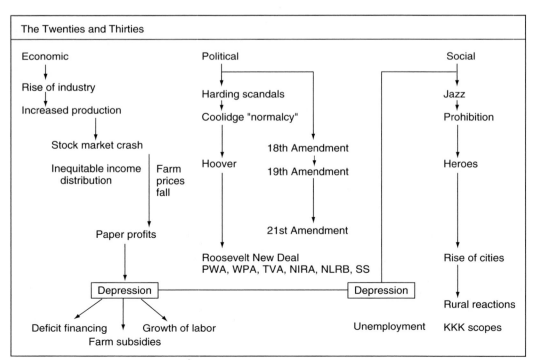

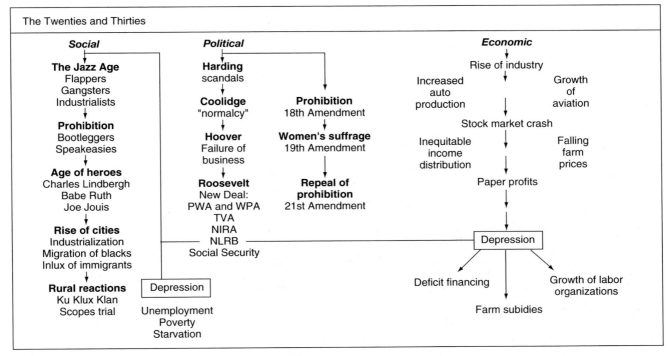

The Twenties and Thirties

Social

The Jazz Age
Flappers
Gangsters
Industrialists

Prohibition
Bootleggers
Speakeasies

Age of heroes
Charles Lindbergh
Babe Ruth
Joe Jouis

Rise of cities
Industrialization
Migration of blacks
Inlux of immigrants

Rural reactions
Ku Klux Klan
Scopes trial

Depression
Unemployment
Poverty
Starvation

Political

Harding
scandals

Coolidge
"normalcy"

Hoover
Failure of
business

Roosevelt
New Deal:
PWA and WPA
TVA
NIRA
NLRB
Social Security

Prohibition
18th Amendment

Women's suffrage
19th Amendment

Repeal of prohibition
21st Amendment

Economic

Rise of industry

Increased auto production

Growth of aviation

Stock market crash

Inequitable income distribution

Falling farm prices

Paper profits

Depression

Deficit financing

Farm subsidies

Growth of labor organizations

FIGURE 7.5

Structured overview: Completed by class.
Prepared by Nancy Bohlander Willis, graduate student, University of New Mexico. Used with permission.

nities for student discussion and thus gives chances for students to learn from each other. At the same time, LGL may provide the teacher with opportunities to redirect misconceptions and/or supply information that addresses gaps in student knowledge.

Guidelines for Preparing and Teaching with List-Group-Label

1. *List:* Select a topic from the materials the students will read. Write this topic (one or two words) on the board or on an overhead. Students brainstorm a **list** of words and phrases related to the topic. The class should generate a list of at least 25 words. The teacher then reads and records all words onto the master list on the overhead or board. This reading is done aloud so that each student has the chance to hear the correct pronunciation. The teacher may use this opportunity to clarify the meaning of words on the master list, correct misconceptions or incorrect information, and/or to provide additional background information.

2. *Group*: Students are asked to **group** the words from their list into smaller categories. Each group of words should have something in common with one another. Ask, "Which of these items go together because they are alike in some way?" Ask "why" often. Each group of words should also have at least three words. Students may add words if they wish. A "miscellaneous" pile may be used for words that don't fit into any other group. A "misinformation" pile might be created for words that they have learned don't belong on any list because they are incorrect or irrelevant to the topic. Once all the words from the original list have been grouped into smaller lists, move to label.

3. *Label*: Students are asked to study their categorized lists and give each list a **label**. This label or title should reflect what each item on the list has in common. Ask students "why" they think this label is a good one.

A completed LGL example may be seen in Figure 7.6.

Anticipation/Reaction Guides

One effective means to activate prior knowledge, and at the same time focus readers' goals for comprehension, is to challenge readers' preconceived notions. **Anticipation guides** (Herber, 1978) are a series of five to seven controversial or debatable statements to which readers respond before they read. The statements are carefully worded with two goals in mind: (1) to get readers to think about what they know about the topic, and (2) to arouse curiosity and interest about whether or not their preconceived notion will be substantiated in the text they are about to read.

Preconceived notions may be correct; however, often they are misconceptions. When reading factual material, especially in science and math, confronting misconceptions early and directly can be helpful in bringing about new understandings (Guzzetti, Snyder, Glass, & Gamas, 1993). Similarly, readers of the social sciences must compare the perspective(s) of an author with their own. To meet these needs many content teachers construct anticipation/reaction guides.

An **anticipation/reaction guide** requires students to respond to the five to seven statements *both before and after* reading the document. As described above, readers

FIGURE 7.6

List, Group, and Label (a sample of a grouped word list)

Attackers and Their Friends	**Targets of Attackers**
Terrorists	World Trade Center, New York City
Osama Bin Laden	The Pentagon, Washington, D.C.
Hijackers	Those who "worked for capitalism"
Taliban in Afghanistan	Military planners
Saddam Hussein?	The White House (instead a field in Pennsylvania)
Victims and Heroes	**Weapons Used**
Those who worked in the buildings	Box cutters
Firefighters who tried to help	4 hijacked planes full of explosive fuel
Police who tried to help	Surprise attack (like Pearl Harbor?)
People near the buildings	Anthrax? (in post office)
Airplane passengers	
People who breathed the air (later on)	**Misc.**
Those on plane in Pennsylvania	Tons of rubble
	Early in the morning
What America Did Next	American flag
National Emergency	Mayor Giuliani
American flags everywhere	
Searched for trapped people	**Misinformation**
Set up Homeland Security	Missiles were fired at the Pentagon
Froze all money assets of enemies	
Attacked Afghanistan	
Attacked Iraq	

complete the anticipation guide marking their answers in the "before reading" columns. The reaction section of the guide requires the readers to complete the "after reading" columns. These columns require the readers to indicate whether or not the author agrees with each statement, and in some cases to provide evidence or substantiation of the author's point of view from the reading itself. For example:

(BEFORE reading)   A = Agree   D = Disagree   **(AFTER reading)**

(Your opinion)   (The author's point of view)

A	D		A	D	Author's evidence	Page #
		Fat is bad for you.				
		A gram of fat contains more than two times as much energy as a gram of carbohydrate (starch or glucose) or protein.				
		If you want to lose weight, you should cut out all fats and carbohydrates.				
		Over the long-term, "carbo-loading"—the consumption of large quantities of carbohydrates by athletes before a big race can result in consequences that make this practice unhealthy.				
		Apples contain fat.				
		Too much cholesterol will lead to a stroke or heart attack.				

This strategy may also be used before and after listening to lectures, watching videos, interacting with instructional software, or combinations of all of the above.

Guidelines for Preparing and Teaching with an Anticipation/Reaction Guide

1. Identify the major ideas or concepts and relevant supporting details in the text.
2. Create five to seven controversial or debatable statements. (See sample above.) Doing so will require that you keep your audience in mind. Don't write statements about content your students know nothing about. After all, one needs at least a little bit of background knowledge to agree or disagree. Avoid statements that can be answered true or false. The best statements are those that require students to evaluate their knowledge, beliefs, and opinions (Readance, Moore, & Rickelman, 2000). Johns and Berglund (2002) suggest that teachers use a variety of words for the columns that students check. For example:

Agree	Tend to Agree	Likely	Disagree	Tend to Disagree	Unlikely

3. Write these statements on an overhead. Before reading, have students respond to these statements. (This may be done with the group as a whole, or by dividing into smaller groups.) If you want to collect individual responses and read this prior to

discussion, have students answer on a sheet of paper and leave space for students to provide you with written rationalizations of their answers.

4. Discuss student responses with the group as a whole. Then summarize their opinions, leaving room for controversy, doubt, and thus, questions, to be answered from the reading itself.

5. Read the text. Those completing an anticipation/reaction guide should complete the after-reading reaction column.

6. Engage students in a follow-up discussion to determine whether or not their ideas have changed and why.

Collateral Pre-Reading

Collateral reading is the use of any media (textual or nontextual) that supports, enriches, or broadens the experience of the reader (Haag, 1992). **Collateral pre-reading** is the use of such media to activate/acquire relevant background knowledge, identify and organize ideas and vocabulary unique to the content, and trigger questions that may guide the comprehending process when reading the intended text itself. Crafton (1983) demonstrated that students who read two different articles on the same topic dramatically improve their comprehension on the second article. This is the principle by which some teachers invite "Cliff Notes" and/or "SparkNotes" into their classrooms. Yes, we know that some students have substituted the reading of these study guides for the actual text. When readers do so, they are not doing collateral reading; they are substituting one text for the other.

Used properly as a pre-reading tool, media can help prepare students for text they wish to read. Think of the millions of books sold after a movie becomes popular. The background knowledge gained from the movie fosters interest and ability to comprehend text with the same topic. Using a mixture of content-rich electronic text from CD-ROM or Internet websites, video from public or cable television offerings, or any article from a popular magazine or local newspaper can help your students develop the background knowledge needed to read material about the topic with greater comprehension.

Workshop 7.5	**Using Pre-Reading Strategies** Gather together with three or four of your colleagues. Consider the six pre-reading strategies described above. Collectively, select a passage from a book in one of your respective disciplines. Plan together how you might use a pre-reading strategy to help students better comprehend this passage.

During-Reading Strategies

Pre-reading strategies are helpful to set the stage for such reading. Once these are completed, it is time to read. However, when reading material is difficult, that is, when the readability of the material is beyond the reading abilities of the students, teachers need to help students learn to select strategies to aid in comprehending. Five such strategies are described in this chapter. The first two may be used when teachers cannot be present. These are especially helpful if the reading is assigned to be done as homework. The remaining techniques are especially effective if done in class.

1. Glossing or gloss booklets
2. During-reading guides
3. ReQuest
4. Slicing
5. Metacognitive scripts

Glossing or Gloss Booklets

Have you ever read from an annotated text? Popular Bible study/commentaries and some textbook study guides are set up this way. The text appears in the center of the page. In the margins are definitions of words, important background information, explanations of hard-to-grasp concepts, and/or sources for additional information. Reading from a text with annotations is like having a teacher sitting in the margins. Perhaps this is why hypertext, which is often set up this way, is becoming so popular. As you read the passage, there are "hot-links" to definitions and additional information. In an ideal world any text that a student was required to read independently would be annotated. Students who read the text easily can, if they wish, choose to ignore most glosses.

We don't yet live in an ideal world, but we can construct a gloss for hard-to-read chapters and source documents. One popular way to do this is to create a gloss booklet. To construct a gloss booklet, do the following:

1. Read the chapter carefully, identifying difficult vocabulary, requisite background information, hard-to-grasp concepts and sources of additional information.

2. On separate pages that you can duplicate, identify page numbers. Some gloss creators split the glossing page in half, writing information for one textbook page on one side, and the next textbook page on the other. (See photos in Figure 7.7.) This allows students to insert each copy in their text opposite the page to be read.

3. Using page and/or line numbers, provide readers with the information needed to better comprehend the passage. (See Figure 7.8 for an example of a gloss.)

4. Remember to personalize your gloss with what you know about your students and your courses. That is, refer to what you know they have already read, studied, or discussed in or out of class (e.g., use inside jokes when they are appropriate).

 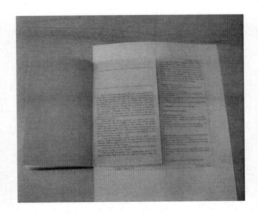 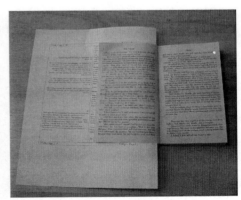

 FIGURE 7.7

A sample part of a gloss for one page of Elie Wiesel's *Night* (1982).
See Figure 7.8 for a detailed example of this gloss.

The "I" in this story is the author, Elie Wiesel. As we have discussed in class, he is a survivor of the Holocaust. It took him ten years to write this book. As you read, try to figure out why it was so hard for him to write about what happened to him, to his family, and to his neighbors. On this first page, read to find out how old he was at the start of the story. Also read to find out about Moshe, the man to whom he introduces us on the first page.

They called him Moshe the Beadle, as though he had never had a surname in his life. He was a man of all work at a Hasidic synagogue. The Jews of Sighet—that little town in Transylvania where I spent my childhood—were very fond of him. He was very poor and lived humbly. Generally my fellow townspeople, though they would help the poor, were not particularly fond of them. Moshe the Beadle was the exception. Nobody ever felt encumbered by his presence. He was a master in the art of making himself insignificant, or seeming invisible.

Moshe—Hebrew for Moses. A **beadle** is a helper, in this case, a person who helped around the synagogue. A **surname** is a person's last name. Does the author ever tell you Moshe's last name? Why do you think that is?

A **synagogue** is a Jewish house of worship. Hasidic is a form of Judaism. To read more about Hasidic Judaism, go to this URL http://religiousmovements.lib.virginia.edu/nrms/hasid.html

Why do you think the townspeople never felt encumbered (bothered) by Moshe being around?

Physically, he was as awkward as a clown. He made people smile, with his waiflike timidity. I loved his great, dreaming eyes, their gaze lost in the distance. He spoke little. He used to sing, or rather, to chant. Such snatches as you could hear told of the suffering of the divinity, of the Exile of Providence, who, according to the cabbala, awaits his deliverance in that of man.

A **waif** is a stray person. **Timid** means lacking courage or self-confidence. So we know that he is clumsy, timid, and waiflike. This didn't seem to bother Elie. What did Elie like about Moshe's appearance?

← In these sentences Elie tells about Moshe's religious practices.

Divinity comes from the word divine. What do you think it means?

The "**cabbala**" is an ancient and mystical form of prayer. You will read more about the cabbala later in this chapter.

I got to know him toward the end of 1941. I was twelve. I believed profoundly. During the day I studied the Talmud, and at night, I ran to the synagogue to weep over the destruction of the Temple. . . .

Think about what you have learned about WWII. When did it start? When did it end? When is this book taking place?

The **Talmud** is a book of Jewish religious study.

1

FIGURE 7.8

A sample of part of a gloss for page one of Elie Wiesel's *Night* (1982). On the left is the actual text, and the gloss has been inserted on the right.

Glossing as a Pre-reading Activity: If your students own copies of what they are reading and you have instructional time, one alternative to duplicating a gloss on separate paper is to "dictate" to students what they should mark in their margins before they read. Add in a little discussion and you've got a complete pre-reading activity. In doing so, you are not only preparing them for what they are about to read, but you are also showing them how to "make books their own" by writing notes in the margins. As you probably know from your own studying experiences, these margin notes can also be very helpful when post-reading for a test.

Glossing as a Post-Reading Activity: Groups of students may construct glosses for future classes. This in-class after-reading activity benefits teachers who teach the same course in successive semesters. The first time the instructor teaches a text she might provide her class with a gloss for the first chapter. For the second chapter she would use a different during-reading strategy. Upon completion of the second chapter, students are divided into groups assigning different pages to each group. The instructor provides students with blank paper and asks them to construct a gloss for their section. (Imagine how you might introduce this gloss booklet for this chapter to your next semester of students: "The students in last year's class decided that there were many things that would be helpful to you when you read the next chapter. To make sure that you got the help you needed, they constructed the gloss booklet for Chapter Two.")

During-Reading Guides

Like gloss booklets, reading guides are designed to help students with vocabulary and content by having them answer questions as they read their text. These teacher-made instructional materials resemble student worksheets in workbooks, however, they are *not* the same! Most workbook worksheets are designed to measure comprehension *after* reading. A reading guide, on the other hand, is designed to be used *while* the student is reading (Herber, 1978; Manzo & Garber, 1995). This enables the teacher to provide students with structure, background information, and vocabulary as they read.

Creating a reading guide can be an insightful experience for content-area teachers. In order to construct one you must read the selection carefully, putting yourself in the students' place. While doing so, we must ask ourselves: What does the student need to know to understand this passage? What are the essential concepts that need to be grasped and in what order must they do so? What is confusing about how this is written and how can I clear up that confusion? What can I say before I ask the question that will guide my students to better understanding? Like gloss booklets, students may construct reading guides for future students as a post-reading activity.

Figure 7.9 on page 256 contains questions from a reading guide written to help students understand an especially difficult passage from a middle school history textbook.

ReQuest

The ReQuest procedure was developed by Manzo (1969) to improve reading comprehension and help students develop questioning techniques. It is a way to show students how to read for comprehension, instead of telling them what to do. Unlike a gloss booklet or reading guide, ReQuest requires that the teacher be present and interact with the student or students. This method is especially effective with dense or highly technical materials. This highly interactive technique provides students with a model of how to think critically and formulate questions about difficult material. Figure 7.10 on page 257 illustrates the ReQuest procedure.

Name_____   Date_____

Directions: This worksheet will help you read and take notes on pages 218 and 219 of your textbook.

1. Look at the title: "Why People Left the Midwest." Has your family ever moved from one area to another? Why did you move? (Perhaps you have never moved. In that case, do you know anyone, from somewhere else, who has moved to where you now live? Why did they move here?)

_____

_____

_____

_____

Our book is about to describe why some families decided to move from the Midwest to the Pacific Northwest. As you read, think about what these families hoped would happen when they got to their new homes.

2. Read the first sentence. It describes the beginning and end of the Oregon Trail. Then complete this analogy: Fort Vancouver is to the end of the trail as _____is to the beginning.

3. Cholera is a disease that spreads because water is not clean. Cholera is not a problem today because we have water treatment plants. To *ford* a river means to go across the river by foot or by horseback. Today we would drive our cars on a bridge over a river. Read the next three paragraphs. As you read you will learn about the many hardships that the travelers faced. When you are done, list three causes of death for people and/or their cattle.

   a) _____

   b) _____

   c) _____

4. Read the next section. It will explain how much it cost to take this trip. It will also explain how much money a person could earn in a day. When you are finished, answer this question: How many days of work would it take to earn enough money to buy a wagon? Assume that all money earned could be saved.

_____

_____

_____

_____

5. Read the next section. Look at the picture in the right-hand corner. Use what you see in the picture to answer this question. Why were the Eastern farmers such tough competitors for the Midwestern farmers?

_____

_____

_____

_____

FIGURE 7.9
Reading Guide for a Middle School History Book

T: You should all have copies of the movie review. Is there anyone who does not?

Yesterday we created a structured overview of the movie. (Shown on overhead.) Note that those of you who have seen this movie helped us to list and describe each of the main characters. You also helped us to get an idea about the plot and setting. Now we are going to read a review by someone who writes in a very complicated fashion. His audience is readers of the *New York Times*. Many of these readers appreciate complex sentences full of multisyllabic words. Let's use ReQuest to see if we can make sense out of it. Please read the first sentence silently to yourself. (Pause while students read.) Would someone please read aloud for us?

S: "For all the impressive innovations in the field of 3-D computer-generated animation, the old-fashioned flat kind, with its warm colors and artful perspectives, has not lost its appeal."

T: O.K.! Now you get to ask me any questions you want about this sentence. You may ask me about the meaning of vocabulary words, or if you prefer, you may ask how I figured out what this sentence means.

S1: What the heck is he saying?

T: Would you please ask me a more specific question?

S1: What is a "3-D computer-generated animation"?

T: I'm not an expert on this, but I think he is talking about cartoons that are generated by computers. Back before my time, cartoons were drawn by hand. Now cartoon makers use software that not only helps them draw the characters and their movements, but adds dimension that makes it look like they are really on the screen.

S2: Then why does the author say, "3-D computer-generated animation, the old fashioned kind"?

T: That's another good question. Anyone want to take a shot at that?

S3: That is old-fashioned! They now have cartoons that are like holograms!

T: What other questions do you have? This is your chance to play stump the teacher.

S4: Yeah. What are "warm colors and artful perspectives"?

T: I was hoping you would ask that. Those of you who have seen the movie can help me with this. Some warm colors are yellow and orange and red. Picture a sun setting into the ocean. There are a few clouds in the sky, just enough to mix the colors. It's warm and there is a nice ocean breeze blowing off the water. In the foreground is the silhouette of a palm tree. Got it? Now that is warm color and artful perspective!

T: Let's move on to the second sentence. Read it to yourself silently. (Pause) Now I need a volunteer to read it out loud.

S5: *Lilo and Stitch*, the new Disney cartoon adventure that was written and directed by Chris Sanders and Dean Deblois, is hardly a work of state-of-the-art virtuosity, but rather an example of quiet, confident craftsmanship that tells a sweet, charming tale of intergalactic friendship.

T: Thank you. This time it is my turn to ask you questions about the sentence. Raise your hand if you think you know the answers. The author says that this movie ". . . is hardly a work of state-of-the-art virtuosity." Does anyone know what the word "virtuosity" means? (No response) Has anyone ever heard of the terms "state-of-the-art" or "virtual reality?"

S1: Isn't that when they use computers to create something that is not real, yet seems like it is?

T: Not exactly, however you are using what you know to figure out what the author is trying to say. How might the movie have been different if it was "state-of-the-art virtuosity"?

S1: Well, they would have all kinds of special effects that are the most modern, the most up-to-date.

T: Good. Now look back at the first sentence. Do you see where the author talks about the "old-fashioned flat kind" of animation? Is the movie *Lilo and Stitch* old-fashioned, computer-generated, or state-of-the-art?

S6: Old-fashioned. It says so right here. It says ". . . the old-fashioned kind, with its warm colors and artful perspectives, has not lost its appeal."

T: Excellent. You've just done a good job of tying what you understood from the first sentence to what you are reading in the second one. So we have a movie that uses animation, but not the most skillful and up-to-date (state-of-the-art) animation. What else does the author tell you about the craftsmanship used to make this movie?

S3: He says that it is "quiet" and "confident."

T: Yes, you are correct! I'm now going to ask a question that will require you to think about what we have already written on our structured overview. To what is the author referring when he describes this movie as a ". . . sweet charming tale of intergalactic friendship"?

S2: He's talking about Lilo and Stitch and their friendship.

T: Yes, I agree with you. Tell me then, how is this friendship "intergalactic"?

S2: Stitch is a being from another planet.

T: Yes, you are doing a very good job of tying together what we talked about yesterday when we put together the structured overview, with what we are reading now. Let's move on to the next sentence. . . .

FIGURE 7.10

The ReQuest Procedure used for a ninth-grade English class of the first paragraph of "Escaping Deep-Space Exile and Making Friends in Hawaii," a review of the movie *Lilo and Stitch* by A. O. Scott. (*New York Times*, June 21, 2002)

Guidelines for Preparing and Teaching Using the ReQuest Procedure

1. Have copies of the selection available for everyone.

2. Each member of the class reads the first sentence silently. Then one student reads it aloud. Students ask the teacher questions about that sentence. They should be questions about vocabulary, or the meaning of the sentence, or how the teacher was able to figure out the meaning of the sentence.

3. Teachers answer the questions. (Often teachers use metacognitive scripting, as described later in this chapter.)

4. After all the students' questions have been answered, the students read the second sentence as they had the first. This time the teacher asks questions of students. (The teacher may have to use the slicing technique described later in this chapter.)

5. As questions from the second sentence are answered, the teacher also asks questions that require integration of ideas from both sentences. The teacher should remember to ask students about *how* the students came to their conclusions about these interrelationships.

6. This procedure is continued until the students can read all the words in the first paragraph, can show literal comprehension of what is read, and can formulate a reasonable purpose for reading the rest of the selection.

Slicing: A Technique for Modeling Questioning

Techniques like the ReQuest procedure require teachers to ask questions in order to facilitate the process of comprehending. In so doing, teachers anticipate where students might have difficulty and model asking those types of questions their students might have as they read. During this modeling the teacher might ask a complex question, only to get the response of utter silence. What does this mean? Did the class understand the question? Are they afraid to hazard an answer? Or do they really need additional guidance? One way to find out is to "slice" the question.

Slicing (Pearson & Johnson, 1978) is very much what it sounds like: chopping a larger question into smaller units. There are two ways to "slice": (1) restate the question asking for a smaller part of the total issue, or (2) change the task required to answer the question to selecting from one of several smaller recognizable alternatives. In the ReQuest procedure example used above, students who had read the first sentence were required to ask questions.

T: O.K.! Now you get to ask me any questions you want about this sentence. You may ask me about the meaning of vocabulary words, or if you prefer, you may ask how I figured out what this sentence means.

S1: What the heck is he saying?

T: Would you please ask me a more specific question?

S1: What is a "3-D computer-generated animation"?

Note how the teacher asked the student for something more specific and got it. This was a good example of the student slicing his own bigger question. Teachers can model this same process when their questions are greeted with silence as did happen later in the same scenario:

T: The author says that this movie ". . . is hardly a work of state-of-the-art virtuosity." Does anyone know what the word "virtuosity" means? (No response) Has anyone ever heard of the terms "state-of-the art" or "virtual reality"?

The teacher did get a response to the second slice, and although it might not have been exactly what the teacher had in mind, she was able to use it to ask another question. But what was the teacher to do if the next question is greeted with "no response"? The answer: Slice again!

T: Does anyone know what the word "virtuosity" means? (No response) Has anyone ever heard of the terms "state-of-the art" or "virtual reality"? (No response) Does anyone own a "state-of-the-art" computer? (No response) If a computer is "state-of-the-art," does that mean that it is fast? Runs all the latest software? Is nearly brand new?

If these slices are not small enough, the teacher could ask one of the students to use the dictionary.

S1: The dictionary says that state-of-the-art means "relating to the highest level of development at any particular time."

S2: And "virtuosity" means "great technical skill in a practice of fine art."

T: Thank you. So what is an example of a state-of the-art television?

S1: A Sony HDTV with plasma screen and surround sound.

T: Yes. That television does have the highest level of development at this time. May I ask you another question?

S1: My uncle has one of those. Go for it.

T: Great. Tell me then, are all cartoons that you watch on that Sony HDTV, with that plasma screen and surround sound, the same, or are some of them more "state-of-the-art" than others?

S1: No, not many cartoons are high definition and you can tell. The colors aren't as bright and the images not as crisp.

T: Indeed! So let's try to put this together. In the first sentence the author talks about "old-fashioned 3-D computer-generated animation." In this second sentence he tells us that this movie might not be the highest level of development or of great technical skill. Tell me, from what we've read so far, do you think this movie contains some of the newest uses of state-of-the-art technology? How would it look on that Sony television? What words in this sentence help you come up with the answer?

When slicing, it is important to remember not to slice again until students have had sufficient time to formulate their answers to the current question. *Wait time* is the educational term for the silence the teacher creates by quietly waiting while students formulate their answers. The tougher the question, the more thinking is necessary and the longer the *wait time* should be. Therefore, the teacher should not slice to the next level until it appears that students have had time think it through. Also, let us not forget there is an affective dimension to volunteering answers to any question. Students should feel they can risk being wrong without being embarrassed or humiliated. The teacher who makes students uncomfortable will get less and less participation.

Slicing takes preparation and practice. New teachers are well advised to script a series of slices to higher-level questions before reading text aloud to their students. Those teachers who play the game "Guess what's in my head, and if you don't get it, I'll tell you" are not teaching, they are telling. Better to *show* students how to think about what they've read by pausing and slicing again.

Metacognitive Scripts

Effective readers monitor their own comprehension by making decisions at all stages of their reading. They understand the processes needed for comprehending in order to reach a specific learning goal (Tonjes, 1985). How can we make the process of reading for understanding more concrete? We can model what we do by verbalizing our own metacognitive dialogue while reading from the text.

As a content teacher, you may be the first, perhaps the only, expert who is knowledgeable and/or excited about what they are asked to read. Why not share your expertise by articulating, for your students, the process you would use if you were reading the text for the first time? Why not share your excitement for your subject by reading with enthusiasm, "thinking out loud" as you read?

You may show your students how you read for understanding by using the metacognitive scripting technique, also called mental modeling (Roehler & Duffy, 1986). This technique requires the teacher to think out loud and narrate the strategies that they used to understand the text while reading that text aloud (Harvey & Goudvis, 2000).

Figure 7.11 is an example of a metacognitive script provided by a seventh-grade teacher as he started to read Elie Wiesel's *Night* to his history class. Wiesel's text is in regular type, the teacher's script, in italics. Note how the teacher models his thinking as he reads, illustrating how he uses his background knowledge to make predictions, define words using the context, and sets his purpose for reading:

FIGURE 7.11

A metacognitive script of the first paragraph of *Night*.

They called him Moshe the Beadle,

What a name?!? I'm not even sure how to pronounce it. But I'll read on hoping it will make sense.

as though he had never had a surname in his life. He was a man of all work at a Hasidic synagogue. The Jews of Sighet—that little town in Transylvania where I spent my childhood—were very fond of him.

Surname . . . his last name. He was Moshe. He had no last name. Was Beadle his nickname? Sort of like Alexander the Great? He worked in a synagogue. I don't know what Hasidic means. It sounds like a kind of Judaism. I'll read a bit further to see if the author tells me. If not, I will need to look that up. Sighet, Transylvania—is there really such a place? Two things to find out. If the author doesn't tell me where this place is, I can use the atlas to find out.

He was very poor and lived humbly.

So I know that Moshe is poor. The author says he lived humbly. I'm not sure I know what "humbly" means. I think it means that he doesn't have a lot of stuff. But I will read further to see if that is accurate.

Generally my fellow townspeople, though they would help the poor, were not particularly fond of them. Moshe the Beadle was the exception. Nobody ever felt embarrassed by him.

Moshe was an exception. Was he an exception because nobody every felt embarrassed by him? Or was he an exception because the townspeople were fond of him? Maybe being humble has something to do with never embarrassing others?

Nobody ever felt encumbered by his presence. He was a past master in the art of making himself insignificant, of seeming invisible.

I don't know what "encumbered" means. I think I've heard the word "cumbersome." In PE the teacher used to say that wearing jewelry while working out was cumbersome. I'd better look up that word. As I go into the next paragraph I am looking for two things: the meaning of Hasidic and the location of Sighet, Transylvania.

Using During-Reading Strategies

Meeting in groups of three or four, consider the six during-reading strategies described above. Collectively, select a passage from a book in one of your respective disciplines. Plan together how you might use a during-reading strategy to help students to better comprehend this passage.

Workshop 7.6

Post-Reading

"Books are wastepaper unless we dedicate time to thinking about what we learned from reading them." This quote, attributed to George Washington, speaks to the value of committing time and effort, after we read, to make sure we have thought about what we have just read. Pre-reading and reading without post-reading is like picking your favorite fresh ingredients for a salad, washing, slicing and tossing them thoroughly, but not taking the time to sit down to thoroughly enjoy their taste.

This final stage of a directed reading-thinking post-reading activity is an important stage because it empowers readers to apply, analyze, synthesize, and evaluate the meanings of what they have just read. Often post-reading activities provide the "comprehension products" used to measure student understanding.

Postreading activities described in this chapter include:

1. Cinquains as Summaries
2. Plus, Minus, Interesting (PMI)
3. Classroom Discussion
4. Simulation/Role-Playing
5. Imaging
6. Collateral (Reiterative) Post-Reading/Viewing
7. Remembering Strategies

Workshop 7.7

What Do We Learn from Answering Comprehension Questions

A number of years ago, Kenneth Goodman developed a nonsense passage followed by typical textbook comprehension questions. Read about the "marlup poving his kump" and then write your answers to the four questions. As you work on the questions keep track of how you figure out your answers. We predict that most of you will get a score of between 50% and 75% "comprehension," some even 100%, on material you really know nothing about!

A marlup was poving his kump. Parmily a narg horped some whev in his kump. "Why did vump horp whev in my frinkle kump?" The marlup juf'd the narg. "Er'm muvvily trungy," the narg gruped. "Er hashed vump norpled whev in your kump. Do vump pove your kump finkle?"

1. What did the narg horp in the marlup's kump?

   _____

2. What did the marlup juf the narg?

   _____

3. Was the narg trungy?

   _____

4. How does the marlup pove his kump?

   _____

To which questions were you able to guess the answers? In what ways did your facility with language help you? If you were an English language learner, would this exercise be easier or more difficult? Why? How did you use syntax and grammar to derive answers? Do you really know what this passage is about?

The first three questions required you to answer "lower-level," explicitly stated facts. The fourth is not directly stated and hence requires readers to make an inference. You may want to discuss the strategies you used to make sense out of the nonsense. For example, did you try substituting real nouns or verbs for the nonsense ones?

Before you go on, consider this: Can your students answer the comprehension questions you assign without having any idea about what they are reading? Well-written questions require that students make meaning of what they read.

Source: Text and questions reprinted from *The Psycholinguistic Nature of the Reading Process,* 1968, pp. 23–24, by Kenneth S. Goodman, editor. By permission of the Wayne State University Press.

Cinquains as Summaries

Vaughan and Estes (1986) describe an interesting strategy for synthesizing or summarizing what one has read by using cinquains. Cinquains are five-line poems with specific limitations:

Line 1   One-word title
Line 2   Two-word description of topic
Line 3   Three words expressing action
Line 4   Four words showing feeling for a topic
Line 5   One-word synonym, restating the essence of the topic

This strategy provides students with a powerful tool to synthesize the "gist" of what they have read.

For example:

Line 1   Volcano
Line 2   Red hot
Line 3   Erupting from within
Line 4   Nature's furnace of fire
Line 5   Inferno

At first, students might benefit from working in pairs or triads to develop cinquains on what they have read. With time and practice, most students will be able to write these on their own. Please note that each chapter of this text ends with a cinquain as summary.

Analyze This!: Plus, Minus, Interesting (PMI)

Plus, Minus, Interesting (deBono, 1985) is a post-reading strategy that students can use to analyze the ideas they get from their readings. Instead of just deciding whether or not they like an idea about which they just read, this strategy encourages students to find the good points (P = Plus), the bad points (M = Minus), and the points that are neither good nor bad but instead are worth further investigation (I = Interesting). A PMI is never intended to indoctrinate one's thinking, but instead to ensure that both sides of a matter are considered. This strategy may also be used to breathe life into ideas that are presented passively in textbooks.

Guidelines for Teaching with a PMI

1. Addressing the class as a whole, ask students how they usually treat new ideas. For example, what do they think about laws against skate boarding, school rules about the clothes they may not wear, or the use of cell phones? Help them to realize that there is a tendency to either like or dislike ideas without thinking carefully about both sides of that rule or idea.

2. Explain that a PMI is a way to treat ideas. When we use a PMI, we decide whether or not we like an idea after we have analyzed it, instead of before. We do this by making sure we have made a list of as many of the good (P), bad (M), and interesting (I) about that idea.

3. Just because we can provide reasons why an idea can be good *and* bad *and* interesting doesn't mean that we agree with any one position. The idea is to generate a complete analysis.

4. After having read from a text, divide students into small groups. Ask them to come up with an important and potentially controversial idea from what they have read.

5. Have one student take notes. Ask students to list what the P, M, and I about the idea they have listed. Help them to realize that if everyone agrees that an idea is positive, and no one sees a possible negative or interesting one, there is a high likelihood that they are not thinking analytically.

Here are two examples of topics for PMI analysis.

From a science textbook:

"Mercury is a naturally occurring substance that can cause serious health and ecological problems when released into the environment through human activities. Large amounts of mercury become airborne when coal, oil or natural gas is burned as fuel." Students come up with this idea for analysis: Stricter laws prohibiting the burning of large amounts of coal, oil, or natural gas need be passed and enforced.

From a social studies textbook:

"John Adams was asked by the British officers and soldiers to serve as attorney for the British troops that killed colonists at the Boston Massacre." Students come up with this idea for analysis: Should John Adams defend these soldiers?

Classroom Discussion

Classroom discussion (Larson, 2000) is an effective technique to help students interpret, analyze, and evaluate what they have read. It is also an effective means to unite the cognitive and social aspects of a classroom. Class discussion requires students to explain their thoughts and ideas within the context of the thoughts and ideas of others. Immediate feedback is possible, as students can explain what they don't understand, and choose to agree or disagree with points of view of classmates. Obviously, discussion also requires listening and questioning skills. Engle and Ochoa (1988) suggest there are four types of questions that teachers and their students may use to help define the purpose of a discussion:

1. What does that mean? (definitional questions)
2. What reasons can you give for your beliefs? (evidential questions)
3. What if that hadn't happened? (speculative questions)
4. What should be done? (policy questions)

Frequently, especially when discussing controversial topics, students will disagree. When controversial issues are discussed in a respectful and orderly fashion, students develop skills in considering opposing opinions, understanding alternative points of view, and identifying commonalities. What is more, discussion can motivate students to do additional reading in order to discover relevant information.

Respectful and orderly discussion of controversial issues requires:

- Commitment by all students to abide by ground rules established prior to discussion.
- A teacher or other group leader committed to impartiality and respectful interaction.
- An understanding that students may disagree with the idea expressed by another, but not with the person expressing that idea.

Simulations/Role-Playing

A *simulation* represents a real experience artificially, putting together a contrived series of activities to approximate a situation or process as closely as possible. Unlike the purely cerebral character of reading for facts, this is a "you are there" type of phenomenon. For example, to make the reading of stock market reports more meaningful, students might simulate the buying and selling of shares in corporations so as to follow the progress as if these were their investments. Or students might be asked to simulate osmosis, with some students playing the role of water molecules, others the role of cell membranes, or simulate the wave activity of the ocean.

A dimension may be added by asking students to play the roles of people in these games. In fact, *role-playing* games have long been a staple of education. For example: It is 1962. You are an advisor to John Kennedy, president of the United States, and you have just learned that the Soviets have introduced medium-range missiles into Cuba. You are an advisor to Fidel Castro, the Communist leader of Cuba and you have good reason to believe that without these missiles, America will attack you militarily. You are an advisor to Nikita Khrushchev, Russian leader, and so forth. The idea is that students can take what they have read about people, their characteristics, and those things learned about the challenges they faced and portray their interactions in simulated events.

Role-playing *is not* appropriate for portraying every event, and discretion in role selection is of utmost importance. For example, most would agree that it would not be appropriate to ask three black students in a history class to play the roles of students at the Woolworth's lunch counter while white students are asked to play the role of Klu Klux Klan members.

FROM THE CONTENT CLASSROOM

Poor Use of Simulation/Role-Playing

Attempting to make his ninth-grade students understand the horrors of the Holocaust, a social studies teacher created a space in his classroom the size of a cattle car, like those used to transport prisoners to the concentration camps. The teacher then assigned students roles as mothers, children, grandmothers, and grandfathers. The students complied and squeezed themselves into the space provided; however, to their teacher's dismay, many were smiling, several giggled, and when one girl exclaimed that the boys next to her had "better keep their hands to themselves," the entire class laughed.

This particular simulation/role-play was disrespectful to the memories of the real victims who had suffered so greatly and disrespectful to the students who were asked to play these roles. In fact, asking them to imagine what it was like was an unreasonable expectation. (This simulation violated two of the three tenets of the three "R's" mentioned in Chapter Four and therefore a poor use of simulation/role-playing.)

Imaging

Painting mental pictures in the mind enables students to make content easier to remember by helping them "see it" as more realistic. Imaging helps integrate information (Pressley, 1977), detect inconsistencies (Gambrell & Bales, 1986), enhance comprehension (Gambrell & Jawitz, 1993), and increase retention (Sadowki, Goetz, Olivarez, Lee, & Roberts, 1990). By helping students place themselves in the scene, and by helping them use their prior knowledge to create vivid pictures, readers learn to think actively about what they are reading.

Reread a short passage from a text and ask students to close their eyes, listen carefully and ask themselves what sounds, smells, or tastes come to mind. When you are done, ask each student to sketch what they saw in their mind's eye. Have them share these illustrations with each other to enlarge their understanding of how differently people can perceive the same input.

Workshop 7.8

The Power of Imaging

It takes two to complete this activity: One to read the directions, the other to follow them. Or the instructor might choose instead to read these directions to the class as a whole.

Directions: Extend both of your hands out in front of you. Your palms should be up, your elbows fully extended. Your hands should be parallel with the ground, chest high. Now close your eyes. Picture me walking over to you with a big bunch of helium balloons. There must be fifteen or more of them. They are all attached to the same cord. I am tying that cord to your left hand. Can you feel the balloons pulling your hand up. Concentrate on imaging the fifteen balloons, tied to a cord, tied to your hand. Feel your left hand being pulled up.

Keep your eyes closed. I am coming to you again. Don't lose track of those balloons. Picture this. I have a large backpack. In that backpack are several heavy bricks. Can you image it? I'm coming to you and placing the straps of that backpack on your right hand. Can you feel the weight of those bricks pulling your hand and arm down? It is pulling down on your right hand and arm. Is your right arm getting tired?

Now open your eyes. If you are like others who have done this exercise, you may find that your left arm is higher than your right.

Collateral (Reiterative) Post-Reading/Viewing

Earlier in this chapter we encouraged the pre-reading and/or viewing collateral materials in order to activate the background knowledge needed to read a text with understanding. Collateral reading and/or viewing may also be used to support, broaden, or enrich the experience of the reader *after* reading the assigned text. For example, documentary and/or instructional videos can reinforce concepts acquired during reading. Novels and trade books on the same theme may provide students with further elaboration and reinforcement of concepts learned. Repetition in multiple formats is one of many strategies that help students understand and remember what they have read.

Workshop 7.9

Using Post-Reading Strategies

With your assigned group, consider the five post-reading strategies described above. Collectively, select a passage from a book in one of your respective disciplines. Plan together how you might use a post-reading strategy to help students better comprehend this passage.

Strategies to Enhance Retention of What Is Read

To succeed in school, students must do more than learn material, they must remember it. There are many books full of strategies to help one remember what one reads. Most of these strategies require the reader to do five things:

1. *Visualize*: Know what it is that you need to remember and picture it in your mind.
2. *Concentrate*: We remember what we understand. We understand what we pay attention to. We pay attention to what we want to know. Consciously choose to remember. Pay attention.
3. *Look for a Pattern*: Relate ideas and information you wish to remember to each other and to ideas and information that you already know.
4. *Organize the Pieces*: Place the pieces that you are trying to remember into some type of organizing system.
5. *Repeat*: Go over the material several times to over learn it. Say or write it in your own words.

Mnemonics

Mnemonics is a term that refers to methods that we can use to help us remember better. The ones we remember best are usually funny, silly, or ridiculous and usually have a rhyming structure. Whenever we construct a mnemonic, we are forced to visualize, concentrate, look for a pattern, organize, and repeat. For example:

- When the face is red, raise the head. When the face is pale, raise the tail (for first aid).
- I before e, except after c, or when sounded like a, as in neighbor or weigh (for spelling).

Other mnemonics include **acronyms, acrostics,** and **peg words**.

An **acronym** is a word that is made by taking the first letter from each word that you want to remember and making a new word from all those letters. For example:

- HOMES (The Great Lakes: Huron, Ontario, Michigan, Erie, Superior)
- ROY G BIV (The colors of visible light in the spectrum in the order that they appear: Red, Orange, Yellow, Green, Blue, Indigo, Violet).

An **acrostic** is a sentence that is made by taking the first letter from each word or symbol that you want to remember and then inserting another word beginning with that same letter. For example:

- Every Good Boy Does Fine, or Every Good Boy Deserves Fudge (the names of the notes on the lines of the treble clef)
- P. Cohn's Café stands for the chemical shorthand for the elements most common in the human body (Phosphorus, Carbon, oxygen, hydrogen, nitrogen, sulfur, calcium [Ca], and iron [Fe])
- Kings Play Cards On Fairly Good Soft Velvet—biology classifications (kingdom, phylum, class, order family genus, species, variety)

Peg words are words that are easily associated with numbers and are useful in memorizing long lists in specific order. Peg words should be nouns so that the reader can link action to them. You can use the rooms of your house, parts of your body, or any series of objects that is firmly fixed in your mind (Sandstrom, 1990). Here is one set of peg words from a nursery rhyme:

One-Sun, Two-Shoe, Three-Tree, Four-Door, Five-Hive, Six-Sticks, Seven-Heaven, Eight-Gate, Nine-Line, Ten-Hen.

Suppose we read a passage about the Bill of Rights, the first ten amendments, and we want to remember what they guaranteed. Here is a list of what the first five guarantees:

One:	freedom of religion, assembly, petition, speech
Two:	right to bear arms
Three:	no quartering of soldiers
Four:	search and seizure
Five:	trial and punishment, personal property

The objective is to link the first peg word with the guarantees of the first amendment. We do this by imagining a ridiculous picture or action in our mind that shows both the peg word and the guarantee. For example: One is sun, and the amendment guarantees freedom of *R*eligion, *A*ssembly, *P*etition and *S*peech. So we might imagine a preacher with sunglasses, preaching in the hot sun, preaching that they must not forget—**R**eligion, **A**ssembly, **P**etition, and **S**peech—**RAPS!!**

Two is a shoe and the right to bear arms. We might visualize a bare right arm sticking out of someone's shoe and in the hand of that arm is a pistol. Three is for tree and soldiers quarters. We can try to picture soldiers setting up camp in some kid's tree house and offering him 50 cents (quarters) as rent. Four is door and search and seizure. We can try to imagine what it would be like to have the police pounding on the door with a search warrant. Five is for hive and trial/punishment and private property. Act this one out if you will: An abusive government official breaks into a home to take someone away without a trial, and bumps into a beehive.

With the peg system, as with all remembering strategies, the keys are to visualize, concentrate, look for the pattern, organize the pieces, and repeat as often as possible. Note that with each of the above there is the opportunity to tie in one of Gardner's multiple intelligences. We can sing the raps, wave the arm from our shoe, offer quarters, knock on the door, and reach for the hive.

Putting Them All Together

The two strategies that follow—K-W-L Plus and PLAN—empower students to utilize the three-stage process of the Directed Reading-Thinking Activity.

K-W-L Plus

The K-W-L Plus strategy (Carr & Ogle, 1987) follows the same general reading-thinking path as the Multiple Reading Process and the Directed Reading-Thinking Activity. K-W-L Plus is designed to be a group activity, however, it can be adapted to be done individually.

K—What I Already Know (Pre-reading)

Brainstorm what the class already knows about the topic to be read, recording responses on the board or in their notes. Be specific as to the concept selected. If there is little response, slice back to a more general question and then ask if these new facts can apply to the original concept. Ogle suggests that volunteers be asked where they learned their fact or how it could be proved. Have students look at their list on the board of what they already know and group items into general categories.

W—What Do I Want to Learn?

The teacher then moves the discussion to aspects of the topic that the students do not know. Students are helped to state these as questions and write them into their notes. They should set their reading purpose by asking, "What do I want to learn?"

L—What I Learned (Post-Reading)

Students read the passage. During reading they pause to write the answers to any of their "want to know" questions. New questions and answers may be added as they are discovered. Once done, the teacher leads a discussion about the answers to their questions and knowledge acquired.

The Plus

The teacher creates a recall diagram (see Chapter One) of the information gathered by the class.

PLAN

Caverly et al. (1995) devised a strategy to help poor readers learn to read strategically using the three-stage process of pre-reading, reading, and post-reading. Students are taught to PLAN: Predict, Locate, Add, and Note. In brief:

- Predict, before reading, the content and structure of the text. To do so, create a prediction map using the chapter title at the center and subtitles, words highlighted, and graphics for major and minor branches.
- Locate, before reading, known and unknown information on this map, placing checks next to familiar concepts and question marks by unknown ones so that the readers have assessed their own prior knowledge. This should help them adapt their reading rate to the passage to be read.
- Add, while reading, any and all words or phases to their map that explain the unknown concepts or confirm known ones. This fosters metacognition because if they can't identify information they know they didn't understand that part of the text. Teachers or other students can help by encouraging rereading, use of the dictionary, or dismissing the missing information as unimportant.
- Note, after reading, the understandings they now have. Have they met their purpose? Students may want to redraw the map if predictions were off. They can redraw the map from memory if preparing for an objective test. They can write a learning log entry if their task was to evaluate or react to the content. They can discuss to confirm, refine, or enrich their ideas, or they can write a summary to recall information for an essay test.

 ## Cinquain as Summary

Comprehending
Ongoing Process
Pre-reading, During Reading, Post-reading
My Thoughts Are Important!
Understanding

Summary

Comprehending written discourse is a complex, interactive process. When readers are fully engaged, they must activate background knowledge, read with a purpose, and adjust strategies to text difficulty. Comprehending involves the mental actions of predicting, interpreting, organizing, synthesizing, revising, and evaluating.

Comprehension is the end product of comprehending. The product depends on the process. Many youngsters read mostly narrative materials until upper-elementary years; consequently, they may require explicit instruction in mastering expository text. The reader's role is that of active learner; the teacher's role is that of a tour guide through the process; the writer's role is that of an architect who designs and builds messages; and the text serves as a blueprint for meaning.

An adaptation of three taxonomies (Bloom's, Sanders's, and Barrett's) includes the comprehending categories of literal, interpretive/applied, evaluative/critical, and creative/personal. Gardner's Eight Ways of Knowing gives us six other ways to look at the processes by which we get to know something besides the verbal/linguistic and logical/mathematical, which unfortunately are the ones stressed most often.

Numerous strategies for pre-reading, during-reading, and post-reading can be adapted to various content areas. These include parts of the text pre-reading guides, advance organizers, graphic representations, list-group-label, anticipatory guides, collateral pre- and post-reading/viewing, glossing booklets, reading guides, the ReQuest procedure, slicing, classroom discussion, metacognitive scripts, cinquains as summaries, simulations/role-playing, plus/minus/interesting, imaging, and retention strategies. Two strategies, KWL and PLAN, encourage students to thoughtfully use pre-reading, reading, and post-reading strategies.

Answers to Workshop 7.3

Passage A: Driving a manual transmission (stick shift) vehicle.
Passage B: The menace of e-mail spam.

References and Recommended Readings

Afflerbach, P., & Johnson, P. (1986). What do expert readers do when the main idea is not explicit? In J. F. Baumann (Ed.), *Teaching main ideas comprehension.* Newark, DE: International Reading Association.

Albright, L., & Ariail, M. (2005). Tapping the potential of teacher read-alouds in middle schools. *Journal of Adolescent and Adult Literacy, 48*(7), 582–591.

Alverman, D., & Boothby, P. (1982). Text differences: Children's perceptions at the transition stage of reading. *The Reading Teacher, 28*, 298–302.

Ausubel, D. (1968). The use of advance organizers in the learning and retention of meaningful verbal material. *Journal of Educational Psychology, 51*, 267–272.

Barrett, T. (1968). Taxonomy of cognitive and affective dimensions of reading comprehension. In Robinson, H. (Ed.), *Innovation and change in reading instruction.* Chicago: University of Chicago Press

Barron, R., & Stone, V. (1974). The effect of student-constructed graphic post-organizers upon learning vocabulary relationships. In P. Nacke (Ed.), *Twenty-third yearbook of the National Reading Conference* (pp. 172–175).

Beck, I., & McKeown, M. (2002). Questioning the author: Making sense of social studies. *Educational Leadership, 59*(3), 44–47.

Belk, C., Seed, A., & Abadi, W. (2005). Content reading strategies. *Science Scope, 28*(6), 44–45.

Blachowizc, C., & Ogle, D. (2001). *Reading comprehension: Strategies for independent learners.* New York: Guilford.

Bloom B. (1956). *Taxonomy of educational objectives: Handbook I, cognitive domain.* New York: Longman.

Brown, R. (2002). Straddling two worlds: Self-directed comprehension instruction for middle-schoolers. In C. Block & M. Pressley (Eds.), *Comprehension instruction: Research-based best practices* (pp. 337–350). New York: Guilford.

Cantrell, R. (2003). Action strategies for deepening comprehension. *Journal of Adolescent and Adult Literacy, 47*(4), 356–357.

Carr, E., & Ogle, D. (1987). K-W-L-Plus: A strategy for comprehension and summarization. *Journal of Reading, 30,* 626–631.

Casteel, C. A. (1993). Basal sidenotes: Do they affect the comprehension of poor readers? *Reading Improvement, 30*(2), 122–124.

Caverly, D., Mandeville, T., & Nicholson, S. (1995). PLAN: Study reading strategy for informational text. *Journal of Adolescent and Adult Literacy, 39*(3), 190-199.

Council of Chief State School Officers. (2005). *INTASC Standards.* Retrieved March 21, 2005, from http://www.ccsso.org/projects/Interstate_New_Teacher_Assessment_and_Support_Consortium/

Crafton, L. (1983). Learning from reading: What happens when students generate their own background information? *Journal of Reading, 26,* 586–592.

deBono, E. (1985). *CoRT thinking teacher notes: Breadth.* New York: Pergamon Press.

Durkin, D. (1978–1979). What classroom observations reveal about reading comprehension instruction. *Reading Research Quarterly, 14,* 481–538.

Engle, S., & Ochoa, A. (1988). *Education for democratic citizenship: Decision making in the social studies.* New York: Teachers College Press.

Fournier, D., & Graves, M. (2002). Scaffolding adolescents' comprehension in short stories. *Journal of Adolescent and Adult Literacy, 46,* 30–39.

Gambrell, L., & Bales, R. (1986). Mental imagery and the comprehension monitoring performance of fourth and fifth grade poor readers. *Reading Research Quarterly, 21,* 400–404.

Gambrell, L., & Jawitz, P. (1993). Mental imagery text illustrations and children's story comprehension and recall. *Reading Research Quarterly, 28*(3), 454–464.

Gardner, H. (1983). *Frames of mind: The theory of multiple intelligences.* New York: Basic Books.

Greenleaf, M., Juel, C., & Graves, B. (2001). Reclaiming secondary reading interventions: From limited to rich conceptions, from narrow to broad conversations. *Reading Research Quarterly, 37,* 484–496.

Guzzetti, B., Snyder, T., Glass, G., & Gamas, W. (1993). Promoting conceptual change in science: A comparative meta-analysis of instructional interventions from reading education and science education. *Reading Research Quarterly, 28,* 116–159.

Haag, E. (1992). Enriching content classrooms through collateral reading. In M. Tonjes, & M. Zintz, *Teaching reading/thinking/study skills in content classrooms* (3rd ed., pp. 339–382). Dubuque, IA: Wm. C. Brown Publishers.

Harvey, S. (1998). *Nonfiction matters: Reading, writing and research in grades 3–8.* York, ME: Stenhouse Publishers.

Harvey, S., & Goudvis, A. (2000). *Strategies that work: Teaching comprehension to enhance understanding.* Portland, ME: Stenhouse Publishers.

Herber, H. (1978). *Teaching reading in content areas* (2nd ed.). Upper Saddle River, NJ: Prentice Hall.

Horn, E. (1937). *Methods of instruction in social studies.* New York: Scribners.

Huffman, L. (1996). What is in it for you? A student-directed text preview. *Journal of Adolescent and Adult Literacy, 40,* 50–57.

International Reading Association National Council of Teachers of English. (1996). *Standards for the English language arts.* Urbana, IL: NCTE/IRA.

Johns, J., & Berglund, R. (2002*). Strategies for content area learning.* Dubuque, IA: Kendall/Hunt.

Keene, E. O., & Zimmermann, S. (1997). *Mosaic of thought: Teaching comprehension in a reader's workshop.* Portsmouth, NH: Heinemann.

Larson, B. (2000). Thinking about classroom discussion as a method of instruction and a curriculum outcome. *Teaching and Teacher Education, 16,* 661–677.

Lloyd, S. (2004). Using comprehension strategies as a springboard for discussion. *Journal of Adolescent and Adult Literacy, 48*(2), 114–124.

Manzo, A. (1969). The ReQuest procedure. *Journal of Reading 13,* 123–126.

Manzo, A., & Garber, K. (1995). Study guides. In A. Purves (Ed.), *Encyclopedia of English studies and language arts* (pp. 1124–1125). New York: Scholastic.

Massey, D., & Heafner, T. (2004). Promoting reading comprehension in social studies. *Journal of Adolescent & Adult Literacy, 48*(1), 28–40.

Mastropieri, M., & Scruggs, T. (1997). Best practices in promoting reading comprehension in students with learning disabilities, 1976–1996. *Remedial and Special Education, 18*(4), 197–213.

National Board for Professional Teaching Standards (2005). *Adolescent and young adult/science standards* (2nd ed.). Retrieved March 28, 2005, from http://www.nbpts.org/candidates/guide/whichcert/19AdolYoungScience2004.html

Naughton, V. M. (1994). Creative mapping for content reading. *Journal of Reading,* 37(4), 324–326.

Pearson, P. D., Dole, J., Duffy, G., & Roehler, L. (1992). Developing expertise in reading comprehension: What should be taught and how should it be taught? In A. Farstrup & S. J. Samuels (Eds.), *What research has to say about the teaching of reading* (2nd ed.). Newark, DE: International Reading Association.

Pearson, P., & Johnson, D. (1978). *Teaching reading comprehension.* New York: Holt, Rinehart & Winston.

Pressley, M. (1977). *Advances in learning and behavior disorders.* Greenwich: JAL Press.

Readence, J., Bean, T., & Baldwin, R. (1995). *Content area literacy: An integrated approach* (5th ed.). Dubuque, IA: Kendall/Hunt.

Readence, J., Moore, E., & Rickelman, R. (2000). *Prereading activities for content area reading and learning* (3rd ed.), Newark DE: International Reading Association.

Roehler, L., & Duffy, G. (1986). Studying qualitative dimensions of instructional effectiveness. In J. V. Hoffman (Ed.), *Effective teaching of reading.* Newark DE: International Reading Association.

Sadoski, M., Goetz, E., Olivarez, A., Lee, S., & Roberts, N. (1990). Imagination in story reading: The role of imagery, verbal recall, story analysis and processing levels. *Journal of Reading Behavior, 22*(1), 55–70.

Sanders, N. (1966). *Classroom questions: What kinds?* New York: Harper and Row.

Sandstrom, R. (1990). *The ultimate memory book.* Granada Hills, CA: Stepping Stone.

Smith, F. (1978). *Reading without nonsense.* New York: Teachers College Press.

Taba, H. (1967). *Teacher's handbook for elementary social studies.* Reading, MA: Addison-Wesley.

Tonjes, M. J. (1981). Using advance organizers to enhance the processing of text. In J. Chapman, (Ed.), *The reader and the text* (pp. 131–141). London: Heineman Educational Books.

Tonjes, M. J. (1985). Metacognitive strategies for active reading. *The New Mexico Journal of Reading* (6), 5–8.

Tovani, C. (2000). *I read it, but I don't get it: Comprehension strategies for adolescent readers.* Portland, ME: Stenhouse Publishers.

Vaughn, J., & Estes, T. (1986). *Reading and reasoning beyond the primary grades*. Newton, MA: Allyn and Bacon.

Wiesel, E. (1982). *Night*. New York: Bantam.

Worst, D., Jones, D., & Moore, J. (2005). Art supports reading comprehension. *School Arts, 104*(5), 44–45.

Ziegert, S. (1994). Reflection: A step beyond the reading of a chapter. *Journal of Reading, 38,*(2) 132–134.

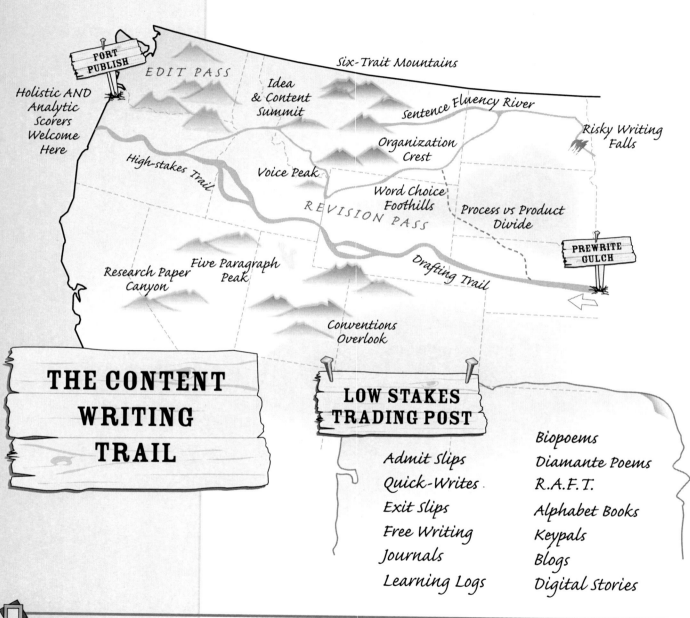

The Content Writing Trail

FORT PUBLISH

Holistic AND Analytic Scorers Welcome Here

EDIT PASS

Six-Trait Mountains

Idea & Content Summit

Sentence Fluency River

Risky Writing Falls

High-stakes Trail

Organization Crest

Voice Peak

Word Choice Foothills

REVISION PASS

Process vs Product Divide

PREWRITE GULCH

Research Paper Canyon

Five Paragraph Peak

Drafting Trail

Conventions Overlook

THE CONTENT WRITING TRAIL

LOW STAKES TRADING POST

Admit Slips
Quick-Writes
Exit Slips
Free Writing
Journals
Learning Logs

Biopoems
Diamante Poems
R.A.F.T.
Alphabet Books
Keypals
Blogs
Digital Stories

FIGURE 8.1

The Content Writing Trail—A Cognitive Map

Writing Process, Traits, and Patterns for Content Area Learning

8

Outline

- Anticipatory and Review Questions
- A Sampling of National Performance Standards
- Introduction
  - Why We Teach Writing Within and Across the Disiciplines
  - The Reading and Writing Connection
  - Teaching Writing: Teacher as Writer
- The Writing Process
  - Product Writing vs. Process Writing
  - Writing Forms
    - *Workshop 8.1: Using Writing Forms to Enhance Content Learning*
  - The Five Stages of Process Writing
    - Pre-writing
    - Drafting
    - Revising
      - Language, Culture, and Writing
    - Editing
      - The Importance of Correct Punctuation
    - Publishing
- The Link Between Assessment and Writing to Learn
- Analytic Traits of Writing
  - Ideas and Content (Details, Development, and Focus)
  - Organization (Internal Structure)
    - *Workshop 8.2: Practice in Assessing Writing for Ideas and Organization*
  - Voice (Tone, Style, Purpose, and Audience)
  - Word Choice (Precise Language and Phrasing)
    - *Workshop 8.3: Practice in Assessing Writing for Voice and Word Choice*
  - Sentence Fluency (Correctness, Rhythm, and Cadence)
  - Conventions (Mechanics)
    - *Workshop 8.4: Practice in Assessing Writing for Sentence Fluency and Conventions*
  - Nonstandard Dialects and Conventions

- *Workshop 8.5: Errors in Conventions or Cultural Sensitivity?*
- From the Content Classroom: "Each Has Its Proper Time and Place"
  - Electronic Connections: To Six-Traits and More
- Content-Area Writing Tasks, Assignments, and Activities
  - Low-Stakes Writing Activities
    - Admit Slips, Quick-Writes, and Exit Slips
    - Free Writing, Journals (Personal, Dialogue, and Double-Entry), and Learning Logs
- From the Content Classroom: Learning Notebooks in a Middle School Science Classroom
    - Biopoems, Diamante Poems, RAFT, and Alphabet Books
    - Key Pals, Blogs, and Digital Stories
      - One More Thought on Technology and Content Writing
- High-Stakes Writing
  - The Five-Paragraph Essay
    - An Alternative Approach to the Five-Paragraph Essay for Struggling Writers
  - The Research Paper
  - TER: A Technique for Helping Students Select Topics for Essays
- Writing and Second Language Learners in the Content Classroom
- Risky Writing
- Cinquain as Summary
- Summary
- From the Pages of Our Lives: *Writing My Way to My Family's History*, by Kie Relyea
- References and Recommended Readings
- Chapter 8 Appendices
  - Appendix 8A: Answer Keys for Workshops 8.2, 8.3, and 8.4
  - Appendix 8B: Five-Paragraph Essay Rubric
  - Appendix C: TER Worksheet and Instructions

"The longer I write and read the more I learn, writing and reading are life long apprenticeships."

Donald M. Murray

"Theorists are fond of saying that learning a discipline means learning its discourse. That is, students don't know a field until they can write and talk about what is in the textbook and the lectures in their own lingo, in their informal home or personal language."

Peter Elbow

Anticipatory and Review Questions

Literal

1. Name and describe five stages of process writing.

2. Describe six traits of analytic assessment of writing.

Interpretative/Applied

3. Use the strategy Target, Expand, Restrict to select a relevant topic for a paper in your content area.

4. Think of a paper that you wrote in high school or college for one of your content area classes. Was it scored holistically or analytically? What feedback did you get on your writing? How did you feel about this feedback? Was it helpful or not? Why?

Evaluative/Critical

5. After analyzing the informal writing strategies described in this chapter, decide which might be useful to you in your work with students and which would not. Describe how you would use them and tell why some would not meet your requirements.

6. List cultural factors that teachers should consider when assessing student writing in your class.

Creative/Personal

7. How would you respond to a colleague who claimed that the teaching of writing is the sole responsibility of those who teach English?

8. You and a team of colleagues have been assigned to plan and direct a workshop on writing across the curriculum. Describe your overall plan with key topics, organization, and basic essentials that you would cover in this workshop.

A Sampling of National Performance Standards

- Capable writers themselves, accomplished practitioners teach students to approach writing as a process of communication to others and to themselves (National Board for Professional Teaching Standards, 2001, p. 13).
- Students employ a wide range of strategies as they write and use different writing process elements appropriately to communicate with different audiences for a variety of purposes (International Reading Association/National Council of Teachers of English, 1996, p. 35).
- The student demonstrates effective scientific communication . . . in a form suited to the purpose and the audience, such as by writing instructions that others can follow; critiquing written and oral explanations; and using data to resolve disagreements (National Center on Education and the Economy and the University of Pittsburgh, 1997, p. 95).

Introduction

President Thomas Jefferson could write! Here are his words describing the confidence he had in Meriwether Lewis, days before Lewis and fellow officer William Clark, set out in a canoe for St. Louis:

> Of courage undaunted, possessing a firmness and perseverance which nothing but impossibilities could divert from its direction . . . of sound understanding and a fidelity to truth so scrupulous that whatever he should report would be as certain as if seen by ourselves, with all these qualifications . . . I could have no hesitation in confiding the enterprise to him. (Ambrose, 1996, p. 8)

And Thomas Jefferson could teach! During the two years that Lewis lived in the White House as Jefferson's confidant and personal secretary, Jefferson encouraged Lewis to expand his understanding of philosophy, literature, and history. At Jefferson's behest, Lewis enriched his scientific education—learning to use new tools of navigation and meeting with experts on birds, animals, and plant life. Most relevant to the topic of this chapter, with Jefferson's help, Lewis also improved his ability to write. Modern-day historian Stephen Ambrose explains:

> A distinct difference is evident between Lewis' writing before 1800 and after 1802. His sense of pace, his timing, his word choice, his rhythm, his similes and analogies all improved. He sharpened his descriptive powers. He learned how to catch a reader up on his own response to events and places, to express his emotions naturally and effectively.
>
> Though his sentences remained convoluted and cried out for punctuation, he managed to carry them off . . . in a way that can be compared to the stream of consciousness of James Joyce or . . . Gertrude Stein—only better, because he was not making anything up, but describing what he saw, said and did (p. 67).

Lewis's journals describing the Missouri River, Rocky Mountains, and Oregon wilderness country of 1804–1806 are a priceless gift to us all. Countless gifts of observation, explanation, insight, and reflection by explorers, historians, physicists, chemists, biologists, astronomers, mathematicians, economists, sociologists, psychologists, artists, musicians, physicians, athletes, and naturalists fill our libraries and populate our websites. Where would we be if biologist Rachel Carson had not written about the web of life, art historian A. Hyatt Mayor had not written about the lithographs of Toulouse-Lautrec, Maria Sklodowska-Curie had not written about radium and radioactivity, Elizabeth Stanton and Susan B. Anthony had not written about woman's suffrage, Roger Sessions had not written about the mysteries of musical composition, or Bill Wilson had not written about twelve-step recovery from alcoholism? What if Albert Einstein, Dorris Kearns-Goodwin, Booker T. Washington, Will and Ariel Durant, Judith Herman, and W. E. B. Dubois had not learned to write about the content they knew best? Jefferson played an important role in fostering Lewis's content-area writing skills. What role might you play with your students?

Why We Teach Writing Within and Across the Disciplines

One need not have a future Rachel Carson and Meriwether Lewis in class to fully appreciate the value of writing within and across the disciplines. As William Zinsser (1988) explains, "Writing . . . . isn't a special language that belongs to English teachers and a few other sensitive souls who have a 'gift for words.' Writing is thinking on paper. Anyone who thinks clearly should be able to write clearly—about any subject at all" (p. 11). Writing provides students with opportunities to organize and clarify their thoughts. As the reader may recall from Chapter One, on taking and making notes, writing can help students recall what they know and think about what they need to know.

Evidence-based research supports the commonly held belief that writing provides students with opportunities to synthesize and integrate what they have learned. In one study Langer (1986) found that essays provided opportunities for integration of content: "When writing essays, students seem to step back from the text after reading it—they reconceptualize the content in ways that cut across ideas, focusing on larger issues or topics. In doing this, they integrate information and engage in more complex thought" (p. 406). In follow-up studies Langer (1987) established that when it comes to learning, not all writing is equal. Nonetheless, she concludes: "In general, any kind of written response leads to better performance than does reading without writing" (p. 130).

The Reading and Writing Connection

Reading and writing are reciprocal processes that result in improved construction of meaning. Proficiency in one affects the other. Consider some of the connections between reading and writing:

- Writers compose, putting their thoughts into written words that carry meaning. Readers compose too—as they compose their own meanings.
- Writers plan by gathering information according to purpose. Good readers also plan their reading by first recalling what they already know about the topic, having a purpose that determines how to read the material.
- Writers revise their writing through a multiple writing process. Readers revise meanings mentally as they use a multiple reading process.
- Advances in technology have made reading and writing a multimedia and multigenre process. For example, reading from a web page may require us to read and write in variety of forms and genres. Yes, we may read the electronic text, but at the same time links may require that we read (view/listen) and write (compose, digitally transcribe) music, take photographs, or create paintings or drawings in order to fully comprehend or express meaning.

When we read like a writer, we anticipate what the author has to say. Conversely, when we write for a reader, we gain perspectives on our subject, our audience, and ourselves. For example, consider what we learned from evaluating the readability of text in Chapter Five. The writings we teachers compose for our university history professors needs to be different than the assignments we write for our sixth-grade social studies students to read. Just as important, whether we are writing journals for ourselves, or assignments for others, returning a day or so later to what we have written, enables us to examine our own thinking with a critical eye. Obviously, if our students are to make reading-writing connections, they need both to see themselves as authors and to see the authors behind their reading (Calkins, 1986).

Teaching Writing: Teacher as Writer

There is a commonly held misconception that the teaching of writing is the sole responsibility of those who teach English. Teachers of literature and composition do educate

4th through 12th grade students in the art of honing well-crafted sentences with proper punctuation. They work with students to improve the organization, word choice, and voice of their papers. However, the content of these papers is usually a reflection of the content of their classes—literature. If you are not an English teacher, please consider what types of text constitute the literature of your discipline. In what ways do you, an expert in your discipline, utilize thinking/writing skills that are different than your colleagues who teach English? How might you model for your students the writing skills they need to develop?

In earlier chapters we spoke of the virtues of reading to and with your students. Good things also happen when teachers write with their students. Spandel and Stiggens (1990) suggest this is true because:

- Students need to see us wrestling with ideas, making connections, clarifying, finding the right word, learning as we go, succeeding, failing, and overcoming the failure. The more we share, the more they learn.

- When we write with our students and give them a chance to review and comment on what we've written, we learn to respect their feelings as writers and show respect for their critical opinions. They in turn come to feel the same towards us.

- When students do not perform well or do not do what you have expected, sometimes it's the fault of the assignment: It wasn't clear; it was too broad, too narrow, or too irrelevant, or it was simply a dumb idea. When we write with our students, we will learn that some of our assignments just aren't worth doing.

- Our students will see that we value writing and think it's important—important enough to do, not just to assign. So important, in fact, that we give class time to drafting and revising. So important that we are writing with them. (pp. 139–141)

The Writing Process

Product Writing vs. Process Writing

Product writing is teacher-centered writing. In a linear fashion, students are required to write essays and exams designed by their teachers who pick the topics and the format by which students put the content they have learned onto paper. In the vast majority of cases, the audience for student writing is the teacher (Applebee, 1981). Product writing dominated instruction for many years.

In the 1970s researchers Emig (1971), Britton and colleagues (1975), and Graves (1975) studied the ways in which elementary and secondary students tackled writing assignments. Shortly thereafter, Flower and Hayes (1975, 1981, 1986) studied college students' writing, asking them to talk about their thought processes while they were writing. From these studies, and many others, the concept of process writing is derived. *Process writing* is recursive and student-centered. When doing process writing, students write to learn, write for multiple audiences, and choose from a variety of writing products.

Table 8.1 summarizes the differences between process and product writing.

An integrated approach to content-area writing must be process-oriented, because process writing provides students with a wide choice of forms. Multiple forms can give students broader opportunities to establish relevant connections to their own sociocultural backgrounds.

TABLE 8.1

Process Writing Instruction	Product Writing Instruction
Recursive (draft, edit, revise, etc.)	Linear
Freedom	Constraint
Variety of products	Protocol provided for a specific product
Student-centered	Teacher-centered
Student choice	Teacher control
Emphasis on generating ideas in text	Emphasis on perfecting through proofreading
Writing to learn	Learning to write
Multiple audiences	Teacher audience
Writing as a cognitive process	Writing as a response

Writing Forms

Process writing takes many forms and can result in many products. Table 8.2 provides a partial list of some of these forms.

TABLE 8.2

- advertisements	- dramatic monologues	- magazine articles	- research
- anecdotes	- editorials	- memos	- resumes
- aphorisms	- essays	- monographs	- reviews
- applications	- fantasy	- newspaper articles	- riddles
- autobiographies	- fiction	- observations	- satires
- ballads, songs	- film scripts	- pamphlets	- science observations
- biographical sketches	- flyers	- photo-essays	- scripts
- cartoons	- graffiti	- plays	- sketches
- children's literature	- historical "You are there"	- poetry	- slide show scripts
- commentaries	scenarios	- posters	- short stories
- commercials	- story problems	- prophecies	- summaries
- conversations	- interviews	- profiles	- telegrams
- dialogues	- jokes	- propaganda	- TV or radio scripts
- diaries	- journals	- reminiscence	- thumbnail sketches
- directions	- letters	- requests	- written debates

Workshop 8.1	Using Writing Forms to Enhance Content Learning
	In groups of four or five take a few minutes to review the list of writing forms in Table 8.2. Check off any of the forms that could be fit into a unit plan for your content area. When you are done, pick one that might be considered unusual or creative (e.g., a script for a play about photosynthesis, a debate between two mathematicians on the best way to solve a problem, etc.). Come up with a concrete example of a lesson into which this might be used. Share your ideas with your colleagues. Select one to share with the class.

The Five Stages of Process Writing

Process writing generally includes five stages: pre-writing, drafting, revising, editing, and publishing. Since process writing is recursive (the same text is returned to many times) and fluid (readily reshaped or changed), these stages need *not* be worked in order. As you will see later in this chapter, several content writing activities do not include all the stages. However, there are elements of each of these stages whenever students are asked to compose a piece of writing. Here is an overview:

Pre-writing

The objective of the *pre-writing* stage is to help students get ready to write by exploring or *brainstorming* the content of a subject. "Getting ready" requires gathering background knowledge through teacher-guided activities on a topic, such as collateral reading, video viewing, reflection, and/or discussion with peers.

However, getting ready goes beyond gathering acorns of information. Students must start to think (the "brain" in the "brainstorm") about their topic with written reflection. Journal entries, free-writes, the TER method, and/or other personal reflections (described later in this chapter) are often a part of pre-writing.

When students haven't spent enough time brainstorming, they may either feel like they have nothing to put on paper, or resort to what Mary K. Healey calls "dump truck writing"—picking up a clump of words, dropping those words onto paper, and then acting genuinely surprised when their teachers accuse them of plagiarism (Fletcher, 1993, p. 76). While it is important to be vigilant about plagiarism, the antidote can be found in a toolbox full of teacher-guided brainstorming activities.

One after-taste of the product writing approach is the expectation that teachers should provide students with topics for their writing. Yes, teachers must help their students focus with prompts and activities; however, students are more likely to feel ownership of topics they have come upon themselves. Regrettably, students may not have the confidence or content knowledge to do so. Teachers may start out by providing lists of suggestions to trigger ideas. However, over the course of the term, teachers should gradually release the responsibility of writing topics to their students.

Drafting

The objective of the *drafting* stage is to get ideas down on paper. Often teachers encourage students to print the words "ROUGH DRAFT" at the top of the page. This label indicates to the writer, and anyone else who reads what is written, that emphasis has been placed on content, not mechanics. This label also helps students remember that perfection is rarely achieved at inception. Students will refine their writing later through a series of drafts.

During the drafting stage, it is the teacher's job to observe facial expressions to see who needs help and to move around the room in such a fashion that students can easily ask for assistance. Getting started is difficult for some students. Teachers can be helpful by reminding students of their audience. Are they writing for themselves, to express and clarify their own ideas and feelings, or are they writing for others like their classmates, friends, or the teacher? What does this audience need to know? Why?

Often students will "get stuck" on opening sentences, what writers call the "lead" or "hook." Fletcher (1993) suggests we help students explore several types of introductions, not all of which start at the beginning. For example, writers can create immediacy by starting in the midst of a dramatic scene, or beginning at the end and explaining how such an ending came about. However, getting the perfect beginning to one's writing or producing "clean copy" is not the objective of the draft stage. When in this stage, students need to be encouraged to put words to paper that begin to express and organize their ideas.

During the drafting stage, students should be given opportunities to collaborate, bouncing ideas off a partner, reading drafts aloud, and pumping each other for new ideas. Improvement in the writing product will come later, during the revising and editing stages.

Revising

Very few writers say, on their first try, exactly what they want to say. Therefore, writing must be viewed as an "evolving organism" (Zinsser, 1988, p. 15). Hence, the objective of the *revising* stage is to clarify and refine ideas. Taken literally, the word *revision* means to look again. Time and distance are necessary for revision. By putting the rough draft aside for a day or so, the writer creates the distance necessary to objectively review what was written with fresh perspective.

During this stage, teacher-guided individual and group activities allow writers to critique and improve upon what they have written by adding, substituting, deleting, and rearranging material. Students should be encouraged to work individually, in pairs, and/or in small groups. They may work silently, or they can read their work to others allowing listeners opportunities to compliment, make suggestions, and answer questions. Often reading aloud to a supportive audience will help writers discover poor word choice or sentence structure.

Teachers who provide time for peer-editing often provide a checklist or rubric to guide feedback. The six-trait analytic assessment tool, described later in this chapter, was developed for this purpose and may be modified to suit the needs of an assignment.

While revision is a necessary stage, it is not necessary for everything we write. Personal journals or quick-writes may not require revision. However, revision and editing are strongly recommended if writers plan to distribute, to others, what they have written. For example, imagine the embarrassment experienced by one supervisor when he learned that a sentence in his recently distributed interoffice had been misunderstood. It read: "I am requesting a list of all employees broken down by sex."

Language, Culture, and Writing

Pragmatics is a term used by linguists to describe how people use language socially to apologize, tell someone what to do, get a point across, demonstrate intelligence, or display status (Meier, 1998b, p. 122). Pragmatics can easily become the source of misunderstanding within or between communities. For example, James Tiffany (2003), editor of the Spanish newspaper *El Mundo*, explains how Mexicans and Americans can become "uncomfortable neighbors" by virtue of their cultural communicative style. (If you find yourself uncomfortable or desiring to revise the prose that follows, consider first whether your response to his writing is an example of a cultural conflict of pragmatics.)

> The American has a "direct style", while the Mexican has an "indirect" communication style. . . . The American's direct style, of getting to the point quickly with no "beating around the bush," is an inheritance from northern Europe. . . .
>
> Many societies in the world are indirect communicators, where lots of information, relevant and not, gets shared, and where due respect must be shown . . . before getting down to business.
>
> In the direct style, the most important thing is the point to be communicated; and the speaker is responsible for getting that done efficiently. In the indirect style, the most important thing is preserving respect among the participants; and the listeners are responsible for getting the point.

For the American, it's no problem being asked *do you understand?* because the speaker is responsible for communicating the point; and if the answer is *no*, then he will make a greater effort to communicate.

But for the Mexican, *do you understand?* sounds slightly offensive; since this question is for children or the feebleminded who have problems reasoning (p. 127).

Wu and Rubin (2000) documented similar pragmatics in the writing of Taiwanese, English language learners who ". . . tended to use more proverbs and to express humaneness, collective virtues, and limited use of personal anecdotes" (p. 148). In their writing, these students were more likely to draw upon values related to family and society, preferring the pronoun "we" to "I."

When providing counsel to students in the revising stage of their writing, teachers must carefully consider cultural context before advising a student to "write right to the point," teachers would be wise to consider the pragmatics of the student's culture of origin as well as the envisioned audience for whom the student may be writing. Consider Tiffany's point about sounding offensive before asking: "Do you understand?" Later in this chapter we will discuss the pragmatics of African American oral and written language. We will also consider effective ways to provide second language learners editorial feedback.

Editing

The objective of the *editing* stage is to put the piece of writing into its final form. During this stage, students develop their ability to *proofread*. Proofreading is a unique form of reading in which students read one-word-at-a-time to hunt for errors. This is the stage when the student must use their red pen, spellchecker/dictionary, and style manual to find and correct errors in capitalization, punctuation, spelling, sentence structure, usage, and formatting considerations.

During the middle school years, and in many content classrooms, many teachers provide their students with "style sheets" designed specifically to subject matter and grade level. These include guidelines for mechanics and lists of frequently misspelled words. For example, in science and math, the correct way to notate formulae and abbreviations might be listed along with rules about format. Mechanics are taught in most English classes; however, research has shown that students will only transfer these skills to their other writing when they are required to do so in their content-area classes (Fearn & Farnan, 1998; Hillocks, 1986).

The Importance of Correct Punctuation

Ever had a student who did not appreciate the value of correct punctuation? Share the two versions of the following note by Gloria for John:

Dear John:

I want a man who knows what love is all about. You are generous, kind, thoughtful. People who are not like you admit to being useless and inferior. You have ruined me for other men. I yearn for you. I have no feelings whatsoever when we're apart. I can be forever happy—will you let me be yours?

Gloria

Dear John:

I want a man who knows what love is. All about you are generous, kind, thoughtful people, who are not like you. Admit to being useless and inferior. You have ruined me. For other men, I yearn. For you, I have no feelings whatsoever. When we're apart, I can be forever happy. Will you let me be?

Yours,

Gloria

Publishing

Publishing, for all intents and purposes, is a post-writing activity. The objective of this stage is to disseminate the finished product to the audience for whom it was written. Most often, the audience is the teacher. Whenever possible, the audience should be peers, other students, parents, or other community members because students can better understand reasons for careful writing when they know others are going to read it for information or entertainment.

When teachers expand the forms of writing used by their students, they can provide them with authentic opportunities to publish. For example, members of a shop class can publish instructions for building a bird feeder from scraps of lumber. Students in a health and fitness class can publish information for athletes on how diet can enhance performance. Students in a history class can publish information pamphlets on local historical events. Students in a math class can publish information on the probability of a city's sports team improving their record. Publishing on school, class, or personal web pages has become common; however, teachers need to make sure that student work is edited and meets school district requirements before placing these on the World Wide Web.

 ## The Link Between Assessment and Writing to Learn

The use of a common vocabulary to enhance communication is essential for teachers or peers to provide students with feedback on their content writing. Let us start with the word *assessment*. As mentioned in the chapter on matching print with reader, *assessment* is rooted in the Latin word *assidere*, which means "to sit next to." When we assess writing we are sitting, sometimes literally—sometimes figuratively, next to writers and listening to their thinking put into writing. Our job is to provide feedback on content and style. Speaking in broad terms, there are two types of writing assessment: holistic and analytic.

Holistic assessment involves giving feedback based on a general or whole impression. Since the whole is greater than the sum of its parts, all aspects of a piece of writing, its content, organization, voice, mechanics, etc., are considered together. The focus is on how the writing addresses its objective, as a whole.

Often, when writing is scored holistically, anchor papers are used. Student writings can thus be compared to these exemplars of strong, acceptable, and weak writing. For example, a science teacher may collect lab reports from her students. During her first reading, she makes corrections about content, method, and/or glaring mechanical errors. Then, sometimes using exemplars from previous classes, sometimes not, she creates five piles, from strongest to weakest. Papers receive grades from "A" to "F" accordingly. Suffice to say, reliability of holistic scores is tricky to attain. More important, without analysis and specific comments about content, organization, word choice, voice, etc., the students may view their teacher's assessment as arbitrary or capricious. (One paper that receives a high score may have strong voice but weak mechanics, while another paper that receives a high score may have strong mechanics but weak voice.) In some cases, students can develop poor self-image about their writing because the specifics of what they can do to improve their performance has not been provided.

Analytic assessment is based on the idea that there are multiple traits in good writing. Papers assessed in this fashion provide feedback on each trait separately, thereby recognizing relative strengths and weaknesses within the paper. Analytic assessment is frequently used in the revision and editing stages of process writing. Diederich (1974) developed one of the first analytic scoring systems for high school and college students.

He divided writing performance into two main categories, general merit (ideas, organization, wording, and style) and mechanics (usage, sentence structure, punctuation, capitalization, spelling, and neatness). Other analytic tools have been developed since. One of these is the Six-Trait Assessment Tool (Culham, 2003) originally developed for 4th through 12th grade students peer editing. When the same students have teachers from different disciplines who use the same analytic categories, students not only benefit from consistency, but also learn to apply these concepts in their writings across the curriculum.

When using analytic assessment, content teachers need not address all six traits at the same time. Instead they may pick from those that are most relevant to the assignment. Returning to the example of the science teacher scoring lab reports, the teacher would pass out the directions for her assignment and include a checklist or rubric. This checklist would explicitly articulate those traits she intends to use in order to score their papers (e.g., content, organization, word choice, proper scientific notation, etc.). After students have created a draft of their lab reports, they would meet in pairs and peer-edit, using the rubric or checklist to provide feedback. Finally, after students have had the opportunity to improve upon their writing, these papers are collected by the teacher and scored. The teacher may choose to weight traits differently in assigning the final grade, and provide trait scores and a holistic final score. In the end, papers returned to students have specific feedback about the strengths and weaknesses of their papers (e.g., ideas are good but organization made it difficult to understand the content) so students will have a better idea what to do to improve next time.

Analytic Traits of Writing

A six-trait model for describing and assessing writing was originally developed to train students to be self-assessors of writing (Arter, Spandel, Culham, & Pollard, 1994) and with refinement has become a widely used system to help teachers and students name and assess the relative strengths and weaknesses in their writing. The descriptions that follow are adapted for assessment of content writing from the work of the Northwest Educational Regional Laboratories (2004), Culham (2003), and Spandel (2000).

Ideas and Content (Details, Development, and Focus)

When speaking with students about their content-writing assignments, this trait is nearly always relevant. When assessing this trait, we ask the following:

Positive	In Need of Improvement
Is the information provided sufficient in length and content and is that content accurate? Are readers' questions anticipated and answered?	Is the length inadequate to fully provide an answer? Is some of the information inaccurate? Is the reader left with unanswered questions?
Are details provided to support main ideas? Are these details relevant, telling, of good quality?	Are the ideas a simple restatement of the topic or an answer to a question with little or no attention to detail in the answer? Does the writer have trouble going from general observations to specifics?
Does the writing provide focus and insight? Has the writer chosen to include content that is clearly significant?	Is the text repetitive? Does the data supported appear to be a collection of disconnected, random thoughts with no discernible point?

Organization (Internal Structure)

Organization is the internal structure of a piece of writing. Some writing products require a specific form of organization; others do not. For example, chronology is often important in scientific or historical writing, however, a narrative recount might include flashbacks so that the reader can better understand the relationship of events to a central theme. When assessing this trait, we ask the following:

Positive	In Need of Improvement
Is the structure that the writer uses to sequence events or details logical and effective? Does the writing have a flow that smoothly guides the reader through the content?	Does the sequence or lack of a sequence distract the reader from the content of the writing? Does it seem as if sometimes the reader is forced to lunge ahead too quickly or is being dragged along too slowly?
Are thoughtful transitions provided to show how ideas between paragraphs or sections are connected?	Are transitions from one idea to the next either missing or unclear? Is it difficult to discern how ideas from one sentence, or paragraph, to the next sentence/paragraph are connected?
Does the writing have a clear beginning and ending? When appropriate, does the writer choose to use a title that captures the central theme of the writing?	Does the writer fail to provide a clear lead to help the reader know what will follow, and/or is there no clear conclusion or end to the piece? Does the title (when appropriate) match well with the content?

Workshop 8.2

Practice in Assessing Writing for Ideas and Organization

The following is a copy of part of a persuasive letter written by a sixth-grade student to her teacher. The writer's intent was to convince the teacher that she would be the best candidate to be the "Tech. Maven" in their classroom. Read it once for content and ideas, and then again for organization. Consult the tables above. With regards to these two traits, what could you tell this student was positive about the first three paragraphs of her persuasive essay? What suggestions would you make for improvement? (Some sample answers may be found in Appendix 8A at the end of this chapter.)

Just imagine this, you getting a whole bunch of e-mails about having a problem with someone's computer or they need pictures for a class project that they are working on. I can imagine that you will feel like e-mailing them and telling them that they can ask someone else to do it because you are tired of being their slave. Well, don't because I have a solution for you. I could be a Tech. Maven this trimester. I am responsible. I have had experience and I love technology.

I'll start with responsibility. I think I served Acme Elementary well. I took pictures and printed them for Mrs. Chase. I did a section of the Veteran's Day slide show. I also made part of the mini DYB. Did you notice that I got all that stuff done on time while keeping my grades high? If I needed to I would take the project home and work on it.

I think Tech. Mavens also need a lot of experience. Well I fit that criteria too. I remember when I was three and I turned on the computer for my mom because she didn't know how. That would make it eight years (almost nine years) of experience. To me that sounds like a quality that a Tech. Maven would need. . . .

Voice (Tone, Style, Purpose, and Audience)

Have you ever read a piece by Garrison Keillor, Carl Sagan, or Dave Barry? Did you really need to read the byline to identify the author? Writers with "voice" speak directly to readers in a way that is individual, engaging, and yet respectful. However, there are many types of content writing (e.g., historical and scientific accounts) for which there is the expectation of objectivity, and hence voice is considered inappropriate. When assessing this trait, we ask the following:

Positive	In Need of Improvement
Can the reader sense the personality of the writer behind the words?	Does the writer weigh ideas so carefully that they discard personal insights in favor of safe generalities?
If narrative, does the text seem honest, personal, and from the heart? If expository or persuasive, does the text seem to reflect a strong commitment or degree of caring about the subject?	If narrative, does the text lack honesty and passion? If expository, does the writer fail to consistently engage the topic sufficiently to build credibility?
Does the author use literary devices such as metaphor, simile, hyperbole, or personification to communicate the ideas of the text?	Does the text appear more technical or jargonistic than necessary? Does the writing appear lifeless or mechanical? Is the text more objective than necessary? Does the writer use so many stylistic phrases that they interfere with reading?

Word Choice (Precise Language and Phrasing)

When speaking with students about their content-writing assignments, this trait is also nearly always relevant. In good descriptive writing, strong word choice clarifies and expands ideas. Word choice involves colorful and precise use of vocabulary. Please remember that the use of multisyllabic words will not necessarily improve clarity. In fact, it often obfuscates discernment (*smile!*). When assessing this trait, we ask the following:

Positive	In Need of Improvement
Are words specific and accurate, natural and not overdone? (e.g., The deep indigo and vibrant orange of this morning's sunrise were awe-inspiring.)	Are words vague and general? (e.g., The wonderful colors of this morning's sunrise were really cool and neat. I mean really, really cool!)
Does the author use lively verbs and descriptive adjectives that create pictures in the readers' minds?	Are words used incorrectly making the message harder to understand? Does limited vocabulary or misuse of parts of speech impair understanding?
Do striking words or phases catch the reader's eye? Is it obvious to the reader that the author is being precise in description?	Does jargon or use of cliché distract or mislead the reader? Does redundancy in word choice distract the reader?

Workshop 8.3

Practice in Assessing Writing for Voice and Word Choice

Find below a copy of part of a persuasive letter written by a sixth-grade student to her teacher. Like the previous author, this writer's intent was to convince the teacher that she would be the best candidate to be the "Tech. Maven" in their classroom. Read it once for voice and then again for word choice. Consult the tables above. With regards to these two traits, what could you tell this student was positive about the first paragraph of her persuasive essay? What suggestions would you make for improvement? (Some sample answers may be found in Appendix 8A at the end of this chapter.)

> When your brain is popping, bopping and swirling around with frustration from a locked out computer you probably thinking "I need HELP!", and when you are overwhelmed with projects and you have absolutely not time to do them you are probably also thinking "I need HELP!" And then you start thinking about details like what kinds of qualities will this "Helper" have to have? They would probably have to be smart. They would have almost all A's in school, have experience with technical stuff, and be willing to do any project that is needed. Well my friend, you have just described the perfect job for me! And that is why you are reading this letter. I am applying to be your tech maven. Now, if you already have your heart set on a few kids to be tech maven then I suggest, HIGHLY suggest, that you DON'T read this letter, because it will be so convincing that you will never see what hit you. . . .

Sentence Fluency (Correctness, Rhythm, and Cadence)

Sentence fluency is the rhythm and flow of the language. This trait is especially important when working with students who are writing for oral presentation. Fluency is also important when revising text. When assessing this trait, we ask the following:

Positive	In Need of Improvement
Are sentences constructed in ways that underscore and enhance meaning? Do these sentences vary in length and structure?	Are sentences choppy, incomplete, or awkward? Do many sentences start and end in the same way?
Does the writing include appropriate connectives (e.g., however, therefore, on the other hand, first of all, finally, etc.) to show how ideas in one sentence are related to the next?	Does the reader have to hunt for clues as to how sentences interrelate? Or, does the writer use so many of the same connectives that there is a massive jumble of language?
Does writing have a cadence that invites oral reading? Does the phrasing sound natural? Has the writer attended to how the words will sound when read aloud?	Would a reader have trouble reading this aloud? Do sentences have a stiff or choppy quality? Would expressive reading of this text sound awkward?

Conventions (Mechanics)

Fail to attend to the conventions of any distributed piece of writing, by teacher or student, and that teacher and/or their supervisor will receive an abundance of complaints. This is because many parents, and the public in general, believe that mechanics is the most important trait of good writing. Writing that is strong in conventions has been proofread and edited with care. When assessing this trait, we ask the following:

Positive	In Need of Improvement
Did the writer consistently use spelling, punctuation, capitalization, grammar, and usage correctly?	Does the writing contain frequent and noticeable errors in spelling, punctuation, grammar, and usage? Must the reader reread parts of the document several times just to decode?
Does the writer manipulate conventions (e.g., colloquial language/spelling/sentence structure) for stylistic effect and, if so, does this work?	Does the intentional inclusion of colloquial language/spelling/sentence structure make the writing overly difficult to understand? Does it distort the intended meaning?
Is this "copy clean enough" to be published and distributed to the public?	Is extensive editing and polishing needed before it may be published? What would we want to improve before we shared this with those outside our classroom?

Workshop 8.4

Practice in Assessing Writing for Sentence Fluency and Conventions

Find below a copy of part of a persuasive essay written by a fifth-grade reluctant writer. At the suggestion of his teacher he is writing about why he doesn't like writing. Read it once for sentence fluency and then again for conventions. Consult the tables above. With regards to these two traits, what could you tell this student was positive about the first paragraph of his persuasive essay? What suggestions would you make for improvement? (Some sample answers may be found in Appendix 8A at the end of this chapter.)

> Okay, you like writing well I don't. You probably wouldn't like my essay. I'm writing this because I had not ideas on what to write, which brought me to my point. We write too many essays around here.
>
> My first reason that I think I shouldn't write this essay is that I don't like writing essays. I don't like it because I don't get ideas in my head as fast as others. After all the frustration I fall behind and end up with a sloppy essay. When I have a sloppy essay I know that there's no way you are going to choose my essay.
>
> I just like to write my own things. When you tell me what to write, I feel frustrated because I know write better if I just started writing. When we just start writing it makes me feel so good because I know I'll write better and have way more fun.

Nonstandard Dialects and Conventions

Reading *The Story of English* (McCrum, Cran, & MacNeil, 1986) can lead one to the conclusion that there is no such thing as "standard English," that everyone speaks a dialect or variety of speech. Nonetheless, there are varieties of dialect, such as "news broadcast-type" English that are considered more standard than others. Many have argued that if students are to have access to opportunities in mainstream society, they must master standard English.

Over the last decade highly charged debates have been waged over the use of nonstandard varieties of English dialect, such as Ebonics and Spanglish, in American classrooms. Many have attempted to correct misinformed assumptions that nonstandard dialects are somehow defective representations of English. In fact, many researchers, like Meier (1998a), have shown that dialects like Ebonics have highly developed phonological and structural rules associated with Black oral and written traditions. These include ". . . intonational patterns; metaphorical language; concrete examples and analogies to make a point; rhyme, rhythm, alliteration, and others forms of repetition, including word play; use of proverbs, aphorisms, biblical quotations and learned allusions . . ." (p. 99).

This brings us back to the idea of evaluating student papers for conventions. Whose dialectic code for proper spelling and syntax should the teacher follow when noting errors in spelling, grammar, or usage? Certainly all teachers should be knowledgeable in the conventions of standard English. However, should they also know enough of the dialect of their students to recognize, appreciate, and acknowledge its proper use? In weighing this question, we hope that teachers will keep in mind what Delpit (1998) tells us about these cultural dialects:

> . . . the linguistic form a student brings to school is intimately connected with loved ones, community, and personal identity. To suggest that this form is "wrong" or, even worse, ignorant, is to suggest that something is wrong with the student and his or her family. To denigrate your language is, then in African American terms, to "talk about your mama." Anyone who knows anything about African-American culture knows the consequences of that speech act (p. 19).

Workshop 8.5

Errors in Conventions or Cultural Sensitivity?

After reading the passage and considering your answers to the questions that follow, form small groups and share your answers and perspectives.

African American student, Charice, shares a paper with you, her teacher, for input. Content and ideas are relevant and abundant, however, errors in conventions, like the ones in the summary sentences that follow, attract your attention:

> *As you can see, when it comes to challenging the racist hatred of Apartheid in South Africa, Mandela be looking good. He be looking good in prison. He be looking good as President. He be looking good. He be free.*

Using standard English conventions, what error(s) do you see? Before you take out your red pen, consider one of the important syntactical conventions of Standard Black English—the use of "be" to convey habitual action (Honegger, 2001, p. 102). Within this conventional use, "I *be* going to church" means that I go to church every Sunday. On the other hand, "I go to church" means that I may have gone last week, but that isn't always the case. In Charice's sentences about Nelson Mendela, "*be*" may have been used to communicate that Mendela was not just "looking good" on one day, but looking good has been his state of affairs for some time. Correcting ". . . Mendela be looking good" to ". . . Mendela looks good" would change the meaning of the sentence to ". . . Mendela looks good today."

In small groups discuss your answers to the following questions:

- Would you point out Charice's errors in usage? Why, or why not?
- If the answer to the previous question is "yes" how would you do so? How would you acknowledge/honor the concerns that her parents and/or community member might bring to your attention about her dialectical heritage? If the answer is "no," how would you acknowledge/honor the concerns of an administrator and/or parent who finds fault with your decision because they are concerned that she might not pass the standardized test required for graduation?
- When grading papers written by students from cultures other than your own, are there questions about dialectical meaning and conventions that you need to learn? If so, how and where would you gather this information?

FROM THE CONTENT CLASSROOM

"Each Has Its Proper Time and Place"

A Black middle school principal came to speak to a university class of future student teachers. The principal spoke with a soft "cultured" Bahamian accent, his English "standard and refined." Willie, a black intern, listened respectfully but not enthusiastically. Suddenly and without warning, the principal broke into a Black dialect. Willie perked up, but didn't seem as entertained as his White classmates. After class, Willie approached the administrator. "With all due respect, what were you trying to prove?" he asked. Making direct eye contact, the principal answered, "My work requires that I speak 'standard English,' but that doesn't mean that I stop using the language of my family, friends and community. Each has its proper time and place. I model this for my students and today I modeled it for you. If you want to come to teach at my school, I would hope that you could do the same."

Electronic Connections: To Six-Trait Analysis and More

North West Regional Educational Lab: links to loads of research-based writing resources:
http://www.nwrel.org/comm/topics/writing.html

Six-Trait Writing Links and Lessons:
http://www.holbrook.k12.az.us/sixtrait/sixindex.html

Ginny's Educational Web Pages:
http://www.ginnyhoover.com/

Content-Area Writing Tasks, Assignments, and Activities

The tasks, assignments, and activities that follow are divided into two broad categories, *low-stakes-writing*—most often informal and used formatively, and *high-stakes-writing*—more formal in nature and usually assessed in a summative fashion.

Low-Stakes Writing Activities

Low-stakes writing tasks tend to appear in multiple forms and include journals, logs, quick writes, and biopoems. Researchers like Peter Elbow (1997) have established that low-stakes writing can help students become more involved in the ideas or subject matter of a course. This is because low-stakes writing helps them find their own language for the issues they are studying as ". . . they stumble into their own analogies and metaphors for academic concepts." Doing so enables students to ". . . write and talk about what is in the textbook and the lectures in their own lingo, in their informal home or personal language" (p. 7).

Admit Slips, Quick-Writes, and Exit Slips

Often teachers will begin a class by asking, "What questions do you have about the assigned reading?" These same teachers often end a class by asking, "Are there any questions?" In both cases, student responses tend to vary from silence to the minimal. Consider instead the versatile strategies *Admit/Exit Slips* and/or *Quick-Writes.*

Admit Slips (Andrews, 1997): Upon arrival in class students are given an index card, on which they are asked to respond, anonymously, to a question or to provide the teacher and class with questions of their own. The teacher collects these cards, and before starting the planned lesson, selects several to read aloud to the class. Here are a few examples of admit slip questions:

- What was the main idea in what you read last night? What was the most confusing point? What questions do you have?
- Describe what was easy and what was difficult for you in solving the 10 math problems you had for homework last night. What questions do you have?
- Based on what you read last night, do you think the pituitary gland is the most important gland in the endocrine system? What questions do you have?
- I asked you last night to watch the president's speech. In that speech he talked a great deal about "freedom." Before we get started, please write what you think the word *freedom* means. What questions do you have about this?

Quick-Writes (Andrasick, 1990): These 3- to 5-minute writing activities may be used to activate prior knowledge, establish personal relevancy, and/or build communities of understanding. During the time period students are encouraged to keep their pens and pencils moving, writing whatever comes to mind and not stopping to correct what they have written. Quick-writes are not collected. Instead, students are asked to talk about what they had written. When the time is up, students are asked to share ideas with their classmates, either in pairs, small groups, or with the class as a whole. Sample quick-write prompts may include:

- We are about to read a short story in which the main character has a very hard decision to make. Think of a time when you were faced with a hard decision. What was that like for you? Did you make the right decision? Why, or why not?
- What does the term *manifest destiny* mean to you? What do you think it might mean to a Native American or Mexican American? Why?

Quick-writes may be used before or after a reading, video, or class discussion. They may also be a helpful means to circumvent a discussion that is being dominated by one or two students, or to help the class refocus a class discussion that is rambling.

Exit Slips (Andrews, 1997): These activities may be used to bring closure to a lesson. Responding to prompts, students reflect on what they just learned, or ask questions about what they find confusing. Once again, no names are used. These cards, collected as students exit the classroom, can provide invaluable information about the success of a lesson and guide the review portion of the next day's lesson. Here are three sample exit prompts:

- Why is sunlight needed to maintain an ecosystem? Why are there no tall trees in the desert? What questions about today's lesson for the teacher?
- Do you think that the eleven southern states were justified in seceding from the Union? Why, or why not? What questions about today's lesson for the teacher?
- Why are humans not considered good organisms for genetic studies? What questions about this do you have for the teacher?

Please note that *Admit/Exit Slips* and *Quick-Writes* are products of the drafting stage of the writing process. Students need not print the words "Rough Draft" at the top of their cards, however, they will need to be reminded that their emphasis should be on content, not mechanics.

Free Writing, Journals (Personal, Dialogue, and Double-Entry), and Learning Logs

Free Writing (Macrorie, 1970): Times have changed since the free thinking late 1960s and early 1970s, and standards-driven learning requirements rarely permit teachers the luxury of allotting students time to write "freely." Nonetheless, providing students short periods of time to privately, and confidentially, write their thoughts and feelings on a topic may be especially helpful to those in need of time for reflection on learning. Perhaps "focused-free writing" is an oxymoron; nonetheless, quick-writes, journals, and reading/learning logs are focused extensions of the idea of free writing.

Journal writing may take many forms. Herein we will discuss three: personal journals, dialogue journals, and double-entry journals.

Personal Journals (Tompkins, 2000): All sorts of people—explorers, artists, biologists, dancers, mathematicians, musicians, and athletes have kept journals to "record the everyday events of their lives and the issues that concern them." Many young people become acquainted with personal journals by reading the poetic journal entries of black rapper Tupac Shakur (1999), Holocaust victim Anne Frank (1953), or Sarajevo child-survivor Zlata Filipovic (1994). In order to better make the reading/writing connection, students can be encouraged to keep personal journals, or diaries, in which they recount the events in their lives.

As one can see by the name, personal journals are personal, hence most times private. Nonetheless, personal journals may be used in the academic setting. If a teacher will be collecting and/or reading student journals, she should let them know so that they can exclude information or thoughts they wish to be kept private. Entries about illegal or safety issues such as child abuse, sexual activity, or drug use may require teacher action. These issues and others related to *risky writing* are discussed later in this chapter.

Dialogue Journals: A dialogue is a conversation between two or more people. Dialogue journals were used originally to respond to literature, however, over the last decade, applications to other content reading have grown exponentially. Dialogue journals provide students and their teachers with opportunities to write back and forth in a journal format. Nancy Atwell (1987), a pioneer in this technique, asked her middle school students to talk about what they had read telling what they thought and felt and why. She asked them what they liked and what they didn't and why. She asked them to write about what their books said and meant to them and in their writing to share their feelings, ideas, experiences, and questions.

Atwell collected these, and then wrote back to her students. Her responses were neither judgmental nor critical. Instead she used these exchanges to connect personally with her students, encouraging them to voice their opinions and thus expand on the meaning of the text. Dialogue journals are most effective when teachers accentuate the positive of what was written, responding with sincerity, and always protecting the feelings of their students (Nistler, 1998).

Teacher responses need not be lengthy; a sentence or two is often enough. When responding, teachers should write less than the students, making sure not to ask too many questions. Instead, teachers should encourage students to ask questions of them.

Double-Entry Journals: As the name implies, double-entry journals (Calkins, 1986) require students to divide their journal pages in half designating one side for taking notes (copying verbatim) quotations, definitions, or other information directly from the text, and the other for making notes (written reflection) in the form of thoughts, questions, or comments. (For more information on taking and making notes, see Chapter One.) This format encourages students to have a written conversation with themselves about the meaning of what they have noted in their first column.

This technique is ripe for modification as needed in the content areas. For example, Tobias (1989) encourages math teachers to have their students use double-entry journals to solve word problems. In one of the columns students show their work by writing their solution to a problem, but as they do so, they write about what they are doing and why they are doing it in the other column. Students whose teachers want them to focus on the comprehension skill of prediction can use the left-hand column to write down predictions of what they think will happen on the next page or chapter, and then the right-hand column to document what really happened (Macon, Bewell, & Vogt, 1991).

Learning Logs: Learning logs are notebooks kept in content classrooms in which students record their learning before and after reading, observing, or participating in an activity. This simple strategy, when used regularly, can be an effective means to get students to record ideas, questions, and reactions to what they have read or observed in class.

FROM THE CONTENT CLASSROOM

Learning Notebooks in a Middle School Science Classroom

One middle school science teacher has his students record all of their questions, observations, data, and conclusions in science notebooks that they keep in the classroom. His seventh graders' notebooks are entitled: Scientific Investigations into the Properties of Matter. Below the title they are instructed to write: "If it isn't written down, it isn't science."

The structure and sequence of what they do makes their writing self-generating. In the very beginning the teacher proposes a question. Students are asked to write the question as well as what they already know that might help them find an answer. Next, students are asked to generate and record a hypothesis that may be tested. The teacher then informs his students what materials are available and they are then encouraged to generate an experiment to test their hypothesis. Students complete their experiment and record their results.

Finally, students write a conclusion, recommendations, and/or new questions. First, they are asked to determine, in writing, if the results of their experiment answered the question with which they started. Next, students generate recommendations for further experiments. Most end up with new questions, from which the teacher directs students to further experiment, thus using the inquiry method to master the learning objectives. Entries in these notebooks influence learning by helping students document their work, the reasoning behind it, and their process of learning.

Biopoems, Diamante Poems, RAFT, and Alphabet Books

Biopoems (Gere, 1985): Somewhat similar to the idea of using cinquains as summaries (see Chapter Seven), a *biopoem* allows students to reflect and synthesize large amounts of material within a poetic form. In English, social studies, or science, a biopoem might be about a person or character—fictional or real life. Here is an example of a biopoem format (feel free to modify) as well as a completed history biopoem:

Line 1:	Name
Line 2:	Four traits that describe the character or entity
Line 3:	Country, time period, or relative of
Line 4:	Enjoys (list three things or people)
Line 5:	Who/which feels (list three emotions)

Line 6:   Who/which needs (list three)
Line 7:   Who/which fears (list three)
Line 8:   Who/which gives or acts (list three)
Line 9:   Resides in
Line 10:   Synonym, describing person or entity as a whole (e.g., historian, amphibian, classic, etc.)

Janusz Korczak,
A devoted physician and doctor who ran an orphanage.
Lived in Warsaw, Poland, during the Holocaust
Loved children, especially orphans, and telling stories
He felt compassion, responsibility, understanding and hope.
His children needed nurturing, support, and guidance.
He feared for their health, for their safety, for their lives.
When given the chance to escape he said, "You don't leave a sick child home alone, and you don't leave children at a time like this."
He and his children died at the concentration camp at Treblinka
He was a hero.

Diamante Poems: Similar in concept and purpose to cinquains and biopoems, students who write diamante poems get to reflect their understanding of how two opposite ideas are part of a larger concept. A diamante poem begins with one subject at the top of its diamond shape and ends with an opposite subject at the bottom. It has seven lines and does not rhyme.

Lines 1 and 7 name the opposites.
Lines 2 and 6 describe the opposite subjects.
Lines 3 and 5 list action words about each opposite.
The first have of line 4 lists nouns related to the first subject, the second half lists nouns related to the second.

For example:

City
Noisy, busy
Growing, crowding, moving
Building, streets, trees, barns
Charming, mellowing, relaxing
Slow, peaceful
Country

To see another example of a diamante poem, used in this instance, to summarize a chapter, turn back to the end of Chapter Six.

RAFT—Role, Audience, Form, and Topic (Santa, Havens, & Harrison, 1996): This writing strategy helps students personalize the concepts they are learning by transforming their perceptions of the topic. When using the RAFT acronym, students are encouraged to brainstorm.

Role: Is the author a thing, a concept, or a person or an animal? What do I already know about this role? What do I need to know?

Audience: To whom are you writing? What do I already know about this audience? What do I need to know?

Format: What form do you want your writing to take? (See Table 8.3)

Topic: With regards to topic, what do you want to write about?

TABLE 8.3 Examples of R.A.F.T. Forms

Role	Audience	Format	Topic
Seismologist	A concerned group of citizens	A newspaper article	The dangers of living on the San Andreas Fault
Propagandist	Unwitting citizenry	Information pamphlet	The powers under a dictatorship
Repeating decimal	Set of rational numbers	Petition	Prove you belong to this set
Huck Finn	Jim	Letter	What I learned on my trip
News Reporter	TV audience	Script	The process of amending the Constitution
Salmon	Self	Diary	Spawning
Carrot	Other carrots	Travel guide	Journey through the digestive system
Author	Children	Historical fiction	An account of surviving the Titanic
Debater	Mathematicians	Persuasive essay	Should "0" be considered a number?

Alphabet Books: Oftentimes, when presented with a great number of items to organize, showcase, or demonstrate, we place these items in alphabetical order—hence, the idea of an *alphabet book.* Cutting pictures from magazines or drawing illustrations of their own, students, working individually or in small groups, can construct an alphabet book about almost anything. When the gym in not available, health and fitness teachers can have students construct alphabet books about sports, their teams, and heroes. The science teacher can have students create alphabet books about plants, animals, arthropods, insects, and combinations of these.

One excellent way to get students started is to show them some alphabet books that have been published. Here is a short list of some of our favorites:

- *Navaho ABC: A Dine Alphabet Book* by Luci Tapahonso and Eleanor Schick, Simon and Schuster, 1995.
- *Hieroglyphs From A to Z: A Rhyming Book With Ancient Egyptian Stencils* by Peter Der Manuelian, Boston, Museum of Fine Arts, 1991.
- *Alison's Zinnia* by Anita Lobel, Mulberry Books, 1990 (flowers).
- *The Handmade Alphabet* by Laura Rankin, Puffin Pied Piper Books, 1991 (American Sign Language).
- *A Bold Carnivore: An Alphabet of Predators* by Consie Powell, Roberts Rinehart, 1995.
- *Alaska ABC Book* by Charlene Kreeger and Shannon Cartwright, 1985, 4th printing; Box 5-000-90, Wasilla, Alaska 99687.
- *New Mexico A to Z*, by Dorthy Weaver, Northland Publishing, 1996.
- *The Ultimate Alphabet* by Mike Wilks, New York: Henry Holt, 1986. (A journey through the English language—reading the pictures—with workbook)

Key Pals, Blogs, and Digital Stories

Key Pals: To the chagrin of most teachers, students write, pass, and read notes incessantly. Creative teachers have learned that, with a little planning and with careful supervision, this negative may be turned into a positive by using the 21st century adaptation of the pen pal, the *key pal*.

A quick web search can help a teacher connect with another teacher in just about any region, state, or country in the world. Think of how much more powerful it is to study about the geography or climate of a region when you can e-mail someone who lives there. Think about how meaningful reading and writing in French, or another language, can be when you correspond with someone from Paris. Or consider the value of sharing lab data with students who are completing the same experiment in another region.

From among the burgeoning literature of educational e-mail correspondence are studies of bridges built between cultures and generations, many connected for a first time via the Internet. For example, Pirrone (1998) and McClanahan (2001) had students communicating with distant peers (across and between continents, respectively), giving and receiving information that both requested and needed about their lives and about what they were reading and writing. Britsch and Berkson (1997) enabled mainstream students to correspond with students with handicaps. Wolpow, Neff, and Neff (2002) successfully linked rural students with preservice teachers who mentored their middle school key pals in writing while helping them consider high school and college possibilities. At the same time, the authors linked sixth-grade rural students who were studying the Holocaust with a survivor who lived miles away.

Some of the **benefits** of key-pal exchanges include:

- Opportunities to write for authentic audiences about authentic content.
- E-mail is asynchronic communication. That is, students can take however long they need to revise and edit before sending their messages. This can be especially advantageous to second language learners and students with learning difficulties.
- Opportunities to gain an understanding, through written communications, of diverse uses of language, such as differing patterns and dialects across cultures and ethnic groups.

Some of the **challenges** of key-pal exchanges include:

- Most schools do have policies about the use of e-mail accessed within their campuses. However, there is nothing to prevent a student from taking home an e-mail address and corresponding independently. While in most cases this can be a positive, there is the potential for unsupervised inappropriate and/or illegal communication that could result in harm.
- Absences and or unequal access to the Internet by one key pal may result in breakdowns in communication and thus student frustration.
- Comfort with audience can lead to less attention to conventions.

Blogs: A *blog*, or *web log*, is a personal website updated frequently with links, commentary, and anything else the writer likes. New items go on top and older items flow down the page. Blogs can be political journals and/or personal diaries; they can focus on one narrow subject or range across a universe of topics. People maintained blogs long before the term was coined, but the trend gained momentum with the introduction of automated published systems. One form of a blog can be a web page, maintained by the content teacher, of the writings and significant web links collected by students as they study an issue. Or, the teacher can subscribe to a published system. Either way, educators would be wise to consult their school's policy on using blogs before endeavoring to create a class blog.

Digital Storytelling: Projects that incorporate *digital storytelling* are limitless and range from telling a personal story to capturing the essence of a community through its stories. For example, students might interview Vietnam veterans (or even World War II vets), successful alumni, or community leaders to capture and present a story about their school and community. They would take both notes and digital pictures. Next they might prepare a script for a 2 to 4 minute movie. Using I-Movie or Movie Maker2 they combine narration of the script, appropriate music, and their digital images. These movies may be played for their classmates and/or posted to the Web. For more information visit the Center for Digital Storytelling: http://www.storycenter.org/index.html

One More Thought on Technology and Content Writing

James J. Duderstadt observes that the average student burns up hours of spare time playing video games on an Xbox, and perhaps more important, "Xbox gaming consoles have more processing power than most [university] faculty have ever seen in their lifetime" (confer Carlson, 2004, pp. A34–35). The authors wish to acknowledge that the readers of this text are more likely to be aware of current-day applications of technology than we are. Working in consort with your colleagues, students, and their parents, you may conceive of new applications of applying technology to enhance content writing. A Web search will often reveal many opportunities to obtain funding for classroom projects of this nature. As you plan such a project, make sure to: (1) remain cognizant of what you have learned about writing forms, the stages of the writing process, and the link between assessment and writing to learn; and (2) secure the approval and support of your administrators and parent association.

High-Stakes Writing

One of the most complex tasks that a teacher can give students is to write a formal essay or a research paper. These tasks require students to combine information gathered from multiple sources. Scores on these essays and reports usually constitute a significant portion of a class grade, and hence are considered "high stake." The formats for these tasks are usually more rigid and formal.

The Five-Paragraph Essay

A traditional format for writing a short paper, the five-paragraph essay, may be expository (giving information, explaining a topic), persuasive (convincing the reader that a point of view is best), or narrative (recounting a personal story). Each of the five paragraphs has a specific purpose. Before they start to write, students should decide on their *thesis* (main idea to be explained or advocated by the writer) and the three most important pieces of evidence or support they will use to substantiate it.

The first or *introductory paragraph* tells the reader what the paper is about. It should contain the *thesis statement*. The introductory paragraph should also include a mini-outline of the paper, introducing the three arguments or evidences that will be developed in paragraphs two, three, and four. Four or more well-written sentences usually present these arguments. By the time the readers have finished this paragraph, their interests should have piqued. Finally, this first paragraph should contain a transition sentence that "hooks" the reader into reading the next paragraph.

Paragraph two usually contains the most significant piece of information, most persuasive argument, or most obvious beginning point to the story. The topic for this paragraph should be in the first or second sentence and it should tie directly to the thesis. Three to four sentences usually elaborate upon this topic. The last sentence in this paragraph should transition the reader to the next point.

Paragraphs three and four usually contain the second and third most important pieces of information, second most persuasive arguments, or obvious follow-up to the earlier narrative. The first sentence in each paragraph should have a reverse hook, that is, it should tie to the transition provided in the previous paragraph. The topic of each of these paragraphs should be in the first of second sentence and it should relate directly to the thesis. Three to four sentences usually elaborate upon this topic. The last sentence should be a transition that hooks the reader into reading the next paragraph.

The *concluding paragraph* usually contains three or more sentences that creatively wrap up the essay in a clever or sophisticated fashion. This last paragraph should restate the thesis statement with a "twist," that is, it should restate without using the same exact words that appeared in the introduction. This paragraph should summarize the three main points from the body of the essay without providing any new evidence. The final sentence should signal to the reader that the essay has concluded. This can take the form suggesting the readers seek additional evidence, take action, or seek an experience of their own.

While most content-area teachers will grade these essays for subject content, the *Five-Paragraph Essay Rubric* (Appendix 8B at the end of this chapter) may be used to help younger students learn to write within this format.

An Alternative Approach to the Five-Paragraph Essay for Struggling Writers

It is not unusual for some students to find it difficult to organize content for a five-paragraph essay. One means to help struggling students get started is use of the PMI comprehension strategy described in Chapter Seven.

Each struggling student selects a topic, for example, whether or not skateboarding should be legal on the school grounds. The writer then makes a statement about what he or she believes should happen. This becomes the thesis statement. The writer then meets with a team of two or three students that she or he believes can present arguments. (This works best when the writer chooses team members who don't agree with each other.) The writer then asks each member of the team for plus arguments, minus arguments, and interesting arguments.

Introductory Paragraph	Whether or not skateboarding should be legal on campus is a controversial issue. I believe this is a good idea because all students will benefit from a change in this rule. First I will explain why making skating legal on campus is a good idea. In the next paragraph I will explain several reasons why this may not be such good idea. Then I will present several interesting questions that can't be answered at this point in time. Finally, I will explain why legalizing skating on campus is truly in the best interest of all students.
Paragraph #2	3 or 4 plus arguments
Paragraph #3	3 or 4 minus arguments
Paragraph #4	3 or 4 interesting questions
Concluding Paragraph	Summary of all arguments and conclusions

The Research Paper

When it comes to high-stakes writing tasks, the research paper can be found near the top of the pyramid. Some teachers call these research papers "term papers," a name that alludes to the idea that they represent many weeks of work over a term of study.

Consequently, many teachers, especially high school teachers, give substantial weight to scores on these papers when assigning semester grades. From the plethora of suggestions that students may find on the Web by searching on the topic "research papers," here are a few suggestions for the teachers who choose to assign them:

- Always review key terminology used in their assignment prompts. For example, teachers should make sure their students know what is meant by the terms *examine, analyze, compare, evaluate,* or *review.* (Definitions of these terms may be found on Table 10.1 of Chapter Ten.)

- Before going to the library, provide students with explicit help in selecting a topic. One method of doing so is TER, described below.

- Give students explicit assistance in locating relevant information for their report. Librarians can be incredibly helpful in this endeavor. Share your assignment with your school librarian ahead of time and have her or him help you design a lesson for your students on accessing appropriate references. Before going to the library, review methods for taking and making notes and for summarizing. (See Chapter One.)

- Model the process. Provide models of exemplary research reports for students to use as references. If the majority of students in your class have never written a term paper, do a cooperative report with your class. In this cooperative report the class completes the TER form as a group, researches answers to questions, then goes through all the necessary steps to complete the paper. This cooperative paper then becomes the exemplar for individual papers.

- Require that students do "process writing" and encourage them to use this process by assigning deadlines for pre-writing, drafting, revising, editing, and publishing. Collect artifacts from students at each stage and provide your students with feedback at each stage. For instance, collecting the TER worksheets early in the process will assure that students have formulated a topic and related questions.

- Once they have chosen a topic, teachers may help students draft a preliminary outline of their papers. One helpful format is to have students use questions in this outline. This will decrease "dump truck writing." By looking to find relevant information that answers these questions, students may be encouraged to write about what they have found instead of simply copying.

- Once students have their topic and an outline, encourage them to start writing early. Collect drafts of the paper. Get extra help to those students who are struggling early on.

- Allot class time for students to peer-edit using a rubric, such as the Six-Trait Rubric described above.

- Encourage students to revise extensively. Once they have a draft that is fairly complete and well organized, help them focus on transitions.

- Encourage students to find someone to proofread their final copy.

- Many teachers require students to submit drafts with their final copy. Some give points to students who can show that their writing evolved from one draft to the next.

TER: A Technique for Helping Students Select Topics for Essays

Adapted from Edward deBono's (1987) problem-solving tactic, this highly structured strategy is designed to help reluctant students brainstorm specific topics for their papers. Students are asked to direct their thinking at a definite *Target* by picking-out, identifying, or defining five specific subtopics and then *Expanding* upon this thinking by generating three questions for each of these five specific topics. Finally, students are asked to *Restrict*, by simplifying or condensing this series of 15 questions by creating a revised general topic in the form of a question. See Appendix 8C at the end of this chapter for samples of this method.

Writing and Second Language Learners in the Content Classroom

As mentioned in earlier chapters, students who speak a language other than English at home and whose proficiency in English is limited are the fastest-growing group of K–12 students in the United States. Gersten and Baker (2000) identified five specific instructional components in a program for English language learners: (1) vocabulary as a curricular anchor, (2) visuals to reinforce concepts and vocabulary, (3) cooperative learning and peer-tutoring strategies, (4) strategic use of the native language, and (5) modulation of cognitive and language demands.

Keeping these in mind, here are several general suggestions for working with students who are emerging bilingual writers:

- When writing prompts, keep them simple. Use direct language. Avoid jargon, figurative language, idioms, and cultural references with which non-English speakers will not be familiar. Use visuals (illustrations) to support the written word.
- Provide generous amounts of wait time. This will benefit all students but especially those less familiar with English.
- To help convey their ideas, English language learners may be encouraged to use illustrations and/or words from their native languages to supplement their writing.
- Encourage students, especially those who have already developed bilingual skills, to work cooperatively on writing assignments.
- Students who are literate in the native language may be encouraged to use their native language when given assignments like quick-writes. This is what is meant by "modulating cognitive demands." Underdeveloped mastery of English can leave language learners void of opportunities to show how well they can think. Besides, a quick-write can take forever if you don't know the English word for an idea.
- When grading ELLs' journal writing, teachers should rephrase students' errors to clarify ideas, providing essential input on the grammatical form, or suggesting a more appropriate word or phrase. Ignoring errors entirely or correcting all errors directly on the journal entry is not productive.

However, content teachers would be badly mistaken if they were to believe that practicing the above items alone will meet the needs of English language learners in their classrooms. Harper and de Jong (2004) point out that well-intentioned but counterproductive efforts to include English language learners in content classroom learning activities are often based upon four misconceptions.

1. Exposure and interaction will result in English language learning.
2. All ELLs learn English in the same way and at the same rate.
3. Good teaching for native speakers is good teaching for ELLs.
4. Effective instruction means nonverbal support.

Yes, all four are misconceptions. Yes, emerging an ELL student in a mainstream class does provide opportunities to use and develop language through its purposeful use. However, the main teaching purpose in a content classroom is mastery of the curriculum content. Consequently, most of the writing activities described throughout this chapter are examples of ways to use writing to help students master that content, in English. This is not enough.

If you are having trouble conceptualizing this, imagine traveling to a country where they don't speak your language. Imagine being invited into a classroom where an expert lectures on content with which you are only vaguely familiar and strongly suggests that you take notes. Imagine trying to make sense of the question-and-answer period at the end of the lesson. Worse yet, imagine what it would be like if you were expected to write an exit slip, in the native language, before you leave. If that's not bad enough, imagine having to complete, within the next 10 weeks, a high-stakes research paper in this language in order pass the class.

For the bilingual emerging student to be successful, language and content learning goals for ELLs need be coordinated with, not subsumed by, those of native speakers of English. In other words, we teachers who want to help ELL students succeed need to be aware not only of the language of our subject areas but also of the process of second language development. Doing so requires that we be aware of the role and interaction of learner variables and the complex ways in which they can influence the process of learning a second language and succeeding in school. Unfortunately, this content exceeds the scope of this book; however, teachers who haven't yet done so are strongly advised to read and engage in the content of ESL textbooks and coursework.

Risky Writing

In his book of the same title, Jeffrey Berman (2001) documents the healing power of writing about depression, divorce, alcoholism, and sexual abuse in a university classroom. Using sample essays written by his students he makes a case for learning to write about personal trauma so as to overcome barriers to intellectual development. In "Strong in the Broken Places," Wolpow and Askov (1998) document how a high school teacher working with a student dealing with the trauma of physical and sexual abuse could use newly acquired writing skills to confront her abuser. In like fashion, Mark Salzman (2003) poignantly transcribes the redemptive power of writing among inmates at Los Angeles' Central Juvenile Hall. In the writing of these adolescent inmates we readers can witness how writing helps these troubled adolescents come to terms with their crime-ridden pasts while searching for reasons to believe in their future selves. For example, one adolescent wrote:

> I can lie in my bed knowing I may never be physically free again, but the Lord allows me to be at peace and have that sense of freedom. Writing also helps me be free. I can create anything with my imagination, pencil and paper, and before I know it I've created something that was in me the whole time, my pencil and paper just helped me let it out freely. (p. 98)

Most readers will consider the examples listed above as beyond the purview of how secondary teachers might use content writing to teach in their classrooms, and understandably so. Nonetheless, the prevalence of student perpetrators and victims of trauma and abuse in secondary classrooms comes as no surprise to most veteran teachers, and these same teachers will tell you that students find it difficult to learn when they are facing unresolved emotional challenges. Hence, the authors would be remiss if we were not to at least mention the genre of "risky" writing and provide these references. On that note, one last suggestion for those better inclined to learn through personal discourse: Talk with any adult member of a twelve-step program recovering from alcohol and/or drug addiction about "writing steps" and ask about the healing power of confidential step-writing. Listen with respect and without passing judgment. Doing so may very well change your understanding of the value of writing.

 ## Cinquain as Summary

Writer

Descriptive, Insightful

Understanding with Voice

Knowledgeable, Discerning, Detailed, Expressive

Author

 ## Summary

Standards call for teachers to be capable writers themselves and to help their students learn to employ a wide range of writing strategies and process elements to communicate with different audiences for a variety of purposes. Doing so requires educators to understand how reading and writing are reciprocal processes—how proficiency in one affects the other. An integrated approach to content-area writing must be process oriented. This is in part because process writing takes many forms and can result in many products. Process writing generally includes five stages: pre-writing, drafting, revising, editing, and publishing. At all stages, but especially in the revision stage, instructors must carefully consider pragmatics and cultural context.

There is an essential link between writing assessment and writing to learn. An analytic approach to writing assessment looks at six writing traits: ideas and content, organization, word choice, voice, sentence fluency, and conventions. A number of low-stakes and high-stakes writing activities are recommended. Instructional components necessary for the success of English language learners are suggested.

FROM THE PAGES OF OUR LIVES
Writing My Way to My Family's History

by Kie Relyea

Journalist, Kie Relyea, fled Vietnam 30 years ago with her family. She hopes to one day return with her momma and document her homecoming.

I write the story of people's lives. I come into their homes, I ask questions, I listen, I take the bits and pieces of their existence, and I craft them into newspaper stories—from a survivor of the Holocaust who tells of reciting poetry in the midst of horror, to a troupe of actors resurrecting the radio dramas of old on air, to two men on two continents trying to stave off AIDS.

It's something I've been doing since age 17, when my English teacher at West High School in Bakersfield, Calif., Mr. Rosenberg, encouraged me to write for the school newspaper. High school journalism being what it was then, I didn't write hard-hitting exposes. But I did write about homelessness and about how children of my generation were grappling with their parents' divorces—accounts buttressed by interviews with the real people who were affected. I had read about these people in books or magazines and now I was adding to the writing on those social issues.

I don't remember Mr. Rosenberg's specific advice, or those of other teachers who helped me on my journey into journalism. But somewhere along the way, they taught me the importance of asking questions, lots of them, to get into people's lives and into their hearts, and to place them into the collective history.

Reporting fed me the raw pieces of their existence, writing helped me see them. And one day in 2000, writing helped me find my way to my own family.

About a month before the 25-year anniversary of the fall of Saigon, my editor at *The Bellingham Herald* in Washington state asked me to write a first-person narrative about my family's escape from Vietnam as the communists advanced. I pooh-poohed the idea at first. After all, I flew over on a cargo plane and into middle class life in Bakersfield, complete with a swimming pool. I was 7. I didn't remember all that much. Given the proliferation of stories about Vietnam's boat people and their life-and-death struggles to come to this, their new homeland, I felt embarrassed by his suggestion.

Besides, my momma rarely talked about that time. My daddy even less. I grew up in a family that had willed itself a shared amnesia about our past. I doubted they would talk now.

"It's a non-story," I told my editor.

"I'm sure you'll find something if you dig deep," he countered.

Which is what editors always say to their reporters.

I didn't expect him to be right.

Over the ensuing weeks, I interviewed my daddy, my momma and my uncle, who had immigrated to the states just a few months prior to head up a Vietnamese Buddhist temple in Long Beach, California. I didn't know what I was looking for. As a reporter, I simply was digging for the facts that would provide a context for a tumultuous time in America's history. How did we fit into world events? As a daughter and a niece, I wanted to break the silence that had engulfed my family. And because I finally asked, my parents finally answered.

I learned about my daddy's tour of duty in Vietnam, and the terrifying nights he spent as a 21-year-old flying "firefly" missions—duties that left him with bullet scars on his back and groin. I learned about him meeting my momma in 1968, the first year of my life. (He's actually my stepfather but I know little about my biological father, other than he was an American G.I.). I learned of our homes in Saigon, Da Lat, Sa Dec and in Buon Me Thuot, in the Central Highlands of Vietnam.

They told me about our escape, stirring memories of how they came for me in the night as I slept in the family home in Sa Dec, and of my aunt's admonishment to "Pray to Buddha so you don't fall out of the sky" shortly before we boarded the plane, which teemed with people who sat against walls and lolled on mattresses on the floor. My momma shared that she thought the United States was actually quite close and that we would return home to Vietnam after six months.

My great-grandmother, the one with whom I'd had the closest bond, knew better. But she kept silent because she feared that her half-white and half-Vietnamese grandchildren, my brother Bernie was not yet 1, would be persecuted by North Vietnamese forces. My daddy kept quiet, too, to spare my momma anguish.

Through their memories, I wandered once again in the Vietnam of my childhood, including the parts I didn't remember. My uncle, my momma's brother, told of taking me on an outing and having a bomb explode 2 1/2 miles from us. My daddy recalled how the company he worked for—after his tour of duty ended, he returned to Vietnam and landed a job as a helicopter mechanic—kept moving our family south as the North Vietnamese advanced. As they talked, I found my way to the few remaining memories of my own.

A yellow-colored river in Sa Dec, the pungent stink of fish in an open-air market, the dripping sweet mess of a bitten mango, the scent of earth and sky in the countryside before a downpour, the bright marigolds in a park, the white sands of a beach, the sticks of burning incense at a Buddhist alter on some country road.

I remembered the ugliness of my youth, as well. Having to fight in Vietnam because I was half-white and in the states because I was half-Vietnamese. An adult yelling "Viet Cong bitch" at me. Yet, I can't deny the opportunities I've been given in this country. What would have befallen my brother and I if my daddy hadn't brought us to the United States with him? Here, I have financial independence, growing up free of the poverty that dogged my momma as a child. I grew up with a chance at an education denied to my momma since age 9, after the death of her own mother. I grew up with parents who made it clear I could be whatever I wanted.

But I knew none of this, truly, until I wrote the article, which appeared on the front pages of *The Herald* on April 30, 2000. The act not only allowed me to ruminate about my family's history, long marked by silence, but also helped place our lives within the larger context of world history—to my surprise. Perhaps I shouldn't have been, but growing up Vietnam was a far-away place and a long-ago time. My parents wanted to focus on life today, and my momma wanted her children to integrate into mainstream society as quickly as possible. And as an American soldier, my daddy struggled with the shame heaped upon those returning home from the war.

The writing allowed me to finally see my parents as people, and history as flesh and blood. Vietnam and the war weren't just blips in time. They didn't end with the last helicopter flight out of a devastated country. They live on in the lives of my family in the United States and of the family I have still in Vietnam, the ones who remember me as a child and who ask about me still. And they will continue to live on, as long as students are given assignments that require them to talk to the human embodiment of history.

Recently, the daughter of another editor asked to interview me for her high school history project. She asked me about my life in Vietnam, my family's escape during those final chaotic days, and the lessons I may have learned along the way. I couldn't give her much about memories of war, shielded as I was from its bullets and its bombs and the dying. But I could share thoughts of life—of a little girl grown to a woman who still recalls the tangy sweet taste of a coconut plucked from a tree, the scent of country air, the sight of a golden river tinged by sunset.

I didn't read her report. In the writing of it, I hope she found her way to history inhabited by real people, of men and women who survived separation and destruction to create new legacies—and new stories.

Questions for Reflection and Discussion

1. Teachers often ask students to interview people who have lived the stories we read about in textbooks. As a student, did you ever conduct such an interview? Who did you interview? What was that like for you? Did you write about it? How did you prepare? What worked? As a teacher, what can you do to help students prepare for such an assignment?

2. Ms. Relyea writes, "Reporting fed me the raw pieces of their existence, writing helped me see them." Have you ever used writing to help sift or sort through raw pieces of content to make meaning? Was this in your subject area or in your personal life? How might you demonstrate or explain this use of writing to your students so that they might do the same?

3. Take a few minutes to reread Ms. Relyea's writing. Using the categories of six-trait assessment, what are some of the salient strengths in the piece? Why do you think this is so?

4. In the end of her story, Ms. Relyea says that she didn't read the report written by the daughter of an editor. Why do you suppose she made that decision? What does that tell you about her perspective on the writing process?

References and Recommended Readings

Ambrose, S. (1996). *Undaunted courage: Meriwether Lewis, Thomas Jefferson, and the opening of the American west.* New York: Simon & Schuster.

Andrasick, K. (1990). *Opening texts: Using writing to teach literature.* Portsmouth, NH: Heinemann.

Andrews, S. A. (1997, October). Writing to learn in content area reading. *Journal of Adolescent and Adult Literacy, 41*(2), 141–142.

Applebee, A. (1981). *Writing in the secondary school: English and the content areas.* Urbana, IL: National Council of Teachers of English.

Arter, J., Spandel, V., Culham, R., & Pollard, J. (1994, April 4–8). *The impact of training students to be self-assessors of writing.* Paper presented at the annual meeting of the American Educational Research Association, New Orleans, LA.

Atwell, N. (1987). *In the middle.* Portsmouth, NH: Boynton/Cook.

Atwell, N. (1989). *Coming to know: Writing to learn in the intermediate grades.* Portsmouth, NH: Heinemann.

Baines, L., & Kunkel, A. (Eds.). *Going Bohemian: Activities that engage adolescents in the art of writing well.* Newark, DE: International Reading Association.

Berman, J. (2001). *Risky writing: Self-disclosure and self-transformation in the classroom.* Amherst, MA: University of Massachusetts Press.

Bright, R. (1995). *Writing instruction in the intermediate grades: What is said, what is done, what is understood.* Newark, DE: International Reading Association.

Britsch, S. J., & Berkson, R. (1997). I am that . . . kid tha (sic) acts weird: Developing e-mail education in a third grade classroom. *Teaching Education, 8*(2), 97–104.

Britton, J., Burgess, T., Martin, N., McLeod, A., & Rosen, H. (1975). *The development of writing abilities* (11–18). London: McMillan.

Calkins, L. (1986). *The art of teaching writing.* Portsmouth, NH: Heinemann Educational Books.

Carlson, S. (2004, October 29). Technology threatens colleges with extinction, ex-president warns. *The Chronicle of Higher Education,* L1(10) A34–35.

Culham, R. (2003). *6+1 Traits of writing: The complete guide (grades 3 and up).* Scholastic.

Daisey, P. (2003). The value of writing a "how-to" book to reduce the writing apprehension of secondary preservice science and mathematics teachers. *Reading Research and Instruction, 42*(3), 75–111.

Delpit, L. (1998). What should teachers do? Ebonics and culturally responsive instruction. In T. Perry & L. Delpit (Eds.), *The real Ebonics debate: Power, language and the education of African-American children.* (pp. 17–26). Boston: Beacon Press.

deBono, E. (1987). *Action: CoRT thinking student textbook #6.* Elmsford, NY: Pergamon Press.

Diederich, P. (1974). *Measuring growth in English.* Urbana, IL: National Council of Teachers of English.

Elbow, P. (1997). High stakes and low stakes in assigning and responding to writing. In M. Sorcinelli & P. Elbow (Eds.), *Writing to learn: Strategies for assigning and responding to writing across the disciplines* (pp. 5–13). San Francisco: Jossey-Bass Publishers.

Emig, J. (1971). *The composing processes of twelfth graders.* Champaign, IL: National Council of Teachers of English.

Fearn, L., & Farnan, N. (1998). *Writing effectively: Helping children master the conventions of writing.* Boston: Allyn & Bacon.

Filipovic, Z. (1974). *Zlata's diary.* New York: Penguin Books.

Frank, A. (1953). *The diary of a young girl.* New York: Pocket Books.

Gere, A. (1985). *Roots in sawdust: Writing to learn across the curriculum.* Urbana, IL: National Council of Teachers of English.

Gersten, R., & Baker, S. (2000). What we know about effective instructional practices for English language learners. *Exceptional Children, 66,* 454–470.

Graves, D. H. (1975). An examination of the writing processes of seven-year-old-children. *Research in the Teaching of English, 9,* 227–241.

Hammann, L., & Stevens, R. (2003). Instructional approaches to improving students' writing of compare-contrast essays: An experimental study. *Journal of Literacy Research, 35,* 731–756.

Harper, C., & de Jong, E. (2004). Misconceptions about teaching English-language learners. *Journal of Adolescent and Adult Literacy, 48*(2), 152–162.

Hillocks, G. (1986). *Research in written composition: New directions for teaching.* Urbana, IL: ERIC Clearinghouse on Reading and Communications Skills.

Honegger, M. (2001). ESL and dialects in the writing classroom. In M. Warner (Ed.), *Winning ways of coaching writing: A practical guide for teaching writing* (pp. 87–104). Needham Heights, MA: Allyn & Bacon.

International Reading Association/National Council of Teachers of English. (1996). *Standards for the English language arts.* Urbana, IL: Authors.

Langer, J. (1986). Learning through writing: Study skills in the content areas. *Journal of Reading, 29,* 400–406.

Langer, J. (1987). *How writing shapes thinking: A study of teaching and learning.* Urbana, IL: National Council of Teachers of English.

Macon, J., Bewell, D., & Vogt, M. E. (1991). *Responses to literature, grades K–8.* Newark, DE: International Reading Association.

Macrorie, K. (1970). *Telling writing.* New York: Hayden Book Co.

Maxwell, R. (1996). *Writing across the curriculum in middle and high school.* Boston: Allyn & Bacon.

McClanahan, L. (2001). *E-pals: Examining a cross-cultural writing/literature project.* (Unpublished doctoral dissertation, Ohio State University).

McCrum, R., Cran, W., & MacNeil, R. (1986). *The story of English.* New York: Viking.

Meier, T. (1998a). Kitchen poets and classroom books: Literature from children's roots. In T. Perry & L. Delpit (Eds.), *The real Ebonics debate: Power, language, and the education of African-American children* (pp. 94–104). Boston: Beacon.

Meier, T. (1998b). Teaching teachers about black communications. In T. Perry & L. Delpit (Eds.), *The real Ebonics debate: Power, language, and the education of African-American children* (pp. 117–125). Boston: Beacon.

National Board for Professional Teaching Standards. (2001). *Middle childhood generalist standards for teachers of students 7–12.* Washington DC: Author.

National Center on Education and the Economy and The University of Pittsburgh. (1997). *Performance standards: Vol. 1. Elementary school.* Washington, DC: New Standards.

Nistler, R. (1998). Preservice teachers, sixth graders and instructors use dialogue journals to extend their classroom communities. *Reading Horizons, 39,* 203–216.

Northwest Educational Regional Laboratory. (2004). *Assessment.* Retrieved October 20, 2004, from http://www.nwrel.org/assessment/

Perl, S. (1994). *Landmark essays on the writing process.* Davis, CA: Hermagoras Press.

Pirrone, J. (1998). Literacy lessons across the lines: E-mail exchange in English class. *Teacher Research, 5*(2), 92–106.

Salzman, M. (2003). *True notebooks: A writer's year at juvenile hall.* New York: Vintage Books.

Santa, C., Havens, L., & Harrison, S. (1996) Teaching secondary science through reading, writing, studying and problem-solving. In D. Lapp, J. Flood, & N. Farnan (Eds.), *Content area reading and learning: Instructional strategies* (2nd ed., pp. 165–180). Boston: Allyn & Bacon.

Shakur, T. (1999). *The rose that grew from concrete.* New York: MTV/Pocketbooks.

Spandel, V. (2000). *Creating writers through 6-trait writing assessment and instruction* (3rd ed.). Boston: Allyn & Bacon.

Spandel, V., & Stiggens, R. (1990). *Creating writers: Linking assessment and writing instruction.* White Plains, NY: Longman.

Tiffany, J. (2003). *Uncomfortable neighbors: Cultural collisions between Mexicans and Americans.* Rochester, WA: Gorham Printing.

Tobias, S. (1989). Writing to learn science and mathematics. In P. Connolly & T. Vilardi (Eds.), *Writing to learn mathematics and science* (pp. 246–280). New York: Longman.

Tompkins, G. (2000). *Teaching writing: Balancing process and product.* Upper Saddle River, NJ: Prentice-Hall.

Unrau, N., & Ruddell, R. (1995). Interpreting texts in classroom contexts. *Journal of Adolescent and Adult Literacy, 39*(1), 16–27.

Wolpow, R., & Askov, E. (1998). Strong at the broken places: Literacy instruction for survivors of pervasive trauma. *Journal of Adolescent and Adult Literacy, 34*(1) 50–57.

Wolpow, R., & Askov, E. (2001). School violence and trauma demand widened frameworks and practice: From bibliotherapy to the literacy of testimony and witness. *Journal of Adolescent and Adult Literacy, 44*(7), 606–609.

Wolpow, R., Neff, G., & Neff, S. (2002). High tech—high touch: Utilizing technology to foster meaningful intergenerational literacy connections. Yearbook of the American Reading Forum, Volume 22. Retrieved June 15, 2005 from http://www.fd.appstate.edu/arfonline/02_arfyearbook/volume02toc.htm#wolpow

Wu, S., & Rubin, D. (2000). Evaluating the impact of collectivism and individualism on argumentative writing by Chinese and North Amercian college students. *Research in the Teaching of English, 35,* 148–178.

Young, A. (1997). Mentoring, modeling, monitoring, motivating: Response to students' ungraded writing as academic conversations. *New Directions for Teaching and Learning, 69,* 27–39.

Zarnowski, M. (2003). *History makers: A questioning approach to reading and writing biographies.* Portsmouth, NH: Heinemann.

Zinsser, W. (1988). *Writing to learn: How to write-and think-clearly about any subject at all.* New York: Harper & Row.

Appendix 8A: Answer Keys for Workshops 8.2, 8.3, and 8.4

Answer Key for Workshop 8.2: Ideas and Organization

You kept a good focus on what you want and your reason here!

You showed your reader that you thought from their perspective here!

You've written three very good reasons why you should be tech maven.

These transitions help your reader make sense of your ideas!

These two sentences make a good transition between ideas!

Just imagine this, you getting a whole bunch of e-mails about having a problem with someone's computer or they need pictures for a class project that they are working on. I can imagine that you will feel like e-mailing them and telling them that they can ask someone else to do it because you are tired of being their slave. Well, don't because I have a solution for you. I could be a Tech. Maven this trimester. I am responsible. I have had experience and I love technology.

I'll start with responsibility. I think I served Acme Elementary well. I took pictures and printed them for Mrs. Chase. I did a section of the Veteran's Day slide show. I also made part of the mini DYB. Did you notice that I got all that stuff done on time while keeping my grades high? If I needed to I would take the project home and work on it.

I think Tech. Mavens also need a lot of experience. Well I fit that criteria too. I remember when I was three and I turned on the computer for my mom because she didn't know how. That would make it eight years (almost nine years) of experience. To me that sounds like a quality that a Tech. Maven would need. . . .

When I read this, I was left with a few questions. Remember, you need to explain to your reader as if they have never met you . . .

What about taking pictures? Why is that important?

What is a mini DYB? Tell me more.

Tell me more about keeping your grades high. . . .

I don't have a picture in my head about this . . . show me what you were like as a little kid who loved technology.

Also, what did you learn over those 8 years that would help you?

Answer Key for Workshop 8.3: Voice and Word Choice

These sound words grab my attention.

I can see your personality in these words.

Great word choice!

You speak directly to your reader! This shows us a little of what you are like as a person.

When your brain is popping, bopping and swirling around with frustration from a locked out computer you probably thinking "I need HELP!", and when you are overwhelmed with projects and you have absolutely not time to do them you are probably also thinking "I need HELP!" And then you start thinking about details like what kinds of qualities will this "Helper" have to have? They would probably have to be smart. They would have almost all A's in school, have experience with technical stuff, and be willing to do any project that is needed. Well my friend, you have just described the perfect job for me! And that is why you are reading this letter. I am applying to be your tech maven. Now, if you already have your heart set on a few kids to be tech maven then I suggest, HIGHLY suggest, that you DON"T read this letter, because it will be so convincing that you will never see what hit you. . . .

You effectively use your voice to entice the reader into reading the thesis of your letter.

Avoid using words that don t have any specific meaning. What is "stuff"?

You did a great job of speaking directly to your reader. Do you really want to highly suggest that the read not read your letter? Doing so could be seen as a negative.

Answer Key for Workshop 8.4: Sentence Fluency and Conventions

Good compound sentence! You follow it with a short sentence that gets right to the point.

For the most part your spelling is good. So is your overall punctuation!

Okay, you like writing well I don't. You probably wouldn't like my essay. I'm writing this because I had no ideas on what to write, which brought me to my point. We write too many essays around here.

My first reason that I think I shouldn't write this essay is that I don't like writing essays. I don't like it because I don't get ideas in my head as fast as others. After all the frustration I fall behind and end up with a sloppy essay. When I have a sloppy essay I know that there's no way you are going to choose my essay.

I just like to write my own things. When you tell me what to write, I feel frustrated because I know write better if I just started writing. When we just start writing it makes me feel so good because I know I'll write better and have way more fun.

Punctuation needed here.

brings

Note that each sentence in this paragraph starts and ends in like fashion: "The first reason I think I shouldn't write this essay is that I . . . I don't like it because I . . . After all the frustration I . . . When I have a sloppy essay I. . . ."

Punctuation needed here.

Your last two sentences are written in the same format.

Appendix 8B Five-Paragraph Essay Rubric*

	Beginner	Intermediate	Advanced	Professional
Introductory Paragraph	One or two sentences. May not make total sense to the reader. May not mention the POINT! (thesis)	Several sentences. The reader may have to do some work to figure out the meaning. It mentions the point of writing.	Three to four related sentences. Very clearly written. The reader would understand easily.	Four or more good sentences that weave in the point (thesis) with a larger idea. The reader's interest is piqued! There is a transition to the first idea.
Paragraph #2	One or two sentences that state the reason with no detail.	Two or more sentences that state the reason, but leave the reader with questions like How? When? Why?	Three or more sentences that clearly tell the reader how this reason goes with the essay.	Four or more sentences that SHOW the reader what you mean and leave no doubts in their mind, and transition the reader to the next point.
Paragraph #3	One or two sentences that state the reason with no detail.	Two or more sentences that state the reason, but leave the reader with questions like How? When? Why?	Three or more sentences that clearly tell the reader how this reason goes with the essay.	Four or more sentences that SHOW the reader what you mean and leave no doubts in their mind and transition the reader to the next point.
Paragraph #4	One or two sentences that state the reason with no detail.	Two or more sentences that state the reason, but leave the reader with questions like How? When? Why?	Three or more sentences that clearly tell the reader how this reason goes with the essay.	Four or more sentences that SHOW the reader what you mean and leave no doubts in their mind.
Conclusion	One sentence that says something like "Thank you . . ." or "Well, that's my essay . . ."	Two to three sentences that tie up the essay, but use limited creativity. The point is not restated.	Three or more sentences that clearly wrap up the essay and leave the reader with complete understanding. The point is restated, but the exact words are used.	Three or more sentences that creatively wrap up the essay. Restates the point with a twist. A suggestion or call to action.

*Developed by Diane Leigh, teacher at Acme Elementary School in the Mount Baker School District, Acme, Washington.

Appendix 8C: TER Worksheet Instructions

Before you go to the library, you must think about your topic. You can do this in three steps:

1. TARGET
2. EXPAND
3. RESTRICT

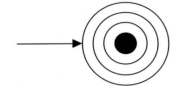

1. **TARGET**

Define
Pick out
Identify
Focus
Aim

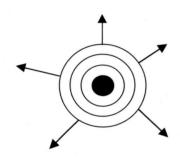

The first thing you must do is direct your thinking at a definite target. Your target may have many parts. These parts may be divided into general or specific. (See Example.)

    A. Write your general topic on your worksheet.
    B. Now write five specific topics on your worksheet.
If you get stuck, you can either: *Look in your class notes.*
                                    Ask your teacher.
                                    Look in your textbook.

2. **EXPAND**

Open up
Think some more
Elaborate
Explore
Go into detail
What else is involved?
Why is this important?

Step 2 is **expand your topic**. This is when it gets interesting.

    A. Look at your worksheet.
    B. For each specific topic ask three questions. Write these in the space provided on your worksheet. (See example)
If you get stuck, you can: *Look in your class notes.*
                          Ask your teacher.
                          Look in your textbook.

3. **RESTRICT**

Simplify
Condense
Reduce
Summarize
Select
Pick out
Narrow
Contract

   Amazing! From one general idea you thought of five specific ideas or questions. From these you came up with as many as 15 ideas or questions. You've done a lot of thinking already. Now it is time to restrict. It is time to simplify, condense, and narrow.

    A. Look at your worksheet. Circle the key words in your 15 questions.
    B. Think about revising your general topic. Make your topic into a question you want to answer. Write that revised general topic in the space provided on your worksheet. (See example)
    C. It is good to have some preferred subtopics. Choose two of these from your list of specific topics. Write these in the space provided on your worksheet. (See example)

Bring your completed worksheet with you to the Library.

Appendix 8C: TER Worksheet

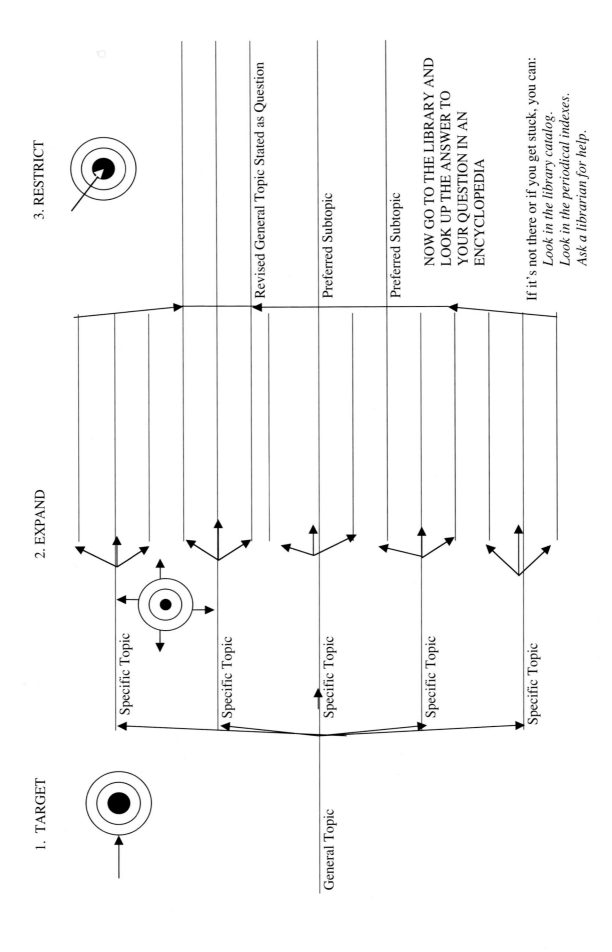

1. TARGET

2. EXPAND

3. RESTRICT

General Topic

Specific Topic
Specific Topic
Specific Topic
Specific Topic
Specific Topic

Revised General Topic Stated as Question

Preferred Subtopic

Preferred Subtopic

NOW GO TO THE LIBRARY AND
LOOK UP THE ANSWER TO
YOUR QUESTION IN AN
ENCYCLOPEDIA

If it's not there or if you get stuck, you can:
Look in the library catalog.
Look in the periodical indexes.
Ask a librarian for help.

Appendix 8C: TER Worksheet: Example

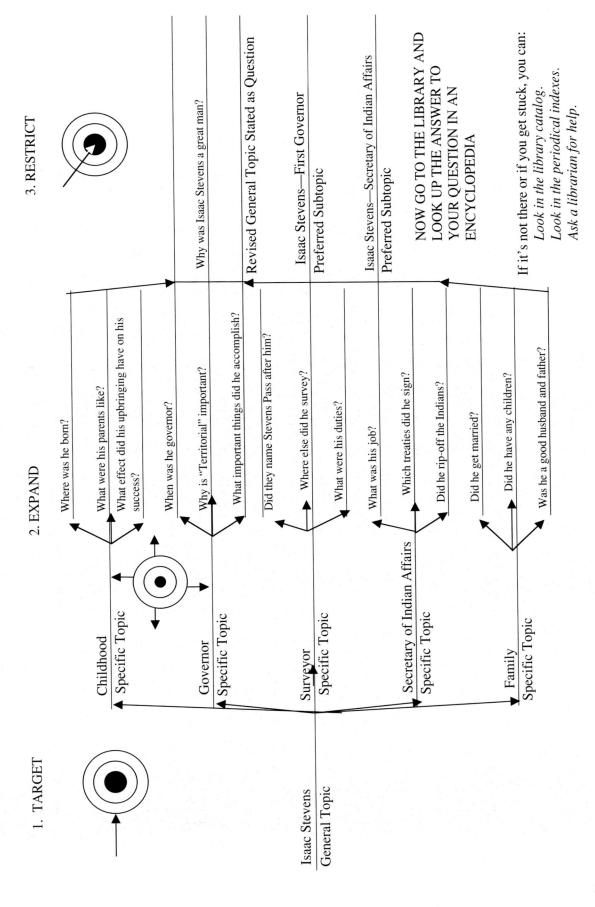

1. TARGET

2. EXPAND

3. RESTRICT

Isaac Stevens
General Topic

Childhood
Specific Topic

Where was he born?
What were his parents like?
What effect did his upbringing have on his success?

Governor
Specific Topic

When was he governor?
Why is "Territorial" important?
What important things did he accomplish?

Surveyor
Specific Topic

Did they name Stevens Pass after him?
Where else did he survey?
What were his duties?

Secretary of Indian Affairs
Specific Topic

What was his job?
Which treaties did he sign?
Did he rip-off the Indians?

Family
Specific Topic

Did he get married?
Did he have any children?
Was he a good husband and father?

Why was Isaac Stevens a great man?

Revised General Topic Stated as Question

Isaac Stevens—First Governor
Preferred Subtopic

Isaac Stevens—Secretary of Indian Affairs
Preferred Subtopic

NOW GO TO THE LIBRARY AND
LOOK UP THE ANSWER TO
YOUR QUESTION IN AN
ENCYCLOPEDIA

If it's not there or if you get stuck, you can:
Look in the library catalog.
Look in the periodical indexes.
Ask a librarian for help.

PART

III

Specialized Tools for Content Needs

FIGURE 9.1

Vocabulary: Building Blocks to Understanding and Enjoyment—A
Cognitive Map

Vocabulary: Building Blocks to Understanding and Enjoyment

9

Outline

- Anticipatory and Review Questions
- A Sampling of National Performance Standards
  - *Workshop 9.1: Getting a Mental Set*
- From the Content Classroom: Benefits of Teaching Vocabulary
- Introduction
- From the Content Classroom: Values Voting and Vocabulary
  - *Workshop 9.2: Words with Multiple Meanings*
- From the Content Classroom: Adventures of the CIMTE 538 Class by a Graduate Student
  - *Workshop 9.3: Key Words*
- Language Acquisition and Word Study
  - Some Potential Stumbling Blocks
  - Levels of Knowing a Word
  - Definitions vs. Meanings
  - Size and Type of Vocabulary
  - Etymology (Word Origins and Histories)
    - *Workshop 9.4: Spectre*
  - Home Economics for Food Lovers
  - Amelioration and Pejoration
  - Denotations and Connotations
  - Coining New Words
- Specific Types of Word Study
- CSSD for Attacking New Words in All Content Areas
  - Context (The Intelligent Guess)
  - Structural Analysis (Meaningful Word Parts)
  - Sound (Phonics—Symbols, Syllables, and Sounds)
  - The Dictionary: A Multipurpose Tool

- Thesaurus: A Storehouse of Information
  - *Workshop 9.5: Strategy Selection*
- From the Content Classroom: Antidisestablishmentarianism
- Teaching Strategies: Before, During, and After
  - Before
    - Word-of-the-Day
    - Synonym Clusters
    - List/Group/Label Concept Development
    - Cognitive Maps
    - Student-Selected Key Words
  - During (While Reading)
    - Modified CLOZE Technique
    - Think-Alouds
  - After (To Confirm, Clarify Meanings, Extend)
    - OPIN
    - Semantic Feature Analysis (SFA)
    - TOAST: A Vocabulary Study System
- Playing with Words: Fun for All!
  - Collective Nouns
  - Mistaken Clichés
  - Palindromes, Pangrams, Anagrams, and Spoonerisms
  - Different Definitions
  - Word Pairs
- Ten Things to Remember
- Vocabulary Tools and Games on the Internet
- Cinquain as Summary
- Summary
- References and Recommended Readings

"One forgets words as one forgets names. One's vocabulary needs constant fertilizing or it will die."

Evelyn Waugh

"The genius of democracies is seen not only in the great number of new words introduced but even more in the new ideas they express."

Alexis de Tocqueville

321

Anticipatory and Review Questions

Literal

1. What are three ways in which we acquire language?

2. What are two stumbling blocks for acquiring new terms?

Interpretative/Applied

3. Select one teaching strategy you believe will be most useful in enhancing technical vocabulary in your class. Explain why you chose it.

Evaluative/Critical

4. The most frequently used method to have students learn technical vocabulary are long lists of words, copied definitions, and words then used in sentences. Why do so many teachers choose to use this method? What could they do instead?

Creative/Personal

5. Develop a unique written lesson plan in your content area in which you incorporate instruction in vocabulary learning. Make sure your plan is culturally relevant and responsive.

6. Describe an experience you had in which you learned a new word, the regular use of which has brought new meaning into your life.

A Sampling of National Performance Standards

- Students adjust their use of spoken, written, and visual language (e.g., conventions, style, vocabulary) to communicate effectively with a variety of audiences and for different purposes (International Reading Association/National Council of Teachers of English, 1996, p. 33).
- The mathematical vocabulary identifies words and phrases that children need to understand and use if they are to make good progress in mathematics (The Department for Education and Skills, 2005).
- The professional educator understands and uses a variety of instructional strategies to encourage students' development of critical thinking, problem solving, and performance skills (Council of Chief State School Officers, 2005).

Workshop 9.1

Getting a Mental Set

Ask yourself the following:

1. Make a list of the ways you were taught technical vocabulary in secondary school. What worked for you? What didn't? Why? Why not?
2. What do you want to learn about teaching vocabulary to your students? Why?
3. What are your thoughts now about the best ways to learn new words?
4. Do you have any word study books in your personal library? If so, which is your favorite and why? Be ready to bring it in later to share.

You may want to discuss this with a partner.

FROM THE CONTENT CLASSROOM

Benefits of Teaching Vocabulary

Good teachers are always ready to learn something new and readily admit past problems. One outstanding secondary English teacher, Alan, had taught for many years but when he took a content-area reading class he admitted to one and all that he had been an assumptive teacher with his students as to their vocabulary knowledge. He had assumed, previously, that they already knew words like fortnight. Some students pictured a fort at night so they didn't bother to look it up. When Alan actually tested that knowledge, he discovered that many had only one general meaning for a word; also they misused the dictionary and ignored the glossary. He became an instant believer in the benefits of teaching vocabulary skills and strategies.

 ## Introduction

There is a cyclical effect between word learning and knowledge. Our knowledge of word meaning affects our comprehension, which in turn affects our knowledge base and may return to increase our word knowledge. It has been said that every content-area teacher must also be a teacher of reading. Texts from each discipline demand content knowledge that only a specialist in that content area will possess. For example, every content area has its own technical language that distinguishes it from other subjects. To master a content area means mastering that area's technical vocabulary. For many, technical vocabulary can be like a second language. For example, in some classes students are asked "compare and contrast" ideas. However, if you look in a dictionary, you will find these directions confusing. The word compare means to "note the similarities and differences." The word contrast means "to show or emphasize differences." Imagine how confusing this would be to a second language learner!

Just as important as these cognitive considerations are the feelings students have about word learning in general. We want our students to experience the fun of building vocabulary and learn to value this lifelong skill. This is an important objective of this chapter.

Vocabulary research over the years has shown that we need a balance between cognition, motivation, and affect, not just an emphasis on the cognitive. Since most words are learned in context, we need to encourage wide reading. Incorporating more senses leads to better word learning. It is also better to learn fewer words in depth with shades of meaning than long lists to look up and use in a sentence. Students need reminders of the various ways to attack unknown works. All students, especially those who are second language learners or from the culture of poverty can derive benefit from early, direct vocabulary instruction. Finally, we need to foster student awareness and responsiveness to words and their meanings in culturally responsive ways.

For example, Graves and Watts-Taffe (2002) base their vocabulary program on: wide reading; many encounters with new terms including definitional and contextual definition given; word learning strategies; and last but not least, fostering word consciousness (awareness, motivation, interest and sense of purpose for words, and their meanings) and enjoyment. They emphasize a need for balance between cognitive and affective factors.

FROM THE CONTENT CLASSROOM

Values Voting and Vocabulary

As a key part of teaching integrated content literacy for many years, I (Tonjes) have taught important sessions on vocabulary development. I predicted that my students would not be enthusiastic about this topic, based on their own past experiences in secondary schools, and therefore planned a session that was mostly affective in nature, one where we would all have fun while still learning.

When students first arrived I told them that my overall goal was to change attitudes, and we would start with a simple values clarification technique. I could see from their expressions that they were not all that happy to be here for this session; instead of the usual cheery greetings there were frowns on their faces and they avoided eye contact. It was, "Oh, here we go again, word study, oh no." I explained the values voting process: When I gave the signal, all those who were wildly excited about word study as taught in schools were to raise their hands and wave them furiously. If they were indifferent, they should only half raise their arm, but not move it; and if they were negative, they should vigorously point thumbs down. I demonstrated

these responses and explained that this was a good way to get class reaction overall without embarrassing anyone. In values clarification there are no put downs. All responses are accepted. The students must do their own clarifying.

"Okay, how did you feel in school about studying words?—Everyone at once! Now look around you and get an overall feel of the class." As expected, most were negative, some apathetic, only one or two enthusiastic. I asked any who had had a positive response to share what their teachers had done or how they had come to feel the way they do. Those who felt negative agreed that they had been exposed to the deadening tasking of long lists of terms on the board to be looked up and then used in a sentence. They also said they just grabbed the first meaning whether it fit the context or not.

We proceeded to many of the activities found in this chapter and at the end of class I asked them to voluntarily give their opinions and feelings now about word study—either in class or written in their response journals. Nearly all were positive, and most swore they would never fall into the "long lists" trap. I was content.

Workshop 9.2	**Words with Multiple Meanings**

With a partner, discuss the general everyday meanings for the following underlined words. Do as many as possible without looking at a reference (e.g., Note: a musical symbol designating pitch and rhythm, writing something down to remember it, or a short letter written to a parent).

1. a <u>run</u> on the bank
2. a three <u>point</u> basket
3. the <u>root</u> of the problem
4. the <u>radical</u> sign
5. the <u>surf</u> was up
6. <u>capital</u> punishment
7. trimming the <u>hedge</u>

FROM THE CONTENT CLASSROOM

Adventures of the CIMTE 538 Class by a Graduate Student

Each class day student pairs did a summary presentation of the previous class. This student was responsible for this vocabulary day summary, where the major objective was to excite students to the power and playfulness and potential of words.

These are the records of the adventures of the CIMTE 538 Class. A group of 18 dedicated adults working to increase their knowledge of content instruction for their teaching careers. They have all traveled different paths but for some higher purpose they have assembled together for an amazing journey through reading instructional techniques. Their leader has had an amazing journey of her own, and has taken it upon herself to lead this courageous and dedicated group. With her help and guidance, will they make it to their final destination? This is just one part of their educational journey, however, they shall make it together. . . . Let's continue with their journey. . . .

Thursday, July 18, 2002
  Today was an adventure to another island. I believe this island was called the "game of words." Everywhere

we turned we were surrounded by a word in some format or phrase. First we ran into Ambiguous who greeted us as we stepped onto the island shore. He told us that by the end of the day we would know what he was doing there. He led us to a group of words that were in the middle of a secret ritual. We were invited to join them—however, if we met the Ghost of the day we were eliminated.

  Our leader guided us through the many groups of animals that were present. We met the parliament of owls, the exaltation of larks, and even the clowder of cats. She led us through the swamp of similes and over the mountain of metaphors. We clustered around the synonym rock and found out that learning more information about one word can help us learn others that are similar. As we continued our journey we went through the valley of antonyms we hooked on to the many "S" words that guided us through the narrow path.

  We thanked the words on "Game of Words" island for allowing us to share in the many uses of vocabulary and as we climbed back into the boat we heard the Spoonerisms chanting a Warewell Fish. (Farewell Wish). Until our next adventure. . . .

Key Words

This is an ongoing activity to apply what you learn from what you read. Using a content-area textbook, select a chapter at random. Skim it to select ten key technical vocabulary words you believe are most important for your students to know. As you read this chapter on vocabulary, refer back to this key word list and apply what you have learned to teaching these words to your students. You should aim to use a different strategy or activity with each word. When you are done, compare your list and teaching strategies with a partner or small group.

Workshop 9.3

Language Acquisition and Word Study

The relationship between reading and vocabulary acquisition is twofold: (1) When the meanings of words in context are clear, we effectively comprehend connected discourse; and (2) when reading, we acquire new words and expand and refine shades of meaning. These are mutually reinforcing, and good readers continually grow; however, those with problems keep slipping behind. It is our job to help students to master key terminology in our content areas. This integration of literacy strategy and content learning is vital because it enables students to clarify concepts essential to the content itself. Teaching content vocabulary is teaching our subject.

Some Potential Stumbling Blocks

Some textbooks read like the following: "His refractory attitude would seem to militate against a palliation of the opprobrium directed toward a lugubrious being." Do you, the reader agree or not? We don't need a readability formula to know that this sentence is hard to understand! How do you feel when faced with a text loaded with unknown words? Students handed a two-pound book with over 600 pages of this kind of writing will either tune-out or turn-off. Some enterprising students will seek out a video, the Cliff Notes, or a website, but most will choose to act-out or drop-out. Can we really blame them?

What are some basic stumbling blocks for acquiring new terms? In literature we often find *obsolete words* such as "hooch," "artics," "nosegay." We find *colloquial* words, words known to people in one region but not in another, such as "flapjacks," used to give flavor. In subjects like science, math, or economics, you find words with specific meanings for a particular subject—*the technical terms* that were discussed earlier. For example "root" and "hedge" mean different things in each of the subjects mentioned. Thus, words with multiple meanings can confuse. For example, many readers, especially English language learners, often have trouble with:

- General words like "eloquent"
- Prose words like "hence forth"
- Content-specific words like "ecological"
- Words with inflectional endings like foolish*ness*, demonstra*ting*, strapp*ed*

Levels of Knowing a Word

Jot down a word that you recently learned. _____ Now define it, giving meanings and uses if you can. Refer back to this word after reading this section to see how well you really know this new word.

1. At the *lowest* level, we never saw the word before, and we have no knowledge of it. For example:

    "Zabunc" (a nonsense word)

2. At the next, or *specific* level, we know it in a general way. For example:
    "Serendipity" (a pleasant word)

3. At the *functional* level, we use the word appropriately when speaking or writing and we know how it is used. For example:

    "Serendipity" (a state of discovering good things by accident)

4. Finally, at the *conceptual* level, we can use it properly in all forms ("It was a serendipitous experience.") and may even know how it came about (from the story "The Three Princes of Serendip"—coined by Horace Wolpole—because these princes kept coming upon pleasant things by accident).

Definitions vs. Meanings

Students often make the mistake of thinking if they look up the definition of a word in the dictionary they will understand its meaning. Perhaps this is true because their teachers taught them this way of learning vocabulary. Definitions by themselves do not interpret meaning because they are not self-contained pieces of knowledge. There must be both an affective and cognitive connection, after all, meanings reside in our hearts as well as our minds. We create our own meaning from what we already know and feel. It is within this largely personal framework that humans interpret language. It therefore follows that when readers have little background for new words, they will have trouble associating them in a meaningful way to their own life experiences.

Size and Type of Vocabulary

Until reading is a strong habit, children learn new words orally through conversation, TV, DVDs, videos, movies, etc. Therefore, the listening and speaking vocabularies of young children are greater than their reading and writing ones. Authorities do not always agree on the actual size of vocabularies at different ages. The variance is due to differences in procedures and what constitutes a distinct word. Anderson and Nagy (1992) state that the average 12th grader may know 80,000 words—almost half of an abridged dictionary. They also believe students may learn 4,000 to 6,000 new words each year, mostly through incidental or natural learning. Direct instruction may account for learning only a few hundred new words a year. This shows the importance of allowing for fiction and nonfiction reading, including newspapers and magazines to ensure incidental or natural learning.

Etymology (Word Origins and Histories)

The history of words can prove to be a fascinating study for student and teacher alike. The term *etymology* comes from the Greek *etymon* meaning true or original meaning, and *ology*, which means the science or study of. Each word originally had just one meaning, but with use meanings were expanded. An extreme example is the word *run*, which is said to have up to 132 meanings. Examples include: run a race, run its course, fence runs east, run out of money, run up a hill, run across an old friend, a home run, a run on the bank, note a common run of people, run to seed, run in her stocking, etc.

The English language comes from the Anglo-Saxon language (Germanic origin and other Northern European languages). The oldest recorded languages of the Indo-European family are Sanskrit (2000 B.C.E.), Greek (1400 B.C.E.), and Latin (500 B.C.E.). Approximately one-half of earth's population speaks some derivative of Indo-European language and most English vocabulary can be traced back to it. Anglo-Saxon was the major language in England during the 5th century A.D. When the Normans invaded in the 11th century they brought their language derived from Old French, Greek, and Latin, which became high-society's language. Between the 12th and 16th centuries, the two languages (Anglo-Saxon and Norman) merged to form what we call "English."

A few words in our modern language traced to preclassical tongues include:

wine (Latin "vinum")—Etruscan
mules (Sumarian "mulus")—house slippers
gum (Greek "kommi")—ancient Egyptian "gnit"
eeny, meeny, miney mo—numerals used by ancient Welsh tribes
ten (Indo-European)—a compound of "two" and "hand" and "five-finger"
Over time some words have changed from their original meanings. For example:
school (Greek)—leisure—having time to think and learn
reading—to guess, to riddle

Tracing a word back to its origin can give "concreteness" to a concept because often a mental image is associated with the word. The saying "A picture is worth 1,000 words" can be seen in this graphic of the proper ending for the word "Alumni," depending on number and gender.

alumnus   **alumna**   **alumni**   **alumnae**   **alumni**

FIGURE 9.2

A graphic worth one-thousand words (*An Ed Leek illustration, University of New Mexico alumnus.*)

Let us look at a few examples of word histories in different content areas, taken from Funk and Wagnalls, W. U. Funk and Dale and O'Rourke. These may liven up a serious class or increase interest.

For Math, Calculate: Ancient Romans had an instrument called a hodometer or road measurer, which was quite like our taxi meters. Imagine a tin can with a revolving cover holding a quantity of pebbles. Each time the wheel of the carriage turned, the metal cover revolved and a pebble dropped through the hole into the can. At the destination the driver then counted the number of pebbles and "calculated" the bill. (The Latin word for "pebble" was *calculus!*)

In Social Studies: When studying military battles and men, can you guess where or how we got the terms *lieutenant, captain, and colonel? Lieutenant* comes from the French words *lieu* (in place of) and *tenir* (to hold). A lieutenant, then, is one who takes the place of the captain when the captain is not around. *Captain* comes from the Latin *caput,* or head. *Colonel* comes from *columna* (Latin for column), so this name is derived from the column being led.

Conspirator: In the light of recent politics and government, this is an interesting word taken from Latin *spirare* (to breath) and the prefix *con* (to gather). Truly, conspirators breathe together. (Sometimes they "sing" together, too!)

Capital punishment: Originally from death by one means only: severing the head from the body. The Latin word for head, *caput,* is the base for this term. Today, of course, the meaning has been broadened to include execution by any means.

Mnemonic: Achilles (the Greek hero of Homer's Illiad with a vulnerable heel) had another problem too—remembering things. He solved this by keeping Mnemon near him as a companion to remember things for him. The name Mnemon means "mind" or "memory"; thus, a mnemonic device such as a string on your finger aids memory.

Curfew: This comes from the French *couvir* (cover) and *feu* (fire). In olden days the curfew bell meant "put out or cover up the fire and go to bed."

Sombrero: From sunny Spain the benefit of this hat when worn is to give shade from the hot sun with its wide brim. The Spanish for "shade" is *sombra.*

Did you know that:

1. The American slang word *guy* is from Guy Fawkes, the historic British conspirator who tried to blow up the House of Lords?
2. *Bonfire* was once a *bonefire*, often made of bones of heretics in the Middle Ages?
3. *Amnesty* (which we now think of as a pardon for offense) actually came from a Greek word meaning "loss of memory"? When we ask for amnesty, we are actually asking the judge to have amnesia—to forget it.
4. *Senate* literally means "a group of old men"; Latin *senex* means an old man.
5. *Tammany* Hall was actually named after an Indian saint of the 17th century, Chief Tammany

For these and other examples, see Wilfred Funk's (1968) *Word Origins and Their Romantic Stories*, especially the two chapters on political and war words.

Workshop 9.4	**Spectre** The branches of word study can be found in the Latin word *spectre* (to look). More than words have sprouted from this base, words such as spectator, spectacle, inspect, introspection. How many others can you think of offhand? List them, create a cognitive map, or draw a recall diagram. Compare your work with the work of others in your class.

Home Economics for Food Lovers

Here is a fun activity that requires knowledge of multiple cultures. Have students fill in the blanks below with the nationality of the people who originated the following foods, or the country from which they came. (Underlined answers have been given here.)

1. *Tortilla* is a (<u>*Mexican*</u>) word for "pancake."
2. *Macaroons* were first baked by (<u>*Italians*</u>).
3. Twice-baked bread, called *Zwieback*, got its name in (<u>*Germany*</u>).
4. The *meringue* of whipped egg whites is a (<u>*French*</u>) word.
5. *Chocolate* is a (<u>*Spanish*</u>) word that comes from the Nahuatl Indian language.
6. The (<u>*Hungarians*</u>) gave us *goulash*.
7. *Minestrone* is a thick (<u>*Italian*</u>) vegetable soup.
8. *Sukiyaki* is a (<u>*Japanese*</u>) dish.
9. *Poi* comes from the (<u>*Hawaiians*</u>).
10. *Oatmeal* originated in (<u>*Scotland*</u>).

Did you realize that we actually control our own language? We have invented over 600,000 usable English words, with others taken directly from foreign languages, such as *bouquet* from the French. We ourselves have devised the queer spellings and pronunciations of our English language. Some of our spellings are due to errors made by uneducated typesetters centuries ago. We have actually honored their misspellings by continuing to use them!

Much of our language today was yesterday's slang, usually cropping up in slum areas. Purists and highbrows, although protesting, have eventually had to give in and agree to include these words in the dictionary. Two hundred thirty years ago slang words included *bubble, sham, bully, hips*. Other past slang included *gin, boycott, cab, greenhorn,* and *hoax*. When these words are included in the dictionary, their definitions actually come from the sentences or context in which the new word appeared.

Amelioration and Pejoration

Amelioration (the up-elevator) and pejoration (basement bound) are terms concerned with the changes in meaning up and down the social scale over a period of time. See the chart below for some examples of amelioration, where the connotation of the word has been elevated today. Pejoration, on the other hand, is concerned with words that now have a negative connotation.

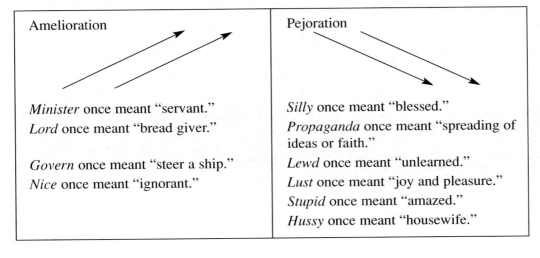

Amelioration	Pejoration
Minister once meant "servant." *Lord* once meant "bread giver." *Govern* once meant "steer a ship." *Nice* once meant "ignorant."	*Silly* once meant "blessed." *Propaganda* once meant "spreading of ideas or faith." *Lewd* once meant "unlearned." *Lust* once meant "joy and pleasure." *Stupid* once meant "amazed." *Hussy* once meant "housewife."

It has been said that Sir Christopher Wren, the great architect of St. Paul's Cathedral in London, was told by King George I that Wren's work was "amusing, awful, and artificial." Wren was delighted with this royal compliment because 300 years ago *amusing* meant "amazing," *awful* meant "awe-inspiring," and *artificial* meant "artistic"! This again shows us how meanings of words can change drastically over time.

Denotations and Connotations

Denotations of words refer to the literal or scientific meanings of words. Most technical terms, especially in science or mathematics, have very precise definitions; there is no ambiguity about which meaning they portray.

Connotation refers to the interpretative or emotional meanings of words. What does yellow mean to you? Your definition will depend on your point of view or the context. Do you have a green thumb? Am I referring to the color of your thumb or your ability to grow plants? If the latter, that is the connotation.

Coining New Words

Blending the first part of a word with the last part of another is one way to coin a new word. Two well-known examples are *smoke + fog = smog*. Other examples include:

American + Asian = Amerasian	grit + slime = grime
dictation + telephone = dictaphone	squirm + wriggle = squiggle
motor + calvacade = motorcade	Europe + Asia = Eurasia
14 + night = fortnight	combine + mingle = commingle
binary + digit = bit	TV + marathon = telethon

From Lewis B. Carroll's *Alice in Wonderland*, we find:

slimy + lithe = slithy	chuckle + snort = chortle
flimsy + miserable = mimsy	

Building new words from parts of old words is another way new words are coined:

astro—astrodome, astrometeorologist	metropolitan—megalopolis
biochemistry—bionic	panorama—cinerama
consort—consortium	medicine—medicare
	culture—acculturate

Shakespeare coined over 1,700 words, many of which still survive today. For example:

suspicious	monumental	hurry
lonely	dwindle	bump
laughable	critical	barefaced
castigate	leapfrog	

During World War II, British fliers coined *gremlin*—a goblin accused of playing tricks on planes. Other words to come out of that war were *radar, flak, gastapo,* and *blitzkreig.* Those familiar with Ebonics will recognize these newly coined words:

phat—nice or very appealing
crib—a house or living quarters
phat crib—a nice house

Specific Types of Word Study

Figures of speech most commonly found in text include metaphors, idioms, euphemisms, onomatopoeias, and oxymorons. In this section on kinds of word study, we will also discuss acronyms, homonyms, and analogies.

You may recall that a *simile* is an analogy where two unlike things are compared using "like" or "as." Simile comes from Latin *similia*, meaning "like." Some examples, which are now clichés (overused): fought like a tiger, easy as pie, sure as shootin', quick as a wink, slow as molasses in January, as smart as a whip, as right as rain, as cute as a button.

On the other hand, *metaphor* comes from Greek *metaphora*, meaning transfer, from *meta* (over) *pherein* (to carry). Metaphors draw a comparison directly between two things without using "like" or "as." "All the world's a stage" (Shakespeare). "No man is an island" (Donne). "Words are weapons" (Santayana). "The road was a ribbon of moonlight," Alfred Nayes, "The Highwayman."

Idioms are difficult for English as second language learners. Some examples using body parts are: don't split hairs, lend an ear, keep a stiff upper lip, finger in every pie, browbeating, nose to the grindstone, without batting an eyelash, giving an arm or a leg, button your lip, rocks in his head, catch her eye, green thumb, by the skin of your teeth.

A *euphemism* is a pleasant term for something considered unpleasant. Students will enjoy adding to these lists or creating their own.

Unpleasant Situation	Euphemism
1. overdrawn bank account	negative saver
2. fired from a job	terminated
3. old people	senior citizens
4. janitor	sanitation maintenance superintendent
5. to die	pass away
6. draft	selective service
7. quiz, test, exam	educational opportunity

Onomatopoeia refers to words resembling the sounds they refer to, (e.g., bleep, blip, boom, bong, chirp, chug, clong, clatter, crunch, slurp, squeal, squish). English teachers might use this idea in a poetry writing assignment.

An *oxymoron* is a figure of speech where words of almost opposite meaning are used together for effect. Writers will use these for the strong effect that comes from putting together words not in harmony. The word *oxymoron* comes from the Greek *oxys* (sharp) and *moros* (foolish). By combining the opposites of *sharp or bright* with *dull or foolish*, you get an oxymoron.

Examples of Oxymorons

free agent	infinitely small	golden ghetto
peace warrior	honest thief	gigante chiquito
dictatorial democracy	icy heat	progressive regression
absolute possibility	bittersweet	jumbo shrimp
restless quiet	sublime folly	organized mess
wonderfully stupid	dynamic bore	brilliant failure
favorite enemy	pure evil	elementary calculus
good war	vast minority	definite maybe
still life	absolute relativity	deafening silence
broadly ignorant	permanent change	gentle strength
political scientist		

A contest or "oxymoron for the day" activity in a middle or high school class has proved to be a successful motivator. Each teacher should consider teaching the oxymorons most commonly used in their own discipline.

Acronyms are words that are formed from the first letters of several words. (Acronym is derived from two Greek words: *akros,* meaning extreme or at the very beginning, and *onyma,* meaning name. *Onyma* is also used in the words antonym and synonym.) In polite society, SNAFU stands for "situation normal: all fouled up." Other acronyms include:

MIA	missing in action
POW	prisoner of war
AIDS	acquired immune deficiency syndrome
SIDS	sudden infant death syndrome
POSH	port out starboard home
RADAR	radio detecting and ranging
LASAR	light amplification by stimulated emission of radiation
NATO	North Atlantic Treaty Organization
LEM	lunar excursion module
WASP	white Anglo-Saxon Protestant
NOW	National Organization for Women
TESOL	teaching English to speakers of other languages
RSVP	respondez s`il vous plait (please reply)
NBA	National Basketball Association
WNBA	Women's National Basketball Association
CSSD	context, structure, sound, dictionary

And then we have special words that can cause problems with meaning, spelling, or pronunciation.

Homonyms have the same sound and spelling, but different meaning (e.g., bank = river of or money). *Homophones* have the same sound, but different spelling and meaning. (e.g., new, knew, gnu, or fair, fare, or to, two, too). *Homographs* have the same spelling, but different meaning and sound (e.g., read—present or past tense).

Analogies are a powerful thinking tool to help see conceptual connections in all content areas. Usually a complete connection is given in the first pair of words and choice of words is given to complete the companion pair. First, you must identify the kind of relationship found in the first pair (e.g., qualitative or quantitative; concrete or abstract; dealing with events, actions, people, or conditions). You select a word from the choice given to fill out the second pair to make it the same or similar to the first. For example:

Clutch: transmission :: Key:_____.
(Starter, engine, exhaust)

Read this "clutch is to transmission as key is to ____*(choose one)*____. The answer is "starter."

: = is to

:: = as

This is a part to whole analogy. A measurement example might be:

Minutes : clock :: _____ : temperature.
(liters, degrees, gradations)

A clock measures minutes; temperature measures degrees.

The Miller Analogies Test is often required for entrance into graduate school. There is a self-help manual that can be used for practice or just for fun.

Here are a few more to try:

- Triangle : 3 :: square : _____
  (4) (12) (1)
  Hint: This has to do with geometric figures with number of sides.

- Water : dehydration :: vitamins : _____
  (measles, typhoid fever, deficiency diseases)
  Hint: What does water do for dehydration?

- Grim Reaper : death :: _____ : sleep
  (Father time, Sandman, Jack Frost)
  Hint: symbols

E. D. Hirsh in his controversial book, *Cultural Literacy* (1988), had an interesting list of vocabulary terms, idioms, names, and historical events that "every American should know." A fun activity is to use these terms in a game like "Trivial Pursuit" to test our knowledge of what is thought by some to be essential cultural knowledge. However, keep in mind that idioms are confusing and can be especially so for English language learners. For example, people do not really "turn green with envy," or "burn the candle at both ends!" If you are fortunate enough to have students from other cultures in your classes, you will find that all students can benefit if you take time to learn their idiomatic expressions and at the same time, help them to learn those recommended by Hirsch.

CSSD for Attacking New Words in All Content Areas

CSSD is a general word attack strategy to identify, pronounce, and get meaning of unknown words in print. Many students tend to rely on a single method and give up if that doesn't work. Letting students know of other ways helps them to develop more independence. Usually, good readers first try to figure out the meaning of an unknown word in its context—looking at the words around it for hints. When not certain they may try taking the word apart into meaningful segments (structural analysis). Roots and affixes (prefixes and suffixes) are looked at for meanings. These meaningful segments are also referred to as morphemes. If words don't lend themselves to breaking into meaningful parts, then they can be broken into syllables with each one sounded out (phonics—or looking at the sound—symbol relationship). As a last resort or when verification or clarification of meaning is needed, readers refer to a dictionary or glossary. Readers may try these four aspects in any order depending on the task at hand.

Let's try it. Look at this underlined new word in the sentence. "He became overly zealous and <u>sesquipedalianist</u> about vocabulary development." How would you go about deriving meaning? Apply what you just read.

Now let's look at each of these four word attack areas in a bit more detail.

Context (The Intelligent Guess)

This can be a powerful tool, especially when combined with any of the other three, and is often used by mature readers when encountering new words. Figuring out the meaning of a word by the words around it may well be a reason that avid readers have a larger vocabulary than reluctant ones. At times this may give a closer meaning than merely looking it up in the dictionary in which a variety of definitions are listed from which to choose.

Steps in context analysis are as follows:

1. Decide on the *syntax* or function of the unknown word as used in the sentence. Is it a noun, verb, adjective, adverb, etc.? Knowing which part of speech it is will cut down on the possible meanings.

2. Using your knowledge of types of context clues (see the list below) try to decide its meaning from the words around it.

3. Check the *semantics* or meaning of substituting a synonym for the unknown word and see if it makes sense here. Try it with these examples.

   a. The thief made a *surreptitious* movement, stealthily pocketing the money.

   _____

   b. It was a *maudlin* performance, sentimental to the extreme.

   _____

   c. Her *sardonic* or bitter expression told the story.

   _____

In our secondary classes we found that many students rarely use context clues knowingly, because they have learned to rely too heavily on other strategies. Major types of clues included in table 9-1.

TABLE 9.1 Semantic Context Clues

Clue	Example
1. Definition	To expire is to die.
2. Restatement	The cliché or stereotyped phrase
3. Example	"It's a great life if you don't weaken."
4. Comparison/Contrast	A harpsichord, like a piano . . . She was quiet in class, but extremely loquacious with her peers.
5. Description	A ginkgo is a shade tree found in eastern China that has leaves in the shape of a fan.
6. Synonyms/Antonyms	To vindicate or justify his actions.
7. Familiar Expressions or Experience	"The Emancipation Proclamation was . . ." helps to understand an emancipated woman.
8. Association	It was as airy and buoyant as a feather.
9. Reflection of Mood	He was aggravated by the constant raspy whine and the repetition of complaints.
10. Summary	She was despondent, could not sleep or eat, cried much of the time, and could not keep her mind on her work.
11. Punctuation	Phobias—irrational fears

Structural Analysis (Meaningful Word Parts)

The structural analysis approach to word attack divides a word into its meaning-bearing parts or morphemes, root words, prefixes, and suffixes. For example: *underhandedness.* The root is *hand*, the prefix is *under*, and the two suffixes are *ed* and *ness.*

For structural analysis to be a successful strategy, students must have some knowledge of meanings of common *affixes* (prefixes and suffixes). Because many English root words and affixes are derived from Latin and Greek, reviewing those common to your content area is time well spent.

The precise technical terminology of the sciences lends itself to this strategy. See Appendix D for a listing of common roots and affixes used in science. Using this list as a reference, students may unlock meanings of long technical scientific terms. One way to become familiar with meanings of word parts such as *bi* or *corpus* is to use them in coining new words. Students must get at the meaning of referring to the list. For example, what is a *"chlor dermato bi capit corpus"*? (It is a coined word for "green-skinned two-headed body." *Chlor* means "green," *dermato* is "skin," etc.)

TABLE 9.2 Numerical Word Elements Activity

Can you mathematicians unlock the mysteries of these words? Any problems? Counting from one to ten in Latin or Greek may help.		
	Latin	**Greek**
1. monolithic	unos	mons
2. dichotomy	duo	dyn/dy/di
3. triptych	tres	tn
4. quadrennial	quattuor	tetra
5. quintessence	quinque	penta
6. hexagon	sex	hexa
7. hebdomadal	septem	hepta
8. octava	octo	octo
9. novena	novem	ennea
10. decalogue	decem	deca/deka

Sound (Phonics—Symbols, Syllables, and Sounds)

Most secondary teachers will not be teaching phonics as that is not usually the content-area teacher's job, but a few hints to troubled readers can really help them. Whether or not you believe that phonics is the panacea for helping troubled readers, it does have its place as one avenue toward meaning even for adults. But don't forget, even if you can sound out a word, if that word is not in your listening vocabulary, the word will have no meaning for you. Even if this word exists in your listening vocabulary, you must also be aware of possible connotations and special meanings for specific content areas. We need but look at examples such as "to *house* the guest" versus "entering a *house*," or "the square *root*" versus "the *root* of the problem" to see this is true. Decoding "house" or "root" doesn't necessarily give the appropriate meaning even if the word is in our original vocabulary.

A few phonic generalizations may help those students who didn't master them in early elementary grades. For those who wish a more detailed explanation of phonics, as well as context, structural analysis, and dictionary, we highly recommend Rinsky's (1997) *Teaching Word Recognition Skills.*

Basic to phonics is knowledge of consonant and vowel sounds. In English it's the vowel sounds that vary most, consonants are generally constant—long vowels in open syllables with a vowel at the end sound their own name—but short vowels, which are more common and appear in closed syllables, are more difficult to remember for some. Note: Bag, beg, big, bog, bug—each has a single vowel between two consonants closing in the vowel. To remind students of short sounds, they are easier to hear when appearing at the beginning of a word. A chart like this one below can act as a quick reference.

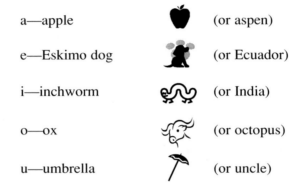

a—apple   (or aspen)

e—Eskimo dog   (or Ecuador)

i—inchworm   (or India)

o—ox   (or octopus)

u—umbrella   (or uncle)

Long vowels appear in open syllables (bi, be, bo) and say their own name (open, item, even). Vowels have other sounds, depending on how they are combined in words with other letters (worm, heard, bread) or depending on different dialects (egg = aig, oil = earl, house = hoose). You may wish to remind students to sound it out one way and if it does not make sense in the sentence try another way.

The schwa sound is designated by an inverted e (∂), which has the "uh" sound heard in a nonaccented or nonstressed syllable.

about   respiration   corolla

Look-alike words may be pronounced differently with different meanings.

Also mispronunciation of words can lead to spelling errors such as histry for history, liberry for library.

The rule of silent e can be depended upon to give correct pronunciation. If a word ends in a silent e, the vowel before it is long. Look at the closed syllable of bit with its short vowel as shown with simply a dot above it. Now take "bit," add "e," and you have "bīte" with the macron over the vowel to show it is now long. Try this now with fin, mat, kit, cut, then eliminate the final e in words hate, cane, and time.

The Dictionary: A Multipurpose Tool

How many uses can you think of for a dictionary? Brainstorming with others, you might be able to come up with a multitude of responses beyond the three obvious ones of meaning, pronunciation, and spelling. The dictionary has been described as being more like an abridged encyclopedia or history book than a law book. It is certainly an important but often misused tool. Acquiring meanings of new words strictly from the dictionary rather than from the context in which they appear is a rote memorization exercise not likely to remain in our long-term memory.

The plethora of definitions for each word may also serve to confuse rather than clarify. It is a misuse to select the first definition, as some students automatically do. Synonyms are not much help to a student when neither word is known, such as the example of "to disparage is to denigrate."

A dictionary is an important tool for vocabulary development, which, unfortunately, many students never master. In order to use a dictionary, students need to:

- use knowledge of alphabetical order beyond the first letter of a word.
- use the guide words for speedier locating.
- locate root words, variants, and derivatives.
- interpret accent marks.
- use the pronunciation key and interpret phonetic spellings.

Because there is likely to be a very broad range in reading achievement in any one content classroom, it is helpful to have some dictionaries at a variety of levels.

Earlier, in Chapter Six, we suggested that Part II of a CIRI (content informal reading inventory), the skills section, might include a subtest on using the dictionary. If you don't have CIRI data, and you are uncertain about your students' skill in this area, it will be worth your time to design a very brief diagnostic "pretest." The results may surprise you. Here is an example of the kinds of questions you might choose to ask of students in a 10th or 11th grade class:

1. Look up the word _____. What are the guide words on that page? (Students may not know what a guide word is.)

2. What does _____ mean? (Students may only give you the first definition.)

3. Where would you find the pronunciation for _____?

4. What is a synonym for _____?

5. What is an antonym for the word _____?

6. What is the derivation of the word _____?

7. What part of speech is the word _____?

8. How is _____ spelled phonetically?

9. How many syllables are in the word _____?

10. Which syllable in the word _____ receives the primary accent?

For an example of how this type of subtest may be incorporated into a CIRI (content informal reading inventory), please see Appendix A.

Thesaurus: A Storehouse of Information

A thesaurus is another handy tool. Whereas dictionaries give us meanings for given words, a thesaurus gives us words for given meanings—that is, synonyms (words that mean the same) and antonyms (words whose meanings are the opposite). The term *thesaurus* comes from Latin and means "a storehouse of information." You may find an abbreviated form of a thesaurus on most word-processing programs. Unfortunately, most of these programs tell you very little about the shades of meaning of the choices provided. You may find more complete versions of this storehouse on the Web (e.g., http://thesaurus.reference.com/), or in print. In the *Random House Webster's Thesaurus* (1997) each entry begins with sample sentences to help pinpoint shades of meaning. For example, for the word *abandon* the entry begins "she abandoned her child on the doorstep of the church," followed by the synonyms. The second sentence, "The scientist abandoned his research for lack of funds." In this case it meant stop or dropped, where as the first meant leave or forsake.

Workshop 9.5

Strategy Selection

Now with this brief background of the basic decoding strategies (CSSD), read over the following vocabulary strategies and select your three favorites. Discuss choices in your group and try to read a consensus of the three most valuable to your group. You may wish to rank order them 1, 2, 3.

Next within the group, with a partner or triad, develop a brief lesson plan in a chosen content area using one of the three strategies along with an appropriate reading selection. These can then be handed in for teacher feedback or feedback from another group.

FROM THE CONTENT CLASSROOM

Antidisestablishmentarianism

With a non-college-bound 10th-grade class at a local Southwest high school, one teacher started her discussion of structural analysis with the following word stretched out across the entire board. Most of these students were reading between a third- and fifth-grade level, and when encountering big words they simply would give up.

"Antidisestablishmentarianism" has 28 letters and was allegedly coined by Gladstone.

First, she divided the word into morphemes (meaningful parts).

Anti / dis / establish / ment / arian / ism

Asked for the root word many said "establishment." She boxed in "establish." Now starting from the end she showed them the meaning of each part.

Anti / dis / establish / ment / arian / ism

Against   not   in the state   one who is   system of
                of being

"A system of one who is in the state of being against establishing." Or, in true translation—opposition to the idea that the church should cease to be formally recognized by the state.

My, her students got a kick out of this extreme example. Some requested that she put some more words on the board to dissect. Student confidence in attacking technical vocabulary words, in history and later in science, had changed, and this had only taken a few minutes.

Teaching Strategies: Before, During, and After

Before

Activating Prior Knowledge, Making Connections, Predicting and Setting a Purpose

Word-of-the-Day (Tonjes & Zintz, 1981)

Write a significant content word on the board before class and circle it. As students come in and while roll is taken, they can try to decode it and think of all possible meanings. In a sophomore English class with low-achieving readers, the word one day was *ambiguous*. No one knew what it meant, then context clues were given and someone asked, "Does it mean 'not clear'?" After discussion, the definition, and with a sentence as an example, the students' assignment with that word was to use it three times before the next class, both in writing and orally. The next day when the word was reviewed, a student reported that it was a dangerous word. He had told his science teacher that his lecture was ambiguous and incurred the teacher's wrath. Needless to say, the student never forgot that word!

Synonym Clusters (Tonjes & Zintz, 1981)

Select a key term or concept to appear in the upcoming chapter. Explain that you want students to understand major concepts with all their shades of meaning, and one way is through synonym clustering.

What is the differences between "guilt" and "remorse"?

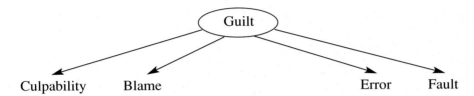

A feeling of responsibility or self-reproach for offenses committed.

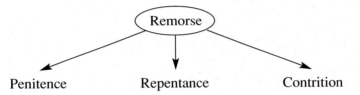

- Regret for one's sins or for acts that wrong others
- Distress arising from a sense of guilt

I'm responsible for it = guilt
I feel bad about it = remorse

List/Group/Label Concept Development (Taba, 1967)

This classification technique activates prior knowledge prior to reading and is a good strategy to find out the depth of class initial knowledge on a particular topic or concept.

a. Brainstorm with the class but always reviewing brainstorming rules (all responses accepted, no put downs or praise of any response). "What are ways of transportation?" or "What were modes of transportation in the 1800s in the United States?" (These are examples only.) The class responds without raising hands, and as quickly as you can, write their responses on the board.

b. When responses flag, stop and ask "Which three of these things can go together because they are alike in some way?" Take the first group of three and ask why they were put together. Write the reason beside the three. Continue with others.

c. When most are grouped or discarded, ask the class to label each group of three based on the reason given for why they are alike. This is an excellent thinking activity, and not as easy as it may appear because of having to justify responses.

More on this strategy may be found in Chapter Seven.

Cognitive Maps

We want our students to make sure they have clear criteria for choosing the words that they do. We also want them to make connections among major concepts. One way to show them how to do this is to model how you map your own connections. We have done this for each of our chapters. You may want to do the same with the units they are studying. As with many other strategies, once you have modeled and provided some guided practice, let students try their hand at it. Have them get into small groups and do the following:

a. Start by listing all key terms of your topic and then placing them in superordinate and subordinate relationships. Group those that are alike in some way, giving labels for each.

b. Playfully start placing categories on a sheet of paper or with your computer (Inspiration Software is discussed in Chapter One), rearranging many times until it gels. Sometimes putting the title or main idea in the center of the page helps.

The cognitive maps in this text have undergone numerous revisions, so do not expect to get it right away the first time. You can judge their effectiveness if they help as a reading pre-organizer to see how major facets will interact in the chapter or unit. It is much more interesting if your diagram reflects the general idea or feeling for the topic.

Student-Selected Key Words

In a subject such as science or social studies, as a review at the end of the course, ask students to decide key words to remember. Have them list these first individually, then meet in small groups to compare. Finally each group reports to the total class. Teachers should have their lists ready, too, so that the similarities and differences can be discussed. The important thing to remember is not simply the word itself, but the reason why the students felt it was one to remember. This can be an excellent synthesis activity, because decisions must be made about what is important and why.

During (While Reading)

Modified CLOZE Technique

The term "CLOZE" stands for a procedure where every fifth word is deleted from a selection of more than 250 words to give 50 blank spaces. The first and last sentences of the excerpt are left intact. Readers must fill in the blanks (12 spaces in length) with the exact word replacement, after carefully reading over the entire piece. (More about this may be found in Chapter Six.)

This modified version uses CLOZE for teaching, not testing, and can be both playful and purposeful. Decisions can be made as to which words to delete, how many and what hints to give such as supplying the first letter of each deleted word, adapting the length of the blank to fit the word, or using a dash to stand for each letter as we once did in "Hang the Man." Sometimes all deleted words are placed at the bottom of the page for reference.

Try putting answers in the left-hand column along the line where words are removed. This column is then folded back until readers are ready to self-check.

Fold Back	Let us look at schema theory:
cognitive what, idea is, reality	A schema is a _____ structure, an organization of _____ we know about an _____, concept or thing. It ____as basic abstraction of _____ (note that space lengths coincide with word length as hints) Here are a number of things teachers can do to help.
reading connections knowledge organizer	Prior to _____, build up and make c_____ with students' background k_____ using some form of advance _____. (Here only key words were deleted, which would be more difficult. Giving the first letter to each would help.)

Think-Alouds

Think-Alouds may be especially helpful for English language learners or struggling readers. You model aloud what you are thinking as you read from the text. You may suggest ways to get at word meanings—questions you ask yourself, reminders of the purpose for reading this, and any known strategies. This is a mature reader sharing insights.

After (To Confirm, Clarify Meanings, Extend)

OPIN

OPIN, created by Green in 1978, stands for opinion or open vs. closed, and combines prior knowledge with context clues. It is more concerned with *why* we select a certain word as the best word for a particular context. The main requirement is a rational defense of the choice made. The four steps are:

1. Students individually read given sentences to fill in the best word they can think of for each blank.
2. In triads they discuss each other's words, trying to convince others that their word is best and always giving a reason for their choice. They then try to reach consensus of the best word.
3. Each triad next meets with another triad to discuss and try to convince that their triad's word is best.
4. The teacher then asks each group of six to share results with the rest of the class, allowing for further arguments.

At each point it is all right to change an answer or adopt another triad's reasons. Workshop 3.1, back in Chapter Three, is a modified OPIN activity.

Examples of sentences for an OPIN exercise may include:

a. Everyone _____ that Columbus discovered America.

b. Today has been an absolutely _____ day so far.

c. The Super Bowl last January was _____ and _____ compared to other years.

d. Chopin's nocturne was played with _____ and _____.

You will find students excitedly arguing for "their" content word—a nice activity on a late Friday afternoon.

Semantic Feature Analysis (SFA) (Anderson & Bos, 1986)

Here is a popular way to establish links between students' prior knowledge and words that are conceptually related. The grid is used to display likenesses and differences. The first step is to select a topic or category, listing related words down the left-side column. Across the top of the grid place features or properties that are shared by some of the words in the column. The students decide which are related by placing a "+" in that square, leaving blank those that are not related or placing a question mark. This can be done first on the board for the whole class and later on individual handouts.

An example follows:

EARLY CIVILIZATIONS	Educated	War-Like	Democratic
1. Roman	+	+	?
2. Greek	+		+
3. Egyptian	+		?
4. etc.			

TOAST: A Vocabulary Study System

Dana and Rodriguez (1992) developed this vocabulary study system for content areas. Students do the following:

T = *Test*:	Self-test to see which words they can't define or use.	
O = *Organize:*	Put words into related categories such as parts of speech, those that sound alike, or are somewhat familiar.	
A = *Anchor:*	Place words into long-term memory by giving them a caption or picture, putting on cards and ordering from easy to hard, tape recording them with definitions and in context.	
S = *Say:*	Review meanings, uses in sentences for 5 minutes at the end of the lesson.	
T = *Toast:*	Self-test through thinking or writing silently from memory.	

Playing with Words: Fun for All!

Collective Nouns

For over 50 years amateur semanticists have been engaged in coining terms for collective nouns. Most were codified around 400 years ago, when the English language was expanding and exploding. A parliament of owls is one example.

   The following "nouns of multitude," or assemblage (Lipton, 1977), may be used by all ages as a general vocabulary incentive. This can be played in relay teams or just as a general class activity. It is strictly a motivator and could be a fill-in at the end of a class. Ask what a group of owls is called. The collective noun is "a parliament" of owls. Continue with others from this list below or find new ones.

What is a group of?	Collective Noun	What is a group of?	Collective Noun
• geese	• gaggle	• walrus	• pod
• leopards	• leap	• seals	• trip
• fish	• school	• wolves	• pack
• crows	• murder	• turtles	• glag
• cats	• clowder	• gorillas	• troup
• lions	• pride	• larks	• exaltation
• donkeys	• pace	• owls	• parliament
• insects	• swarm	• nightingales	• watch
• bears	• crowd/sloth	• bananas	• hand
• beavers	• colony	• bicycles	• wobble
• jellyfish	• smack	• dermatologists	• rash
• cardiologists	• flutter		

Mistaken Clichés

Mistaken clichés are overused phrases, words, or sentences. They are often used in error. Try these with your class as a 5 minute filler:

1. Pride goeth before _____? (*destruction*, students may say "the fall." Proverbs 16)

2. To _____ the lily? (*paint*, students may say "gild." King John, Shakespeare)

3. A little _____ goes a long way. (*knowledge*, students may say "learning.")

4. Ask me no questions, I'll tell you no _____? (*fibs*, students may say "lies." Goldsmith)

5. Give him an inch, he'll take _____? (*an el*, students may say "a mile.")

6. _____ is the root of all evil? (*The love of money*, students may say "money.")

Palindromes, Pangrams, Anagrams, and Spoonerisms

Palindromes (Greek) means running back again. These are words and sentences spelled the same way backwards and forwards (e.g., radar, eve, kayak, rotor, "Madam, I'm Adam.", "A man, a plan, a canal, Panama!"). This is merely a playful activity mainly for language arts classes.

Finding the perfect *pangram* is an obsession with some people. Their goal is to compose a sentence containing every letter of the alphabet—preferably using each letter only once. This is especially difficult with vowels. A sentence that has every letter but multiple vowels is "A quick brown fox jumps over the lazy dog."

Anagrams or juggling letters around you come up with another word or phrase that is connected in some way. For example:

1. Angered—(another word meaning the same thing)—*Enraged*
2. Train—(two words that can be said about it)—*It ran*
3. Agitator—(four words)—*I got a rat*
4. Punishment—(two words)—*Nine Thumps*

Perhaps you have heard of the term "*spoonerisms*." It comes from the Reverend Wm. Archibald Spooner, Warden (Head) of New College Oxford from 1903 to 1924. He had the habit of transposing letters at beginnings of words. When toasting the dear Queen it came out "Here's to our *queer dean*." When expelling a student (sending him down, as they say at Oxford) he meant to say "You have missed my history lectures. You have wasted a whole term. You will leave Oxford on the next down train." Instead he said, "You have *hissed* my *mystery* lectures, you have *tasted* a whole *worm*. You will leave Oxford on the next *town drain*." Just imagine the fun his students had awaiting his next revelation! Picture him now as he actually was—short, nearsighted, but shrewd, humorous, and with great personal dignity (which made it all the better!).

Different Definitions

We can have fun with different definitions. Here are a few examples:

- *Liberty*—the right to do what the law permits.
- *Autobiography*—an unrivaled vehicle for telling the truth—about other people.
- *Time*—nature's way of ensuring that everything doesn't happen at once.
- *Slang*—a language that rolls up its sleeves, spits on its hands, and goes to work. (Carl Sandburg)
- *Burglar Alarm*— a protection racket.
- *Profit Sharing Plan*—two people seeing a guru at the same time.
- *Home*—"is the place where, when you have to go there they have to take you in." (Robert Frost, "Death of the Hired Man")
- *Courage*—is fear that has said its prayer.
- *Character*—"is like a tree and reputation like its shadow. The shadow is what we think of it, the tree is the real thing." (Abraham Lincoln)
- *Conformity*—"is the jailer of freedom and the enemy of growth." (John F. Kennedy)
- Your Word and Definition

Word Pairs

"Word pairs to see relationships" can be a nice filler for the last 5 minutes of class. Tell one word that fits both words.

For example: jewelry and bell—ring

emerald and rookies = green	cigarette and tree = ash
clothes and law = suit	candy and money = mint/bar
river and money = bank	sum and nobility = count
duel and time = second	

Do you want more word study? If so, see Appendix E for further word study books.

Ten Things to Remember When Teaching Vocabulary

1. Select fewer words for direct teaching and find ways to give them shades of meaning. If it is a content-specific term, be sure it doesn't have a general meaning too.

2. Encourage outside recreational and collateral reading with the same content theme (e.g., an historical novel of the place and time period being studied).

3. Plan to teach key vocabulary daily, introducing new terms before the reading.

4. Connect between new and known words through such activities as classifying, synonyms, and antonyms, having students restate meanings in their own words and connecting to their personal experiences if possible.

5. Use words in context—at least in a short phrase—and be sure that when they need to check in the dictionary that they find the appropriate definition, not just the first one.

6. Start now to build up your own personal reference library for vocabulary.

7. Avoid mindless drill.

8. Be enthusiastic; show personal interest.

9. *Make it fun*, encouraging students to be collectors of favorite words, word histories, oxymorons, fun definitions, etc. An example of a fun definition is home—"the place where when you have to go there they have to take you in." (Robert Frost, "Death of the Hired Man")

10. Remember—definitions do not necessarily connect to meanings.

Vocabulary Tools and Games on the Internet

Most are amazed when they find out how many sites there are online that may be used for vocabulary study. Here are four of our favorites:

- http://www.dictionary.com

  A popular dictionary and thesaurus.

- http://www.onelook.com/

  This website provides comprehensive word definitions by providing links to multiple dictionaries from multiple disciplines. For example, type in the word vocabulary and you'll get 24 links to different dictionaries with definitions, including medicine, art, and science.

- http://www.educationworld.com

  This is Education World's Site. Type the word vocabulary into its search engine and you'll get links to hundreds of vocabulary lessons and activities.

- http://www.vokabel.com

  Vocabulary training exercises in French, Spanish, and German.

Cinquain as Summary

Vocabulary
Word Play
Addictive Once Started
Joyful, Mind-expanding, Productive, Challenging
Lexicon

Summary

National standards suggest that the professional educator must understand and use a variety of instructional strategies to encourage students' development of critical thinking, problem-solving, and performance skills. This is especially true when it comes to teaching vocabulary, because students must master the specialized vocabulary of each content area in order to comprehend its concepts and major ideas. Vocabulary words are the building blocks for comprehending. Knowing their specialized meanings promotes better understanding. Definitions are not enough, we must also associate meanings based on our background knowledge.

Levels of knowing a word range from not recognizing it to having a general idea of it, being able to use it (functional level), and finally at the conceptual level we use it comfortably in all its forms. Four types of vocabulary include listening, speaking, reading and writing. Since direct instruction may account for only a small fraction of the actual new vocabulary words learned each year, it is important to encourage wide reading. Vocabulary study may be made more interesting by including word origins, idioms, euphemisms, oxymorons, acronyms, or coining new words. As with teaching all reading skills, think of instruction within the model of "before, during, or after reading." Specific strategies can then be adapted to your field as needed for learning and enjoyment. When you turn students on to the fun and utility of learning words, you have given them a great gift for a lifetime.

References and Recommended Readings

Anderson, P. L., & Bos, C. S. (1986, April). Semantic feature analysis: An interactive strategy for vocabulary development and text comprehension. *Journal of Reading, 29,* 610–616.

Anderson, R. C., & Nagy, W. E. (1992, Winter). The vocabulary conundrum. *American Educator, 16(4),* 14–18, 44–47.

Balchowicz, C. L. Z., & Fisher, P. (2000). Vocabulary instruction. In M. L. Kamil, P. B. Mosenthal, P. D. Pearson, & R. Barr (Eds.), *Handbook of reading research: Vol. III,* (pp. 503-523). Mahwah, NJ: Erlbaum.

Baumann, J. F., Kameenui, E. J. (1991). Research on vocabulary instruction: Ode to voltaire. In J. Flood, J. M. Jensen, D. Lapp, J. R. Squire (Eds.), *Handbook of research on teaching to English language arts.* New York: MacMillan.

Beck, I. L., & McKeown, N. G. (1991). Conditions of vocabulary acquisition. In R. Barr, M. L. Kamil, P. B. Bosenthal, & P. D. Pearson (Eds.), *Handbook of reading research, Vol. II* (pp. 789–814). New York: Longman.

Blake, M. E., & Majors, P. L. (1995, October). Recycled words: Holistic instruction for LEP students. *Journal of Adolescent and Adult Literacy, 39*(2), 132–137.

Bransford, J. D., Brown, A. L., & Cocking, R. R. (2000). *How people learn: Brain, mind, experience and school* (Expanded edition). Washington, DC: National Academy Press.

Bremiller, A. (2001, Spring). Teaching vocabulary: Early, direct and sequential. *American Educator, 25*, 24–28, 47.

Cantrell, R. J. (1994, December; 1995, January). Enhancing the spelling/meaning connection through crossword puzzles. *Journal of Reading, 38*(4), 310–311.

Chase, C., & Deffelmyer, F. (November 1990). VOCAB-LIT: Integrating vocabulary study and literature study. *Journal of Reading, 34*, 188–193.

Council of Chief State School Officers. (2005). *INTASC standards*, Retrieved March 21, 2005, from http://www.ccsso.org/projects/Interstate-New_Teacher_Assessement_and_Support_Consorttium

Coxhead, A. (2000). A new academic word list. *TESOL Quarterly, 34* (2), 213–238.

Dana, C. & Rodriguez M. (1992). TOAST: A system to study vocabulary. *Reading Research and Instruction, 31*(4), 78–84.

Department for Education and Skills. (2005). *The Standards site*. Retrieved June 28, 2005, from http://www.standards.dfes.gov.uk/primary/publications/mathematics/vocabulary/

Dole, J. A., Cloan, C., & Trathen, W. (1995, March). Teaching vocabulary within the context of literature. *Journal of Reading, 38* (6), 452–460.

Farstrup. A. E., & Samuels, S. J. (Eds.). (2002). *What research has to say about reading instruction* (3rd ed.). Newark, DE: International Reading Association.

Funk, W. (1968). *Word origins and their romantic stories*. New York: Funk and Wagnalls.

Gauthier, L. R. (1991). The effects of vocabulary gain upon instructional reading level. *Reading Improvement, 28*, 195–202.

Gonzalez, O. (1999, November). Building vocabulary: Dictionary consultation and the ESL student. *Journal of Adolescent and Adult Literacy, 43*, 264–270.

Graves, M. F., & Watts-Taffe, S. M. (2002). The plan of word consciousness in a research based vocabulary program. In A. E. Farstrup & S. J. Samuels, (Eds.), *What research has to say about reading instruction* (3rd ed.). Newark, DE: International Reading Association.

Green, F. (1978, April). Unpublished presentation given at Western Washington University, Bellingham, Washington.

Hague, S. (1987). Vocabulary instruction: What L2 can learn from L1. *Foreign Language Annals, 20*, 217–225.

Harmon, J. M. (May 2000). Assessing and supporting independent word learning strategies of middle school students. *Journal of Adolescent and Adult Literacy, 43*(6), 518–527.

Harris, T. L., & Hodges, R. E. (Eds.). (1995). *The literacy dictionary: The vocabulary of reading and writing*. Newark, DE: International Reading Association.

Hennings, D. G. (Nov 2000). Contextually relevant word study: Adolescent vocabulary development across the curriculum. *Journal of Adolescent and Adult Literacy, 44*(3), 268–279.

Hirsh, E. D. (1988). *Cultural diversity: What every American needs to know*. Visalia, CA: Vintage Press.

Hopkins, G., & Bean, T. W. (1998–1999). Vocabulary learning with the verbal–visual word association strategy in a Native American community. *Journal of Adolescent and Adult Literacy, (42)4*, 274–281.

Huckin, T., Haynes, M., & Coady, J. (Eds.). (1993). *Second language reading and vocabulary learning*. Norwood, NJ: Ablex.

International Reading Association and National Council of Teachers of English Joint Task Force on Assessment. (1994). *Standards for the assessment of reading and writing*. Newark, DE: International Reading Association.

Johnston, F., Bear, D., & Invernizzi, M. (2006). *Words their way: Word sorts for derivational relations spellers*. Upper Saddle River, NJ: Pearson, Merrill, Prentice Hall.

Kibby, M. W. (1995, November). The organization and teaching of things and the words that signify them. *Journal of Adolescent and Adult Literacy, 39*(3), 208–223.

Konopak, B. C. (1991). Teaching vocabulary to improve science learning. In C. M. Santa & D. E. Alvermann, *Science learning process and applications*, Ch. 14.

Kuhn, M., & Stahl, S. (1998). Teaching children to learn word meaning from context: A synthesis and some questions. *Journal of Literacy Research, 30*(1), 119–138.

LaFlamme, J. G. (1997, February). The effect of the multiple exposure vocabulary method and the target reading/writing strategy on test scores. *Journal of Adolescent and Adult Literacy, 40*(5), 372–381.

Lipton, J. (1977). *An exaltation of larks*. New York: Penguin Books.

McKeown, M. G. (1993). Creating effective definitions for young word learners. *Reading Research Quarterly, 28*, 16–31.

Memory, D. M. (1990). Teaching technical vocabulary before, during and after reading assignment. *Journal of Reading Behavior, 22*, 39–53.

Mountain, L. (2002, September). Flip a chip to build vocabulary. *Journal of Adolescent and Adult Reading, 46*(1), 62–68.

Nagy, W. E., & Scott, J. A. (2000). Vocabulary processes. In M. L. Kamil, P. B. Mosenhnall, P. D. Pearson, & R. Barr (Eds.), *Handbook of reading research, Vol. III* (pp. 269–284).

Nilsen, A. P., & Nilsen, D. L. F. (2002, November). Lessons in the teaching of vocabulary from September 11 and Harry Potter. *Journal of Adolescent and Adult Literacy, 46*(3), 254–260.

Nist, S. L., & Olejnik, S. (1995). The role of context and dictionary definitions on varying levels of word knowledge. *Reading Research Quarterly, 30*, 172–193.

Random House. (1997). *Random House Webster's college thesaurus*, J. Stein, S. Berg Blexner, & F. Sutherland, (Eds.). New York: Random House.

Rapp-Haggard Ruddell, M. (1992). Integrated content and long term vocabulary learning with the vocabulary self-selection strategy. In E. K. Dishner, T. W. Bean, J. E. Readence, & D. W. Moore (Eds.), *Reading in the content areas: Improving classroom instruction* (3rd ed., pp. 190–195). Dubuque, IA: Kendall-Hunt.

Rinsky, L. (1997). *Teaching word recognition skills* (6th ed.). Upper Saddle River, NJ: Prentice Hall.

Rosenbaum, C. (2001, September). A word map for middle school: A tool for effective vocabulary instruction. *Journal of Adolescent and Adult Literacy, 45*, 44–49.

Ryder, R. J., & Medo, M. A. (1993). The effects of vocabulary instruction on readers' ability to make causal connections. *Reading Research and Instruction, 33*, 119–134.

Shu, H., Anderson, R. C., & Zang, H. (1995). Incidental learning of word meanings while reading: A Chinese and American cross-cultural study. *Reading Research Quarterly, 30*, 76–95.

Stahl, S. A. (1999). *Vocabulary development*. Cambridge, MA: Brookline Books.

Taba, H. (1967). *Teacher's handbook for elementary social studies*. Reading, MA: Addison-Wesley

Taylor, W. (1953, Fall). CLOZE procedure: A new tool for measuring readability. *Journalism Quarterly, 30*, 415–533.

Tompkins, G., & Blanchfield, C. (2004). *Teaching vocabulary: 50 creative strategies, grades k–12*. Upper Saddle River, NJ: Pearson, Merrill, Prentice Hall.

Tonjes, M. J., & Zintz, M. (1981). *Teaching reading/thinking/study skills in content classrooms.* Dubuque, IA: Wm. C. Brown Company Publishers.

Tonjes, M. J., & Tonjes, J. C. (1993). Enriching stupidity. In V. Milicic (Ed.)., *Symposium on stupidity* (pp. 125–129). Bellingham, WA: Western Washington University.

Unsworth, L. (2001). *Teaching multi-literacies across the curriculum changing contexts of text and image in classroom practice.* Buckingham, England: Open University Press.

White, T. C., Graves, M. F., & Slater, W. (1990). Development of recognition and reading vocabularies in diverse sociolinguistic and educational settings. *Journal of Educational Psychology, 82,* 281–290

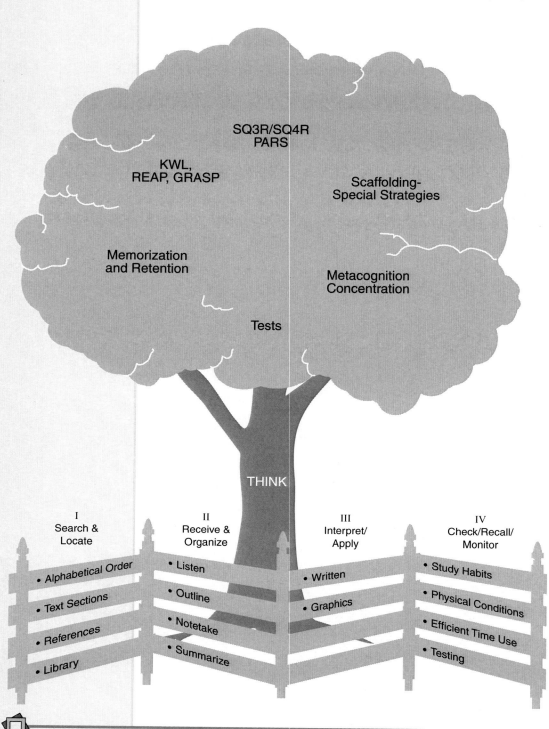

FIGURE 10.1

Study Learning—A Cognitive Map

Within the figure:

SQ3R/SQ4R
PARS

KWL,
REAP, GRASP

Scaffolding-
Special Strategies

Memorization
and Retention

Metacognition
Concentration

Tests

THINK

I
Search &
Locate

II
Receive &
Organize

III
Interpret/
Apply

IV
Check/Recall/
Monitor

- Alphabetical Order
- Text Sections
- References
- Library

- Listen
- Outline
- Notetake
- Summarize

- Written
- Graphics

- Study Habits
- Physical Conditions
- Efficient Time Use
- Testing

Study Learning

10

Outline

- Anticipatory and Review Questions
- A Sampling of National Performance Standards
- Introduction
  - *Workshop 10.1: Study Learning Checklist*
- Search and Locate Information
  - General and Specific References
  - Internet Search Form
  - Library Scavenger Hunt
- Receive and Organize Information
- Interpret and Apply Information
  - Written Language
  - Graphics
    - Types of Graphics
    - Charts and Diagrams
    - Graphs
    - Tables
    - Maps
    - Pictures/Illustrations
    - Cartoons
    - Graphic Information Lesson
    - Teaching Tips
  - *Workshop 10.2: Interpreting Charts*
  - *Workshop 10.3: Interpreting Maps*
- Special Strategies
  - Scaffolding Strategies in General
  - SQ3R/SQ4R
  - PARS
  - *Workshop 10.4: Preparing a Learning Center*
  - K-W-L
  - *Workshop 10.5: K-W-L*

- REAP
- Guided Reading and Summary Procedures: GRASP
- Check/Recall/Monitor Information
  - Establishing Study Habits for Better Concentration
  - Physical Conditions
  - Frame of Mind
  - Efficient Use of Time
  - Time Schedules
  - Memory: Forgetting and Remembering
  - Memorizing: Some Personal Reminiscences
  - Retention
  - Concentration Aids
  - *Workshop 10.6: Practicing Concentration*
- Pulling It All Together
  - Thematic Teaching Units
  - Predict, Verify, Judge, and Extend
- Testing
  - Preparing for Tests
  - Writing Essay Tests
  - Objective Tests
  - Taking the Objective Test: A Worksheet for Students
  - *Workshop 10.7: Teaching Test-Taking Skills*
- Cinquain as Summary
- Summary
- References and Recommended Readings

"Never regard study a duty, but as the enviable opportunity to learn to know the liberating influence of beauty in the realm of the spirit for your own personal joy and to the profit of the community to which your later work belongs."

Albert Einstein

"Study without reflection is a waste of time. Reflection without study is dangerous."

Confucius

"There is no limit to how complicated things can get."

E. B. White

Anticipatory and Review Questions

Literal

1. What are the four steps of the overall study learning process described in this chapter?

2. Which sections of a text should students preview before starting to read or study from it?

Interpretive/Applied

3. A small group of students approach you claiming to have test-taking anxiety. For some reason they have trouble answering multiple choice and true/false questions. How would you help them overcome this anxiety? What guidelines and practice might you provide?

4. Suppose students were having trouble reading graphic aids from you textbook. How would you help them master this important skill in your content area?

Evaluative/Critical

5. Select one specific study strategy that you believe would be most effective for study in your content area. Explain and justify your answer.

6. Do you think it would be wise to review SQ3R/SQ4R each year with a group of high school students? Defend your position, stating your criteria for judging.

Creative/Personal

7. Design your own cognitive map, as seen throughout this text, for a unit in your content area, using a playful representation.

8. A small group of students approach you for help with time management problems. Between school, club or athletic participation, home responsibilities, and their part-time jobs, they don't seem to be able to get all their homework and studying done. Their grades are dropping. What procedures would you use to help this student get control of their time and their lives?

A Sampling of National Performance Standards

- The professional educator understands and uses a variety of instructional strategies to encourage students' development of critical thinking, problem-solving, and performance skills (Council of Chief State School Officers, 2005).
- Students apply a wide range of strategies to comprehend, interpret, evaluate, and appreciate texts (International Reading Association/National Council of Teachers of English, 1996, p. 31).

◈ Introduction

A major goal of teaching is to help students become independent and willing learners, ready to apply knowledge when and where needed. In our rapidly changing world the processes for obtaining, integrating, and reviewing information are crucial and just memorizing facts to give back on a test is not sufficient. That is not to say that memorization does not have its place—it does, as you will see later. Study learning just involves more than mere memorization.

Once a problem has been defined or an assignment given, students must then search for and locate information, then receive and organize it, interpret what it means and apply it to the task at hand, and finally check, recall, and monitor what they have done. This is the overall study learning process that forms the outline for this chapter.

How unfortunate it is that many students finish high school without having learned to read comprehensively or use appropriate study strategies. Study learning is still not a consistent part of a regular curriculum throughout the grades. Perhaps the responsibility for teaching it has not been clearly defined. Every content area can benefit from reviewing strategies with their students that will enhance overall learning.

After reexamining the cognitive map at the beginning of this chapter (Figure 10.1) read Workshop 10.1. The map and the workshop checklist serve as two kinds of advance organizers to aid you in retaining the information in this chapter.

Study Learning Checklist

Workshop 10.1

As you read, try to determine how well you know the following, using the criteria below. "Superior" would mean that you feel comfortable teaching it to your students.

1—Superior	4—Very poor
2—Adequate	5—Don't know
3—Below average	

I. Search and locate needed information using the following:

_____ Alphabetical order to the third letter

_____ Sections: Table of Contents, Index, Appendices

_____ References: Dictionary, Encyclopedias, Almanac, Card Catalog, Reader's Guide, CD-ROM

II. Receive and organize information gathered

_____ Through listening, outlining, note taking, summarizing

III. Interpret and apply this information

_____ Written language (comprehension)

_____ Graphics (charts, graphs, tables, maps, diagrams)

_____ Special strategies, tips

IV. Check, recall, and monitor this information

_____ Study habits (memory, concentration, memories)

_____ Prepare/take notes

Search and Locate Information

The basic skill areas here are alphabetical order, book parts, references, and the school library.

Alphabetical Order is a basic skill for all reference activities and requires alphabetizing beyond the first letter. All content teachers requiring research from students should check on ability here. A few speed drills when necessary would be helpful.

Text Sections, or parts of the book, is an often ignored search skill that should be renewed at the beginning of the term. This strategy is in Chapter Two. (See Workshop 2.5.) It was placed there so readers could practice and use the ideas given as they progressed through Chapters Three through Twelve.

1. *Title page* tells subject, authors, and publisher and often tells what the book is about.

2. *Copyright*, usually found on the back of the title page, indicates how up-to-date the information is. If it's beyond a first edition, it also tells how well received the text has been. Copyright date is more crucial for science classes because of new discoveries.

3. *Table of Contents* gives us a complete outline of the entire text, usually showing main categories and subcategories. It is a map of the domain, a framework that should be studied before reading the first chapter.

4. *Preface* gives the authors' purpose for writing, what they believe to be important, how this text differs, and perhaps some suggestions on how best to read

5. *Appendices* can contain a wealth of supplementary materials that should enrich what was described in the text.

6. *Glossary* is better than a dictionary for a particular content area's technical terminology because it is less confusing, having only one specific meaning.

7. *Index* is an alphabetical listing of specific topics and authors, showing page numbers for rapid location. Cross-referencing is an important skill here because if the item is not there, they must think of a synonym or a larger category.

8. *Bibliography or References* gives a complete record of other authors who were used as references.

9. *Recommended Readings* are particularly helpful for students who want to further pursue a particular topic.

10. *Questions and Activities*, usually found at the end of each chapter, include what the authors felt was most important. By reading these questions before reading the chapter they can serve as an advance organizer. Activities often serve as enrichment.

General and Specific References

1. *Dictionary and Thesaurus* are excellent tools for vocabulary development. Dictionaries go from words to meanings, whereas a thesaurus takes meanings and provides synonyms for each.

2. *Encyclopedias* are often the first resource for investigating a topic. From there it is possible to move on to specialized encyclopedias, atlases, yearbooks, and almanacs.

3. *School Libraries and Media Centers* can play a vital role in enriching content. CD-ROM is a computerized way you are all familiar with to access topics and materials. School libraries are a great help in reviewing procedures with classes and helping to locate appropriate materials.

Internet Search Form (Gunning, 2005)

Be very specific about the question you want answered (e.g., How do manufacturers use robots to make cars?).

- Underline the key words and give synonyms in your question (e.g., cars—autos, vehicles; robot manufacturers—assemblers).

Taking just your key words you will ask your search engine to find:

cars or (autos or vehicles) and robot and manufacturers or (assemblers)

You put parentheses around synonyms, join words with "or" and put "and" between key words. Use an asterisk (*) to signal a search for different forms of a word (e.g., car*auto, autos, automobile).

It is so easy to become overloaded with information that it is important for students to learn how to select the best combination for their purpose.

Subject directories and indexes are good sources of information because they arrange information by categories. You can examine and click on categories or you can enter key words. An advantage of using directories is that students only need to have a general idea of what they are looking for. Some useful subject directories are:

Librarians' Index: http://www.lii.org

Open Directory Project: http://dmoz.org/

WWW Virtual Library: http://www/vlib.org/

Library Scavenger Hunt

Cocking and Schafer (1994) devised a way to improve instruction in use of the library by holding a library scavenger hunt. Later students in small groups were able to develop their own. Five steps for teaching are listed below.

1. *Discuss.* Using a graphic organizer discuss kinds of library resources with the class. The librarian may perform this step with the teacher present.
2. *Complete a hunt.* This is a teacher- or librarian-guided scavenger hunt with a simple walk-through for practice.
3. *Attend a library orientation* given by the librarian who may use a slide presentation or other visual aids. The purpose is to show location of materials, possibly setting up a CD-ROM search and using an online catalog.
4. *Design their own hunt.* In small groups each group designs their own hunt, which will take more than one class session to complete.
5. *Solve another group's hunt.* Groups exchange projects. Give full credit when a hunt can be completed. Also take into account the number of items in the hunt. Each group should give the teacher a copy with the answer.

Two possible designs of hunts are flow chart and work/sentence. The flow chart pattern uses clues to lead from one source to another. Choose a starting source and locate a clue from that source which will lead to the next one. As an example, a starting source might be like the following hunt:

1. Go to government documents.
2. Locate the report on *(give the title)*_____.
3. Find the first word of the subheading on page 9.
4. Write that word on your handout.

To design the word or sentence hunt:

1. Choose the number of sources you want to include and put them in order, for example, 8.
2. Find a word with 8 letters or compose a sentence or use a quote with 8 words.
3. Use a theme or topic to guide the search; or randomly choose materials from each source.
4. Go to each source and choose a clue to help complete the word or sentence. You may find that you will need to change the order of your sources.

Receive and Organize Information

This section, concerned with listening, outlining, note taking, and summarizing, can be found in Chapter One. It was placed there so that readers could practice and use the ideas given throughout the text.

Interpret and Apply Information

Written Language

(See Chapter Seven on Making Meaning, Reflecting, and Remembering)

Graphics

Graphics or visual aids are the focus of this section because it is an often neglected area. As the saying goes, "a picture is worth a thousand words." And yet students often think, when assigned 30 pages of text, "Thank goodness for those pictures, charts, graphics! I can skip them so there will be much less to read."

Look at Figure 10.2, which depicts a visual image for the term "The Broad-Based Constituency." As you read the description, do you find yourself associating the words with the gross image? This was done to assist the reader in forming a clearer understanding of the political concept.

FIGURE 10.2
Broad-based
constituency.
From *A Political
Bestiary,* by Eugene
McCarthy and James
Kilpatrick. Copyright
© 1978. Reprinted by
permission of the
McGraw-Hill
Companies.

A cow never voluntarily sits down. Because it has several stomachs, when it lies down it does so first with its front half and then with its rear half. The Broad-Based Constituency, on the contrary, never voluntarily stands up. Its strength and appeal lie in its broad base. Its movement consists principally in a slow pivot on its nether quarters.

Politicians constantly make the mistake of seeking Broad-Based Constituencies. The thought is that a BBC is reasonably stable and not likely to wander off, as narrow-based or narrow-hipped Constituencies often do. In time, however, Broad-Based Constituencies become a burden on their owners. As they become broader and broader their mobility decreases until in some cases they cannot move, even in search of food. They have to be fed incessantly.

Possessors of Broad-Based Constituencies frequently develop nervous habits. They worry whether the Constituency is happy, whether it needs water, or more food, or just reassurance. Often they will leave in the middle of a party just to run home and give the Constituency a few biscuits and kibbles and a glass of cold milk.

In consequence of its sedentary existence, the Broad-Based Constituency suffers from nerve and muscle deterioration in its lower back and demands to be regularly stroked or massaged. BBCs also become calloused and insensitive in their basic areas, developing an ailment comparable to bargeman's bottom, which is in turn comparable to housemaid's knee or barfly's elbow. It is very painful—so painful that it sometimes drives a Broad-Based Constituency to overcome its inertia and move—leaving the politician who has nurtured it, bereft.

Types of Graphics

Graphic aids may include charts, diagrams, graphs, tables, maps, pictures, and cartoons.

Charts and Diagrams

Charts and diagrams organize information by focusing on relationships. They are particularly valuable when used with information that is constantly changing. One step beyond a drawing, they coordinate words and graphics in a summary or overview fashion. Types of charts include: flow, tree, stream, time, comparison, sequence, process, organization, and diagram. Several of these charts appear in Figures 10.3, 10.4, and 10.5.

FIGURE 10.3
Tree chart.

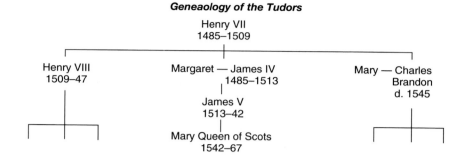

Geneaology of the Tudors

Henry VII
1485–1509

Henry VIII
1509–47

Margaret — James IV
1485–1513

James V
1513–42

Mary Queen of Scots
1542–67

Mary — Charles
Brandon
d. 1545

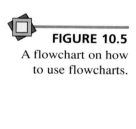

FIGURE 10.4
Stream chart.

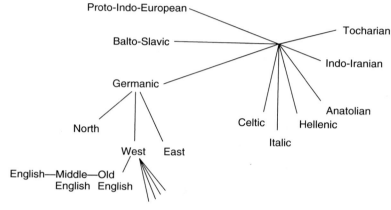

Development of the English Language

Proto-Indo-European

Balto-Slavic

Tocharian

Indo-Iranian

Germanic

North

West   East

Celtic   Hellenic

Italic

Anatolian

English—Middle—Old
English English

FIGURE 10.5
A flowchart on how
to use flowcharts.

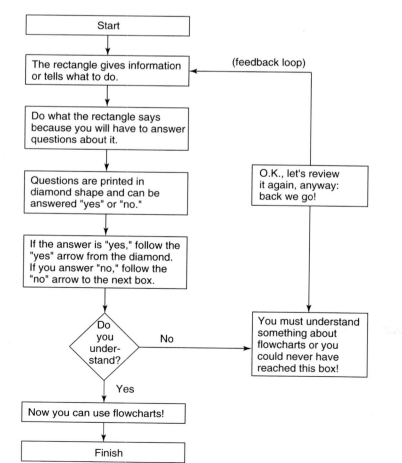

Start

The rectangle gives information
or tells what to do.

(feedback loop)

Do what the rectangle says
because you will have to answer
questions about it.

Questions are printed in
diamond shape and can be
answered "yes" or "no."

O.K., let's review
it again, anyway:
back we go!

If the answer is "yes," follow the
"yes" arrow from the diamond.
If you answer "no," follow the
"no" arrow to the next box.

Do
you
under-
stand?   No

You must understand
something about
flowcharts or you
could never have
reached this box!

Yes

Now you can use flowcharts!

Finish

Graphs

Graphs compare things and show quantitative information in a more dramatic fashion. Because they are a visual representation, size and shape may sometimes give an inaccurate impression if not pointed out. A graph enables us to see trends, positions, or history, at a glance.

Types of graphs include bar, circle or pie, line, and pictographs. A *bar graph* is shown in Figure 10.6. Note how the bars are used to compare quantities of items or changes in size of those quantities. A *circle* or *pie* graph is shown in Figure 10.7. Note that the circle represents the total value and percentages of that total are slices in the pie.

FIGURE 10.6
Bar graph.

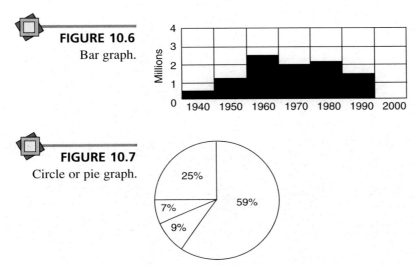

FIGURE 10.7
Circle or pie graph.

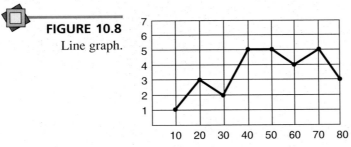

Line graphs (Figure 10.8) can be the most accurate type of graph and are used to show the relations between two variables. They have vertical and horizontal axes and points are plotted along these.

FIGURE 10.8
Line graph.

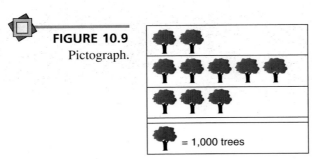

Pictographs are more pleasant to view and easier to read; however, they may not be as accurate as other types of graphs. A common type is the repeated symbol pictograph like the one shown in Figure 10.9.

FIGURE 10.9
Pictograph.

Tables

Tables contain information arranged in columns and rows in systematic fashion. They have become increasing popular with the advent of modern word-processing software. An example of a table may be seen in Figure 10.10.

Year	Cost	% change
1970	10.40	. . . .
1975	10.00	−3.8
1980	9.75	−2.5
1990	9.24	−5.2

FIGURE 10.10

Table.

Maps

Maps are important tools for aiding understanding in many content areas and are essential in daily life. (See Figure 10.11.) They are the oldest written language, having been tracked back, in the West, to Babylonian times. Examples of the wide variety of maps include road maps, physical maps, political maps, historical maps, and weather maps. Students need to be aware of the type of map, title, legend, direction, distance, scale, and location.

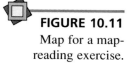

FIGURE 10.11

Map for a map-reading exercise.

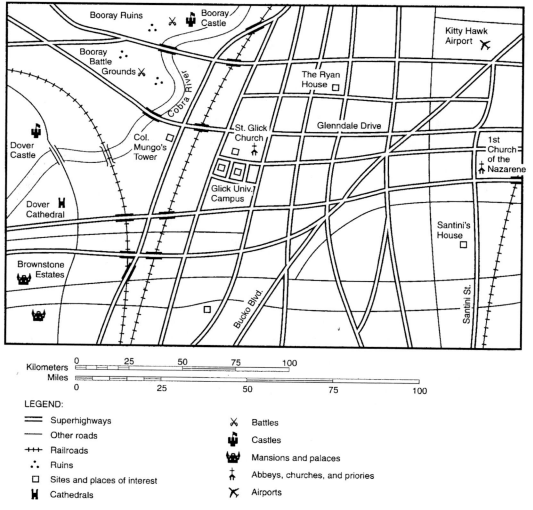

Pictures/Illustrations

Most content texts today contain pictures that motivate, increase interest, or extend the knowledge of readers. Effective illustrations enable students to recognize the subject of the picture, examine details, make inferences, or form generalizations. Figure 10.12 shows one example of how illustrations can extend or clarify information, in this case, meanings of the word *trunk*.

FIGURE 10.12
Multiple meanings of "trunk": illustration that extends and clarifies information. Images © Clipart.com

Pictures
Trunk

Trunk in automobile storage compartment

Suitcase trunk

Swimming trunk

Elephant trunk

Tree trunk

Trunk line railroad switch

Another type of illustration is seen in the Frost/Jeffers children's edition of *Stopping by Woods on a Snowy Evening* (See Figure 10.13). This is a beautiful example of enhancing imagery through illustration, and it is ageless. Jeffers has captured the essence of Frost's message. Readers may well feel as if they physically enter the snowy world she depicts.

FIGURE 10.13

Illustration that enhances imagery. From *Stopping By Woods on a Snowy Evening* by Robert Frost, illustrated by Susan Jeffers, copyright © 1978 by Susan Jeffers, illustrations. Used by permission of Dutton Children's Books, A Division of Penguin Young Readers Group, A Member of Penguin Group (USA) Inc., 345 Hudson Street, New York, NY 10014. All rights reserved.

The woods are lovely, dark, and deep.

Cartoons

One should never underestimate the power of a cartoon, whether it appears in a comic book, on the editorial page of a newspaper, or is used as literature. Cartoons are used for humor, for entertainment, and/or for the purpose of promoting propaganda. To interpret cartoons, the readers need to decide: (1) What assumptions are being made by the cartoonist? (2) Are the symbols used clear and appropriate? (3) Are the facts accurately portrayed? (4) Did the cartoonist overgeneralize, and if so, was it effective? Take a look at the cartoon in Figure 10.14. What assumptions did the artist make about the background knowledge you bring to the drawing? Are the symbols used clear? Appropriate? Are the facts accurately portrayed? If not, was this done intentionally? Did the cartoonist overgeneralize? If so, why? Did this work for you the reader?

FIGURE 10.14
Illustration that may contain bias or propaganda.
Images © Clipart.com

Graphic Information Lesson

There is a need for instructional activities that help students make connections among elements of the text, the graphics, and the reader's prior knowledge. A graphic information lesson includes five steps (Reinking, 1986):

1. Select maps, charts, or graphs that are important to understanding major concepts.
2. Explain why these are important to understanding major concepts so that students can transfer this knowledge when reading on their own.
3. Model for them your analysis of the graphic—whether the title is accurate, what the basic message is, how the information is organized, and any problems with possible interpretation.
4. Show how the information gleaned from the graphic supports a main concept or idea, citing the supporting evidence.
5. Group students and have them go through the whole process with another graphic, their goal being to try to reach consensus.

Teaching Tips

When having students examine various types of graphics, remember to help them to recognize what kind of graphic and its features by asking:

What type of graphic is this? What is the title? Are there subheadings? What special devices of symbols are used? What kind of information might you be asked to find in this graphic? What is the significance of _____ ?

Having recognized the various elements to be interpreted, they are then ready to seek the deeper meanings, generalizations, and conclusions that may be drawn. Here students can be asked:

What are the relationships between or among these elements that are here? What inferences might you make? What conclusions can you draw?

**Workshop
10.2**

Interpreting Charts

The following activity is taken from a discussion of how the polls predicted the 1976 presidential election. It is used here as an excellent example of how it is possible to obtain more relevant information from a graphic than from the print describing that graphic—in this case a chart.

In his final sample for TIME, completed Oct. 19, Pollster Daniel Yankelowich found Jimmy Carter ahead of Gerald Ford, 45% to 42%. That lead was precisely the margin by which the Democrat, according to nearly complete returns, won the popular vote (51% to 48%). George Gallup continued polling until three days before the election and gave Ford an edge of 47% to 46%. Louis Harris wound up a day later and found Carter ahead by 46% to 45%. Given the standard 3 point margin for error, all three polling organizations did well in detecting a close race.

In their final soundings, both Gallup and Harris termed the election too close to call. Each had given Carter a lead of 30 or so points immediately after the Democratic National Convention in July, and each had traced the steady—and inevitable—erosion of that lead. Yankelowich did not poll immediately after the Democratic Convention, when Ford had not yet been chosen, and consequently never found more than a 10-point lead for the Democrat. Nonetheless, he too picked up the falling-off to a dead heat but also registered Carter's rebounding to the 3% lead.

The singularities of the 1976 election—with two candidates who displayed well-developed capacities for blundering—gave pollsters their sternest test. They appear to have earned good grades.

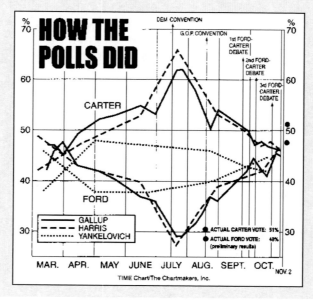

(continued)

Here is an opportunity to practice and compare findings with classmates. Take ten minutes to: (refer to the Carter-Ford chart)

1. Study the chart and key individually.
2. Write three comments or conclusions.
3. Read the text above the graphic.
4. Compare conclusions with the class.

A sample of comments and conclusions for the *Time* chart might be:

1. Carter and Ford started out in March fairly close according to three major polls.
2. The gap widened by the July Democratic Convention, with Carter having a thirty-point lead.
3. The gap quickly narrowed to a photo finish. Overall the polls did very well in their predictions.
4. Overall the polls were very accurate.
5. Other _____

Interpreting Maps

This activity was designed to give students an opportunity to enjoy working with maps in a creative manner before exposing them to the possible drudgery of tracing and drawing maps of countries about which they know little and may care even less. Students are given a chance to exercise their skills in both areas of interpretation: written language and graphics. The directions can be modified to fit different skill levels, student needs, content areas, or a combination of these.

STEP I WRITTEN DESCRIPTION

Students are asked first to fold their paper in thirds and put their name on the top. Then they are asked to write a one- or two-paragraph description of a mythical country of their own creation. The description might include approximate or exact size and shape of country, large cities, natural formations, and border countries and their locations in respect to one another. The directions can be specific or vague according to your content objective. An English teacher might stress use of unusual adjectives and descriptive imagery, whereas a geography or history teacher might ask for mileage scales and concrete data.

STEP II SKETCH

The students now pass their completed descriptions to the student on the left. Each student then draws a map of this fictional country according to the details given. Let them choose their own symbols for such things as major highways, cities, and natural formations. They use the second third of the paper for this.

STEP III WRITTEN DESCRIPTION

When the maps are completed, students fold down the first third and pass them (without their original descriptions) to the person on their left. The students will now write a description of that country using the map only. They should include all the details that the drawings include. When they have finished this written description, have students compare the original description to the one based on the maps. The class can then discuss the results and see how differently people interpret written and graphic material.

For example:

"My country is actually a small island off the Bahamas, of approximately twenty-five square miles. It is subtropical and has many indented coves; white, soft, sandy beaches; and crystal clear aqua-purple water. The foliage is dense because of the amount of rainfall. There are two small villages on opposite sides of the island with a total population of 150. My plantation is on a hill in the center of the island with a 360-degree view of the water. One deeply indented cove is directly in front of the main house.

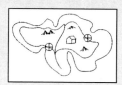

Special Strategies

Scaffolding Strategies in General

Students need guidance and support in choosing appropriate strategies for specific tasks. We as teachers need to note their prior knowledge, their cultural understandings, their language proficiency, their reading ability, and don't ever forget the importance of their attitude and interests. Scaffolding is a way then to support their efforts by showing or modeling what strategies to use when and how.

Ask first of all how much help will be needed before, during, and after reading. Provide a study guide initially, gradually decrease aid, and eventually remove.

Prompts are one important way to assist—in math, for example, a prompt to solve word problems might be a poster on the wall showing steps.

WORD PROBLEMS

1. Survey problem
2. Decide what is given, what is asked for
3. Decide which operations to use, when to use them
4. Estimate your answer
5. Solve the problem
6. Decide if your solution is reasonable

Once students have internalized these steps, you should remove the poster.

Analogies may also be helpful—like comparing students to detectives, because both look for clues, form hunches, and then support their findings. Ask students what analogies they can think of for a particular concept.

When modeling a strategy, use a simple, familiar piece, or something they already know from the past or have studied recently. In a secondary English classroom studying plot, a teacher might start out using *The Three Little Pigs*, then transfer to *The Island of the Blue Dolphins*, and finally to Shakespeare's *The Tempest*.

It's a good idea to check strategies from time to time. Ask before reading: "How will you be able to recall this later?" After reading, ask: "How did you figure that out? or "Why do you say that?"

SQ3R/SQ4R

A number of study learning strategies have been developed by reading authorities; the forerunner and foundation was SQ3R. Francis P. Robinson developed SQ3R in 1941 because he was concerned about the lack of reading comprehension and memory of his high school students. The typical reader remembered one-half of what was asked for on a quiz immediately following the reading assignments. This was found to be true for average and superior students.

Thus, Robinson devised the SQR (survey, question, read), but found it was not totally satisfactory because 80% of what the students read was forgotten within two weeks. By adding a test type of review, RR (recite and review), forgetting was reduced significantly.

Among other strategies inspired by SQ3R are: (1) PQRST, for science—the steps for which are preview, question, read, summarize, and test; and (2) SQRQCQ, for math—survey, question, read, question, compute, and question.

The SQ3R (SQ4R) method is described here.

1. *S—Survey* (or preview). Read the title, the introductory paragraph, the headings and subheadings; look at pictures and other graphics, reading the explanation beneath each; read the summary and questions. Ask yourself what major points are to be developed. Have an overall picture or map in your mind.

2. *Q—Question.* Turn each subheading into a question. Avoid closed questions that can be answered by a mere yes or no. Instead ask the "who," "what," "where," "why," or "how" types of questions.

3. *R—Read.* Read to find the answer to your first question. This is active reading. Reading for your own purposes (to answer your own question) keeps your mind on the material at hand. Be aware that your question may not cover all the important material so that you may have to add a question or revise your original one.

4. *R—Recite.* Cover up what you have just read under the first subheading and try to answer your question from memory. Check back on those items that you do not remember. Always master one section before moving on to the next one. Repeat steps 2, 3, and 4 with each successive section.

5. *R—Review.* Upon completion of the chapter, spend a few minutes going back over the text and your notes to try to get the overall picture. Knowing that some forgetting will always occur, occasional review keeps this to a minimum.

To this basic strategy some have added a sixth step, *reflect.*

6. *R—Reflect.* Personalizing what has just been learned by mentally manipulating ideas, reorganizing into larger or smaller categories, playing with these categories, and tying them to existing knowledge make it possible for knowledge to be retained more effectively.

PARS

Using the five steps in SQ3R may be too complicated or time-consuming for some students. Thus, a simpler alternative strategy, PARS, is presented here. The four steps are:

1. Set a purpose.
2. Ask questions related to the purpose.
3. Read to find answers to the questions.
4. Summarize in your own words what you have learned.

Workshop 10.4

Preparing a Learning Center

SQ4R CENTER

SUPPLIES NEEDED: LONG OR ROUND TABLES AND FOUR CHAIRS

- Next chapter xeroxed—four copies
- General instructions on folded cardboard with colorful design
- Specific worksheets in packets
- Two timers, four pencils, two stopwatches

The purpose of this center is to help you master the next assigned chapter in our text. There will be a short multiple-choice quiz in class after we have completed the chapter. This session will take twenty-five minutes. You can return tomorrow if you need more time.

STEP ONE—SURVEY

1. Take out the first sheet marked "survey."
2. Set the timer for five minutes. Be sure to note if you finished earlier, or if you needed more time, how much. Write your actual survey minutes in the space provided at the top right of your sheet.

STEP TWO—QUESTION/READ

Return to the beginning of the chapter and change the first heading into your own question; write it in the space provided.

3. Question:_____

3. Revision:_____

If working cooperatively with a partner, check each other's questions as you go along. *Read* to answer your question. You may have to revise your question to take in all of the information.

STEP THREE—RECITE

1. Cover up the text page and recite your answer to your question. If you don't recall the complete answer, look at your text immediately to find it. Mark that one with a highlighter pen.
2. As a check of comprehension continue through the chapter turning each sub-heading into a question, reading to answer your question, and reciting the answer without looking at the text.

STEP FOUR—REVIEW/REFLECT

1. Set your timer for five minutes and review by looking again at each sub-heading to see if you can still recall answers comfortably, paying special attention to those you checked. Note your time.
2. Reflect on the significance of this information. In a phrase or sentence write what was most important.

K-W-L

Step One—What Do You Already Know?

Quickly read the bold headings and examine pictures and other graphics (charts, maps, etc.). Decide what you already know and what this is all about or what you will learn and what you want to learn. Fill in each column

What I know already	What I will learn in general	My questions

Step Two—Question/Read

Return to the beginning of the chapter and turn the first heading into your own question and write it in the space provided.

Question: _____

Revision: _____

If working cooperatively with a partner, check each other's questions as you go along.

Read to answer your question. You may have to revise your question to take in all the information.

Step Three—Recite

- Cover up the text page and recite your answer to your question. If you don't recall the complete answer, look at your text immediately to find it. Mark that one with a check mark or highlighter pen.
- Continue through the chapter turning each subheading into a question, reading to answer your question and reciting the answer without looking at the text as a check of comprehension.

Step Four—Review/Reflect

- Set your timer for 5 minutes and review by looking again at each subheading to see if you still can recall answers comfortably, paying special attention to those you checked. Note your time.
- Reflect on the significance to you of any of this information. Write what was most important in a phrase or sentence.

**Workshop
10.5**

K-W-L

In one of your content area texts, quickly read the bold headings, and examine the pictures and other graphics (charts, maps, etc.). Decide what you already know and what this is all about, or what you will learn and what you want to learn. Fill in each column and then compare your results with your group's results.

What I know already	What I will learn in general	My questions

REAP

REAP, devised by Eanet and Manzo (1976) as a strategy for improving reading/ writing/study skills. It was based on the idea that you must process information and organize it in a way that is useful to you as well as to others. The steps in this strategy are:

1. *R—Read* to discover author's message.
2. *E—Encode* the message by putting it into your own words.
3. *A—Annotate* by rewriting the message in notes for yourself or for others.
4. *P—Ponder* or process the message by thinking about it yourself or discussing it with others.

The key step in REAP is annotation, where readers differentiate the writer's ideas, translate them into their own language, and then summarize the results in writing. Of the seven kinds of annotation, three examples are:

1. *Summary,* or condensing in a concise manner. In nonfiction, main ideas are stated to make relationships clear but no details are given.
2. *Thesis,* a clear statement, much like a telegram.
3. *Questions,* or stating significant questions that the reader thinks the author is addressing and directing attention to the answers given.

The sequence of steps for teaching students how to write annotation is as follows:

1. *Recognize and define.* Students read a selection while the teacher writes a summary annotation on the chalkboard. This is then discussed with the students when they have finished reading.
2. *Discriminate.* Students read a second selection, and this time several summary annotations are presented, one good and the others poor. Students must select the best and defend their choice, explaining why the others are not satisfactory.
3. *Model.* Students read a third selection, and the teacher shows them how to get at the summary annotation by thinking aloud and noting their thought processes when trying to pull out the main ideas and how they are related. They write one together and then rewrite for more exactness or conciseness.

4. *Practice*. With the fourth selection students write their own summary annotation. Then they pair off to compare and come up with the best annotation possible.

In teaching these strategies, you must lead students through the various steps until they can begin to see the value of the strategy. As an aid in taking more precise notes, you may wish to hand out in advance an outline such as the "notes facilitator" in figure 10.15. Students taking notes are then more aware of any key points that they may have missed.

FIGURE 10.15
REAP: Using a notes facilitator.

This is an example of a notes facilitator. Students must complete the outline as they listen to a lecture. They can return later to study these notes more easily for a test.

Eanet and Manzo (1976) developed a strategy for improving reading/writing/ study skills, based on the idea that we need to process information and organize it so that it is useful to ourselves and others. Use the existing spaces to take notes as we talk about each aspect.

Steps

R—(read)—
E—(encode)—
A—(annotate)—
P—(ponder)—

Types of Annotations (samples):

1. Summary—   2. Thesis—   3. Questions—

Steps for teaching students to write summary annotations:

1. Recognize and define—   3. Model—
2. Discriminate—   4. Practice—

Guided Reading and Summary Procedures: GRASP

The Guided Reading and Summary Procedures (GRASP: Hayes, 1989) process uses direct instruction and student input. (1) First, tell students that the purpose is to give them skills in writing, understanding, and showing their knowledge. (2) Next, give a text reading assignment of about 500 words (for middle school) to 1500 words (for high school). Tell students to read to recall as much as possible. Then ask them to tell what they recall, make a list on the board. They then reread to complete what is missing or incorrect. (3) Have students organize the information on the board into complete sentences, identifying main categories and labeling them. They can also list subsets. (4) Give them three basic rules for summarizing—include only important data, compress by combining, and add words or phrases only if needed for clarity and coherence (Brown and Day, 1983). (5) Model the process by turning data into sentences, showing why certain items are omitted, and explaining how ideas can be combined and why added words are useful. (6) Students are now ready to produce their own summaries for the next assignment.

Check/Recall/Monitor Information

Establishing Study Habits for Better Concentration

What conditions do you think are most conducive to study? Before reading this section, list a few that come immediately to mind:

_____	_____
_____	_____
_____	_____
_____	_____

Physical Conditions

Finding a specific spot associated only with study is important to concentration. Students should select a spot in an environment that is completely quiet, free from disruption, comfortable in terms of ventilation and temperature, well lighted without glare, furnished with desk or table and comfortable chair, and supplied with all needed equipment such as sharpened pencils, note-book paper, 3 X 5 cards, dictionary, clock and calendar.

Specific study site. Psychologists have found that there can be a conditioning effect between students and the study location. If students allow themselves to daydream a great deal at the desk, then the desk can be a cue for daydreaming. To avoid negative conditioning, students should plan that only work and study be done there. If their minds start to wander, suggest that they get up and go elsewhere for a brief change of pace.

Noise versus quiet. Most studies support the thesis that the quieter the spot, the more efficient it is for study. Many students, however, claim that background music helps them concentrate by blotting out intermittent sounds. Even the soft background music used in industry to alleviate the boredom of repetitious chores is still noise and may interfere with higher cognitive learning tasks. Music of any kind requires expending extra energy to keep one's mind on the studies rather than on the music.

Light. Poor lighting with little contrast causes eye strain, headaches, and fatigue. This in turn can interfere with concentration. Good lighting is glare- and flicker-free. A good shade over the bulb should eliminate glare. Two lights (e.g., ceiling and desk) are recommended to control contrasts or shadows, and a two-tube rather than a one-tube fluorescent lamp is recommended to eliminate flicker.

Comfort and equipment. Real concentration means becoming unaware of the physical surroundings. This is easier to attain when the student is physically comfortable. Also, having needed equipment on hand ahead of time saves wasted minutes and unwanted interruptions later on.

Frame of Mind

More important to concentration than all the physical conditions mentioned above is mental attitude toward the subject and studying in general. If students are really interested in a subject, they will not have difficulty studying it. But what can they do about required courses? And how can teachers help generate interest?

1. Students may ask what benefits they can accrue from mastery in a particular content area. It can be pointed out that good grades in all subjects will help later in the job market.

2. When students ask questions about the courses—and then read to find the answers to their own questions—they often find that the more they learn about a subject, the more interesting it becomes. So, encourage them to ask questions.

Other factors interfering with interest and concentration are poor health, fatigue, and personal problems. Remind students that it is possible to study in spite of these problems if they are willing to persevere. When they are tired, suggest that they take short breaks, such as a brief walk, to change the activity. Study time can be spread out, and a temporary switch can be made to another subject when interest lags. Study can actually be a temporary escape from pressing personal problems.

Efficient Use of Time

A dictionary definition of *study* is "the process of applying the mind to acquire knowledge." The term *process* tells us that study is not one activity but a series of activities. Organization is always necessary wherever steps in a process are involved.

Ask your students if they recognize themselves in either or both of these situations.

"I must turn down a fascinating invitation because there was no extra time left to study for an exam. While studying my mind kept wandering, thinking about the fun I might have had."

or,

"I accept the fascinating invitation but do not enjoy it because I feel guilty thinking of how I should really be studying for that exam."

Better organization and planning could have eliminated either unhappy situation.

Time Schedules

The following activity works well with middle school and high school students. Ask your students if they are able to account for the amount of time they spend on different activities. Suggest as an experiment that they try the following activity for one week. When this activity was used with a number of classes at a local high school, the students were amazed to discover how much time was unaccounted for and how little time was actually spent studying (See Figure 10.16).

Students should fill in the chart keeping a daily record and total each day in the right-hand column. At the end of the week, they total each activity along the bottom row. When completed, they are led to think about the conclusions to be drawn about efficient use of time.

At this point they are then ready to set up a schedule to fit their own specific needs. Characteristics of a good schedule include:

1. Time allotted for all activities.
2. Enough time for studying each subject (on the average of one-half to one hour daily per subject for high school; two hours for every credit hour for college).
3. Efficient use of small slots of "free" time for study, such as while waiting for a bus.
4. Scheduling study time according to the laws of learning, studying a subject as soon as possible after class with a brief review just before the next class, "overlearning by frequent review," and alternating types of material to be studied, such as math and literature.
5. Time for relaxation and rewards for diligence.

Instruct students to first fill in the blocks in Figure 10.17 with fixed activities, then fill in study sessions, recreation and other flexible activities. Check it against the list of characteristics of a good time schedule, try it out for one week and revise where need-

FIGURE 10.16

Time study blank.

One week schedule	\multicolumn{13}{c}{Hours devoted to:}
	Sleeping	Eating	Home chores	Outside jobs	Travel to and from school	Classes	Extra cur. school actv.	Studying	TV/movies	Other recreation	Total	Unaccounted for time	Grand total (Must equal 24 hours)
Monday													
Tuesday													
Wednesday													
Thursday													
Friday													
Saturday													
Sunday													
Total hours spent per week													

ed. They should remember to break up long study periods into blocks of forty-five minutes to an hour each, with a short break in between of five to ten minutes. This will prevent boredom or tiredness and will allow time to absorb what they have been learning.

The students should spend the first few minutes in a warm-up, where they review the previous assignment and rapidly reread their latest notes. This mastery technique helps bridge the gap between old and new material and will help them see existing relationships.

FIGURE 10.17

Trial schedule.

Time	Mon.	Tues.	Wed.	Thurs.	Fri.	Sat.	Sun.
7:00 a.m.							
8:00							
9:00							
10:00							
11:00							
12:00							

etc.

Some people find it beneficial to estimate before starting how much time will be needed for a specific assignment and then work to complete it within the allotted time—a "beat the clock" game.

Memory: Forgetting and Remembering

Memory is *a process,* a complex system concerned with selecting, acquiring, retaining, organizing, retrieving, reconstructing and using our knowledge and beliefs about the world, including our past experience.

Forgetting is one of the biggest problems that students face in school. By understanding more about this phenomenon, students should be able to lessen its impact. As Pauk states, the fact that we have a memory of a previous experience shows us that the brain does keep a record, or a neural trace. But, like the traces on a recording tape, the brain traces can be erased.

Without periodic review, what we learn fades away over time. Hermann Ebbinghaus, the German psychologist, used nonsense syllables in his research to show how rapidly forgetting takes places. In only four weeks' time we lose 80 percent of the total sum of ideas entering our brain. He also concluded that the greatest amount of forgetting happens immediately after completing the learning task, and then the forgetting process slows down. He constructed the first curve of forgetting, based on years of research and statistics. Figure 10.18 shows this curve. Other more recent studies, using regular words, have come to the same conclusions.

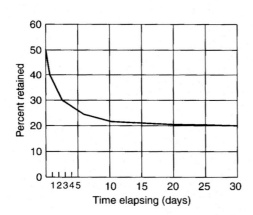

FIGURE 10.18

Curve of retention (Ebbinghaus) for nonsense syllables after various time intervals.
From Henry E. Garrett, *Great Experiments in Psychology* (New York: Appleton-Century-Crofts, 1941), p. 273.

Of the various theories of forgetting, Pauk describes only one, the "interference theory." This theory demonstrates *retroactive interference,* where new learning interferes or covers up the old, and *proactive interference,* where earlier learning interferes with later learning. (This is also referred to as *proactive inhibition.*)

Retroactive interference operates when students learn certain facts at the beginning of the course and do not review them. After a week of learning newer material, they can only remember a few of those initial facts.

An example of proactive interference is learning French and then switching to Spanish and confusing the two.

Memorizing: Some Personal Reminiscences

Many schools today appear to have strayed from requiring students to memorize poetry or prose. We need to ask ourselves if we are actually robbing our students of a lifetime of enjoyment, as well as denying them valuable practice in memory training. For example, as I (M. Tonjes) walked through England's Lake District for the first time, I was enraptured with the golden scenery. Suddenly, seemingly out of nowhere came the words of Wadsworth's poem:

> "I wandered lonely as a cloud
> That floats on high o'er vales and hills
> When all at once I saw a crowd,
> A host of golden daffodils;"

He had said it so much better than I could ever do. The next summer I was on a coastal steamer to the North Cape of Norway when, in order to get my "diploma" showing I had crossed the Arctic Circle, I was required to sing with four German passengers who spoke little English. Thank heaven for that secondary music teacher who taught us "Silent Night" in German—even though it was July. The audience loved it.

Finally, I did not appreciate it at the time when my senior high English teacher required all of us to memorize and recite to her 150 lines of *Macbeth*. But some 40 years later they were still with me and made my viewing of *Macbeth* at Stratford-on-Avon a special joy, as I sat there silently mouthing the words along with the actors.

Retention

For students who want to remember, here are some suggestions based on learning theory that you may share with them:

1. *Purpose.* Always have a purpose in mind when reading study materials. When not stated in the text or by the teacher, you must set your own purpose to ensure that the material has meaning for you in order to be remembered longer.

2. *Author's organization.* Try to grasp how the concepts are organized and what the main ideas and supporting details are. A helpful procedure is to outline the chapter first.

3. *Notes.* Jot down important points to help fix them in your memory. The act of writing aids memory. It is easier to remember what you have *read* than what you have *heard*.

4. *Summarize.* Upon completion of the chapter, summarize it in your own words. This indicates that you have the main ideas in mind and understand their relationships.

5. *Discuss or recite.* Talking about the material to yourself or to classmates is another way to enhance your memory of it. This should be done as soon as possible after reading it.

6. *Apply.* Interacting with the material and applying the concepts also facilitates retention.

We need to remember the psychologist's edict, "No learning takes place without a motive." Then we should be ingenious in generating learning that will be of real interest. One way to make a subject come alive is to find two other students who are enthusiastic and meet with them to discuss assignments. Their attitude may rub off. Another way is to find an alternate text written in an easier style and read the topic from that text before reading your own assignment.

Concentration Aids

When we really concentrate, we focus so strongly that we block out the rest of the world around us. Concentration then means sustained attention, which demands a mental set or attitude as well as a determination to allow nothing to interfere with the task at hand. We are actively involved and alert.

Two aspects of memory are short-term and long-term. Short-term or working memory holds information temporarily until it is either processed into long-term memory or is erased to make room for new information. Short-term has a limited capacity and lasts only briefly, whereas long-term or permanent memory has an infinite capacity for storing all our past knowledge and experience in a highly organized way. Long-term has one limitation—it is relatively slow in processing new information, depending on how meaningful that new information is to us.

As we can attest, it is possible to concentrate and comprehend material read or heard at the time, and then promptly forget it. For example, when reading purely for pleasure or relaxation, we can follow the plot and characters with no problem while we read, but later if unexpectedly called on to share some detailed information, we might be hard pressed to do so. Thus, when learning needs to go into long-term memory, we need to take steps to ensure retention. The mnemonic device CAPS is one way (Graham & Robinson, 1984).

1. *Categorizing*: Placing information into a larger framework, making connections to what we already know.
2. *Applying*: Making a model, map, or project.
3. *Personalizing*: Associating new information with our own personal experiences, like connecting a particular adjective to someone we know.
4. *Self-reciting*: Using all sensory channels through repetition silently and aloud, and using acronyms—the first letter of each word. Examples: RSVP: *Respondez sil vous plait* (French for reply if you please) or NATO: North Atlantic Treaty Organization.

The Russian psychologist, Smirnov (1973) discussed ways to aid concentration and retention that can serve as a model by using the acronym "GRIPP it."

Group thoughts
Relate to background knowledge
Image—use imagery
Paraphrase in your own words
Ponder significance (Tonjes, 1981)

We all tend to lack concentration when any of the following conditions prevail.

- We are anxious as a result of procrastinating.
- We are distracted by outside noise.
- We allow our minds to wander to more pleasurable thinks like a sports event or dance on the weekend.
- We study without breaks for long periods of time.

To concentrate more effectively, we need to ask at first ourselves *why* we are doing it, *what* we should be doing, and *how* best to do it. It is helpful for teachers to remind students for the why, what, and how.

Workshop 10.6 presents a workbook page addressed to college freshmen on practicing concentration.

**Workshop
10.6**

Practicing Concentration

The following activities will help you develop your ability to concentrate more effectively.

1. Close your eyes and picture a large blackboard in your mind. Visualize numbers being written on the blackboard one at a time: 100, 200, 300, and so on. See how far you can get before stray thoughts push the number pictures from your mind. Then start over again, concentrating harder, and try to get farther the second time, and still farther the third time.

2. Concentration is an important part of careful observation and is essential for good remembering. Look at a picture of a group of people in a magazine or newspaper. Read the caption that gives the names of the people. Study the picture and caption for thirty seconds, concentrating on them as intensely as you can. Without looking at the picture, name and describe each person.

3. Many popular meditation systems promote deep relaxation by teaching you how to concentrate on relaxing. Because everyone's concentration wanders after a time, a preselected number, word or nonsense syllable can be used to return your concentration to what you are attempting to master. Try the following procedure at a time when you are reasonably alert. (If you are tired, concentrating on relaxing will probably put you to sleep!)

   a. Sit in a comfortable position with your eyes closed. Choose any word, name, number, or nonsense syllables—*Shangri-la* would do, for example.

   b. Concentrate on relaxing every muscle in your body, starting with your scalp and moving slowly down to your toes.

   c. Once completely relaxed, think of something pleasant—a friend, or a country scene. You will find you cannot concentrate on the subject very long before distracting or unpleasant thoughts push it from your mind and your relaxed muscles begin to become tense again. This is when you use your word or number.

   d. Drive out the distracting thoughts by saying the word or number until you can return your concentration to relaxing and your pleasant thought. Each time you try, you will find your span of concentration becomes longer.

4. Check the quality of your concentration with and without distractions. Select any two illustrations in this book that have similar subjects. Study one of them for one minute in a quiet atmosphere. Write as complete a description of the illustration as you can under the same quiet circumstances. Do the same with the second, but have loud music playing all the time. Which is the better description? Which took longer?

Pulling It All Together

Two strategies to pull the process of studying together are presented below. These include *Thematic Teaching Units* and *Predict, Verify, Judge, and Extend*.

Thematic Teaching Units

One way to pull the study skills process together is to teach a thematic unit. Meeks (1999) provides examples for a 10th-grade poetry unit on conditions for language learning.

- Immerse students in poetry, choosing favorites to copy for inclusion in their portfolio and/or to share with the class on large charts.
- Share your own favorite poems.
- Show how to read and write poems and let them practice.

- Students are given responsibility for choosing their groups, which poets to study, what topics for their writing assignments, and how to present to the class or world.
- Students may share with senior citizens in a rest home, or post them on the Internet.
- Respond with sticky notes to parts and have students respond to each other.

Overall Unit (1 day)

- Graphic organizer
- Major concepts
- Main resources—Text, fiction, etc.
- Instructional activities
- Three-level study guide—literal, inferential, personal

1st Topic (2 days)

- Major concepts in sentences (e.g., survival was a priority)
- Main resources—text, fiction
- Instructional activities—read, introduction, discuss, review, etc.

2nd Topic (3 days)

3rd Topic (2 days)

4th Topic (1 day) Final Resolutions

Conclusion (3 days)

- Review, K-W-L chart, Mock Trial, Impersonate, Reflect, Graphic Organizer
- Response groups use bulletin board displays, drama, book jackets

Predict, Verify, Judge, and Extend

Find, below, an example from a handout that may be used with a new unit or difficult chapter.

Name: _____

Date: _____

Content Area Reading and Writing—
A Listening/Reading Guide
and a Notes Facilitator

As this class starts, read over this page in order to predict and get an overview of what you will be asked to do towards the end of class today. This page will be handed in.

1. *PREDICT*

    After looking at the title in the syllabus for today's class (or skimming our next assigned chapter), predict a learning generalization or major idea you think will be addressed in class.

    _____

    _____

2. *VERIFY*

After listening, reading, or discussing look back at your initial response to #1 and note how accurate your prediction was. Circle one.

Very   Partly   Not at all

3. *JUDGE*

Now support or prove what you did learn. Back it up with a quote or paraphrase from this session or chapter.

_____

_____

_____

4. *EXTEND / INTERCONNECT / APPRECIATE*

   A. Connect what you have just learned to what you now see as the total overall picture of the topic. How does it all fit? You may wish to try to diagram the big picture here.

Testing

Testing in some form is generally a part of classroom learning. Students are rarely ecstatic and about this state of affairs; nevertheless, there can be significant benefits for students as well as for teachers. Good teachers test to find out which students have learned what and to discover how well they have taught. For the results of tests to be a true reflection of what has occurred, students should have been shown how to study as well as how to prepare for and take a test. It is remarkable how many students have learned this only by a process of trial and error. The greatest advantage to students is that, forced to review and reorganize material they might never have looked at again, they are able to remember the ideas over a long term.

Assuming that your students have been introduced to the study skills previously discussed and that they have learned how to organize their time, listen or read efficiently, take good notes, use a study strategy to enhance concentration and memory, and periodically review their readings and notes, it is now time to help them study for the test.

Preparing for Tests

Remind students that the ideal time to organize and consolidate learnings is several days prior to taking the test. This means that all material should have been read, all notes are in order, and other assignments are completed and turned in—a clearing of the deck, so to speak.

They must synthesize, find the organizing principals, and see relationships in order to successfully handle large bodies of material. If they have not been reviewing the material periodically, they will be forced to "cram," which will work only if they are able to select the vital information. Trying to memorize too much detail in a short time can lead to a failure to remember any of it well. The best they can do is skim over the text and their notes and make a summary sheet of key points with supporting details, then use this for study, reciting the material over and over again.

In preparing for the day of the test, students should get a good night's sleep and get up early enough to avoid rushing. For those who dislike eating breakfast, this is the day to make an exception. They should be sure to include protein, which is nourishing, whereas coffee and a sweet roll are not.

Some tension is good in that it will keep the students alert, but too much tension is a distraction. If panic arises, tell them to talk positively to themselves and take a few deep breaths and hold them for a short count.

Writing Essay Tests

Many students dislike essay-type tests because they involve much writing, composition, spelling, and punctuation. However, essay tests offer several advantages to students once they have learned some techniques. First, because of time limitations the number of questions will be limited, and those included will cover the most important points. Second, a choice of questions is often given, thus allowing them to write on the areas they know best. Third, it is possible to prepare many answers in advance, because only major ideas are usually included (See Table 10.1).

TABLE 10.1 Key Words for Essay Questions

Clue Words	Meaning

1. Describe
   define
   trace
   discuss
   examine
   analyze
	Give in words a picture of an idea, a concept or an object. Give clear, concise definitions. Record careful observation. Give the important ideas and show how they are related.

2. Compare and contrast
   differentiate
   distinguish
	Give likenesses and differences. Show differences between items, groups, or categories.

3. Enumerate outline	Use lists, outlines, main and subordinate points, and details.
4. State relate	Write concisely and clearly, connecting ideas or concepts Use chronology of events or ideas where it applies.
5. Prove justify	Use facts, or logic, or cite authorities to justify your thesis.
6. Evaluate criticize	Make value judgments but use logic to explain. Criticize—pro or con—the merits of a concept or a theory.

7. Review
   summarize
   synthesize
	Summarize main points concisely, restate judgments or conclusions, integrate arguments from different sources.

There are three major tasks involved in taking an essay test: recalling material, organizing it, and writing (ROW). Note that writing comes last, after time for thinking about the answer and organizing it into an outline. The following steps are suggestions for writing successful essay questions.

1. *Estimate the time.* Look over the entire test and the amount of credit allowed for each question. Spend proportionately more time on the ones that are worth more. (This might seem too obvious, but it is amazing how many students will agonize over initial questions, leaving little or no time for the all-important thirty-point question at the end.)

2. *Outline all answers before writing.* Using only headings and subheadings, quickly write the key points in the sequence to be used. (This step cannot be overstressed, because it is essential to well-organized writing and will demonstrate to the reader a control over the material.)

3. *Writing.* Starting with the easiest question first, begin writing with a thesis statement. For example, "There are many useful suggestions for taking exams," or "Comparing and contrasting *x* with *y*, many similarities and several differences can be found." Then fill in from this outline the supporting details, leaving a blank space for whatever detail cannot be remembered at the moment. Use transitional words such as *thus* to lead the reader from one idea to another. Finish the essay with a summary statement.

4. *Review.* Try to leave a few minutes at the end of the test period to read over the paper, inserting a missing word or phrase and correcting misspelling or punctuation.

Objective Tests

Objective tests require short answers about specific facts. This kind of test includes true/false, multiple choice, matching, and completion or fill-in questions. Students often prefer this kind of test, thinking that it is easier to answer and that they do better on it. Actually they have more control over their grade with essay questions. Where essay tests can only cover major ideas, objective tests can probe for the minutest of details.

1. *True/false.* These questions are absolutely true or false, so look for the clue words to see how they change the meaning:
   a. Extreme expressions, such as *none, all, never, always, every* ("Women are *never* taller than men"), are often false.
   b. More moderate expressions, such as *many, some, few, rarely, often, usually* (*"Some* women are taller than men"), are often true.

   There will generally be more true questions than false, and longer questions are more likely to be true. The reasoning behind this is that test-makers dislike taking up too much space with negative learning.

2. *Multiple choice.* If one thinks of these as being a series of true/false questions, then the choices that are clearly false can be eliminated first (usually three of the possible responses), narrowing the field down to the best answer and the almost correct one. This gives a fifty-fifty chance of being correct rather than a 20 percent chance!

3. *Matching.* In linking up two items of information, first read both columns quickly. Starting at the top of the left column compare it with each item on the right until a match is reached, then fill in the correct letter of the right column by the one in the left. Cross out the matched items as you go along.

4. *Completion or fill-ins.* Here the missing word(s) are supplied in the sentence provided. The whole sentence should be read first to determine what is being asked for, such as a number in the item "A U.S. senator serves a _____ year term."

Advantages to teachers of objective tests are that they are easy to correct using a scoring key and that once constructed they can be reused if copies are numbered and collected. The major disadvantage is the difficulty in constructing valid, reliable test items. The major advantage to students is that the test is scored objectively, with no room for misinterpretation or bias on the part of the scorer. When reviewing with the class for this type of test, let them know the type of question you, the teacher, favor, such as multiple choice or fill-in. It is also helpful to give them one or two examples.

Taking the Objective Test: A Worksheet for Students

1. *Read directions carefully.* This is the most crucial point and one where students most often have problems. Find out, for example, how to mark the true/false, whether more than one multiple choice answer is correct, or if more than one word is allowed in a fill-in.

2. *Skim the entire test* to determine what types of questions are asked and what type of information is sought. Some students have been known to "freeze" when confronted with the first question when they think they do not know the answer to it, thus wasting precious time.

3. *Allot time* to different sections, depending on the number of points. Maintaining a schedule keeps you from spending too much time on one area and running out of time to complete the test.

4. *Answer easy questions first.* Moving rapidly, answer those you feel comfortable with, leaving a small mark by the ones you need to return to. Often the answers will come to you after having gotten into the test.

5. As a rule, *do not change the first answer* to any question unless you are very certain it is incorrect. Statistics indicate that the first hunch is usually better than the second guess.

Teaching Test-Taking Skills

A small group of students approach you claiming to have test-taking anxiety. These students ask you for help. They are especially poor at answering multiple choice and true/false questions. Provide them with guidelines to help them answer these types of questions. Then, provide them with one sample multiple choice question and a sample true or false question that can be answered solely by following these guidelines. Your two questions should not require content knowledge to deduce the correct answer. For example:

Multiple Choice

1. Railroads played an important role in American history because

    a. they transported all of the country's supplies.
    b. they never broke down.
    c. they were often late so people started taking airplanes.
    d. they provided efficient transportation for people and supplies.

True/False

2. Slaves in America, thought bitterly resentful, never openly rebelled.
3. Good athletes always learn their sport when they are very young.

Workshop 10.7

Cinquain as Summary

Study—Learning
Complex Independent Thinking
Scaffolding Strategies Support Learning
Crucial for Success
Independent—Learner

 Summary

Study learning is as immense and diverse as shown in the cognitive map and chapter outline at the beginning of the chapter. Our model for study learning is fourfold and includes: (1) search and locate information, (2) receive and organize it, (3) interpret and apply it, and finally (4) check, recall, and monitor it. We need to remind students of the usefulness of alphabetical order for speed in locating data, the uses of various text sections, and how to master references, the library, and CD-ROM. Once they have found and processed the information through listening, outlining, note taking, and summarizing, their third major task is to interpret what it means and then apply what they have gathered from writings and graphics. They then decide on which special strategies they might need to apply to fit the task at hand. If needed here teacher scaffolding applies. Lastly they check recall and monitor information, using good study habits, preparing for tests, and using time management wisely. They understand the importance of concentration and memory and will be successful study learners in the future. National standards suggest that students be able to apply a wide range of strategies to comprehend, interpret, evaluate, and appreciate texts. When professional educators understand and teach study strategies, they are giving their students the tools needed to enhance their critical thinking, problem-solving, and performance skills.

References and Recommended Readings

Anderson, E., & Guthrie, J. T. (1996). Teaching with CORI: Taking the big jump. *NRRC News, 3,* 1–3.

Barton, M., Heidema, C., & Jordan D. (2002). Teaching reading in math and science. *Educational Leadership, 60*(3), 24–28.

Bean, T. W., & Ericson, B. O. (1989). Test previews and three level study for content area critical reading. *Journal of Reading, 32,* 337–341.

Berlin, D. F., & Hillen, J. A. (1994). Making connections in math and science: identifying student outcomes. *School Science and Mathematics, 94,* 283–390.

Brown, A. L., & Day, J. D. (1983). *Macrorubs for summarizing text: The development of expertise.* Urbana-Champaign, IL: Center for the Study of Reading, University of Illinois.

Burrell, K. I., & McAlexander, P. J. (1998). Ideas in practice: The synthesis journal. *Journal of Developmental Education, 22,* 20–30.

Call, P. E. (1991, September). SQ3R + What I know sheet=one strong strategy. *Journal of Reading, 35,* 1, 50–52.

Carver, R. P. (1982). Optimal rate of reading prose. *Reading Research Quarterly, 18,* 56–88.

Cocking, T. S., & Schafer, S. A. (1994). Scavenging for better library instruction. *Journal of Reading, 38*(3), 164–170.

Council of Chief State School Officers. (2005). *INTASC standards.* Retrieved March 21, 2005, from http://www.ccsso.org/projects/Interstate_New_Teacher_Assessment_and_Support_Consorti um/

Davey, B. (1993). Helping middle school learners succeed with reading assignments: A focus on time planning. *Journal of Reading, 37*(3), 170–173.

Eanet, M., & Manzo, A. (1976). REAP: A strategy for improving reading/writing/studyskills. *Journal of Reading, 19*, 647–652.

Fay, L. (1965). Reading study skills: Math and science. In J. Allen Figuro (Ed.), *Reading and inquiry.* Newark, DE: International Reading Association.

Fine, J. (2004). *Reciprocal mapping: Scaffolding students' expository writing.* Paper given at the American Reading Forum, December 2004, Marco Island, Florida.

Fry, E. (1981). Graphic literacy. *Journal of Reading, 24*, 383–390.

Graham, K. G., & Robinson, H. A. (1984). *Study skills handbook: A guide for all teachers* (pp. 100–101). Newark, DE: International Reading Association.

Gunning, T. C. (2005). *Creating literacy: Instruction for all students.* Boston: Allyn & Bacon.

Hanf, M. B. (1971, January). Mapping: A technique for translating reading into thinking. *Journal of Reading, 14*, 224–230, 270.

Howard, J. (2001). Graphic representations as tools for decision-making. *Social Education, 65*, 220-223.

International Reading Association/National Council of Teachers of English. (1996). *Standards for the English language arts.* Urbana, IL: Authors.

James, E., James, C., & Barkin, C. (1998). *How to be school smart: Super study skills.* New York: Beech Tree Books.

Manzo, A., Manzo, U. C., & Thomas, M. M. (2005). *Content area literacy: Strategic teaching for strategic learning* (4th ed.). Hoboken, NJ: John Wiley and Sons, Inc.

Meeks, L. L. (1999). Making English classrooms happier places to learn. *English Journal, 88*, 73–80.

Nishet, J., & Shucksmith, J. (1986). *Learning strategies.* London: Routledge & Kegan Paul.

Ogle, D. M. (1986, February). K-W-L: A teaching model that develops active reading of expository text. *The Reading Teacher, 39*, 564–570.

Ogle, D. (1989). The known, want to know, learn strategy. In K. D. Muth (Ed.), *Children's comprehension of text* (pp. 205–223). Newark, DE: International Reading Association.

Pauk, W. (1989). *How to study in college* (4th ed.). Boston: Houghton Mifflin.

Pearson, J. W., & Santa, C. M. (1995). Students as researchers of their own learning. *Journal of Reading, 38*(6) 462–469.

Peresich, M. L., Meadows, J. D., & Sinatra, R. (1990). Content area cognitive mapping for reading and writing proficiency. *Journal of Reading, 33*(6), 424–432.

Randall, S. N. (1996). Information charts: A strategy for organizing student research. *Journal of Adolescent and Adult Literacy, 39*(7), 536–542.

Reinking, D. (1986). Integrating graphic aids into content area instruction: The graphic information lesson. *Journal of Reading, 30*, 146–151.

ReKrut, M. D. (1999). Using the Internet in the classroom instruction. *Journal of Adolescent and Adult Literacy, 42*, 546–557.

Roberts, P. L., & Kellough, R. D. (2000). *A guide for developing interdisciplinary thematic units* (2nd ed.). Upper Saddle River, NJ: Merrill.

Robinson, D. H. (1998). Graphic organizers as aids to text learning. *Reading Research and Instruction, 37*, 85–106.

Robinson, F. P. (1970). *Effective study.* New York: Harper Row.

Rosenshine, B., & Meister, C. (1992). The use of scaffolds for teaching higher level cognitive strategies. *Educational Leadership, 49*, 26–33.

Rozakis, L., & Cain, D. (2003). *Super study skills: The ultimate guide to tests and studying.* New York: Scholastic Reference.

Ryder, R. J., & Graves, M. F. (1996). Using the Internet to enhance students' reading, writing and information-gathering skills. *Journal of Adolescent and Adult Literacy, 40*(4), 244–255.

Simmers-Wolpow, R., Farrell, D., & Tonjes, M. (1991). Implementing a secondary reading study skills program across the disciplines. *Journal of Reading, 34,* 590–594.

Smirnov, A. A. (1973). *Problems of psychology of memory.* New York: Plenum Press.

Strichart, S. S., & Mangrum, C.T. (2001). *Teaching study strategies to students with learning disabilities* (3rd ed.). Boston: Allyn & Bacon.

Tonjes, M. J. (1981). Selected instructional strategies for promoting content reading and study skills. In A. Hendry (Ed.), *Teaching reading: The key issues* (pp. 97–106). London: Heinemann Educational Books.

Tonjes, M. J. (1986). Reading and thinking skills in the subject classroom. In B. Gillam (Ed.), *The language of school subjects* (pp. 68–75). London: Heinemann Educational Books.

Tonjes, M. J. (1991). *Secondary reading, writing and learning.* Needham Heights, MA: Allyn & Bacon.

Wade, S. E., Trathem W., & Schraw, G. (1996). An analysis of spontaneous study strategies. *Reading Research Quarterly, 25,* 147–166.

Wong, L. (2002). *Essential study skills* (4th ed.). Boston: Houghton Mifflin.

Wood, K. D., Lapp, D., & Flood, J. (1992). *Guiding readers through text: A review of study guides.* Newark, DE: International Reading Association.

Wooten, S. (1996). *Study skills: Making the most of your human computer.* Dubuque, IA: Kendall/Hunt.

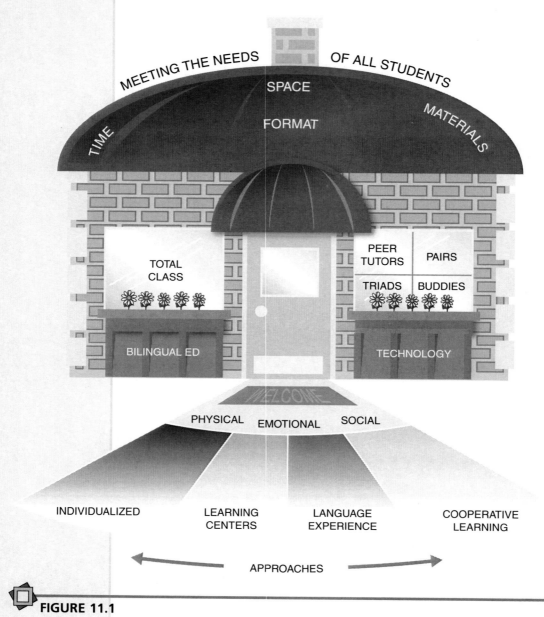

FIGURE 11.1

Classroom Organization and Approaches—A Cognitive Map

Classroom Organization and Approaches

Outline

- Anticipatory and Review Questions
- A Sampling National Performance Standards
- Introduction
- Organizational Concerns
  - Time
  - Space
  - Materials
  - *Workshop 11.1: Flexible Time Plans, Designing Space, and Organizing Materials*
- Teaching Formats
  - Total Class
  - Flexible Small-Group Instruction
- From the Content Classroom: The Freedom of Using Small Groups
  - Triads or Buddy System
  - Peer-Tutoring or Pairs
- Approaches
  - Individualized/Personalized Learning
  - Language Experience Approach (LEA)
- From the Content Classroom: Dream Car

- Learning Centers for Content Areas
  - *Workshop 11.2: Mini-Learning Centers*
  - Cooperative Learning
- Organizing for Diversity Responsive Instruction
  - Planning for a Responsive Environment
  - Planning What We Teach
  - Planning How We Teach
- Approaches to Bilingual Education
- Technology: Organizing Instruction with Old Friends
  - *Workshop 11.3: Old Technology at Wegotnonewtechno High*
- Cinquain as Summary
- Summary
- From the Pages of Our Lives: *My High School's Transformational Power*, by Carole H. Tyson
- References and Recommended Readings

"I hold before you my hand with each finger standing erect and alone, and as long as they are held thus, not one of the tasks that the hand may perform can be accomplished. I cannot lift. I cannot grasp. I cannot hold. I cannot even make an intelligible sign until my fingers organize and work together. In this we should also learn a lesson."

George Washington Carver

"If there is anything less scientific than one-size-fits-all curriculum, I'm not sure what it might be . . . . Effective reading instruction provides a balance of whole-group, small-group and side-by-side lessons every day."

Richard L. Allington

Anticipatory and Review Questions

Literal

1. To meet your goals, what are five basic decisions you must make in order to have a well-organized classroom?

2. In planning for diversity responsive teaching, what are the three main categories for which we plan?

Interpretative/Applied

3. Select three of the small-group formats and describe how you would incorporate each into a weekly lesson plan outline.

4. Describe how you might use three different "older" technologies to teach your content.

Evaluative/Critical

5. In just a few sentences discuss the strengths and weaknesses of two of the different approaches (e.g., individualized/personalized learning, language experience, cooperative learning) to meet student content learning needs.

6. Do you agree or disagree with those who say that how a classroom is organized is as important as what is being taught?

Personal

7. Some classrooms are welcoming and well organized. Others are not. From your own personal experiences, describe an example of each. Explain the strengths and weaknesses of each learning environment.

8. What was the single most important learning for you from this chapter? Explain why.

A Sampling of National Performance Standards

- The professional educator understands how students differ in their approaches to learning and creates instructional opportunities that support their intellectual, social, and personal development (Council of Chief State School Officers, 2005).

- Accomplished teachers establish a caring, inclusive, stimulating, and safe school community where students can take intellectual risks, practice democracy, and work collaboratively and independently (National Board of Professional Teaching Standards, 2005a).

- Accomplished teachers of linguistically and culturally diverse learners establish a caring, inclusive, safe, and linguistically and culturally rich community of learning where students take intellectual risks and work both independently and collaboratively (National Board of Professional Teaching Standards, 2005b).

Introduction

Classroom organization is a crucial aspect of effective instruction. To try to move toward or meet content literacy goals, teachers need to consider the vast variety of individual differences found in most content classrooms. These differences include, but are not limited to background knowledge, abilities, interests, and needs. As George Washington Carver so eloquently points out, we cannot use our hands until we get each of our fingers organized so that they may work together. Analogously, we have to organize time, space, materials, and teaching formats to best meet student needs. However, there is even more. We must make decisions about large- and small-group activities. In the event we choose small-group assignments, we must decide whether to have students work in triads, with the buddy system, peer-tutoring, or simply in pairs. Approaches to teaching include *individualized/personalized learning, learning centers, language experience*, and *cooperative learning*. In this chapter we also touch on an approach to diversity responsive teaching and the use of technology to better meet student needs. A thoughtful, personal mixture of approaches, formats, and organizational concerns will generally benefit most students and will lead to more effective, motivated learning.

Organizational Concerns

Time

How many more slow-learning students might master the content if given more time? How many more gifted students might be less bored and extend their knowledge if given the choice of spending less time (but all that is needed) on the required task and the rest of the time on some type of enrichment activity? How many students of normal learning aptitude have short attention spans that cause them to tune out halfway though a forty-minute lecture? Questions such as these are important to teachers who hope to reach most of their students.

A traditional time plan for a week of fifty-minute science classes might have a lecture on Monday, lab on Tuesday, lecture-discussion on Wednesday, lab on Thursday, and a test on Friday. This plan does not allow for student flexibility in pursuit of learning goals. All students must do the same things, at the same time, for the same amount of time, whether or not it meets their individual needs. This sequence built into traditional classroom organization means that when a student misses a class or daydreams through a lecture, it is often impossible to recapture the information. On the other hand, the same science class could be organized around a flexible time plan, where specified activities must be completed by Friday but students have some choice as to how much time is spent on each activity.

Here is a possible time plan that allows for some flexibility.

Assignments for the Week:

1. Perform labs 24 and 25 and write up in lab workbook.
2. Read chapters 9 and 10 and outline main ideas.
3. Complete study guide pages 17 to 21 and check it with your buddy.

TABLE 11.1 Flexible Time Plan

Time	Monday Tuesday	Wednesday Thursday	Friday
9:00–9:05	Vocabulary activity ————————————————————————————		Quiz or small group contest or game, short film
9:05–9:15	Summarize previous week's learning or return quiz and answer questions	Small groups meet for developing questions, getting classifications, planning, helping each other, correcting other group's work	
9:15–9:45	Mini-lecture Labs—in pairs Relistening (could be on tapes at listening posts) Outside reading Work on study guides		Go over study guides or advance organizers for next week's reading assignment
9:45–9:50	Cleanup, questions, hand in assignments		

This week's tasks, topics: _____ _____

Space

A classroom should be designed to emphasize its function as a workroom. This requires a division of space that is often quite different from the traditional rows of desks and chairs. There could be stations or learning centers, a large group meeting area with demonstration facilities, a reference corner and some privacy spaces. Committee or group work is best accomplished in small circles or four desks pushed together—two facing the other two. See Figure 11.2.

To assist in making these divisions, it is helpful to have movable dividers, homemade folding screens, bookcases, carrels, a portable chalkboard and small and large tables.

An English class held in the basement of a San Diego area high school made use of huge supporting pillars to divide usable space. In the creative writing area there were numerous homemade carrels, whereas the general discussion area in the center was filled with overstuffed sofas and chairs donated by parents. Long tables around the periphery served as learning centers for small group discussion. This was an exciting yet relaxed classroom.

Materials

Another important consideration is the collection and organization of materials. Collateral, or outside, materials should be collected for the unit. These might include a special film or video, historical novels or articles from popular magazines. Students may view or read them during free reading time or for extra credit.

Another area might contain materials to enhance skill development, such as booklets on map-reading skills for social studies or programmed workbooks on basic computational skills for a math class.

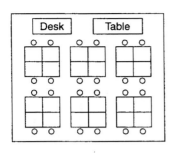

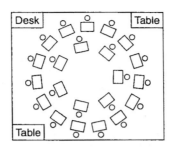

FIGURE 11.2
Space suggestions.

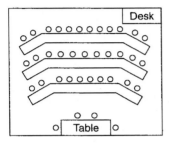

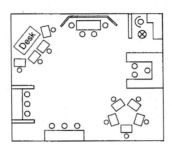

It is helpful to students when some sort of readability designation is made for reading materials, if not by grade level, then at least by the three categories of *introductory*, *average*, and *advanced*. These levels can be designated by labels or stickers placed on the book spine and may be color coded. The school librarian will be ready to assist and make suggestions for each individual classroom.

Flexible Time Plans, Designing Space, and Organizing Materials

1. Working in small groups of not more than five, develop a flexible time plan for one week in your subject area. Put this on an overlay for the overhead projector to explain to the class.

2. In pairs, design an ideal content classroom plan. Show how furniture can be moved and label key areas of the room for different functions.

3. Individually start a content materials file based on one unit, using the assistance of the curriculum librarian and a computer search. Materials should include films, tapes, and videos. Try to find a topic that is written at several levels to meet individual needs.

Workshop 11.1

Teaching Formats

Let us now look at several teaching formats for the content classroom. Table 11.2 provides an overview of these formats.

Total Class

Even though there is usually an extreme range of knowledge, skills and attitudes in any given content class, thee are still many times when it is more efficient and effective to use the total class mode of instruction. This includes large blocks of time for lecture, lecture-discussion, demonstration, student presentation, evaluation, field trips, outside speakers and viewing audiovisual presentations. It also includes the smaller segments of time devoted to such things as announcements, directions, explanations, brainstorming, sharing, or summarizing. Total class activities, then, are numerous and necessary.

TABLE 11.2 Teaching Formats

Type	Description		Activities/Materials
Total Class (30 +)	Large time blocks		Lecture, lecture discussion, demonstration, student presentation, debate, panel discussion, diagnosis, evaluation, field trip, outside speaker, viewing audiovisual presentations
	Smaller segments of time		Announcements, directions, explanations, brainstorming, sharing, summarizing
Small Groups (4–10)	General types	Achievement Skill Social interest	Research/information search, role playing, simulation, discussion, project construction, workshops
	Both homogeneous and heterogeneous		
Triads	Permanent heterogeneous helping groups		Correct and/or review each other's work before handing in, generally assisting each other in problem solving
Pairs	Pairs—random temporary assignment solve specific problem		Problem solving
Peer Tutors	Peer tutoring—heterogeneous pairing where stronger helps the weaker		Skills
Buddy Systems			General help
Individualized/Personalized	Working alone, self-seeking, self-selecting, self-pacing, within content area limits		LAPS (learning activity packets) Developing research papers
Learning Centers	Individual or small group works around a table that includes instructions and materials for independent activities		Task cards, learning packets, listening posts, schedule, check sheets
Cooperative Learning	Used with any of the above groupings		Peer teaching, noncompetitive tasks

Flexible Small Group Instruction

Breaking up the class into small groups of around five students each is an important consideration for any content teacher. Two advantages of small groups for student learning are: (1) more opportunity for active student participation; and (2) more ways to meet student needs.

There are numerous ways to group students: by achievement, skill or social needs, and interests. The student makeup of these groups may be heterogeneous (at different levels) or homogeneous (at the same level). It is a good thing to change groups from time to time to avoid labels and for variety.

FROM THE CONTENT CLASSROOM

The Freedom of Using Small Groups

Recently, one teacher was heard to say, "When I stopped talking at the whole class and let groups work together to get their reports ready to present to the class, I found that I had freed myself to circulate, answer questions, an make suggestions. I also found I was not having to spend so much time disciplining." Breaking up the class into small groups means that the teacher is changing the method to *how* students will learn, rather than *what* they will learn.

Students reading at approximately the same levels (as determined in the initial diagnosis when the informal tests and Content IRI were administered) may be grouped homogeneously at times so that they may share the same reading materials. At times it might be a more advantageous for groups to consist of a variety of achievement levels so that a cross-sharing or pooling of information occurs.

All content subjects have specific skill areas needed for knowledge mastery, for example, interpreting diagrams in an auto mechanics class; knowing and interpreting meanings of Italian words used in music; spelling in a composition class; or using a microscope in a science class. Because some students will have already mastered these particular skills, it would be a boring waste of time to practice them in a whole-class setting. Instead, skill groups can be organized to give everyone something they need to work on. For the gifted, some type of enrichment activity or advanced skill practice may be devised. This type of grouping is always a temporary one—as soon as the particular skills are mastered, the group is disbanded.

Grouping by social needs can be extremely beneficial to students' interpersonal development. One way to develop leadership qualities in the more reticent students might be to place them together in a group where, of necessity, some must take on the leadership responsibility. Class leaders, on the other hand, might learn cooperation strategies if placed together. Cultural or social cliques can be broken up by dispersing members among groups.

An important grouping consideration is the students' own interests as they relate to the subject in question. An English class studying short stories can be successfully subdivided into groups based on areas of interest—mysteries, adventure, romance, or sports. Each group has certain tasks to perform in reading and processing learnings, then the groups come together for total class session to compare and contrast their learnings. To find out students' subject-related interests, a simple, brief interest inventory can be administered, asking if they would like to read about specific things.

Triads or Buddy System

Smaller groups/triads can be a specific type of permanent grouping that involves three students in each heterogeneous group. The main task for triads is for members to care for each other for the duration of the term, for example, by correcting and reviewing each other's papers before handing them in. It also means answering many of the minor questions that continually appear, and it can be especially helpful to shy students who rarely ask questions in front of the whole class. This triad support system works well when students understand their cooperative roles—that no one student is to be leaned on to do most of the work, and that it is a shared responsibility. Another option is to arbitrarily assign buddies (two people) to carry some responsibility for each other during the term, such as sharing notes when one is absent.

Peer Tutoring or Pairs

Many processing tasks assigned in class can be handled well by allowing students to work in pairs. At times this means one student helping the other, but often it should be a two-way street. The pairs should be changed often so that students have the opportunity of being the helper, the helped, or the equal.

Approaches

Individualized/Personalized Learning

At times students benefit from the opportunity to work alone on a task. *Individualized instruction* means that students are allowed to seek their own area of interest within the content structure, selecting their own materials, and working at their own rate. A key to this type of instruction is the individual conference with the teacher, when progress is checked and questions are dealt with. In content classrooms, there is usually a limit to this absolute freedom of choice, so for that reason, it is often termed *personalized* rather than strictly *individualized*.

Language Experience Approach (LEA)

The *language experience approach (LEA)* is related to individualized or personalized classrooms. Used successfully for many years by primary teachers, it has been adapted by some content teachers of older students. LEA combines listening, speaking, writing, and reading with an instructional sequence some-thing like the following:

1. Generate or evoke the memory of an experience.
2. Stimulate analysis of that experience through questions and probes.
3. Elicit oral statements from students about the experience.
4. Record these statements.
5. Use the written record for group practice or review.
6. Illustrate, tape, dramatize, make a book, etc.
7. File and reuse the written record for individual rereading, reference, or future classes.

Some applications of this approach follow:

In an English class, LEA can be an appropriate vehicle for creative writing; in social studies for critical thinking analysis; in a science class (following a field trip), for group summary and categorization of key concepts observed; or in any content class as a readiness technique before reading a difficult text assignment. Severely disabled readers can be helped when time and student resources are allotted for dictating and typing main ideas from a lecture to be used later for review.

Students involved in a language experience listen, think, speak, write, read, illustrate, share and sometimes tape what they have learned. Generally, they remember these experiences positively in the future.

FROM THE CONTENT CLASSROOM

Dream Car

Students in a non-college-bound eleventh-grade English class, most not reading above a fourth-grade level, listened to a short story entitled *Dream Car*. Following a general discussion, students made elaborate plans and sketches of their own dream car. They then wrote descriptions to accompany their final drawings and presented them to the class. The results were then posted around the room. These "turned-off" students became highly motivated with this project and hidden talents emerged. The school posted these final products in the Learning Activity Center, which was a special recognition for most of these potential dropouts.

Learning Centers for Content Areas

Learning centers vary according to purpose (see Figure 11.3). They may teach a specific skill like summarizing, they may be a practice center for specific needed skills, or they may stress developing higher level thinking processes (e.g., creative writing, problem solving). Learning centers usually motivate reluctant students because students must become active participants.

In elementary classrooms, learning centers might offer quiet reading, creative and technical writing, science exploration, a social studies "You Are There," or a listening center—in other words, anything across the curriculum—perhaps even integrating math and art.

Secondary content classrooms might have one center for optional skill practice or reward for completing work early, or an entire term can be taught through multiple centers, as one tenth-grade biology class did successfully in San Diego.

A center may have a colorful, eye-catching backdrop made from a large appliance carton; materials could include folders, envelopes, paper, colored pencils or crayons, scissors, glue, rulers, etc. Activities are described, directions are given, self-correcting devices worked out and reading materials gathered—in other words, all the tools, activities and directions needed to make students independent of the teacher.

Teacher work time is heaviest when putting centers together. Once completed, centers can be used for many years with only a few updates. Teachers then become facilitators—available for consultation and guidance as needed.

It is usually better to start out with one center, possibly for practicing a skill; then add a second one, working out directions for moving from one center to the other. A center should never have more than a few students at a time. All students need to be very clear about what the rules are and what will happen if they break a rule. With only part of a class at a center at one time, it should not be a noisy one that would disturb the rest of the class.

FIGURE 11.3
Learning centers in content classrooms.

Purposes/Advantages	Physical Setup
Meets diverse needs. Provides variety. Individualizes learning, encourages independent study. Reinforces learnings. Introduces new concepts. Allows for investigation, exploration, decision making, active involvement. Motivates. Encourages student responsibility.	Use tables, chairs, desks pushed together, walls, floor, bookcases, bulletin boards, folding screens. Arrange for small group or individual work.

Learning Components	Steps in Developing
1. Introductory poster explaining learning tasks in general. 2. Center rules—directions for proper use. 3. Resource materials including pictures for advertising. 4. Learning activity packets, task cards, readings. 5. Schedule for use by assignment, self-selection contract, or rotation. 6. Check sheets for record keeping.	1. Select topic or concept: e.g., Math: computational shortcut English: humor in poetry History: the roaring twenties Science: arthropods 2. Decide on main ideas within the topic selected. 3. Develop or gather materials to teach these ideas at the knowledge, interpretive, and applied levels. 4. Develop evaluative criteria. 5. Decide on rules and regulations for use of center, best done in cooperation with students. This includes traffic patterns and amount of talking allowed when working.

Workshop 11.2

Mini-Learning Centers

1. Pass around a sign-up sheet with general topic headings such as technical vocabulary development, critical-creative comprehension, adaptable rates, locational study skills, organizational study skills, and motivational strategies, or as an alternative, allow groups to form according to content areas and let them decide their theme (e.g., American Revolution, math shortcuts, comparative short stories).

2. The task for each group is to develop a mini-learning center on the general topic, but using its content specialty; for example, the technical vocabulary of biology for the science teacher, figures of speech for English teachers, or rules for the game for the physical education teacher.

3. Allow thirty minutes of class time initially for small group planning. Have outside reading resources available to be checked out or have them on reserve in the library. Large posters of pictures showing examples of a learning center would be helpful.

4. At the next class session allow fifteen minutes for groups to reconvene and refine their plans, including individual task responsibilities.

5. During a later class session, each group might set up the center and briefly describe it to the rest of the class in three minutes. The last time segment might be reserved to allow each group to try out one other center. As an alter-native, show the need to be concerned with efficient *traffic patterns* from one center to another by demonstrating this to the class. Assign groups to centers and allow them several minutes to examine the material. Ring a bell or make some signal that they have two minutes to "clean up" and then move to the next center.

6. Follow up with general evaluative discussion of merits and disadvantages of using learning centers in content classrooms.

Cooperative Learning

Much has been said about the value of cooperative learning for both elementary and secondary students. Students are placed together in pairs, triads, or small groups to work toward common goals. This allows for high social inter-action, more individual emotional involvement, and more possibility of risk taking. *Cooperative processes* mean that students learn how to work productively with others, receiving the support of the study group; they can share what they have learned, hear others, opinions and teach and be taught by peers.

Some advantages of cooperative learning include higher test scores, greater motivation to learn, more positive attitudes, general academic improvement and decreased dependence on teachers.

Organizing for Diversity Responsive Instruction

In Chapter Three we reviewed schemata for literacy and a schema for diversity. We also argued that literacy and culture are inseparable. If we want to teach all of our students how to acquire new content knowledge, we must include the knowledge and experiences our students use to make meaning. This is what we mean when we say that content literacy instruction must be relevant and responsive to the cultural diversity of our individual students.

Appropriate methods to effectively assess (Chapters Five and Six) and teach (Chapters Seven through Ten and Twelve) for diversity are presented throughout this text. However, in this chapter on organization, let us look at how we might organize our teaching so that it is responsive to diversity.

Price and Nelson (2007) suggest that in order to organize our teaching so that it is responsive to the many dimensions of culture (e.g., abilities/skills, ethnicity, language, gender, socioeconomic class, religion, immigrant status, sexual orientation, age, family structure), we need to plan in three categories: (1) planning the environment, (2) planning what we teach, and (3) planning how to teach.

Planning for a Responsive Environment

A responsive environment is safe, supportive, and respectful on three levels: physical, social, and emotional. On the *physical level*, such an environment contains objects and materials (e.g., photographs, posters, music, books, games, artifacts, recordings) that are fully representative of each of the dimensions of diversity. The very presence of these objects and materials should stimulate students to learn about diverse groups and individuals. On the *social level* we need to plan friendly and respectful interactions. For example, we need to create rules about name calling, and group students in ways that encourages full inclusion and integration. Among other things, this planning will require the teacher to learn how to correctly pronounce all names and greet students in a variety of languages. On the *emotional level* teachers need to plan activities that are sensitive to the cultures of students and their families. For example, in their planning, teachers need to be sensitive to holidays that are celebrated or observed outside of those of the predominant culture. Finally, planning involves sensitivity to cultural needs. For example, time demands may make homework difficult at certain times of the week or year. Assignments where students are asked to document family events need be sensitive to varied family structures.

Planning What We Teach

When planning what we teach, we need to make sure that the content is complete—not Eurocentric in approach. We need plan to include ideas and examples that connect directly to students' lives. When doing so we plan to include all-important contributors to the field, incorporate varied voices, and emphasize similarities as well as differences. There are several real-world examples of this documented in this book. For example, think back to Evangelina (*Evangelina Can Read*—Chapter Three). Evangelina discovered she could read in English when the traditional texts that she was assigned were supplemented with texts that were grounded in her own culture. Completeness of content was also a significant factor in the literacy learning lives of the writers of *A Weekend with My Grandfather* (Chapter Two), *Sharing Is Healing* (Chapter Four), *Writing My Way to My Family* (Chapter Seven), and *The Truth, Whispered or Shouted . . .* (Chapter Twelve). A responsive environment includes instruction on the dimensions of diversity themselves, as well as the skills needed to resolve the conflicts that often arise between cultures.

Planning How We Teach

With a responsive environment and relevant content, the planning piece that makes responsive teaching complete is planning the *how* of teaching. The author of *My High School's Transformative Power,* at the end of this chapter, provides an excellent example of how teaching can and does have profound and lasting consequences. The "how" of teaching should include universal design principles, that is, variety in presentation of information as well as in the ways that students are encouraged to express their learning. As we consider how our students are different, we include individual modifications and accommodations. We do this by including specialized materials, equipment, and technology and by adjusting assessment and evaluation so that it is culturally meaningful and fair.

Approaches to Bilingual Education

English is not the first language of a growing number of students in American schools. In the year 2000, there were 18% of the households in the United States that were language minority households. Consequently, a significant percentage of secondary students arrive in our classes in need of support. There are six approaches to providing that support: Four are versions of the bilingual education approach, and the other two are versions of English as a second language (Ernst, 1994; Guldin, 2002). The six approaches are summarized below:

- *Structured Immersion*—where the instructor speaks the student's native language but teaches mostly in English, providing minimal if any ESL supporting instruction.

- *Transitional Bilingual Education*—in which students are instructed in their native language but are rapidly transitioned to English literacy. This transition occurs within 3 years; hence, this approach is also called "early-exit bilingual education."

- *Bilingual/Bicultural Education*—which aims to maintain and enrich students' knowledge and skills in the original language while promoting development of English. This is also called "dual immersion."

- *Two-way Bilingual Education*—in which both languages are used equally to teach a class of native English speakers as well as native speakers of the second language, across the curriculum. This is also sometimes called "developmental bilingual education" and is seen more often in elementary schools than at the secondary level.

- *English as a Second Language*—in which compensatory language instruction is offered entirely in English with an aim that the student acquires oral English proficiency.

- *Sheltered English/Alternate Immersion*—in which science, math, and social studies are taught with ESL techniques. The idea here is that students acquire language by receiving instruction that is sheltered from input that is beyond their comprehension.

Technology: Organizing Instruction with Old Friends

Many of today's students are accustomed to working in a technological environment that exceeds what is present in most classrooms. Beyond their cellular phones, some students own hand-held wireless devices that combine telephone, text messaging, Internet access, multiple software applications, and more computer memory than most teachers will ever see on the computers in their classrooms. Nonetheless, a significant percentage of the millions of students who access the Internet do so from their schools and classrooms.

Unfortunately, there are still many schools where the majority of classrooms don't have access to the Internet. We do not have suggestions as to how to overcome this disparity. Moreover, we learned an important lesson in our last edition. The information we provided on newer technologies were nearly out of date before our new text hit the shelves of local bookstores. Given the rate of growth of technology, we are instead going to focus on some old familiar friends, older technologies that are less expensive and more readily available. We will now focus on organizing instruction with transparencies, videotapes, and audiotapes.

Transparencies may be used as overlays, thereby allowing presentation of a complex subject as several individual strands that may be combined towards the end of a lesson. For example, when teaching the writing process, the teacher may use a series of overheads to demonstrate what the writing sample may look like at different stages of the composition. Remember, overhead pens come in many colors and each layer of the overlay may be in a different color. Yes, a computer with a projector may be a preferred instructional tool; however, overhead projectors are usually readily available and transparencies are inexpensive and may be washed and reused.

By preparing overhead transparencies before class, teachers can avoid having to write and rewrite information on the board. However, there is still something to be said for writing notes on blank transparencies during class, thereby presenting material without having to turn their backs to their students.

Transparencies may also be used by groups of students to illustrate the cognitive maps they construct from a reading. Those students who learn best with visual illustrations will benefit from this method. Cognitive maps constructed by each group can then be shared with the class as a whole and if desired, paper copies may be made for distribution.

Televisions and videotape players are often available to teachers and their students. Teachers who plan ahead can work with and record PBS and cable shows on videotape for use in the classroom. **Be forewarned**, however; teachers must carefully adhere to their district's policy for getting approval to show videos that they have taped, and stay within copyright laws applicable for such showings.

Although in the average home television is on more than 6 hours per day, few if any of these viewing hours are for learning. Often the television provides background sounds and images or is used purely for amusement. Realizing this, many teachers provide schematic organizers and/or worksheets with questions to answer while watching a video. These teachers then use the pause button to provide students with time to reflect, discuss, and write about what they have seen. Videos also provide students with opportunities to demonstrate the skills they have learned about taking and making notes (see Chapter One).

More and more students have access to camcorders that may be used to produce videocassette tapes of their own. Consider having groups of students write and produce a documentary on a topic about which they are reading for viewing by the class as a whole.

Finally, audiocassettes and tape recorders are available for use by most students. Teachers may prerecord information on audiocassette tapes for student use during or after class. (This is an excellent way to accommodate students who have special needs.) If they don't have the time to do so, they may ask parent and/or student volunteers to tape significant passages from textbooks and novels. Students who anticipate extended absences due to travel or illness may be provided with copies of these audiocassettes for listening while traveling or recuperating. Students may also be encouraged to use tape recorders to practice oral reports they must give in class.

Workshop 11.3	**Old Technology at Wegotnonewtechno High**
	Here's a scenario. Get into groups of three to five and play out this scenario:
	You get a teaching job at Wegotnonewtechno High. Unfortunately, you have no access to computers or the Internet in your classroom. However, there is literally a storeroom of unused old technology available for checkout. There are extra transparencies and overhead projectors, old cassette tape recorders, lots of old video players, an old video camcorder, and other such goodies. Describe how you might integrate the use of this technology into your classroom to organize student learning of difficult concepts from your content area.

Cinquain as Summary

Classroom
Formats, Approaches
Time—Space—Materials
Crucial Attention to Diversity
Organization

 ## Summary

Content teachers face many organizational decisions for their classroom. Based on their content goals and the needs and abilities of their students, they first must consider flexible time plans, designing classroom space, and gathering and organizing resource materials. Their students may be a mixture of gifted, average, unmotivated, at-risk, and culturally diverse. The format of how teachers plan instruction will hopefully include both total class instruction and flexible small groups. These small groups of about five each change periodically and include achievement or ability, skill needs, social needs, and interests. Small groups include triads, the buddy system, peer-tutoring, or pairs.

Several approaches to be considered are individualized/personalized learning, language experience approach, learning centers, and cooperative learning. In order to organize our teaching so that it is responsive to the many dimensions of culture (e.g., abilities/skills, ethnicity, language, gender, socioeconomic class, religion, immigrant status, sexual orientation, age, family structure), we need to plan in three categories: (1) planning the environment, (2) planning what we teach, and (3) planning how to teach. Given the rate of growth of technology, some old familiar friends, older technologies that are less expensive and more readily available, such as transparencies, videotapes, and audiotapes can help teachers organize and present vital content.

FROM THE PAGES OF OUR LIVES
My High School's Transformational Power

by Carole H. Tyson

Dr. Carole H. Tyson is currently president and founder of Henderson's Global Voices, LLC, a bureau of speakers and experts on international affairs and has traveled to more than 60 foreign countries. She served as a senior U.S. Foreign Service officer in the Department of State and the U.S. Agency for International Development for 20 years. In her essay, Dr. Tyson describes what it was like to be an African American high school student from racially segregated Atlanta, Georgia, in the days when Rosa Parks refused to relinquish her bus seat and Emmett Till was murdered. She expresses gratitude to the teachers whose acts of love and compassion erased the damage caused by years of hatred.

My high school radically changed my life through the strong leadership of its headmistress, the love and dedication of its teachers, and the values on which the school stood.

As an African American girl from racially segregated Atlanta, Georgia, I arrived at St. Mary's In-The-Mountains Episcopal school for girls in Littleton, New Hampshire in the fall of 1957. There I joined one other colored girl along with the otherwise all-white student body. 1957 was just two years after Rosa Parks refused to relinquish her bus seat to a white man in segregated Montgomery, Alabama; two years after the lynching of sixteen-year-old Emmett Till by a group of white men in Mississippi; and it was the year of enactment as the Civil Rights Act of 1957, all serving to spark the modern civil rights movement in the United States. It was also two years after my mother and father founded the first African American travel agency in America for the purpose of exposing black people to the freedoms in Europe and Africa that they were not entitled to at home in America.

In the 1950's, my Atlanta, Georgia, was a cocoon of black people surrounded by a vast circle of hostile white people. Virtually every white person I encountered disliked me because of my color and refused to allow me and people like me to participate in their world of schools and universities, shops and businesses, banks, hospitals, hotels, restaurants, neighborhoods and churches. However, within my cocoon where my community maintained a parallel set of the same amenities, I was safe. This was the Atlanta of Martin Luther King, Jr. and Coretta Scott King, Vernon Jordan, David Abernathy, Andrew Young, Benjamin Mays, Whitney Young, Sam Westerfield, Herman Russell, and Charlayne Hunter-Gault. These names are now familiar to many of us because of their contributions to ending racial segregation.

When I left Atlanta and arrived in New England, I thought I was in a foreign country because everything was different for me. The people were different, and so were their color, their culture, their way of speaking, their everyday activities, the environment, the food, the weather. Having later had a career in international affairs, I am fond of saying that New Hampshire was indeed my first international experience because no culture could have been more different.

Ms. Mary Harley Jenks was the undisputed leader and headmistress of St. Mary's In-The-Mountains. She set the tone, ensured that rules were followed, and led by example. She, a white woman, treated me, a colored girl, with equanimity, care and love. This was the first time I experienced this from a white person. She carefully picked staff who shared her and the Episcopal school's values of learning about God, caring for others, contributing to the community, and excelling in scholastic work. My French teacher, for example, was from France and considered me exactly the same as she did all other students. I excelled in Madame Raphael's course.

My ballet teacher, Alice Reisz, was a Hungarian woman who had recently escaped from the Hungarian Uprising of 1956 and was formerly a prima ballerina with the Russian Bolshoi Ballet Company. Since I had taken ballet for ten years prior to arriving at St. Mary's, she and I enjoyed one another and I became one of her star pupils and later went on to teach ballet myself. Mr. Kilde, from Norway, taught me soccer, which I had barely heard of before, and whom I remember as a happy, competent athletic instructor. One male teacher from the area did not take too much care with me and I remember him because of that, but he was the only one who stands out for such feelings and actions. I graduated from St. Mary's, studied languages at Tufts University, earned a doctorate in Anthropology at Harvard University (in part based on my early exposure to other languages and culture at St. Mary's) and spent a twenty year career with the U.S. Department of State (U.S. Agency for International Development), serving as Director or Deputy Director of several of our foreign assistance programs in west and southern Africa and the Caribbean.

A mere three years at St. Mary's In-The-Mountains washed away fifteen previous years of racial intolerance and bigotry toward me and from me. At sixty-two years of age now, I am still benefiting from my three years of high school. These three years taught me from that time forward that leadership can and does have profound and lasting consequences, that hatred can be easily erased with love, and that teachers are extremely important in students' lives and that their actions have lifelong effects on their students.

Discussion Questions

1. In the first paragraph, Dr. Tyson writes about how administrative leadership, teacher love and dedication, and school values radically changed her life when she entered high school. What examples of leadership, of teacher love and dedication, and of school values did you find in this essay?

2. Dr. Tyson writes, "I thought I was in a foreign country because everything was different for me." She was explaining what it was like to move from a school in Georgia to one in New Hampshire in 1957. Think for a moment of the experience you had in high school. Did any students relocate to your school? What challenges did they face? What did teachers and students do to make them feel welcomed and safe? Presented with students who are making a transfer into a school where you teach, what might you do to help them make the transition?

3. Dr. Tyson's "cocoon," in part, was the love and dedication of her teachers. As we organize and plan for diversity responsive instruction, what kinds of choices might we make that will have "lifelong effects" on our students? Relate this, if you will, to how you teach or will teach content literacy.

References and Recommended Readings

Allington, R. L. (2005, June/July). The other five pillars of effective reading instruction. *Reading Today*, 3.

Bates, G. W. (1984). Developing reading strategies for the gifted: A research-based approach. *Journal of Reading, 27*, 590–593.

Buell, C., & Whittaker, A. (2001). Enhancing content literacy in physical education. *Journal of Physical Education, Recreation and Dance, 72*, 32–37.

Campbell, J., Hombo, C., & Mazzeo, J. (2000). *NAEP trends in academic progress: Three decades of student performance*. Jesup, MD: U.S. Department of Education.

Conley, M. W. (1985). Promoting cross-cultural understanding through content area reading strategies. *Journal of Reading, 28*, 600–605.

Council of Chief State School Officers. (2005). *INTASC standards*. Retrieved March 21, 2005, from http://www.ccsso.org/projects/Interstate_New_Teacher_Assessment_and_Support_Consortium/

Davey, B. (1993). Helping middle school learners succeed with reading assignments: A focus on time planning. *Journal of Reading, 37*(3), 170–173.

Echevarria, J., Vogt, M., & Short, D. (2000). *Making Content Comprehensible for English Language Learners: The SIOP Model*. Needham Heights, MA: Allyn & Bacon.

Emmer, E. T., Evertson, C. M., & Worsham, M. E. (2000). *Classroom management for secondary teachers* (5th ed.). Boston: Allyn & Bacon.

Ernst, G. (1994). Beyond language: The many dimensions of an ESL program. *Anthropology & Education Quarterly, 25*(3), 321–325.

Guldin, G. E. (2002). *Cultural diversity in school: A guide for school board members and school administrators*. Olympia, WA: Washington State School Directors' Association.

Harper, C., & deJong, E. (2004). Misconceptions about teaching English language learners. *Journal of Adolescent and Adult Literacy, 48*, 152–162.

Jacobson, J., Thorpe, L., Fisher, D., Lapp, D., Frey, N., & Flood, J. (2001). Cross-age tutoring: A literacy improvement approach for struggling adolescent readers. *Journal of Adolescent and Adult Literacy, 44*, 528–536.

Johannessen, L. R. (2004). Helping struggling students achieve success. *Journal of Adolescent and Adult Literacy, 47*, 638–647.

Judy, J. E., et al. (1988). Effects of two instructional approaches and peer tutoring on gifted and nongifted sixth grade students: Analogy performance. *Reading Research Quarterly, 23*, 236–256.

Kagan, S. (1994). *Cooperative learning.* San Juan, CA: Kagan Cooperative Learning.

Kasper, L. F. (1994). Improved reading performance of ESL students through academic course pairing. *Journal of Reading, 37*, 376–385.

Kasten, W. C., & Wilfong, L. G. (2005). Encouraging independent reading with ambience: The book bistro in middle and secondary school classes. *Journal of Adolescent and Adult Literacy, 48*(6), 656–664.

Kline, A. A. (1972). Individualizing chemistry: A method used in an open high school. *Science Teacher, 39*, 61–62.

Marlett, P. B., & Gordon, C. J. (2004). The use of alternative texts in physical education. *Journal of Adolescent and Adult Literacy, 48*, 226–237.

National Board for Professional Teaching Standards. (2005a). *English as a new language: Adolescence and young adult standards* (2nd ed.). Retrieved July 7, 2005, from http://www.nbpts.org/candidates/guide/whichcert/06AdolYoungEnglish2004.html

National Board for Professional Teaching Standards. (2005b). *Middle school generalist standards* (2nd ed.). Retrieved March 28, 2005, from http://www.nbpts.org/candidates/guide/whichcert/02MiddleChild2004.html

Nelson, K. L., & Price, K. M. (2005, March). *Diversity responsive teaching.* Paper presented at Western Washington University, Bellingham, WA.

O'Byrne, B. (2003). The paradox of cross-age, multicultural collaboration. *Journal of Adolescent and Adult Literacy, 47*, 50–83.

Price, K. & Nelson, K. (2007). Daily planning for today's classroom: A guide for writing lesson and activity plans (3rd ed.). Belmont, CA: Wadsworth/Thomson Learning.

ReKrut, M. D. (1994). Peer and cross-age tutoring: The lessons of research. *Journal of Reading, 37*, 356–363.

Sanacore, J. (1997). Students diversity and learning needs. ERIC digest. Bloomington, IN: Eric Clearing House on Reading, English and Communication.

Simmers-Wolpow, R., Farrell, D., & Tonjes, M. (1991). Implementing a secondary reading/study skills program across the disciplines. *Journal of Reading, 34*(8), 590–594.

Slavin, R. E. (1989). Research on cooperative learning: Consensus and controversy. *Educational Leadership, 47*, 52–54.

Slavin, R. E. (1995). *Cooperative learning* (2nd ed.). Needham Heights, MA: Allyn & Bacon.

Stallman, J. A. (1986). Effective use of time in secondary reading programs. In J. K. Hoffman (Ed.), *Effective teaching of reading: Research and practice.* Newark, DE: International Reading Association.

Steuben, S. J. (1978). Learning centers in the secondary school. *Journal of Reading, 22*, 134–139.

Swafford, J. (1995). I wish all my groups were like this one—Facilitating peer interaction during group work. *Journal of Reading, 38*, 626–631.

Wheeler, P. M. (1982). Matching abilities in cross-age tutoring. *Journal of Reading, 26,* 404–407.

Williams, M. (2001). Making connections: A workshop for adolescents who struggle with reading. *Journal of Adolescent and Adult Literacy, 44,* 588.

Wood, K. D. (1987). Fostering cooperative learning in middle and secondary classrooms. *Journal of Reading, 31,* 10–18.

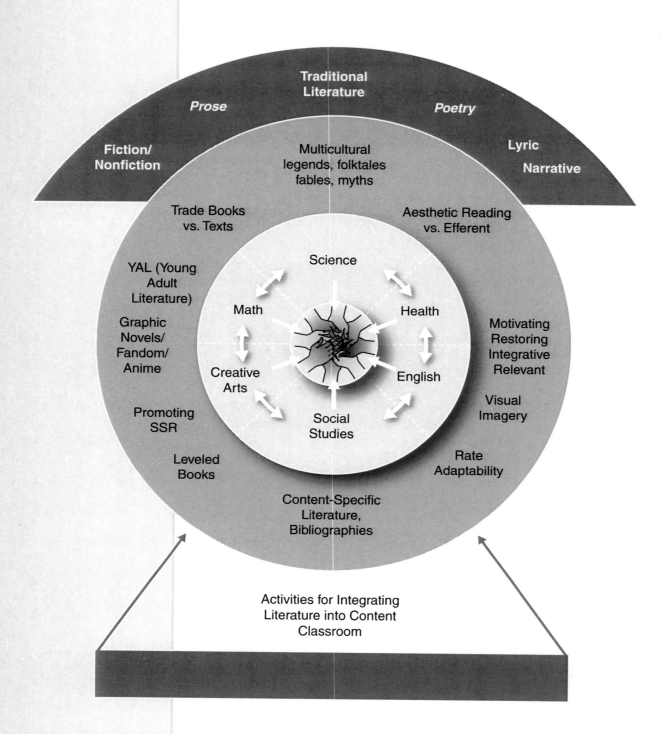

Traditional
Literature

Prose

Poetry

Fiction/
Nonfiction

Multicultural
legends, folktales
fables, myths

Lyric

Narrative

Trade Books
vs. Texts

Aesthetic Reading
vs. Efferent

YAL (Young
Adult
Literature)

Science

Math

Health

Motivating
Restoring
Integrative
Relevant

Graphic
Novels/
Fandom/
Anime

Creative
Arts

English

Visual
Imagery

Promoting
SSR

Social
Studies

Rate
Adaptability

Leveled
Books

Content-Specific
Literature,
Bibliographies

Activities for Integrating
Literature into Content
Classroom

FIGURE 12.1

Integrating Literature into Content Classrooms—A Cognitive Map

Integrating Literature into Content Classrooms

12

Outline

- Anticipatory and Review Questions
- A Sampling of National Performance Standards
- Introduction: Looking at Literature
  - *Workshop 12.1: In the Beginning*
- Rosenblatt's Efferent and Aesthetic Reading: Reader Response Theory
- Motivating and Restorative Qualities of Literature
- Importance of Reading Rate Adaptability
- Multicultural Literature for Understanding and Transformation
- From the Multicultural Classroom: The Correct Answer Is Wrong
  - Empowering Minority Students
- From the Multicultural Classroom: The Tree of Life
  - Two Poems: "The Beads of Life" and "We Wear the Mask"
  - Integrating Folklore into a Middle School Cross-Cultural Unit
    - *Workshop 12.2: A Classroom Visit*
    - *Workshop 12.3: Sharing Multicultural Understandings*
- Locating Appropriate Materials
  - Text vs. Trade Books
  - Using Trade Books in Content Classrooms
  - Leveled Books
- Other Sources of Help in Selecting Appropriate Trade Books
  - A Guide to Locating Content-Specific Literature

- A Guide to Locating Multicultural Literature
- A Guide to Locating Young Adult Literature
- An Annotated Literature Bibliography: Some Personal Choices
- Content-Specific Websites with Literature Resources
  - A Guide to Trade Book Selection Guides
- Graphic Novels, Fandom, and Anime
- Content Classroom Activities
  - Read-Alouds
  - Book Talks
  - Text Walk
  - Picture Books for Adolescents
  - Sustained Reading and Writing
- From the Content Classroom: Promoting SSR
  - Study Reading Circles (Literature Circles)
  - Response Journals (RJ)
  - Curriculum-Based Readers Theatre (CBRT)
    - *Workshop 12.4: Select a Strategy*
  - Here's a Checklist for You
- Cinquain as Summary
- Summary
- From the Pages of Our Lives: *The Truth, Whispered or Shouted . . . ,* by Janice Brendible
- References and Recommended Readings

"Reading is the sole means by which we slip involuntarily, often helplessly, into another's voice, another's soul."

Joyce Carol Oates

"Reading makes immigrants of us all. It takes us far from home, but more important, it finds homes for us all."

Hazel Rochman

Anticipatory and Review Questions

Literal

1. What is meant by "efferent" and "aesthetic"?

2. Describe SSR and DEAR in a content classroom as used here.

Interpretative/Applied

3. How might you apply activities like "read-alouds" and "book talks" in your own classroom?

4. How will you integrate Content Literature into your own classroom? What will you select or omit? And why?

Evaluative/Critical

5. In what ways will literature inclusion increase student motivation, interest, and positive attitudes?

6. Discuss the importance and significance of including multicultural literature in your class.

Personal/Creative

7. What one piece of literature has helped you to improve your understanding of your subject area? Describe the book and how it affected you.

A Sampling of National Performance Standards

- Students read a wide range of print and nonprint texts to build an understanding of texts, of themselves, and of the cultures of the United States and the world; to acquire information; to respond to the needs and demands of society and the workplace; and for personal fulfillment. Among these texts are fiction and nonfiction, classic and contemporary works (International Reading Association/National Council of Teachers of English, 1996, p. 27).

- Accomplished teachers select, adapt, and foster rich and varied sources for social studies and history and use them productively (National Board for Professional Teaching Standards, 2005).

- The professional educator understands and uses a variety of instructional strategies to encourage students' development of critical thinking, problem-solving, and performance skills (Council of Chief State School Officers, 2005).

Introduction: Looking at Literature

What is a chapter on literature doing in a content literacy methods text? Integrating content literature into your class can be a powerful motivator, especially for those students who have difficulty seeing relevance and application of school subject matter in their "real worlds." Content literature can be not only informative but also enjoyable, relevant, restorative, and even integrative. What is more, this literature may go a long way in helping to develop lifetime readers. Reading to escape, to find comfort from others' trials and solutions, to travel to distant places without leaving your arm chair, and yes to learn, are just a few of the things literature can bring to our lives.

The recent bestseller, Dan Brown's *The Da Vinci Code* is just one example of learning much about art and codes from a suspense novel. A reader may read it once rapidly to follow the story line and then return to carefully savor all the meaningful revelations intermixed with the action as pictured events as if one were there. With that in mind, let's give this chapter a try.

In the Beginning Meeting with your class-assigned partner (or newly assigned one), start out by sharing and comparing literature you both have particularly enjoyed. What was it about them that captured your interest? To what content areas were they connected? In what ways (e.g., science fiction for science, sports hero for health and fitness, historical biography of a great woman or man from math or history)? From your compiled lists, together rough out a unit you might teach in the future, emphasizing the outside readings to go with the topic. Share this with the whole class.	**Workshop 12.1**

Rosenblatt's Efferent and Aesthetic Reading: Reader Response Theory

Let us look now for a moment at a theory that has had a profound effect on literature study in general and can be readily adapted to content-area literature. It should point out how important it is to start including more aesthetic or affective considerations into our own disciplines.

Louise Rosenblatt (1978) described reading as a complex transaction between reader and text. A reader's purpose and stance influences how they get meaning and respond. Two stances defined by Rosenblatt (1985) are **efferent** and **aesthetic**. In the efferent stance readers focus on retaining information, being able to recall, paraphrase, analyze, or act on it. Most content classroom teachers emphasize the efferent stance. Both literary and informational text should also have affective (aesthetic) responses. Aesthetic readers focus on their feelings while reading, experiencing what is personally significant. It is not an all-or-nothing choice between the two stances but should fall somewhere on a continuum, as there is a need for both. Using reading and writing strategies found in Chapters Seven and Eight, such as role-play, PMI, RAFT, and digital stories can help bridge the gap.

When discussing aesthetic response, teachers should listen carefully for reactions and assure students that there is no one right answer. Ask questions like: "What interested you most? Why?" Based on their own experiences, ask them to help us see why they feel that way. "What annoyed you? Frightened you? What was familiar or weird?" This helps students to discover what has special meaning for them. We are so polished in emphasizing the efferent and may well be surprised at how motivating it can be for students to express their feelings in an aesthetic stance. Aesthetic responses are personal and cannot in most cases be considered wrong. "That's an interesting way to look at it" is better than "Who has a better idea?" or "No, that's not it!"

Motivating and Restorative Qualities of Literature

We strongly agree with Rosenblatt that there is or can be a motivating/restorative quality to reading literature. How many times have we ourselves found comfort in a book, or found escape from today's turmoil. We want this for all readers and it can often be found through a variety of content-specific literature books, also referred to as trade books. This reading can enlarge on issues or events to bring them to life; textbooks do not have the time or space to deal with such things. More students can be reached because they can find material at their own reading level, which can bring to life content concepts in a concrete way.

As discussed in Chapter Four, the use of bibliotherapy (therapy through books) by teachers who are not therapists has been brought into question. Students who have been through significant traumas such as violent assault or sexual abuse need to work with trained mental health professionals, not simply be given books by teachers to read. Even so, reading and writing may bring comfort to those dealing with problems ranging from the death of a pet, the difficulties that result from moving to a new community, or the death of a loved one. As long as teachers remember that they are *not* therapists and remain teaching professionals, they can share books or suggest ideas to write about. For more on this, read the section on "risky writing" in Chapter Seven, or Noémi Ban's essay, "Sharing Is Healing," at the end of Chapter Four. The ways in which Mrs. Ban and her father used reading and writing to help heal their wounds is testimony to the restorative qualities of literature and journaling.

Whether a situation is a simple classroom problem or life-threatening, whether the book in which it is described is autobiographical or "true-to-life" fiction, ability to empathize with protagonists' situations, to see how they handle their challenges, may be helpful. Also the realization that others have similar problems and have persevered, finding hope despite desperation, can be reassuring. That is why we asked Noémi Ban, Leila Flores-Dueñas, Kie Relyea, Carole Tyson, and Janice Brendible to share stories from the pages of their lives and have included them in this book.

Importance of Reading Rate Adaptability

In Chapter Two you were introduced to reading rate adaptability. The emphasis in this chapter was primarily on expository (nonfiction) text. However, this approach may be modified to read fiction. One reason we stress reading rate adaptability is that the plodding word-by-word readers may be unable to truly enter the world of fiction, because they are bogged down in the struggle to read every word, from the beginning of book, one word at a time, to the end. Leisure reading, to be pleasurable, must flow smoothly and fairly swiftly so the words on the page blend into mental thoughts and images. It is the ideas that count. Readers must adapt their reading by adjusting rate to accommodate their familiarity with the text and/or their purpose for reading it. Consider returning to Chapter Two, if you wish, to reexplore these possibilities.

 ## Multicultural Literature for Understanding and Transformation

Culturally diverse students often make up more than half of a school's population. This can provide teachers with incredible opportunities, but only if we are willing to develop a better understanding of diverse cultures. Doing so requires that we develop a curriculum that is culturally relevant, and that we teach it in a culturally responsive manner. There is much to learn here, and reading literature written by authors from different cultures can be helpful. As you read ask yourself how the culture depicted is the same or different from your own. Even with differences, what do you have in common? What follows are some examples from my (Tonjes's) experiences teaching overseas:

 ## FROM THE MULTICULTURAL CLASSROOM

The Correct Answer Is Wrong

While teaching at the University of Guam for a year, at first I had trouble understanding my Palauan student helper. She was extremely quiet and shy, answered only in monosyllables and never questioned anything, even when she didn't understand. I decided to attend an all-university lecture with the intriguing title "The Correct Answer Is Wrong"—given by a renowned Palauan authority. Thus, I began to see where my student helper was coming from. She had been taught never to stand out or speak out—that quietly cooperating with her peers was the only way to be. In class she didn't answer a question even when called on—even when she knew the correct answer. With respect I allowed her and others to write out their answers if they chose or to discuss them within their small groups.

We need to learn more about others' beliefs and values and respect those differences, and when possible, find alternative ways to assess their knowledge and learning.

Empowering Minority Students

To empower minority students we should thus consider how much their language and culture are part of our school curriculum. Whatever existing skills and knowledge they have are the foundation for becoming literate and successful in our language. For example, if Spanish is their first language and they are fluent in it, they can use this to begin to master reading and writing in English (Cummins, 1994).

Getting community participation and collaboration is important too. Parents should be warmly welcomed both in the classroom and out. In the classroom, genuine dialogue between students and teachers both oral and written should be encouraged, as well as cooperative learning with other students. Lectures should play a small role if at all. Avoiding labels is also important.

Labels such as "Hispanic" or "Asian" can hide the actual diversity of immigrants from Mexico, Honduras, Puerto Rico, Vietnam, Korea, Cambodia, China, Japan, and others. Celebrating the diversity all around us can and should be an enriching experience for all.

The Tree of Life

Again at the University of Guam, there were very few Anglo mainlanders, mostly Filipinos, Chamorans, Japanese, Micronesians, and Chinese. I soon discovered that they knew very little about each other's culture so I asked each one to select one aspect of their culture to share with the class—a 20-minute presentation each. This turned out to be an astonishing experience for all of us and one of the highlights of my year there in terms of multicultural understanding. Shown at right is one product of my graduate student, Sisinio, from Truk, Micronesia, and it shows what he considered to be a crucial part of his culture that he wanted to share.

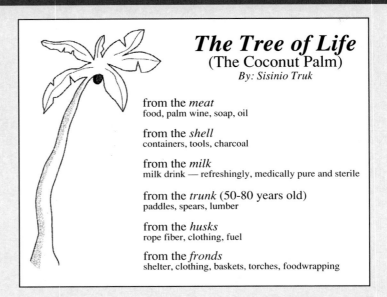

The Tree of Life
(The Coconut Palm)
By: Sisinio Truk

from the *meat*
food, palm wine, soap, oil

from the *shell*
containers, tools, charcoal

from the *milk*
milk drink — refreshingly, medically pure and sterile

from the *trunk* (50-80 years old)
paddles, spears, lumber

from the *husks*
rope fiber, clothing, fuel

from the *fronds*
shelter, clothing, baskets, torches, foodwrapping

Two Poems: "The Beads of Life" and "We Wear the Mask"

Have you ever read something that touched you deep down and that you could never forget? Here is a bit of Native American wisdom that we want to share with you.

The Beads of Life
Nancy Woods

The space between events is where
most of life is lived. Those half-remembered moments
of joy or sadness, fear or disappointment, are merely
beads of life strung together
to make one expanding necklace of experience.

The space between events is where
we grow old. From sunrise to sunset one day lives
as another day emerges from the fluid womb of dawn,
the first bead strung upon
the everlasting thread of life.

The space between events is where
knowledge marries beauty. In quiet reflection
we remember only the colored outline of events,
the black and white of war, the rosiness
that surrounded our first love.

The space between events is why
we go on living. The laughter of a child or
the sigh of wind in a canyon becomes the music
we hear expanding in our hearts each time
we gather one more bead of life.

Frank Howell

From *Dancing Moons* by Nancy Wood and Illustrated by Frank Howell, copyright Illus. © 1995 Frank Howell. Used by permission of Random House Children's Books, a division of Random House, Inc.

In the spirit of her friends and teachers of the New Mexico pueblos, the noted, award-winning poet shares her knowledge of Native American wisdom. Her poems show her deep appreciation of the magical and complex world around us. Frank Howell is a well-known Southwestern artist who can evoke the grandeur of nature and ourselves.

Another great poet, Paul Lawrence Dunbar, gives us a powerful message. Here is something to ponder as you read it—this poet is African American. How might this affect the meaning here? We might decide he is speaking mostly for the down-trodden, like so many of the blacks in the era in which he lived. Knowing about a poet's life helps us to read between the lines, inferring meanings not always directly stated.

We Wear the Mask

We wear the mask
  That grins and lies
It hides our cheeks
  And shades our eyes—
This debt we pay to human guile
With torn and bleeding hearts
  We smile
And mouth with Myriad Subtleties.

Why should the world be over-wise
In counting all our tears and sighs?
Nay, let them see us while we wear
the mask.

We smile, but O great Christ, our cries
To thee from tortured souls arise.
We sing, but oh, the clay is vile.
Beneath our feet, and long the miles.
But let the world dream otherwise.
We wear the mask.

Integrating Folklore into a Middle School Cross-Cultural Unit

Unit study is a vital part of many content-area classrooms. As you already know, the first thing in planning a unit is to establish a theme and a rationale; then identify important concepts. Each concept can then be divided into subtopics, deciding which are most crucial, relevant to the theme. A list of related literature (trade books) is made and a variety of activities are designed for each. Finally, a calendar of events that includes these activities is developed including the chosen literature.

An integrated cross-cultural study combining English and social studies classes in middle school, for example, can be a significant learning experience. Traditional literature shows us cultural and psychological beliefs of our own as well as cultures around the world. Folk literature or folklore, mythology, legends, fables all give us a glimpse into past beliefs and what might have been. The style used rich language and many language patterns that need to be retained. Major themes are usually the power of love or mercy or kindness. Motifs or patterns, the smallest part of a tale, can exist independently. Comparing these motifs to other cultures' folktales can be an interesting beginning to cross-cultural studies. Here are some examples:

- *Germany*—wicked enchantments and magical transformation often with elves, dwarfs, and devils.
- *Scandinavia*—often reflect the harsh elements of the northern climate.
- *French*—the earliest recorded and the most sophisticated and adult, usually not of the poor (considered by some to be the soap operas of that day).
- *Russian*—contains tasks, tricks, and transformations and are often longer, more complicated, filled with stories of poor but lucky men.
- *Jewish*—have poignancy, wit, ironic humor unmatched in other folklore.
- *Middle East and India*—the cradle of civilization and the birthplace of many of our stories, such as Arabian Nights and Aladdin.
- *Asia*—an increasing number of folktales from Japan, China, Korea, and Vietnam.
- *Africa*—a rich bounty of tales with more Caldecott awards for illustrations than any other culture. Storytelling is highly developed especially in West Africa, with an aural cadence that is unique.
- *North America*—Native American, Eskimo and Hawaiian tales—all originally from here. African American tales came from West Africa originally. There are modified tales from Europe. Originating here are tall tales, legends, and other Americana (e.g., Davey Crockett, Buffalo Bill, Johnny Appleseed).

Workshop 12.2	**A Classroom Visit** Visit a content classroom at the level you now teach or intend to teach. After observing for one period, ask the teacher what specific strategies are used to meet the diversity of cultures in the student population. What works? Why? What doesn't work? Why? Write a brief report of what you observed and what the teacher shared with you, including your reactions. Bring this to the next class to discuss with your group. Have a recorder list what appeared to be successful strategies for meeting and celebrating diversity. The designated artist in your group can then make a poster for this list.

Sharing Multicultural Understandings

Following an introduction (preferably by a librarian) on what to look for in reading various multicultural trade books and after students have had the opportunity to explore some of the titles listed later in this chapter, divide into groups of no more than five. Each participant selects a trade book title representing another culture from the others and with the librarian's help obtains a copy for reading. Two weeks later each group meets again in a Content-Area Literature Circle to discuss their particular insights into the various cultures. Notes are taken by a designated recorder and the reporter then shares highlights from the notes with the entire class. A large wall chart might then be assembled to assimilate data.

Locating Appropriate Materials

Text vs. Trade Books

Our content texts give us a distilled version of concepts and general information. The emphasis is on key facts, general effects, and a broad view of the topic at hand. *The Celestine Prophecy* by James Redfield (1998) could have been dull and dry, except that interwoven throughout was an adventure/mystery story that was hard to put down. You had to find out what was happening next. How many texts do we feel that way about?

Because youngsters learn to read mostly from stories, it is not surprising that in the transition to expository (seeking to explain) writing some find it difficult to make the transfer.

Using Trade Books in Content Classrooms

We use trade books in content classrooms:

- To increase vocabulary.
- To bring text information up to date.
- To build interest—writing styles, formats can be entertaining as well as informative.
- To extend ideas in the text—filling out details, content.
- To enhance content schema and make connections to their other reading.
- To meet the needs of diverse learners—trade books are found at many reading levels.

Most teachers have these objectives in mind but find it difficult to implement. You may say, "But I don't have the time." The answer is to choose key themes and concepts upon which to concentrate. By doing this, some text sections will not then be stressed over others. The upside is that readers will have a clearer, more detailed grasp of what you have deemed most important, and will be more interested and motivated than before.

One way to use trade books with texts is to activate students' mental schema (picture in their head) when previewing a unit or lesson. You read a section aloud or show a picture book to capture their attention and begin to build on what they already know. You may ask them to speculate about the topic, sharing what they do know. One way is to use the strategy K-W-L explained in Chapter Seven.

You might try to collect sets of books, which include some of the major concepts you will be stressing—such as civil rights, uses of the environment, fun with math puzzles, sports heroes, renaissance artists. The sets might include novels, photo essays, journals, biographies, and picture books, as well as informational texts written at a lower level.

Leveled Books

In Chapter Five, the chapter on assessing the readability of a text, we discussed three computer-generated readability assessment systems that are available online. They are the *Lexile Scale* (http://www.lexile.com) operated by Metametrics Inc., the Degrees of Reading Power (http://tasaliteracy.com) operated by Touchstone Applied Science Associates Inc., and the ATOS Readability Formula (http://www.renlearn.com/) a product of Renaissance Learning, the same company that created Accelerated Reader. All three of these companies are vying for classroom teachers who are looking for guidance in choosing books that are appropriate for their students. With all three systems, books are rated at different ability levels, which may then be matched to the ability levels of students as determined by their scores on reading tests. The term, leveled books, at least in theory, means that by matching students' scores with book readability scores, a match is made and the reading field is leveled.

For example, many trade books today are designated by Lexile levels. For example: 850–1000 = sixth-grade reading level such as C. S. Lewis, *The Lion, the Witch and the Wardrobe*. An example of grades seven, eight, and nine is *Island of the Blue Dolphins*, grades nine and ten *The Hobbit,* and eleven and twelve *Navaho Code Talkers.* Fountas and Pinnell (2001, pp. 590–630) has an extensive listing of these books for reference and planning purposes. However, before you go online to learn your options, please do take a few minutes to review the strengths and weaknesses of readability formulae, as detailed in Chapter Five.

While you are in Chapter Five, do note that there are several other tools you may use to match print with reader, such as the Fry Readability Graph, the ICL Checklist Buffet, the Qualitative Assessment of Text Difficulty, and, when in a pinch, Allington's Quick Check. Yet another alternative is Marie Clay's Reading Recovery Approach. Her seven factors relating to text difficulty are listed here:

1. *Book and Print Features*—Book length, print size, amount of print on page, illustrations, diagrams
2. *Content*—Familiar topic and student interest
3. *Vocabulary*—Range and variety of words, phonetically regular, technical, multi-syllabic—of Latin/Greek origin
4. *Complex Language*—Similar to student's oral language, longer sentences, figurative language, symbolism
5. *Sentence Complexity*—Sentence length with imbedded clauses
6. *Text Structure*—Genre (type), complex text structure, complicated plots, abstract
7. *Themes and Ideas*—Mature themes, ideas

When considering levels of informational texts, look for these four qualities:

1. Accuracy—Facts current and complete
2. Organization—Information clear, logical
3. Design—Eye-catching, appropriate illustrations with explanations for each
4. Style—Lively, stimulating, engaging, curiosity and wonder

When selecting trade books for English language learners, we need to consider not only students' reading level, but also their interest level. This is true for both text and trade books. When time is limited, eyeball the text—look at length, print size, amount of print on a page, graphics, topic familiarity, word length, high-frequency words, and interest.

Informational books are organized around description, sequence, compare/contrast, cause/effect, and problem/solution. These may be helpful in making selections, and then, if illustrated to students, helpful to improve their understanding of what they read. Here are a few schematics that illustrate their organization:

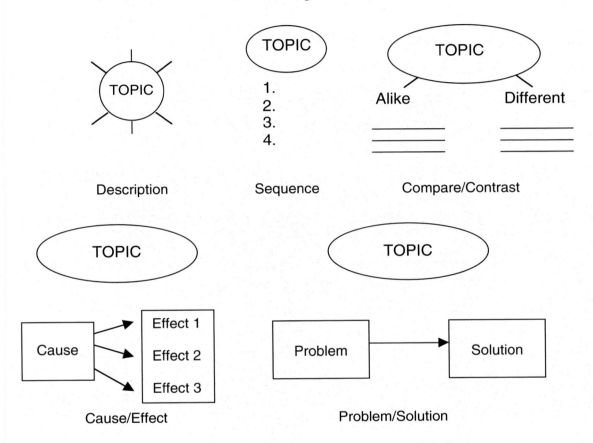

Other Sources of Help in Selecting Appropriate Trade Books

A Guide to Locating Content-Specific Literature

To find current high-quality trade books in your content area, here are a few suggestions:

Social Studies

The annual listing of notable children's trade books in the field of social studies. April/May issue of *Social Education* or http://www.ness.org/resources/notable/home.html

Making multicultural connections through trade books, http://www/mcps.k12md.us/curriculum/socialstudiesMBD/Books-begin.html

Science

Published yearly in the March issue of *Science and Children* is a list of excellent science books, or from the National Science Teachers Association: NSTA Outstanding Science Trade Books for Students K–12, http://www.nsta.org/ostbc

From Reading Online, a review of 13 trade books for use in the content area of science, http://www.readingonline.org/reviews/literature/andersen

Math

http://www.luc.edu/schools/eduation/csipdc/2bib.htm
This is a bibliography written for young people that teaches and reinforces math concepts organized by topics (e.g., algebra, geometry, miscellaneous).

Mathematician Bibliographies online:
http://www.groups.dcs.st-and.ac.uk/~history/brogindex.html
Biographic and historic information on mathematicians from ancient time to the present.

Mr. Brandenburg's Books About Math, http://mathforum.com/t2t/faq/brandenburg.html
An extensive collection of math and related trade books to supplement high school math.

Language Arts

Association for Library Service to children:
http://www.ala.org/ala/alsc/alscresources/forchildren/childrenfamilies.htm
Information on collections of most highly regarded children and adolescent literature and trade books.

A Guide to Locating Multicultural Literature

African American

Angelou, M. (1994). *Maya Angelou poems.* New York: Random House.

Busby, M. (1992). *Daughters of Africa: An international anthology of words and writings by women of African descent from the ancient Egyptian to the present.* New York: HarperCollins.

Giovanni, N. (1994). *Racism 101.* New York: HarperCollins.

Haley, A. C. (1976). *Roots.* New York: Dell.

Hansberry, L. (1959). *A raisin in the sun.* New York: Random House.

Haskins, J. (1987). *Black music in America: A history through its people.* New York: Crowell.

McKissack, P. (1989). *Jesse Jackson.* New York: Scholastic.

Morrison, T. (1987). *Beloved.* New York: Knopf.

Myers, W. D. (2001). *Monster.* New York: Harper.

Payton, A. (2003). *Cry the beloved country.* New York: Scribner.

Sterling, D. (1987). *Freedom train: The story of Harriet Tubman.* New York: Scholastic.

Taylor, M. (1996). *Roll of thunder hear my cry.* New York: Dell.

X., Malcom. (1987). *The autobiography of Malcom X.* New York: Ballantine.

Asian American

Crew, L. (1989). *Children of the river*. New York: Dell.

Huynh, Q. N. (1986). *Land I lost: Adventures of a boy in Vietnam*. New York: Harper & Row.

Lee, M. (2001). *Finding my voice*. New York: Trophy.

Sone, M. (1979). *Nisei daughter*. Seattle: University of Washington Press.

Tan, A. (1990). *The joy luck club*. New York: Ivy Books.

Yep, L. (1990). *Child of the owl*. New York: Harper & Row.

Hispanic American

Anaya, R. (1972). *Bless me ultima*. Berkeley, CA: TQS Publications.

Bernardo, A. (2003). *Jumping off to freedom*. Houston: The Gale Group.

Carlson, L. (1994). *Cool salsa: Bilingual poems on growing up in the United States*. New York: Ballantine Publishing Group.

Cisneros, S. (1991). *The house on mango street*. Houston: Reed Business Information.

Cruz, V. H. (1988). *Rhythm, content & flavor*. Houston: Arte Publico Press.

Day, F. A. *Latino and latina voices in literature for children and teenagers*. Portsmouth, NH: Heinemann.

Garver, S., & McGuire P. (1981). *Coming to North American from Mexico, Cuba, and Puerto Rico*. New York: Delacorte Press.

Mohr, N. (1999). *Felita*. New York: Dell.

Soto, G. (1993). *Small faces*. Houston: Laurel Leaf Books.

Islamic American

Idilibi, U. (1999). *Grandfather's tale*. London: Quartet Books.

Staples, S. (1989). *Shabanu: Daughter of the wind*. New York: Laurel Leaf Books.

Jewish American

Brooks, J. (1990). *Naked in winter*. New York: Orchard Books.

Frank, A. (1993). *The diary of a young girl*. New York: Bantam Books.

Grossman, M., & Dabba, F. (2000). *My secret camera: Life in the Lodz Ghetto*. New York: Gulliver Books.

Klein, G. W. (1995). *All but my life*. New York: Hill & Wang.

Mazer, N. F. (1999). *Good night maman*. New York: Harcourt Children's Books.

Potok, C. (1987). *The chosen*. New York: Fawcett Publications.

Sanfield, S. (1991). *The feather merchants and other tales of the fools of Chelm*. New York: Orchard Books.

Weidman, J. (1961). *My father sits in the dark and other selected stories*. New York: Random House.

Native American

Bouchard, D. (2003). *The elders are watching*. Vancouver, BC: Raincoast Books.

Bruchac, J. (1977). *The dreams of Jesse Brown*. Austin: Cold Mountain Press.

Erdoes, R., & Ortiz, A. (1984). *American Indian myths and legends*. New York: Pantheon Books.

Hernandez, I. (1992). *Heartbeat drumbeat*. Houston: Arte Publico.

Morris, N., & Morris, T. (1985). *Featherboy and the buffalo: Tales of the Native Americans*. Englewood Cliffs, NJ: Silver Burdett Press.

Thom, J. (1990). *Panther in the sky*. New York: Ballantine Books.

Americans with Disabilities

Crutcher, C. (2002). *Athletic shorts*. New York: Harper Tempest.

Dorris, M. (1990). *The broken cord*. New York: HarperCollins.

Koertge, R. (2002). *Stoner and spaz*. Cambridge: Candlewick.

Jones, R. (1976). *The acorn people*. New York: Dell.

Philbrick, R. (1993). *Freak the mighty*. New York: Scholastic.

Rubio, G. H. (1998). *Icy sparks*. New York: Penguin Books.

A Guide to Locating Young Adult Literature

Any literature read by young adults is considered Young Adult Literature (YAL). The world of books written for teens and preteens is exceptionally rich. They can do many things for young people such as what Miller (1993) found: YAL improved at-risk students' achievement and self-concepts by enlarging on basic text facts. These books include positive qualities as well as social issues, which are addressed.

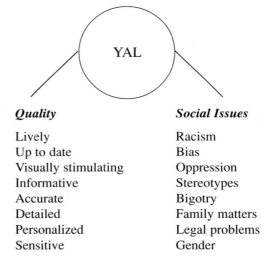

The November issue each year of the *Journal of Adolescent and Adult Literacy* publishes an annotated list of books chosen by a team of young adults. These include math, social studies, English, science, art, music, and sports. A sample for ages 12–20 is given on the next page.

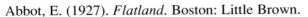

Abbot, E. (1927). *Flatland*. Boston: Little Brown.

Adair, G. (1989). *George Washington Carver*. Broomal, PA: Chelsea House.

Anno, M. (1983). *Anno's USA*. New York: Phibomel. (a picture book)

Christopher, M. (1999). *At the plate with Mark McGuire*. Boston: Little Brown.

Corbett, S. (1998). *Venus to the hoop: A Gold medal year in women's basketball*. New York: Anchor Books.

Croll, C. (1996). *Redoute: The man who painted flowers*. New York: Putnam.

Downing, J. (1991). *Mozart tonight*. New York: Simon & Schuster.

Duplacey, J. (1999). *Muhammad Ali: Athlete, activist, ambassador*. Warwick, CA: Woodside Publishing.

Dygard, T. (1999). *Forward pass*. Minneapolis, MN: Econ-clad Books.

Herrin, L. (1989). *The unwritten chronicles of Robert E. Lee*. New York: St. Martins Press.

Hoffman, P. (1998). *Archimedes revenge—The joys and perils of mathematics*. New York: Fawcell.

Horosko, M. (1994). *Sleeping beauty: The story of the ballet*. New York: Atheneum.

Kalman, E. (1995). *Tchaikovsky discovers America*. New York: Scholastic.

Kidd, R., Kessler, J., Kidd, J., & Morin, K. *Scientists of the 20th century*. Phoenix: Ory Press.

LeTord, B. (1995). A *blue butterfly: A story about Claude Monet*. New York: Doubleday.

Macy, S. (1996). W*inning ways: A photo history of American women in sports*. New York: Henry Holt.

Manceux, M. (1994). *Jazz: My music, my people*. New York: Alfred Knopf.

Mandela, N. (1996). *Mandela: An illustrated autobiography*. Boston: Little Brown.

Pappas, T. (1991). *Math talk: Mathematical ideas in poems for two voices*. San Carlos, CA: Wide World/Tetra.

Peat, F. D. (1989). *Cold fusion: The making of a scientific controversy*. Chicago: Contemporary Books.

Preston, R. (1994). *The hot zone*. New York: Random House (Ebola Virus).

Schattschneider, P. (1990). *Visions of symmetry: Notebooks, periodic drawings and related works of M. C. Escher*. New York: W. H. Freeman.

Skills, L. (1993). *Visions: Stories about women artists*. Morton Grove: Albert Whitman.

Stanley, D. (1996). *Leonardo da Vinci*. New York: Morrow.

Thomas, D. (1995). *Math projects in the computer age*. New York: Watts.

Thompson, W. (1990). *Ludwig von Beethoven*. New York: Penguin.

Van Cleave, J. (1989). *Chemistry for every kid: 101 experiments that really work*. New York: Wiley.

Warr, J. (1990). *Designing for a livable planet: The eco-action guide to positive ecology*. New York: Harper Collins.

An Annotated Literature Bibliography: Some Personal Choices

The following is a brief annotated bibliography of books for secondary students. Some are more difficult than others.

Math/Science

- Abbott, E. A. (1884). *Flatland: A parable of spiritual dimensions.* Rockport, MA: One World Publications.

This classic science fiction novel portrays a strange land whose inhabitants consist of two-dimensional geometric figures. This allegory is a humorous lesson in Geometry, a creative exploration of high dimensions—psychological and religious. Here the world of mathematics comes to life and expands our way of thinking and experiencing the world. *Flatland* was first published under the title *A. Square. The Saturday Review of Literature* called it "One of the best things of its kind ever written."

- Devlin, K. (2002). *The math gene: How mathematical thinking evolved and why numbers are like gossip.* New York: Basic Books.

This is essential reading for those fascinated, angry at, or frightened by mathematics. *The Math Gene* tells us how our pattern-making abilities allow us to do mathematical reasoning. For the teacher, the author suggests ways to improve our mathematical skills and offers some intriguing puzzles to solve. *Discover* magazine calls this one of the best science books of 2000.

- Livio, M. (2002). *The golden ratio: The story of phi, the world's most astonishing number.* New York: Broadway Books.

The history and mystery of the remarkable number phi ("fee") serves as a springboard to the amazing world of math. It is described so that both math lovers and haters can enjoy the wonder. The number 1.6180339887 is called the "Golden Ratio," defined by Euclid over 2,000 years ago. It has appeared in mollusk shells, crystals, psychology experiments, Leonardo da Vinci's *Mona Lisa.* Debussy was a phi-fixated musician. The author quotes from Shakespeare, Keats, Einstein, and Galileo and the writing of Pythagoras, Kepler, and others. Livio is head of the Science Division of the Space Telescope Science Institute.

- Sacks, O. (2002). *Uncle Tungsten: Memories of a chemical boyhood.* New York: Vintage Books.

This eloquent and charming memoir weaves together chemistry and boyhood experiences of the author with ease and humor. Written by a practicing New York neurologist, it tells of his love affair with science from early years of an often harrowing childhood. It was chosen as *The New York Times* Book Review—Editors Choice. Young Oliver is exiled to a sadistic, dreary boarding school to escape the World War II London blitz. Returning four years later, he visits his "Uncle Tungsten" whose factory produces tungsten-filament lightbulbs. Oliver then proceeds to set up his own home chemical laboratory.

- Seife, C. (2000). *Zero: The biography of a dangerous idea.* New York: Penguin Books.

This is the story of Zero and its power from its birth in ancient times to its growth in the East, its struggle for acceptance to its present threat to modern physics. Infinity and Zero are inseparable and essential to math. Today Zero is at the core of the largest scientific controversies ever—the quest for the theory of everything. Written with elegance and wit, it is truly enlightening. A *New York Times* Notable Book and Winner of the Pen/Martha Albrand Award.

Social Studies

- Chavez, D. (1994). *Face of an angel*. New York: Warner Books.

Rudolfo Anaya, author of *Bless me, Ultima,* called this award-winning novel "as delicious as a hot New Mexican meal." *The Dallas Morning News* exclaimed it as "Read-it Again, Read-it Aloud, Tell-all-Your friends fabulous." It is the raucous story of an Hispanic family in a small New Mexican town. Her characters stay with you long after you have finished the book. Winner of the American Book Award and Alternate Selection of Book of the Month Club.

- Flake, S. G. (1998). *The skin I'm in*. New York: Hyperion Books.

A black girl, Maleeka, with low self-esteem encounters her new teacher who she feels is worse off than she. Miss Saunders has a rare, blotched skin condition and serves as a mirror to Maleeka. Maleeka has to stand up to other students, learn to accept friendship, and accept her own skin color. Winner of the 1999 Coretta Scott King John Steptoe Award for new authors. ALA Best Book for Young Adults, 1999. This funny, clever story shows adolescent readers a world rarely represented in secondary fiction.

- Kingsolver, B. (1998). *The poison wood Bible*. New York: New Directions.

The story is told by five female narrators—a missionary's wife and daughters in the Congo in 1960 to "Convert the African heathens." The story shows the effects of colonialism on the country and society. Her use of language is beautiful; character development is outstanding with their complex interrelationships. Critics call this a modern parable.

- Klein, G. W. (1957). *All but my life*. New York: Hill and Wang.

This powerful book is a true story about survival by hope alone. The Nazis took from Gerda all but her life—every family member, every friend died in the concentration camps. Despite terrible experiences like being forced on a thousand mile winter march, she was able to begin a new life based on faith and love. Some critics compare this to The Diary *of Anne Frank.*

- Morris, N. (2003). *The atlas of Islam: People, daily life and traditions.* New York: Barron's Educational Series.

A laviously illustrated atlas that depicts the development of a great world faith from the Prophet Muhammad to today. Covered are basic beliefs, forms of worship, geography, historical figures, empires, festivals, music, art, and more. This is an easy study of a world we all need to know more about today. It is appropriate for all ages and contains a wealth of information.

- Paulsen, G. (1987). *The crossing*. New York: Dell.

This is a life and death novel of a Juárez, Mexico orphan who decides to risk an illegal crossing of the Rio Grande to the United States where he has an explosive encounter with a Vietnam veteran. In terse prose Paulsen shows the abject poverty, acceptance of life's inequities.

- Rees, C. (2002). *Sorceress*. Cambridge: Candlewick Press.

This novel follows the collection of documents known as "The Mary Papers," which were hidden inside a colonial-era quilt. Mary Newbury's diary gives us a clear account of a 14-year-olds' life in the New England Puritan Settlement. Mary was forced to flee from England in 1659 after seeing her grandmother executed for witchcraft. Relive those days in this well-written, well-documented account of life over 400 years ago. This is a sequel to the best-selling novel, *Witch Child.*

- Soto, G. (2000). *Nickle and dime*. Albuquerque: New Mexico Press.

The detailed lives of three Hispanic men are vividly described by Gary Soto. He does not fall into the trap of politicizing his subjects, having them blame the church, or Anglos, or anyone for what happens. Out of a job, Roberto ends up in an abandoned Quonset hut and then the street. He meets poet Silver Mendoza and Gus Hernandez, also down on their luck. He brings to life their dauntless optimism, their desperate ingenuity, their hunger. The men are always looking for a way just to earn enough for a cup of coffee, with lots of cream and sugar. The author is Distinguished Professor of Creative Writing at the University of California, Riverside.

- Yen Mah, A. (1999). *Chinese Cinderella: The true story of an unwanted daughter*. New York: Dell Laurel.

The author returns to her roots to show us an authentic portrait of 20th century China. Adeline's powerful family considers her bad luck after her mother dies in childbirth. When her father remarries, her stepmother treats her with disdain. This detailed, true story describes the author's childhood up to age fourteen. It has been chosen as an ALA Best Book for Young Adults.

Content-Specific Websites with Literature Resources

Arts

- The Kennedy Center's Arts Edge
  http://www.artsedge.kennedycenter.org/artsedge.html

- The National Endowment for The Arts
  http://www.arts.endow.gov/

English

- Literature Resources
  http://vos.ucsb.edu/shultle/eng-mod.html

- Public Broadcasting Service (PBS) website
  http://www.pbs.org/

Foreign Language

- Elementary Spanish Curriculum
  http://www.veen.com/veen/leslie/curriculum/

Mathematics

- Math Ed.: Mathematics Education Resources
  http://www-hpcc.astro.washington.edu/scied/math.html

- Math Magic
  http://forum.swarthmore.edu/mathmagic/

Science

- Environmental Education
  http://www.eelink.net.

- The Official Website of NASA
  http://www.nasa.gov/

Social Studies

- Russian History
  http://www.friends-partners.org/oldfriends/mes/russia/history.html

- Interactive Egyptian History Site
  http://www.iwebquest.com/egypt/ancientegypt.htm

Vocational Education

- Office of Vocational and Adult Education (OVAE)
  http://www/ed.gov/offices/OVAE

- Links to Vocational Education Resources
  http://pegasus.cc.ucf.edu/~sorg/vocation.html

A Guide to Trade Book Selection Guides

The Alan review. Urbana, IL: National Council of Teachers of English. Published three times a year.

Book links: Connecting books, libraries and classrooms. American Library Association. Published six times a year.

Books for the teenage. Office of Adult Services, New York Public Library. Published annually.

Christenbury, L. (Ed.). (1995). *Books for you: A book list for senior high students* (11th ed.). Urbana, IL: NCTE.

Gillespie, J. T. (1991). *Best books for junior high readers.* New Providence, NJ: Bowker.

Helbig, A., & Perkins, A. R. (1994). *This land is your land: A guide to multicultural literature for children and young adults.* Westport, CT: Greenwood Press.

Montenego, V. J., O'Connell, S. M., & Wolff, K. (1986). *AAA's science book list: 1978–1986.*

Notable children's trade book in the field of social studies. National Council for the Social Studies. Published in the Spring issue of *Social Education.*

Walker, E. (Ed.). (1988). *Book bait: Detailed notes on adult books popular with young people* (4th ed.). Chicago: American Library Association.

Williams, H. E. (1991). *Books by African-American authors and illustrators for children and young adults.* Chicago: American Library Association.

Young adults choices list. International Reading Association.

Graphic Novels, Fandom, and Anime

As part of an increasingly visual culture, we might consider the idea of using graphic novels in our classes (Schwarz, 2002). These include both fiction and nonfiction text with pictures—"comics" in book format, and offer variety that appeals to students. They may introduce students to literature and be a bridge to other classics. They also can inspire writing assignments useful in social studies, art, science, math, and English classrooms.

The 101 Best Graphic Novels, edited by Stephen Weiner (2001) describes and rates novels for age appropriateness.

A recent addition to multi-literacies is fan fiction, a popular cultural phenomenon involving electronic exchanges between teenagers (Manzo, Manzo, & Thomas, 2005).

It is built around the new art form, "Anime"—a Japanese animation. It offers a common frame of reference and social connection for those young people of different linguistic and cultural backgrounds.

There is a question as to whether we as teachers should consider getting involved in something that may pass quickly or that teens do not wish us to be involved in, but it is good to be aware of this pop fiction, available in comics, video, etc.

 ## Content Classroom Activities

Several activities that may help in integrating literature into content classrooms are described below. These include Read-Alouds, Book Talks, Text Walk, Anticipation Guides, Picture Books for Adolescents, SSR and DEAR, Study Reading Circles, Response Journals, and Curriculum-Based Reader's Theatre (CBRT).

Read-Alouds (Richardson, 2000; Trelease, 1995)

When teachers talk about trade books in class and read aloud from them, they are modeling how experts in that particular field enjoy reading. There are a number of reasons to use this activity for 10 to 20 minutes, perhaps once a week.

- Introduce a topic
- Develop interest in the study topic
- Add variety
- Tie to practical applications
- Focus attention and thought
- Extend student knowledge
- Share humor when it exists
- Show importance of literacy

It is important to select what you like and think your students will enjoy—something perhaps with unusual action, humor, or strong emotion. You may edit out too lengthy descriptions, and should note what might be discussed afterwards. This means previewing the book in question.

As you read, make eye contract with each student at some point, standing where all can see you.

Practice reading aloud with expression, varying intonation, and never rushing. For ELLs, Read-Alouds introduce students to syntactic patterns, idioms, and general vocabulary as well as important cultural information. Furthermore, intonation of voice and gesture help with comprehension.

Here are a few suggestions for grades 6, 7, and 8 that have proven to be appropriate and of interest to students when teachers read aloud.

Grade 6

L'Engle, M. (1962). *A wrinkle in time*. New York: Dell.
Lowry, L. (1989). *Number the stars*. New York: Dell.
Lowry, L. (1999). *The giver*. New York: Dell.

Grade 7

Lewis, C. S. (1994). *The lion, the witch and the wardrobe*. New York: Harpertrophy.
Sachar, L. (1995). *Holes*. New York: Random House.

Grade 8

Clark, T. (1992). *The house that crack built*. San Francisco: Chronicle Books.
Frank, A. (1993). *Ann Frank: The diary of a young girl*. New York: Bantam Books.
Taylor, M. (1991). *Roll of thunder, Hear my cry*. New York: Penguin Books.

Book Talks (Alverman and Phelps, 2002, p. 384)

Book talks can replace Read-Alouds or be combined to capture students' attention and interest in a forthcoming topic. Like Read-Alouds this can be very brief, not taking up much class time, but can pay dividends in terms of motivation and willingness to delve deeper into a topic. Sometimes it may be appropriate to give a brief author biography. Here is an example of an author talk that you might give to your class. Many of your students will already know his famous short poem.

Carl Sandburg—Born January 6, 1878 in Galesburg, Illinois, died July 22, 1967. Known as one of our greatest writers, his poetry is a celebration of America. He saw poetry in everything from the common place to the majestic. He wrote more than 800 poems. Some were probing like "When ice turns back into water does it remember it was ice?" Some were whimsical—"If you ask your mother for one fried egg and she gives you two —who is better at arithmetic—you or your mother?" He can be funny, serene, serious, or sad. Here is his most famous poem.

FOG

The fog comes
On little cat feet.

It sits looking
Over harbor and city
On silent haunches
And then moves on.

During his lifetime he worked as a laborer, secretary, newspaper reporter, political organizer, historian, lecturer, and collector and singer of folksongs.

He spent 30 years preparing the huge six-volume biography of Abraham Lincoln and in 1940 received the Pulitzer Prize in History for the last four volumes—*Abraham Lincoln: The War Years*. In 1951 he received his second Pulitzer for *The Complete Poems*. We think you will enjoy reading more of his works.

Or perhaps, if you are lucky, you have met a writer and can create a poster to share with your students. For example:

Robert Frost
1874–1963
"America's Best Loved Poet"

The Pasture (Inviting us—"you come too")
Mending Wall ("good fences make good neighbors")
The Death of the Hired Man (A story—167 lines)
The Road Not Taken ("I took the one less traveled by, and that has made the difference")
Christmas Trees (A Christmas circular letter)
Birches (A boy swinging birches down—but not to stay as ice storms do)
Two Witches—I—The Witch of Coos (A scary Halloween story)
Fire and Ice ("Some say the world will end in fire, some say in ice")
Stopping by Woods on a Snowy Evening ("the woods are lovely, dark and deep")

Robert Frost was born in San Francisco, but moved east to Massachusetts when he was eleven, after his father died. As a young man he started work as a

(continued)

(continued from previous page)

farmer but never liked it. It was 1894 when his first poem appeared in national publication. He was working on his final volume just before his death in 1963. That means that more than 350 poems, some lengthy, were published during three quarters of a century.

I knew Robert Frost, but at age 17 I had not yet fully realized the significance of that fact. When I was in boarding school in Littleton/Bethlehem, New Hampshire, he lived nearby and was invited to school to spend the weekend with us—58 girls and faculty. It was winter with deep snow on the ground and bitter cold. When he arrived, we were having lunch and I happened to be at the round table facing a small garden. Across the way was the window to the Bishop's guest bedroom. Not aware that he could be seen, my first glimpse of the great poet was in his long woolen underwear, with a foot on a hassock, cutting his toenails! (I really could not have made that up.) Over the years my students of all ages have loved that story as he was real to them. It was a thrill to sit in the music room after dinner, with Robert Frost seated in a deep arm chair, his beloved dog lying quietly by his side while he read some of his favorite poems to us—an unforgettable time.

Marian J. Tonjes, 2004

Text Walk

Here is a scaffolding technique to guide your students through a piece of literature or text chapter so that they have key concepts, a general picture, and important vocabulary before reading. This sets up readers who are having difficulties with reading to succeed.

Teachers can:

1. Read the text to get an overview of key ideas, terms, storyline, etc.
2. Using pictures or graphics as prompts ask students to predict what it will be about using some of the key words they will need.
3. Go through the text telling key ideas.

This strategy is especially useful for those who need more support. By observing responses you will have a valuable assessment tool. It can be adapted to all grade levels.

Picture Books for Adolescents

This is an area that social studies, foreign language, and English teachers especially can consider. Take John Goodall's (1978) *The English Village*, a wordless picture book that is historically accurate according to many English historians. Starting in 1400 every 100 years the same two scenes depict the changes of the village square, castle, church, and home, also showing costumes and customs. It requires comparing and contrasting as we study each page and half page, returning to earlier centuries to note the changes. This book can leave a lasting mental image and speculation as to whether some things have really improved or deteriorated over time. Many picture books will appeal to adults as well as secondary students. Here is a sampling:

Picture Books for Adolescents

Anno, M. (1982). *Anno's counting house*. New York: Philomel.

Anno, M. (1989). *Anno's math games II*. New York: Philomel.

Chekhov, A. (1991). *Kashtanka*. Orlando, FL: Harcourt Brace & Company.

Goodall, J. (1979). *The story of an English village.* New York: Atheneum.

Macauley, D. (1973). *Cathedral.* New York: Houghton Mifflin.

Macauley, D. (1975). *Pyramid.* New York: Houghton Mifflin.

Macauley, D. (1977). *Castle.* New York: Houghton Mifflin.

Maruki, T. (1982). *Hiroshima no pika.* New York: Lothrop, Lee & Sheppard.

Schwartz, D. M. (1985). *How much is a million?* New York: Scholastic.

Schwartz, D. M. (1989). *If you made a million.* New York: Scholastic.

Ventura, P. (1987). *Venice, birth of a city.* New York: Putnam.

Wisniewski, D. (1996). *Golem.* New York: Clairon.

Sustained Reading and Writing

Research shows that most American students spend less than 20 minutes a day reading printed materials outside of school. It is difficult to develop an appreciation for something we don't do. Studies have shown that providing a fixed period of time for students to read materials of their own choosing, either for pleasure or for information, improves students' attitudes toward reading (Yoon, 2002). With the goal of cultivating a love of reading, the in-class activities named Sustained Silent Reading (SSR) was invented. In each case, there are three guiding principles that are usually followed: (1) students are free to select their own reading materials; (2) teachers model the value of reading by participating during the time allotted; and (3) accountability for what has been read is not required. See what one high school did with SSR:

FROM THE CONTENT CLASSROOM

Promoting SSR

A high school in the Northwest decided some years ago to promote SSR (Sustained Silent Reading) throughout the school. The reading specialist started a campaign with parents to collect appropriate paperbacks for every classroom and content area. Part of the summer was spent with helpers, sorting and distributing books—sports stories to PE classes, stories set in France or Spain to foreign language classes, science fiction to science, books like *Flatlands* to geometry, contemporary novels to English. SSR tee shirts and buttons were distributed. Twenty minutes Monday, Wednesday, Friday were set aside for the entire school to read silently—staff and all. Signs at the doors said, "Do Not Disturb from 10–10:20 for SSR." After a few weeks the kitchen staff complained they didn't have enough time to prepare lunch so they were excused. Then shortly thereafter, they came back to say they missed it and would like to resume. The librarian noted an increase in library use for pleasure reading, and one formerly obsteferous student had discovered the author Robert Ludlum and no longer made trouble because his nose was in the suspense thriller.

Today it is often called DEAR (Drop Everything and Read) but it is almost the same idea. No one interrupts or leaves their seats. The teacher also reads for pleasure, a timer is used if a school bell isn't available and no book reports or accountability is required. Excluding magazines is an option.

SSR and DEAR are practiced from elementary school through college, thus there are several variations on the sustained reading theme. There is Sustained Reading and Writing (SSR+W) where students are given time to read and/or write and in some instances, they are asked to voluntarily share their writings with their peers. For example, in one diverse inner-city high school students were grouped into smaller learning communities. For SSR time, students were encouraged to choose books from which they could make "real-life" connections. Students were encouraged to keep SSR logs in which they shared their successes and struggles with reading, and the meaning they found in what they had read. The emotional support that students gave and received helped to develop strong bonds in the classroom (Waff & Connell, 2004).

The guiding principle that accountability for reading should not be required is not always followed. For example, in one middle school, teachers contracted with students to encourage them to start and finish "good books" and help regular conferences with them during which student and teacher discussed reading progress (Akmal, 2002). Perhaps this movement towards accountability is because many teachers believe that practice in reading will lead to progress. While we can agree with this viewpoint, it is important to remember that the purpose of SSR is to cultivate a love for reading. Doing so requires that students have time to freely choose those books they want to read, in whatever fashion they enjoy reading them. When teachers and peers model concentration and reflection, without being disturbed or distracted by some other task or requirement, the message that reading is something worth doing is discovered and reinforced.

Study Reading Circles (Literature Circles)

When content classrooms include content literature there are several ways to do it leading to success. First of all you may set up study reading circles that use student-directed cooperative learning groups for reading and sharing. It is necessary to collect sets of four to five appropriate trade books, which you introduce though brief book talks, giving an overview with some possible tantalizing tidbits. Students select one of four sets to form their own cooperative groups. When a group fills up, they must move to another group. Each group helps set up an independent reading schedule and a daily homework assignment is given connected to the reading. At first you lead the discussion until students become more practiced in running their group. Students are given specific roles at first, which may rotate later. Roles can be adapted to a specific content area. Here are a few suggestions. These can be typed as handouts.

a. Discussion Director—Formulates three to five questions for the group to address. These will tie the reading to the text topic and also elicit personal feelings and opinions (e.g., "How did this strengthen your knowledge of our theme?" "What happened that might have further explained this?" "What do you suppose the underlying cause was?" "How did you feel when _____?" "Who can predict what happens next and how it will tie in with our study?").

b. Recorder—Jots down key points only of discussion.

c. Reporter—The group selects one or two points for the reporter to share later with the whole class, using the recorder notes if necessary.

d. Vocabulary Enricher or Word Wizard—Prepares a list of several unfamiliar terms, choosing the best definition in context using the text glossary, dictionary, or thesaurus or getting the group to guess first.

e. Checker—Asks each member whether they completed the assignment and keeps a record, urges active participation, and evaluates each participation using a checklist (e.g., name, job, completed, cooperated, etc.).

f. Creative artist—Uses sketch, song, poem, or skit to enrich or bring closure to the session. They share their vision and images held as they read.

g. Researcher (Investigator)—Expands knowledge of the topic by using the library or the Internet to provide further details or an opposing view.

h. Time and Task—Keeps group focused and watches the time allotted.

   i. Connector—Makes personal life connections "Reminds me of . . . " or connections to the outside world.

   j. Summarizer—Tells main ideas from discussion and summarizes two or three key points in no more than two minutes.

The crucial roles are the discussion leader, recorder, and reporter. Other roles may be added as fits your purpose. The main thing is to give each group member some responsibility for a smoother running group. There is much less chance then of "goofing off." Roles can be rotated daily or weekly.

These circles can be a powerful way to build thinking skills, leadership, and cooperation. Students learn from others what was significant to them, what strategies were used to solve problems, what connections could be made to their own lives, and group process decision making and self-responsibility.

Response Journals (RJ)

Chapter Eight, "Writing to Learn," provides ample information on this classroom activity. We won't go into it here, but please do turn back to Chapter Eight on writing to learn to find meaningful suggestions. RJs personalize learning.

Curriculum-Based Readers Theatre (CBRT)

Flynn (2005) describes an informing and entertaining way to address standards by developing a Curriculum-Based Readers Theatre Script. This approach integrates drama, theatre, writing, reading, speaking, listening, *and* content learning.

Students are asked to create a short script in a particular content area that informs as well as entertains through dialogue. The script is rehearsed and read aloud (not memorized), with emphasis on spoken words and possible gestures.

CBRT scripts are based on content-area topics and written to address prescribed standards—local, state, and national—that require writing in various formats and styles.

Through repeated rehearsals and performance students are able to read text fluently, smoothly, and with expression and this repetition enhances retention.

Start by determining what standards students are required to meet, what they need to know. Distribute a fact sheet or text page or instructions, and ask students to create a context to present the facts through dialogue. Tell them to assign lines to narrators and characters, individual and group voices. This is a creative and challenging endeavor as the script must be interesting, possibly humorous, or containing contemporary references.

Before beginning, students use pre-writing strategies such as clustering, mindmapping, making lists, organizing ideas, etc.

After the first draft is read and critiqued by the teacher and class, it undergoes editing. The final typed draft is photocopied and distributed with individual parts highlighted by the students. These scripts are usually not more than two to three pages, or 5 to 10 minutes performance time.

Initially the rehearsal focus is on reading lines correctly, listening for cues, then moving on to volume and expression. When ready they perform for selected audiences—in science, math, and history—whatever. The students are involved with meeting challenges, moving around, making discoveries, doing interesting things. When you hear enthusiastic voices exclaiming that "This is *fun!*," you can assume that CBRT has been a successful learning endeavor.

Workshop 12.4	**Select a Strategy**
	Having just read eight various literature strategies for content areas, with a small group in the same or similar subject, select one and develop a lesson plan for teaching it together in your classroom. Fill in details of how you will do it and what you will say. Hand in a typed copy for your instructor to combine with others with everyone getting a copy. Be sure to put your names on it for credit!

Here's a Checklist for You

1. Create a classroom library where students can check out books.
2. Put enticing readings on display connected to your unit of study.
3. Make sure you vary the reading levels and genres.
4. Share some of your favorite books through book talks.
5. Give students a chance to recall past book talks—titles and authors.
6. Give students a choice whenever possible for their outside reading (not a textbook).
7. Use writing to reflect, explore, explain, and express.
8. Writing should have a real purpose and be aimed at a real audience.
9. Talk and listen to one another in study reading circles.
10. Provide students with background knowledge when needed.
11. Motivate them to explore and think critically.
12. Use visuals and media to enhance topics.
13. Have students use sticky notes for important pages they may want to refer to in their discussion circles.
14. Reader response—Have them summarize, make personal associations, and synthesize.

    Literal Level: What did the author say about _____?

    Interpretive Level: What did the author mean by _____?

    Applied Level: How can you apply this to your own life?

    See Chapter Seven on comprehension for more details.
15. Read the trade books yourself to discover how enjoyable they can be.

Cinquain as Summary

Content Literature
Integrating Diversity
Motivating, Restoring, Respecting
Making Lifetime Reading Lovers
Trade Books

 ## Summary

Integrating literature (trade books) into content classrooms while respecting diversity can be an enriching experience for teacher and student alike. Rosenblatt's Efferent and Aesthetic Reading are two reading stances in her Reader Response Theory. Aesthetic responses mean focusing on feelings, while the efferent is concerned with getting the facts. Using literature in any content field can be motivating and at times restorative. An important consideration is the use of multicultural literature for understanding and possible transformation. Reading rate adaptability is also important as it affects comprehension and is based on purpose and material difficulty. Advantages of using trade books are many. Locating appropriate materials to fit your content field is facilitated by bibliographies for young adult literature, picture books for adolescents, websites across the curriculum, multicultural literature, annotated literature for content area, content-specific literature, and a selection guide for trade books. Activities for classrooms include Read-Alouds, Book Talks, Text Walk, Anticipation Guides, Picture Books for Adolescents, SSR/DEAR, Study Reading (Literature) Circles, Response Journals, Curriculum-Based Readers Theatre, and Integrating a Cross-Cultural Unit for Middle School. All content teachers need to consider the importance of integrating literature into their classes.

FROM THE PAGES OF OUR LIVES
The Truth, Whispered or Shouted . . .

by Janice Brendible

Born and raised in southeast Alaska, Janice Brendible is a Tsimshian in the Raven Clan. She taught special education classes at a reservation school and has just completed her principal's credentials. Using anecdotes from her own life experiences, Ms. Brendible encourages teachers to choose literacy materials and activities that sustain and promote the integrity and dignity of their students.

I learned to read from my mother. She loved to read. She would read to us and we would be transported to other places all together. My brother, my sister and I would be lifted from our home as our mother started yet another book as we fell under the spell of her soft voice. Reading in school was another thing entirely. I was one of those people that grew up reading about Dick, Jane and Sally. It still amazes me that someone in education, whether the principal or teacher, thought a Native girl growing up on a remote island in Alaska, a fishing community at that, had anything in common with Dick and Jane.

Dick, Jane and Sally wore their church clothes every day! Imagine that! Jane's mother never left the kitchen! Didn't this woman have better things to do? The father wore church clothes every day to work! My dad wore work boots, blue jeans, a Pendleton shirt and a hard hat. What on earth did that dad do? Maybe he worked in a funeral parlor or a church. Even their yard was mysterious. It had short, short green grass evenly cut along the walk way. Our yard had, and still has, several lilac trees, gooseberry bushes, strawberries, blueberry bushes, raspberry bushes, and a smoke house for smoking salmon. The life of Dick and Jane was a curiosity that was never discussed in class. We all dutifully read, "See Dick run. Run Dick run." But we never discussed why Dick was running. Was his father after him? Were some kids trying to beat him up? Was he late getting home? This was not important to the teacher and it was a book we simply read. Their lives seemed so foreign and yet so clean that it was hard to imagine anyone having a life like Dick and Jane.

Dad loved to read as well. He read mostly stories of the "Old West." When I was a little girl, my dad told me about the Navajo code talkers. Dad and one of my uncles had served in the United States Army. Another of my uncles served in the Marines. And yet, the country they fought for refused to acknowledge Native American accomplishments in its history books. In all the history books that I read when I was in school, there was no mention of Native Americans except for the first Thanksgiving. Engraved in my brain is: "Christopher Columbus sailed the ocean blue in 1492 with the Nina, the Pinta and the Santa Maria." The Navajo code talkers weren't even discussed in public until 30 years after my dad first told me what these people, the Navajo, did for

their country. I wondered, still do, what others who read these same history books with the same factual omissions thought. It seems to me that these books leave the impression that this country was empty before the settlers came. One would also believe that god gave them this country. Of course, neither of these is true.

My sister who was two years older tended to share reading material when she thought something was exceptional. One day she said, "You have to read this, it's really good." The story came from her school reading book and it was called, "The Man without a Country." "The Man without a Country" was about a man who said things about his country that he probably shouldn't have said. As a result, he was no longer considered a citizen of that country and was punished to live on a boat forever. What could this man have possibly said to have to spend the rest of his life on a boat? And for that matter, who says that living on a boat is punishment? He had a pretty big boat with a full crew, all the necessities that he needed and could see the world! Who cared if the country liked him? He could probably go somewhere else and the new country might love what he had to say.

In two years time, it was my turn to study that same short story. "A Man without a Country" by Edward Everett Hale was assigned reading with some questions as homework. I dutifully reread the story. Again, the same questions came up, "This is a man put to sea in a huge ship! He isn't alone on a rowboat! He has every luxury available to him! The only thing he lacks is validation from one person, just one! What's the problem here?" The size of the man's boat had to be big enough to accommodate both him and his crew, so the galley, storage, all had to be pretty big. The picture showed him with his head down standing sadly on a huge ship. In a fishing community, like the one I am from, punishing a man to live on a boat is the same as locking a kid in a candy store. Being Native American the feeling of being without a country is a given. It's the daily trying to be a part of the country, the inclusion that is the toughest part. It would be so much easier to sail away on a boat forever and a lot more peaceful too. I did my homework and the next day in school there was no discussion. All the teacher directed questions checked whether or not we had really read the story. The very same questions of substance can be drawn from a reading of Dick and Jane. What is the name of the brother? Who is the older sister?

In middle school, I asked a substitute in our history class, a Native man, what he thought the United States would look like if the white people hadn't come and taken everything, not discovered—but took. He said that life would have gone on, that the different Native peoples would have continued to live as they had for hundreds of years. Life would have gone on. This life was never mentioned in the history books. The only appearance of the Native American was at the Thanksgiving table with the pilgrims. "Hi! We brought the corn!" Ever notice that no particular tribe is even mentioned, only that the Native Americans attended (bringing corn)? I'm a Tsimshian from S.E. Alaska and I'm pretty sure we were not at that Thanksgiving table. So which people attended exactly? The history books did not distinguish between all the nations and wrote about us as if all Native Americans have the same shared culture and beliefs. I have come to understand that the "pan" Indian was created to remove the identity of all the nations hurt by the "birth" of this nation. The Tsimshian are a different people, from the Haida, and the Tlingit, but we all supposedly fall under the umbrella of "Native American." But my dad knew our history, and shared it with me. He gave me validation for being who I am. I knew my history whether it was in the books or not. Dad would often say, "The truth whispered or shouted is still the truth." These words reverberate within me.

After my dad passed on, a friend, who is a teacher, told me about a new program. Those who run this program are looking for Native Americans who are interested in becoming teachers. The idea appeals to me. I place an initial call of inquiry, knowing all the while that signing up means that I would have to move and start somewhere new.

The first person I run this by is my mother. She is little and round but she stands tall and straight. Her cheeks are round and full like the rest of her lovely body. Her warm, brown eyes are always ready to share smile or a tear. We are in her kitchen, the kitchen where we, my brother and sister and I, as kids hid in the cabinets and under the table playing "hide and seek." The same kitchen where I learned to cook and bake and we would have lists of recipes that mom planned for the holidays. My mother kept all her recipes in an empty candy box. I keep all my recipes in an empty candy box. I look into her eyes and explain that I want to become a teacher, and that I am going to sign up for this program. I wait for the words to sink in. She sets her coffee down and looks startled at me, a deep wailing sound comes from her throat, "What are you doing? A teacher? You know better, don't you?" She has anger, fear, hurt and pain in her eyes. She glares at me as tears start to form. Mom quietly studies me. I am standing before her but say nothing.

Not all Americans view teaching as an honorable profession. Just one generation away, mom attended a Native American boarding school. Her journey started in Alaska and ended in Oregon. Imagine a government official showing up at your door demanding your kids. Imagine him taking your children from your home and bringing them to another state, a place many days travel away, a place where the teachers will force them to learn a new language, a language that you didn't know. If and when you saw your child in the summer, you will be forbidden to speak in your language to your child and your child is forbidden to respond in your language. Imagine the penalty for violating this rule is to have your child taken from the home permanently. As a result, my mother can understand Tsimshian when it is spoken to her, but she cannot speak it. This is part of my mother's history of education and it is part of *my* history of education.

I grew up hearing my family's stories about teachers and what they did to Tsimshian kids and other natives too. I can repeat the stories verbatim for my own children. We know the dangers of education. My mother studies me. Resolute and with respect she speaks. "If you do go into teaching, don't you become like them. It's not your job to change children, to tell them that how they live and what they believe is wrong. You accept them for where they are."

I did become a teacher. Like most teachers I have continued my studies so that I can do a better job of teaching my students to read. My studies most recently led me to the position statement written by Moore, Bean, Birdyshaw and Rycik (1999) for the Commission on Adolescent Literacy of the International Reading Association. Principle Six reads, "Adolescents deserve teachers who understand the complexities of individual adolescent readers, respect their differences, and respond to their characteristics." The Commission goes on to explain, ". . . adolescents deserve more than a centralized one-size-fits-all approach to literacy. They deserve teachers who . . . move into individuals' worlds with respect, choice and support; and move out to allow growth" (pp. 8–9) As a Native American woman in education, I ask myself what this has to do with the reality of what is going on in our schools.

When I consider the reading material I was required to read as an adolescent in school, and compare it to my life at the time, I see a difference as great as night and day. My life today hasn't come close to the life of Dick and Jane, has yours? The books we use contain the values our students are expected to accept without question. Or do they? Schools reflect the faces of society. Yet the school continues to fool itself that all students come from only one house, the house of Dick and Jane. I know for a fact this didn't work for my mom, even when they took her and placed her where the house would be closer to this concept in education. I understand what it means to be different, not to be part of the status quo. I know there are lots of kids thinking about a particular story and are wondering why it seems so foreign.

As a student, parent, teacher and Native American I am still guided by what I learned from my mother and father. It's not my job to change children. It is my job to accept them for where they are, to ask what they "thought" about the story, to listen to them describe how the story made them "feel," to help them figure out what parts of the story have to do with their lives whether dad wears a funeral suit or a blue jeans and a hard hat. This is the truth, whispered or shouted.

Questions for Reflection and Discussion:

1. Ms. Brendible's father said, "The truth, whispered or shouted, is still the truth." Name some of the truths Brendible discusses in her essay.

2. Ms. Brendible refers to a position statement published by the Commission on Adult Literacy of the International Reading Association. What do you think it takes to ". . . move into individuals' worlds with respect, choice and support; and move out to allow growth"?

3. Leila Flores-Dueñas' essay *Evangelina Can Read* tells the story of a young Latina struggling to negotiate the culturally different literacy expectations of school and home. If you haven't read it yet, you may want to turn to the end of Chapter 3 to do so. If you have read both, take a moment to compare the truths that are spoken in each. How are they the same? How are they different?

Reference

Moore, D., Bean, T., Birdyshaw, D., & Rycik, J. (1999). *Adolescent literacy: A position statement for the Commission on Adolescent Literacy of the International Reading Association.* Newark, DE: International Reading Association.

References and Recommended Readings

Adams, P. (1990). Teaching Romeo and Juliet in the non-tracted English classroom. *Journal of Reading, 38*, 424–432.

Adamson, L. (1997). *Literature connections to American history 7–12: Resources to enhance and entice.* Englewood, CO: Libraries Unlimited.

Adamson, L. (1999). *World historical fiction: An annotated guide to novels for adults and young adults.* Phoenix, AZ: Oryx Press.

Akmal, T. (2002). Ecological approaches to sustained silent reading: Conferencing, contracting, and relating to middle school students. *The Clearing House, 75*(3), 154–158.

Alverman, D., & Hagood, M. (2000). Fandom and critical media literacy. *Journal of Adolescent and Adult Literacy, 42*, 436–440.

Alverman, D., & Phelps, S. (2002). *Content area reading and literacy: Succeeding in today's diverse classrooms* (3rd ed.). Boston: Allyn & Bacon.

Anzaldua, G. (1988). The path of the red and black ink. In S. Walker & R. Simonson (Eds.), *The Gray Wolf annual five: Multicultural literacy* (pp. 13–28). St. Paul, MN: Graywolf Press.

Austin, P. (1998). Math books as literature: Which ones measure up? Use of trade books rather than text books in school. *New Advocate, 11*, 119–133.

Barry, A. (1998). Hispanic representation in literature for children and young adults. *Journal of Adolescent and Adult Literacy, 41*, 630–637.

Bean, T., Kile, R., & Readence, J. (1996). Using trade books to encourage critical thinking about citizenship in high school social studies. *Social Education, 60*, 227–230.

Bean, T. W., & Moni, K. (2003, May). Developing students' critical literacy: Exploring identify construction in young adult fiction. *Journal of Adolescent and Adult Literacy, 46*, 638–648.

Biloff, E. (1996). The killer angels: A case study of historical fiction in the social studies curriculum. *Social Studies, 87*, 19–23.

Bitz, M. (2004, April). The comic book project: Forging alternative pathways to literacy. *Journal of Adolescent and Adult Literacy, 47*, 574–586.

Bohnring, G., & Radencich, M. (1989). Informational action books: A curriculum resource for science and social studies. *Journal of Reading, 82*, 434–438.

Borasi, R., Sheedy, J. R., & Siegel, M. (1990). The power of stories in learning mathematics. *Language Arts, 67*, 174–189.

Brown, K. (1998). *Verse and universe: Poems about science and mathematics.* Minneapolis: Milkweed.

Burns, B. (1998). Changing the classroom climate with literature circles. *Journal of Adolescent and Adult Literacy, 42*, 110–113.

Carr, E., & Ogle, D. (1987). K-W-L Plus: A strategy for comprehension and summarization. *Journal of Reading, 30*, 626–631.

Carter, B., Estes, S., & Waddle, L. (2000). *Best books for young adults* (2nd ed.). Chicago: American Library Association.

Cena, M., & Mitchell, J. (1998). Anchored instruction: A model for integrating the language arts through content area study. *Journal of Adolescent and Adult Literacy, 41*, 559–561.

Chandler-Olcott, K., & Mahar, D. (2003, April). Adolescents anime-inspired fanfictions, an exploration of multi-literacies. *Journal of Adolescent and Adult Literacy, 46*, 556–566.

Clay, M. (1993). *Reading recovery: A guidebook for teachers in training.* Portsmouth, NH: Heinemann.

Commeryras, M., & Alverman, D. (1996). Reading about women in world history textbooks from one feminist perspective. *Gender and Education, 8*(1), 31–48.

Cornett, C. E. (1999). *The arts as meaning makers.* Upper Saddle River, NJ: Prentice Hall.

Council of Chief State School Officers. (2005). *INTASC standards.* Retrieved March 21, 2005, from http://www.ccsso.org/projects/Interstate_New_Teacher_Assessment_and_Support_Consortium/

Cullinan, B. E. (1993). *Fact and fiction: Literature across the curriculum.* Newark, DE: International Reading Association.

Cummins, J. (1994). The acquisition of English as a second language. In K. Spangenber-Urbschat & R. Pritchard (Eds.), *Kids come in all languages: Reading instruction for ESL students* (pp. 36–62). Newark, DE: International Reading Association.

Daniels, H. (1994). *Literature circles: Voice and choice in the student-centered classroom* (p. 10). York, ME: Stenhouse.

Daniels, H., Bizar, M., & Zemelmann, S. (2000). *Rethinking high school: Best practices in teaching, learning, and leadership.* Portsmouth, NH: Heinemann.

Drew, B. (1997). *The 100 most popular young adult authors: Biographical and bibliographies.* Englewood, CO: Libraries Unlimited.

Dunbar, P. L. (1913). We wear the mask. *The complete poems of Paul Lawrence Dunbar.* New York: Dodd, Mead.

Erickson, B. (1996). Read alouds reluctant readers relish. *Journal of Adolescent and Adult Literacy, 40*, 212–214.

Flynn, R. M. (2005). Curriculum-based theatre: Setting the stage for reading and retention. *The Reading Teacher, 58*(4) 360–365.

Fountas, I., & Pinnell, G. (2001). *Guiding readers and writers: Grades 3–6: Teaching comprehension genre and content literacy.* Portsmouth, NH: Heinemann.

Fuhler, C. J. (1994). Response journals: Just one more time with feeling. *Journal of Reading, 37*, 400–405.

George, M., & Stix, A. (2000). Using mulitlevel young adult literature in middle school American studies. *The Social Studies, 91*, 25–31.

Gonick, L. (1994). *The cartoon history of the universe.* New York: Broadway Books.

Gonick, L., & Smith, W. (1993). *The cartoon guide to statistics.* New York: Harper Perenial.

Goodall, J. (1978). *The story of an English village.* New York: MacMillan.

Grant, C. A., & Gomez, M. L. (Eds.). (2001). *Campus and classroom: Making schooling multicultural* (2nd ed.). Upper Saddle River, NJ: Prentice Hall.

Grisham, D. (1999). Literacy partners: Supporting literacy innovation in a teachers study group. *Journal of Reading Education, 2*, 1–8.

Hadaway, N., & Mundy, J. (2000). Children's informational picture books, visit a secondary ESL classroom. In D. Moore, D. Alverman, & K. Hinchman (Eds.), *Struggling adolescent readers: A collection of teaching strategies*, (pp. 83–95). Newark, DE: International Reading Association.

Hancock, J. (Ed.) (1999). *Teaching literacy using informational technology.* Newark, DE: International Reading Association.

Hill, B. C., Johnson, N. J., & Schlick-Noe, K. (2000). *Literature circle resource guide.* Norwood, MA: Christopher Gordon.

Hopkins, L. B., & Alcon, S. (2000). *My America: A poetry atlas of the United States.* New York: Simon & Schuster.

Hopkins, L. B., & Barbour, K. (Eds.). (1997). *Marvelous math: A book of poems.* New York: Simon & Schuster.

Hopkins, L. B., & Halstead, V. (Eds.). (1999). *Spectacular science: A book of poems.* New York: Simon & Schuster.

Howes, E. V., Hamilton, G. W., & Zaskoda, D. (2003, March). Linking science and literature through technology: Thinking about interdisciplinary inquiry in middle school. *Journal of Adolescent and Adult Literacy, 47*, 494–504.

Johnson, H., & Freedman, L. (2005). *Content area literature circles: Using discussion for learning across the curriculum.* Norwood, MA: Christopher Gordon.

Jones, T. G., & Fuller, M. L. (2003). *Teaching Hispanic children.* Boston: Pearson Education Inc.

Kane, S., & Rule, A. C. (2004, April). Poetry connections can enhance content area learning. *Journal of Adolescent and Adult Literacy, 47*, 658–669.

Katz, B. (1998). *American history poems.* New York: Simon & Schuster.

Klug, B., & Whitfield, P. (2003). *Widening the circle: Culturally relevant pedagogy for American Indian children.* New York: RoutledgeFalmer.

Lev, D. J., Jr., & Leu, D. D. (2000). *Teaching with the Internet: Lessons from the classroom* (3rd ed.). Norwood, MA: Christopher Gordon.

Lombard, R. (1996). Using trade books to teach middle level social studies. *Social Education, 60*, 223–230.

Lott, C., & Wasta, S. (1999). Adding voice and perspective: Children's and young adult literature in the civil war. *English Journal, 88*, 56–61.

Manzo, A., Manzo U. C., & Thomas, M. M. (2005). *Content area literacy: Strategic teaching for strategic learning* (4th ed.). Hoboken, NJ: Wiley Jossey-Bass.

McMahon, S. I., & Raphael, T. E. (Eds.). (1997). *The book club connection.* New York: Teachers College Press.

Miller, D. E. (1993). The literature project: Using literature to improve the self-concept of at risk adolescent females. *Journal of Reading, 36*, 442–446.

Miller, T. (1998). The place of picture books in middle level classrooms. *Journal of Adolescent and Adult Literacy, 41*, 376–381.

Moore, D. W, Bean, J. W., Birdyshaw, D., & Rycik, J. R. (1999). Adolescent literacy: A position statement. *Journal of Adolescent and Adult Literacy, 43*, 97–112.

Nagy, N. M., Campenni, C. E., & Shaw, J. N. (2000). *Reading online.* Retrieved March 21, 2005, from http://www.readingonline.org/articles/nagy/ssr.html

Nagy, N. M., Campenni, C. E., & Shaw, J. N. (2000). A survey of sustained silent reading practice-for Professional Teaching Standards. (2005). Adolescence and young adulthood/social studies-history standards for teachers. Retrieved March 21, 2005, from http://www.nbpts.org/pdf/mcya_ssh.pdf

National Council of Teachers of English/International Reading Association. (1996). *Standards for the English language arts.* Urbana, IL: Authors.

Noll, E. (1994). Social issues and literature circles with adolescents. *Journal of Reading, 38*, 88–93.

Nye, N. S. (1998). *The space between our footsteps: Poems and paintings from the Middle East.* New York: Simon & Schuster.

Palmer, R. G., & Stewart, R. A. (1997). Nonfiction trade books in content area instruction: Realities and potentials. *Journal of Adolescent and Adult Literacy, 40*, 630–641.

Pappas, C., & Barry, A. (2001). Examining language to capture scientific understandings. *Science and Children, 38*, 26-29.

Paxton, R. J. (1999). A deafening silence: History textbooks and the students who read them. *Review of Educational Research, 69*, 315–330.

Pilgreen, J. (2000). *The SSR handbook: How to organize and mange a sustained silent reading program.* Portsmouth, NH: Boynton/Cook.

Poitras, G. (2001). *Anime essentials: Everything a fan needs to know.* Berkeley, CA: Stone Bridge Press.

Rasinski, T. V. (2000). Speed does matter in reading. *The Reading Teacher*, 54, 146–151.

Redfield, J. (1998). *The celestine prophecy: An adventure.* New York: Warner Books.

Reynolds, F., & Pickett, I. (1989). Read! Think! Write! The response journal in the biology classroom. *The American Biology Teacher, 51*, 435–437.

Richardson, J. (2000). *Read it aloud! Using literature in the secondary content classroom.* Newark, DE: International Reading Association.

Rosenblatt, L. (1978). *The reader, the text, the poem: The transactional theory of the literary work.* Carbondale, IL: Southern Illinois University Press.

Rosenblatt, L. (1985). Transaction versus interaction—A terminological rescue operation. *Research in the Teaching of English, 19*, 96–107.

Schwarz, G. E. (2002 November). Graphic novels for multiple literacies. *Journal of Adolescent and Adult Literacy, 46*, 262–265.

Stover, L. (1988). What do you mean, we have to read a book for art class? *Art Education, 41*(5), 8–13.

Sullivan, E. (2001). Some teens prefer the real thing: The case for young adult non-fiction. *English Journal, 90*(3), 43–47.

Tiedt, I. M. (1995). *Teaching with picture books in the middle school.* Newark, DE: International Reading Association.

Trelease, J. (1995). *The new read-aloud handbook* (3rd ed.). New York: Penguin.

Waff, D., & Connell, P. (2004). Trenton Central high school SSR: A case study. *English Journal (High school edition), 93*(5), 13–16.

Weiner, S. (2002). Beyond superheroes: Comics get serious. *Library Journal, 127*(2), 55–58.

Westcott, W., & Spell, J. (1999). Tearing down the wall: Literature and science. *English Journal, 89*, 70–76.

Wood, N. (1995). The beads of life. In F. Howel (Illustrator), *Dancing moons*, (p. 55). Doubleday.

Worthy, J., Moorman, M., & Turner, M. (1999). What Johnny likes to read is hard to find in school. *Reading Research Quarterly, 34*(1), 12–27.

Yoon, J. (2002). Three decades of sustained silent reading: A meta-analytic review of the effects of SSR on attitude toward reading. *Reading Improvement, 39*(4), 146–196.

Young, T. A., & Vardell, S. (1993). Weaving readers' theatre and non-fiction into the curriculum. *The Reading Teacher, 46*(5), 396–406.

Directed Reading/ Thinking Activity

APPENDIX

A

Text: *The Wind in The Willows*
Author: Kenneth Grahame
Publisher: Charles Scribner's Sons

Objectives:
1. To enrich literary appreciation.
2. To stimulate creative imagination.
3. To entertain.
4. To improve vocabulary skills.

Time	Student Activities	Teacher Activities	Materials Needed
9 minutes	Listen	*Part I: Preparation/Motivation* Today we are going to take a look at the personalities of Mole, Rat, Toad, and the Badger in *The Wind in the Willows*. Let's brainstorm for a while and list some characteristics of these animals on the board. We'll begin with Mole.	
	Respond	What kind of an animal do you think Mole is? (inexperienced, eager, happy, curious, blissful, impetuous, good-natured, friendly, conscientious)	
	Respond	Good! Let's do the same with Rat. (very considerate, sensitive, intelligent, neat, soft-hearted, patient, perceptive, warm)	
	Respond	Great! How about the Badger? (wise, respected, feared, paternal, comfortable, gruff, suspicious, kindly, plain, narrow-minded)	
	Respond	And now for Mr. Toad! (arrogant, rich, impulsive, energetic, enthusiastic, jolly, obnoxious, conceited, friendly) Okay, good! We've got a fairly comprehensive list of characteristics for each animal.	

*Pam Merrill (Used with permission.)

Time	Student Activities	Teacher Activities	Materials Needed
6 minutes	Listen Listen Read silently	*Part II: Directed Silent Reading* Please turn to page 105 in our text. Let's take a minute and refresh our memories quickly. Prior to this part of the story, the Toad has been wildly gallivanting around the countryside wreaking havoc in various large and expensive motor cars. His friends, led by Mr. Badger, have decided that enough is *enough!* The Toad has gotten completely out of hand with his enthusiastic and furious driving habits. He's been giving the animals in the district a bad name, having rows with the police, and squandering his father's money. His friends decide to stop this nonsense once and for all. I want you to read beginning with "The hour has come!" on page 105, continue on to page 107, and stop where it says "His hearty accents faltered and fell away . . . and his invitation remained unfinished." *(Purpose statement)* Be thinking about the action that is happening in this passage and the purpose of the visit by Mole, Rat, and Badger to Toad Hall. When you finish reading, you'll break up into small groups in order to act out a short skit involving this visit. I'll tell you more about that when you finish.	Text: *The Wind in the Willows,* p. 105
5 minutes	Listen	*Part III: Reflections/Enrichments/Applications* I'd like you now to get into your small groups as soon as I've finished explaining what we're going to do. Within your group, each person will take the role of one of the animals in the story. Since there are four animals, the fifth person in your group will be the narrator. I have index cards with the animal names on them. You'll each draw a card to determine which role you'll play. Then you must collectively decide on what happens in the next scene that will begin exactly where our reading left off. The jolly Toad is standing on the steps faced by his three friends who are silently and sternly staring at him. What's next? It's up to you to decide! You have approximately 10 minutes to write and rehearse your skit. Each skit should last about three minutes.	

Time	Student Activities	Teacher Activities	Materials Needed
	Listen	Then, each group will present their skit to the class with each student in the role of an animal or narrator. Don't be afraid to get into the spirit! Adopt voices like you'd imagine your character would have. What's his posture like? We've listed some personality characteristics—use them if you can!	
		To make it just a bit more interesting, I'm going to ask that each of you speak at least two lines in the skit. And . . . somewhere in those lines, you must use ONE vocabulary word from this handout. To ensure that there's no confusion about the meaning of these words, I've included a brief definition. Now when you're speaking your lines and you come to your vocabulary word, really let us know that's YOUR word! Yell it out or emphasize it in some way! And try not to use the same word that someone else in your group will be using.	Vocabulary Handout (See page 446)
		Write your lines on these index cards so you can refer to them if necessary during your skit.	
		I've also brought along a few props for your skits. Feel free to grab what you need and we can all trade off between skits so everyone gets a chance to use them.	Props: four loud and colorful jackets, fur hat, striped hat, racecar hat, military hat, goggles, gloves, red model car, scarves
	Ask questions	Now, what question do you have?	
		In 10 minutes then we'll reconvene and Group 1 will take center stage.	
10 minutes	Work in small groups	(Circulate among groups to answer questions, clarify vocabulary definitions, etc.)	
		(Call group 1.)	
	Group 1 stages skit	(Narrator faces class, with actors facing blackboard. Actors turn around and face class when narrator finishes introduction.)	
20 minutes	All other group skits	(Groups 2, 3, 4, and 5 perform skits.)	
		(Lead round of applause for all groups!)	
	Listen	(Closing remarks:) I've finished reviewing your Content IRIs from last Friday. I've added some comments and you may keep these if you'd like. There is a score at the top which I used to tabulate the results for my class at WWU.	Content IRIs
		Thank you all very much! You were first class all the way!	
		Applause!!!	

Evaluation

The DRTA lesson was taught on Friday, February 21, to Miss Tony Smith's 6th period Honors English class at North Mason High School, Belfair, Washington. This same class had completed the Content IRI the previous Friday.

Positive Notes:

When students first entered the room and saw the pile of silly costumes on Miss Smith's desk, they were immediately curious and interested in knowing "what we were going to do today."

The brainstorming session went very quickly as students were eager to participate and to see their contributions listed on the blackboard. The adjectives came so fast and furiously I could hardly write them all down.

When I announced the purpose of the Directed Reading Thinking Activity, students were quick to roll their eyes and giggle at each other. I interpreted this as a good sign that they were receptive to performing the skits.

I allowed ten minutes preparation time for the groups to write and rehearse their skits. Group 1, however, was ready before the ten minutes had passed and jumped up asking "Can we get dressed now?" These kids "broke the ice" and set the level of enthusiasm on high when they donned their costumes and took center stage. (We had cleared the center of the classroom for the performances.)

Students showed an amazing amount of imagination and creativity in this exercise. They went beyond the box of props and costumes and implemented some of their own props from within the classroom, such as four desks used as a car, a stool used as a motorcycle, a pointer used as a weapon, etc.

I had been concerned about completing the activity by the end of the hour, but we finished with two minutes to spare. Students were eager to see how they'd done on their Content IRIs and many came forward after the class ended to ask questions.

All in all, it was a wonderful experience that I wouldn't hesitate to do again. Miss Smith even had the school photographer come in and take pictures of the kids in costume!

A. VOCABULARY LIST

Each Mole, Rat, Badger, Toad, and Narrator should use one word from this list in the group skit. Try not to use the same word that someone else in your group has chosen.

array—to dress in splendid or impressive attire (She wanted to array herself in diamonds and silk.)

bluster—to talk or act with noisy swaggering threats (He blustered under pressure.)

artful—wily, crafty, sly (The artful hamster outsmarted the child.)

assail—to attack violently with blows or words (She assailed her boss for assigning overtime.)

caustic—incisive, biting wit (His caustic attitude caused him trouble.)

comrade—friend, companion (They were comrades for life.)

eloquent—marked by fluid expression (She spoke eloquently to the group.)

exploit—a notable or heroic act (Her exploits made her famous.)

folly—foolish act or idea (His folly prevented his promotion.)

gaiters—a cloth or leather leg covering reaching from instep to midcalf (He wore his gaiters with pride.)

Content IRI Report*

Date Administered: Friday, February 14, 1998
North Mason High School
Belfair, Washington
6th Period
Honors English (Grades 9–12)
Miss Toni Smith, Instructor

As I entered the classroom, I sensed a stirring of anticipation and excitement. "Great," I thought to myself, "the kids know what's happening today and they're anxious to begin!" Next, Miss Smith, the teacher, informed me that all during sixth period today, students will be delivering "sweet-o-grams" in honor of Valentine's Day. These kids were anticipating goodies from their friends and sweethearts! "This should be interesting," I quivered. So let's begin!

Miss Smith had announced my presence with a scribble on the blackboard that said: "Nice Mrs. Merrill is here today to give us a reading test." I began the hour by erasing "reading test" and substituting "Content Informal Reading Inventory (Content IRI)." I explained to the students that the Content IRI was not a test, but rather a diagnostic tool that is meant to ascertain how well they are able to handle a text and what skills need to be improved. In this class, the text used for my Content IRI was *The Wind in the Willows,* by Kenneth Grahame.

I followed this introduction with a short personal introduction of myself. I told the students I was a student at WWU in Bellingham and that I was studying to be a teacher. I also told them a little bit about Education 484 to explain further why I was in their classroom today.

Next, I passed out the Content IRI with the intention of beginning my verbal run-through on Parts I and II. Suddenly, the door to the classroom was flung wide and in marched three giggling freshmen girls carrying trays of pink-frosted cupcakes stuck with giant red paper hearts. With Miss Smith's assistance, the pink cakes were deposited quickly and quietly on her desk, while my students eyed them hungrily. "We'll distribute these *AFTER* the Content IRI," winked Miss Smith.

I proceeded to explain Part I. I told the students to read the excerpt and then answer the questions on the next page. One student asked what the *V, L,* and *I* meant opposite each question. I answered that there are vocabulary, literal and inference questions in

*Pam Merrill. Used with permission.

this section. The literal question indicates that the answer is to be found verbatim in the excerpt. The inference questions are intended to determine the student's ability to reason the answer, based on what she has read.

Moving on to Part II, I remarked that Section A is intended to measure their comprehension skills. After reading the paragraph, students should answer the questions on the following page and try to avoid rereading if possible.

"Section B is designed to measure the rate at which you can comprehend what you've read," I stated. "These are timed readings, which we will all do together after I finish explaining Section C." (moan, groan) "How much time do we get?" they asked. "10–15 seconds," I answered calmly. (louder groans and whimpers) "Section C," I bravely countered, "is a Content-Specific Vocabulary section. The words I have chosen are taken directly from the text. All you need to do is match each word with its correct definition in the opposite column. What questions do you have?" There were none.

Back to Section B. I instructed everyone to turn to page 5 and when I said "Begin!" they were to read the first paragraph. Fifteen seconds later I called "Stop!" and the surprised students quickly answered the question. I allowed 10 seconds each for the second and third paragraphs, and each time the students responded easily.

Now back to Part I. I told the students they could have the rest of the hour to finish the Content IRI. "What questions do you have?" I asked. Again, there were none. "When you finish, please bring your content IRI to Mrs. Merrill," interjected Miss Smith, "and then come and claim your treats!"

I should note that there were two more brief interruptions during this hour. Once, for the delivery of long-stemmed pink carnations, and once for the delivery of several pink love-notes. These items were duly added to the cupcake pile on Miss Smith's desk, for later distribution.

All students finished with a minimum of five minutes to spare. Over the din of disappearing cupcakes, I explained that I would return the following Friday with the completed Content IRIs and that we would then do an activity based on the skill need determined today. "Okay, fine, whatever you say," the students happily answered. I guess it's not every day they get to eat pink-frosted cupcakes delivered with love from a fellow classmate.

P.S. The visiting teacher was handed a spare cupcake from one popular girl who received eight! Who said Friday afternoon 6th period wasn't going to be fun!

TABLE A4.1 Content IRI class profile

Name of Student	Part I			Part II			
	Vocabulary (2 of 3)	Literal (3 of 4)	Inference (2 of 3)	Comprehension Skills	Adaptable Rate	Content-specific Vocabulary	Individual Needs
1. Kenda C.	✓	✓	✓	✓	✓	✓	no
2. Sasha O.		✓	✓	✓			yes
3. Michele Z.		✓	✓				yes
4. Larissa U.			✓	✓	✓	✓	yes
5. Samantha L.		✓	✓		✓		yes
6. Tara W.	✓	✓	✓	✓	✓		no
7. Tim N.		✓	✓	✓	✓	✓	no
8. Regina L.		✓	✓	✓	✓		yes
9. Shannon A.		✓	✓		✓	✓	yes
10. Janelle D.		✓	✓	✓	✓	✓	no
11. Scott E.		✓	✓	✓		✓	yes
12. Heidi H.		✓	✓	✓	✓		yes
13. Shannon C.		✓	✓		✓	✓	yes
14. Scott S.		✓	✓	✓	✓		yes
15. Chris J.	✓	✓	✓	✓	✓	✓	no
16. Amy E.			✓	✓	✓		yes
17. Keri A.		✓	✓	✓	✓	✓	no
18. Dana M.		✓	✓		✓	✓	yes
19. Tom D.		✓	✓		✓		yes
20. Gene S.		✓	✓		✓	✓	yes
21. Sarah J.		✓	✓		✓		yes
22. Tim B.	✓	✓	✓	✓	✓	✓	no
23. Lori T.	✓	✓	✓	✓	✓	✓	no
24. Katie W.		✓	✓	✓	✓	✓	no
25. Tabby R.	✓	✓	✓	✓	✓		no
26. Will H.		✓	✓	✓	✓	✓	no
Overall Class Needs	Yes	No	No	Yes	No	Yes	

Key: ✓ means skill mastery

Class _____

Date _____

Content IRI

Wind in the Willows

Part 1: Reading

PURPOSE/MOTIVATION STATEMENT

This excerpt is taken from Chapter 1, when Mole has decided to give himself a holiday from his whitewashing task. Read it to find out how Mole felt when he first discovered the river.

It all seemed too good to be true. Hither and thither through the meadows he rambled busily, along the hedgerows, across the *copses,* finding everywhere birds building, flowers budding, leaves thrusting—everything happy, and progressive, and occupied. And instead of having an uneasy conscience pricking him and whispering 'Whitewash!' he somehow could only feel how jolly it was to be the only idle dog among all these busy citizens. After all, the best part of a holiday is perhaps not so much to be resting yourself, as to see all the other fellows busy working.

He thought his happiness was complete when, as he meandered aimlessly along, suddenly he stood by the edge of a full-fed river. Never in his life had he seen a river before—this sleek, *sinuous,* full-bodied animal, chasing and chuckling, gripping things with a gurgle and leaving them with a laugh, to fling itself on fresh playmates that shook themselves free, and were caught and held again. All was a-shake and a-shiver—glints and gleams and sparkles, rustle and swirl, chatter and bubble. The Mole was bewitched, entranced, fascinated. By the side of the river he trotted as one trots, when very small, by the side of a man who holds one spellbound by exciting stories; and when tired at last, he sat on the bank, while the river still chattered onto him, a babbling procession of the best stories in the world, sent from the heart of the earth to be told at last to the *insatiable* sea.

As he sat on the grass and looked across the river, a dark hole in the bank opposite, just above the water's edge, caught his eye, and dreamily he fell to considering what a nice snug dwelling-place it would make for an animal with few wants and fond of a bijou riverside residence, above flood level and remote from noise and dust. As he gazed, something bright and small seemed to twinkle down in the heart of it, vanished, then twinkled once more like a tiny star. But it could hardly be a star in such an unlikely situation; and it was too glittering and small for a glow-worm. Then, as he looked, it winked at him, and so declared itself to be an eye; and a small face began gradually to grow up round it, like a frame round a picture.

A brown little face, with whiskers.

A grave round face, with the same twinkle in its eye that had first attracted his notice.

Small neat ears and thick silky hair.

It was the Water Rat!

TABLE A4.2

Directions: Now that you have finished reading the selection, write your answers to the following questions.

(V) 1. Never in his life had he seen a river before—this sleek, *sinuous,* full-bodied animal . . .

  Sinuous means: _____

  _____

(L) 2. What did the Mole consider the best part of holiday? _____

  _____

(I) 3. What season of the year do you think it is and why? _____

  _____

  _____

  _____

(L) 4. How does the author compare the river to a book of stories? _____

  _____

  _____

  _____

(V) 5. Hither and thither through the meadows he rambled busily, along the hedgerows, across the *copses* . . .

  Copses means: _____

  _____

(L) 6. How did the Mole react to his first glimpse of the river? _____

  _____

  _____

  _____

(I) 7. Why do you think the Mole had never seen the river before? _____

  _____

  _____

(L) 8. What did the Mole see in the dark hole on the opposite bank of the river?_____

  _____

(I) 9. Do you think the Mole wanted to live by the river? Why? _____

  _____

  _____

  _____

(V) 10. . . . a babbling procession of the best stories in the world, sent from the heart of the earth to be told at last to the *insatiable* sea.

  Insatiable means:_____

  _____

Part II: Reading/Study Skills

A. *Comprehension Skills*

  Read this paragraph and then turn the page to answer the questions.

  The pattering increased till it sounded like sudden hail on the dry-leaf carpet spread around him. The whole wood seemed running now, running hard, hunting, chasing, closing in round something or—somebody? In panic, he began to run too, aimlessly, he knew not whither. He ran up against things, he fell over things and into things, he darted under things and dodged round things. At last he took refuge in the deep dark hollow of

TABLE A4.2 *Continued*

an old beech tree, which offered shelter, concealment—perhaps even safety, but who could tell? Anyhow, he was too tired to run any further and could only snuggle down into the dry leaves which had drifted into the hollow and hope he was safe for the time. And as he lay there panting and trembling, and listened to the whistlings and the patterings outside, he knew it at last, in all its fullness, that dread thing which other little dwellers in field and hedgerow had encountered here, and known as their darkest moment—that thing which the Rat had vainly tried to shield him from—The Terror of the Wild Wood!

1. What is the main idea of this paragraph? _____
   _____
   _____

2. What three facts support the main idea? _____
   _____
   _____
   _____

3. List the events in the order in which they occurred. _____
   _____
   _____
   _____
   _____

4. What conclusion can you draw from the last sentence in the paragraph? _____
   _____
   _____

5. Determine the cause and effect of the concluding statement. _____
   _____
   _____
   _____
   _____
   _____
   _____
   _____

B. *Adaptable Rate*
   (15 seconds)
   Read this paragraph to tell why Toad spoke mainly to the Mole.

   _____

   _____

During luncheon—which was excellent, of course, as everything at Toad Hall always was—the Toad simply let himself go. Disregarding the Rat, he proceeded to play upon the inexperienced Mole as on a harp. Naturally a voluble animal, and always mastered by his imagination, he painted the prospects of the trip and the joys of the open life and the roadside in such glowing colours that the Mole could hardly sit in his chair for excitement. Somehow, it soon seemed taken for granted by all three of them that the trip was a settled thing; and the Rat, though still unconvinced in his mind, allowed his good nature to override his personal objections. He could not bear to disappoint his two friends, who were already deep in schemes and anticipations, planning out each day's separate occupation for several weeks ahead.

TABLE A4.2

(10 seconds)

Skim this paragraph to tell who "they" are. _____

_____

They waited patiently for what seemed a very long time, stamping in the snow to keep their feet warm. At last they heard the sound of slow shuffling foot-steps approaching the door from the inside. It seemed, as the Mole remarked to the Rat, like some one walking in carpet slippers that were too large for him and down-at-heel; which was intelligent of Mole, because that was exactly what it was.

(10 seconds)

Read this paragraph to define *emancipated*. _____

_____

This day was only the first of many similar ones for the emancipated Mole, each of them longer and fuller of interest as the ripening summer moved onward. He learnt to swim and to row, and entered into the joy of running water; and with his ear to the reed-stems he caught, at intervals, something of what the wind went whispering so constantly among them.

C. *Content-Specific Vocabulary.* Match the words with the definitions by writing the correct letter from the column on the right next to the number of the left.

1. _____ Divine	a. wandered aimlessly or casually
2. _____ Imperious	b. an animal in the brown summer coat
3. _____ Contemptuous	c. a dam in the stream
4. _____ Meandered	d. supremely good
5. _____ Sculled	e. made or done on the spur of the moment
6. _____ Forbearance	f. marked by arrogant assurance
7. _____ Stoat	g. noisy commotion
8. _____ Weir	h. manifesting lack of respect or reverence
9. _____ Impromptu	i. propelled with oars
10. _____ Rumpus	j. patience, leniency
	k. point of origin, fountainhead
	l. tightly controlled, restrained
	m. differing from one another, unlike

CIRI for Chemistry and Math: For Use in Triangulation of Assessments

Logan O'Sliabh
Sec Ed 525
11/17/04

Text:
It's About Time, Inc. (2003). *Active Chemistry* (1st ed.). Armonk, NY: Author.

Intended Audience:
This textbook is intended for use in a 9th/10th-grade chemistry class.

I. Introduction

The pages that follow contain a Content Informal Reading Inventory (CIRI). A CIRI is an assessment tool used by teachers to evaluate their students' abilities to read with comprehension from a particular textbook. In addition, it provides a way to measure several different literary skills (e.g., locating reference materials, interpreting graphics, taking and making notes from a lecture, etc.) that are necessary to perform well in certain classroom settings. The results of a CIRI help teachers to design better lesson plans and also to identify areas where students may need additional help.

II. CIRI Format

This CIRI is constructed in two parts. Part I focuses on reading with comprehension, and it contains a short (262 words) sample from the textbook, *Active Chemistry*. After reading the passage, students are asked to answer ten questions, which take a variety of forms. Literal (L) questions measure students' abilities to locate and transcribe specific details contained in the selection. Contextual Vocabulary (V) questions, on the other hand, demonstrate how well students can infer word definitions that are not explicitly stated. Finally, Inferential (I) questions call upon students to deduce answers based on information in the text and/or infer answers by applying their background knowledge.

Part II of this CIRI evaluates literary skills in three different areas: (1) interpreting graphics; (2) following written directions; and (3) conducting Internet searches. The first two skills are critical for succeeding in any high school chemistry class, and the third is becoming increasingly more important (and will be used specifically in my classroom setting). Students are prompted to answer five to six questions in each of these subtests.

III. Use of Results

After administering this CIRI on the first day of the term to all of my 9th/10th-grade chemistry students, I will compile the results in a Class Profile Sheet similar to the one on page 458. By displaying mastery in each of the assessment areas, this scoring summary will show me at a glance where my students' strengths and weaknesses lie (in this CIRI), both individually and overall as a class. I will then be able to plan my lessons accordingly and also provide help to those students who need it.

Please note that a CIRI is *not* a norm-referenced test, and therefore results have little meaning outside of the classroom in which it is administered. The results can be extremely valuable for teachers, however, to improve their instruction in this specific setting.

IV. Role of the CIRI in Determining Textbook Readability

In order to match a textbook properly to a group of students, three different types of measures are usually necessary (this is called triangulation of data). The three corners of this triangle are readability formulas (e.g., Fry Readability Graph, Flesch Reading Ease, etc.), readability checklists (e.g., Marshall's or the ICL Checklist Buffet), and student feedback. The first corner of the triangle gives an unbiased assessment of the approximate grade level at which the text reads, and this is the first tool that I used to evaluate *Active Chemistry*. According to the Fry Readability formula, this textbook reads somewhere between the 13th and 15th grade levels. By itself, this assessment is worrisome because the textbook is intended for 9th and 10th-grade students. However, we still have two more corners to examine.

The second part of triangulation calls for the use of a checklist to reveal the ease or difficulty of a text. This type of assessment considers many other factors (that formulas do not) such as the context and intended audience. Since this measure is highly subjective, however, it is recommended that several teachers from differing disciplines rate the same material. Below are the results of a Marshall Readability checklist that I completed for *Active Chemistry*. Although other content teachers' input still needs to be included, the text received high marks overall on this list.

Marshall's Readability Checklist for Comprehensibility of Active Chemistry

		Well Done + Average 0 Poor –
Main Ideas	1. a. Are major points stated clearly?	+
	b. Are chapter titles and headings meaningful?	+
	c. Do titles outline major points clearly?	+
Vocabulary	2. a. Are key vocabulary terms defined clearly when the subject is new?	+
	b. Are these terms used in a variety of contexts meaningful to the reader?	0
Concepts	3. a. Are new concepts introduced in the context of familiar concepts?	+
	b. Are they well defined in the text?	+
Related Ideas	4. a. Are ideas clearly related to each other?	+
	b. Will the reader be able to understand relationships among ideas?	0
	c. Could the reader illustrate these graphically?	
Referents	5. a. Are pronouns used unambiguously?	+
	b. Do they usually refer to referents no more than one sentence away?	+
Audience	6. Has the author addressed the audience intended?	–

Because *Active Chemistry* displays low readability (high difficulty) by the Fry Formula yet high readability (low difficulty) in the Marshall Checklist, the third corner of the assessment triangle becomes especially important. That's where student feedback is considered, and the CIRI represents one way to obtain that feedback. If my students perform well overall on the CIRI that I designed, then I feel confident that the textbook will be appropriate for the class (despite the high grade level determined by Fry). If, on the other hand, most students struggle on this assessment, I will need to modify my curriculum significantly to adjust for a difficult-to-read textbook.

V. *Relationship of the CIRI to Washington State Learning Standards: Essential Academic Learning Requirements (EALR's)*

Another important influence on the design of my CIRI was the Essential Academic Learning Requirements (EALRs) outlined by the Office of the Superintendent of Public Instruction of Washington State. Each question posed in my assessment addresses one or more of the EALRs in reading, writing, communication, and/or science. The following chart displays these relationships.

EALR's Addressed	Questions
Reading 1.1 (word recognition)	Part I: 1–10 and Part II: A: 1–5, B: 1–6, C: 1–5
Reading 1.2 (building vocabulary)	Part I: 5–7 and Part II: C: 3–5
Reading 2.1 (comprehend ideas)	Part I: 1–10 and Part II: A: 2–5, B: 1–6, C: 3–5
Reading 2.2 (text components)	Part I: 8, 9 and Part II: A: 1–5, C: 1–5
Reading 2.3 (expand comprehension)	Part I: 8–10 and Part II: A: 2–5
Reading 3.1 (new information)	Part I: 1–4, 8–10 and Part II: A: 1–5
Reading 3.2 (perform task)	Part II: B: 1–6 and C: 1–6
Science 1.1 (properties)	Part I: 1–9 and Part II: A: 1–5
Science 1.2 (systems)	Part I: 1, 3, 4, 6–9 and Part II: A: 1–5
Science 1.3 (matter & energy)	Part I: 3, 7 and Part II: A: 1, 5
Science 3.2 (human endeavors)	Part I: 10 and Part II: C: 5

VI. *Aggregating, Disaggregating and Displaying Data*

Once students have completed this CIRI I will record their scores on the profile sheet on the next page. This chart provides a concise picture of the strengths and weaknesses of the class as a whole and of each individual student. Both parts of the CIRI are listed along with the different tests and subtests. Below the name for each test or subtest is the criteria a student must meet to pass to demonstrate mastery. For example, under Part I, there are literal, vocabulary and inferential sub-tests. I have determined that students should be able to answer all three literal questions, hence the notation of (3/3). I believe they need to be able to answer at least three of the four vocabulary questions (3/4) and two of the three inferential questions (2/3).

CIRI Class Profile Sheet

Student Name	Part I			Part II			Overall Individual Needs
	Literal (3/3)	Vocabulary (3/4)	Inferential (2/3)	Graphics (4/5)	Directions (5/6)	Internet (4/5)	
1							
2							
3							
4							
5							
6							
7							
8							
9							
10							
11							
12							
13							
14							
15							
16							
17							
18							
19							
20							
Class Skill Needs							

Explanation:

Scoring each section: To receive a "x" for a section of the CIRI, a student must meet or exceed the minimum score indicated inside the parentheses in the columns above. An "x" mark in one of the skill boxes indicates that a student has mastered that particular skill.

Meeting individual needs: If a box in one of the columns does not have a "x," then the student has not mastered that skill and needs more instruction in that particular area. If a student has three or more boxes without a "x," then that student is a candidate for individual skill instruction in those particular skill areas. This may be accomplished through peer tutoring, grouping or individual instruction.

Meeting overall class needs: If more than half of the students within a class do not attain skill mastery on any or all of the skills, then extra instruction needs to be given to the class as a whole in that particular skill area.

What follows are the pages I would copy and present to my students.

CIRI for Chemistry

Welcome to Chemistry 101!

I'm looking forward to working with all of you this semester as we put on our lab coats and goggles and unravel the mysteries of the physical world. Because I want you all to succeed in this course, I'd like you to spend today's class working on the following assignment. This is an evaluation tool called a Content Informal Reading Inventory (CIRI).

This is **not** a test, and you will **not** receive a grade. However, I will give you points for completing the CIRI. Your answers will help me design better lessons in the future. The results of this CIRI will also show me your strengths and where you might need additional help when reading our textbook. If you have any questions during the assignment, please raise your hand or come up to my desk.

Thanks for your help,

Mr. O'Sliabh

PART I—Comprehension

The following passage is from your text, *Active Chemistry*. This text provides an interesting and fun introduction to the world of chemistry. Each chapter is divided into several activities where you will get a chance to perform real experiments for yourself. After each activity there is a short section explaining some of the principles behind the experiment. The selection that you are about to read was taken directly from one of those sections. Pay close attention to the concepts of elements and compounds.

Read the selection below entitled, "The Structure of Matter," and take a look at the table provided on the next page. Then answer the questions that follow. You do **not** need to answer in complete sentences. Feel free to go back to the passage as often as you want.

The Structure of Matter

Hydrogen and oxygen are elements. An **element** is any material that cannot be broken down into simpler materials by chemical means. You are probably familiar with many elements like hydrogen, oxygen, zinc, gold, or helium. Other elements like strontium and beryllium are more *exotic* and less likely to be familiar to you. Every kind of *matter* you observe in your everyday life is made up of the chemical elements. There are only about a hundred different kinds of chemical elements. This is an amazing discovery of chemistry—everything you observe in the world is made of different combinations of a hundred elements. Chemistry is the study of how these elements combine and the characteristics of these combinations.

Elements are represented by symbols. The symbol is one, two, or three letters that represent the name. It's easier to write O than to write oxygen. It's easier to write H than to write hydrogen. The symbols come from many different sources. However, the same symbols are used for each element in all countries of the world.

When elements combine they form new substances called **compounds**. These compounds have entirely new *characteristics*. It is like combining the letters of the alphabet to make words. Twenty-six letters can be combined to make thousands of different words.

Water is an example of a compound. A water molecule, H_2O, is composed of two atoms of hydrogen and one atom of oxygen. (For now, think of an atom as the smallest particle of an element and a molecule as the smallest unit of a compound.)

Symbols for Some Elements

Name of Element	Symbol	Name of Element	Symbol
Aluminum	Al	mercury	Hg
Bromine	Br	neon	Ne
Calcium	Ca	nickel	Ni
Carbon	C	nitrogen	N
chlorine	Cl	oxygen	O
copper	Cu	phosphorus	P
gold	Au	potassium	K
helium	He	silicon	Si
hydrogen	H	sodium	Na
iodine	I	sulfur	S
iron	Fe	tin	Sn
lead	Pb	zinc	Zn
magnesium	Mg		

Directions: Answer the following 10 questions to the best of your ability. You do *not* need to answer in complete sentences. Feel free to go back to the selection and/or the table as often as you want.

(L)   1. What is an element?

(L)   2. How many different kinds of chemical elements are there?

(L)   3. When elements combine, they form new substances called _____.

(L)   4. What is a water molecule composed of?

(V)   5. In the first paragraph of the selection, the following statement appears: "Other elements like strontium and beryllium are more *exotic* and less likely to be familiar to you." In the context of this sentence, what do you think the word "exotic" means?

(V)   6. Also in the first paragraph, you will find the statement, "Every kind of *matter* you observe in your everyday life is made up of the chemical elements." How would you define the word "matter" as used here?

(V)   7. The second sentence in the fourth paragraph reads, "These compounds have entirely new *characteristics*." In this sentence what do you think the word "characteristics" means?

(I)   8. Is Aluminum (Al) an element or a compound?

(I)   9. What are the names of the two elements in the compound NaCl?

(I)   10. Why do you suppose the same symbols are used for each element in all countries of the world?

Congratulations on finishing Part I! When you're ready, turn the page and begin Part II.

PART II—Skill Areas

A. Interpreting Graphics

In Part I of this CIRI you learned a little bit about chemical elements. You may remember, for instance, that there are approximately 100 of them. An easy way to display information about all of the elements at once is with a chart called a **Periodic Table of the Elements**. [The chart that I will give my students is in color.] Because we will use the Periodic Table frequently during this course, it is important that you know how to find information on it.

The next page contains the Periodic Table from your textbook, *Active Chemistry*. Take a moment to look at it and then return to this page when you're finished. . . .There's a whole lot of crazy stuff on that thing, *isn't there*? Don't be alarmed! It's really quite simple to use a Periodic Table once you've learned how.

Each box on the Periodic Table contains some basic information about one of the elements. The legend at the top of the chart explains how to find that information (using hydrogen as an example). Use the Periodic Table and its legend to answer the five questions below.

Directions: Answer the following 5 questions to the best of your ability. You do *not* need to answer in complete sentences. Refer to the Periodic Table and legend found on the next page.

---

1. What *color* is used to denote *gases at room temperature*?

2. Of the choices below, what type of element occurs most frequently on the Periodic Table? (circle one answer only)

    A) Metals

    B) Metalloids

    C) Nonmetals

3. What is the atomic number of Helium (He)?

4. What is the average atomic mass of Potassium (K)?

5. What are the only two elements that are liquids at room temperature?

Periodic Table of the Elements

KEY

1 ← Atomic Number
H ← Symbol
1.00794 ← Average Atomic Mass
1s¹ ← Electron Configuration
Hydrogen ← Name

Gases at room temperature
Liquids at room temperature
Solids at room temperature

Metals
Metalloids
Nonmetals

GROUP

	IA/1A Alkali Metals	IIA/2A Alkaline Earth Metals											IIIA/3A	IVA/4A	VA/5A	VIA/6A Chalcogens	VIIA/7A Halides	VIIIA/8A or 0 Noble Gases
	1	2	3	4	5	6	7	8	9	10	11	12	13	14	15	16	17	18

PERIOD

1
1 H 1.00794 1s¹ Hydrogen
2 He 4.002602 1s² Helium

2
3 Li 6.941 [He]2s¹ Lithium
4 Be 9.012182 [He]2s² Beryllium
5 B 10.811 [He]2s²2p¹ Boron
6 C 12.011 [He]2s²2p² Carbon
7 N 14.00674 [He]2s²2p³ Nitrogen
8 O 15.9994 [He]2s²2p⁴ Oxygen
9 F 18.998403 [He]2s²2p⁵ Fluorine
10 Ne 20.1797 [He]2s²2p⁶ Neon

3
11 Na 22.98977 [Ne]3s¹ Sodium
12 Mg 24.3050 [Ne]3s² Magnesium
13 Al 26.981539 [Ne]3s²3p¹ Aluminum
14 Si 28.0855 [Ne]3s²3p² Silicon
15 P 30.973762 [Ne]3s²3p³ Phosphorus
16 S 32.066 [Ne]3s²3p⁴ Sulfur
17 Cl 35.4527 [Ne]3s²3p⁵ Chlorine
18 Ar 39.948 [Ne]3s²3p⁶ Argon

IIIB/3B IVB/4B VB/5B VIB/6B VIIB/7B VIIIB/8B IB/1B IIB/2B

Transition Metals

4
19 K 39.0983 [Ar]4s¹ Potassium
20 Ca 40.078 [Ar]4s² Calcium
21 Sc 44.95591 [Ar]4s²3d¹ Scandium
22 Ti 47.867 [Ar]4s²3d² Titanium
23 V 50.9415 [Ar]4s²3d³ Vanadium
24 Cr 51.9961 [Ar]4s¹3d⁵ Chromium
25 Mn 54.93805 [Ar]4s²3d⁵ Manganese
26 Fe 55.847 [Ar]4s²3d⁶ Iron
27 Co 58.93320 [Ar]4s²3d⁷ Cobalt
28 Ni 58.6934 [Ar]4s²3d⁸ Nickel
29 Cu 63.546 [Ar]4s¹3d¹⁰ Copper
30 Zn 65.39 [Ar]4s²3d¹⁰ Zinc
31 Ga 69.723 [Ar]4s²3d¹⁰4p¹ Gallium
32 Ge 72.61 [Ar]4s²3d¹⁰4p² Germanium
33 As 74.92159 [Ar]4s²3d¹⁰4p³ Arsenic
34 Se 78.96 [Ar]4s²3d¹⁰4p⁴ Selenium
35 Br 79.904 [Ar]4s²3d¹⁰4p⁵ Bromine
36 Kr 83.80 [Ar]4s²3d¹⁰4p⁶ Krypton

5
37 Rb 85.4678 [Kr]5s¹ Rubidium
38 Sr 87.62 [Kr]5s² Strontium
39 Y 88.90585 [Kr]5s²4d¹ Yttrium
40 Zr 91.224 [Kr]5s²4d² Zirconium
41 Nb 92.90638 [Kr]5s¹4d⁴ Niobium
42 Mo 95.94 [Kr]5s¹4d⁵ Molybdenum
43 Tc 98.9072 [Kr]5s²4d⁵ Technetium
44 Ru 101.07 [Kr]5s¹4d⁷ Ruthenium
45 Rh 102.90550 [Kr]5s¹4d⁸ Rhodium
46 Pd 106.42 [Kr]4d¹⁰ Palladium
47 Ag 107.8682 [Kr]5s¹4d¹⁰ Silver
48 Cd 112.411 [Kr]5s²4d¹⁰ Cadmium
49 In 114.82 [Kr]5s²4d¹⁰5p¹ Indium
50 Sn 118.710 [Kr]5s²4d¹⁰5p² Tin
51 Sb 121.757 [Kr]5s²4d¹⁰5p³ Antimony
52 Te 127.60 [Kr]5s²4d¹⁰5p⁴ Tellurium
53 I 126.90447 [Kr]5s²4d¹⁰5p⁵ Iodine
54 Xe 131.29 [Kr]5s²4d¹⁰5p⁶ Xenon

6
55 Cs 132.90543 [Xe]6s¹ Cesium
56 Ba 137.327 [Xe]6s² Barium
57 *La 138.9055 [Xe]6s²5d¹ Lanthanum
72 Hf 178.49 [Xe]6s²4f¹⁴5d² Hafnium
73 Ta 180.9479 [Xe]6s²4f¹⁴5d³ Tantalum
74 W 183.85 [Xe]6s²4f¹⁴5d⁴ Tungsten
75 Re 186.207 [Xe]6s²4f¹⁴5d⁵ Rhenium
76 Os 190.23 [Xe]6s²4f¹⁴5d⁶ Osmium
77 Ir 192.22 [Xe]6s²4f¹⁴5d⁷ Iridium
78 Pt 195.08 [Xe]6s¹4f¹⁴5d⁹ Platinum
79 Au 196.96654 [Xe]6s¹4f¹⁴5d¹⁰ Gold
80 Hg 200.59 [Xe]6s²4f¹⁴5d¹⁰ Mercury
81 Tl 204.3833 [Xe]6s²4f¹⁴5d¹⁰6p¹ Thallium
82 Pb 207.2 [Xe]6s²4f¹⁴5d¹⁰6p² Lead
83 Bi 208.98037 [Xe]6s²4f¹⁴5d¹⁰6p³ Bismuth
84 Po 208.9824 [Xe]6s²4f¹⁴5d¹⁰6p⁴ Polonium
85 At 209.9871 [Xe]6s²4f¹⁴5d¹⁰6p⁵ Astatine
86 Rn 222.0176 [Xe]6s²4f¹⁴5d¹⁰6p⁶ Radon

7
87 Fr 223.0197 [Rn]7s¹ Francium
88 Ra 226.0254 [Rn]7s² Radium
89 **Ac 227.0278 [Rn]7s²6d¹ Actinium
104 Rf 261 [Rn]7s²5f¹⁴6d² Rutherfordium
105 Db 262 [Rn]7s²5f¹⁴6d³ Dubnium
106 Sg 263 [Rn]7s²5f¹⁴6d⁴ Seaborgium
107 Bh 262 [Rn]7s²5f¹⁴6d⁵ Bohrium
108 Hs 265 [Rn]7s²5f¹⁴6d⁶ Hassium
109 Mt 265 [Rn]7s²5f¹⁴6d⁷ Meitnerium
110 Uun 271 [Rn]7s²5f¹⁴6d⁸ Ununnilium
111 Uuu 272 [Rn]7s¹5f¹⁴6d¹⁰ Unununium
112 Uub 277 [Rn]7s²5f¹⁴6d¹⁰ Ununbium
113
114 Uuq 289 [Rn]7s²5f¹⁴6d¹⁰7p² Ununquadium
115
116
117
118

*Lanthanide Series
58 Ce 140.115 [Xe]6s²4f² Cerium
59 Pr 140.90765 [Xe]6s²4f³ Praseodymium
60 Nd 144.24 [Xe]6s²4f⁴ Neodymium
61 Pm 144.9125 [Xe]6s²4f⁵ Promethium
62 Sm 150.36 [Xe]6s²4f⁶ Samarium
63 Eu 151.965 [Xe]6s²4f⁷ Europium
64 Gd 157.25 [Xe]6s²4f⁷5d¹ Gadolinium
65 Tb 158.92534 [Xe]6s²4f⁹ Terbium
66 Dy 162.50 [Xe]6s²4f¹⁰ Dysprosium
67 Ho 164.93032 [Xe]6s²4f¹¹ Holmium
68 Er 167.26 [Xe]6s²4f¹² Erbium
69 Tm 168.93421 [Xe]6s²4f¹³ Thulium
70 Yb 173.04 [Xe]6s²4f¹⁴ Ytterbium
71 Lu 174.967 [Xe]6s²4f¹⁴5d¹ Lutetium

**Actinide Series
90 Th 232.0381 [Rn]7s²6d² Thorium
91 Pa 231.03588 [Rn]7s²5f²6d¹ Protactinium
92 U 238.0289 [Rn]7s²5f³6d¹ Uranium
93 Np 237.0482 [Rn]7s²5f⁵ Neptunium
94 Pu 244.0642 [Rn]7s²5f⁶ Plutonium
95 Am 243.0614 [Rn]7s²5f⁷ Americium
96 Cm 247.0703 [Rn]7s²5f⁷6d¹ Curium
97 Bk 247 [Rn]7s²5f⁹ Berkelium
98 Cf 251 [Rn]7s²5f¹⁰ Californium
99 Es 252 [Rn]7s²5f¹¹ Einsteinium
100 Fm 257 [Rn]7s²5f¹² Fermium
101 Md 258 [Rn]7s²5f¹³ Mendelevium
102 No 259 [Rn]7s²5f¹⁴ Nobelium
103 Lr 262 [Rn]7s²5f¹⁴6d¹ Lawrencium

B. Following Directions

Frequently during the year we'll be doing experiments in the lab, and you and your lab partner will be given a set of procedures to follow. It is critical that you follow these instructions exactly as written. A simple mistake (such as doing step #4 before step #3) could ruin an entire day's work. Because we will be using real chemicals, this might even be dangerous!

The following directions are from an activity you will do later this year. Please read the procedure carefully, and then answer the 6 questions that follow. Some of the words in the directions may be unfamiliar to you. Don't worry! You won't need to know their meanings right now to answer the questions.

1. Check your balance to make sure that it reads zero with nothing on it. Then measure the mass of a 50-mL beaker.

    a) Record the mass in your *Active Chemistry* log.

2. Measure out approximately 0.20 g of aluminum foil into the empty beaker. Try to get your mass measurement close to the assigned value.

    If you have a centigram balance, you'll need to adjust the balance to read 0.20 more grams than the beaker alone. Then add pieces of aluminum foil until it rebalances.

    If you have an electronic balance, simply add pieces of aluminum foil until the display indicates 0.20 g more than the empty beaker.

    a) Record the value that you obtain, even though you might not hit the target value.

3. Measure the mass of a piece of weighing paper.

    Place approximately 2.00 g of copper (II) chloride on the weighing paper. (The chemical elements you would expect to find in copper (II) chloride are copper and chlorine.) Again, remember that your target value is 2.00 g and that you may be slightly over or under this value.

    a) Record the masses in your *Active Chemistry* log.

4. Add the copper (II) chloride to the beaker.

    Next add water to the beaker until it is approximately half full.

    a) Record your observations in your *Active Chemistry* log.

Directions: Answer the following 6 questions to the best of your ability. You do *not* need to answer in complete sentences. Feel free to go back to the selection as often as you want.

1. In step #1 of the procedure on the previous page, what's the very first thing you need to do?

2. In step #2 how much aluminum foil do you need to measure out into the empty beaker?

3. In step #2 of the procedure, what do you need to do if you have a centigram balance?

4. In step #3 of the procedure, *after* measuring the mass of a piece of weighing paper, what compound do you place on the weighing paper?

5. In step #4 what do you need to do *before* you add water to the beaker?

6. Where should you record your observations in step #4?

You're almost through! Now turn the page to complete the last section.

C. Conducting Internet Searches

Occasionally during the year, I will ask you to look up some information on the Internet. You'll easily be able to complete these assignments if you have some basic web navigation skills. The tool that you will use to find things on the Internet is called a search engine. There are many different search engines. One of the most popular is Google, which you can find online at http://www.google.com

The next two pages show the results of an Internet search that I conducted on Google. Briefly look over these results, and then answer the 5 questions below.

> **Directions: Answer the following 5 questions to the best of your ability. You do *not* need to answer in complete sentences. Refer to the Google search results on the following two pages.**

1. What 2 key words did I use to start the search?

2. About how many results did Google find?

3. The 3ʳᵈ result is titled, "It's Elemental—The Element Strontium." What is the complete Internet address (also called a URL) for this result?

4. Out of the 10 results displayed, what is the *title* of the one where you would most likely find information on how the element Strontium got its name?

5. To the right of the first result ("Visual Elements—Strontium"), there is a smaller entry entitled "Strontium Support." It contains a description that reads, "The New Bone Health Mineral Supports Bone Structure & Function." If you were to click on this link, do you think you would more likely find valuable information about Strontium *or* an advertisement for a product? Why?

Congratulations! You've completed the CIRI. Thank you for helping me with this project. If there is any time left over, feel free to work quietly on whatever you'd like.

Web Images Groups News Froogle **more »**

element strontium

Search Advanced Search
Preferences

Web

Results **1 - 10** of about **141,000** for element strontium. (**0.35** seconds)

Visual **Elements** - **Strontium**
... in 1808 by Sir Humphry Davy in London, UK Origin : The
element is named after the village of Strontian in Scotland,
where **strontium** ore was first found. ...
www.chemsoc.org/vis**elements**/pages/**strontium**.html - 25k -
Nov 12, 2004 - Cached - Similar pages

Visual **Elements**: **Strontium**
Strontium - Sr General Information Discovery **Strontium** was isolated by Sir Humphry
Davy in 1808 in London, but recognised as an **element** by A. Crawford in 1790. ...
www.chemsoc.org/vis**elements**/ pages/data/**strontium**_data.html - 24k -
Cached - Similar pages
[More results from www.chemsoc.org]

It's **Elemental** - The **Element Strontium**
... 87.62. **Strontium**. Atomic Number: 38. Atomic Weight: 87.62. ... Density: 2.64 grams per
cubic centimeter. Phase at Room Temperature: Solid. **Element** Classification: Metal ...
education.jlab.org/its**element**al/ele038.html - 14k - Nov 11, 2004 - Cached - Similar pages

Periodic Table of **Elements**: **Strontium** - Sr (EnvironmentalChemistry ...
Comprehensive information for the **element Strontium** - Sr is provided by this page
including scores of properties, **element** names in many languages, most known ...
environmentalchemistry.com/yogi/periodic/Sr.html - 52k - Nov 12, 2004 -
Cached - Similar pages

Periodic Table of the **Elements** - **Strontium**
... Search. Chemistry Periodic Table of the **Elements Strontium**. Sr. Atomic Number: 38.
Symbol: Sr. Atomic weight: 87.62. Discovery: Davey ...
chemistry.about.com/library/blsr.htm - 22k - Cached - Similar pages

Chemistry : Periodic Table : **strontium** : index
... **Element** bond length, **strontium**. Enthalpy of atomization, **strontium**. Enthalpy of fusion,
strontium. ... History of the **element**, **strontium**. Ionic radii (Shannon), **strontium** ...
www.web**elements**.com/web**elements**/**element**s/text/Sr/ - 43k - Nov 12, 2004 -
Cached - Similar pages

Chemical **Elements**.com - **Strontium** (Sr)
... MLA Format for Citing This Page. Bentor, Yinon. Chemical **Element**.com - **Strontium**.
<http://www.chemicalelements.com/**elements**/sr.html>. ...
www.chemical**elements**.com/**element**s/sr.html - 9k - Cached - Similar pages

ScienceDaily -- Browse Topics: Science/Chemistry/**Elements** ...
... properties of the **element**. Wikipedia: **Strontium** - Properties of the **element**, including
its history, applications, and charateristics. ...
www.sciencedaily.com/directory/ Science/Chemistry/Elements/Strontium - 42k - Nov 12,
2004 - Cached - Similar pages

Periodic Table of the **Elements**: **Strontium**
... Next **element**. ...
www.tabulka.cz/english/**element**s/show.asp?id=38 - 20k - Cached - Similar pages

ELEMENT: STRONTIUM
... differing from other barium minerals. Forms **Element** Displays**Strontium** is found chiefly
as celestite and strontianite. The metal can be ...
www.radiochemistry.org/periodictable/**element**s/38.html - 7k - Cached - Similar pages

Result Page: 1 2 3 4 5 6 7 8 9 10   **Next**

 element strontium   Search

Search within results | Language Tools | Search Tips | Dissatisfied? Help us improve

Google Home - Advertising Programs - Business Solutions - About Google

©2004 Google

Structural Analysis: Words and Affixes

Some Common Root Word and Affixes often found in scientific terms.

Root or Affix	Meaning	Example
a-, an	without	anaerobic
ab-	away from	abnormal
ad-	to, toward	adhere
aero-	air	aerobic
ambi-	both	ambidextrous
ante-	before	anterior
anthropo-	man, human	anthropology
anti-	against, opposite	antigen
aqua-	water	aquatic
astro-	star	astronomy
auto-	self	automatic
avi-	bird	aviary
baro-	pressure	barometer
bene-	good	benefit
bi-	two, twice	biped
bio-	life	biology
capit,	head	decapitate
cardio-	heart	cardiogram
carni-	flesh	carnivorous
chlor	green	chloroplast
chrom-	color	chromatin
chrono-	time	chronology
circum-	around	circumference
com-	together, with	combine
contra-, contro	against	contraception
corpus	body	corpse
cyclo-	circular	cyclotron
cyto-	cell, hollow	cytoplasm
derm	skin	epidermis
di-, dis-	two	dissect

From Pierce, D. *Reading Activities in Content Areas: An Ideabook for Middle and Secondary Schools.* Published by Allyn & Bacon, Boston, MA. Copyright © 1976 by Pearson Education. Reprinted by permission of the publisher.

Some Common Root Word and Affixes often found in scientific terms (continued).

Root or Affix	Meaning	Example
dorsi-, dorso-	back	dorsal
entomo-	insect	entomology
epi-	upon, outer	epidermis
erg-	work	energy
ex-	out, form	excrete
eu-	good	euphoria
frater	brother	fraternal
gen-	race, kind born, produce	generation
geo-	earth	geology
germ-	sprout	germinate
graph-	write, record	graphite
gyn-	female	gynecology
helio-	sun	heliograph
hemi-	half	hemisphere
hemo-	blood	hemoglobin
herb-	plant	herbivorous
hetero-	mixed	heterogeneous
hexa-	six	hexagon
homo-	same, alike	homogeneous
hydr(o)-	water	dehydrate
hyper-	over, excess	hyperactive
hypo-	under, less	hypodermic
ichthyo-	fish	ichthyology
in-	not	insomnia
in-	into	inbreed
inter-	between	intercellular
intra-	within	intramuscular
iso-	equal	isometric
-itis	inflammation	tonsillitis
junct-	join	junction
kine-	movement	kinetic
lact(o)-	milk	lactic
-logy	science, study of	biology
lunar-	moon	lunarian
-lysis	break up	analysis
macro-	large	macroscopic
magni-	great, large	magnitude
meta-	change, beyond	metaphase
-meter	measure	altimeter
micro-	small	microscope
mono-	one, single	monocyte
morpho-	form	metamorphosis
mortal	death	mortality
multi-	many	multicellular

Some Common Root Word and Affixes often found in scientific terms (continued).

Root or Affix	Meaning	Example
natal	birth	postnatal
nubul	cloudy	nebulous
neuro-	nerve	neuron
non-	not	nonnitrogenous
octo-	eight	octopus
oculo-	eye	oculist
omni-	all	omnivorous
ornitho-	bird	ornithology
ortho-	straight	orthopterous
osteo-	bone	osteopath
patho-	disease, feeling	pathology
pedi-, pod	foot, footed	anthropod
per-	through	permeate
phono-	sound, voice	phonograph
photo-	light	photosynthesis
physio-	organic	physiology
poly-	many, much	polyembryony
pos, pon	place, put	position
post-	after	postnatal
pre-	before	prediagnosis
pro-	for	pro bono
pseudo-	fake	pseudopod
psycho-	mind	psychology
pteron	winged	lepidoptera
quad-	four	quadruped
retro-	backward	retroactive
rhodo	rose, red	rhodolite
-scope	view, examine	microscope
-sect	part, divide	dissect
som(a)	body	chromosome
somn	sleep	insomnia
son(i)	sound	supersonic
sphere	round, globe	spherical
sub-	under	subconscious
syn-	together, with	synthesis
tele-	far, distant	telescope
ten-	to hold	tenaculum
thermo-	heat	thermometer
trans-	across	transmutation
un-	not	undeveloped
under-	below	underactive
vita-	life	vitamin
-vor(e)	eat	herbivorous
zo-	animal	zoology

Word Study References

APPENDIX

E

Allen, M., & Kelsch, J. (1997). *Challenging word games.* New York: Sterling.

Ammer, C. (1989). *Fighting words: From war, rebellion and other combative capers.* New York: Dell.

Asimov. (1959). *Words of science and the history behind them.* Boston: Houghton-Mifflin Co.

Asimov, I. (1961). *Words from myths.* Boston: Houghton-Mifflin Co.

Asimov, I. (1962). *Words on the map.* Boston: Houghton-Mifflin Co.

Asimov, I. (1968). *Words from history.* Boston: Houghton-Mifflin Co.

Asimov, I. (1972). *More words of science.* Boston: Houghton-Mifflin Co.

Augarde, T. (1984). *The Oxford guide to word games.* New York: Oxford University Press.

Bierce, A. (1978). *The devil's dictionary.* Owings Mills, MD: Stemmer House.

Blumenfeld, W. (1989). *Pretty ugly: More oxymorons and other illogical expressions that make absolute sense.* New York: Putnam.

Boatner, T., & Gates, E. (1975). *Dictionary of American idioms* (Rev. ed.). Edited by Adam Makkai. Woodbury, NY: Barron's Educational Services, Inc.

Bowler, P. (1979). *The superior person's book of words.* Boston: David R. Godine Publisher.

Brandreth, G. (1980). *The joy of lex: How to have fun with words.* New York: William Morrow and Company, Inc.

Cutler, C. (1994). *O brave new words: Native American loan words in current English.* Norman: University of Oklahoma Press.

Dale, E., & O'Rourke, O. (1971). *Techniques of teaching vocabulary.* Palo Alto, CA: Field Educational Publications.

de Bono, E. (1977). *Word power: An illustrated dictionary of virtual words.* New York: Harper Colophon Books.

Donaldson, G., & Setterfield, S. (Eds.). (1986). *Why do we say that?* New York: Penny farthing Editions, Dorset Press.

Freeman, M. S. (1985). *The story behind the word.* Philadelphia, PA: ISI Press.

Funk, C. E. (1948; Reprinted in 1985). *A hog on ice.* New York: Warner Publishing, Inc.

Funk, C. E. (1968). *Word origins and their romantic stories.* New York: Funk and Wagnalls.

Funk, C. E. (1985). *Thereby hangs a tale: Stories of curious word origins.* New York: Harper & Row.

Funk, C. E. (1986). *Heavens to Betsy! and other curious sayings.* New York: Harper & Row.

Funk, C. E., & Funk, C. E., Jr. (1986). *Horsefeathers.* New York: Harper Paperback Library.

Golick, M. (1987). *Playing with words.* Markham, Ontario: Pembroke Publishers.

Grambs, D. (1986). *Dimboxes, epopts, and other quidams: Words to describe life's indescribable people*. New York: Workman.

Grothe, M. (2004). *Oxymoronica: Paradoxical wit and wisdom from history's greatest wordsmiths*. New York: Harper-Collins.

Harris, T. L., & Hodges, R. E. (1995). *The literacy dictionary: The vocabulary of reading and writing*. Newark, DE: International Reading Association.

Hendrickson, R. (1994). *Grandslams, hat tricks, and alley-oops: A sports fan's book*. New York: Prentice Hall.

Lederer, R. (1987). *Anguished English*. Charleston: Wyrick & Company.

Lederer, R. (1989). *Crazy English: The ultimate joy ride through our language*. New York: Pocket Books.

Lederer, R. (1990). *The play of words: Fun and games for language lovers*. New York: Pocket Books.

Lederer, R. (1996). *Pun and games: Jokes, riddles, daffnitions, tairy fales, rhymes and more word play for kids*. Chicago: Chicago Review Press, Inc.

Lipton, J. (1977). *An exaltation of larks*. Westford, MA: Penguin Books.

Makkai, A. (Ed.). (1975). *A dictionary of American idioms* (Rev. ed.). Woodbury, NY: Barron's Educational Series, Inc.

Marks, W., & Marks, M. (1971). *Dictionary of words and phrase origins*. New York: Harper & Row, vol. 1, 1962, vol. 2, 1967, vol. 3, 1971.

Major, C. (1994). *Juba to jive: A dictionary of African-American slang*. New York: Viking.

McCutcheon, M. (1992). *Descriptionary: A thematic dictionary*. New York: Checkmark Books.

Mills, J. (1993). *Woman words: A dictionary of words about women*. New York: Henry Holt.

Parlett, D. (1981). *Botticelli and beyond: Over 100 of the world's best word games*. New York: Pantheon.

Pei, M., & Romodicio, S. (1974). *Dictionary of foreign terms*. New York: Dell, Laurel Edition.

Saffire, W. (1978). *Saffire's political dictionary* (Rev. ed.). New York: Random House.

Shaw, H. (1987). *Dictionary of problem words and expressions*. New York: McGraw-Hill.

Smith, J. (1982). *How to win a pullet surprise: The pleasures and pitfalls of our language*. New York: Franklin Watts.

Sperling, S. (1977). *Poplollies and belibones: A celebration of lost words*. New York: Clarkson N. Potter, Inc.

Winokur, J. (Ed.). (1987). *The portable curmudgeon*. New York: New American Library.

Religion in the Public School Curriculum: Questions and Answers

(Reprinted with permission of the American Association of School Administrators from the Publication, *Religion in the Public School Curriculum: Questions and Answers*.)

Growing numbers of people in the United States think it is important to teach about religion in the public schools.[1] But what is the appropriate place to put religion in the public school curriculum? How does one approach such issues as textbook content, values education, creation science, and religious holidays?

The following questions and answers are designed to assist school boards as they make decisions about the curriculum and educators as they teach about religion in ways that are constitutionally permissible, educationally sound, and sensitive to the beliefs of students and parents.

There are other questions concerning religion and the schools not addressed here, including school prayer, equal access, and how schools accommodate diverse religious beliefs and practices. For a full discussion of these broader issues, please contact the sponsors listed on the back of this publication.

Q: Is it constitutional to teach about religion in public schools?

A: Yes. In the 1960s school prayer cases (which ruled against state sponsored school prayer and Bible reading), the U. S. Supreme Court indicated that public school education may include teaching about religion. In *Abington v. Schempp,* Associate Justice Tom Clark wrote for the Court:

> [I]t might well be said that one's education is not complete without a study of comparative religion or history of religion and its relationship to the advancement of civilization. It certainly may be said that the Bible is worthy of study for its literary and historic qualities. Nothing we have said here indicated that such study of the Bible or of religion, when presented objectively as part of a secular program of education, may not be effected consistently with the First Amendment.

---

[1] Teaching about religion includes consideration of the beliefs and practices of religions; the role of religion in history and contemporary society; and religious themes in music, art and literature.

Reprinted by permission of the American Association of School Administrators from the publication, *Religion in the Public School Curriculum: Questions and Answers.*

Q: What is meant by "teaching about religion" in the public school?

A: The following statements distinguish between teaching about religion in public schools and religious indoctrination:

- The school's approach to religion is *academic*, not *devotional*.
- The school may strive for student *awareness* of religions, but should not press for student acceptance of any one religion.
- The school may sponsor *study* about religion, but may not sponsor the *practice* of religion.
- The school may *expose* students to a diversity of religious views, but may not *impose* any particular view.
- The school may *educate* about all religions, but may not *promote* or *denigrate* any religion.
- The school may *inform* the student about various beliefs, but should not seek to *conform* him or her to any particular belief.[2]

Q: Why should study about religion be included in the public school curriculum?

A: Because religion plays a significant role in history and society, study about religion is essential to understanding both the nation and the world. Omission of facts about religion can give students the false impression that the religious life of humankind is insignificant or unimportant. Failure to understand even the basic symbols, practices and concepts of the various religions makes much of history, literature, and contemporary life unintelligible.

Study about religion is also important if students are to value religious liberty, the first freedom guaranteed in the Bill of Rights. Moreover, knowledge of the roles of religion in the past and present promotes cross-cultural understanding essential to democracy and world peace.

Q: Where does study about religion belong in the curriculum?

A: Wherever it naturally arises. ON the secondary level, the social studies, literature, and the arts offer many opportunities of the inclusion of information about religions—their ideas and themes. On the elementary level, natural opportunities arise in discussion of the family and community life and in instruction about festivals and different cultures. Many educators believe that integrating study about religion into existing courses is an educationally sound way to acquaint students with the role of religion in history and society.

Religion also may be taught about in special courses or units. Some secondary schools, for example, offer such courses as world religions, the Bible as literature, and the religious literature of the West and of the East.

Q: Do current textbooks teach about religion?

A: Rarely. Recent textbook studies conclude that most widely used textbooks largely ignore the role of religion in history and society. For example, readers of high school U.S. history texts learn little or nothing about the great colonial revivals, the struggles of minority faiths, the religious motivations of immigrants, the contributions of religious groups to many social movements, major episodes of religious intolerance, and

---

[2] The answer is based on guidelines originally published by the Public Education Religion Studies Center at Wright State University.

many other significant events of history. Education without appropriate attention to major religious influences and themes is incomplete education.

Q: How does teaching about religion relate to the teaching of values?

A: Teaching about religion is not the same as teaching values. The former is objective, academic study; the latter involves the teaching of particular ethical viewpoints or standards of behavior.

There are basic moral values that are recognized by the population at large (e.g., honesty, integrity, justice, compassion). These values can be taught in classes through discussion, by example, and by carrying out school polices. However, teachers may not invoke religious authority.

Public schools may teach about the various religious and non religious perspectives concerning the many complex moral issues confronting society, but such perspectives must be presented without adopting, sponsoring, or denigrating one view against another.

Q: Is it constitutional to teach the biblical account of creation in the public schools?

A: Some states have passed laws requiring that creationist theory based on biblical account be taught in the science classroom. The courts have found these laws to be unconstitutional on the ground that they promote a particular religious view. The Supreme Court has acknowledged, however, that a variety of scientific theories about origins can be appropriately taught in the science classroom. In *Edwards v. Aguillard*, the Court stated:

> [T]eaching a variety of scientific theories about the origins of humankind to school-children might be validly done with the clear secular intent of enhancing the effectiveness of science instruction.

Though science instruction may not endorse or promote religious doctrine, the account of creation found in various scriptures may be discussed in a religious studies class or in any course that considers religious explanations for the origin of life.

Q: How should religious holidays be treated in the classroom?

A: Carefully. Religious holidays offer excellent opportunities to teach about religions in the elementary and secondary classroom. Recognition of and information about such holidays should focus on the origin, history, and generally agreed-upon meaning of the observances. If the approach is objective, neither advancing nor inhibiting religion, it can foster among students understanding and mutual respect within and beyond the local community.

Religion in the Public School Curriculum: Questions and Answers—sponsored jointly by:

American Academy of Religion
Department of Religion
501 Hall of Languages
Syracuse University
Syracuse, New York 13244-1170
http://www.aarweb.org/

American Association of School Administrators
801 N. Quincy Street, Suite 700
Arlington, VA 22203
http://www.aasa.org/

American Federation of Teachers
555 New Jersey Ave., N.W.
Washington, DC 20001
http://www.aft.org/

American Jewish Congress
http://www.ajcongress.org/

American United Research Foundation*
900 Silver Spring Ave.
Silver Spring, MD 20910

Association for Supervision and Curriculum Development*
125 N. West Street
Alexandria, VA 22314-2798
http://www.ascd.org/portal/site/ascd/index.jsp/

Baptist Joint Committee on Public Affairs
200 Maryland Ave., NE
Washington, DC 20002
http://www.bjcpa.org/

Christian Legal Society
P.O. Box 1492
Merrifield, VA 22116
http://www.clsnet.org/

The Church of Jesus Christ of Latter-day Saints
http://www.lds.org/

First Amendment Center
http://www.firstamendmentcenter.org/

The Islamic Society of North America
http://www.isna.net/clear.gif

National Association of Evangelicals
1430 K Street, NW
Washington, DC 20005
http://www.nae.net/

National Conference for Community and Justice
71 5th Avenue
New York, NY 10003
http://www.nccj.org/

---

*These organizations have materials available for teaching about religion in the public school curriculum.

National Council of Churches of Christ in the USA
475 Riverside Drive
New York, NY 10115
http://www.ncccusa.org/

National Council for the Social Studies*
3501 Newark St., NW
Washington, DC 20016
http://www.ncss.org/

National Education Association
1201 16th St., NW
Washington, DC 20036
http://www.nea.org/index.html

National School Boards Association
1680 Duke St.
Alexandria, VA 22314
http://www.nsba.org/site/index.asp

---

*These organizations have materials available for teaching about religion in the public school curriculum.

Using Advance Organizers to Enhance the Processing of Texts

by Marian J. Tonjes

> . . . The most important single factor influencing learning is what the learner already knows. Ascertain this and teach him accordingly.
>
> D.P. Ausubel (1968) *Educational Psychology: A Cognitive View,* New York: Holt, Rinehart and Winston, p. vi.

Introduction

The topic of advance organizers fits in quite well with the second major strand of this conference, that of "Reading to Learn." In this paper I would like to describe, first of all, the notion of an advance organizer as a preinstructional strategy. Second, I will touch on some major research findings on the effectiveness of advance organizers in enhancing text comprehension. Third, I will report on a research study completed in May 1980 at Western Washington University with graduate student in reading, Richard Gigo. Finally, I will suggest some needed changes and applications for advance organizers if they are indeed to enhance the processing of text.

The notion of an advance organizer

Let me say here at the onset that I am using the term "advance organizer," to describe a particular type of preinstructional reading strategy, one that is written at a more *general, inclusive* and *abstract* level than the text itself. Its purpose is to assist the reader in the mastery of forthcoming concepts by providing a framework or scaffolding prior to the reading assignment. This notion is based on Ausubel's (1960) theory of meaningful learning and his delineation of what constitutes an advance organizer, hereafter to be referred to as an "AO."

Original Published Source:

Tonjes, M. J. (1981). Using advance organizers to enhance the processing of text. In J. Chapman (Ed.), *The reader and the text* (pp. 131–141). London: Heineman Educational Books.

The following examples were designed to illustrate two major types of AO's, textual and schematic. As you will see, the textual may be further subdivided into preinstructional materials that are either expository or comparative in nature.

The first example, an expository organizer, is used when the forth-coming material is completely unfamiliar, the intent being to familiarize the reader with overall basic concepts and their interrelationships for organizational purposes.

The second example, a comparative organizer, should be given when the general idea of the topic to be read is already familiar. In this example an AO is compared and contrasted with other types of preinstructional activities.

One type of schematic or graphic organizer is shown next; in this case it is a type of cognitive map or representation which attempts to show interrelationships of major facets of an AO. As you will note, the subsumers move from the more general to the specific and attempt to show interrelationships among points.

When they can't see the forest for the trees: three examples of advance organizers

I. An expository organizer (with unfamiliar material)

Each of us has in his brain a structure or framework which reflects all of our previous meaningful learnings. New material, to be meaningful and retained, must be associated in some way with that structure of prior knowledge. Preinstructional strategies which attempt to lay the groundwork for processing this new material include pretests, learning objective, previewing, purpose statements, survey-questions, structured overviews and advance organizers (AO's). As a preinstructional strategy an AO assists the learning of factual material when the text does not already contain built-in organizers. To be effective the main concepts to be encountered and their interrelationships must be stated clearly and precisely. By speaking or writing in more general (broader in scope) inclusive (comprehensive) and abstract (concentrated) terms we create a subsumer, or category heading, under which new information may be placed. Thus, information may enter long-term memory and be readily recalled when the subsumer is presented. The two basic types of AO's are textual, which include expository and comparative; and schematic, which includes pictures, maps and charts.

II. A comprehensive organizer (with familiar material)

All preinstructional activities have the purpose of facilitating text comprehension by alerting readers as to what is to follow, while providing a framework or scaffolding into which new information may be categorized. Pretests, learning objectives, previewing, purpose statements, survey-questions and structured overviews are similar to advance organizers (AO's) in that they generally state or search for main points while omitting details. An AO differs as a preinstructional strategy in that it shows interrelationships between points (the organizing elements) making use of the prior knowledge, integrating unfamiliar information with what is already known.

III. A schematic organizer

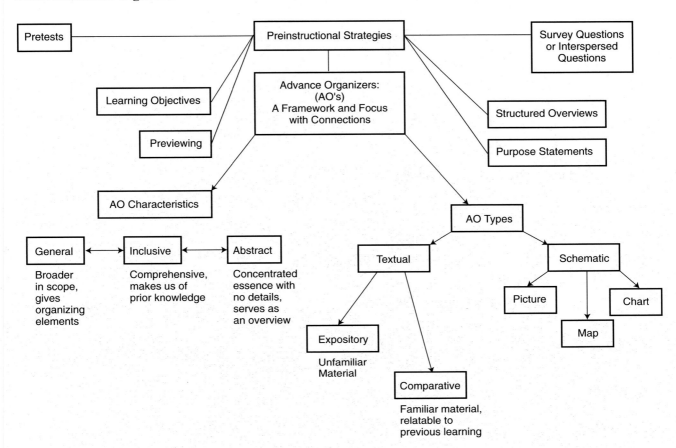

Thus, comprehending written text depends on our prior knowledge: what kind, how much *and* how well organized it is. Any new information must be related or integrated in some way into what we already know. It must not only be reconciled with what we know, but also differentiated to avoid any confusion. This is the intent of the advance organizer. As the length and syntactic complexity of the text increases there is a greater need for this type of learning assistance.

Research findings

For twenty years extensive research has been conducted on how AO's affect learning and retention. Much of this research has been based on David Ausubel's (1960) theory of meaningful learning, within which he developed the strategy of providing the reader with higher order explanatory material prior to the text. Early studies involving his subsumption theory consistently reported significant results. (e.g., Ausubel, 1960; Ausubel and Fitzgerald, 1962).

Since that time, however, reports of effectiveness in a variety of subject areas have shown mixed results—both facility (e.g., Mayer, 1978, 1979; Lawton, 1977; Gardner and Schumacher, 1977; Scandura and Wells, 1967)—and non-significant or impeding (e.g., Rickards and McCormick, 1977; Clawson and Barnes, 1973; Caponecchi, 1973). An intensive debate was started by investigators Barnes and Clawson in 1975 questioning the value of AO's as a teaching device. A reply from Lawton and Wanska in 1977 demonstrated the superior effectiveness of AO pre-lessons which presented high-order content and process concepts and were constructed to point out crucial relationships between the actual structural requirements and the content of the learning material.

In another example, Rickards (1976) found that interspersed AO's yielded greater recall of information from the passage than either interspersed post-organizers or interspersed coordinate *(not* super-ordinate) prestatements or poststatements. The interspersed AO's engendered a subsumptive process with the information presented, as there was a substantially greater amount of recall of concepts and related facts.

On the other hand, Bransford and Johnson (1973) had found no difference in passage recall between a pre-theme or AO group and the control group. It has been suggested that this discrepancy could be related to differences in passage length and complexity, as Bransford and Johnson used short passages of approximately 190 words, centered on only one theme. Thus, the processing demands here were considerably less, perhaps even making the addition of an AO immaterial.

In an important recent review of AO research Luiten and others (1979) examined 135 studies using Glass's technique of meta-analysis. Variables included grade (age level), subject area, presentation mode of the organizer and ability level. A majority of these studies showed AO's to have a facilitative effect on learning and retention. What I found most interesting was that the AO's effect on retention increased with time. Also, the learning effect was more pronounced with college students and with special educational areas that in primary and secondary schools. However, primary school subjects did show a greater retention increase. Within subject areas the size of the effect was positive, especially for learning in social studies, and for retention in physical sciences.

In 1978 Kozlow also performed a meta-analysis of selected AO research reports from 1960 to 1970. His report found only a tendency for AO's to show facilitative effects. Among several conclusions formed were that:

1) Some of the reported facilitative effects may have been due to the AO's contribution to answering the test questions or due to an inequality of study time for treatment groups.

2) Some of the non-significant findings might have resulted from students inability to understand the AO information. (That is why it is so important to have a simply and clearly state AO!)

3) Comparative AO's may be more effective than expository ones. (I would suggest that this might very well have more to do with the background knowledge the reader brought to the reading task!)

So, as you can see, research results have been inconclusive, at least on the surface.

The effect of two pre-instructional strategies on learning and retention

A study conducted in the spring of 1980 at Western Washington University by Gigo and Tonjes was the second in a projected series on the topic of Advance Organizers. The first—Karahalios, Tonjes and Towner (1979)—found a significant difference in comprehension between the AO group and the control group, using 76 seventh grade science students and a text unit on measurement of mass and length.

The purpose of the present study was to investigate the effect of two types of pre-instructional strategies on short term learning and retention. The hypotheses were that given a text segment of sufficient length written at an advanced readability level there would be a significant difference in learning and retention between:

1. the group that received a written advance organizer (AO group) and the control group (C);
2. the group given an explanation of the survey and question steps of SQ3R (the SQ group) and a control group;
3. the AO group and the SQ group.

Method

Sample

The subjects were university student volunteers from four sections of a predominantly sophomore class, 'Introduction to Psychology.' This course was selected in an attempt to rule out prior knowledge or instruction in the topic to be read, i.e. types of research methods. The total number in the sample was 30.

Material

The single test segment, given to all three groups, consisted of an expositiory description, approximately 2,500 words in length, of five research methods—historical, descriptive, correlational, causal-comparative and experimental—taken from Gay's *Educational Research* The estimate of readability level using Fry's (1978) graph on three sections of the excerpt, was found to be beyond 17th grade level or outside the upper limits of the graph. The only subheadings in the text segment were those merely identifying the type of research to be discussed.

An objective test of twenty items was constructed to measure literal recall of information without referring back to the material read. One question was inadvertently omitted when the test was administered. The two types of questions asked were completion and identification.

Procedure

Thirty volunteer subjects were randomly assigned to one of three color-coded groups. All subjects were told that the purpose of this exercise was a reading experiment. They were asked at the onset to agree to return in three days for a follow-up, to do the best they could, and to not discuss the material in the interim.

It was explained that their task would be to read a five page text and respond to questions about it. Subjects were given sixty minutes to read and respond to the questions. All completed the assignment within forty-five minutes. All groups were given the identical written instructions to turn in their pamphlet when they had finished reading and pick up a like-coloured test. The terms 'data' and 'hypothesis' were also defined for each group.

Group I: Advance Organizer (AO) subjects were given a brief overview type of paragraph, written in simple terminology at a higher level of generality, inclusiveness and abstraction, so as to build a cognitive framework for classifying details when reading. (The expositiory type of organizer was used rather than a comparative one because the learning material was considered to be unfamiliar to the readers.) Readers were also instructed in writing to keep in mind while reading that they would be expected to identify the different research methods and the characteristics of each.

Group II: The Survey-Question (SQ) group were instructed to do three things: first, to skim to get a basic understanding, second, to rephrase each subheading, turning it into a question, and third, to read to answer their question.

Group III: The control Group (C) were given no additional instructions. Three days later the test was administered again to each group.

Results

Table I shows the number of participants in each group, the mean and mean square for each for immediate and delayed recall.

TABLE I

Mean score summary

Group	Immediate Recall			Delayed Recall		
	N	X	X²	N	Y	Y²
AO	11	9.09	68.92	9	9.44	24.19
SQ	9	8.44	176.19	4	6.25	18.74
C	10	6.6	40.4	9	6.22	63.57

T tests for independent samples, randomly formed, were used because they make adjustments for such small samples, which become increasingly different from the normal distribution as the size becomes smaller. As can be seen in Table II, the AO group showed a significant difference over the control group in immediate recall at the $<.05$ level; while delayed recall was significant at the $<.01$ level. There was a high mortality rate of the SQ group, which makes other comparisons questionable.

Limitations

Along with statistical limitations mentioned previously, the material itself did not contain subheadings conducive to conversion into meaningful guide questions. Also, the test, while carefully developed, was not pilot tested with a large group to determine reliability and validity.

It was speculated that the SQ group might have had a greater return of participants if there had been some previous practice with the SQ method. Informal observation of their initial behaviour suggested possible annoyance or frustration with the task, which may have accounted for the small number willing to return.

TABLE II

Results of T test comparisons

Group	Immediate Recall	Delayed Recall
AO vs C	HØ = rejected p .05 df = 19 t = 2.382	HØ = rejected p .01 df = 16 t = 2.927
AO vs SQ	HØ is not rejected df = 18 t = .394	HØ is rejected df = 11 t = 2.687
SQ vs C	HØ is not rejected df = 17 t = 1.125	The difference between the means is negligible.

Recommendations

Future research might well focus more on the quality of the AO itself, that it does in fact meet the criteria of being written at a higher level of generality, abstractness and inclusiveness. As you may recall, when an AO is generalized it gives organizing elements; when it is abstract it gives the reader an overview beforehand, and when written at a higher level of inclusiveness it makes use of the reader's established knowledge. It goes almost without saying that to be useful AO's must be learnable and stated clearly and precisely in familiar terms. An AO that bridges this gap while connecting the links in some meaningful way should always be a powerful tool.

Another area which should be given greater consideration is the nature of the text material itself. If a text of factual material is already well organized and proceeds from lesser to greater differentiations (higher to lower inclusiveness), there is much less need for an AO. Material should be lengthy enough, too (i.e., 2,000 or more words) so that there is a need for an AO to assist the reader in processing information.

I would suggest too that additional research in comparing the effectiveness of written versus graphic organizers should prove informative.

Some suggested applications

If the AO first delineates clearly, precisely and explicitly the subsuming concepts to be learned it should lead the reader to mastery of the contents with fewer ambiguities, competing meanings or misconceptions. Writing such an organizer is not a simple task. Teachers may well say, "I haven't the time," or they might even think to themselves, "I *can't do that* properly . . ." I have found, however, that they indeed *can* do it with practice, in their subject matter, and do it well. I ask my students to try two kinds of AO's on their material and invariably they discover that in the process of doing it there may be holes in their logic or mental connections, and that when worked out, their lectures or discussions with students are much improved.

Teachers should not forget that, because of the wide variety of background experiences and the uniqueness of cognitive structures, students will often have difficulty with shared meaning. Using an AO will help to bridge this gap by giving all a common focus and framework.

Finally, it should not be forgotten that some material does not lend itself to the need for an AO. If, for example, the author has organized the text from the general to the specific, making explicit the connecting links among concepts, themes and chapters; and if the information is clearly and simply stated, it would seem a waste of time and effort to develop and include the additional reading of an advance organizer.

References

AUSUBEL, D.P., NOVAK, J., and HANESIAN, H. (1978) *Educational Psychology: A Cognitive View* 2nd ed., New York: Holt, Rinehart, and Winston.

AUSUBEL, D.P. (1978) 'In defense of advance organizers, a reply to the critics,' *Review of Educational Research 48, 2,* pp. 251-257, Spring.

AUSUBEL, D.P. and FITZGERALD, D. (1962) 'Organizer, general background and antecedent variables in sequential verbal learning,' *Journal of Educational Psychology,* p. 243, December.

AUSUBEL, D.P., and ROBINSON, F.G. (1969) *School Learning: an Introduction to Educational Psychology.* New York: Holt, Rinehart and Winston.

AUSUBEL, D.P. (1963) *The Psychology of Meaningful Verbal Learning.* New York: Grune and Stratton.

AUSUBEL, D.P. (1960) 'The use of advance organizers in the learning and retention of meaningful verbal material,' *Journal of Educational Psychology.* 51, pp. 267-272.

BAKER, R.L. (1977) 'Meaningful reception learning.' In H.L. Herber and R.T. Vacca (eds.) *Research in Reading in Content Areas: The Third Report.* Syracuse, New York: Syracuse University Reading and Language Arts Center.

BARNES, B.R. and CLAWSON, E.U. (1975) 'Do advance organizers facilitate learning? Recommendations for further research based on an analysis of 32 studies.' *Review of Educational Research,* 45, 4 pp. 637-659, Fall.

BARRON, R.R. (1971) *The Effects of Advance Organizers on Reception, Learning and Retention of General Science Content* (Final Report) Department of Health, Education and Welfare Project No. 1B-030; Grant No. OEG-2-710030, November (ERIC Document Reproduction Service No. ED 061 554).

BRANSFORD, J.D. and JOHNSON, M.K. (1973) 'Considerations of some problems of comprehension,' In W.Chase (ed.) *Visual Information Processing,* New York: Academic Press, pp. 383-438.

CAPONECCHI, W.P. (1973) 'A comparative study of an advance organizer in mathematics to determine its effectiveness on knowledge acquisition and retention.' *Dissertation Abstracts International 34,* 5644A (University Microfilms No. 73-31, 468).

CLAWSON, E.U. and BARNES, B.R. (1973) 'The effects of organizers on the learning of structured anthropology materials in the elementary grades.' *Journal of Experimental Education 42,* pp. 11-15.

FRY, E.B. (1977) 'Fry's Readability Graph: clarification, validity and extension to Level 17,' *Journal of Reading* 21, pp. 242-252.

GARDNER, E.T. and SCHUMACHER, G.M. (1977) 'Effects of contextual organization on prose retention.' *Journal of Educational Psychology* 69, 2, pp. 146-195, April.

GAY, L.R. (1976) *Educational Research.* Charles Merrill Publishing Company, pp. 9-13.

KARAHALIOS, S.M., TONJES, M.J. and TOWNER, J.C. (1979) 'Using advance organizers to improve comprehension of a content text,' *Journal of Reading* 22, pp. 706-708, May.

KOZLOW, M.J. (1978) 'A meta-analysis of selected advance organizer research reports from 1960-1977.' Doctoral Dissertation. The Ohio State University: ED 161755 SE 025245.

LAWTON, J.T. and WANSKA, S.K. (1977) 'Advance organizers as a teaching strategy: a reply to Barnes and Clawson,' *Review of Educational Research* 47, pp. 233-244.

LAWTON, J.T. (1977) 'Effects of advance organizer lessons on children's use of the causal and logical because,' *Journal of Experimental Education* 46, pp. 41-46 (b).

LAWTON, J.T. (1977) 'The use of advance organizers in the learning and retention of logical operations and social studies concepts.' *American Educational Research Journal* 14, pp. 25-43 (a).

LUITEN, J. and others (1979) 'The Advance Organizer: a review of the research using Glass's technique of meta-analysis.' Paper presented at the Annual Meeting of the American Educational Research Association (63rd, San Francisco, California, April) ERIC ED 171803 TM 009515.

MAYER, R.E. (1978) 'Advance Organizers that compensate for the organization of text.' *Journal of Educational Psychology* 70, 6, pp. 880-886, December.

MAYER, R.E. (1979) 'Twenty years of research on advance organizers: assimilation theory is still the best predictor of results.' *Instructional Science* 8, 2, pp. 133-167, April.

PICHERT, J.W. and ANDERSON, R.C. (1977) 'Taking different perspectives on a story.' *Journal of Educational Psychology* 69, 4, pp. 309-315, August.

RICKARDS, J.P. (1975-1976) 'Processing effects of Advance Organizers interspersed in text.' *Reading Research Quarterly* XI, 4, pp. 599-622.

RICKARDS, J.P. and McCORMICK, C.B. (1977) 'Whole versus part presentation of Advance Organizers in text.' *Journal of Educational Research* 70, 3, pp. 147-149, January-February.

SCANDURA, J.M. and WELLS, H.N. (1967) 'Advance Organizers in learning abstract mathematics.' *American Educational Research Journal* 4, pp. 295-301.

WEISBERG, J.S. (1970) 'The use of visual Advance Organizers for learning earth science concepts.' *Journal of Research in Science Teaching* 7, pp. 161-165.

Glossary

accountability   The responsibility of educators to provide evidence to taxpayers and citizens that education dollars are being well-spent.

acronyms   Words formed from the first letters of several words, e.g., NATO, WASP.

ADHD, ADD   Once called hyperkinesis, the constitutional impairment of a student's attention mechanism (ADD) often accompanied by hyperactive behaviors (ADHD).

admit slips   A writing to learn activity. Upon arrival in a class, students are given an index card on which they are asked to respond, anonymously, to a question or to provide the teacher or class with questions of their own. Contrast with *quick writes* and *exit slips*.

advance organizers   A pre-reading comprehension strategy. A brief summary provided as an introduction, usually at a higher level of abstraction. Advance organizers may be used with unfamiliar, new material to provide perspective or to relate new material to previous learned ideas.

affect   A measure of a person's emotional response to any situation (feelings, interests, attitudes already learned). As contrasted to *cognition* (knowing and understanding) *affect* refers to personal responses to whatever is read.

affective domain   Those human interactions that are measured by feelings, emotions, values, interests and attitudes. The affective domain includes students' enthusiasm or boredom, involvement, or noninvolvement in everyday learning activities. Contrast with *cognitive domain*.

affixes   Prefixes and suffixes attached to root words.

aggregate   In assessment, the process of collecting data together in order to make a more general statement. Contrast with *disaggregate*.

aliteracy   Lack of the habit of reading in those capable of doing so. Contrast with *illiteracy*.

amelioration   Words that once had a negative meaning which now have a positive meaning. Contrast with *pejoration*.

anagram   A word or phrase formed by reordering the letters of another word or phrase.

analytic assessment   In writing, assessing multiple traits separately, thereby recognizing relative strengths and weaknesses within a paper. Contrast with *holistic assessment*.

aphorism   A brief statement of a principle, truth or opinion, a maxim or saying.

assessment   Gathering data to find strengths and weaknesses of students either informally or formally. Rooted in the Latin word "assidere" which means, "to sit next to." With regards to writing to learn, see *holistic assessment* and *analytic assessment*.

assessment standards   Statements setting forth guidelines for evaluating student work.

at-risk students   Students in danger of not succeeding in school often due to socio-economic factors, ethnicity, language, or other factors are rarely well served by their schools.

audience   The collection of intended readers, listeners or viewers for a particular work or performance. With written texts, the audience and the writer are separated by time and distance.

authentic   In assessment, those tasks based on the actual ("real world") experiences that students encounter in their lives.

benchmark   A reference point used when measuring or assessing.

bibliotherapy   The use of well chosen books to ease suffering and aid healing.

blogs   A web log (we…blog) or personal web site updated frequently with links, commentary and anything else the writer cares to include.

brainstorming   Generating many different ideas with minimal inhibition.

BRI   Basic Reading Inventory; a tool to measure the independent, instructional and frustration reading levels of a student grades pre-primer through twelve.

CAI   Computer Assisted Instruction. Use of computers to assist instruction.

canon   The body of literary or other artistic works that a given culture defines as important at a given time.

CBRT   Curriculum-Based Reader's Theatre; an adaptation of reader's theatre for all content areas. See *reader's theatre*.

censorship   The act, process, or practice limiting access to the ideas and/or images in certain books, magazines or films.

checklist   A systematic means for recording qualitative reflections about textbooks.

cinquain   Five-line poems with specific limitations, used here as a summary technique.

civic literacy   Knowledge of governments and ways of acting in the political sphere, and the ability to read to acquire such knowledge.

cliché   A trite or overused expression or idea.

CLOZE   A measure of ability to restore omitted words in a passage by carefully reading the remaining text.

cognition   The mental process of knowing, including aspects such as awareness, perception, reasoning or judgment.

cognitive domain   All the learning that has to do with acquiring the academic content of the curriculum. Contrast with *affective domain*.

cognitive map   A diagram that gives students a visual overview of the structure of a larger text such as a chapter or unit. The purpose is to help clarify relationships among words that represent key concepts. It provides a framework to which new information or concepts can be added or subsumed.

computer literacy   Knowledge about and ability to use computers for a variety of purposes.

conspiracy days   An across the curriculum strategy where teachers "conspire" to teach and reinforce the same reading/study skill in all their classes.

comprehending   The process by which readers utilize prior knowledge and experience to construct or reconstruct meaning while interacting with text. The product of comprehending is *comprehension*.

comprehension   The construction of intended meaning of a communication, an accurate representation of an understanding of text; the product of comprehending.

concept load   The density of ideas given in a text in relation to text length.

content literacy   The ability to use reading and writing for the acquisition of new content in a given discipline.

Content IRI   Content Informal Reading Inventory; a teacher-constructed curriculum-based assessment tool used to determine the ability of a group of students to read, with understanding, from a specific content area text with understanding.

collateral reading   Materials related to the main topic or theme being studied which supports, broadens, or enriches the experiences of the reader. When used prior to reading to activate/acquire relevant background knowledge we call this collateral pre-reading. When used after reading, to broaden or reinforce understanding, we call this collateral post-reading.

connotation   The meaning of a word which is in addition to, or apart from, the thing explicitly named or described by the word; its *denotation*.

context   The setting, physical or linguistic, in which words occur.

context clue   Identification of a new word in context by anticipation of its meaning from the adjacent words and ideas.

Cornell notes   A note taking and making system with two columns developed at Cornell University.

CoRT   Cognitive Research Trust; an organization founded by alternative thinking strategist Edward DeBono that publishes instructional materials for teaching thinking.

conventions   The accepted practice in a spoken or written language.

criterion   A standard by which a test may be judged; a set of scores, rating etc. (Plural form is criteria.)

criterion-referenced test   A test that compares student's scores to a pre-determined criteria that serves as a *benchmark* of performance. Contrast with a *norm-referenced* test.

cultural literacy   The knowledge of concepts, items, or facts a person needs to succeed in a cultural context.

DaNOTES   A note evaluation strategy used to evaluate the quality of one's notes. This acronym stands for Date, Name, Organized, Trimmed, Essential points highlighted, and Source.

DEAR   A take-off on sustained silent reading (*SSR*). This acronym stands for Drop Everything And Read.

decode   To analyze spoken or graphic symbols. Used here to mean the recognition of letters and other word parts and then assembling of them into wholes. Contrast with *encode*.

denotation   The literal definition of a word as might be found in a dictionary. Contrast with *connotation*.

diagnosis   The act or process of identifying or determining the nature or cause of a learning problem through assessment. Conclusions are used to facilitate a plan for assistance to the learner.

diamante   A seven line contrast poem in diamond shape that helps students apply knowledge of a concept by describing its opposites.

disaggregate   In assessment, to subgroup scores to see how smaller groups performed within a larger group. Contrast with *aggregate*.

domain   In learning theory, a sphere of activity, concern or function, as in *cognitive domain or affective domain*. In computer science, the unique name that identifies an Internet site.

ELL   Acronym for English Language Learners; those who are learning to communicate in English.

encode   To make meaning from spoken or graphic symbols that have been decoded. Contrast with *decode*.

engaged reader   One who is emotionally involved (absorbed) in responding to the content of reading.

EQ   Emotional Quotient; involves how well we understand our own feelings, our empathy for others' feelings and our ability to regulate emotions for enhanced living.

ethnicity   A group of people who believe that they have a common origin and believe they have distinctive cultural patterns which distinguish them from others.

etymology   The study of word origins.

euphemism   A pleasant term for something considered unpleasant.

exit slips   A writing to learn activity. Responding to prompts, students anonymously write about what they have learned, and/or asking questions about what they find confusing about that same content. Contrast with *admit slips* and *quick writes*.

expository text   Oral or written text that sets forth meaning or intent, explaining and defining information.

extrinsic motivation   Behaviors directed toward achievement in anticipation of an overt reward.

fandom   Fan fiction involving electronic exchanges between teenagers.

Ferndale notes   A system for taking and making notes that used three columns as developed by teachers in Ferndale, Washington.

format   In readability analysis, the way a page is laid out and how this layout affects comprehension.

formative assessments   Tools used by teachers to help students "form" or develop their skills. Data from these assessments are used by teachers while students are working on projects. Contrast with *summative assessments*.

figurative language   Figures of speech (simile, metaphor, irony, hyperbole, personification, synecdoche, oxymoron, metonymy) that create vivid mental pictures.

fixation   The coordinated positioning and focusing of the eyes on an object. In reading rate adaptability, the pause for the selection of visual information as the gaze rests in one place in the text.

fluency   The ability to read with accuracy, expression, phrasing and appropriate rate.

Fry Readabililty Graph   A formulaic method of estimating the difficulty level of reading materials based on the number of syllables and sentences in 100 word samples.

frustrational reading level   The level at which no reasonable amount of instructional assistance is sufficient to bridge the gap between a reader's abilities and the author's expectations.

functionally illiterate   One who is unable to read at a fourth-grade level or above.

Gardner's Intelligences   Howard Gardener's eight ways of knowing. (See *multiple intelligences*.)

gender   Refers to the social, cultural and psychological constructs (masculine and feminine) that society has assigned to the biological reproductive forms of male and female. See *sexual orientation*.

genre   A category used to classify literary and other works, usually by form, technique, or content. Categories of fiction like science fiction, romance, adventure, and mystery are considered genres.

giraffe talk   Rosenberg's paradigm for assertive language: "When I observe . . . . I feel . . . . Because I imagine . . . . Would you . . . .

GIST   Generating Interactions between Schemata and Text; a method for teaching students to write progressively more condensed summaries of a selection.

glossing   The technique of using marginal notes of explanation to improve comprehension, directing attention to both content and process, teaching a skill.

graphic organizer   A visual aid that illustrates relationships among key concepts with the intent of making abstract materials more concrete.

GRIPP   A memory enhancing study strategy; Group thoughts, Relate to background knowledge, Image, Paraphrase in your own words, and Ponder significance.

high stakes test   A test whose outcome serves as a decision point for some concrete outcome for an individual, a school or a school district.

holistic assessment   In writing, giving feedback based on a general or whole impression. Since the whole is greater that the sum of its parts, all aspects of a piece of writing are considered together. Contrast with *analytic assessment.*

Home Page (also Homepage)   The web page that one's browser is set to use when it starts up or the main web page for a business, organization or person.

hypertext   Any text on the Internet that contains links to other documents. Words or phrases in the document that can be chosen by a reader and which cause another document to be retrieved or displayed.

I.E.P.   Individualized educational program. A learning plan for any student that includes objectives, methodology, specific curriculum changes, and any classroom adjustments.

illiteracy   Inability to read or write. Contrast with *aliteracy.*

imagery   The process or result of forming mental images while reading or listening to a story that may aid in comprehension and retention. (Also called *visual imagery.*)

inclusiveness (inclusivity)   The practice of teaching and using instructional materials that embrace the background, culture and hence the needs of all students.

independent reading level   The level at which readers can read text for understanding without outside help.

inferential-connection questions   Questions that require readers to derive a conclusion or consequence from facts or premises within the text. To do so readers must use their own experiences along with the facts within the text to make an inference. Contrast with *inferential-reflection questions.* See also *QARs.*

inferential-reflection questions   Questions that require using the text and the reader's background knowledge to travel into new tracts of thought. Answers to these questions are personal and creative. Contrast with *inferential-connection questions.* See also *QARs.*

informal diagnosis   Any non-standardized measure teachers administer to students to judge or evaluate students' abilities to handle text material.

inquiry   A mode of interest driven by a desire to look deeply into a question or an idea that is of interests.

Inspiration 7.0   A note taking and making software tool that combines the function of a *cognitive map* or *recall diagram* and a standard outline.

instructional reading level   The level at which the readers' vocabulary, skills, and/or conceptual awareness fall slightly below the writer's expectations.

integrated content literacy   Bringing together concepts, skills and values usually taught separately in various subjects.

intrinsic motivation   Behaviors directed toward achievement based on a personal, internal drive or wish to succeed.

IRA   International Reading Association; a professional organization founded in 1956 for those involved in teaching reading to learners of all ages.

jargon   In readability analysis, the specialized or technical vocabulary of a subject area.

journal writing   Journal writing may take many forms including personal journals for personal reflection, dialogue journals for a written exchange of ideas between the student and the teacher, and double-entry journals where students take and make notes on separate parts of the page.

KWL   Strategy useful for identifying purposes for reading expository material (what I **K**now, what I **W**ant to know, and what I have **L**earned).

language diversity   Variety in both national languages and dialects or codes within national languages. These varieties carry historical, cultural, religious and personal meanings.

learning center   An area within a classroom with materials provided for following preset directions for meeting predefined objectives. Such centers provide for different ability levels and student self-checking.

learning logs   A writing to learn activity. Notebooks kept in content classrooms in which students record their learning before and after reading, observing, or participating in an activity.

leveled books   A collection of books grouped together according to approximate level of difficulty.

lexical complexity   In readability analysis the level of difficulty of the vocabulary.

linguistics   The study of the nature and structure of language and languages.

listening   Making a conscious effort to hear. Listening implies connecting with the speaker by attempting to make personal meaning from what is being said.

literacy   Defined by the National Literacy Act of 1991 as "…an individual's ability to read, write and speak in English, and compute and solve problems necessary to function on the job and in society, to achieve one's goals, and develop one's knowledge and potential." See also: *aliteracy, content literacy, civic literacy, computer literacy, cultural literacy,* *illiteracy, math literacy, religious literacy, scientific literacy, visual literacy,* and *musical literacy.*

literal-explicit questions   Questions for which the answers may be found and stated word-for-word in the text. Contrast with *literal-implicit* questions. See also *QARs.*

literal-implicit questions   Questions that require readers to provide answers that can be understood but are not stated directly in any one section the text. Contrast with *literal-explicit* questions. See also *QARs.*

literature   Imaginative writing in prose or verse such as poems, plays, novels and short stories.

math literacy   Also called numeracy; the ability to quantify or express oneself with numbers and mathematics.

mature reader   One who has mastered the basic "how to read" skills and has developed higher-level reading, attitudes, and behavior in reading.

meaning   A relative term; the interpretation that the reader places on the text, and/or the interpretation that an author or third party expects a reader to place on the text.

metacognition   Thoughts about one's own thinking, understanding or learning.

metacognitive   Thinking about thinking necessary to direct learning. Includes learning strategies such as thinking about what you know or need to learn, keeping a journal and/or self-evaluation.

metacognitive scripting   An instructional method used to improve student comprehension in which teachers share the thought processes they are using to understand what they are reading while they are actually doing that reading. Also called "mental modeling."

metaphor   A figure of speech in which a comparison is implied by analogy but is not stated.

mature readers   Those who have achieved a high and wide degree of literacy and are able to read efficiently and to find pleasure in doing so.

mnemonic   A type of strategy used to improve memorizing or recall.

morals   The rules of behavior, or of right and wrong, that are accepted within a social group.

morpheme   The smallest unit of meaning in words.

motivation   The forces that work within us to arouse and direct behavior. The inner force that causes us to do the things we do.

MRP   Multiple Reading Process; a three staged reading strategy that includes (1) previewing or pre-reading; (2) reading; and (3) post-viewing of postreading.

multiple intelligences   Howard Gardner's postulate that there are eight ways by which the human brain/mind system approaches the task of solving problems or making something meaningful. These eight are: linguistic, logical/mathematical, visual/spatial, body kinesthetic, musical/rhythmical, interpersonal, intrapersonal, and naturalist.

musical literacy   Ability to view and create music by recognizing and analyzing the different elements of sound, relating them to each other and thus creating meaning.

narrative text   Written or oral text that recounts events or tells a story.

National Assessment of Educational Progress (NAEP)   A U.S. federal program that regularly tests students nationwide in reading, writing, mathematics, science and other subjects.

network   The connection of two or more computers together so they can share resources.

No Child Left Behind Act (NCLB)   The revised (2001) Elementary and Secondary Education Act. This law sets deadlines for states to expand the scope and frequency of student testing, revamp their accountability systems and guarantee that every teacher is qualified in their subject area. NCLB also requires states to make demonstrable annual progress in raising the percentage of students who are proficient in reading and math, and in narrowing the test-score gap between advantaged and disadvantaged students.

norm-referenced test   A test that used to compare a student's scores to the scores of other students. Usually results in a ranking. (e.g., A group of 20 students run a mile. Did one student come in first or 20th in the field?) Contrast with *criterion-referenced* test.

note making   Reviewing, analyzing and reflecting upon information noted after note taking.

note taking   Writing down the main ideas and supportive details while listening or reading from a text.

objective tests   Tests that usually have only one correct answer per given question.

onomatopoeia   The formation or use of words in imitation of natural sounds (e.g., *buzz* or *hiss*).

OPIN   A vocabulary teaching/learning technique for selecting and defending word choices.

outcome   Knowledge, skills and/or understandings that students gain from learning experiences.

oxymoron   A figure of speech where words of almost opposite meaning are used together for effect.

palindrome   A word, phrase or number with the same sequence of letters or numbers whether read from right to left or left to right. (e.g., Go hang a salami - - - I'm a lasagna hog.)

paraphrasing   A three step process: (a) reading or listening; (b) asking oneself what was read or heard; and (c) putting the above into one's own words.

PARS   A study strategy; Set **P**urpose. **A**sk questions related to purpose. **R**ead to find answers to questions. **S**ummarize in your own words what you have learned.

pejoration   In linguistics, a change of meaning for the worse. Contrast with *amelioration.*

performance standards   Statements that specify the quality of student performance at various levels of competency in subject area.

"person first" language   The practice of portraying people who have disabilities in respectful and realistic ways, thus a person who has cerebral palsy; not a spastic.

people with disabilities   Those who have disabilities that may, or may not, require support or accommodation (e.g., Down syndrome, learning disability, physical disability).

phoneme   The smallest unit of speech.

phonics   The study or teaching of reading and spelling stressing symbol-sound relationships. Phonics begins with the understanding that each letter (or grapheme) of the alphabet stands for one or more sounds (phonemes).

plain language laws   State laws that consumer contracts be written in language that is easy to read and understand.

PMI   Plus, Minus, Interesting; a post-reading strategy requiring readers to analyze the positive, negative, and interesting aspects of an idea.

portfolio   A selective collection of student work in progress gathered over time in collaboration with teacher and parents. Contains reflective comments and student self-assessment.

pragmatics   A term used by linguists to describe how people use language to apologize, tell someone what to do, get a point across, demonstrate intelligence, or display status.

prefix   A syllable before the root word that usually changes the meaning.

prior knowledge   Knowledge that comes from previous experience.

process writing   Student centered writing tasks. Students choose from a variety of writing products and write for multiple audiences. Contrast with *product writing.*

product writing   Teacher designed and centered student writing tasks usually written for teacher as sole audience. Contrast with *process writing.*

QARs   Question and Answer Relationships; when teachers write comprehension questions it is helpful to look at the two major types of questions and their subdivisions: *literal-explicit, literal-implicit, inferential-connection,* and *inferential-refection.*

quick writes   A writing to learn activity. Three to five minute writing activities used by content teachers to activate prior knowledge, establish personal relevancy, and or build communities of understanding. Contrast with *admit slips* and *exit slips.*

RAFT   **R**ole, **A**udience, **F**orm and **T**opic; a writing strategy that helps students to personalize the concepts they are learning by transforming their perceptions of the topic.

reading rate adaptability   The ability to adjust rate of reading in order to respond to the purpose, type and difficulty of the text.

reading   The International Reading Association defines reading as the "complex recursive process through which we make meaning from texts, using semantics; syntax; visual, aural and tactile cues; context; and prior knowledge."

readability   The overall difficulty or ease with which material can be read by a given audience. Used here to mean the level of difficulty of a book or article as measured through the *triangulation* of data from formulae, checklists and student/parent input.

reader's theater   A reading activity in which students, while reading directly from scripts, are able to tell a story in a most entertaining form, without props, costumes, or sets. This activity may be used as a means to develop oral interpretation, analysis. This technique may also be used as a writing activity by having students develop their own scripts. See *CBRT.*

recall diagrams   A schematic method for relating associated memories enabling students to recall information in the way that is easiest for them. Also called "thought mapping."

recursive   Moving back and forth through a document when reading or writing it. (e.g., rereading earlier passages in light of later ones or rewriting a paragraph to improve its clarity.)

referencing   In assessment, choosing a framework for interpreting something. See *norm-referenced* and *criterion-referenced.*

reliability   One of the two cornerstones of accuracy in testing and measurement. (See *validity* for the other.) Whether the same measurement will give the same results for the same data every time.

religious literacy   Ability to read and understand the scriptural teachings of a religion.

retention   The ability to remember what has been read.

resiliency   The self-righting mechanism within every person that enables us to withstand difficulty and survive traumatic events. See *risky writing* and *bibliotherapy.*

response theory As used here, Rosenblatt's Response Theory posits that reading is a transaction between reader and text in which our purpose influences how we focus attention.

risky writing The use of writing to foster *resiliency* among students dealing with issues like depression, divorce, and/or sexual/physical/emotional/drug and alcohol abuse. Considered risky to do in a school classroom without the help/guidance of trained counselor or mental health professional.

root A basic word from which new words are developed by the addition of suffixes or prefixes.

rubric A graduated chart or table that describes the traits or characteristics at different levels of proficiency. Using rubrics, evaluators examine each piece of student work to find the level at which the descriptors best fit the skill level.

scaffolding During instruction, teachers assist and guide students so that they can read, learn, and respond to text in ways they may not be able to do without support. Teachers continue to provide this support until students are able to effectively read or write independently. Scaffolding student learning is especially important when students are reading a challenging text or writing a difficult piece.

scanning A rapid search for specific details

schemata A series of ideas or concepts in a structure or framework into which information can be assimilated or categorized. (Singular form is schema.)

schematic organizer A type of *advance organizer* that takes the form of a diagram, flowchart, table, or map.

scientific literacy The ability to access and process core knowledge in science.

schwa An unaccented vowel. Written as an upside down "e". Has the sound of "uh" as in *a*bout.

SDQA San Diego Quick Assessment; a quick reading-level screening tool which requires students to decode words to determine level. No comprehension of the meaning of those words is required.

semantics The study of the meaningful aspect of language.

semantic feature analysis A strategy that helps reinforce vocabulary by building a grid in which words are listed vertically and their features are listed horizontally. Students then use the grid to indicate whether each word possesses the stated feature or is related to the categorized ideas.

semantic mapping Graphic display of a cluster of related words often used in the prereading and vocabulary building phase of content reading.

search engine A web page that creates an index when searching for a key word or phrase on the World Wide Web.

sexual orientation The way in which people view and express the sexual component of their personality. See *gender.*

slicing A comprehension improvement strategy in which the teacher simplifies a question by asking a smaller part of the answer.

Spoonerisms Words of phrases in which letters or syllables get (by a slip of the tongue) unintentionally swapped. (e.g., Wave the sails—Save the whales.)

SQRRR or SQ3R Survey, Question, Read, Recite, Review; a general study method.

standards Statements about what is valued in a given field and/or descriptions of what is considered quality work.

standard deviation How much variation there is in a group, also used to describe how much someone differs from the average.

standard English English as it is spoken and written by those groups with social, economic and political power in the United States.

standardized For a test, developed appropriately (questions carefully generalized, analyzed, tried out and revised) and administered under consistent conditions (time, instructions, role of administrators).

study guides A set of suggestions designed to direct students' attention to the key ideas in a reading and to suggest ways to study this material more effectively.

simile Direct comparison using like or as.

six-trait analytical writing assessment model an *analytic assessment* rubric for evaluating writing which examines 1)ideas and content, 2) organization, 3) voice, 4) word choice, 5) sentence fluency, and 6) conventions.

skimming A very rapid form of over-viewing a selection to get the gist, skipping over unneeded information.

SSR Sustained Silent Reading; Practice in independent silent reading.

story grammar A grammar that delineates relationships between episodes in stories and makes possible the setting of rules for generating new stories.

structural analysis Analysis of words by affixes or roots.

structured overview A visual or verbal representation of key vocabulary and concepts, similar to an *advance organizer* in that it helps to relate pertinent new information to existing knowledge in a hierarchical form. It differs in that students participate in its construction.

study guide   A series of problems, directions, or thought-provoking questions given to students to encourage efficient study habits and mastery of subject matter.

study learning   Study skills; techniques and strategies to help read, listen and remember information.

subjective tests   Usually essay tests; answers are not merely right or wrong.

summarizing   Concisely restating what an author has said or written.

summative assessments   Tools used by teachers "summarize" the learning of student projects and activities. These include grades on assignments, tests and projects. Contrast with *formative assessements.*

survival literacy   Ability to perform reading, writing and numerical tasks necessary for daily living.

synonym   A word that has the same, or nearly the same, meaning as another word.

synonym clustering   A vocabulary building technique used to help students understand shades of meaning.

syntactical complexity   The difficulty level of sentence structure or writing style.

syntax   The grammar of language, that is, the rules by which sentence structure is regulated.

synthesis   The process of putting together information from various sources in a new, creative way, a higher level of comprehension.

tachistoscope   In reading rate adaptability, a projector or other viewing device with a shutter or timer controlling the presentation of visual information for brief periods of time.

taxonomy   A classification in a hierarchy of an area of study or body of knowledge specifying its components and their relationships

TER   Target, Exand, Restrict; a writing to learn strategy used by students to pick the topic for a paper.

thematic teaching unit   A series of lessons or class activities organized around a them, a literary form, or a skill.

TOAST   Test, Organize, Anchor, Say, Toast; a vocabulary study system for content areas.

trade books   Books published by commercial "trade" publishers that may be used to supplement instruction in content reading.

triangulation   In assessment, the use of at least three different perspectives and measures of data to provided a balanced representation.

validity   One of the two cornerstones of accuracy in testing a measurement. (See *reliability* for the other.) Whether a test measures what it says it measures.

values clarification   A technique used to help students identify their own values, think about them, clarify their positions, and act on their beliefs when appropriate.

vicarious experience   An experience that is not firsthand; that is, one that is formed using the imagination while or after observing a picture, film, or reading a story.

visual literacy   Ability to view and create art by recognizing and analyzing different elements, relating them to each other and thus creating meaning.

visual imagery   See *imagery* above.

vocabulary   Those words known or used by a person or group, including technical, regional or slang uses.

word identification or word attack   Analyzing a new word into known elements for the purpose of identifying it and discovering meaning through phonics, structural analysis, context clues and/or dictionary.

wait time   The period of time a teacher waits between asking a question and providing further prompts for an answer.

WRAT   Wide Range Achievement Test; a standardized norm-referenced word assessment tool to ascertain approximate reading levels.

writing process   The steps used to create written communication including brainstorming or pre-writing, drafting, revising, editing and publishing.

writing to learn   Using writing to help with content learning. Helping students explore, clarify and think of concepts and ideas when reading.

YAL   Young Adult Literature; includes literature for ages 12–20.

Author Index

Adler, M. J., 41
Akmal, T., 432
Allington, R., 154
Alvermann, D., 84, 138, 236
Ambrose, S., 279
American Educational
  Research Association, 202
Anderson, P. L., 342
Anderson, R. C., 327
Andrasick, K., 294
Andrews, S. A., 293, 294
Applebee, A., 281
Arter, J., 287
Askov, E., 136, 304
Atwell, N., 295
Ausubel, D. P., 246, 483, 485

Bader, L., 84
Baker, S., 303
Bales, R., 267
Banks, J., 83
Barnes, B. R., 485
Barrera, I., 93
Barrett, T., 237, 272
Barron, R., 247
Bean, J. W., 438
Beers, K., 133
Benard, B., 135
Berglund, R., 251
Berkson, R., 299
Berman, J., 304
Bewell, D., 296
Bicknell, J., 77
Bijou, A., 203
Birdyshaw, D., 438
Bissex, G., 175
Bloom, B., 119, 237, 272
Bond, E., 84
Bond, G., 84
Boothby, P., 236
Bos, C. S., 342
Bransford, J. D., 486
Braun, T. J., 139

Breese, 154
Britsch, S. J., 299
Britton J., 281
Brophy, T., 84
Brown, A. L., 371
Brown, K., 139
Burgess, T., 281
Burnman, W., 154

Calkins, L., 280, 295
Campbell, J., 91
Caponecchi, W. P., 485
Carlson, S., 300
Carr, E., 270
Castle, M., 133
Caverly, D., 271
Chall, J., 169, 175
Chissom, B. S., 169
Ciliberti, B., 77
Clancy, M., 77
Clawson, E. U., 485
Cocking, T. S., 355
Conard, S., 175
Conley, M., 84
Connell, P., 432
Cotter, R., 136
Council of Chief State
  School Officers, 4, 40, 76,
  112, 196, 232, 322, 352,
  390, 410
Crafton, L., 252
Cramer, E. H., 133
Cran, W., 291
Culham, R., 287
Cummins, J., 413
Cunningham, J., 26

Dale, E., 169
Dana, C., 342
Day, J. D., 371
de Jong, E., 303
deBono, E., 265, 302
Delpit, L., 292

Diederich, P., 286
Dole, J., 235
Duffy, G., 235, 260
Dunbar, P. L., 415
Durban, K., 94
Durkin, D., 236

Eanet, M., 370, 371
Elbow, P., 293
Emig, J., 281
Engle, S., 266
Ernst, G., 400
Estes, T., 265
Eubanks, P., 84

Farnan, N., 285
Farrell, D., 28
Fearn, L., 285
Feingold, I., 136
Filipovic, Z., 295
Fishburne, R., 169
Fitzgerald, G., 485
Fletcher, 283
Flower, 281
Flynn, R. M., 433
Forgan, H., 167
Fountas, I., 418
Fox, K., 135
Frank, A., 295
Friere, P., 84
Fry, E. B., 161, 162, 487
Funk, W., 328

Gamas, W., 250
Gambrell, L., 267
Garber, K., 255
Gardner, E. T., 485
Gardner, H., 238, 272
Gay, L. R., 487
Gere, A., 296
Gersten, R., 303
Giroux, H. A., 84
Gittelman, R., 136

Glass, G., 250
Goetz, E., 267
Goleman, D., 120
Goodall, J., 430
Goodlad, 132
Goodman, K., 263
Goudvis, A., 235, 260
Graham, K. G., 377
Graves, D. H., 281
Graves, M. F., 324
Gray, W., 84
Green, F., 341
Guldin, G. E., 91, 400
Gunning, T. C., 355
Gunning, T. G., 221
Guzzetti, B., 250

Haag, E., 252
Hallowell, E., 137
Harper, C., 303
Harris, T., 133
Harrison, S., 297
Harris-Sharples, S., 175
Harvey, S., 235, 260
Havens, L., 297
Hayes, D., 281
Heafner, T., 248
Heitzmann, K. A., 136
Heitzmann, W. R., 136
Herber, H., 250, 255
Hillocks, G., 285
Hirsch, E., 83
Hirsh, E. D., 333
Hodges, R., 133
Hombo, C., 91
Honegger, M., 292
Hoobler, D., 61
Hoobler, T., 61
Horabin, I., 170
Howe, L., 130

International Reading
  Association, 178

International Reading
  Association/National
  Council of Teachers of
  English, 4, 40, 76, 112,
  135, 152, 200, 232, 278,
  322, 352, 410

Jawitz, P., 267
Johns, J., 207, 251
Johnson, D., 208, 258
Johnson, M. K., 486
Justak, J. R., 203

Karahalios, S. M., 486
Katz, C., 139
Katz, R., 29
Kincaid, J., 169
Kirschenbaum, H., 130
Klein, D., 136
Kozlow, M. J., 486
Krathwohl, D., 119
Kuby, S. A., 139

Langer, J., 280
LaPray, M., 203
Larson, B., 266
Lawton, J. T., 485
Lee, S., 267
Lent, R. C., 94
Lipton, J., 343
Lyman, F. T., 138

MacNeil, R., 291
Macon, J., 296
Macrorie, K., 295
Mandeville, T., 271
Mangrum, C., 167
Manzo, A., 255, 370, 371,
  427
Manzo, U. C., 427
Marshall, N., 171
Martin, N., 281
Martorella, P., 83
Masia, B., 119
Massey, D., 248
Massie, M. J., 139
Mayer, R. E., 485
Mazzeo, J., 91
McClanahan, L., 299
McCormick, C. B., 485
McCrum, R., 291

McLeod, A., 281
McPherson, G., 84
McTighe, J., 138
Meeks, L. L., 378
Meier, T., 284, 291
Miller, D. E., 422
Millus, A., 153
Moore, D. W., 84, 438
Moore, E., 251

Nagy, W. E., 327
National Board for
  Professional Teaching
  Standards, 112, 152, 196,
  232, 278, 390, 410
National Center for
  Educational Statistics, 91
National Center on Education
  and the Economy and the
  University of Pittsburgh,
  278
National Council for the
  Social Studies, 132
National Institute of Mental
  Health, 136
Neff, G., 299
Neff, S., 299
Nelson, K., 399
Neuman, S., 94
Nicholson, S., 271
Nistler, R., 295
Northwest Educational
  Regional Laboratories,
  287

O'Matz, M., 153
Oboler, E., 94
Ochoa, A., 266
Office of the Superintendent
  of Public Instruction, 40
Ogle, D., 270
Olivarez, A., 267

Pardeck, J., 136
Pauk, W., 6
Pearce, D., 84
Pearson, P. D., 208, 235, 258
Pennac, D., 124
Pinnell, G., 418
Pipkin, G., 94
Pirrone, J., 299

Pollard, J., 287
Pressley, M., 267
Price, K., 399

Readence J., 84, 251
Redfield, J., 417
Reinking, D., 363
Richardson, J., 428
Rickards, J. P., 485
Rickelman, R., 84, 251
Rinsky, L., 336
Roberts, N., 267
Robinson, F. P., 367
Robinson, H. A., 377
Rodriguez, M., 342
Roehler, L., 235, 260
Rogers, R. L., 169
Rosen, H., 281
Rosenberg, M., 140
Rosenblatt, L., 411
Ross, R., 203
Rubin, D., 285
Rycik, J. R., 438

Sadowki, M., 267
Salzman, M., 304
Sanders, N. 237, 272
Sandstrom, R., 269
Santa, C., 297
Scandura, J. M., 485
Schaefer, C., 185
Schafer, C. A., 355
Schumacher, G. M., 485
Schwarz, G. E., 427
Shakur, T., 295
Siegel, A., 153
Simmers-Wolpow, R., 28,
  135
Simon, S., 130
Simpson, J. A., 77
Sleator, E. K., 136
Smirnov, A. A., 377
Smith, D., 170
Smith, F., 45, 236
Smith, M., 170
Snyder, T., 250
Spandel, V., 281, 287
Sprague, R. L., 136
Stedman, L., 78
Stenner, A. J., 170
Stiggens, R., 281

Stone, V., 247
Styslinger, M., 140
Swafford, J., 84

Taba, H., 247, 248, 339
Taylor, W., 221
The Department for
  Education and Skills, 322
Thomas, M. M., 427
Tiffany, J., 284
Tillman, C. E., 136
Tobias, S., 296
Tompkins, G., 295
Tonjes, M. J., 28, 94, 124,
  260, 338, 339, 377, 486
Tovani, C., 17
Towner, J. C., 486
Trelease, J., 428

United States Bureau of the
  Census, 91
United States Department of
  Education, 91

Vaughan, J., 265
Venezky, R. L., 77
Vogt, M. E., 296

Waff, D., 432
Wagner, D., 77
Walker, F., 77
Wanska, S. K., 485
Watts-Taffe, S. M., 324
Webster, 29
Weiner, E. S., 77
Weiner, S., 427
Weist, L., 167
Wells, H. N., 485
Werner, E., 135
Wilde, S., 202
Wolpow, R., 136, 299, 304
Wood, N., 414
Wu, S., 285

Yoon, J., 431

Zinsser, W., 279, 284
Zintz, M., 338, 339

Subject Index

A

Abbreviations, 27
Abstractness, 157
Acronym, 269, 332
Acrostics, 269
Adler's levels of reading; *see* Reading levels
Admit slips, 293–294
Advance Organizer (AO), 246–247, 483–489
  comprehensive organizer, 484
  expository organizer, 484
  research findings, 485–486
  schematic organizer, 485
Aesthetic stance, 411
Affective domain
  categories, 121
  taxonomy, 119–120
Aliteracy, 133
Alphabet books, 298
Amelioration, 329
Anagrams, 344
Analogy, 332–333
Analytical reading level, 42
Anime, 428
Anticipation/reaction guides, 250–252
Assembling directions, 33
Assessment
  community input, 224
  parent input, 223–224
  portfolios, 224–226
  student input, 223
Assessment data
  aggregating, 199
  collection, 199
  disaggregating, 199–200
  triangulating, 202
Assessments; *see also* Classroom assessments; Informal whole-class assessment
  criterion-referenced, 198, 199
  formative, 198
  high-stakes, 198
  norm-referenced, 199
  performance-based, 198
  standardized, 198–199
  standards, 200–201, 202
  students, 197
  summative, 198
  tests, 197
Assessments of readability; *see* Tools for measuring readability
ATOS™ readability formula, 171, 418
At-risk students, 134–135
Attention deficit disorder (ADD), 136–137
Attention deficit hyperactivity disorder (ADHD), 136–137
Attitudes
  assessing, 123–125
  building positive attitudes, 123–124
  reading attitude survey, 125
Audiocassettes, and instruction, 402
Authentic assessment, 197

B

Background knowledge and comprehension, 243
Bar graph, 359
Basic reading inventory, 207
"The Beads of Life," 414
Bibliotherapy, 136, 412
Bicultural education, 401
Bilingual education, 401
  approaches, 400–401
Biopoems, 296–297
"The Blind Man and the Elephant," 44
Blogs, 299
Bloom's taxonomy of the cognitive domain, 237
Book talks, 429–430
Brainstorming, 283
Buddy system, 395

C

Cartoons, 362
Censorship, 94–95
  censored books, 95
Charts, 357–358
  flowchart, 358
  interpreting, 364–365
  stream chart, 358
  tree chart, 258
Checklists for measuring readability
  ICL checklist buffet, 172–174
  Marshall's checklist, 171–172
Cinquains as summaries, 265
Circle graph, 359
CIRI; *see* Content IRI
Civic literacy, 83
Class profile sheet, 458
Classroom assessments
  basic reading inventory, 207
  and English language learners, 206
  individual quick classroom screening, 203
  San Diego Quick Assessment (SDQA), 203–207
  wide-range achievement test, 203
Classroom discussion, 266
Classroom organization
  materials, 392
  space, 392, 393
  time plan, 391, 392
Clay, Marie, 418
Clichés, 343
CLOZE technique
  administering, 221–222
  constructing, 221
  modified, 340–341
  procedure, 221–223
  scoring, 221–222
Cognitive maps, 247, 340
Collateral (reiterative) post-reading/viewing, 268
Collateral pre-reading, 252

Collective nouns, 343
Communication
    giraffe talk, 140–141
    nonviolent, 140–141
    violent, 140–141
Completion tests, 382
Comprehending process, 235
    Bloom's taxonomy of the cognitive
        domain, 237
    DRTAs, 240–241
    Gardner's eight ways of knowing,
        238–240
    taxonomies, 237–238
Comprehension, 236–237; *see also*
        comprehending process
    and advance organizers, 483
    levels of, 237
    narrative vs. expository, 236–237
    types of, 239–240
Comprehensive organizer, 484
Computer literacy, 83
Concentration aids, 376–378
Concept load, 157
Connection constructors, 17–18
Connotations, 330
Content classroom activities
    anticipation guides, 250–252
    book talks, 429–430
    Curriculum-Based Reader's Theatre
        (CBRT), 433
    DEAR, 431–432
    picture books for adolescents,
        430–431
    read-alouds, 428
    response journals, 433
    SSR, 431–432
    study reading circles, 432
    text walk, 430
Content Informal Reading Inventory
        (CIRI); *see* Content IRI
Content integration, 139
Content IRI, 177, 210—221, 337; *see
        also* Content IRI report; Content
        IRI subtests
    for chemistry and math, example of,
        455–469
    comprehension section, 211–214
    displaying and using data, 220–221
    scoring profile, 211, 214, 220–221
Content IRI report, example of, 447–453
Content IRI subtests, 214–221
    defining or applying content-specific
        vocabulary subtest, 219
    following directions subtest, 218
    graphics subtest, 216
    locating and/or using reference
        materials subtest, 217–218
    outlining, taking, and making notes
        subtest, 217
    parts of the text subtest, 217

translating symbols and formulae
        subtest, 219
Content literacy, 84
Context, and vocabulary instruction,
        333–334
Contextual vocabulary questions, 210,
        213
Conventions
    in writing, 290–291
    nonstandard, 291
Cooperative learning, 399
Cornell notes, 6–7
Criterion-referenced assessments, 198,
        199
Critical literacy, 84
Cross-cultural study, and folklore, 416
CSSD (Context, Structure, Sound,
        Dictionary), 333–338
Cultural literacy, 83
Cultural sensitivity, 292
Curriculum
    community involvement, 413
    minority students, 413
    multicultural, 413
    and religion, 477–481
Curriculum-Based Readers Theatre
        (CBRT), 433

D

Dale-Chall Readability Formula; *see*
        New Dale-Chall Readability
        Formula
DaNOTES, 6, 19–20
DEAR; *see* Drop Everything and Read
        (DEAR)
Decoding, 82
Defining or applying content-specific
        vocabulary subtest, 219–220
Degrees of Reading Power (DRP), 170,
        418
Denotations, 330
Dewey, 234
Diagrams, 15–17, 357, 358; *see also*
        Graphic representations; Recall
        diagramming
Dialects in writing nonstandard,
        291–292
Dialogue journals, 295
Diamante poems, 297
Dictionary, in vocabulary instruction,
        336–337
Digital stories, 411
Digital storytelling, 299–300
Directed Reading-Thinking Activities
        (DRTAs), 240–241, 270
    during-reading strategies, 252–261
    K-W-L Plus strategy, 270–271
    PLAN, 271

post-reading strategies, 262–270
    pre-reading strategies, 241–252
    sample lesson, 443–446
Directions
    assembling, 33
    experimental, 33
    following, 28–31, 33–34
    performing, 33
Disabilities, students with, 92
Discussion web, 138–139
Distractions, and learning, 122
Diversity, 91–94, 413
    and literacy, 91
Diversity responsive instruction
    organizing for, 399–400
    planning for, 399–400
Double-entry journals, 295–296
Drafting, 283–284
Drop Everything and Read (DEAR),
        431–432
DRTAs; *see* Directed Reading-Thinking
        Activities (DRTAs)
During-reading guides, 255, 256
During-reading strategies
    during-reading guides, 255, 256
    glossing, 253–255
    metacognitive scripts, 260, 261
    ReQuest, 255, 257, 258
    slicing, 258–260

E

Ebonics, 291–292
Editing, 285
Efferent stance, 411
Elementary reading level, 41
ELL; *see* English language learner
        (ELL)
Elsner's DaNOTES; *see* DaNOTES
Emotional intelligence, 120
Emotional Quotient (EQ), 120, 122
Encoding, 82
Engaged readers, 113, 117–120
Engagement strategies
    discussion web, 138–139
    gender: dual-voiced journals, 140
    giraffe talk, 140–141
    informational publications, 139
    integrate content, 139
    think-pair-share, 138
Engaging students
    concerns and opportunities, 132–137
    strategies for, 137–141
English as a second language, 401
English language learners (ELL), 17, 41,
        93, 124, 199–200, 206, 285,
        400–401, 419, 428
    teaching strategies, 133
    and writing, 303

Essay tests, writing, 381–382
Ethnicity, 91–92
Etymology, 327–328
Euphemism, 331
Exit slips, 294
Experimental directions, 33
Explicit literal questions, 209
Expository comprehension, 236
Expository organizer, 484
Eye fatigue, 46
Eye fixations, 45–46

F

Family structure, 94
Fan fiction, 427
Ferndale notes, 6, 7–8, 9, 10, 11
Figures of speech, 331
    acronym, 332
    analogy, 332–333
    euphemism, 331
    homonym, 332
    idiom, 331
    metaphor, 331
    onomatopoeia, 331
    oxymoron, 331–332
    simile, 331
Five-paragraph essay, 300–301, 314
Fixations, 45–46
Flesch Reading Ease Score, 168–169,
    456
Flesch-Kincaid Grade Level Score,
    168–169
Flexible small group instruction,
    394–395
Fluency, 177
Folklore, 416
Following directions subtest, 218
Forgetting, 375
    theories of, 375
Format of text, and readability, 157
Formative assessments, 198
Formulae for readability, 161–163, 165,
    167–171
    ATOS™ readability formula, 171
    Dale-Chall Readability Formula,
        169–170
    Degrees of Reading Power (DRP),
        170
    Flesch Reading Ease Score, 168–169,
        456
    Flesch-Kincaid Grade Level Score,
        168–169
    Fry Readability Graph, 161–163, 165,
        167, 418, 456
    Lexile Scale, 170
    and math books, 167–168
Free writing, 295
Frost, Robert, 429–430

Frustrational reading level, 161
Fry Readability Graph, 161–163, 165,
    167, 418, 456
    directions for working with, 162–163
    evaluating shorter passages, 167
Functional literacy, 78

G

G.I.S.T. (Generating Interactions
        between Schemata and Text), 25–26
Gardner, Howard, 238
Gardner's eight ways of knowing,
    238–240
    applying, 240
Gender, 93
    dual-voiced journals, 140
Gender roles, 140
Gender-role stereotyping, 137
Gillette, Mary, 58, 59
Giraffe talk, 140–141
Glossing or gloss booklets, 253–255
Grade level of reading; *see* Readability
Graphic aids, 157
Graphic information lesson, 363
Graphic novels, 427
Graphic representations, 247–248
    cognitive maps, 247
    structured overviews, 247–248, 249
Graphics, 356–366, 463
    cartoons, 362
    charts and diagrams, 357–358
    graphic information lesson, 363
    graphs, 359
    maps, 360
    pictures/illustrations, 361–362
    tables, 360
    teaching tips, 364
Graphics subtest, 216
Graphs
    bar graph, 359
    circle or pie graph, 359
    line graph, 359
    pictograph, 359
GRASP study strategy, 371
Group instruction
    grouping methods, 395
    small groups, 394–395
    triads or buddy systems, 395
Guided Reading and Summary
        Procedures (GRASP); *see* GRASP
        study strategy

H

Harvard notes, 6, 7–8
Headings and subheadings, 157
High-stakes test assessments, 198

High-stakes writing
    five-paragraph essay, 300–301, 314
    research paper, 301–302
    TER, 302–303, 315–317
Homograph, 332
Homonym, 332
Homophone, 332
How to Read a Book, 41
Howell, Frank, 415

I

ICL checklist buffet, 172–174, 418, 456
Ideas and content in writing, 287
Idiom, 331
Illiteracy, 133
    defined, 77
Illustrations, 361–362
Imaging, 267–268
Implicit literal questions, 209
Inclusiveness, 159–160
Independent reading level, 160
Individual quick classroom screening,
    203
Individualized learning, 396
Inferential questions, 208, 213
    connection, 209, 213
    reflection, 209–210, 213
Informal whole-class assessment
    CLOZE procedure, 221–223
    comprehension questions, 208–210
    Content IRI, 210–221
Informational publications, 139
Inspectional reading level, 41–42
Inspiration 7.0™, 23–24
Instructional reading level, 160
Integrated content literacy, goals of
        instruction, 113
Integrating content, 139
Interest inventories, 127–128, 129–130
    creating, 130
Interests, assessing, 124, 129
Internet search, 355

J

Jargon, 158
Journals
    dialogue, 295
    double-entry, 295–296
    personal, 295

K

Key pals, 298–299
Key words, 340
King, Dr. Martin Luther, 132

Krathwohl's taxonomy, 120
K-W-L plus, 369–370, 417
    strategy, 270–271

L

Language acquisition, 325–330
Language Experience Approach (LEA),
    396
Language minorities, 93
Language of feelings, 120
Learning centers, 397–399
Learning environment, 135
Learning logs, 296
Learning strategies; *see* Study strategies
Length of text, and readability, 157
Leveled books, 418
Lexical density, 158–159
Lexile scale, 170, 418
Library scavenger hunt, 355–356
Line graph, 359
List/group/label, 339
Listening, 28–31, 33–34
    instruction in, 29–31, 33
    puzzles, 30–31, 33
    skills, 29, 30, 33
List-Group-Label (LGL), 248–250
Literacy
    content literacy, 84
    definitions of, 77, 78
    functional literacy, 78
    survival literacy, 78
    types of, 83–84
Literacy activities, ineffective, 137–138
Literal questions, 208, 213
Literal vocabulary questions, 210, 213
Literature
    folklore, 416
    leveled books, 418
    multicultural, 413
    qualities of, 412
    sources for locating, 419–427
    sources for secondary students,
        424–426
    websites, 426–427
    young adult, 422–423
Literature circles, 432–433
Literature integration into classroom
    content; *see* Content classroom
    activities
Literature strategies; *see* Content
    classroom activities
    checklist, 434
Locating and/or using reference
    materials subtest, 217–218
Low-stakes writing
    admit slips, 293–294
    alphabet books, 298
    biopoems, 296–297

blogs, 299
diamante poems, 297
digital storytelling, 299–300
exit slips, 294
free writing, 295
journals, 295
key pals, 298–299
learning logs, 296
quick-writes, 294
RAFT—Role, Audience, Form, and
    Topic, 297–298

M

Making notes; *see* Notes
Maps, 360
    interpreting, 365–366
Marshall's readability checklist,
    171–172, 456
Matching tests, 382
Math books, and readability, 167–168
Math literacy, 83
Mature readers, 96
    self-assessment, 97–101
Meaning and reading, 234; *see also*
    Comprehending process
    reader's role, 234
    teacher's role, 235
    writer's role, 235
Mechanics, in writing, 290–291
Memorizing, 375–376
    tips, 376
Memory, 375–378; *see also* Memorizing
    long-term 377
    and repetition, 158
    short-term, 377
Memory strategies, 268–270
    acronym, 269
    acrostics, 269
    guidelines, 269
    mnemonics, 269
    peg words, 269–270
Mental modeling; *see* Metacognitive
    scripts
Metacognitive scripts, 260, 261
Metaphor, 331
Miller analogies test, 333
Minority students, empowering, 412
Mnemonics, 269
Motivating qualities of literature, 412
Motivation, and learning, 122–123
Multicultural curriculum, 413
Multicultural literacy, 83
Multicultural literature, 413
    sources, 420–422
Multicultural understanding, 412–413
    sharing, 417
Multiple choice tests, 382
Multiple intelligences, 238

Multiple Reading Process (MRP),
    57–63, 240–241, 270
    stages of, 57–59
Musical literacy, 84
"My Father's Hands," 81–82

N

Narrative comprehension, 236
National Literacy Act of 1991, 78
New Dale-Chall Readability Formula,
    169–170
Norm-referenced test assessments, 199
Notes, *see also* Outlining
    abbreviation in, 27
    as Connection constructors, 17–18
    Cornell, 6–7
    evaluation of, 19
    Ferndale, 6, 7–8, 9, 10, 11
    Harvard, 6, 7–8
    making, 6–22
    paraphrasing, 25
    roadblocks, 14
    summarizing, 25–26
    symbols in, 27
    taking, 6–22
    and technology, 23–24
Notice of Privacy Act, 153

O

Objective tests, 382–383
    completion, 382
    matching, 382
    multiple choice, 382
    taking, 383
    true/false, 382
Onomatopoeia, 331
OPIN, 341–342
Organization in writing, 288
Outlining, 20–25
    taking, and making notes subtest, 217
    teaching skills, 22–25
Oxymoron, 331–332

P

Palindromes, 344
Pangrams, 344
Paraphrasing, 25
PARS study strategy, 367
Parts of the text pre-reading guides,
    245–246
Parts of the text subtest, 217
Peer tutoring, 396
Peg words, 269–270
Pejoration, 329

Performing directions, 33
Personal journals, 295
Personalized learning, 396
Phonics, 336
Phrase comprehension, 55–56
Piaget, 234
Pictograph, 359
Picture books for adolescents, 430–431
Pictures, 361–362
Pie graph, 359
Plagiarism, 283
Plain language laws, 153–154
Plan, 271
Plus, Minus, Interesting (PMI), 265–266, 411
Portfolios
    and assessment, 224–226
    construction, 224
    sample record sheet, 225–226
Post-reading, 57–58
Post-reading strategies, 262–271
    cinquains as summaries, 265
    classroom discussion, 266
    collateral (reiterative) post-reading/viewing, 268
    imaging, 267–268
    Plus, Minus, Interesting (PMI), 265–266
    remembering strategies, 268–270
    simulations/role-playing, 267
Post-viewing, 57–58
Pragmatics, 284
Predict, verify, judge, and extend, 379–380
Performance-based assessments, 198
Pre-reading; *see also* Previewing
    activity, 115
Pre-reading strategies, 241–242, 245–252
    advance organizers, 246–247
    anticipatory guides, 250–252
    collateral pre-reading, 252
    graphic representations, 247–248
    list-group-label, 248–250
    parts of the text pre-reading guide, 245–246
Previewing, 57, 59
    steps, 60–61
Pre-writing, 283
Print size, 157
Proactive interference, 375
Process writing, 281, 282
Process writing stages
    drafting, 283–284
    editing, 285
    pre-writing, 283
    publishing, 286
    revising, 284
Product writing, 281, 282
Prompts, 366

Proofreading, 285
Publishing, 286
Punctuation, 285

Q

Qualitative Assessment of Text Difficulty (QATD), 175–176, 418
"Quality not Quantity," 58, 59
Question-and-Answer Relationship (QAR), 209–210
Questions; *see* Test questions
Quick check of readability, 177, 418
Quick-writes, 294

R

RAFT——Role, Audience, Form, and Topic, 297–298, 411
Rapid eye movements, 45
Readability; *see also* Reading levels; Textual factors and readability; Tools for measuring readability
    assessing, 154, 155
    assessment triangle, 178, 179
    cheating, 163
    defined, 154
    factors affecting 157–160
    leveled books, 418
    levels of understanding, 160–161
    matching student to textbook, 180–181
    qualitative assessment, 175–176
    trade books, 419
Readability graph; *see* Fry Readability Graph
Read-alouds, 428
Reader response theory, 411–412
Readers, classifying, 133–134
Readers' Bill of Rights, 124
Reading
    attitude survey, 125
    challenges, 134–135
    interest inventory, 129–130
    and learning, 85, 86–87
    making meaning, 234–235
    for pleasure, 122
    reading and writing connection, 280
    restorative qualities, 136
Reading assessment; *see also* Assessments; Informal whole-class assessment
Reading levels, 41–42; *see also* Readability
    Adler's levels of reading, 41–42
    analytical, 42
    and CLOZE scores, 222
    elementary, 41

frustrational reading level, 161
independent reading level, 160
inspectional 41–42
instructional reading level, 160
syntopical, 42
Reading rate adaptability, 41–66
    and fiction, 412
    importance of, 412
Reading rates, 41–44
    eye-mind connection, 45–46
    importance of, 43
    measuring, 42
    misconceptions, 43–44
    Zintz's reading rates, 41–42
Reading recovery approach, 418
Reading strategies; *see* Pre-reading strategies; Post-reading strategies
REAP study strategy, 370–371
Recall diagramming, 13–14, 15–17, 19
    scoring, 19–20
Reference materials, 354–355
Religion, and schools, 132, 477–481
Religion in the Public School Curriculum: Questions and Answers, 132
Religious diversity, 92–93
Religious literacy, 83
Remembering strategies; *see* Memory strategies
ReQuest, 255, 257, 258
Research paper, 301–302
Resiliency, 134–135
Response Journal (RJ), 433
Restorative qualities of literature, 412
Retention, 486; *see also* Memory; Memory strategies; Memorizing
    and CBRT, 433
Retention curve, 375
Retroactive interference, 375
Revising, 284
Risky writing, 295, 304, 412
Role-playing, 267
Rosenblatt's reader response theory
    aesthetic stance, 411–412
    efferent stance, 411-412
Rubric, 198

S

San Diego Quick Assessment (SDQA), 203–207
    administering, 204, 206, 207
    scoring, 206, 207
Sandburg, Carl, 429
Scaffolding, 430
Scaffolding strategies, 366
Scanning, 45–46
    exercise, 47–50
Schematic organizer, 485

Scientific literacy, 83
Scientific terms, common roots and affixes, 471–473
Scoring profile, 211
SDQA; *see* San Diego Quick Assessment (SDQA)
Semantic, 334
Semantic context clues, 334
Semantic Feature Analysis (SFA), 342
Sentence fluency, 290, 291
Sentence length, and readability, 159
Sentence structure, and readability, 159
Sexist Intelligence Quotient (SIQ), 137
Sex-role stereotyping; *see* Gender-role stereotyping
Sexual orientation, 93
Sheltered English/alternate immersion, 401
Shipwreck at the Bottom of the World: The Extraordinary True Story of Shackleton and the Endurance, 139
Simile, 331
Simulations, 267
Six-trait analytical writing assessment model, 287–291
    conventions, 290–291
    ideas and content, 287
    organization, 288
    sentence fluency, 290
    voice, 289
    word choice, 289
Six-trait assessment tool, 287
Skimming, 42
    exercise, 47–50
Slicing, 258–260
Small group instruction, 394–395
Sound, and vocabulary instruction, 335–336
Spanglish, 291
Speed reading, 55
Spoonerisms, 344
SQ3R/SQ4R, 367, 368
SSR; *see* Sustained Silent Reading (SSR)
Standardized test assessments, 198–199
Standards, and assessments, 200–201, 202
Stereotypes, 91, 92, 137
The Story of English, 291
Structural analysis, and vocabulary instruction, 335
Structured immersion, 400
Structured overviews, 247–248, 249
Student assessment; *see* Assessment
Students
    at-risk, 134–135
    resiliency, 134–135
Study habits
    attitude, 372–373
    concentration aids, 376–378

and memory, 375–376
physical conditions, 372
time management 373–374
Study learning; *see also* Listening; Outlining; Notes; Reading; Summarizing
    check/recall/monitor information 372–383
    interpret and apply information, 356–366
    searching and locating information, 354–356
    strategies, 366–371
Study reading circles, 432–433
Study strategies
    GRASP, 371
    K-W-L, 369–370
    PARS, 367
    predict, verify, judge, and extend, 379–380
    REAP, 370–371
    scaffolding, 366
    SQ3R/SQ4R, 367, 368
    thematic teaching units, 378–379
Summarizing, 25–26
    G.I.S.T., 25–26
Summative assessments, 198
Survival literacy, 78
Sustained reading and writing, 431
Sustained Silent Reading (SSR), 123, 431–432
Syllabification, 158
Symbols, 27
Synonym clustering, 338
Syntax, 334
Syntopical reading level, 42

T

Tables, 360
Tachistoscopes, 55
Taking notes; *see* Notes
Taking objective tests, 383
Taxonomies
    Bloom's taxonomy of the cognitive domain, 237
    for comprehension, 237–238
Teaching approaches
    cooperative learning, 399
    individualized/personalized learning, 396
    Language Experience Approach (LEA), 396
    learning centers for content areas, 397–399
Teaching formats, 393–396
    flexible small group instruction, 394–395
    peer tutoring or pairs, 396

total class, 393
    triads or buddy system, 395
Technological literacy, 83
Technology in the classroom, 401–402
    tape recorders, 402
    televisions, 402
    transparencies, 401–402
    videotape players, 402
Televisions, and instruction, 402
TER (Target, Expanding, Restrict), 302–303, 315–317
Test assessment, 197–199; *see also* Assessment
Test questions
    contextual vocabulary, 210
    explicit literal, 209
    implicit literal, 209
    inferential, 208, 213
    inferential connection, 209, 213
    literal, 208
    literal vocabulary, 210, 213
    writing, 208–210
Tests, 380–383
    essay tests, 381–382
    objective tests, 382–383
    preparing for, 380–381
    teaching skills for taking, 383
Text walk, 430
Textbook analysis, 185, 187–188
Textbook readability; *see* Textual factors and readability; *see also* Textbook analysis
Textbooks
    sections, 354
    surveying, 62–63
    vs. trade books, 417
Textual factors and readability, 456
    abstractness, 157
    concept load, 157
    format, 157
    inclusiveness, 159–160
    length of text, 157
    sentence length, 159
    sentence structure, 159
    vocabulary, 157–158
Thematic teaching units, 378–379
Thesaurus, 337–338
Think-alouds, 341
Think-pair-share strategy, 138
Thought mapping, 13–14
Time management, and study habits, 373–374
Time plan for classrooms, 391, 392
Time schedules, 373–374
TOAST study system, 342
Tonjes Interest Inventory (TII), 127–128
Tools for measuring readability, 161–163
    checklists, 171–176
    formulae, 161–163, 165, 167–171

informal assessments, 177
    student input, 176–178
Total class instruction, 393
Trade books
    in content classrooms, 417–418
    sources for selecting, 419–427
    vs. textbooks, 417
Transitional bilingual education, 401
Translating symbols and formulae
    subtest, 219
Transparencies, 401–402
Triads, 395
Triangulation of assessments, and CIRI,
    455–469
True/false tests, 382
Tutoring, by peers, 396
Two-way bilingual education, 401

V

Values clarification, 130–131
    and religion, 132–133
Values voting, 324
Videotapes, and instruction, 402
Visual discrimination, 55
Visual literacy, 83
Vocabulary; *see also* Language
    acquisition; Words; Word study
    benefits of teaching, 323
    and formulae, 161
    and readability, 157–158
    size, 327
    type, 327
    values voting, 324
Vocabulary instruction
    benefits of, 323
    cognitive maps, 340
    CSSD (Context, Structure, Sound,
        Dictionary), 333–338

guidelines, 345
internet tools, 345–346
key words, 340
list/group/level, 339
modified CLOZE, 340–341
OPIN, 341–342
Semantic Feature Analysis (SFA), 342
synonym clusters, 339
think-alouds, 341
TOAST, 342
word-of-the-day, 338–339
Voice, in writing, 289
Vygotsky, 234

W

Walter Pauk's Cornell System; *see*
    Cornell notes
"We Wear the Mask," 415
Websites, with literature resources,
    426–427
Wide range achievement test, 203
Word choice, in writing, 289
Word study
    etymology, 327–328
    levels of, 326
    references, 475–476
    stumbling blocks, 325–326
    types of, 331–333
Word-of-the-day, 338
Words; *see also* Vocabulary; Vocabulary
    instruction
    amelioration, 329
    common roots and affixes in scientific
        terms, 471–473
    connotations, 330
    definitions, 326
    denotations, 330
    meanings, 326

multiple meanings, 324
construction of new, 330
origins, 327–328
pejoration, 329
phonics, 336
World War II, 55
Writing; *see also* Process writing stages
    analytic traits, 287–291
    and culture, 284
    forms, 282
    narrative vs. expository, 236
    reading and writing connection, 280
    risky, 295, 304
    teaching, 280–281
Writing activities; *see* High-stakes
    writing; Low-stakes writing
Writing assessment
    analytic, 286–287
    holistic, 286
    self-assessment, 287
    six-trait assessment tool, 287
    six-trait model, 287–291
Writing process
    process writing, 281, 282
    product writing, 281, 282
    stages of, 283–285
Writing to learn, 96

Y

Young adult literature, locating, 422–423

Z

Zintz's reading rates; *see* reading rates